1997

WITNESS TO THE HOLOCAUST

ALSO BY MICHAEL BERENBAUM

The Vision of the Void: Theological Reflections on the Works of Elie Wiesel (1979). Reprinted as *Elie Wiesel: God, the Holocaust, and the Children of Israel* (1994).

Editor, *From Holocaust to New Life* (1985).

Coeditor with John Roth, *Holocaust: Religious and Philosophical Implications* (1989).

After Tragedy and Triumph: *Modern Jewish Thought and the American Experience* (1990).

Editor, *A Mosaic of Victims: Non-Jews Persecuted and Murdered by the Nazis* (1990).

The World Must Know: The History of the Holocaust As Told in the United States Holocaust Memorial Museum (1993).

Coeditor with Israel Gutman, *Anatomy of the Auschwitz Death Camp* (1994).

Coeditor with Betty Rogers Rubenstein, *What Kind of God? Essays in Honor of Richard L. Rubenstein* (1995).

WITNESS TO THE HOLOCAUST

MICHAEL BERENBAUM

HarperCollins*Publishers*

HarperCollins books may be purchased for educational, business, or sales promotional use. For information, please write to: Special Markets Department, HarperCollins*Publishers,* Inc., 10 East 53rd Street, New York, New York 10022.

FIRST EDITION

Designed by Irving Perkins Associates

Library of Congress Cataloging-in-Publication Data
    Witness to the Holocaust/Michael Berenbaum, editor.
          p.   cm.
    ISBN 0-06-270108-8
    1. Holocaust, Jewish (1939-1945)—Sources. 2. Jews
Government policy—Germany—History—20th century—Sources.
3. Holocaust, Jewish (1939-1945)—Personal narratives.
I. Berenbaum, Michael, 1945-   .
D804.19.W58   1997
940.53'18—dc20   96-22595

97 98 99 00 ❖/RRD 10 9 8 7 6 5 4 3 2 1

To My Sister and Brother-in-Law

Susan and Uri Mingelgrin

Their Children

David and Miriam, Dan and Hilla

And Their Grandchild

Shira

Named in the Memory of My Father

The First of My Mother's Great Grandchildren

◈ CONTENTS

ACKNOWLEDGMENTS

Words of gratitude are in order.

This book was born at the initiative of my editor Robert Kaplan, who had an inkling of what he wanted and who displayed enthusiasm and patience—perhaps too much patience—during the time the work was in process. Without him and the fruitful professional collaboration of my friend and able agent Ronald Goldfarb this work would never have come to fruition.

Witness to the Holocaust was made possible—and nearly impossible—because of my work at the United States Holocaust Memorial Museum and its Research Institute. No one told those of us who created the museum that we would have to run it as well. Six million visitors have come in the first three years: ordinary people and heads of state, scholars of renown, politicians, artists, writers, and other notables. Among them have been friends who have touched my life during each of its stages. The pressure of daily work, the pleasure of greeting friends and notables, the privilege of sharing with them the permanent exhibition and other parts of the museum, and the urgency of a hectic daily schedule made it more and more difficult to write. It is often felt that life is a series of interruptions, most of them wonderful, almost all interesting and irresistible.

And yet being in the Research Institute where, almost daily, new documents are discovered and new research revealed, where colleagues learn and teach and are dedicated to knowing more about the Holocaust, has kept me engaged in the field. My thanks to Drs. Brewster Chamberlain, Radu Ioanid, Sybil Milton, Joan Ringelheim, and Severin Hochberg; to Raye Farr, Genya Markon, Benton Arnovitz, Mark Ziomek, and our colleagues with whom I am fortunate to work day by day. Dr. Wesley Fisher, Deputy Director of the Research Institute, does so much so well, and so unassumingly, that I can contemplate writing even while at work—albeit for only the briefest of moments.

Deirdre McCarthy's gentle prodding and graceful way with people makes the difficult seem possible and much else easy. Dan Stiles replaced Deirdre and learned his tasks well and so very quickly. Scott Miller and Aleisa Fishman offered criticism and insight. They are all people of intellectual integrity. Five assistants—Laura Surwit, Billy Mann, Patricia O'Connell, Steve Friesen, and Joshua Grey—worked on this work as part of their internships. For much that I have learned I can credit them. I alone am responsible for the shortcomings of this work. I would like to thank Dr. Michael Newman and his wonderful staff, most especially Brent Putman, at the Computer Center of Georgetown University for their assistance in scanning documents, and to thank Jennifer Schansberg and Toni Green for assistance in keyboarding those documents that could not be scanned. Thanks also to Kate Brannan who performed the difficult task of proofreading.

I have been blessed with wonderful children—Ilana and Lev—who have grown up with Holocaust research and often found in my work a rival for attention that was most properly due them. They have been understanding and rightfully demanding of time that should have been theirs. Ilana has now written an honors thesis at Brown and better understands the craft and the demands of scholarship. Lev has traveled to Poland; he has stood with me at Auschwitz and Majdanek and journeyed directly from Treblinka to the Western Wall, so he understands the burdens of memory and the privilege of living Jewish history. Melissa has entered my life and given me perhaps as much tranquility as I can endure, and significant joy; a different context in which to work, to write, to live. She has made it inviting and welcoming to walk away from the study of death.

This has been a year of enormous blessing: the graduation of a child from college, my marriage, the birth of my mother's first great grandchild, Shira, and the marriage of her other Israeli grandson, my nephew Dan Hillel. Such milestones of life occurring one after another have made me appreciate once again the magnitude of loss and the possibility of grace in personal life.

It has been a time in which one may hope that the Jewish people will experience peace and an end to the vulnerability that has characterized the struggles of the past century. Thus, perhaps, for one people the era of the Holocaust may be at an end.

But it has also been a time of Bosnia and Rwanda, tragic events which appear before our eyes daily in our CNN era, and echo anew the urgency of this study. We must learn from this past and salvage from the ashes lessons for our collective future.

MICHAEL BERENBAUM

WASHINGTON, D.C.

INTRODUCTION

Witness to the Holocaust presents in specific detail—in documents, diaries, letters, and testimony—the evolution of the Holocaust. The power of the work lies in its details, so too perhaps its shortcoming, for it may be possible for the casual reader to misplace the picture of the whole in the specificity of the facts.

So permit me in this brief introduction to present an overview of an event that unfolded over twelve years in many different countries involving perpetrators, bystanders, victims, resisters, rescuers, and survivors. Such an overview is difficult and by its every nature inadequate. Apologies aside, it is still required. The details will fill out what will surely be but a skeletal depiction of the event.

In his monumental work, *The Destruction of the European Jews*, Raul Hilberg outlined six stages in the destruction process:

Definition
Expropriation
Concentration
Mobile Killing Units
Deportation
Killing Centers

The Nazis came to power in Germany legally; they were elected to the Reichstag. Adolph Hitler assumed office in 1933 as head of a coalition government with his opponents gambling that once in power he would be forced to the center, to moderate or mute the anti-Semitic, racist, and dictatorial aspects of his platform. He spent the first two years of his regime consolidating power, eliminating political opposition, and solidifying his dictatorship.

In the Nuremberg legislation of 1935, German law defined the Jews not by the religion they professed, the values they avowed, the beliefs they practiced, or the identity they affirmed, but biologically, based on the religion of their grandparents. The enemy was all Jews, religious and secular, ardent or assimilationist, Zionists or German nationalists.

Once established, this definition of Jews was applied in country after country as the Reich expanded its borders and occupied other lands from 1938 onward.

Property was confiscated, civil liberties were abridged and then violated; homes, businesses, possessions, synagogues, public institutions, and private property were all taken from the Jews. At first, it was in an effort to force Jews to emigrate, to make Germany *Judenrein* [free of Jews]; later, confiscation and expropriation became an essential part of the Final Solution. In Germany this policy evolved slowly from 1933–39; it reached a

crescendo in the November pogroms of 1938 known as Kristallnacht in which the synagogues of Germany and Austria were burned, Jewish businesses were looted, Jewish
homes invaded, and almost thiry thousand Jewish men were arrested and sent to concentration camps. The process of eliminating the Jews from society, which had taken years in
Germany, took only months in Austria after its incorporation into the Reich in March 1938,
and, later, oftentimes only weeks in territories occupied by the German expansionism.

Within a month of the beginning of World War II, more than two million Jews came
under Nazi domination when the Germans conquered Poland in September 1939. Forced
emigration of so vast a population became an ever more distant fantasy. Shortly afterwards,
the first killings began, not of Jews but of the mentally retarded and physically disabled
Germans. Hitler personally ordered that "that patients considered incurable according to
the best available human judgment of their state of health, can be granted a mercy killing."
Within two years, six killing centers were established with gas chambers and crematoria.
The physicians who began their service at these centers would later be moved to the death
camps.

GHETTOIZATION AND WAR

Jews in Nazi-occupied Poland were forced to live together in confined areas, ghettos in
the East; with the German invasion of western Europe, transit camps were established in
the West. To the killers, these were temporary measures, pending a determination of some
final policy. The victims thought the ghettos would endure. They imagined some sort of
ongoing subsistence as a permanent underclass, discriminated against and persecuted at
least until the war came to a close.

Just as German policy toward Jews did not remain static, so too German domination of
Europe was an evolving phenomena. The Reich increased in size by incorporating former
German territories; in 1938 Austria, in 1939 the Sudetenland, and then from the fall of
1939 onward expansion by war. Poland fell in September, western Europe—Holland,
France, Belgium, Luxembourg, Denmark, and other countries—in the spring and summer
of 1940, and the Balkans and the Soviet Union in 1941. With each expansion the number
of Jews under German control increased and anti-Jewish policies were immediately
imposed.

Emigration was out of the question. There were too many Jews and they were
unwanted everywhere. Allied countries refused to receive large numbers of Jews even in
peacetime. This position was confirmed at the 1938 conference in Evian and reaffirmed at
the Bermuda Conference of 1943. The Germans perceived Allied reluctance to receive
immigrants as tacit consent. They were confident that the Allies were equally reticent to
implement rescue.

IMPLEMENTING THE FINAL SOLUTION: EINSATZGRUPPEN

Sometime in the winter of 1940–41 a policy decision was made and crowned with the
title "The Final Solution to the Jewish Problem." The "solution" envisioned was all too
final, the murder of all Jews under German domination—men, women, and children. Those
who acted on this policy were certain that they were implementing the Führer's will.

With the invasion of the Soviet Union in June of 1941, the slaughter was undertaken
by mobile killing units, Einsatzgruppen, that accompanied advancing German forces. They

entered town after town, village after village, hamlets, and even large cities, rounded up the Jews, Gypsies, and Soviet Commissars and shot them one by one, bullet by bullet, person after person. This process continued as the army advanced eastward and when the military situation stabilized the killing units returned to finish off what had been left undone. They were to return again in 1943, this time to dig up and burn the bodies in order to wipe out all evidence of their crimes.

Killing was difficult, even for the killers. The killers drank heavily. Alcohol somehow made the work more bearable. They spoke in euphemisms—of special actions, special treatment, executive measures, cleansing, resettlements, liquidation, finishing off, appropriate treatment.

The killers themselves were marked. "Look at the eyes of the men in this kommando, how deeply shaken they are," Himmler was told by one of his Einsatzgruppen commanders. "These men are finished for the rest of their lives. What kind of followers are we training here? Either neurotics or savages."

To deal with this problem, a more impersonal method of killing was sought. If the killers could no longer be brought to the victims in order to slaughter them face to face, the victims must be brought to the killers and disposed of in a way that kept the victims at a distance. Thus a second form of killing was developed—the death camp, where the victims were gassed, and the bodies were then burned.

FROM EINSATZGRUPPEN TO DEATH CAMPS

Railroads were *the* essential link in the killing process. Deportation transformed the ghetto into a transit camp, a way station to contain the captive population until the killing centers were developed and opened for business. Deportation meant the loss of home, the collapse of families, the beginning of a journey to death. Deportation also meant that there was no tomorrow, no hope. It was then, and only then, that several ghettos—Warsaw, Vilna, Bialystock, and many others—rose in revolt.

The timetable was swift. The policy was announced in January 1942 at Wannsee, the death camps were developed that winter and the spring, by the summer of 1942 deportations to death had begun. By 1943 most of the Jews to be killed in the Holocaust were already dead.

Three camps were reserved exclusively for killing: Sobibor, Treblinka, and Belzec. Auschwitz and Majdanek served multiple functions as killing centers, slave labor camps, and concentration camps. Other concentration camps were not solely dedicated to killing, though conditions were so harsh, slave labor so intense, and food so scarce that hundreds of thousands of inmates died or were killed.

The fate of Jews differed country by country, and region by region. What evolved slowly over twelve years in Germany or over three years in Poland, took less than three months in Hungary. The Germans invaded in March 1944. Jews were defined immediately and their property confiscated, by April they were ghettoized; on May 15, the deportation began and by July 8, 437,402 Jews had been deported to Auschwitz on 148 trains.

A MOSAIC OF VICTIMS: JEWS BUT NOT ONLY JEWS

Though the destruction of the Jews was at the center of Nazi ideology, Jews were not the Nazi's only victims. Nazi racism was directed against a mosaic of victims.

Some were targeted for what they did. In the early years trade unionists and political dissidents were incarcerated along with clergy who spoke out. Some were victimized for what they refused to do. Jehovah's Witnesses would not swear allegiance to the state, they would not register for the draft. The words "Heil Hitler" did not leave their lips. Nazi propaganda demonized these targeted groups so as to permit their elimination.

German male homosexuals were targeted and arrested because they would not breed the master race; they were an affront to the Nazi macho image.

In addition to Jews, the Germans systematically killed two groups of victims. Mentally retarded, physically handicapped, or emotionally disturbed Germans were killed in a so-called euthanasia program. They were an embarrassment to the concept of the German master race. Gas chambers and crematoria were developed to kill these Germans. Darwinian ethics were taken to the extreme by the Nazis who believed in survival of the fittest, but were unwilling to wait for natural selection. Certain groups were defined as "life unworthy of living." Roma and Sinti (Gypsies) were also targeted. Their fate most closely paralleled the Jews. The were to be found in ghettos such as Lodz and Warsaw, and they were murdered by the Einsatzgruppen. They too were killed in the gas chambers of Auschwitz—men, women, and children.

During the war, especially the early days of victory, Soviet prisoners of war were targeted for extinction, often by starvation and exposure to the harsh Russian winter. Later, they were allowed to live, sheltered and fed by German officials anxious to use them in forced labor. Slavic nations were heavily decimated. Under the Nazi master plan, they were to become subservient nations to the master race.

WORLD WAR II AND THE WAR AGAINST THE JEWS

The progress of the World War II impacted on the Holocaust. With each German advance more Jews came under Nazi domination; impending German losses often intensified the pace of destruction; each area liberated from German control brought relief to its endangered population—none more endangered than the Jews. In the final months of the war, as camps in the East were being overrun, the Nazis instituted a series of forced evacuations by foot and by rail, hasty retreats of incarcerated concentration camp populations. Few if any provisions were provided; the marches took place in the dead of winter. They were known as death marches, the last ditch effort to keep the living witnesses from being captured by the Allies. For the victims, the struggle was no longer against the Nazis, but against death itself; pushed beyond the limits of endurance, they were forced to draw upon reservoirs of strength.

As the Allied armies swept through Europe in 1944 and 1945, they found seven to nine million displaced people living in countries not their own. More than six million returned to their native lands, but more than one million refused repatriation. Victims became displaced persons, stateless, in search of new homes and new lands. For Jews, there were two types of illegal migration, *Bricha*, the escape from Soviet-held territories to American or British-held territories, and *Aliyah Bet*, efforts to bring displaced persons to Palestine in violation of British policy. With the resettlement of Jews from a trickle in 1945-47 to the mass migrations of 1948 onward, it seemed that the Holocaust had come to its end; the final chapter was written.

I have told a large story in the briefest of outline. Before you are the documents, precise, specific, anguishing. They tell another part, an essential part, of the story. What remains unsaid in these details and what you must bring to this book is an understanding of the human tale, the anguish of the victims, the courage of the resisters, the morality of the rescuers, and the depravity of the perpetrators.

A word about this work. In the library of the Museum's Research Institute there are tens of thousands of pages of Nazi documents that were collected for trials as evidence for the prosecution. Historians have combed the pages of archives to gather collections of documents for scholars. In the Research Institute Archives, the holdings from eastern Europe alone number millions of pages. Obviously, this work makes no claim of inclusiveness. Rather, I have attempted to tell the story of the Holocaust through documents so major elements of what happened can be understood by the reader of the texts.

Throughout, I have tried to help keep the larger issues in perspective. I have endeavored to contextualize the documents you will read, to choose those documents that illustrate the evolution of the Holocaust, and to place them within the evolving history of Nazi policy and within the history of the era so they are understood not in isolation, but as fragments of a whole. Lawyers are prone to say that "the devil is in the details." Nothing could be more true of German policy between 1933 and 1945.

MICHAEL BERENBAUM

WASHINGTON, D.C.

# CHRONOLOGY

1933

Adolph Hitler and Franklin Roosevelt both came to office in 1933 to lead nations uncertain of their future.

In his inaugural address, President Roosevelt told the American people: "We have nothing to fear but fear itself."

Jews in Germany were soon to learn the meaning of fear.

Within Hitler's first month:

> Freedom of speech was suspended.

> Freedom of assembly was restricted.

> Freedom of the press was ended.

Hitler came to power legally. Violence and terror, which had paved the way for his rise, intensified when Hitler became chancellor.

On April 1, 1933, Jewish businesses and offices throughout Germany were boycotted. The attack against Jews had begun.

On April 7, Jews were expelled from the Civil Service.

On May 10, 1933, Nazi students stormed universities, libraries, and bookstores throughout Germany. Hundreds of thousands of books were cast onto bonfires. Some of these books were by Jewish authors. Most were not.

Opposite the main entrance to Berlin University, Propaganda Minister Joseph Goebbels triumphantly proclaimed: "The age of a hairsplitting Jewish intellectualism is dead . . . The past lies in the flames."

A century earlier, Heinrich Heine, a German poet of Jewish origin, had prophesied: "Where one burns books, one will, in the end, burn people."

It took only eight years.

1934

Nazi rule was consolidated and the policies that formed the basis of the German persecution of the Jews were implemented. A stunned Jewish community began the process of adjustment.

As the year begins Germany and Poland signed a ten-year nonaggression pact. An altered curriculum in Jewish schools was designed to nurture both the Jewish and German spirits. Palestine, the Hebrew language, and physical fitness were stressed as never before.

Before the spring semester concluded, non-Aryan medical students were prohibited from taking state medical examinations, and Jewish students in Germany could not receive tuition exemptions.

In June, Hitler ordered SS Chief Heinrich Himmler to purge the SA (stormtroopers) leadership including his closest ally, SA leader Ernst Röhm, in what became known as the "Night of the Long Knives."

By midsummer the commandant of Dachau concentration camp was named inspector of concentration camps and commander of SS guard units, and Austrian Chancellor Engelbert Dollfuss was killed in a failed attempt by Nazis to seize power in Austria.

In August, the German president, Paul von Hindenburg, died; Hitler's dictatorship was firmly set in place.

Within three weeks all officials and soldiers in the Armed Forces had to swear allegiance to Hitler personally, not to the people or the fatherland.

At the September Nazi Party Congress in Nuremberg, Hitler's oratorical powers were on display as he spoke to two hundred thousand political leaders. He proclaimed that the National Socialist Revolution was completed and Germany would not experience another one for the next thousand years.

By December, Bavarian Justice Minister Hans Frank was named to Hitler's cabinet and assigned to bring German law into line with Nazi ideology, to align individuals and institutions with Nazi goals.

1935

At the annual Nazi Party rally in Nuremberg, September 1935, the German parliament decreed the two laws that became the centerpiece of its anti-Jewish legislation: The Law for the Protection of German Blood and Honor and the Reich Citizenship Law.

Citizenship in the Reich was restricted to persons of "German or kindred blood." Only citizens—i.e., racial Germans—had full civil and political rights. Jews could no longer be citizens, merely state subjects.

"To protect German blood and honor" marriages and sexual relations between Jews and "citizens of German or related blood" were prohibited as was the employment of women under the age of forty-five in Jewish households.

Categorization had consequences. Definition was the first step toward destruction.

For the first time in history Jews were persecuted not for the religion they practiced or the beliefs they affirmed, but for the blood of their grandparents.

Thus, under these decrees, Roman Catholic priests and nuns and Protestant pastors who had (or whose parents had) converted to Christianity lost their rights because they were Jews.

Later, the Nazi's imposed the Nuremberg Laws upon the lands they occupied. These regulations served as a "model" for the Nazi's treatment of Gypsies.

1936

The Berlin Olympic Games of 1936 forced Germany to mute some external manifestations of anti-Semitism in an effort to avoid a Western [American] boycott of the games. Hitler was determined to use the games as a means of enhancing his international prestige and his hold on the German people. Still, in March, German forces entered the Rhineland, which had been declared a demilitarized zone and placed under the French sphere of influence in the Treaty of Versailles; the French did not react.

In early May, Ethiopia was attacked and swiftly surrendered to Italy.

In June, Hitler named Heinrich Himmler SS chief and chief of German Police. He swiftly reorganized his empire into the Main Office of the Regular Police (Ordnungspolizei, or Orpo), and the Main Office of the Security Police (Sicherheitspolizei, or Sipo). Orpo comprised uniformed urban, municipal, and rural police. Sipo consisted of the Gestapo and the Criminal Police (Kiriminalpolizei, or Kripo). Each were linked directly to the party, each would play an important role in the Holocaust.

In July, Sachsenhausen concentration camp was established in Germany. Karl Koch was appointed camp commandant. The first fifty prisoners were interned in the camp.

The summer Olympic Games were a smashing success, a propaganda victory for Adolf Hitler despite the four gold medals of American track star Jesse Owens. Marty Glickman and Sam Stollar, two Jewish-American Olympic stars, were benched by U.S. Olympic president Avery Brundage rather than further embarrass Hitler.

Before the school year began, non-Aryan teachers were forbidden to teach and Jews were not to be used as teachers even in private instruction.

By mid-fall, the Berlin-Rome Axis agreement was signed by Hitler and Italian Fascist dictator Benito Mussolini.

The sting of German anti-Semitism is felt even in Warsaw, where the Jewish communal organization, the Kehilla was dissolved for opposing the Polish government's anti-Jewish policies. An appointed commissioner and advisory council were imposed on the community and boycotted by Jewish leadership.

In December the Nuremberg Laws were expanded; a German married to a non-Aryan could not salute the Nazi flag. By the end of the year, the temporary respite was over and the anti-Semitic campaign continued unabated.

1937

In retrospect 1937 appeared as a year of quiet before the storm. In the spring, Pope Pius XI issued the encyclical *Mit brennender Sorge* (With Burning Concern), a statement against racism and extreme nationalism. Shortly thereafter, Jews in Germany were prohibited from giving testimony in courts of law.

In July, a concentration camp at Buchenwald was opened and Karl Koch, commandant of Sachsenhausen concentration camp, was transferred to the new camp.

Nazi anti-Semitism spread to neighboring countries. Attacks on Jews by Poles took place throughout Poland in July; 350 such attacks were recorded.

By the fall, anti-Jewish violence broke out in the Free City of Danzig (a League of Nations–declared international city, between Germany and Poland), directed mainly against Jewish traders and shopkeepers.

Regulations against Jews intensified. Jewish women were arrested for violations of the Nuremberg Law for the Protection of German Blood and Honor which prohibited sexual relations between Germans and Jews. They were sent to concentration camps. By the fall, the German Justice Ministry issued a decree prohibiting Jews from giving the "Nazi salute."

The Interior Ministry decreed that Jews must carry special identity cards when traveling in Germany. The Reich Representation of German Jews (*Reichsvertretung*) publicly summoned the Jews of Germany to demonstrate resoluteness and self-confidence. Such confidence would be shaken in 1938.

In November, Germany and Japan signed a military and political pact. Their alliance was to endure.

1938

Jewish life in Germany came to an end in 1938, so too, the possibility that Germany could be rid of Jews by forced emigration.

On March 12, 1938, Germany entered Austria. Welcomed by the native population, Austria was incorporated into the Reich.

For Jews the annexation spelled doom. The Nazis accomplished within a year what, in Germany, they had failed to achieve in five years—total exclusion from society.

In the five years between 1933–38, more than 150,000 Jews had emigrated from Germany. In one night, 185,000 Jews were added to the Reich's population.

In July, representatives from thirty-two countries gathered at Evian, France for a conference on the Jewish problem convened by President Roosevelt. Pious pronouncements, fancy speeches, but no action resulted.

The United States refugee quotas were rigidly enforced. Britain was unwilling to change its restrictive immigration policies. French transit camps were set up to contain the refugees.

The Germans concluded: "We wanted to get rid of our Jews but the difficulties lay in the fact that no country wished to receive them."

Neutral Switzerland asked that passports of Jews in Germany be marked with the letter J for "Jude."

In November the situation grew more ominous.

On November 9, violence erupted throughout the Reich. Within forty-eight hours, approximately 1,300 synagogues were burned, along with their Torah scrolls, Bibles, and prayer books; 30,000 Jews were arrested and sent to concentration camps; 7,000 businesses were smashed and looted; 236 Jews were killed. Jewish cemeteries, hospitals, schools, and homes were destroyed.

In the aftermath of Kristallnacht, Jews were without illusions. Jewish life in the Reich was no longer possible.

1939

In a speech to the Reichstag on his sixth anniversary in office, the Führer predicted: "The consequence will not be the Bolshevization of the earth and thereby the victory of Jewry, but the annihilation of the Jewish race in Europe."

The British restricted emigration to Palestine.

A piece of paper with a stamp on it was the difference between life and death.

The United States closed its doors to Jewish refugees. The Wagner-Rogers Bill to admit ten thousand refugee children died in Congress.

In May, the S.S. *St. Louis* set sail for Cuba with 936 passengers, most of them Jews. The Cuban government refused to honor their visas.

The captain appealed without avail to the United States for a haven. As the ship sailed off the Miami coast, Coast Guard ships patrolled the waters. The ship returned to Europe.

On September 1, Germany invaded Poland. World War II began. The war was needed, Hitler argued, for *Lebensraum*, living space for the German nation.

More than two million Jews came under Nazi control in September. They were held captive, awaiting a solution more drastic than forced emigration.

Mass murder also began in 1939—not of Jews, but of handicapped and retarded Germans, embarrassments to the master race.

The first killings were by starvation, then injections. Gassing soon became the preferred method of killing. Crematoria were built. Doctors were in charge.

These physicians soon "graduated" at Belzec, Sobibor, Treblinka, and Auschwitz.

1940

On April 9, 1940, Germany invaded Denmark and Norway.

On May 10, German armies approached France through Belgium and the Netherlands in a blitzkrieg, a lightning war. Netherlands and Belgium were conquered. The French Army retreated. On June 10, Paris fell.

Throughout western Europe, the Nazis followed a familiar pattern: Jews were defined, businesses were confiscated, Jews were segregated, marked, and barred from public schools and public places.

In Poland the situation was even more ominous. Within weeks of the Nazi conquest of Poland, Jews were forced to wear the yellow stars. Soon their movements were restricted, local Jewish Councils—*Judenrat*—were formed as instruments of German control.

In 1940, the ghettos of Warsaw and Lodz were sealed. Guards were posted at entrances and exits. Permission forms were required to enter or to leave. These areas were euphemistically called "Jewish residential quarters."

Moving into ghettos was chaotic. In Lodz an area housing sixty-two thousand Jews was set aside as the ghetto. One hundred thousand more Jews had to move into these crowed quarters from other sections of the city. In Warsaw, the ghetto decree was announced on Yom Kippur, the Jewish Day of Atonement. The Warsaw Ghetto contained 30 percent of the city's population on 2.4 percent of the land—an average of 9.2 people per room.

Unlike the earlier ghettos which were permanent, the ghettos in Poland were viewed by the Nazis as a transitional measure. Worse was sure to follow.

1941

The mass murder of Jews began in 1941. On June 21, the German Army invaded Soviet territory; mobile killing units were dispatched on special assignment to kill Jews.

The invasion was followed immediately by the roundup of Jews, Jews but not only Jews; Communists, Gypsies, political leaders, and the intelligentsia were also killed. Those rounded up were marched to the outskirts of the city where they were shot. Their bodies were buried in mass graves—large ditches were filled with bodies of people who had been shot one by one and buried layer upon layer.

Frequently, local pogroms were encouraged especially in Lithuania and Latvia. Auxiliary police comprised of local natives became indispensable. Collaborators volunteered.

On September 19 the German Army captured Kiev. Days later, Kiev's Jews were marched to Babi Yar, two miles from the city center.

Forced to strip, their clothing was gathered and folded. Rings were ripped from fingers of the naked.

Jews were then shot. The dead fell into the ravine. The sounds could be heard in Kiev.

In the days between Rosh Hashanah and Yom Kippur, 33,771 Jews were killed at Babi Yar. And Babi Yar was but one example of the Einsatzgruppen's work.

Before this phase of the killing ended, more than 1.2 million Jews were killed. Yet a new stage of mass killing was only beginning.

In September, there were experiments at Auschwitz with gas chambers and Cyclon-B.

By December 8 actual gassing of Jews had begun in mobile vans at Chelmno death camp. Stationary gas chambers were being erected at Auschwitz and Belzec.

1942

If the Holocaust was a long, seemingly unrelenting journey into darkness, 1942 was the heart of that darkness.

In January 1942, Reinhard Heydrich convened a meeting at a Wannsee Villa. He invited fifteen colleagues, the Reich's best and brightest. More than half of them held advanced degrees from prominent German universities. He announced a change in policy from emigration "to Evacuation to the East," merely a provisional plan for the future "Final Solution to the Jewish problem."

"Evacuation to the East" was a euphemism for concentration camps; "the Final Solution" was systematic murder. The prototypes had already been tested, mobile killing units, gas vans, even plans for Cyclon-B in stationary gas chambers.

The full implications of Wannsee were shown in 1942. During the winter and spring the killing centers of Aktion Reinhard were created—Sobibor, Belzec, Treblinka. They joined Auschwitz, Chelmno, and Majdanek as the six death camps, the Nazi killing centers.

Until 1942, the killers were sent to the victims—after Wannsee the victims were sent to the killers—deportation to death.

In the summer, the ghettos of Poland were emptied. On July 23, the ninth day of the Hebrew month of Av, the anniversary of the destruction of the first and second Temple in Jerusalem in 586 B.C.E. and 70 C.E., deportations began from Warsaw to Treblinka. The ghetto was emptied block by block, building by building. On August 6, 1942, the Nazis struck against the children's institutions in the ghetto. By September, 310,000 Jews from Warsaw had been sent to Treblinka where they were soon gassed; 850,000 Jews were to be killed at Treblinka during the eighteen months it operated.

In early September 1942, the Nazis demanded that all children and old people in the Lodz ghetto be surrendered. Ghetto leader Mordecai Rumkowski complied. "The decree cannot be revoked. It can only be slightly lessened by our carrying it our calmly," he said. In a public speech, he pleaded: "Brothers and sisters, hand them over to me. Fathers and mothers, give me your children."

Throughout the warm summer days and the cool days of autumn, train after train from ghetto after ghetto arrived at the death camps. At Majdanek and Auschwitz there was a *selection*—the old, the infirm and children, mothers and their children were sent to the gas chambers. The able-bodied were to work for a while. At the Aktion Reinhard death camps, the fate of all was equal. There was no reprieve even for those who could work.

And in August, at the height of the deportations from Warsaw, word of the Final Solution reached the United States.

Dr. Gerhart Riegner, the World Jewish Congress representative in Bern, Switzerland, sent a secret cable on August 11, 1942, through secure channels to the State Department and to Rabbi Stephen S. Wise, president of the World Jewish Congress, informing them:

> that there has been and is being considered in Hitler's headquarters a plan to exterminate all Jews from Germany and German-controlled areas in Europe after they have been concentrated in the East. The numbers involved is said to be between three and a half and four million and the object to permanently settle the Jewish question in Europe.

The State Department did not pass on the telegram to Rabbi Wise until he inquired, and when they did they asked him to remain silent until the information could be confirmed. In November, they "regretfully confirmed his darkest fear."

1943

The violence unleashed in the first two years of the Final Solution intensified in 1943.

The Warsaw Ghetto was obliterated after a month of fierce fighting. The ghetto was burned to the ground, block by block, building by building. Mordecai Anielewicz, commander of the Jewish Fighting Organization (ZOB) writes to his colleague, "My life's dream has been realized: I have lived to see Jewish defense in the ghetto in all its greatness and glory."

General Jurgen Stropp wrote to his superiors: "The Jewish Residential Quarter of Warsaw is no longer." In desperation Samuel Zygelbojm, a Jewish representative of the Polish government-in-exile, committed suicide in solidarity with the fighters and to protest the world's silence.

Warsaw was the first ghetto to rise in resistance. By year's end—and on the edge of destruction—Vilna and Bialystock were also to have mass armed public resistance. In August, even in the death camp of Treblinka, the inmates rose in resistance. In the fall, some three hundred Sobibor inmates escaped after a brief resistance. At Janowska labor and extermination camp, a revolt broke out among the Sonderkommando 1005, who had the task of collecting and cremating the bodies of victims. Several camp guards were killed and dozens of prisoners escaped; the majority were caught and shot.

Yet by the time of the revolt, the work of Treblinka and of Sobibor were completed, and the Jews of Poland were decimated. Vilna, Bialystock, and Warsaw were at the end, facing "final liquidation."

It was a year of deportations: the ghettos of Poland were emptied, Jews were deported from Germany, Belgium, the Netherlands, Greece, and Yugoslavia.

On Rosh Hashanah, the Jewish New Year, the order was given to deport the Jews of Denmark, but the Danish population would not consent. In a series of clandestine operations, the Jews of Denmark were ferried to freedom in Sweden.

Bulgaria also protected *its* Jews, but willingly ceded the Jews of Trace and Macedonia.

One after another, mobile killing units reported their great achievements. In the East, the Jews had been annihilated. A special operation was then launched to dig up the bodies that had been buried in mass graves and to burn them; thus to leave no physical evidence of the crime.

U.S. President Franklin Roosevelt and British Prime Minister Winston Churchill met at Casablanca in early winter; the unconditional surrender of Germany was declared a war aim.

The tide of war had shifted after the German Army surrendered to the Red Army at Stalingrad. Allied forces invaded Sicily. For a time, Benito Mussolini fell from power in Fascist Italy.

1944

By the beginning of 1944, one could see the end of the Third Reich. German defeat was inevitable. The Red Army was advancing in the East, the Allies were marching through Italy. The killing of Jews went on unabated, its pace quickened by the looming end.

The United States began its belated rescue efforts only in January 1944 when Secretary of Treasury Henry Morgenthau presented President Roosevelt with decisive new evidence of governmental inaction that Roosevelt knew would be politically explosive if it became public. So the War Refugee Board was established in response to revelations that the United States government had covered up its knowledge of the murder of Jews and actively prevented efforts that might have rescued them.

In March 1944, Germany occupied its ally Hungary. In sixty days, Hungarian Jewry replicated the fate of the Jews of Europe—definition, confiscation of property and possessions, the yellow star, ghettoization, and deportation. Between May 14 and July 8, 437,402 Jews were deported to Auschwitz on 148 trains. Hungary was without Jews, except for the Jews of Budapest.

The War Refugee Board sought international help in an attempt to protect Hungarian Jews. Overtures were made to neutral countries, the Vatican, and the International Red Cross. Only Sweden answered the call.

Raoul Wallenberg was chosen to lead the rescue operation. He was given a diplomatic passport, a large sum of money, and carte blanche to use whatever methods he wished, however unorthodox, to rescue Jews. He immediately began issuing Jews with impressive looking passports bearing the Swedish seal. The first batch of five thousand was only the beginning. Other neutral missions followed Wallenberg's lead.

In November, Eichmann organized a series of forced marches. He ordered the roundup of all Jewish men between the ages of sixteen and sixty. A large group of Jews was marched to the Austrian border in the first of a series of death marches. Wallenberg reacted immediately. He issued thousands of Swedish safe passes, pursued convoys carrying Jews, halted trains about to depart for Auschwitz, and roamed through the city, badgering German and Hungarian officers to release Jews in their custody.

But the War Refugee Board was only partially successful. In the summer of 1944, it asked that Auschwitz be bombed. The response from the War Department was misleading and bureaucratic. Assistant Secretary of War John J. McCloy wrote:

such an operation could be executed only by the diversion of considerable air forces now engaged in decisive operations elsewhere and would be of such doubtful efficacy that it would not warrant the use of our resources. There has been considerable opinion to the effect that such an effort, even if practicable, might provoke even more vindictive action by the Germans.

During the summer of 1944, Soviet forces overran Belzec, Treblinka, and Sobibor, the killing centers which had been closed a year earlier when the annihilation of Polish Jews was virtually complete. The SS had burned Treblinka and turned it into a farm. At Belzec, pine trees had been planted to conceal the camp. Still, soldiers found bones protruding from the ground.

On July 23, 1944, Soviet troops arrived at the death camp of Majdanek, just outside the Polish city of Lublin. As the Red Army advanced to the outskirts of Lublin, the SS hastened to hide, bury, and burn the evidence of their crime. They simply ran out of time. When the Soviets entered they found few prisoners, but ample evidence remained, including a storehouse of eight hundred thousand shoes. And survivors ready to testify.

1945

The final year of the war was a race against time. Defeated in war, the Nazis tried to win the war against the Jews.

Roosevelt, Churchill, and Stalin met for a final time in Yalta, in the USSR, to discuss the postwar aim of "denazifying" Germany.

In January, between ten and twenty thousand Jews of Budapest, the last Jewish community in Europe, were shot along the banks of the Danube River by Hungarian fascists. Protected Jews—Wallenberg Jews—were forced to move into the city's central ghetto. The Swedish diplomat traded food to stop the transfers and intervened to halt attempts to burn the ghetto. Tens of thousands of Jewish lives were saved. As the Soviet army entered Budapest, Wallenberg negotiated to ensure proper care of the liberated Jews. Suspected of spying, he disappeared into the Soviet gulags.

At Birkenau extermination camp, demolition squads frantically hid evidence of mass murder by dismantling crematoria and gas chambers. Storehouses and records were burned. To avoid capture of the inmates—living witnesses—sixty thousand were hastily evacuated to concentration camps in the German heartland. In the harsh Polish winter, they walked inland without food or shelter in death marches.

On January 27, Soviet forces entered Auschwitz. They found 348,820 men's suits, 836,255 woman's coats, 13,964 carpets and more than seven tons of human hair. Since 1942, between 1.1 million and 1.3 million Jews and thousands of Soviet POWs, Poles, and Gypsies were murdered there.

Liberation reveals the magnitude of the loss. In Poland, the Soviets entered Czestochowa and found 800 Jews left in Czestochowa from the city's prewar Jewish population of 28,500. In Kielce, 25 Jews were left from a prewar Jewish population of 24,000. In Kraków, only a few Jews were alive in what had once been the home of 60,000 Jews, and in Lodz 877 Jews were found alive—800 who had been left to clean the ghetto, and 77 in hiding—from a ghetto of 164,000.

The evacuations of concentration camps continued until the end, so too the discoveries. Forty thousand prisoners were force-marched from Gross-Rosen and its satellite camps. Thousands were murdered en route; the remainder arrived at Bergen-Belsen, Buchenwald, Dachau, Flossenburg, Mauthausen, Mittelbau, and Sachsenhausen concentration camps. So too, in Neuengamme and Flossenburg, thousands of prisoners died en route.

As the Soviet army encircled Stutthof concentration camp, the Nazis began the final evacuation of the camp's forty-five hundred remaining prisoners. The prisoners were evacuated on ferryboats by way of the Baltic Sea; two hundred female Jewish prisoners were the first to be driven to the sea shore and shot. Two thousand prisoners were drowned or shot by the Nazis on the open sea.

In April, advancing American and British forces came upon the concentration camps. Buchenwald, Mauthausen, and Dachau were liberated by the Americans. The British army liberated Bergen-Belsen concentration camp and found fifty-eight thousand surviving prisoners, mostly Jews, all in critical condition. Thirteen thousand corpses are found. During the next five days, fourteen thousand prisoners died, and in the following few weeks another fourteen thousand perished.

In April Roosevelt died and Hitler committed suicide. In May, the Germans surrendered to the Allies. Nazi General Alfred Jodl signed an unconditional surrender at the headquarters of U.S. General Dwight Eisenhower.

On May 8, V-E Day, the war in Europe officially ended. Thirty million Europeans, soldiers and civilians, were casualties of World War II. Among these dead were some six million Jews, victims of the Holocaust along with millions of Soviet prisoners of war, hundreds of thousands of Gypsies, Poles, and mentally handicapped, thousands of Jehovah's Witnesses, homosexuals, and others.

The long task of rebuilding began.

Reichminister Joseph Goebbels delivers a speech in the Berlin Lustgarten urging Germans to boycott Jewish-owned businesses. He defended the boycott as a legitimate response to anti-German propaganda being spread abroad by "international Jewry." April 1, 1933. National Archives/Courtesy of USHMM–Photo Archives.

I. THE BOYCOTT

On 10:00 A.M. Saturday April 1, 1933, the Nazis began a boycott of Jewish businesses and offices in cities and towns throughout Germany. It was the first systematic act attacking Jewish economic life in Germany. Storm troopers, the Nazi Party militia, were stationed at the entrances to Jewish shops. The Star of David was painted in yellow and black across thousands of doors and windows. Signs read: "Germans Defend Yourselves! Don't Buy from Jews," "The Jews are Our Misfortune," or "Jude" [Jew].

In the first sixty days of the Nazi regime, most violence against the Jews had been directed against individuals. The boycott was the first nationwide act against the entire German Jewish community.

The decision to boycott was made directly by Hitler. He was stung by criticism of his regime abroad and faced pressure from Nazi Party militants at home. Foreign protests of the Nazi regime had intensified in response to reports of increased violence against German Jews and Jewish businesses. There had also been some discussion of an American boycott of German goods.

With the American threat as pretext, Hitler set the party machinery in motion. Joseph Goebbels, the Minister of Public Enlightenment and Propaganda, was summoned by Hitler on March 26. Of the instructions he received, Goebbels wrote: "We must . . . proceed to a large scale boycott of Jewish businesses in Germany. Perhaps the foreign Jews will think better of the matter when their racial comrades in Germany begin to get it in the neck."

The boycott began within a week.

Scheduled to last for five days, the boycott ended within twenty-four hours. It could be reimposed at a moment's notice.

For many Jews in Germany, the boycott was a sign of things to come.

Some fled. Some took their own lives in despair. Others appealed to the German public's better judgment, urging noncompliance with the boycott through leaflets and advertisements.

Others became defiant. Robert Weltsch, editor of a German-language Jewish newspaper, saw the Star of David used by the boycotters as a sign of shame. He recalled the medieval markings imposed on German Jews and, eerily anticipating future humiliations, he urged his readers: "Wear it with Pride, the Yellow Badge."

One week after the boycott, the government announced the first of a series of laws discriminating against the Jews. Less grandiose, but far more ominous than the boycott, these laws demonstrated the Nazi determination to be rid of the Jews.

In the sections below, we will read an anonymous declaration signed by the "Party Leadership," but reflecting in style and attitude Hitler's initiative. Historians believe that the eleven points of implementation are the work of Goebbels, holder of a Ph.D. in literature and philosophy from the University of Heidelberg, whose task it was to round up support for this effort, and from whose Diary we will read.

We will also read Robert Weltsch's response to the boycott, a call to self-acknowledgment, a call to greatness.

DECLARATION OF THE BOYCOTT BY THE NAZI PARTY LEADERSHIP

MARCH 28, 1933

National Socialists! Party Comrades!

After fourteen years of inner conflict, the German Volk—politically overcoming its ranks, classes, professions, and confessional divisions—has elected an *Erhebung* which put a lightning end to the Marxist-Jewish nightmare.

In the weeks following January 30, a unique military revolution took place in Germany.

In spite of long years of exceedingly severe suppression and persecution, the masses of millions that support the Government of the National Revolution have, in a very calm and disciplined manner, given the new Reich leadership legal cover for the implementation of its reform of the German nation from top to bottom. On March 5 the overwhelming majority of Germans eligible to vote declared its confidence in the new regime. The completion of the national revolution has thus become the demand of the *Volk*.

The Jewish-Marxist *Bonzen* (bigwigs) deserted their position of power with deplorable cowardice. Despite all the fuss, not a single one dared to raise any serious resistance.

For the most part, they have left the masses they had seduced in the lurch and fled abroad, taking with them their stuffed strongboxes.

The authors and beneficiaries of our misfortune owe the fact that they were spared—almost without exception—solely to the incomparable discipline and order with which this act of overthrowing was conducted.

Hardly a hair on their heads was harmed.

Compare this act of self-discipline on the part of the national uprising in Germany with, for instance, the Bolshevist Revolution in Russia, which claimed the lives of over three million people, and you will begin to appreciate what a debt of gratitude the criminals guilty of the disintegration in Germany owe the powers of the national uprising. Compare the terrible battles and destruction of the Revolution of these very November Men themselves—their shooting of hostages in the years 1918 and '19, the slaughtering of defenseless opponents—and you will once again perceive how enormous the difference is between them and the national uprising.

The men presently in power solemnly proclaimed to the world that they wanted to live in international peace. In this, the German *Volk* constitutes a loyal *Gefolgschaft* [following]. Germany wants neither worldwide confusion nor international intrigues. National revolutionary Germany is firmly resolved to put an end to internal mismanagement!

Now that the domestic enemies of the nation have been eliminated by the *Volk* itself, what we have long been waiting for will now come to pass. The Communist and Marxist criminals and their Jewish intellectual instigators, who, having made off with their capital stocks across the border in the nick of time, are now unfolding an unscrupulous, treasonous campaign of agitation against the German *Volk* as a whole from abroad. Because it became impossible for them to continue lying in Germany, they have begun, in the capitals of the former Entente, to continue the same agitation against the young national uprising that they had already pursued at the outbreak of the War against the Germany of that time.

Lies and slander of positively hair-raising perversity are being launched about Germany. Horror stories of dismembered Jewish corpses, gouged-out eyes, and hacked-off hands are circulated for the purpose of defaming the German *Volk* in the world for a second time, just as they had succeeded in doing once before in 1914. The animosity of millions of innocent human beings, i.e., peoples with whom the German *Volk* wishes only to live in peace, is being stirred up by these unscrupulous criminals. They want German goods and German labor to fall victim to the international boycott. It seems they think the misery in Germany is not bad enough as it is; they have to make it worse!

They lie about Jewish females who have supposedly been killed, about Jewish girls allegedly being raped before the eyes of their parents, about cemeteries being ravaged! The whole thing is one big lie invented for the sole purpose of provoking a new world-war agitation!

Standing by and watching this lunatic crime any longer would mean being implicated.

The National Socialist Party will therefore now take defensive action against this universal crime with means that are capable of striking a blow to the guilty parties.

For the guilty ones are among us, they live in our midst and day after day misuse the right to hospitality which the German *Volk* has granted them.

At a time when millions of our people have nothing to live on and nothing to eat, while hundreds of thousands of German brain-workers degenerate on the streets, these intellectual Jewish men of letters are sitting in our midst and have no qualms about claiming the right to our hospitality.

What would America do were the Germans in America to commit a sin against America like the one these Jews have committed against Germany? The National Revolution did not harm a hair of their heads. They were allowed to go about their business as before; but, mind you, corruption will be exterminated, regardless of who commits it. Just as belonging to a Christian confession or our own *Volk* does not constitute a license for criminals, neither does belonging to the Jewish race or the Mosaic religion.

For decades, Germany indiscriminately allowed all aliens to enter the country. There are 135 people to one square kilometer of land in this country.

In America there are less than 15. In spite of this fact, America saw it fit to set quotas for immigration and even exclude certain peoples from immigrating.

Without any regard to its own distress, Germany refrained for decades from instituting these measures. As our reward, we now have a clique of Jewish men of letters, professors, and profiteers inciting the world against us while millions of our own *Volksgenossen* are unemployed and degenerating.

This will be put to a stop now!

The Germany of the National Revolution is not the Germany of a cowardly bourgeois mentality.

We see the misery and wretchedness of our own *Volksgenossen* and feel obliged to leave nothing undone which could prevent further damage to this, our *Volk*.

For the parties responsible for these lies and slander are the Jews in our midst. It is they who are the source of this campaign of hate and lies against Germany. It would be in their power to call the liars in the rest of the world into line.

Because they choose not to do so, we will make sure that this crusade of hatred and lies against Germany is no longer directed against the innocent German *Volk*, but against the responsible agitators themselves.

This smear campaign of boycotting and atrocities must not and shall not injure the German *Volk*, but rather the Jews themselves— a thousand times more severely.

Thus the following order is issued to all party sections and party organizations:

ITEM 1: ACTION COMMITTEES FOR A BOYCOTT AGAINST THE JEWS

Action Committees are to be formed in each *Ortsgruppe* [local chapter] and organizational body of the NSDAP for conducting a practical, organized boycott of Jewish businesses, Jewish goods, Jewish doctors, and Jewish lawyers. The Action Committees shall be responsible for ensuring that the boycott does not do any harm to innocent parties but instead does all the more harm to the guilty parties.

ITEM 2: UTMOST PROTECTION FOR ALL FOREIGNERS

The Action Committees shall be responsible for providing the utmost protection for all foreigners, without regard to their religion and origins or race. The boycott is a purely defensive action that is aimed exclusively at the *Judentum* in Germany.

ITEM 3: BOYCOTT PROPAGANDA

The Action Committees shall immediately popularize the boycott by means of propaganda and enlightenment. Basic principle: no good German is still buying from a Jew or allowing the Jew or his henchmen to offer him goods. The boycott must be a universal one. It will be borne by the entire *Volk* and must hit Jewry where it is most vulnerable.

ITEM 4: THE CENTRAL MANAGEMENT: PG. STREICHER

In cases of doubt, one is to refrain from boycotting businesses until informed otherwise by the Central Committee in Munich. The Chairman of the Central Committee is Pg. Streicher.

ITEM 5: SURVEILLANCE OF NEWSPAPERS

The Action Committees shall keep the newspapers under sharp surveillance in order to ascertain the extent to which they are participating in the enlightenment crusade of the German *Volk* against the Jewish smear campaign of atrocities [*Greuelhetze*] abroad. If newspapers are not doing so or doing so only within a limited scope, it is to be seen to that they are instantly removed from every building inhabited by Germans. No German man and no German business is to continue advertising in such newspapers. These papers must become victims of public contempt, written for fellow members of the Jewish race, but not for the German *Volk*.

ITEM 6: BOYCOTT AS A MEANS OF PROTECTING GERMAN LABOR

In conjunction with the factory cell organizations of the party, the Action Committees must carry the propaganda of the enlightenment concerning the effects of the Jewish smear campaign of atrocities on German labor and thus the German worker into the factories, enlightening the workers in particular as to the necessity of a national boycott as a defensive measure for the protection of German labor.

ITEM 7: ACTION COMMITTEES DOWN TO THE LAST VILLAGE!

The Action Committees must be driven into the smallest villages in order to hit especially the Jewish traders on the flatlands.

As a basic principle, it should be stressed that the boycott is a defensive measure which was forced upon us.

ITEM 8: THE BOYCOTT IS TO COMMENCE ON APRIL 1!

The boycott shall not begin in a dissipated fashion but abruptly. For this reason all preparations are to be made instantly. The SA and SS will be given orders to set up guards to warn the population not to set foot in Jewish shops from the moment the boycott begins. The beginning of the boycott is to be publicized on posters and in the press, in handbills, etc.

The boycott shall commence abruptly at 10:00 in the morning on Saturday, April 1. It will be maintained until an order from the party leadership commands that it be discontinued.

ITEM 9: DEMAND OF THE MASSES FOR RESTRICTED ADMISSION

In tens of thousands of mass assemblies that are to reach as far as the smallest village, the Action Committees shall organize the demand for the introduction of a restriction of the number of Jews employed in all professions which should be relative to their proportion in the German population. In order to increase the impact of the action, this demand is initially to be confined to three areas:

A. admission to the German secondary schools and universities;
B. the medical profession;
C. the legal profession.

ITEM 10: ENLIGHTENMENT ABROAD

Another further task of the Action Committees is to ensure that every German who upholds any connection whatsoever abroad shall make use of this to circulate in letters, telegrams, and telephone calls in an enlightening manner the truth that law and order reigns in Germany; that it is the single most ardent wish of the German *Volk* to be able to pursue its work in peace and live in peace with the rest of the world; and that it is fighting the battle against the Jewish smear campaign of atrocities purely as a defensive battle.

ITEM 11: CALM, DISCIPLINE, AND NO ACTS OF VIOLENCE!

The Action Committees are responsible for ensuring that this entire battle is conducted with the utmost calm and the greatest discipline. Refrain from harming a single hair of a Jew's head in the future as well! We will come to terms with this smear campaign simply by the drastic force of these measures cited.

More than ever before it is necessary that the entire party stand behind the leadership in blind obedience as one man.

National Socialists, you have wrought the miracle of sending the November State cartwheeling in a single offensive; you will accomplish this second task the same way. International *Weltjudentum* should know one thing:

The government of the National Revolution does not exist in a vacuum. It is the representation of the working German *Volk*. Whoever attacks it, is attacking Germany! Whoever slanders it, is slandering the nation! Whoever fights it, has declared war on 65 million people! We were able to come to terms with the Marxist agitators in Germany; they will not force us to our knees, even if they are now proceeding with their renegade crimes against the people from abroad.

National Socialists! Saturday, at the stroke of ten, *Judentum* will know upon whom it has declared war.

National Socialist German Workers' Party/Party Leadership

Extract from Joseph Goebbels's Diary

APRIL 1, 1933

The boycott against the international atrocity propaganda has burst forth in full force in Berlin and the whole Reich. I drive along the Tauentzien Street in order to observe the situation. All Jewish businesses are closed. SA men are posted outside their entrances. The public has everywhere proclaimed its solidarity. The discipline is exemplary. An imposing performance! It all takes place in complete quiet; in the Reich too ...

In the afternoon 150,000 Berlin workers marched to the Lustgarten, to join us in the protest against the incitement abroad. There is indescribable excitement in the air. The press is already operating in total unanimity. The boycott is a great moral victory for Germany. We have shown the world abroad that we can call up the entire nation without thereby causing the least turbulence or excesses. The Führer has once more struck the right note.

At midnight the boycott will be broken off by our own decision. We are now waiting for the resultant echo in the foreign press and propaganda.

APRIL 2, 1933

The effects of the boycott are already clearly noticeable. The world is gradually coming to its

A Jewish-owned store is covered with graffiti and plastered with signs of rhyming anti-Semitic verse. April 1, 1933. Courtesy of USHMM–Photo Archives.

senses. It will learn to understand that it is not wise to let itself be informed on Germany by the Jewish emigrés. We will have to carry out a campaign of mental conquest in the world as effective as that which we have carried out in Germany itself.

In the end the world will learn to understand us.

(Source: J. Goebbels, *Mom taiscrhof zur Reichskanzlei* [From the Emperor's court to the Reich chancellery], Munich, 1937, pp. 291–292.)

"WEAR IT WITH PRIDE, THE YELLOW BADGE"
Robert Weltsch

The first of April, 1933, will remain an important date in the history of German Jewry—indeed, in the history of the entire Jewish people. The events of that day have aspects that are not only political and economic, but moral and spiritual as well. The political and economic implications have been widely discussed in the press, though of course the need for agitation has frequently obscured objective understanding. To speak of the moral aspect, that is our task. For however much the Jewish question is now debated, nobody except ourselves can express what is to be said on these events from the Jewish point of view, what is happening in the soul of the German Jew. Today the Jews cannot speak except as Jews. Anything else is utterly senseless . . . Gone is the fatal misapprehension of many Jews that Jewish interests can be pressed under some other cover. On April 1 the German Jews learned a lesson which penetrates far more deeply than even their embittered and now triumphant opponents could assume . . .

We live in a new period, the national revolution of the German people is a signal that is visible from afar, indicating that the world of our previous concepts has collapsed. That may be painful for many, but in this world only those who are able to look reality in the eye will be able to survive. We stand in the midst of tremendous changes in intellectual, political, social and economic life. It is for us to see how the Jews will react.

April 1, 1933, can become the day of Jewish awakening and Jewish rebirth. If the Jews will it. If the Jews are mature and have greatness in them. If the Jews are not as they are represented to be by their opponents.

The Jews, under attack, must learn to acknowledge themselves.

Even in these days of most profound disturbance, when the stormiest of emotions have visited our hearts in face of the unprecedented display of the universal slander of the entire Jewish population of a great and cultural country, we must first of all maintain: composure. Even if we stand shattered by the events of these days we must not lose heart and must examine the situation without any attempt to deceive ourselves. One would like to recommend in these days that the document that stood at the cradle of Zionism, Theodor Herzl's "Jewish State," be distributed in hundreds of thousands of copies among Jews and non-Jews . . .

They accuse us today of treason against the German people: the National-Socialist Press calls us the "enemy of the Nation," and leaves us defenseless.

It is not true that the Jews betrayed Germany. If they betrayed anyone, it was themselves, the Jews. Because the Jew did not display his Judaism with pride, because he tried to avoid the Jewish issue, he must bear part of the blame for the degradation of the Jews.

Despite all the bitterness that we must feel in full measure when we read the National-Socialist boycott proclamations and unjust accusations, there is one point for which we may be grateful to the Boycott Committee. Para. 3 of the Directives reads: "The reference is . . . of course to businesses owned by members of the Jewish race. Religion plays no part here. Businessmen who were baptized Catholic or Protestant, or Jews who left their community remain Jews for the purpose of this order." This is a [painful] reminder for all those who betrayed their Judaism. Those who steal away from the community in order to benefit their personal position should not collect the wages of their betrayal. In taking up this position against the renegades there is the beginning of a clarification. The Jew who denies his Judaism is no better a citizen than his fellow who avows it openly. It is shameful to be a renegade, but as long as the world around us rewarded it, it appeared an advantage. Now even that is no longer an advantage. The Jew is marked as a Jew. He gets the yellow badge.

A powerful symbol is to be found in the fact that the boycott leadership gave orders that a sign "with a yellow badge on a black background" was to be pasted on the boycotted shops. This regulation is intended as a brand, a sign of contempt. We will take it up and make of it a badge of honor.

Many Jews suffered a crushing experience on Saturday. Suddenly they were revealed as Jews, not as a matter of inner avowal, not in loyalty to their own community, not in pride in a great past and great achievements, but by the impress of a red placard with a yellow patch. The patrols moved from house to house, stuck their placards on shops and signboards, daubed the windows, and for twenty-four hours the German Jews were exhibited in the stocks, so to speak. In addition to other signs and inscriptions one often saw windows bearing a large Magen David, the Shield of David the King. It was intended as dishonor. Jews, take it up, the Shield of David, and wear it with pride! . . .

(Source: *Judische Rundschau*, No. 27, April 4, 1933.)

II. THE FIRST REGULATORY ASSAULT AGAINST JEWS

The April 1 boycott of Jewish businesses was the first step in the disenfranchisement of Jews. Within the month, two major decrees were added that deprived some Jews of their livelihood and pension benefits as well as distanced them from Germans whom the Nazis regarded as Aryan. The law for the Restoration of the Professional Civil Service of April 7, 1933, fired Jewish civil servants. The language was precise: "Civil servants who are not of Aryan descent are to be retired."

As an accommodation to aging President von Hindenburg, a World War I hero, an exception was made for those Jews who had fought at the front during World War I or whose fathers or sons were killed in action, as well as for those who had served since August 1, 1914.

This exempted many German Jews and took some of the sting out of the decree. It also divided German Jews between those who had served their nation and thus proved their Germanness (for a time) and those who had not. German Jews had demonstrated their patriotism during World War I as American Jews were to do in World War II. More than one hundred thousand—one of every six Jews in the population—served in the army, four of five in combat roles. Thirty-five thousand were decorated for bravery, and twelve thousand lost their lives. Under the Weimar Republic, Jews served in high office, held important places in the civil service and the judiciary, and studied and taught in Germany's great universities.

Within the month, the Law Against the Overcrowding of German Schools and Institutions of Higher Learning was promulgated; a quota was introduced restricting the number of Jewish students in secondary and higher education. Here, too, exemptions were made for children of veterans, and additional exceptions were made for children of the intermarried. A student with one Aryan parent or two Aryan grandparents was exempted. After the Nuremberg Laws of 1935, their situation would be compromised.

The end of German Jewry came gradually. In the fall of 1933, non-Aryan editors were fired from newspapers; later, Jews were expelled from the guilds set up under the Reich Chamber of Culture by Dr. Goebbels in order to make sure artists were politically accept-able to the Reich.

LAW FOR THE RESTORATION OF THE PROFESSIONAL CIVIL SERVICE

APRIL 7, 1933

The Reich Government has enacted the following law, promulgated herewith:

1

1. To restore a national professional civil service and to simplify administration, civil servants may be dismissed from office in accordance with the following regulations, even where there would be no grounds for such action under the prevailing law.

Portrait of a Jewish schoolboy. Jews were forced to wear the yellow star in Germany beginning September 1941, two years after the decree was introduced in Poland. Yad Vashem.

2. For the purposes of this law the following are to be considered civil servants: direct and indirect officials of the Reich, direct and indirect officials of the Länder, officials of local councils, and of the federations of local councils, officials of public corporations as well as of institutions and enterprises of equivalent status. . . . The provisions will apply also to officials of social insurance organizations having the status of civil servants. . . .

2

1. Officials who entered service after November 9th, 1918 without having the required or customary education or ability are to be dismissed. Their salaries are to be paid to them for three consecutive months after their dismissal.
2. They have no claim whatever to temporary allowance, pension or sustenance of their survivors nor any claim to remaining in possession of their titles and uniforms.
3. In case of distress, especially if they have to care for poor relatives, they may obtain an annuity up to a third of the salary they received in their last position. This annuity, however, may be withdrawn at any time. They have no claim to being insured ex post according to the provisions of the Reich Social Insurance.
4. The provisions of paragraphs 2 and 3 are similarly to be applied to persons described in paragraph 1 who have retired before this law becomes effective.

3

1. Civil servants of non-Aryan descent must retire; as regards the honorary officials, they must be discharged.

2. The above paragraph does not apply to officials who were already employed as civil servants on or before August 1st, 1914, or who, during the World War, fought at the front for Germany or her allies, or whose fathers or sons were killed in action in the World War.

3. Further exceptions may be granted by the Reich minister of the interior in cooperation with the competent heads of the specific ministries, or by the supreme authorities of the States, as to civil servants working abroad.

4

Officials who, judged from their previous political activity, do not warrant that they will always unreservedly stand for their national country, may be dismissed. For three consecutive months after their dismissal they get their regular salaries. After that time they get three-quarters of their pension and corresponding maintenance of their survivors.

5

1. Every official must consent to being removed to a different office of the same or an equal career, even to an office of a lesser rank and salary, the costs for changing the residence being compensated for, if service demands it. The official who is removed to an office of lesser rank and salary retains his former title and salary.

2. The official may, within one month, demand retirement instead of removal to an office of lesser rank and salary (paragraph 1).

6

For the purpose of simplifying the administration, officials may be retired even if they are not yet unfit for service. When officials are retired for this reason, the vacancy must not be filled.

7

1. Dismissal, removal to another office and retirement are decreed by the supreme authority of the Reich or States which makes final decisions barring the legal way.

2. The provisions according to 2 to 6 must be carried through at the latest by September 30th, 1933. This time may be shortened in cooperation with the minister of the interior, if the competent supreme authorities of the Reich or States declare that within their administration the provisions of this law are carried through.

8

Officials who are retired or dismissed according to 3, 4, are not granted a pension, if they have not at least completed a ten-year service; this also applies to cases where according to the existing provisions of the laws of the Reich and States a pension is being granted after a shorter term of service. Sections 36, 47 and 49 of the Reich Civil Service Law, the law of July 4th, 1921, concerning an increased computation of the term of service during the war (*Reichsgesetzblatt*, page 825) and similar provisions of the Civil Service Laws are not affected hereby.

9

For officials dismissed or retired according to sections 3, 4, the following provisions in regard to pensions are to be applied:

1. According to the existing provisions, only time served in the Reich, States or Communes may be taken into consideration when computing the term of service worthy of pension, beside service completed in the last position. Even computation of this service is only admissible if it is connected with the last position in education and career; such a connection especially is to be found if the elevation of an official from a lesser career to a higher one is to be regarded as a due advancement. If

the official would have obtained a higher pension in a former position duly acquired through education and ability by adding the later years of service, the provision that is more favorable for the official is applied.

2. The computation of the length of service with public law bodies and similar organizations is regulated by the provisions as to the execution of the law.

3. Settlements and promises as to pension for services which do not conform with the execution of the provisions of paragraph 1 become invalid.

4. The minister of the interior in cooperation with the minister of finances may adjust the rigors of the law affecting officials of the Reich and the public law bodies that are subject to supervision by the Reich; rigors affecting other officials may be adjusted by the supreme authorities of the States.

5. Sections 1 to 4 as well as 8 are also to be applied to officials who definitely or temporarily retired before this law becomes effective and to whom sections 2 to 4 could have been applied if the officials had still been in service at the time when this law becomes effective.

The new settlement of the length of service as regards pension and the settlement of the pension proper or of the temporary allowance must be made at the latest by September 30th, 1933, effective October 1st, 1933.

10

1. Directions given as to the amount of the salaries of officials must serve as a basis for fixing the salaries and pensions. If decisions of the competent authorities as to application of the directions are not at hand as yet, they must be made without delay.

2. If officials according to the decision of the competent authority as to the application of the directions have obtained higher salaries than they were entitled to, they have to return the surplus they received since April

1st, 1932 to the pay office from which the salaries were paid. The objection that enrichment no longer exists (section 812 ff, Civil Law Book) is excluded.

3. Sections 1 and 2 also apply to persons who have retired within one year before this law becomes effective.

11

For officials retired from office according to sections 3, 4, the following provisions with regard to pensions are to be applied:

1. If, in fixing the term of service with regard to pension, service outside the territory of the Reich, the States or Communes has been added, the term of service must be fixed anew. Only employment in the service of the Reich, the States, Communes, or public law bodies and similar institutions and organizations, according to the provisions for executing this law, may be computed. The Reich minister of the interior in cooperation with the Reich minister of finances may make exceptions for officials of the Reich, the supreme authorities of the States may make exceptions for other officials.

2. If according to section 1 the term of service with regard to salary is to be fixed anew, the new settlement of pension must be made in the case of officials who have been dismissed or retired according to sections 3, 4.

3. The same applies to persons mentioned in section 9, paragraph 5.

12

1. The salaries of the Reich ministers appointed since November 9th, 1918 that have not been fixed according to the provisions of sections 16 to 24 of the Law Concerning the Reich Ministers, of March 27th, 1930 (*Reichsgesetzblatt* I, page 96), be fixed anew. In making the new settlement, the above provisions of the Law Concerning the Reich Ministers are applied in such a

way, as if they had already been in force at time of the retirement of the minister from office. Accordingly, surplus received since April 1st, 1932 is to be returned. The objection that enrichment no longer exists (section 812 ff, Civil Law Book) is inadmissible.

2. Paragraph 1 applies to members of a State government appointed since November 9th, 1918 with the modification instead of the Law Concerning the Reich Ministers, the respective provisions of the State laws are applied. But salaries may be paid only up to an amount that is in keeping with the rules of sections 16 to 24 of the Law Concerning the Reich Ministers.

3. The new settlement of the salaries must be made not later than December 31st, 1933.

4. Additional payments are not made.

13

The pensions of the survivors are computed by appropriately applying sections 8 to 12.

14

1. Even after dismissal or retirement of officials according to this law disciplinary proceedings may be instituted against them for the purpose of deprivation of pension, sustenance of survivor title and uniform because of crimes committed in office. Proceedings must be instituted at the latest by December 31st, 1933.

2. Paragraph 1 also applies to persons who have retired within one year before this law becomes effective and to whom sections 2 to 4 would have been applicable if these persons had still been in office at the time when this law becomes effective.

15

The provisions concerning officials similarly apply to clerks and workers.

Details are regulated through provisions as to executing the law.

16

If in executing this law there appear unjust rigors, higher salaries or transitional fees may be granted within the scope of the general provisions. Decisions hereto are made by the minister of the interior in cooperation with the minister of finances for officials of the Reich, and by the supreme authorities of the States for other officials.

17

1. The Reich minister of the interior in cooperation with the Reich minister of finances issues the necessary regulations and administrative provisions for carrying out and executing this law.

2. If necessary the supreme authorities of the States issue supplementary regulations. In doing so they must confine themselves to the framework of the regulations of the Reich.

18

At the end of the terms fixed in this law, the general provisions as to the Professional Civil Service will be put into force again without derogation of the measures taken on the basis of this law.

Berlin, April 7th, 1933.
The Reich Chancellor
ADOLF HITLER

The Reich Minister of the Interior
FRICK

The Reich Minister of Finances
COUNT SCHWERIN VON KROSIGK

Law Against the Overcrowding of German Schools and Institutions of Higher Learning

April 25, 1933

The Reich government has enacted the following law, which is promulgated herewith:

1

In all schools except schools providing compulsory education, and in institutions of higher learning, the number of pupils and students is to be limited so as to ensure thorough training and to meet professional needs.

2

State governments will determine at the beginning of each school year how many pupils each school may accept and how many new students each university faculty may accept.

3

In those kinds of schools and faculties whose attendance figures are particularly out of propor-

Jewish children with their teacher. Karlsruhe. 1937.

tion to professional needs, the number of pupils and students already admitted is to be reduced during the 1933 school year as far as this can be done without excessive rigor, in order to establish a more acceptable proportion.

4

In new admissions, care is to be taken that the number of Reich Germans who, according to the Law for the Restoration of the Professional Civil Service of April 7, 1933 (RGBI. I, p. 175), are of non-Aryan descent, out of the total attending each school and each faculty, does not exceed the proportion of non-Aryans within the Reich German population. The ratio will be determined uniformly for the entire Reich territory.

Likewise, in lowering the number of pupils and students according to section 3, a suitable proportion is to be established between the total number of persons attending and the number of non-Aryans. In doing so, a quota higher than the population ratio may be used as a base.

Paragraphs 1 and 2 do not apply to Reich Germans of non-Aryan descent whose fathers fought at the front during the World War for the German Reich or its allies, or to the offspring of marriages concluded before this law took effect, if one parent or two grandparents are of Aryan origin. These also are not to be included in calculating the population ratio and the quota.

5

Obligations incumbent upon Germany as a result of international treaties are not affected by the provisions of this law.

6

Decrees for implementation will be issued by the Reich minister of the interior.

7

The law takes effect on the date of promulgation.

III. EARLY EFFORTS AT SPIRITUAL RESISTANCE

Journalist Robert Weltsch responded to the emergence of the Nazi menace; "wear it with pride," he said of the Jewish star. It was an attitude of defiance that could be summed up in a phrase, but it had yet to be translated into a program.

Martin Buber (1878–1965) was a leading German-Jewish theologian. An internationally known figure, widely respected throughout the world, his reputation had long been established by the time the Nazis came to power. He had been a leading figure in the Jewish community almost since the turn of the century, when, in his early twenties, he edited the Zionist publication *Die Welt* for Theodore Herzl, and took on the founder of the Zionist movement who sought merely a political revolution in the Jewish condition,

Dr. Leo Baeck addresses the meeting of the *Reichsvereinigung der Juden in Deutschland*. Mr. Hirsch, Mr. Stahl, Mr. Meyer, and Mr. Gruenberg are seated at the table. c. 1938. Abraham Pisarek Archive.

Jewish sovereignty in Palestine. Buber sided with the cultural Zionists who saw the political revolution as but one step in the cultural renaissance of the Jewish people, both in their own land and elsewhere.

From Zionism, Buber discovered Hasidism and withdrew from public life for several years while he mastered, translated, and transmitted this mystical religious tradition of the eastern European Jews, to a skeptical, rationalistic German and German-Jewish audience.

His work *I and Thou*, first published in 1923, was widely regarded as a classic in modern religious philosophy, and was influential in Protestant theological circles, even more than among Jews. He became the emblematic Jew, the religious leader who represented Judaism to the non-Jews.

An ardent Zionist and a founder of the Hebrew University, Buber had long thought of emigration to Palestine, but with the onset of Nazism, there was an urgent task to perform among German Jews. Buber urged a mobilization for existence; Jews who were to suffer under Nazi rule needed to know of their past and required the substance of their tradition in order to endure what was to come. The result was the creation of a network of schools for youths and adults. Their task was not only to substitute for the schooling that was denied Jewish youth because of the imposition of quotas and finally their expulsion from German schools, but also to shape a Jewish person capable of spiritually withstanding the assault that was sure to come. Spiritual resistance and spiritual integrity in the face of an uncertain fate was the task, and Buber pursued this task with vigor, bravery, and personal courage. By 1935, he was forbidden to speak in public, and his writings during this period created what his disciple Ernst Simon called a "new Midrash," where the recounting of biblical stories and their commentary was used to speak to contemporary circumstance and to subtly instruct at a time when a word, even to the wise, was dangerous.

In the mid-1930s, he published a collection of twenty-three psalms entitled "Out of the Depths I Cried Onto Thee" (Psalm 130) in which the texts of the collection describe and prescribe the condition of the community of Israel.

The collection of psalms begins with a cry, a lament. They speak of God forgetting and bemoan the oppressor asking "But where is your God?" They bemoan the condition of society. "Vileness is exalted among the children of Adam." They demand of God: "Arise O God and fight your fight." The psalmist bemoans the fact that the enemy imagines God does not see, but concludes with faith in restoration, faith in Zion.

Such were the ways in which Buber could teach, instruct, cajole, and prepare his people for the trials to follow. According to Ernst Simon, Buber taught throughout his five years of sojourn in Nazi Germany the "meaning of spiritual resistance against identification with the aggressor. He was and remained our teacher, not a leader of men."

Buber is often contrasted with the other prominent German-Jewish religious thinker who assumed the burdens of leadership during the assault on Jews in Germany, Rabbi Leo Baeck (1873–1956). Both Baeck and Buber were widely perceived as embodiments of the German-Jewish symbiosis, as it was called, fully at home in German culture, deeply rooted in Jewish tradition, brilliantly learned in both literatures.

The son of an Orthodox rabbi, Baeck studied at the Jewish Theological Seminary at Breslau (a school kindred in spirit to Conservative Judaism's Jewish Theological Seminary of America) before he studied at the Hochschule in Berlin, which was the center of the Wissenschaft movement in Germany. He was ordained in 1897 and served as the rabbi of liberal congregations in Opplen and Düsseldorf before moving to Berlin, where he continued to serve as a rabbi until 1942.

His intellectual reputation was firmly established with the 1905 publication of *The Essence of Judaism*, an important and critical response to Adolph Harnack's portrayal of Judaism in *The Essence of Christianity.* He was to continue as a scholar and rabbi throughout his long career.

When the Nazis came to power in 1933, Baeck assumed an overtly political role as president of the *Reichsvertretung*, the Reich Representation of German Jews. It was in this role that he was to preside over the demise of his community. Baeck served as a political leader of his people, while his fellow Jewish theologian Martin Buber stayed in Germany to teach and to organize adult education until his departure for Palestine in 1938. Baeck was to forgo all entreaties to leave, all opportunities to secure his personal safety, even after he was deported to Theresienstadt along with his community. As a rabbi, he chose to remain with his people, choosing a martyrdom for which he was intellectually prepared and which he regarded as the highest form of religious witness. In *The Essence of Judaism*, Baeck said:

> Martyrdom is the truest sanctification of the Holy Name, the clearest testimony to God. . . . Where there is the unconditional duty to testify to God through faith in Him and obedience to His imperatives, the boundary of our existence is not the boundary of the duty. . . . And to agree with God, man must be able to surrender his will for life.

Even in the concentration camp, he continued to work as a rabbi teaching theology as well as the classical Greek philosophers Plato and Aristotle.

His commitment was tested during his years of leadership. The most controversial action of Baeck's leadership remains very much in dispute. Reports persist that Rabbi Baeck received information in Theresienstadt regarding Auschwitz and kept his knowledge of the lethal happenings to himself. His reasoning behind his actions, it is stated, was compassion for his flock who needed every shred of hope—even false hope—to survive. His respected biographer Albert Friedlander denies the story and Leonard Baker, author of the Pulitzer Prize–winning book *Days of Pain and Sorrow*, remains unconvinced that Baeck ever knew of Auschwitz.

Nothing could be more fitting from a rabbi than to hear words of prayer. The prayer below, composed by Baeck in 1935 in the aftermath of the Nuremberg Laws, was to be read in every synagogue on the evening of the Day of Atonement, the most widely attended service of the year.

In *Persecution and the Art of Writing* Leo Strauss wrote that before we read what an author has written, we must understand what it was he could have gotten away with writing. Understanding a text is impossible without knowing the context within which the author wrote and what he or she was free to say. Thus, the unsaid must be understood in what Baeck said so clearly.

The prayer Baeck wrote is an elaboration of the *Aleinu* prayer, the Adoration, which reads:

> We rise to our duty to praise the Lord of all, to acclaim the Creator. He made our lot unlike that of other people, assigning to us a unique destiny. We bend the knee and

bow, acknowledging the King of Kings, the Holy One praised be He, who spread out the heavens and laid the foundations of earth, whose glorious abode is in the highest heaven, whose mighty dominion is in the loftiest heights. He is our God, there is none other.

Listen to Rabbi Baeck's commentary:

We stand before our God; we draw strength from His Commandments, which we obey. We bow down before Him, and we stand upright before Men.

No one could doubt his meaning. Everyone understood. "The silent worship" was indeed more emphatic than any words could be.

We also present Martin Buber's 1934 lecture at the Lehrhaus in Frankfurt, "The Jew in the World." Speaking to educated German Jews, Buber enunciates some of the meaning of current Jewish life. "Every symbiosis [the Jewish people] enters upon is treacherous." Everyone has an "invisible terminating clause." The Jews cannot be fitted into any scheme, he tells his understanding audience. He then instructs them: "We have only one way to apprehend the positive meaning of this negative phenomenon. The way of faith."

While Buber's concerns were lofty and seemingly revolutionary, and Baeck's concerns were for the fate of his people, throughout the Nazi years religious Jews and their rabbis faced the ordinary problems of daily existence under unusual conditions. How Jews responded can be seen in how Jews behaved, and for Orthodox Jews praxis is directly related to Halakah, to Jewish religious law.

On April 21, 1933, the Nazis abolished Jewish ritual slaughter throughout Germany, but the attack was not quite as direct as in other regulations. Under the guise of preventing cruelty to animals, German law required the stunning of an animal prior to slaughter. By Jewish religious tradition, an animal may not be injured prior to slaughter, lest the animal be rendered *treife*, unkosher, unfit for consumption by a religious Jew.

The question was then posed to Rabbi Yechiel Yaakov Weinberg of Berlin whether the practice of stunning an animal can be compatible with Jewish religious law. At stake was not only the practice of individual Jews who observed the dietary regulations, but communal practices in old-age homes, hospitals, schools, and community centers as well. Another concern was whether such a practice would require the importation of all kosher meats, which could result in an additional drain on communal resources. We shall not reprint the decision. A complete text is available in Robert Kirschner's fine book, *Rabbinic Response to the Holocaust Era.*

Rabbi Weinberg struggled to find a compassionate answer compatible with his religious task. He was certain of the law, but uncertain as to his response. According to his account, he sought advice and was told that it was not "our right to search out grounds for permitting change in the manner of shechitah."

The Orthodox Jews will not want it and will not listen to us. They will suffer and go hungry rather than defile themselves by eating meat slaughtered by the method decreed by the wicked ones. . . . The Jews of Germany must stand up to the trial for the sake of our holy law. We must show the entire world that we are ready to sacrifice ourselves for the sanctity of Israel . . .

In the years to come the questions became more difficult, the answers more impossible and the degree of sacrifice ever more intense.

"THE JEW IN THE WORLD"

A LECTURE BY MARTIN BUBER
DELIVERED AT THE *LEHRHAUS* IN
FRANKFURT
AM MAIN IN 1934

The concept of the "Jew in the world" in its most serious sense did not arise until a certain quite definite juncture. This juncture did not—as one might suppose—coincide with the destruction of the Jewish state by Titus, but with the collapse of the Bar Kokhba rebellion. When Jerusalem ceased to be a Jewish city, when the Jew was no longer permitted to be at home in his own country—it was then that he was hurled into the abyss of the world. Ever since, he has represented to the world the insecure man. Within that general insecurity which marks human existence as a whole, there has since that time lived a species of man to whom destiny has denied even the small share of dubious security other beings possess. Whether or not it is aware of it, this people is always living on ground that may at any moment give way beneath its feet. Every symbiosis it enters upon is treacherous. Every alliance in its history contains an invisible terminating clause, every union with other civilizations is informed with a secret divisive force. It is this inescapable state of insecurity which we have in mind when we designate the Jewish Diaspora as *galut*, i.e., as exile.

What is the cause of this fate of insecurity? The Jewish group plainly cannot be fitted into any known scheme. It resists all historical categories and general concepts; it is unique. This uniqueness of Israel necessarily thwarts the

nations' very natural desire for an explanation, and explanation always implies arrangement in categories. The existence of whatever cannot be cubbyholed and hence understood is alarming. This state of affairs provides a basis of truth

Martin Buber (1878–1965) Jewish theologian, philosopher, and Zionist leader. c. 1930. Jewish National Library.

for the observation that antisemitism is a kind of fear of ghosts. The wandering, roving, defenseless group which is different from any other and comparable to none seems to the nations among which it lives to have something spectral about it, because it does not fit into any other given group. It could not be otherwise. The Jewish people was, indeed, always a "sinister," homeless specter. This people, which resisted inclusion in any category, a resistance which the other peoples could never become quite accustomed to, was always the first victim of fanatical mass movements (the Crusades of the eleventh century, for instance). It was branded as the cause of mass misfortunes ("the Jew is responsible for the 'Black Death'"). No matter how hard it tried, it never quite succeeded in adjusting to its environment. (The Inquisition followed upon Marranism.)

When I say that the nations regard us as a specter—and this myth is symbolized in the form of the wandering Jew—we must distinguish between being and appearance. We ourselves know very well that we are not specters, but a living community, and so we must ask ourselves what our nonclassifiability really signifies. Is it due merely to a lack of vision and insight on the part of the nations? Is it that we can be fitted into a system, only they are not able to do it? Is this resistance of ours to classification merely a negative phenomenon, one that is temporary? Does it simply mean that we cannot be classified until—at some future time—we are?

We have only one way to apprehend the positive meaning of this negative phenomenon: the way of faith. From any viewpoint other than faith, our inability to fit into a category would be intolerable, as something counter to history and counter to nature. But from the viewpoint of faith, our inability to fit into a category is the foundation and meaning of our living avowal of the uniqueness of Israel. We would differentiate this uniqueness from the general uniqueness we attribute to every group and each individual. The uniqueness of Israel signifies something which in its nature, its history, and its vocation is so individual that it cannot be classified.

Moreover, Israel will not fit into the two categories most frequently invoked in attempts at classification: "nation" and "creed." One criterion serves to distinguish a nation from a creed. Nations experience history as nations. What individuals, as such, experience is not history. In creeds, on the other hand, salient experiences are undergone by individuals, and, in their purest and sublime form, these experiences are what we call "revelation." When such individuals communicate their experiences to the masses, and their tidings cause groups to form, a creed comes into being. Thus, nations and creeds differ in the same way as history and revelation. Only in one instance do they coincide. Israel receives its decisive religious experience as a people; it is not the prophet alone but the community as such that is involved. The community of Israel experiences history and revelation as one phenomenon, history as revelation and revelation as history. In the hour of its experience of faith the group becomes a people. Only as a people can it hear what it is destined to hear. The unity of nationality and faith which constitutes the uniqueness of Israel is not only our destiny, in the empirical sense of the word: here humanity is touched by the divine.

Now, in order to understand our position in the world, we must realize that a twofold desire comes to the fore in the history of Diaspora Jewry: the insecure Jew strives for security, the Jewish community which cannot be classified strives to be classified. These two strivings are by no means on a par. Like all human longing for security, this search for security is in itself quite legitimate. Man cannot be condemned to spend his life in insecurity. So the striving toward security is unobjectionable, but the means taken to arrive at this desired end may well be questioned.

The striving for security is familiar to us from the history of the ancient Hebrew state which presaged the insecurity of the Diaspora in a rather curious way. Wedged between Egypt and Babylonia, the two great powers of the ancient Orient, this state attempted time and again to overcome its geographic and political insecurity by employing power politics. Driven by the hope of overcoming its insecurity, it veered and compromised now with the one side, now with the other. The actual political content of the prophets is a warning against such false security. The prophets knew and predicted that in spite of all its veering and compromising Israel must perish if it intends to exist only as a political structure. It can persist—and this is the paradox in their warning and the paradox of the reality of Jewish history—if it insists on its locution of uniqueness, if it translates into reality the divine words spoken during the making of the Covenant. When the prophets say that there is no security for Israel save that in God, they are not referring to something unearthly, to something "religious" in the common sense of the word; they are referring to the realization of the true communal living to which Israel was summoned by the Covenant with God, and which it is called upon to sustain in history, in the way it alone is capable of. The prophets call upon a people which represents the first real attempt at "community" to enter world history as a prototype of that attempt. Israel's function is to encourage the nations to change their inner structure and their relations to one another. By maintaining such relations with the nations and being involved in the development of humanity, Israel may attain its unimperiled existence, its true security.

In the late Diaspora the need for security assumed the anomalous form of a need to be categorized. It was reasoned that if it was our nonclassification which made us seem mysterious to the others, then that characteristic must be removed. This too is presaged in our ancient history, in the wanting to be "like unto all the nations" in the crisis during Samuel's time. But then and ever since then, the inner strength of faith was and is the resisting factor. The need for inclusion does not assume actual historical shape (if only history in caricature) until a late period of the exile, until the Emancipation. The Jews, to be sure, are not primarily to blame for the inadequacy of the Emancipation, for the fact that they were accepted as individuals, but not as a community.

At the beginning of the Emancipation, the nations pondered the question whether this unclassifiable Israel could not, after all, be included in one of the usual categories, and so they asked whether the Jews were a nation or a religion. The discussions which preceded the Emancipation in France anticipate all the later differences of opinion connected with this problem. Among other statements, we find the following words of Portalis, the French minister of education, whom Napoleon had asked to report on the Jews in 1802. What he wrote was: "The Government could not but consider the eternal life of this people, which has been preserved up to the present through all the stupendous changes and all the misfortunes of the centuries, since . . . it enjoys the privilege of having God himself as its lawgiver."

These words might well have been the prelude to the legal recognition of our people as such. But not one of the nations perceived the great task of liberating and accepting the Jewish community as a community sui generis and not a single Jew from out of his age-old awareness thought to exert such a claim upon the unaware nations. Jewry disintegrated into small particles to comply with the nations' demand. The urge to conform became a cramp. Israel lost its reality by becoming a "confession." Our era attempted to counteract this by nationalization. The attempt failed: the one thing that is essential, the element of uniqueness, was ignored.

There is no reestablishing of Israel, there is no security for it save one: it must assume the burden of its own uniqueness; it must assume the yoke of the kingdom of God.

Since this can be accomplished only in the rounded life of a community, we must reassemble, we must again root in the soil, we must govern ourselves. But these are mere prerequisites. Only when the community recognizes and realizes them as such in its own life, will they serve as the cornerstones of its salvation.

Prayer Composed by Rabbi Leo Baeck for All Jewish Communities in Germany on the Eve of the Day of Atonement

October 10, 1935

At this hour the whole House of Israel stands before its God, the God of Justice and the God of Mercy. We shall examine our ways before Him. We shall examine what we have done and what we have failed to do; we shall examine where we have gone and where we have failed to go. Wherever we have sinned we will confess it: We will say "we have sinned" and will pray with the will to repentance before the Lord and we will pray: "Lord forgive us!"

We stand before our God and with the same courage with which we have acknowledged our sins, the sins of the individual and the sins of the community, shall we express our abhorrence of the lie directed against us, and the slander of our faith and its expressions: this slander is far below us. We believe in our faith and our future. Who brought the world the secret of the Lord Everlasting, of the Lord Who Is One? Who brought the world understanding for a life of purity, for the purity of the family? Who brought the world respect for Man made in the image of God? Who brought the world the commandment of justice, of social thought? In all these the spirit of the Prophets of Israel, the Revelation of God to the Jewish People had a part. It sprang from our Judaism, and continues to grow in it. All the slander drops away when it is cast against these facts.

We stand before our God: Our strength is in Him. In Him is the truth and the dignity of our history. In Him is the source of our survival through every change, our firm stand in all our trials. Our history is the history of spiritual greatness, spiritual dignity. We turn to it when attack and insult are directed against us, when need and suffering press in upon us. The Lord led our fathers from generation to generation. He will continue to lead us and our children through our days.

IV. THE NUREMBERG LAWS

At the annual Nazi Party rally in Nuremberg in September 1935, the German parliament decreed the two laws that became the centerpieces of the anti-Jewish legislation: The Law for the Protection of German Blood and Honor and the Reich Citizenship Law.

Citizenship in the Reich was restricted to persons of "German or kindred blood." Only citizens—i.e., racial Germans—had full civil and political rights. Jews could no longer be citizens, merely state subjects.

"To protect German blood and honor" marriages and sexual relations between Jews and "citizens of German or related blood" were prohibited as was the employment of Aryan women under the age of forty-five in Jewish households. Jews were not permitted to fly the Reich flag. Neither the term "Jew" nor the term "German or kindred blood" were defined.

Though these laws may seem innocuous and merely the work of bureaucrats, categorization had deadly consequences. Definition was the first step toward destruction.

At Nuremberg, Jews were defined and persecuted, not for the religion they practiced or the beliefs they affirmed, but by the blood of their grandparents. Thus, under these decrees, Roman Catholic priests and nuns and Protestant pastors who had converted, or whose parents had converted to Christianity lost their rights because they were defined as Jews.

Definition also established a precedent, guidance for the future. Later, the Germans imposed these laws upon the lands they occupied and these regulations served as a "model" for the Nazi treatment of Gypsies.

At Nuremberg the German nation was divided into Germans and Jews. Two terms that were used in the original laws remained undefined—"Jew" and "German or kindred blood." Since the laws contained criminal provisions, the bureaucracy faced an urgent task. Terms had to be defined; within two months they were.

According to Raul Hilberg, the Nazi Party and the civil service clashed in their efforts to define a Jew. The civil service wanted to protect the "German" part of the half-Jew. The Nazi Party viewed the part-Jew as a more serious threat than the full-Jew because in addition to Jewish characteristics, he or she possessed many Germanic ones. The German nation must be protected from racial contamination, they argued.

In the end two categories were developed: full-Jew (any person with three Jewish grandparents) and part-Jew.

In time, the category of half-Jews, or *Mischlinge* (mongrels), was further refined into two classes. First-class *Mischlinge* were those descended from two Jewish grandparents, but not practicing Judaism and not married to a Jewish spouse.

Second-class *Mischlinge* were the descendants of only one Jewish grandparent.

In Germany, church offices rather than the city clerk registered all births until 1875. Once the people learned of the laws, they immediately besieged the church offices with requests for legal documentation of their German (non-Jewish) ancestry. "Licensed family researchers" developed a new enterprise of researching the ancestry of their clientele.

Reaction in the Jewish community was mixed. The Reich Representation of Jews in Germany was reserved, their response restrained. Clarification of the Jewish legal status "must create a basis for a tolerable relationship between the German and Jewish people," they said.

The Zionists understood that "Jews had lost the legal status of equality." But, at the very least, they hoped the Nuremberg Laws would provide a "firm legal basis" for Jewish life.

With the Nuremberg Laws, emancipation, the process by which Jews were given the full rights of citizenship in the lands of their birth, had ended in Germany.

In the readings that follow, we will read the Nuremberg Laws as proclaimed by the Reichstag on September 15 and the supplementary regulations to those laws promulgated sixty days later. We will also read of the response of the *Reichsvertretung*, the Reich Representation.

REICH CITIZENSHIP LAW

SEPTEMBER 15, 1935

The Reichstag unanimously enacted the following law, which is promulgated herewith:

1

1. A subject of the state is a person who enjoys the protection of the German Reich and who in consequences has specific obligations toward it.
2. The status of a subject of the state is acquired in accordance with the provisions of the Reich and State Citizenship Law.

2

1. A Reich citizen is a subject of the state who is of German and related blood, who proves by his conduct that he is a willing and fit faithfully to serve the German people and the Reich.

2. Reich citizenship is acquired through the granting of a Reich Citizenship Certificate.
3. The Reich citizen is the sole bearer of full political rights in accordance with the law.

3

The Reich minister of the interior, in coordination with the deputy of the Führer will issue the legal and administrative orders required to implement and complete this Law.

> Nuremberg, September 15, 1935 at the Reich Party Congress of Freedom
> The Führer and Reich Chancellor
> ADOLF HITLER
>
> The Reich Minister of the Interior
> FRICK

Reichsbürgergesetz.

Vom 15. September 1935.

Der Reichstag hat einstimmig das folgende Gesetz beschlossen, das hiermit verkündet wird:

§ 1

(1) Staatsangehöriger ist, wer dem Schutzverband des Deutschen Reiches angehört und ihm dafür besonders verpflichtet ist.

(2) Die Staatsangehörigkeit wird nach den Vorschriften des Reichs- und Staatsangehörigkeitsgesetzes erworben.

§ 2

(1) Reichsbürger ist nur der Staatsangehörige deutschen oder artverwandten Blutes, der durch sein Verhalten beweist, daß er gewillt und geeignet ist, in Treue dem Deutschen Volk und Reich zu dienen.

(2) Das Reichsbürgerrecht wird durch Verleihung des Reichsbürgerbriefes erworben.

(3) Der Reichsbürger ist der alleinige Träger der vollen politischen Rechte nach Maßgabe der Gesetze.

§ 3

Der Reichsminister des Innern erläßt im Einvernehmen mit dem Stellvertreter des Führers die zur Durchführung und Ergänzung des Gesetzes erforderlichen Rechts- und Verwaltungsvorschriften.

Nürnberg, den 15. September 1935,
am Reichsparteitag der Freiheit.

Der Führer und Reichskanzler
Adolf Hitler

Der Reichsminister des Innern
Frick

Gesetz zum Schutze des deutschen Blutes und der deutschen Ehre.

Vom 15. September 1935.

Durchdrungen von der Erkenntnis, daß die Reinheit des deutschen Blutes die Voraussetzung für den Fortbestand des Deutschen Volkes ist, und beseelt von dem unbeugsamen Willen, die Deutsche Nation für alle Zukunft zu sichern, hat der Reichstag einstimmig das folgende Gesetz beschlossen, das hiermit verkündet wird:

§ 1

(1) Eheschließungen zwischen Juden und Staatsangehörigen deutschen oder artverwandten Blutes sind verboten. Trotzdem geschlossene Ehen sind nichtig, auch wenn sie zur Umgehung dieses Gesetzes im Ausland geschlossen sind.

AREA 12   GERMANY   JEWS, PERSECUTION OF 1935.   THE BASIC "NUERNBERGER GESETZE" (LAWS AGAINST THE JEWS).   OSS 736583

Texts of the "Reich Citizenship Law" of September 15, 1935, and the "Law for the Protection of German Blood and Honor" of September 15, 1935 (Nuremberg Race Laws). National Archives/Courtesy USHMM–Photo Archive.

Law for the Protection of German Blood and German Honor

September 15, 1935

Imbued with the insight that the purity of German blood is prerequisite for the continued existence of the German people and inspired by the inflexible will to ensure the existence of the German nation for all times, the Reichstag has unanimously adopted the following law, which is hereby promulgated:

1

1. Marriages between Jews and subjects of German or kindred blood are forbidden. Marriages nevertheless concluded are invalid, even if concluded abroad to circumvent this law.
2. Only the state attorney may initiate the annulment suit.

2

Extramarital intercourse between Jews and subjects of German or kindred blood is forbidden.

3

Jews must not employ in their households female subjects of German or kindred blood who are under forty-five years old.

4

1. Jews are forbidden to fly the Reich and national flag and to display the Reich colors.
2. They are, on the other hand, allowed to display the Jewish colors. The exercise of this right enjoys the protection of the state.

5

1. Whoever violates the prohibition in paragraph 1 will be punished by penal servitude.
2. A male who violates the prohibition in paragraph 2 will be punished either by imprisonment or penal servitude.
3. Whoever violates the provisions of paragraphs 3 or 4 will be punished by imprisonment up to one year and by a fine, or by either of these penalties.

6

The Reich minister of the interior, in agreement with the deputy of the Führer and the Reich minister of justice, will issue the legal and administrative orders required to implement and supplement this law.

7

The law takes effect on the day following promulgation, except for paragraph 3, which goes into force January 1, 1936.

> *Nuremberg, September 15, 1935 at the Reich Party Congress of Freedom*
> *The Führer and Reich Chancellor*
> ADOLF HITLER
>
> *The Reich Minister of the Interior*
> FRICK
>
> *The Reich Minister of Justice*
> *The Deputy of the Führer and Reich Minister without Portfolio*

RESPONSE OF THE *REICHSVERTRETUNG* TO THE NUREMBERG LAWS

SEPTEMBER 24, 1935

The *Reichsvertretung der Juden in Deutschland** announces the following:

I

The laws decided upon by the Reichstag in Nuremberg have come as the heaviest of blows for the Jews in Germany. But they must create a basis on which a tolerable relationship becomes possible between the German and the Jewish people. The *Reichsvertretung der Juden in Deutschland* is willing to contribute to this end with all its powers. A precondition for such a tolerable relationship is the hope that the Jews and the Jewish communities of Germany will be enabled to keep a moral and economic means of existence by the halting of defamation and boycott.

The organization of the life of the Jews in Germany requires governmental recognition of an autonomous Jewish leadership. The *Reichsvertretung der Juden in Deutschland* is the agency competent to undertake this. It has the support, with few exceptions, of the totality of the Jews and Jewish communities, particularly the State Association of Jewish Communities *[Landesverbande]* and all the city communities, as well as the independent Jewish organizations: Zionist Federation of Germany *[Zionistische Vereinigung fur Deutschland]*, Central Organization of Jews in Germany *[Zentralverein der Juden in Deutschland]*, Union of Jewish Veterans *[Reichsbund Judischer Frontsoldaten]*, Association for Liberal Judaism *[Vereinigung fur das religios-liberale Judentum]*, the Organized Orthodox Community *[die organisierte Gemeinde-Orthodoxie]*, Union of Jewish Women *[Judischer Frauenbund]*, Reich

Committee for Jewish Youth Organizations *[Reichsausschuss der Judischen jugendverbande]*.

The most urgent tasks for the *Reichsvertretung*, which it will press energetically and with full commitment, following the avenues it has previously taken, are:

1. Our own Jewish educational system must serve to prepare the youth to become upright Jews, secure in their faith, who will draw the strength to face the onerous demands which life will make on them from conscious solidarity with the Jewish community, from work for the Jewish present and faith in the Jewish future. In addition to transmitting knowledge, the Jewish schools must also serve in the systematic preparation for future occupations. With regard to preparation for emigration, particularly to Palestine, emphasis will be placed on guidance toward manual work and the study of the Hebrew language. The education and vocational training of girls must be directed to preparing them to carry out their responsibilities as upholders of the family and mothers of the next generation.

   An independent cultures structure must offer possibilities of employment to Jews who are artistically and culturally creative, and serve the separate cultural life of the Jews in Germany.

2. The increased need for emigration will be served by large-scale planning, firstly with respect to Palestine, but also to all other available countries, with particular attention to young people. This includes study of additional possibilities for emigration, training in professions suited for emigrants, particularly agriculture and technical skills; the creation of ways and means to mobilize and liquidate

---

**Reichsvertretung der Juden in Deutschland*—National Representation of the Jews in Germany.

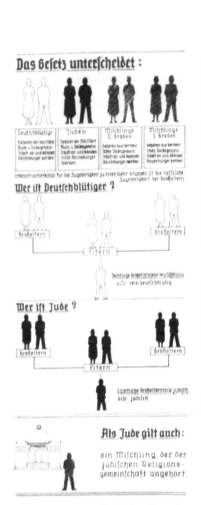

A chart used to distinguish Jews from *Mischlinge* (Germans of mixed blood) and Aryans for purposes of the "Law for the Protection of German Blood and Honor." The white figures represent Aryans; the black figures represent Jews; and shaded figures represent *Mischlinge*. 1935. Stadtarchiv Bielefeld.

the property of persons who are economically independent; the broadening of existing means of transferring property and the creation of additional such means.

3. Support and care of the needy, sick or aged must be assured through further systematic expansion of the Jewish welfare services provided by the communities to supplement government social services.

4. An impoverished community cannot carry out these varied and difficult tasks. The *Reichsvertretung* will try by every means to safeguard the economic position of the Jews by seeking to protect the existing means of livelihood. Those who are economically weak will be assisted by the further development of economic aids as employment bureaus, economic advice, and personal or mortgage loans.

5. We are given strength in the present and hope for the future by the vitality of the progress in the construction of Jewish Palestine. In order to draw the Jews of Germany even more closely into this development, the *Reichsvertretung* itself has joined the Palestine Foundation Fund *[Keren Ha-Yesod]* and appeals warmly to Jewish communities and organizations to follow its example. The *Reichsvertretung* offers its services to establish organizational links between the institutions of the Jews in Germany and the work of reconstruction in Palestine.

In full awareness of the magnitude of the responsibilities involved and the difficulties of the task, the *Reichsvertretung* calls on Jewish men and women, and on all Jewish youth, to join together in unity, to maintain high Jewish morale, to practice strict self-discipline, and show a maximum willingness to make sacrifice.

II

In accordance with a proposal made in the presidium of the *Reichsvertretung*, the *Reichsvertretung*, the state Federations an the communities are requested to cooperate closely in taking such organizational and personnel measures as are required in these Jewish bodies in order to ensure the vigorous and systematic carrying out of the new working program by all Jewish official bodies.

_____

(Source: *Judische Rundschau*, No. 77, September 24, 1935.)

V. THE CONFERENCE AT EVIAN

After the Nazi incorporation of Austria, pressure mounted on President Franklin Delano Roosevelt to do something about the refugee problem. The president decided on a grand gesture.

On March 25, the president invited thirty-three nations to participate in an international conference on the refugee crisis. Sensitive to his guests, the invitation specified that no country would be expected to receive greater numbers of immigrants than was permitted by existing law. Nor would government funds be required—new programs would be financed by private agencies.

Britain received assurances that the question of Palestine would not be discussed; the American quota system would remain in tact.

Two days after FDR announced the Evian Conference, Adolf Hitler gloated:

Lord Winterton, representative of Great Britain, addressing the International Conference on Refugees at Evian les Bains, France. July 19, 1938. Bettmann.

I can only hope that the other world which has such deep sympathy for these crimi-nals [Jews] will at least be generous enough to convert this sympathy into practical aid. We on our part are ready to put all these criminals at the disposal of these coun-tries, for all I care, even on luxury ships.

American representation at Evian was downplayed. The U.S. delegation was not headed by the secretary of state or even the undersecretary. Instead FDR nominated a close friend and business executive.

Foreign leaders understood the president's intentions: the French premier told his British counterpart that the American president was acting to soothe public opinion.

Little was expected. Even less was accomplished.

For nine days delegations from thirty-two nations met at the Hotel Royal on Lake Geneva along with representatives of thirty-nine private relief agencies, twenty-one of which were Jewish. The world press covered the event intensely.

One by one, delegates from each country rose to profess their understanding of the refugees' plight. One by one, they gave excuses why so little could be done.

The United States resorted to euphemism. Speaking of political refugees, it wanted to conceal the Jewish character of its problem.

Britain had no room on the mainland; it would not open Palestine. Canada would accept farmers—small comfort for urbanized Jews fleeing Germany. Holland and Denmark offered temporary refuge for a few.

"Australia does not have a racial problem, and we are not desirous of importing one," its delegate proclaimed.

Colombia's delegate was not "prepared to resign himself to the belief that two thou-sand years of Christian civilization must lead to this terrible catastrophe." Colombia itself could offer nothing.

The delegate from Venezuela was reluctant to disturb the "demographic equilibrium" of his country. In short, no Jewish merchants, peddlers, or intellectuals were wanted in Venezuela.

Only the Dominican Republic offered to receive one hundred thousand Jews. In the end only a few came.

In a formal response to Evian, the German Foreign Office gloated:

. . . since in many foreign countries it was recently regarded as wholly incomprehensi-ble why Germans did not wish to preserve in its population an element like the Jews . . . it appears astounding that countries seem in no way anxious to make use of these element themselves now that the opportunity offers.

The implications for Nazi policy were clear. Forced emigration would not succeed. No one wanted the Jews.

The desperate struggle of the refugees would now be even more difficult.

In one of the readings that follow, German Foreign Minister Joachim von Ribbentrop, in a memo to Adolf Hitler, describes a conversation he had with French Foreign Minister Georges Bonnet:

Bonnet said that in the first place they did not want to receive any more Jews from Germany and [asked] whether we could not take some sort of measures to keep them from coming to France, and in the second place France had to ship 10,000 Jews somewhere else. . . .

I replied to M. Bonnet that we all wanted to get rid of our Jews but that the difficulties lay in the fact that no country wished to receive them . . .

The only victor from Evian was the one country that was not invited to the conference—Nazi Germany. Within months, the Jews in Germany and Austria were to feel the impact of the failure of Evian when, in the pogroms known as Kristallnacht on the night of November 9–10, 1938, their synagogues were burned, their homes invaded, their businesses looted and almost thirty thousand Jewish men were arrested.

Evian marked a bitter moment in Western history. It marked an even more important point in Nazi Germany's policy towards the Jews: as the Nazis began to implement an ideology bent on making the Reich *Judenrein*—free of Jews—emigration was no longer feasible for there was no country was willing to receive Jews.

Surely these nine days were not America's finest hours as a nation, but their recollection has shaped a more humane policy. In 1979, Vice President Walter Mondale invoked the memory of Evian as he called for "a world solution to the world problem of the boat people." The United States took the lead and other Western countries followed. Within months, new homes were found throughout the West for many of the boat people of southeast Asia.

Forty-one years ago this very week, another international conference on Lake Geneva concluded its deliberations. . . .

At stake at Evian were both human lives—and the decency and self-respect of the civilized world. If each nation at Evian had agreed on that day to take in seventeen thousand Jews at once, every Jew in the Reich could have been saved. . . .

At Evian, they began with high hopes. But they failed the test of civilization.

Let us not reenact their error. Let us not be heirs to their shame.

Speech by Myron C. Taylor

July 1938

Mr. Myron C. Taylor (United States of America).

On behalf of my government, I wish to express my gratitude to the government of France and to the distinguished Ambassador of France—who is affectionately remembered in my country—M. Berenger, president of the Foreign Relations Committee of the French Senate, for the hearty collaboration that has been extended in organizing this meeting of governments which has been called on the initiative of President Roosevelt, and for the friendly interest which M. Berenger has manifested in presiding to-day. I also wish to express my personal appreciation of His Excellency's many courtesies to me since I came to the fair land of France.

Mr. Chairman: Some millions of people, as this meeting convenes, are, actually or potentially, without a country. The number is increasing daily. This increase is taking place, moreover, at a time when there is serious unemployment in many countries, when there is a shrinkage of subsistence bases and when the population of the world is at a peak.

Men and women of every race, creed and economic condition, of every profession and of every trade, are being uprooted from the homes where they have long been established and turned adrift without thought or care as to what will become of them or where they will go. A major forced migration is taking place, and the time has come when governments—I refer specifically to those governments which have had the problem of political refugees thrust upon them by the policies of some other governments—must act and act promptly and effectively in a long-range program of comprehensive scale.

Mindful of the harrowing urgency of this situation, President Roosevelt took the initiative of calling this meeting at Evian. The response of thirty-two governments which were invited to participate has been generous and encouraging and the courtesy of the French government in offering the hospitality of its territory to the meeting and in arranging the technical details of our reception calls for deepest appreciation and most profound thanks.

At the outset, we must consider that we are dealing with a form of migration which presents peculiar difficulties. The earliest migratory movements of which we have record consisted in the migration of races which overran western and southern Europe in a concerted hostile movement of whole peoples, advancing as military or political waves on those areas of the world where a high standard of living was already established. Then came the colonization movements, which were largely migrations by organized groups, usually under direct political authorization essentially for governmental purposes. This was followed by the nineteenth- and early twentieth-century migration, which was movement by individuals and families on an enormous scale induced by unsatisfactory economic and living conditions in the countries of origin and promise of a higher standard of living in the countries of settlement. Now, we have a form of compulsory migration, artificially stimulated by governmental practices in some countries which force upon the world at large great bodies of reluctant migrants who must be absorbed in abnormal circumstances with a disregard of economic conditions at a time of stress.

We must admit frankly, indeed, that this problem of political refugees is so vast and so complex that we probably can do no more at the initial intergovernmental meeting than put in motion the machinery, and correlate it with

Delegates at the Evian Conference. *Left to right:* Henri Berenger (France); Myron C. Taylor (U.S.); Lord Winterton (Great Britain). July 8, 1938. National Archives/Courtesy of USHMM–Photo Archives.

existing machinery, that will, in the long run, contribute to a practicable amelioration of the condition of the unfortunate human beings with whom we are concerned. While, for example, our ultimate objective should be to establish an organization which would concern itself with all refugees, wherever governmental intolerance shall have created a refugee problem, we may find that we shall be obliged on this occasion to focus our immediate attention upon the most pressing problem of political refugees from Germany (including Austria). Accordingly, my government, in its invitation, referred specifically to the problem of German (and Austrian) refugees and proposes that, for the purposes of this initial intergovernmental meeting, and without wishing to set a precedent for future meetings, persons coming within the scope of the conference shall be: (a) persons who have not already left Germany (including Austria) but who desire to emigrate by reason of the treatment to which they are subjected on account of their political opinions, religious beliefs or racial origin, and (b) persons as defined in (a) who have already left Germany and are in process of migration.

Doubtless, some delegates will suggest that there is already established under the general provisions of the League of Nations a Commission for political emigrants from Germany and that the Council of the League of Nations on May 14th, 1938, agreed upon a resolution my recommendations with regard to the organization of this Commission and with regard to the Nansen Office, whose distinguished head is the delegate of Norway. It is the firm belief of the American government that the intergovernmental organization which it is proposed to set up at this meeting, the League Commission and the Nansen Office should be complementary and should work together towards a solution of the problem of political refugees in which the fate of so many hapless human beings is at stake. As evidence of my government's intentions in this respect, I should like to propose, before we proceed further, that Sir Neill Malcolm, the League's Commissioner for Refugees from Germany, should be invited by the Intergovernmental Committee to assist in its deliberations. Happily, as I have already observed, Judge Michael Hansson, head of the Nansen Office, is officially in attendance and will, I am sure, give us the benefit of his profound knowledge and wide experience.

I shall not at this point dwell at length upon the technical aspects of the problem with which we shall have to deal. May I merely suggest that it will be advisable for us to exchange, for the strictly confidential information of the Committee, details regarding the number and the type of immigrants whom each government is prepared to receive under its existing laws and practices, details regarding these laws and practices and indications regarding those parts of the territory of each participating government which may be adapted to the settlement of immigrants. Then there will be the problem, which must be carefully considered, of documenting political emigrants who have been obliged to leave the country of their original residence in circumstances which render impossible the production of customary documents. It will also be incumbent upon us to consider the various studies which have been made in the respective countries of the problems of aiding the emigration and the settling and the financing of political refugees. I might observe, in this connection, that President Roosevelt has set up in the United States an Advisory Committee on Political Refugees, whose Chairman, Mr. James G. McDonald, is present at this meeting and will, I know, be prepared to furnish you with detailed information regarding his organization.

You will have noted that my government's invitation to this meeting stated specifically that whatever action was recommended here should take place within the framework of the existing laws and practices of the participating governments. The American government prides itself upon the liberality of its existing laws and practices, both as regards the number of immigrants whom the United States receives each year for assimilation with its population and the treatment of those people when they have arrived. I might point out that the American government has taken steps to consolidate both the German and the former Austrian quota, so that now a total of 27,370 immigrants may enter the United States on the German Quota in one year.

From the inception of this present effort on behalf of political refugees, it has been the view of the American government that the meeting at Evian would serve primarily to initiate the collaboration of the receiving governments in their assistance to political refugees, and that the work would have to be carried forward subsequently in a more permanent form. It is the belief of the American government that this permanent collaboration might be most effectively maintained by the regular meeting of the diplomatic representatives of the participating governments—or such other representative as a participating government may wish to designate—in a European capital, and we hope that the French government will agree that these meetings may take place at Paris. It might be useful if a secretariat were to be established to assist the Intergovernmental Committee in its continued form in caring for administrative details—the expenses of this secretariat to be borne by the participating governments on a basis to be recommended by this initial meeting.

In conclusion, I need not emphasize that discrimination and pressure against minority groups and the disregard of elementary human rights are contrary to the principles of what we have come to regard as the accepted standards of civilization. We have heard from time to time of the disruptive consequences of the dumping of merchandise upon the world's economy. How much more disturbing is the forced and chaotic dumping of unfortunate peoples in large numbers. Racial and religious problems are, in consequence, rendered more acute in all parts of the world. Economic retaliation against the countries which are responsible for this condition is encouraged. The sentiment of international mistrust and suspicion is heightened, and fear, which is an important obstacle to general appeasement between nations, is accentuated.

The problem is alas no longer one of purely private concern. It is a problem for intergovernmental action. If the present currents of migration are permitted to continue to push anarchically upon the receiving states and if some governments are to continue to toss large sections of their populations lightly upon a distressed and unprepared world, then there is catastrophic human suffering ahead which can only result in general unrest and in general international strain which will not be conducive to the permanent appeasement to which all peoples earnestly aspire.

DECISIONS TAKEN AT THE EVIAN CONFERENCE ON JEWISH REFUGEES

JULY 1938

(The Intergovernmental Committee)*
Adopted by the Committee on July 14th, 1938

Having met at Evian, France, from July 6th to July 13th, 1938:

I. Considering that the question of involuntary emigration has assumed major proportions and that the fate of the unfortunate

---

* Proceedings of the Intergovernmental Committee, Evian, July 6 to 15, 1938 . . . Record of the Plenary Meetings of the Conference Resolutions and Reports, London, July 1938.

people affected has become a problem for intergovernmental deliberation;

II. Aware that the involuntary emigration of large numbers of people, of different creeds, economic conditions, professions and trades, from the country or countries where they have been established, is disturbing to the general economy, since these persons are obliged to seek refuge, either temporarily or permanently, in other countries at a time when there is serious unemployment; that, in consequence, countries of refuge and settlement are faced with problems, not only of an economic and social nature, but also of public order, and that there is a severe strain on the administrative facilities and absorptive capacities of the receiving countries;

III. Aware, moreover, that the involuntary emigration of people in large numbers has become so great that it renders racial and religious problems more acute, increases international unrest, and may hinder seriously the processes of appeasement in international relations;

IV. Believing that it is essential that a long-range program should be envisaged, whereby assistance to involuntary emigrants, actual and potential, may be coordinated within the framework of existing migration laws and practices of governments;

V. Considering that if countries of refuge or settlement are to cooperate in finding an orderly solution of the problem before the Committee they should have the collaboration of the country of origin and are therefore persuaded that it will make its contribution by enabling involuntary emigrants to take with them their property and possessions and emigrate in an orderly manner;

VI. Welcoming heartily the initiative taken by the president of the United States of America in calling the Intergovernmental Meeting at Evian for the primary purpose of facilitating involuntary emigration from Germany (including Austria), and expressing profound appreciation to the French government for its courtesy in receiving the Intergovernmental Meeting at Evian;

VII. Bearing in mind the resolution adopted by the Council of the League of Nations on May 14th, 1938, concerning international assistance to refugees:

Recommends:

VII.

A. That the persons coming within the scope of the activity of the Intergovernmental Committee shall be

1. persons who have not already left their country of origin (Germany, including Austria), but who must emigrate on account of their political opinion, religious beliefs or racial origin, and

2. persons as defined in 1) who have already left their country of origin and who have not yet established themselves permanently elsewhere;

B. That the governments participating in the Intergovernmental Committee shall continue to furnish the Committee for its strictly confidential information, with

1. details regarding such immigrants as each government may be prepared to receive under its existing laws and practices and

2. details of these laws and practices;

C. That in view of the fact that the countries of refuge and settlement are entitled to take into account the economic and social adaptability of immigrants, these should in many cases be required to accept, at least for a time, changed conditions of living in the countries of settlement;

D. That the governments of the countries of refuge and settlement should not assume any obligations for the financing of involuntary emigration;

E. That, with regard to the documents required by the countries of refuge and settlement, the governments represented on the Intergovernmental Committee should consider the adoption of the following provision:

In those individual immigration cases in which the usually required documents emanating from foreign official sources are found not to be available, there should be accepted such other documents serving the purpose of the requirements of law as may be available to the immigrant, and that, as regards the document which may be issued to an involuntary emigrant by the country of his foreign residence to serve the purpose of a passport, note be taken of the several international agreements providing for the issue of a travel document serving the purpose of a passport and of the advantage of their wide application;

F. That there should meet at London an Intergovernmental Committee consisting of such representatives as the governments participating in the Evian Meeting may desire to designate. This committee shall continue and develop the work of the Intergovernmental Meeting at Evian and shall be constituted and shall function in the following manner: There shall be a chairman of this committee and four vice-chairmen;

there shall be a director of authority, appointed by the Intergovernmental Committee, who shall be guided by it in his actions. He shall undertake negotiations to improve the present conditions of exodus and to replace them by conditions of orderly emigration. He shall approach the governments of the countries of refuge and settlement with a view to developing opportunities for permanent settlement. The Intergovernmental Committee, recognizing the value of the work of the existing refugee services of the League of Nations and of the studies of migration made by the International Labor Office, shall cooperate fully with these organizations, and the Intergovernmental Committee at London shall consider the means by which the cooperation of the committee and the director with these organizations shall be established. The Intergovernmental Committee, at its forthcoming meeting at London, will consider the scale on which its expenses shall be apportioned among the participating governments;

VIII. That the Intergovernmental Committee in its continued form shall hold a first meeting at London on August 3rd, 1938.

MEMORANDUM BY THE GERMAN FOREIGN MINISTER JOACHIM VON RIBBENTROP TO ADOLF HITLER

PARIS, DECEMBER 9, 1938.

In the course of a second conversation on the following day, December 7, 1938, Bonnet mentioned the following points:

1. The Jewish question. After I had told M. Bonnet that I could not discuss this question officially with him, he said that he only

wanted to tell me privately how great an interest was being taken in France in a solution to the Jewish problem. To my question as to what France's interest might be, M. Bonnet said that in the first place they did not want to receive any more Jews from Germany and [asked] whether he could not take some sort of measures to keep them from coming to France, and in the second place France had to ship ten thousand Jews somewhere else. They were actually thinking of Madagascar for this.

I replied to M. Bonnet that we all wished to get rid of our Jews but that the difficulties lay in the fact that no country wished to receive them, and, further, in the shortage of foreign exchange. While I had always avoided handling this matter with any kind of international committee, and even now did not in any way wish to discuss it, I had, as I wished to inform him confidentially, declared myself to be in agreement that a German well versed in the Jewish problem should sometime confer in a private capacity with a deputy of an international committee, in order to examine the question of the Jewish emigration from Germany in its practical aspects. This conference was, I believe, taking place right now in Switzerland. Furthermore, I told the French Foreign Minister that the resettlement of the Jews was particularly difficult, since the Jews were not willing to undertake any work on the land and, even if the finest resettlement project was carried out today, I was afraid that within only a short space of time everything would be sold again by the Jews, who would once more make their appearance in the capital of the country concerned.

2. M. Bonnet then referred once more to the Spanish question and asked me whether we would not use our influence with Franco in urging him to accept the London plan for combing out volunteers. France would then be prepared without more ado, to accord him belligerent rights.

I told him that Franco had objections to this plan because his volunteers could be located without difficulty, while this would hardly be possible with the Communists, since they all had forged passports, etc. This appeared to me to be Franco's objection. I wanted, however, to examine this question again myself and also to discuss it some time with the Italians. The crux of the matter certainly always seemed to me to be that nobody, including France, wished to see Bolshevism in Spain and that the quickest way to a solution satisfactory all around was therefore to stop completely reinforcements coming through France. No decision of any sort was taken on Spain.

R[IBBENTROP]

VI. THE NOVEMBER POGROMS—KRISTALLNACHT AND ITS AFTERMATH

On the evening of November 9, 1938, anti-Jewish violence erupted throughout the Reich, which, since March 1938, included Austria. The outburst appeared to be a spontaneous eruption of national anger at the assassination of a minor German embassy official in Paris by a seventeen-year-old Jewish youth, Herschel Grynszpan. However, the violence was in fact precisely choreographed. We will trace the evolution of the pogrom in detail. On October 28, Polish Jews living in Germany were expelled from the country. They were not admitted to Poland as the Polish Foreign Ministry invalidated their passports effective October 29. They were forced to live under desperate conditions in a no-man's-land in the border town of Zbnszyn. We will read American cables from Berlin to Washington describing the expulsion. One of the families expelled from Germany were the Grynszpans. On November 3, Herschel received a postcard from his sister Berta describing the family's plight. He was pushed over the edge.

The assassination was the pretext for what was to follow.

At 11:55 on the evening of November 9, Gestapo Chief Heinrich Mueller sent a telegram to all police units: "In shortest order, actions against Jews and especially their synagogues will take place in all Germany. These are not to be interfered with. . . ." Bystanders to the violence, the police were to arrest its victims. Fire companies were instructed to stand by not to protect the synagogues, but to ensure that the flames did not spread to adjacent Aryan property.

Within forty-eight hours, 1,300 synagogues were burned, along with their Torah scrolls, Bibles, and prayer books; 30,000 Jews were arrested and sent to concentration camps; 7,000 businesses were smashed and looted; and 236 Jews were killed. Jewish cemeteries, hospitals, schools, and homes were destroyed.

Hour after hour the pace of the pogrom intensified; minute by minute the damage toll increased. No Jewish institution or business or home was safe. The terror directed at the Jews was often not the action of strangers but neighbors.

In the aftermath of Kristallnacht, the Jews in Germany were left without their synagogues. Many had lost their businesses and their homes. The concentration camps of Buchenwald, Dachau, and Sachsenhausen were overflowing with new Jewish inmates.

As the fury subsided, the pogrom was given a fancy name: *Kristallnacht*—Crystal Night.

Most Jews were without illusions. Jewish life in the Reich was no longer possible.

Many committed suicide. Most desperately tried to leave. Unwanted at home, Jews had only a few havens abroad. They could not stay. They had nowhere to go! We will read the account of Yitzhak S. Herz, the director of a religious orphanage at Dinslaken and learn of the terror, the injustice, and the fear that he and his charges experienced on Kristallnacht and the way he learned of what had happened.

The Nazis, too, had learned important lessons. Because of the bourgeois sensibilities of the urbanized Germans, many opposed the events of Kristallnacht. The sloppiness of the pogroms and the explosive violence of the SA were soon replaced by the cold, calculated, disciplined, and controlled violence of the SS. They would dispose of the Jews out of the view of most Germans.

On November 12, 1938, Field Marshal Goering convened a meeting of Nazi officials to deal with the problems that resulted from Kristallnacht. Historians are fortunate that the stenographic records of that meeting survived, for few documents reveal more candidly and more directly German policy toward the Jews at this transitional moment. Joseph Goebbels, a Ph.D. from Heidelberg, and now minister of public enlightenment and propaganda attended the meeting. Several ministries including the Justice and Economic ministries had urgent matters to discuss, and the insurance industry had much at stake in the outcome of the meeting—it stood to lose huge sums of money if it had to pay claims from those whose property had been destroyed.

Goering was clearly disturbed by the damage of the two-day rampage—not to Jewish shops, homes, or synagogues, but to the German economy. It's insane to burn a Jewish warehouse and then have a German insurance company pay for the loss, he said. We suffer, not the Jews.

The idea was introduced to solve the Jewish problem once and for all, but in 1938, its meaning was in economic terms. Only later, by 1941, would the language be genocidal.

Notice the concern for legality, for maintaining the stability of the economy. Thus, while the economic elimination of the Jews could not be done all at once, the direction of policy is clear. Jews are to disappear from German economic life. When concerns are raised about foreign Jews, the Foreign Ministry expresses interest, not willing to surrender its authority or preeminence. Their concerns are assuaged but not fully satisfied. They will be consulted only for important cases, but not for every case.

There is much give and take at the meeting and some brainstorming. Several concrete results are achieved, all economically lethal to the Jews. The community will be fined one billion reichsmarks; Jews will be responsible for cleaning up their losses; they will be barred form collecting insurance.

Apartheid is introduced. Jews are barred from theaters; they are to travel on separate compartments on trains, they will be denied entry to German schools and parks. By January 1, 1939, Jews are forbidden to operate retail trades.

Concern is expressed for those who looted; the booty in furs and jewels belongs to the state, not to individuals. And in the end Goering expresses regrets over the whole messy business. "I wish you had killed two hundred Jews and not destroyed such value." He concludes on a note of irony, "I would not like to be a Jew in Germany!"

By a series of policy decisions, the Nazis transformed Kristallnacht into a program designed to eliminate Jews from German economic life.

- The perpetrators were not to be prosecuted. They had "no ignoble motives for their excesses."

- Rubble of ruined synagogues had to be cleared by the community. Jewish compensation claims were confiscated by the Reich and Jewish property owners were forced to repair their own property.
- Jews of German nationality could not file for damages.
- A collective fine of one billion reichsmarks ($400,000,000) was imposed on the Jewish community.

On November 15, Jews were barred from schools. Two weeks later, authorities were given the right to impose a curfew. By December, Jews were denied access to most public places.

The November pogroms were the last occasion for street violence against Jews in Germany. While Jews could thereafter leave their homes without fear of attack, a lethal process of destruction that was more effective and more virulent was set in place.

In the readings that follow, we shall see depictions of the event that triggered Kristallnacht—the expulsion of Polish Jews from Germany and their transfer to no-man's-land in Zbyngyn on the Polish-German border where they could neither leave Germany nor enter Poland—in telegrams to the American secretary of state. We shall also read the detailed instructions given to the police by Deputy Chief of the Gestapo Reinhard Heydrich, and the minutes of the November 12 meeting where the impact of the November pogroms was discussed and a policy formulated for the elimination of Jews from German society.

TELEGRAM TO SECRETARY OF STATE

OCTOBER 28, 1938

TELEGRAM RECEIVED
GRAY,
BERLIN
FROM:
DATED OCTOBER 28, 1938
REC'D 5:22 P.M.
SECRETARY OF STATE
WASHINGTON.
578, OCTOBER 28, 8 P.M.

During the course of the day the German police authorities have rounded up a large number of Polish JEWS and are issuing orders for their expulsion to Poland. This has taken place in Berlin and we understand in other big cities in the Reich. As far as we can ascertain only male Polish JEWS have been arrested and none up to this time have actually been sent over the Polish border. We understand that the grounds for the action are a recent Polish decree to the effect that no Polish citizen may reenter Poland after October 30th unless his passport has previously been validated by a Polish consulate or diplomatic mission.

The Polish embassy states that it is negotiating with the Germans in an endeavor to get them to rescind the expulsion orders. American correspondents report: the explanation of the German officials is that the Polish decree produced the probability of Germany having several thousand foreigners without nationality (*staatenlos*) who after October 30th could not (repeat not) be deported. The Polish embassy sometime ago informally estimated that there were 50,000 Polish JEWS in Germany proper

and 5,000 in Austria. More specific information should be available tomorrow.

Repeated to Warsaw and London for Rublee.

WILSON

TELEGRAM TO SECRETARY OF STATE

OCTOBER 29, 1938

TELEGRAM RECEIVED
GRAY,
BERLIN
FROM:
DATED OCTOBER 28, 1938
REC'D 5:22 P.M.
SECRETARY OF STATE
WASHINGTON.
582, OCTOBER 29, 3 P.M.
REFERRING TO THE EMBASSY'S 578,
OCTOBER 28, 8 P.M.

Geist was officially informed today at German police headquarters that on October 6 the Polish government issued a decree by virtue of which all passports of Polish JEWS abroad became invalid on October 29. German authorities state they are convinced this decree was shortly to be followed by another expatriating all such persons. To prevent these thousands of Polish JEWS from becoming stateless and undeportable the German authorities are expelling all Polish male JEWS and expect to finish the deportations by tonight. Women and children are not included, it being assumed they will follow voluntarily their male relatives. Police have assured us that they are not deporting Polish Jews holding American immigration visas.

Repeated to Warsaw and London for Rublee.

RR WILSON

LETTER FROM HERSCHEL GRYNSZPAN

You have undoubtedly heard of our great misfortune. I will give you a description of what happened.

On Thursday night there were rumors circulating that all Polish Jews of a certain city had been expelled. However, we refused to believe them. On Thursday night at 9:00 P.M., a Schupo [local policeman] came to our house and told us we had to go to the police headquarters with our passports. We went just as we were, all together, to the police headquarters, accompanied by the Schupo. There we found almost our entire neighborhood already assembled. A police wagon then took us at once to the *Rathaus* [town hall]. Everyone was taken there. We had not yet been told what it was about, but we quickly realized that it was the end for us. An expulsion order was thrust into our hands. We had to leave Germany before October 29 (Saturday). We were not allowed to return to our homes. I begged to be allowed to return home to get at least a few essential things. So I left with a Schupo accompanying me and I packed a valise with the most necessary clothes. That is all I could save. We don't have a cent.

Mug shot of Herschel Grynszpan (1921–?) after his arrest for the assassination of Ernst vom Rath, third secretary of the German Embassy in Paris. November 14, 1938. Yad Vashem.

Reinhard Heydrich's Instructions for Measures Against Jews

November 10, 1938

Secret

Copy of most urgent telegram from Munich, of November 10, 1938, 1:20 a.m.

To:

All headquarters and stations of the State Police

All districts and sub districts of the SD

Urgent! For immediate attention of the chief or his deputy!

Re: Measures against Jews tonight

Following the attempt on the life of Secretary of the Legation vom Rath in Paris, demonstrations against the Jews are to be expected in all parts of the Reich in the course of the coming night, November 9/10, 1938. The instructions below are to be applied in dealing with these events:

I. The chiefs of the State Police, or their deputies, must immediately upon receipt of this telegram contact, by telephone, the political leaders in their areas—Gauleiter [regional party leader] or Kreisleiter [district party leader]—who have jurisdiction in their districts and arrange a joint meeting with the inspector or commander of the Order Police to discuss the arrangements for the demonstrations. At these discussions the political leaders will be informed that the German Police has received instructions, detailed below, from the Reichsführer SS and the chief of the German Police, with which the political leadership is requested to coordinate its own measures:

A. Only such measures are to be taken as do not endanger German lives or property (i.e., synagogues are to be burnt down only where there is no danger of fire in neighboring buildings).

B. Places of business and apartments belonging to Jews may be destroyed but not looted. The police are instructed to supervise the observance of this order and to arrest looters.

C. In commercial streets particular care is to be taken that non-Jewish businesses are completely protected against damage.

D. Foreign citizens—even if they are Jews—are not to be molested.

II. On the assumption that the guidelines detailed under paragraph I are observed, the demonstrations are not to be prevented by the police, who are only to supervise the observance of the guidelines.

III. On receipt of this telegram, police will seize all archives to be found in all synagogues and offices of the Jewish communities so as to prevent their destruction during the demonstrations. This refers only to material of historical value, not to contemporary tax records, etc. The archives are to be handed over to the locally responsible officers of the SD.

IV. The control of the measures of the Security Police concerning the demonstrations against the Jews is vested in the organs of the State Police, unless inspectors of the Security Police have given their own instructions. Officials of the Criminal Police, members of the SD, of the Reserves and the SS in general may be used to carry out the measures taken by the Security Police.

V. As soon as the course of events during the night permits the release of the officials required, as many Jews in all districts, especially the rich, as can be accommodated in existing prisons are to be arrested. For the time being only healthy male Jews, who are not too old, are to be detained. After the detentions have been carried out the appropriate concentration camps are to be contacted immediately for the prompt accommodation of the Jews in the camps. Special care is to be taken that the Jews arrested in accordance with these instructions are not ill-treated....

SIGNED HEYDRICH,

SS Gruppenführer

KRISTALLNACHT AT THE DINSLAKEN ORPHANAGE
REMINISCENCES*

Yitzhak S. Herz

Early one morning I was awakened by the shrill ringing of the door bell. With a sense of foreboding I opened the front door. Three men, two Gestapo officers and a policeman in mufti, entered announcing: "This is a police raid! We are looking for arms in all Jewish homes and apartments and so we shall search the orphanage too!" The three commenced their task at once. They searched only the ground floor, especially the small office and the children's workroom. In the office they cut the telephone wires and, searching for money, opened the lockers and drawers of the young students. Unobserved for a moment, the Gestapo officer Schneider whispered in my ear: "During the night all the Jewish men in Dinslaken were arrested. But there is no need for you to worry. Nothing will happen to you! You will remain in charge of the children." Schneider, I later found out, was a former Social Democrat and had always been friendly to Jews. After the search which lasted for twenty-five minutes and which—as was to be expected—yielded no tangible results, the Nazi officers left the building and gave the following order: "Nobody is to leave the house before 10 A.M.! All the blinds of the building facing the street must be drawn! Shortly after 10 A.M. everything will be over!"

About one hour later, at 7 A.M., the morning service in the synagogue of the institution was scheduled to commence. Some people from the town usually participated, but this time nobody turned up. Only the teacher of the Jewish primary school and two Polish Jews, who escaped during the Polish action of October, attended the minyan. Then I heard the ringing of the house bell. The sound of the bell, which I hastened to answer, became louder and louder. When I opened the door a strange man faced me. In the dim light of the street lamp I recognized a Jewish face. In a few words the stranger explained to me: "I am the president of the Jewish community of Düsseldorf. I spent the night in the waiting room of the Gelsenkirchen railway station. I have only one request—let me take refuge in the orphanage for a short while. While I was traveling to Dinslaken I heard in the train that anti-Semitic riots had broken out everywhere,

---

* Written originally in German these reminiscences were based on daily notes made by the author in 1938 while at Dinslaken. In 1940, as a refugee in Australia, Mr. Herz submitted a manuscript describing his experiences in Nazi Germany to the Literary Prize Competition conducted by Harvard University Faculty, Cambridge, Massachusetts. His paper, which included this chapter on the Dinslaken Orphanage, was graded among the twenty best out of more than two hundred manuscripts.

and that many Jews had been arrested. Synagogues everywhere are burning!"

With anxiety I listened to the man's story; suddenly he said with a trembling voice: "No, I won't come in! I can't be safe in your house! We are all lost!" With these words he disappeared into the dark fog which cast a veil over the morning. I never saw him again. In spite of this Job's message I forced myself not to show any sign of emotion. Only thus could I avoid a state of panic among the children and tutors. Nonetheless I was of the opinion that the young students should be prepared to brave the storm of the approaching catastrophe. About 7.30 A.M. I ordered forty-six people—among them thirty-two children—into the dining hall of the institution and told them the following in a simple and brief address:

As you know, last night a Herr vom Rath, a member of the German embassy in Paris, was assassinated. The Jews are held responsible for this murder. The tension in the political field is now being directed against the Jews, and during the next few hours there will certainly be anti-Semitic excesses. This will happen even in our town. It is my feeling and my impression that we German Jews have never experienced such calamities since the Middle Ages. Be strong! Trust in God! I am sure we will withstand even these hard times. Nobody will remain in the rooms of the upper floor of the building. The exit door to the street will be opened only by myself! From this moment on everyone is to heed my orders only!

After breakfast the pupils were sent to the large study hall of the institution. The teacher in charge tried to keep them busy.

At 9.30 A.M. the bell at the main gate rang persistently. I opened the door: about fifty men stormed into the house, many of them with their coat or jacket collars turned up. At first they rushed into the dining room, which fortunately was empty, and there they began their work of destruction, which was carried out with the utmost precision. The frightened and fearful cries of the children resounded through the building. In a stentorian voice I shouted: "Children, go out into the street immediately." This advice was certainly contrary to the order of the Gestapo. I thought, however, that in the street, in a public place, we might be in less danger than inside the house. The children immediately ran down a small staircase at the back, most of them without hat or coat—despite the cold and wet weather. We tried to reach the next street crossing, which was close to Dinslaken's town hall, where I intended to ask for police protection. About ten policemen were stationed here, reason enough for a sensation-seeking mob to await the next development. This was not very long in coming; the senior police officer, Freihahn, shouted at us: "Jews do not get protection from us! Vacate the area together with your children as quickly as possible!" Freihahn then chased us back to a side street in the direction of the backyard of the orphanage. As I was unable to hand over the key of the back gate, the policeman drew his bayonet and forced open the door. I then said to Freihahn: "The best thing is to kill me and the children, then our ordeal will be over quickly!" The officer responded to my "suggestion" merely with cynical laughter. Freihahn then drove all of us to the wet lawn of the orphanage garden. He gave us strict orders not to leave the place under any circumstance.

Facing the back of the building, we were able to watch how everything in the house was being systematically destroyed under the supervision of the men of law and order—the police. At short intervals we could hear the crunching of glass or the hammering against wood as windows and doors were broken. Books, chairs, beds, tables, linen, chests, parts of a piano, a radiogram, and maps were thrown through apertures in the wall, which a short while ago had been windows or doors.

In the meantime the mob standing around the building had grown to several hundred. Among these people I recognized some familiar faces, suppliers of the orphanage or tradespeople, who only a day or a week earlier had been happy to deal with us as customers. This time they were passive, watching the destruction without much emotion.

At 10.15 A.M. we heard the wailing of sirens! We noticed a heavy cloud of smoke billowing upward. It was obvious from the direction it was coming from that the Nazis had set the synagogue on fire. Very soon we saw smoke clouds rising up, mixed with sparks of fire. Later I noticed that some Jewish houses, close to the synagogue, had also been set alight under the expert guidance of the fire brigade. Its presence was a necessity, since the firemen had to save the homes of the non-Jewish neighborhood.

At 10.45 A.M. the police commissioner of the town approached me. He had an order—as he expressed it—to discuss the situation with me. The way he talked about the event did not leave the slightest doubt that he was disturbed and shocked. He asked me to accompany him through the orphanage. Meanwhile most of the Nazis had left the building. While we were walking from room to room the officer asked me about my future plans. I answered briefly that I wanted permission from the authorities to leave with the children for Belgium or Holland at the earliest opportunity. As we continued our "inspection," trying to make our way over heaps of rubble and the broken staircase, a young fellow in brown trousers who was wearing a "civilian" jacket shouted at the police commissioner in a coarse voice: "What's this bloody Jew doing near you?" Thereupon the "friendly" police officer gave me the order "to run as quickly as possible to the members of my race." In this situation there was no alternative but to disappear and return to my charges.

In the meantime a large number of police officers had arrived in the backyard. They told me to prepare all the children, older students, and employees of the orphanage for a march to the center of Dinslaken. They held me responsible for getting them ready in the shortest possible time. The news of the *Judenparade* or *Judenzug* (this was the name they mockingly gave it) spread like wildfire through the streets of the town. Three to four rows deep, the Germans filled the pavements of both sides of the street waiting for the procession. Most of them did not make any remarks; many faces revealed obvious disapproval, but even these people turned up for the "show." The "parade" was led by two police officers and was flanked by Nazi Storm Troopers. The small children of the orphanage were forced into a wagon with a long shaft, which was pulled by four teenage boys from the orphanage. Suddenly, from a street corner police officer Freihahn shouted at the brown-shirted guards who marched with us: "Friends, what are you doing accompanying this *Judenzug*? They will and they must know themselves where their stable will be!" Both policemen immediately followed Freihahn's advice and left the procession. They drove us on and pushed us into a schoolyard, close to Dinslaken's synagogue. We were now able to see with our own eyes how a German fire brigade, whose task was to extinguish fires, was ordered to perform legalized arson. I could clearly see how members of the German fire brigade fanned the flames which were consuming the synagogue and Jewish community buildings, while others directed jets of water onto nearby houses belonging to non-Jews.

In the schoolyard we had to wait for some time. Several Jews, who had escaped the previous arrest and deportation to concentration camps, joined our gathering. Many of them, mostly women, were shabbily dressed. They told me that the brown hordes had driven them out of their homes, ordered them to leave everything behind and come at once, under Nazi guard, to the schoolyard. A Storm Trooper in charge commanded some bystanders to leave the schoolyard "since there is no point in even looking at such scum!"

In the meantime our "family" had increased to ninety, all of whom were placed in a small hall in the school. Nobody was allowed to leave the place. Men considered physically fit were called for duty. Only those over sixty—among them people of seventy-five years of age—were allowed to stay. Very soon we learned that the entire Jewish male population under sixty had already been transferred to the concentration camp at Dachau. During their initial waiting period, while still under police custody, the Jewish men had been allowed to buy their own food. This state of affairs, however, only lasted for a few hours.

I learned very soon from a policeman, who in his heart was still an anti-Nazi, that most of the Jewish men had been beaten up by members of the SA before being transported to Dachau. They were kicked, slapped in the face, and subjected to all sorts of humiliation. Many of those exposed to this type of ill-treatment had served in the German army during World War I. One of them, a Mr. Hugo B.C., had once worn with pride the Iron Cross First Class (the German equivalent of the Victoria Cross), that he had been awarded for bravery.

I myself was relatively fortunate. The leader of the "action" informed me that I was to be in charge of the Jews and responsible for order. Furthermore, he appointed me spokesman for all the Jews then in custody. My first job was to prepare a list of those who were in the school hall. This took quite a while. There were frequent interruptions. One woman fainted, another asked for water, a third complained of headaches. The old Jewish teacher, a pensioner, a real gentleman, once a city councilor and principal of a commercial school, was sitting moaning in a corner. His forehead was bleeding from a beating he had received from the Nazis. I found an old envelope, used it as a cup, and brought some water to the suffering old man. Unobserved for a moment, I had been able to steal this water from the tap in the corridor.

A sudden quiet! A Nazi in plainclothes and peaked cap had entered the hall. He was accompanied by a woman in her early forties, most unimpressive in her appearance. The representative of the party "took the floor:"

People, now listen to me! Unknown elements are the culprits responsible for this morning's work of destruction. We must be clear on this. Look! In Düsseldorf a German mother and German father are mourning over a promising son who was murdered by a Jew. You must understand this, people! This woman (pointing at the person accompanying him) is a German. That is already enough reason for her to be regarded as honest and honorable. She is here as a witness to assure you that not one Jew was harmed in the slightest degree.

People! There is no need to live in fear! We are not here in Soviet Russia! The old folks—if they want to—may be taken to the hospital. A physician will come very soon! If you are hungry put your money together—Jews always have plenty! Somebody may go to the shopping center and buy some food!

A few minutes later the representative of the Nazi Party made another announcement:

People! I want to tell you that the cow owned by the orphanage has been transferred to the stable of a German peasant. We ordered him to provide the animal with proper food, because animals should never suffer!

Meanwhile, a doctor had arrived. He treated the elderly with visible sympathy. They were treated for shock and some minor wounds which they had received due to the rough handling meted out by the Nazi rowdies. The afternoon passed quickly, however children and adults began to show signs of despair and depression. On the lips of everyone was a single question: "What will be next?" There were, however, a few small children who obviously did not grasp the gravity of the situation. Some of these—this was my impression—regarded the Nazi fete with a feeling of thrill.

At 6.30 P.M. the Nazi official who had been in charge in the morning "honored" us with another visit. This time he appeared in an elegant uniform. He gave the order that all Jews assembled and in custody were to get ready immediately. We were to be marched off to another hall, which belonged to the owner of an inn. As in the morning the little children were seated on a wagon, which was pulled by four boys: "and all the others—male and female—are to march behind." It took about twenty minutes for the *Judenzug* to reach the other place. As was to be expected, huge crowds waited on both sides of the streets. Most of them were silent onlookers, and from their stern faces I could sense that they did not approve of this type of anti-Semitic demonstration.

We arrived at the building at about 7 P.M. It was normally used as a dance hall but this time it had been prepared for a different purpose. The floor was covered with straw and some cushions, which belonged to the orphanage. Above the stage hung a picture of Adolf Hitler, which had been covered with some cloth shortly before our arrival. The SA man in charge told me that in accordance with my request all prisoners would receive some macaroni with dried fruit, nicely prepared as their evening meal. "The Nazis," so he assured me, "did not put any poison into the food!" An hour later a police officer appeared with yet another order, namely that all boys over fifteen and the Jewish men (mostly invalids of World War I) were to sleep somewhere else. He informed me that the stable of the Jew L. had been chosen as a suitable accommodation for the men and boys, and there they were led.

About 10 P.M. *Feierabend* [the end of the workday] was ordered. All lights were turned off, except those at the two exits. In the hall between the children and women there stood about forty SA and SS men, all of them armed with pistols. Those who took positions along the walls looked like horrible monsters, frightening their Jewish captives. I had to do something to calm the children, who were put in one row against the wall. In a whisper I told them to recite the night prayer with me in a chorus.

I must admit it was a dramatic moment, fraught with religious emotion. Even these coarse Germans in uniform must have been touched for some seconds when they heard the children's voices ringing out in the darkness. Suddenly, the Nazis retreated one by one and left our "protection" to a policeman and a brown-shirted Storm Trooper. Despite repeated assurances from the guard, supported by "words of honor" that nothing would happen, it took a long time for the grown-ups to fall asleep. I myself remained awake and tried to observe our "protectors." I was reminded of the protagonist in Heinrich Heine's *Der Rabbi von Bacharach* and his remark to his wife Sara, while both were walking along the *Judengasse* in Frankfurt: "How badly protected is Israel! False friends guard them from the outside and, their protectors within are guardians of foolishness and fright!" At about three o'clock in the morning three people were driven to the hospital by ambulance. Then silence returned. You could hear only the monotonous steps of the guard walking back and forth. It was night; officially "rest" was declared—and guarded. Tranquillity?—there was none. Nobody really slept.

The next day (November 11) a representative of Dinslaken's town clerk introduced himself as the newly-appointed commissar whose job it was to regulate the food supply for the Jews. He was the prototype of a German public servant, who took his new task extremely seriously. He immediately informed me, that "they" had found 13,250 reichsmarks in the office of the orphanage, and he was ordered to account for each penny to me. There was not the slightest doubt that the man, indeed, meant well. But this type of correctness, when you were forced to make your way over heaps of destruction carried out by vandals, could not convince or deceive me. While I was talking to the man my pupil Arno Bergmann brought me a German twenty-mark note he had found in a heap of debris in a corner of the former office. And yet the Nazi continued to speak of correct bookkeeping.

They gave us permission to do some cooking in the semidestroyed kitchen of the orphanage. The oven and the water pipe were still in order although the rooms, hall, and the staircase of the house were in shambles. As already indicated above, the German vandals carried out their mission of destruction with skillful efficiency. Preserved fruits in jars were used by the Nazis as projectiles and were flung against the walls and doors of the kitchen. Yet it was amazing how quickly we got used to the new situation which had been forced on us.

Some police officers, when they felt safe, i.e., when SA men were not in sight, talked freely to me about the gruesome event. Apologizing profusely they declared that they had nothing to do with these crimes and misdeeds, but as policemen had to fulfill the orders of their superiors. Another member of the police force confided his secret to me, that during the night of November 10, at about four o'clock, he was ordered to come immediately to the Dinslaken town hall to participate in a most important "action." The same officer told me a few hours later that: "Our order for the 10th of November was to leave the streets of Dinslaken completely in the hands of the Nazi Storm Troopers." The police were to appear in streets and public places only at 4 P.M., by which time the "action" would be over.

November 12 (Shabbat). After the so-called breakfast one of my pupils approached me. He wanted to tell me something, but only on condition that I keep it a secret. The boy commenced: "As you know, last night we slept in a horse stable. Suddenly, during the night, an SA man, completely drunk, entered the stable. Although we were under the protection of a police guard, we were forced to listen to the utterances of this brownshirt and to obey his orders. Under his command we were forced to do exercises for nearly an hour. At the end of this type of training we had to sing one stanza of the 'Horst Wessel' song, the anthem of the Nazi Movement." Thus ran the boy's story. As usually happens in such situations someone who was involved in this episode learned that I had been informed of it. The man begged me not to inform the authorities of this "illegal"

incident, which in any case was totally "harmless," as he put it. It had never been my intention to report the misbehavior of one Nazi to another Nazi of a higher rank.

At about 10.30 A.M. I asked two teenagers to follow me. Although we were officially in custody we managed to reach the backyard of the orphanage. It was a foggy morning. The grass was wet and the small lanes very muddy. Why did I ask the two boys to follow me? During the "action" of November 10, I had noticed that the Nazis had thrown all the books, most of them religious, as well as the Torah scroll of the orphanage out of the window. Very shortly after reaching the backyard we discovered the holy scroll on the ground covered with mud and dirt. I still remember that very close to it I noticed Mandelkern's *Concordance* in a new "resting place." But not for long! Without much explanation the boys got hold of the garden tools, dug a deep hole, and buried the scroll. They quickly filled the "grave" with soil. While the boys were working, it was my job to look out for the "enemy." Thank God our plan was executed without incident, and we returned to our hall.

At about seven o'clock in the morning of November 13 a policeman came to our small internment camp and asked me to come to the orphanage at once. He told me that since the official attack on November 10 all the rooms of the building had been guarded day and night to prevent looting. It was a fact that heaps of clothing and linen were still buried under dirt and broken glass. In a voice which revealed his utter despair, the man said to me: "Mr. Tutor, to have put us on guard here was completely senseless. Last night the leader of the local NSDAP [Nazi Party] came to the orphanage with two big trucks, and brownshirts loaded all those goods and chattels which we policemen were supposed to protect onto the vehicles. Before they left they even forced open the safe, then went to the cellar of the house and emptied the contents of about forty bottles of wine, which they found in one case." I replied to the police officer that it was very nice of him to trust me, although I was a Jew and was more or less kept under arrest by the very same people whom he accused of all these misdeeds. I added, candidly speaking, that under the prevailing conditions it would be absurd to make any complaints; complain to whom and against whom? This question the policeman might ask and answer by himself.

At about 11 A.M. on the same day, a car stopped in front of our hall. A well-dressed woman got out. With tears in her eyes, crying and moaning, she ran toward the entrance of our building. Suddenly she shouted: "My husband is dead! After being tortured by the Gestapo he died in one of the prison cells near the border!" Whereupon a policeman remarked: "You mean forced to die!" *(getotet Borden)*. The woman continued: "Yes! My husband must be buried here! I hope it's possible." The policeman next to me could not give any advice. We succeeded, however, in obtaining permission to arrange the burial at the local Jewish cemetery, but no one was allowed to attend the funeral itself.

I had hoped that with this incident the exciting events of the day would be over. But since it was still only midday the rest of November 13 might still hold in store some surprises. They came in the early afternoon, when the commissioner of police appeared in the hall and commanded me to come to the orphanage immediately. The local leader of the Nazi Party wanted all the keys to the building, and insisted that I hand them over personally. I was prepared for an unpleasant scene, full of tension and threats which might, perhaps, end with my being sent to a concentration camp.

We reached the former dining room of the building. About forty policemen, SS and SA officials, all of them in uniform, took up positions along the walls of the room; the wall with the windows faced the backyard. The leader of the district, a former assistant teacher at a primary school, was a lanky man with a stern expression on his face. When I came closer to him he snatched the keys from my right hand and loudly ordered me to leave the room and wait in the yard. In the backyard I turned my face to the wall and the broken windows of the dining room. I also noticed with shock that from every corner of the yard and house Nazis were staring at me. I neither lost my composure nor did I tremble. I must admit that I never was the heroic type. Although my position was quite hopeless I knew my weapon. Gangsters of the Nazi type are impressed to a certain degree if you do not show fear. It is always a good thing to answer the questions of coarse and brutal people evasively, but without hesitation. Religious strength often may help to conquer fear. From an open window the district leader of "Lower Rhine" *(Niederrhein)* leveled two accusations against me: that I had removed the Torah scroll and had complained about the way I was being treated. I denied both charges and towards evening I was allowed to return to the inn.

In the evening an SA man asked me to come to the front room of the tavern and to answer the telephone calls from abroad. Relatives and friends of the children were phoning—from Holland, Belgium, Berlin, Hamburg, Cologne, and other places. All of them wanted to find out how the children were and what had become of them. One Nazi at the table shouted anti-Semitic remarks through the room, but was quickly "reprimanded" by someone else, who told him: "The Jews are human beings like ourselves!"

November 14: No special events or incidents.

November 15: The police informed me that the Jews must return again to their houses or apartments. By 4 P.M. the hall of the inn was to be cleared and made spick-and-span again. Naturally, we were responsible for keeping it clean. Dinslaken's sports association needed the place for the evening's boxing match! It was left to me to make the necessary accommodations—a very hard task, because most of the Jewish homes had been destroyed. I advised the people that for the time being they should live in groups in any rooms which they considered still habitable. I myself "squatted" in the villa of the above-mentioned war veteran (Iron Cross First Class). I now found out that he had been given "accommodation" in a concentration camp. Inside the house practically everything had been destroyed, including the kitchen and the bathroom. Through the windows came the blast of an icy north wind. The floors were covered with rubble. I asked some of the boys to clear up two rooms and to find some cardboard with which to fill up the holes in the windows. Our food reserve had reached a dangerously low level. Before we left for our new quarters, two district leaders of the Nazi Party had prohibited the storekeepers from selling us food or doing us any favors. Furthermore, he ordered that the "junk" we still had (some pots, bags of food, cushions, brooms, etc.) was to be carried by the children. Thus burdened with the remaining belongings of the orphanage, we were forced to march through Dinslaken's main street, and this—as was to be expected—during the peak shopping hours.

The police were ordered to withdraw their men from the villa. Upon being given this information I organized the boys into a "homeguard" of our own. While the younger ones and the older girls were "asleep" we walked around the house throughout the whole night. Although I was aware that in an emergency this protection would have been useless, it gave me a sense of moral satisfaction to do guard duty with the boys.

While we made the rounds I discussed our immediate future with the boys; in other words what to do the next morning? I realized that it was impossible to continue this gypsy life for another day. We were even worse off than Gypsies. They would have been allowed to obtain food, but the Nazis denied this basic right to the Jewish children. "Yes, I must act; I must act immediately," I said to myself time and again. This house, which had once been an elegant villa, was now cold, dirty, wet, and windy. The two toilets were destroyed, and so was the shower and the bathtub. Many parts of the railing on the staircase had been ripped off.

It entered my mind that, in spite of the riots and devastation, there was a slim chance that one of the offices of the Jewish community in Cologne might still be functioning. I went to Dinslaken Post Office and spoke with the director, an elderly gentleman, who not only made the telephone connection for me, but also expressed his disgust with the action of November 10 against the Jews and with the many wrongs perpetrated by the new regime in the name of the German nation.

The person in charge of the remnants of the Jewish community in Cologne advised me to make the arrangements to transfer the children and the remaining members of the staff to the Rhenish metropolis. The next day was *Buss- und Bettag*, an official "Day of Repentance" in Prussia. It was a gray and foggy day. A truck brought the youngsters to Cologne, while I and some boys stayed behind until the empty truck had returned from its seventy kilometer journey. I went to the police and reported the departure of the residents of the former Jewish orphanage to Cologne. I did not fail to notice that in a corner of the magistrate's office silver and many other valuables of the orphanage had been "secured" in large boxes. At about 6 P.M. the truck returned, and with the assistance of the driver I was able to load the vehicle with the few meager bits and pieces which we were allowed to take with us. It was an open truck. I sat in the back surrounded by brooms, buckets, pots, and pans. It was about 8 P.M. when we reached Duisburg. The fog changed to a fine drizzle, but the streets of the big city were filled with people going to the movie theaters, concerts, and cafés. I do not think they were much worried about a Jew, sitting among brooms, who had been driven out of one town, was trying to reach a safe haven, and was not sure whether he would be accepted for any length of time anywhere.

By 1.30 A.M. our truck had arrived in Cologne, and it stopped in front of the Jewish Apprentice Home in old Agrippa Street. From here I was to prepare the emigration of the Dinslaken children to Belgium and Holland; I was also to act as tutor to the thirty Jewish apprentices of the home. Although the institution had escaped the destruction of November 10, the effects of this black day in Jewish history were obvious here, too. Many boys, who could not work in the destroyed school for artisans, had returned to their hometowns and villages. They wanted to find out how the conditions were there and whether their fathers or brothers had been taken to concentration camps. However, after a few days all the boys had returned to Cologne because the conditions "at home" were much worse. The mob had been much more destructive in the smaller places from which most of the boys had come.

During the first two weeks I took advantage of the good meals served in the backyard of a former Jewish organization. There was a long wooden table with benches. Without taking pay a woman, perhaps a Jewish lady whose husband was under arrest, served out the *Eintopfgericht*, a hot soup with barley or noodles in it; in addition everybody received a slice of bread. Here one met all types of citizens. Many of them were elderly people or those who had escaped the Nazi roundup. The chief topic of conversation was, naturally, emigration: "Are you going to America?" "What is your waiting number in Stuttgart?"—seat of the U.S. Consulate. Those who now "enjoyed" their bowls of soup together had previously been complete strangers. Yet they all talked about their common interests—arrests, permits, affidavits, good connections, illegal transfers of money, crossing the border. They talked softly, in whispers. All of them were scared, frightened of Jewish spies paid by the Gestapo. Indeed, they were full of fear. They did not dare to pronounce the name of Hitler; instead they referred to him as "Horowitz."

In the meantime the city of Cologne prepared for the great festival of peace—Christmas. Stores, shops, and streets were decorated with fir trees, electric candles, and the Star of Bethlehem. From some corners loudspeakers blared the famous German *Weihnachtslieder* (Christmas songs) "*Heilige Nacht*" or "*O Tannenbaum, o Tannenbaum, wie grun sind deine Blatter.*" There were many stalls where children in particular could buy candy or ginger-

bread. In front of a large store (Kaufhof) children sang Christmas carols. The air was full of peace and love.

However, any Jew who had experienced November 10 had to be very realistic. Very soon one noticed that Christendom and Nazidom seemed to be in perfect harmony. Many stores exhibited the photo of the Führer next to a scene of Bethlehem and the festivities in this sacred place. Garlands with swastikas and glittering stars, symbols of brutality and peace, were strung side by side across the streets. The sidewalks were teeming with shoppers, the majority were men in gray, black, or brown uniforms. Most of them greeted each other with "Heil, Hitler!" and only rarely with the once-familiar "Frohes Fest!" The facades of the shopping centers, however showed many dark spots. These were Jewish shops, which had been destroyed or closed by the Nazis. Overnight the big stores were all placed in Aryan hands, in accordance with the new legislation enacted in the Third Reich. *Der Stürmer*, Germany's leading anti-Semitic weekly, now an official Nazi organ, had put up special placards in many streets, displaying its chief slogan "The Jews are our misfortune!"

Julius Streicher, chief editor of this gutter-sheet and a well-known personality in the Nazi hierarchy, invited the Germans in his innumerable articles to eradicate the Jews, the "scum of the earth." He told them in special issues, published during Christmas and Lent, that Jews were in the habit of slaughtering Christian girls and using their blood for wine at Passover. I myself saw a *Stürmerspecial* in front of Cologne's Kaufhof, displaying a "Jewish" family seated around the Passover Seder table. Over a large glass of red wine was printed: "Germans, this is not red wine, it is the blood of a little German child, slaughtered by a Jew!" During the same week, in February 1939, the Cologne newspaper printed the following in bold headlines: "Baby disappears in front of Kaufhof." Waves of fear passed through the homes of those Jews who still remained in the city. A constant feeling of dread and insecurity haunted those Jews who had so far avoided being sent to concentration camps. When, a little later, the baby was found safe and sound, an audible sigh of relief was uttered by the anxious Jews.

Despite all this, somehow life continued. The principal of the Apprentice Home and I began to reorganize life and work in the institution. Besides trying to resettle in a German city, I wrestled with the Nazi bureaucracy to arrange the emigration of my former charges. There is no need to give a detailed account of the treatment accorded the Jews by the infallible bureaucracy of the Third Reich....

EXCERPTS FROM "STENOGRAPHIC REPORT OF THE CONFERENCE ON THE JEWISH QUESTION"

Office of the U.S. Chief of Counsel
Stenographic Report on a part
of the Conference on the Jewish Question
under the presidency of Field Marshal
Goering at the Reich Ministry for Air on
12 November 1938—11 o'clock

PART I

GOERING: Gentlemen! Today's meeting is of a decisive nature. I have received a letter written on the Führer's orders by the *Stabsleiter* of the Führer's deputy Borland requesting that the Jewish question be now, once and for all, coordinated and solved one way or another. And yesterday once again did the Führer request by phone for me to take coordinated action in the matter.

Since the problem is mainly an economic one, it is from the economic angle that it shall have to be tackled. Naturally a number of legal measures shall have to be taken which fall into the sphere of the minister of justice and into that of the minister of the interior; and certain propaganda measures shall be taken care of by the office of the minister of propaganda. The minister of finances and the minister of economic affairs shall take care of problems falling into their respective resorts.

The meeting in which we first talked about this question and came to the decision to aryanize the German economy, to take the Jew out of it, and put him into our debit ledger, was one in which, to our shame, we only made pretty plans, which were executed very slowly. We then had a demonstration, right here in Berlin; we told the people that something decisive would be done, but again nothing happened. We have had this affair in Paris now, more demonstrations followed, and this time something decisive must be done!

Because, gentlemen, I have had enough of these demonstrations! They harm not the Jew, but me, who is the last authority for coordinating the German economy.

If today, a Jewish shop is destroyed, if goods are thrown into the street, the insurance company will pay for the damages, which the Jew does not even have—and furthermore goods of the consumer goods belonging to the people, are destroyed. If in the future demonstrations, which are necessary occur, then I pray that they be directed so as not to hurt us.

Because it's insane to burn out and destroy a Jewish warehouse then have a German insurance company making good the loss. And the goods which I need desperately, whole bales of

View of interior of the Nuremberg synagogue after its destruction during the November 1938 pogroms. After November 10, 1938. Yad Vashem.

clothing and whatnot, are being burned, and I miss them everywhere.

I may as well burn the raw materials before they arrive. The people of course, do not understand that; therefore we must make laws which will show the people once and for all, that something is being done.

I should appreciate it very much if, for once, our propaganda could make it clear that it is unfortunately not the Jew who has to suffer in all this but the German insurance companies.

I am not going to tolerate a situation in which the insurance companies are the ones who suffer. Under the authority invested in me, I shall issue a decree, and I am, of course, requesting the support of the competent government agencies, so that everything shall be processed through the right channels, and the insurance companies will not be the ones who suffer.

It may be, though, that these insurance companies may have insurance in foreign countries—if that is the case, foreign bills of exchange would be available which I would not want to lose. That shall have to be checked. For that reason, I have asked Mr. HILGARD of the insurance company, to attend, since he is best qualified to tell us to what extent the insurance companies are protected against damage, by having taken out insurance with other companies. I would not want to miss this, under any circumstances.

I should not want to leave any doubt, gentlemen, as to the aim of today's meeting. We have not come together merely to talk again but to make decisions, and I implore the competent agencies to take all measures for the elimination of the Jew from the German economy and to submit them to me, as far as it is necessary.

The fundamental idea in this program of elimination of the Jew from the German economy is first: the Jew being ejected from the economy transfers his property to the state. He will be compensated.

The compensation is to be listed in the debit ledger and shall bring a certain percentage of interest. The Jew shall have to live out of this interest. It is a foregone conclusion, that this aryanizing, if it is to be done quickly, cannot be made in the ministry for the economy in Berlin. That way, we would never finish.

On the other hand, it is very necessary to have safety precautions so that the lower echelons, Statthalter and Gauleitern, will not do things unreasonably. One must issue correction directives immediately.

The aryanizing of all the larger establishments, naturally, is to be my lot—the ministry for economy will designate, which and how many there are—; it must not be done by a Statthalter or his lower echelons, since these things reach into the export trade, and cause great problems, which the Statthalter can neither observe, nor solve from his place.

It is my lot, so that the damage will not be greater than the profit, which we are striving for.

It is obvious, gentlemen, that the Jewish stores are for the people, and not the stores. Therefore, we must begin here, according to the rules previously laid down.

The minister of economic affairs shall announce which stores he'll want to close altogether. These stores are excluded from aryanizing at once. Their stocks are to be made available for sale in other stores; what cannot be sold, shall be processed through the "Winterhilfe" or taken care of otherwise. However, the sales value of these articles shall always be considered, since the state is not to suffer but should profit through this transformation. For the chain and department stores—I speak now only of that, what can be seen, certain categories have to be established, according to the importance of the various branches.

The trustee of the state will estimate the value of the property and decide what amount the Jew shall receive. Naturally, this amount is to be set as low as possible. The representative of the state shall then turn the establishment over to the "Aryan" proprietor; that is, the property shall be sold according to its real value.

There begins the difficulties. It is easily understood that strong attempt will be made to get these stores to party members and to let them have some kind of compensations. I have witnessed terrible things in the past; little chauffeurs of Gauleiters have profited so much by these transactions that they have now about half a million. You, gentlemen, know it. Is that correct?

[Assent]

Of course, things like that are impossible. I shall not hesitate to act ruthlessly in any case where such a trick is played. If the individual involved is prominent, I shall see the Führer within two hours and report to him.

We shall have to insist upon it, that the Aryan taking over the establishment is of the branch and knows his job. Generally speaking he is the one who must pay for the store with his own money. In other words, an ordinary business transaction is to be sought—one merchant selling, the other one buying, a business. If there are party members among the contenders, they are to be preferred, that is if they have the same qualifications: first shall come the one who had the most damage, and secondly, selection should be according to length of party membership.

Of course, there may be exceptions. There are party members who, as may be proven, lost their business concessions by action of the Schuschnigg or Prague government, and so went bankrupt. Such a man has naturally first option on a store for sale, and he shall receive help if he does not have the means to help himself. The trustee of the state can justify this help, if he is more businesslike in the transfer. This party member should have the chance to buy the store for as cheap a price as possible. In such a case the state will not receive the full price, but only on the amount the Jew received.

Such a buyer may even receive a loan besides, so that he will get off to a good start.

I wish to make it clear that such a proceeding shall only be legal if the party member has once owned such a store. For example, a party member was the owner of a stationery store, and Schuschnigg took away the concession to operate it so that the man lost the store and went bankrupt. Now, if a Jewish stationery store is being aryanized, this party member should get the store on conditions that he'll be able to fulfill. Such a case shall be the only exception though, in all other cases the procedure shall be of a strictly businesslike nature whereby the party member, like I said before, shall have the preference, if he has the same qualifications as any other candidate, who is not a member of the party.

When selling for the actual value we shall find only about sixty Aryans ready to take over one hundred Jewish stores; I don't think that we have a German for every Jewish store. You must not forget that the Jew sees his main activity in the field of trade, and that he owns 90 percent of it. I doubt that we'd have a demand big enough. I even doubt that we'd have enough people, particularly now since everybody has found his field of work.

Therefore, I ask the minister of economy to go beyond what we think ought to be done for the sake of the principle, in liquidating the establishments—I ask him to go further, even though there won't be any candidates. That'll be perfectly all right.

The transfer of stores and establishments shall have to be executed by the lower echelons, not through Berlin but through the Gaue and through the *Reichsstatthalterschaft*. Therein shall be the seat of the members of the Board of Trustees, even if it consists of a few people only. The Statthalter and his people cannot do this job; the trustees will have to tackle it. But the Statthalter shall be the authority which supervises, according to the regulations given him, the trustees, particularly in dealings such as the transfer to party members.

Naturally, these establishments cannot disap-pear all at once but we'll have to start by Monday, in a manner that shall make it obvious that a change has begun to materialize. Besides that, certain stores could be closed which will make things here easier.

Another point! I have noticed that Aryans took over a Jewish store and were then so clever to keep the name of the Jewish store as "formerly," or kept it altogether. That must not be; I can not permit it. Because it may happen—what has just happened—stores were looted because their signboards bore Jewish names because they had once been Jewish, but had been "aryanized" a long time ago. Names of former Jewish firms shall have to disappear completely, and the German shall have to come forward with this or his firm's name. I ask you to carry this out quite definitely. That much then regarding aryanizing of stores and whole-sale establishments, particularly in regards to signboards and of all that is obvious!

Of the consequences resulting from this for the Jew, I shall speak later, because this is connected with other things.

Now for the factories. As for the smaller and medium ones, two things shall have to be made clear.

1. Which factories do I not need at all, which are the ones where productions could be suspended? Could they not be put to another use? If not, the factories will be razed immediately.

2. In case the factory should be needed, it will be turned over to Aryans in the same manner as the stores. All these measures have to be taken quickly, since Aryan employees are concerned everywhere. I'd like to say right now that the Aryan employees shall have to be given employment immediately after the Jewish factory is closed. Considering the amount of labor we need these days, it should be a trifle to keep these people, even in their own branches. As I have just said, if the factory is necessary, it will be aryanized. If there is no need for it, it being abandoned shall be part of the procedure

of transforming establishments not essential for our national welfare into ones that are essential for it—a procedure that shall take place within the next few weeks. For it, I shall still need very much space and very many factories.

If such a factory is to be transformed or razed, the first thing to be done is check the equipment. The questions arising will be: Where can this equipment be used? Could it be used after the place is transformed? Where else might it be needed badly? Where could the machinery be set up again? It follows that aryanizing factories will be an even more difficult task than the aryanizing of stores.

Take now the larger factories which are run solely by a Jewish owner, without control by a board of directors; or take corporations where the Jew might be in the supervisory council or board of directors. There the solution is very simple: the factory can be compensated in the same manner as in the sale of stores and factories; that is, at a rate which we shall determine, and the trustee shall take over the Jew's interest as well as his shares, which he in turn may sell or transfer to the state, which will then dispose of them. So, if I have a big factory, which belonged to a Jew or a Jewish corporation, and the Jew leaves, perhaps with his sons who were employed there, the factory will still continue to operate. Maybe a director will have to be appointed because the Jew has run the factory himself. But otherwise, particularly if the maintenance of the establishment is very essential, everything will run smoothly.

Everything is very simple. I now have his shares, I may give them to some Aryan or to another group or I may keep them. The state takes them over and offers them at the stock market, if they are acceptable there and if it so desires, or it makes use of them in some other way.

Now, I shall talk of the very big establishments, those in which a Jew is on the board of directors, in which he holds shares, etc., and so is either the owner or one of the coowners; in any case in which he is greatly interested. There too, things are comparatively simple; he delivers all of his shares which shall be bought at a price fixed by the trustee. So the Jew gets into the account book. The shares shall be handled like I've just explained. These cases can not be taken care of by the Gaue and Reichsstatthalter, but only by us here on top; because we are the only ones to decide where these factories are to be transferred to, how they may be affiliated with other establishments or to what an extent the state shall keep them or hand them over to another establishment belonging to the state. All this can only be decided here. Of course, the Gauleiter and Statthalter will be to glad to get hold of the shares, and they'll make great promises to beautify our capital cities, etc. I know it all! It won't go! We must agree on a clear action that shall be profitable to the Reich.

The same procedure shall be applied where the Jew has a share in, or owns property of the German economy. I am not competent enough to tell offhand in what forms that may be the case, and to what an extent he'll have to lose it. Anyway, the Jew must be evicted pretty fast from the German economy.

Now, the foreign Jews. There we'll have to make distinctions between the Jews who have always been foreigners—and who shall have to be treated according to the laws we arranged with their respective countries. But regarding those Jews who were Germans, have always lived in Germany and have acquired foreign citizenship during the last year, only because they wanted to play safe, I ask you not to give them any consideration. We'll finish with these. Or have you any misgivings? We shall try to induce them through slight and then through stronger pressure and through clever maneuvering, to let themselves be pushed out voluntarily.

WOERMANN: I'd like the Foreign Office to be included, since a generally valid decision could hardly be made—

GOERING: We cannot consult you in every case, but on the whole we will.

WOERMANN: Anyway, I'd like to make known the claim of the Foreign Office to participate. One never knows what steps may become necessary.

GOERING: Only for important cases! I do not like to take this category under special consideration. I have learned only now to what extent that has been done, particularly in Austria and Czechoslovakia. If somebody was a Czech in Sudetenland, we do not have to consider him at all, and the Foreign Office doesn't have to be consulted because that person now belongs to us. And in Austria and also in Sudetenland, too many become all of a sudden Englishmen or Americans or whatnot—and generally speaking we cannot consider that a great deal.

[PART II IS MISSING]

PART III

FUNK: That is quite a decisive question for us: shall the Jewish stores be reopened?

GOEBBELS: If they will be reopened is another question. The question is will they be restored? I have set the deadline for Monday.

GOERING: You don't have to ask whether they will be reopened. That is up to us to decide.

GOERING: Number two. In almost all German cities synagogues are burned. New, various possibilities exist to utilize the space where the synagogues stood. Some cities want to build parks in their place, others want to put up new buildings.

GOERING: How many synagogues were actually burned?

HEYDRICH: Altogether there are 101 synagogues destroyed by fire, 76 synagogues demolished, and 7,500 stores ruined in the Reich.

GOERING: What do you mean "destroyed by fire"?

HEYDRICH: Partly they are razed, and partly gutted.

GOEBBELS: I am of the opinion that this is our chance to dissolve the synagogues. All those

The broken windows of Jewish photography and printing store in Berlin vandalized during the November 1938 pogroms. After November 9, 1938. World Wide Photo.

not completely intact shall be razed by the Jews. The Jews shall pay for it. There in Berlin, the Jews are ready to do that. The synagogues which burned in Berlin are being leveled by the Jews themselves. We shall build parking lots in their places or new buildings. That ought to be the criterion for the whole country, the Jews shall have to remove the damaged or burned synagogues, and shall have to provide us with ready free space.

Number three. I deem it necessary to issue a decree forbidding the Jews to enter German theaters, movie houses and circuses. I have already issued such a decree under the authority of the law of the chamber for culture. Considering the present situation of the theaters, I believe we can afford that. Our theaters are overcrowded, we have hardly any room. I am of the opinion that it is not possible to have Jews sitting next to Germans in varieties, movies and theaters. One might consider, later on, to let the Jews have one or two movie houses here in Berlin, where they may see Jewish movies. But in German theaters they have no business anymore.

Furthermore, I advocate that the Jews be eliminated from all positions in public life in which they may prove to be provocative. It is still possible today that a Jew shares a compartment in a sleeping car with a German. Therefore, we need a decree by the Reich Ministry for Communications stating that separate compartments for Jews shall be available; in cases where compartments are filled up, Jews cannot claim a seat. They shall be given a separate compartment only after all Germans have secured seats. They shall not mix with Germans, and if there is no more room, they shall have to stand in the corridor.

GOERING: In that case, I think it would make more sense to give them separate compartments.

GOEBBELS: Not if the train is overcrowded!

GOERING: Just a moment. There'll be only one Jewish coach. If that is filled up, the other Jews will have to stay at home.

GOEBBELS: Suppose, though, there won't be many Jews going on the express train to Munich, suppose there would be two Jews on the train and the other compartments would be overcrowded. These two Jews would then have a compartment all themselves. Therefore, Jews may claim a seat only after all Germans have secured a seat.

GOERING: I'd give the Jews one coach or one compartment. And should a case like you mention arise and the train be overcrowded, believe me, we won't need a law. We'll kick him out and he'll have to sit all alone in the toilet all the way!

GOEBBELS: I don't agree. I don't believe in this. There ought to be a law. Furthermore, there ought to be a decree barring Jews from German beaches and resorts. Last summer—

GOERING: Particularly here in the Admiralspalast very disgusting things have happened lately.

GOEBBELS: Also at the Wannsee beach. A law which definitely forbids the Jews to visit German resorts.

GOERING: We could give them their own.

GOEBBELS: It would have to be considered whether we'd give them their own or whether we should turn a few German resorts over to them, but not the finest and the best, so we cannot say the Jews go there for recreation.

It'll also have to be considered if it might not become necessary to forbid the Jews to enter the German forest. In the Grunewald, whole herds of them are running around. It is a constant provocation and we are having incidents all the time. The behavior of the Jews is so inciting and provocative that brawls are a daily routine.

GOERING: We shall give the Jews a certain part of the forest, and the Alpers shall take care of it that various animals that look damned much like Jews—the elk has such a crooked nose—get there also and become acclimated.

GOEBBELS: I think this behavior is provocative. Furthermore, Jews should not be allowed to sit around in German parks. I am thinking of the whispering campaign on the part of Jewish women in the public gardens at Fehrbelliner Platz. They go and sit with German mothers and their children and begin to gossip and incite.

GOEBBELS: I see in this a particularly grave danger. I think it is imperative to give the Jews certain public parks—not the best ones—and tell them: "You may sit on these benches." These benches shall be marked "For Jews only." Besides that they have no business in German parks. Furthermore, Jewish children are still allowed in German schools. That's impossible. It is out of the question that any boy should sit beside a Jewish boy in a German Gymnasium and receive lessons in German history. Jews ought to be eliminated completely from German schools; they may take care of their own education in their own communities.

GOERING: I suggest that Mr. Hilgard from the insurance company be called in; he is waiting outside. As soon as he's finished with his report, he may go, and we can continue to talk. At the time Gustloff died, a compensation for the damage Germany had suffered was prepared. But I believe that at present we should not work it through raised taxes but with a contribution paid only once. That serves my purpose better.

[Hilgard appears]

Mr. Hilgard, the following is our case. Because of the justified anger of the people against the Jew, the Reich has suffered a certain amount of damage. Windows were broken, goods were damaged and people hurt, synagogues burned, etc. I suppose that the Jews, many of them are also insured against damage committed by public disorder etc.

HILGARD: Yes.

GOERING: If that is so, the following situation arises; the people, in their justified anger, meant to harm the Jew, but it is the German insurance companies that will compensate the Jew for damage. This situation is simple enough; I'd only have to issue a decree to that effect that damage resulting from these risks shall not have to

be paid by the insurance companies. But the question that interests me primarily, and because of which I have asked you to come here, is this one; in case of reinsurance policies in foreign countries, I should not like to lose these, and that is why I'd like to discuss with you ways and means by which profit from reinsurance, possibly in foreign currency, will go to the German economy, instead of the Jew. I'd like to hear from you, and that is the first question I want to ask: In your opinion, are the Jews insured against such damage to a large extent.

HILGARD: Permit me to answer right away. We are concerned with three kinds of insurance. Not with the insurance against damage resulting from revolt or from risks. But with the ordinary fire insurance, the ordinary glass insurance, and the ordinary insurance against theft. The people, because of their contracts, who have a right to claim compensation are partly Jews, partly Aryans. As for the fire insurance they are practically all Jewish, I suppose. As for the department stores, the victim is identical with the Jew, the owner, and that applies more to the synagogues, except for neighbors to whose places the fire may have spread. Although the damage done to the latter's property seems to be rather slight according to the inquiries I made late last night.

As for the glass insurance which plays a very important part in this, the situation is completely different. The majority of the victims, mostly the owners of the buildings, are Aryans. The Jew has usually rented the store, a procedure which you may observe all over, for example on Keirfuerstendamin.

GOERING: That is what we've said.

GOEBBELS: In these cases, the Jew will have to pay.

GOERING: It doesn't make sense, we have no raw materials. It is all glass imported from foreign countries and has to be paid for in foreign currency! One could go nuts.

HILGARD: May I draw your attention to the following facts; the glass for the shop windows is not being manufactured by the Bohemian, but by the Belgian glass industry. In my estimation, the approximate money value to which these damages amount is 6,000,000—that includes the broken glass, glass which we shall have to replace, mainly to Aryans because they have the insurance policies.

Of course I have to reserve final judgment in all this, Your Excellency, because I have had only one day to make my inquiries. Even counting on about half of the 6,000,000 being spent in transacting the business—specialists from the industry itself are more confident in this matter than I am—we might well have to import glass for approximately 3,000,000. Incidentally, the amount of the damage equals about half of the whole year's production of the Belgian glass industry. We believe that half a year will be necessary for the manufacturers to deliver the glass.

GOERING: The people will have to be enlightened on this.

GOEBBELS: We cannot do this right now.

GOERING: This cannot continue! We won't be able to last with all this. Impossible! Go on then! You suggest that the Aryan is the one who suffers the damage, is that right?

HILGARD: Yes, to a large extent, as far as the glass insurance goes.

GOERING: Who would have to replace the glass.

HILGARD: Yes. Of course there are cases in which the Aryan, the owner of the store is identical with the owner of the building. That is so with all department stores. In the case of the department store in Israel, the owner is the Jew.

GOERING: And now the third category.

HILGARD: Under this fall the victims of thievery.

GOERING: I have to ask you a question. When all kinds of goods were taken away from the stores and burned in the streets, would that also be thievery?

HILGARD: I don't think so.

GOERING: Could that be termed as "Riot"? . . .

V. KROSIGK: I have no idea about the extent.

HEYDRICH: 7,500 destroyed stores in the Reich.

DALUEGUE: One more question ought to be cleared up. Most of the goods in the stores were not the property of the owner but were kept on the books of other firms, which had delivered them. Then there are the unpaid for deliveries by other firms, which definitely are not all Jewish but Aryan, those goods that were delivered on the basis of commission.

HILGARD: We'll have to pay for them too.

GOERING: I wished you had killed two hundred Jews, and not destroyed such values.

HEYDRICH: There were thirty-five killed.

KERL: I think we could do the following: Jews we don't pay anyhow. As for Aryans, payment shall be made; the insurance company may contact us through the *Reichsgruppe* and we shall investigate each case. I am thinking of the small reciprocity companies; it should be easy to find out whether they are capable of paying or not. In their cases, the amounts involved are not too large. We may find an arrangement for this later on; I am thinking of one in which the insurance companies arrange for compensation exclusively to Aryans, and once they know the results of their inquiries, contact us. We shall then find a way out for these small companies. Of course only in cases where it is absolutely necessary.

FUNK: That is not necessary. I'd like to refer to what I've said before about the decree. That seems to be the easiest solution.

GOERING: We cannot do that. These people make a point of their ability to pay.

FUNK: If the Jews pay for it, the insurance companies don't have to pay.

GOERING: Right, well, gentlemen, this is all very clear. We'll stick to it. At this moment every insurance company, except Mr. Hilgard who is here, counts on having to pay for the damage. They want to pay, too, and I understand this very well. They'll have to want that, so they cannot be reproached for not being secure enough to pay. The glass insurance, and a point was made of that, has brought the highest profits so far. That means they have enough surplus money, and if they haven't divided it all up in dividends, they'll have savings enough for the compensation. Such an insurance company will have to be in a position to pay for a damage of ten, twelve, fifteen million, that is three times the amount paid in the normal year. If they are unable to do that, then we'll have to wonder whether we should let small companies live at all. It would be insane to keep insurance companies which would be unable to pay for such damage. To permit an insurance company like that to exist would simply mean to cheat the people. I suggest now the following. The damage shall be determined in each case. And for the time being, the insurance companies shall have to honor their contracts in every respect and shall have to pay.…

HEYDRICH: I'd like to say one more thing of primary importance. In the decree we should not mention the confiscation. We can do that easily.

GOERING: No, you cannot do that tacitly. A clear legal procedure will have to be employed there. But that is not what Mr. Woermann means, he is talking about those foreign Jews who are not insured. As far as they are insured, they are covered. This here concerns those who are not insured. That may be the case here and there.…

GOERING: Like the Führer says, we'll have to find a way to talk this over with the countries which also do something against the Jews. That every dirty Polish Jew has a legal position here and we have to stand him, that ought to cease. The Führer was not very happy about the agreement that was made with the Poles. He thinks we should take a few chances and just tell the Poles: all right, we are not going to do that; let's talk over what we may be able to accomplish

together; you are doing something against your own Jews in Poland; but the minute the *Itzig* has left Poland, he should suddenly be treated like a Pole! I'd like to disregard these stories from foreign countries a little.

WOERMANN: It ought to be considered whether or not, the U.S. might take measures against German property. This question cannot be handled equally for all countries. I have to make a formal and general reservation.

GOERING: I have always said and I'd like to repeat it that our steamship companies and German companies in general should finally catch on and liquidate their investments in the U.S., sell them, etc. That country of scoundrels does not do business with us according to any legal rules. Once before they stole everything from us, that is why I don't understand how we could do it again, just for some temporary profit. It is dangerous. You can do it with a regular country but not with one that cares for the right as little as the U.S. The other day I had the American ambassador with me, we talked about the zeppelin and I told him: "We don't need any helium, I fly without helium but the prerequisite will have to be that this ship will be flying to civilized countries where the right prevails. It goes without saying that one cannot fly to such gangster states." He had a rather silly look on his face. One ought to tell these Americans. But you are right, Mr. Woermann, it ought to be considered.

WOERMANN: In other words, the foreign office is granted the right to be consulted.

GOERING: Granted, but I'd like to avoid mentioning the foreign Jews as long as we can help it. We'd rather have the foreign office take part in those cases where that question becomes acute, so that some compromise can be reached.…

WOERMANN: Generally, and in particular cases.

FUNK: The decisive question is: Are the Jewish stores to be reopened or not?

GOERING: That depends on how big a turnover

these Jewish stores have. If it is big, it is an indication that the German people are compelled to buy there, in spite of it's being a Jewish store, because a need exists. If we'd close all Jewish stores which are not open right now, altogether before Christmas, we'd be in a nice mess....

HEYDRICH: Through the Jewish *Kulturgemeinde*, we extracted a certain amount of money from the rich Jews who wanted to emigrate. By paying this amount, and an additional sum in foreign currency, they made it possible for a number of poor Jews to leave. The problem was not to make the rich Jew leave but to get rid of the Jewish mob.

GOERING: But children, did you ever think this through? It doesn't help us to extract hundreds of thousands from the Jewish mob. Have you ever thought of it that this procedure may cost us so much foreign currency that in the end we won't be able to hold out.

HEYDRICH: Only what the Jew has had in foreign currency.

GOERING: Agreed.

HEYDRICH: This way, may I propose that we set up a similar procedure for the Reich, with the cooperation of the competent government agencies, and that we then find a solution for the Reich, based on our experiences, after having corrected the mistakes the General Field Marshal has so rightly pointed out to us.

GOERING: Agreed.

HEYDRICH: As another means of getting the Jews out, measures for emigration ought to be taken in the rest of the Reich for the next eight to ten years. The highest number of Jews we can possibly get out during one year is eight to ten thousand. Therefore, a great number of Jews will remain. Because of the aryanizing and other restrictions Jewry will become unemployed. The remaining Jews gradually become proletarians. Therefore, I shall have to take steps to isolate the Jew so he won't enter into the German normal routine of life. On the other hand, I shall have to restrict the Jew to a small circle of consumers, but I shall have to permit certain activities within professions; lawyers, doctors, barbers, etc. This question shall also have to be examined.

As for the isolation. I'd like to make a few proposals regarding police measures which are important also because of their psychological effect on public opinion. For example, who is Jewish according to the Nuremberg laws shall have to wear a certain insignia. That is a possibility which shall facilitate many other things. I don't see any danger of excuses, and it shall make our relationship with the foreign Jews easier.

GOERING: A uniform!

HEYDRICH: An insignia. This way we could also put an end to it that the foreign Jews, who don't look different from ours, are being molested.

GOERING: But, my dear Heydrich, you won't be able to avoid the creation of ghettos on a very large scale, in all the cities. They shall have to be created.

HEYDRICH: As for the question of ghettos, I'd like to make my position clear right away. From the point of view of the police, I don't think a ghetto, in the form of completely segregated districts where only Jews would live, can be put up. We could not control a ghetto where the Jews congregate amidst the whole Jewish people. It would remain the permanent hideout for criminals and also for epidemics and the like. We don't want to let the Jew live in the same house with the German population; but today the German population, their blocks or houses, force the Jew to behave himself. The control of the Jew through the watchful eye of the whole population is better than having him by the thousands in a district where I cannot properly establish control over his daily life through uniformed agents.

GOERING: We'd only have to forbid long distance calls.

HEYDRICH: Still I could not completely stop the Jews from communicating out of their districts.

GOERING: And in towns all of their own?

HEYDRICH: If I could put them into towns entirely their own, yes. But then these towns would be such a haven for criminals of all sorts that they would be a terrific danger. I'd take different steps. I'd restrict the movement of the Jews and would say: In Munich, the government district and the district—

GOERING: Wait a minute! I don't care so much for it that the Jews don't appear in spots where I don't want them. My point is this one; if one Jew won't have any more work, he'll have to live modestly. He won't be able to go far on his 3½ percent, to restaurants, etc. He'll have to work more. That'll bring about a concentration of Jewry which may even facilitate control. You will know that in a particular house only Jews are living. We shall also have concentrated Jewish butchers, barbers, grocers, etc. in certain streets. The question is of course whether we want to go on tolerating that. If not, the Jew shall have to buy from the Aryan.

HEYDRICH: No, I'd say that for the necessities in daily life, the German won't serve the Jew anymore.

GOERING: One moment. You cannot let him starve. But there'll be the following difficulty. If you say that the Jews will be able to have so and so many retail stores, then they'll again be in business, and they'll continually have to sell for the wholesaler.

SCHMER: In a small town that wouldn't work at all.

GOERING: It could only be worked out if you'd reserved in advance whole districts or whole towns for the Jews. Otherwise, you'll have to have only Germans do business, and the Jew shall have to buy from them. You cannot set up a Jewish barbershop. The Jew will have to buy food and stockings.

HEYDRICH: We'll have to decide whether we want that or not.

GOERING: I'd like to make a decision on that right now. We cannot make another subdivision here. We cannot argue: so and so many stores will remain for the Jew because then again no control will be possible since these stores in turn would have to work with wholesale stores. I'd say, all stores should be Aryan stores, and the Jew may buy there. One may go one step further and say that these and these stores will probably be frequented mostly by Jews. You may set up certain barbershops operated by Jews. You may make concessions in order to channel certain professions into certain streets for certain tasks. But not stores.

HEYDRICH: What about the ghetto? Would the Jew have to go to an Aryan district to buy.

GOERING: No. I'd say that enough German storekeepers would love to dwell in the ghetto if they could do some business there. I wouldn't alter the principle that the Jew shall have no more say in German economy.

HEYDRICH: I shouldn't like to comment on that. Now a few things which are important also form a psychological angle.

GOERING: Once we'd have a ghetto, we'd find out what stores ought to be in there, and we'd be able to say: You, the Jew so and so, together with so and so, shall take care of the delivery of goods. And a German wholesale firm will be ordered to deliver the goods for this Jewish store. This store would then not be a retail shop but a cooperative store. A cooperative one for Jews.

HEYDRICH: All these measures will eventually lead to the institution of the ghetto. I'd say one shouldn't want to build a ghetto. But these measures, if carried through as outlined here, shall automatically drive the Jews into a ghetto.

FUNK: The Jews will have to move quite close together. What are three million? Everyone will have to stand up for the next fellow. The individual alone will starve.

GOERING: Now, as to what Minister Goebbels has said before, namely compulsory renting. Now, the Jewish tenants will be together.

HEYDRICH: As an additional measure, I'd propose to withdraw from the Jews all personal papers such as permits and driver's licenses. No Jew should be allowed to own a car, neither should he be permitted to drive because that way he'd endanger German life. By not being permitted to live in certain districts, he should be furthermore restricted to move about so freely. I'd say the Royal Square in Munich, the Reichsweihestatte, is not to be entered any more within a certain radius by Jews. The same would go for establishments of culture, border fences, military installations. Furthermore, like Minister Dr. Goebbels has said before, exclusion of the Jews from public theaters, movie houses, etc. As for the cultural activities I'd like to say this: cultural activities in holiday resorts may be considered an additional feature, not absolutely necessary for the individual. Many German *Volksgenessen* are unable to improve their health through a stay at a resort town. I don't see why the Jew should go to these places at all.

GOERING: To health spas, no.

HEYDRICH: Well, then I'd like to propose the same thing for hospitals. A Jew should not lie in a hospital together with Aryan *Volkgenessen*.

GOERING: We'll have to manage that gradually.

HEYDRICH: The same applies to public conveyances.

GOERING: Are there no Jewish sanitariums and Jewish hospitals? [Remarks—Yes!] We'll have to finagle all this. These things will have to be straightened out one right after another.

HEYDRICH: I only meant to secure your approval in principle so that we may start out on all this.

GOERING: One more question, gentlemen: What would you think the situation would be if I'd announce today that Jewry shall have to contribute this one billion as a punishment?

BUEREKEL: The Viennese would agree to this wholeheartedly.

GOEBBELS: I wonder if the Jews would have a chance to pull out of this, and to put something on the side.

BRINKMANN: They'd be subject to punishment.

V. KROSIGK: Mr. Fisdiboeck, one question: Could this authorization be ordered without their closing out their securities?

FUNK: They are all registered. They'll also have to register the money.

V. KROSIGK: But for the time being they may dispose of it.

GOERING: It won't help them to cash them at all. They can't get rid of the money.

FUNK: They'll be the ones to have the damage if they sell their stocks and bonds.

FISDIBOECK: There is a certain danger, but I don't think it is very great. But only then, when all the other measures shall definitely be carried out during next week.

V. KROSIGK: They have to be taken during the next week at the latest.

GOERING: I would make that a condition.

FISDIBOECK: Maybe it is good that we put ourselves under pressure this way.

GOERING: I shall close the wording this way; that German Jewry shall, as punishment for their abominable crimes, etc., etc. have to make a contribution of one billion. That'll work. The pigs won't commit another murder. Incidentally, I'd like to say again that I would not like to be a Jew in Germany.

V. KROSIGK: Therefore, I'd like to emphasize what Mr. Heydrich has said in the beginning; that we'll have to try everything possible, by way of additional exports, to shove the Jews into foreign countries. The decisive factor is that we don't want the society-proletariat here. They'll always be a terrific liability for us.

FRICK: And a danger.

V. KROSIGK: I don't imagine the prospect of the ghetto is very nice. The idea of the ghetto is not a very agreeable one. Therefore, the goal must be, like Heydrich said, to move out whatever we can!

GOERING: The second point is this. If, in the near future, the German Reich should come into conflict with foreign powers, it goes without saying that we in Germany should first of all let it come to a showdown with the Jews. Besides that, the Führer shall now make an attempt with those foreign powers who have brought the Jewish question up, in order to solve the Madagascar project. He has explained it all to me on 9 November. There is no other way. He'll tell the other countries. "What are you talking about the Jew for?—Take him!" Another proposal may be made. The Jews, gotten rid of may buy territory for their "coreligionists" in North America, Canada or elsewhere. I wish to summarize: The minister of economic affairs shall direct the committee and he shall in one form or another, take all steps necessary within the next few days.

BLERNING: I fear that during the next few days, beginning Monday, the Jews will start to sell bonds on internal loans for hundreds of thousands, in order to provide themselves with means. Since we hold the course of the internal loan in order to sell more bonds, The Reich Treasury, Loan Committee, or the Reich minister of finances should have to back this internal loan.

GOERING: In what way could the Jew bring his bonds on the market?

REMARK: Sell them.

GOERING: To whom?

REMARK: On the stock market. He orders a bank to do it.

GOERING: Well, I'll prohibit selling internal loan bonds for three days.

BLERNING: That could be done only through a decree.

GOERING: I can't see any advantage for the Jew. He won't know himself how and he'll have to pay. On the contrary, I believe he won't move.

GOEBBELS: For the time being he is small and ugly and stays at home.

GOERING: I don't think it would be logical. Otherwise we'll have to do it. The reason why I want this decree in a hurry is that for the time being we have peace but who can guarantee that there won't be new trouble by Saturday or Sunday. Once and for all I want to eliminate individual acts. The Reich has taken the affair in its own hand. The Jew can only sell. He can't do a thing. He'll have to pay. At this moment, the individual Jew won't think of throwing anything on the market. There'll be some chatter first, and then they will begin to run to us. They'll look for those great Aryans with whom they'll think they may have some luck, the so-called various mailboxes of the Reich with whom they can lodge their protests. These people will run my door in. All that takes some time, and by then we'll be ready.

DALUEGUE: May we issue the order for confiscating the cars?

GOERING: Also the Ministry of the Interior and the police will have to think over what measures will have to be taken. I thank you.

[Conference closed at 2:40 P.M.]

VII. THE BEGINNING OF GHETTOIZATION

A secret memo issued on September 21, 1939, by Reinhard Heydrich, the chief of the Security Police to the chiefs of all task forces operating in the conquered Polish territory, established the basic outlines of German policy in the territories.

Heydrich distinguishes between the ultimate goal (*Endziel*), which will require some time to implement, and the intermediate goals which must be carried out in the short term. He said some goals could not yet be implemented for technical reasons and some for economic reasons. Room was left for innovation.

He writes: "The instructions and directives below must serve also for the purpose of

Jews from Lodz, Poland, forced to move into the ghetto. March 1940. Bundesarchiv.

urging chiefs of the Einsatzgruppen [mobile units] to give practical consideration to the problems involved."

His language is specific: the *Endziel*, the final goal, must be distinguished from the language that is later to be used, the *endlossen*, or Final Solution, a polite euphemism for the murder of Jewish men, women, and children. The ultimate goal is unarticulated; it may be assumed and yet remains undefined.

The first intermediate goal is concentration. Jews are to be moved from the country-side into the larger cities. Certain areas are to become *Judenrein*, free of Jews, and smaller communities are to be merged into the larger ones.

Heydrich orders local leaders to establish a Council of Jewish Elders, twenty-four men to be appointed from the local leaders and rabbis that is to be made *fully responsible*, "in the literal sense of the word" to implement future decrees. A census must be taken and leaders are to be personally responsible for the evacuation of Jews from the countryside. It was unnecessary to indicate what personal responsibility implied.

Due priority is given to the needs of the army and to minimize economic dislocation, not of the Jews, but of industries essential to German economic interest. Businesses and farms are to be turned over to the locals, preferably Germans, and, if essential and no Germans are available, even to Poles.

And the Einsatzgruppen are to issue reports, a census of people, an inventory of resources, industries, and personnel.

It is within this framework that the Jewish Councils were established and that the work of securing the occupied territory began.

A second decree dated two months later and signed by Hans Frank, the head of the General Government further specified the role of the Jewish Council, which was to have a chairman and a deputy.

"The Jewish Council is obliged to receive through its chairman and his deputy the order of the German official agencies. Its responsibility will be to see that the orders are carried out completely and accurately." Jews are ordered to obey the orders of the Jewish Councils.

In Lodz, two additional documents specify the nature of the authority of the *Judenrat*. The town commissar, Leister, named Mordecai Chaim Rumkowski as Elder of the Jews. His power is extensive, but derivative. He is given the power of taxation, con-trol over existing institutions, and sole responsibility for the ghetto. His orders are to be obeyed unconditionally. Any opposition will be punished by Leister.

In April 1940 when the ghetto is sealed, Rumkowski's power is extended. Rumkowski is to safeguard order in "the economic life, food supply, utilization of manpower, public health and public welfare." He may confiscate property and distribute all supplies. He may conscript labor. In short, he has derivative dictatorial power, which may be exercised as instructed and as required. And Rumkowski was to indeed exercise these powers as instructed and as required.

Perhaps the clearest way to understand the evolving policy toward the Jews is to look at a third document, a secret memo handed to Hitler by Himmler on May 25, 1940, in which he articulates German policy toward the Poles. On schooling, Himmler writes:

For the non-German population of the East there must be no higher school than the four-grade elementary school. The sole goal of this school is to be simple arithmetic—up to five hundred at the most; writing of one's name; the doctrine that it is a divine law to obey the Germans and to be honest, industrious, and good. I don't think that reading is necessary.

He suggests a policy of aryanization, parents must give up elite children in order for them to get an education. And thus, no leadership class can emerge. Laborers without leader, he calls them, at the disposal of the German people.

Shortly, thereafter, a key difference will emerge in the policy toward the Jews and the "subhuman populations in the East." Jews are to be killed—all Jews, the elite as well as the ordinary—and even Jewish labor is to be devalued.

INSTRUCTIONS BY REINHARD HEYDRICH ON POLICY AND OPERATIONS CONCERNING JEWS IN THE OCCUPIED TERRITORIES
SEPTEMBER 21, 1939

The Chief of the Security Police.
Berlin, September 21, 1939
Schnellbrief
To: Chiefs of all Einsatzgruppen of the Security
   Police
Subject: Jewish Question in Occupied Territory

I refer to the conference held in Berlin today, and again point out that the planned total measures [i.e., the final aim—*Endziel*] are to be kept strictly secret.

Distinction must be made between:

1. the final aim (which will require extended periods of time) and
2. the stages leading to the fulfillment of this final aim (which will be carried out in short periods).

The planned measures require the most thorough preparation with regard to technical as well as economic aspects.

It is obvious that the tasks ahead cannot be laid down from here in full detail. The instructions and directives below must serve also for the purpose of urging chiefs of the Einsatzgruppen to give practical consideration [to the problems involved].

I

For the time being, the first prerequisite for the final aim is the concentration of the Jews from the countryside into the larger cities.

This is to be carried out speedily.

In doing so, distinction must be made:

1. between the zones of Danzig and West Prussia, Poznan, Eastern Upper Silesia, and
2. the other occupied zones.

As far as possible, the areas referred to under 1) are to be cleared of Jews; at least the aim should be to establish only few cities of concentration.

In the areas under 2), as few concentration centers as possible are to be set up, so as to facilitate subsequent measures. In this connection it should be borne in mind that only cities which are rail junctions, or are at least located on railroad lines, should be selected as concentration points.

On principle, Jewish communities of less than five hundred persons are to be dissolved and transferred to the nearest concentration center.

This decree does not apply to the area of Einsatzgruppe 1, which is situated east of

Kraków and is bounded roughly by Polanice, Jaroslaw, the new line of demarcation, and the former Slovak-Polish border. Within this area only an approximate census of Jews is to be carried out. Furthermore, Councils of Jewish Elders, as outlined below, are to be set up.

II

Councils of Jewish Elders

1. In each Jewish community a Council of Jewish Elders is to be set up which, as far as possible, is to be composed of the remaining authoritative personalities and rabbis. The council is to be composed of up to twenty-four male Jews (depending on the size of the Jewish community).

   The council is to be made fully responsible, in the literal sense of the word, for the exact and prompt implementation of directives already issued or to be issued in the future.

2. In case of sabotage of such instructions, the councils are to be warned that the most severe measures will be taken.

3. The *Judenrate* (Jewish Councils) are to carry out an approximate census of the Jews of their areas, broken down if possible according to sex (and age groups): a) up to sixteen years, b) from sixteen to twenty years, and c) above twenty years; and also according to the principal occupations. The results are to be reported in the shortest possible time.

4. The Councils of Elders are to be informed of the date and time of the evacuation, the means available for evacuation, and, finally, the departure routes. They are then to be made personally responsible for the evacuation of the Jews from the countryside.

   The reason to be given for the concentration of the Jews in the cities is that the Jews have taken a decisive part in sniper attacks and plundering.

5. The Councils of Elders in the concentration centers are to be made responsible for the appropriate housing of the Jews arriving from the countryside.

   For reasons of general police security, the concentration of the Jews in the cities will probably call for regulations in these cities which will forbid their entry to certain quarters completely and that—but with due regard for economic requirements—they may, for instance, not leave the ghetto, nor leave their homes after a certain hour in the evening, etc.

6. The Councils of Elders are also to be made responsible for the suitable provisioning of the Jews during the transport to the cities.

   There is no objection to the evacuated Jews taking with them their movable possessions in so far as that is technically possible.

7. Jews who fail to comply with the order to move into cities are to be given a short additional period of grace where there was sufficient reason for the delay. They are to be warned of the most severe penalties if they fail to move by the later date set.

III

All necessary measures are, on principle, always to be taken in closest consultation and cooperation with the German civil administration and the competent local military authorities.

In the execution [of this plan], it must be taken into consideration that economic requirements in the occupied areas do not suffer.

1. Above all, the needs of the army must be taken into consideration. For instance, for the time being, it will scarcely be possible to avoid, here and there, leaving behind some trade Jews who are absolutely essential for the provisioning of the troops, for lack of other possibilities. But in such cases the prompt aryanization of these enterprises is to be planned and the removal of the Jews to be completed in due course, in cooperation with the competent local German administrative authorities.

2. For the preservation of German economic interests in the occupied territories, it is obvious that Jewish-owned war and other essential industries, and also enterprises, industries and factories important to the Four Year Plan, must be maintained for the time being.

In these cases also, prompt aryanization must be aimed at, and the removal of the Jews completed later.

3. Finally, the food situation in the occupied territories must be taken into consideration. For instance, as far as possible, land owned by Jewish settlers is to be handed over to the care of neighboring German or even Polish farmers to work on commission to ensure the harvesting of crops still standing in the fields, and to carry out replanting.

With regard to this important question, contact is to be made with the agricultural expert of the chief of the Civil Administration.

4. In all cases in which it is not possible to coordinate the interests of the Security Police on the one hand, and the German civil administration on the other, I am to be informed by the fastest route and my decision awaited before the particular measures in question are carried out.

IV

The chiefs of the Einsatzgruppen are to report to me continuously on the following matters:

I. Numerical survey of the Jews present in their areas (according to the above classifications, if possible). The numbers of Jews evacuated from the countryside and of those already in the cities are to be listed separately.

II. Names of the cities which have been designated as concentration centers.

III. The dates set for the Jews to move to the cities.

IV. Surveys of all the Jewish [owned] war and other essential industries and enterprises, or those important to the Four Year Plan, in their areas.

If possible, the following should be specified:

A. Type of enterprise (with a statement on possible conversion to really vital or war-important enterprises or ones of importance to the Four Year Plan);

B. which factories should be most urgently aryanized (in order to forestall possible losses);

What kind of aryanization is proposed? Germans or Poles? (the decision to depend on the importance of the enterprise);

C. The number of Jews working in these factories (specify those in leading positions).

Can operations at the enterprise be continued without difficulty after the removal of the Jews, or will it be necessary to allocate German or possibly Polish workers in their place? In what numbers?

If Polish workers have to be used care should be taken that they are drawn mainly from the former German provinces so as to begin to ease the problem there. These matters can be carried out only by means of coordination with the German Labor Offices which have been set up.

V

In order to reach the planned aims, I expect the fullest cooperation of the whole manpower of the Security Policy and the SD.

The chiefs of neighboring Einsatzgruppen are to establish contact with each other immediately in order to cover the areas in question completely.

VI

The High Command of the Army; the Plenipotentiary for the Four Year Plan (attention: Secretary of State Neumann), the Reich Ministry for the Interior (attention: State Secretary Stuckart), for Food and the Economy (attention: State Secretary Landfried), as well as the Chiefs of Civil Administration of the Occupied Territories have received copies of this decree.

SIGNED HEYDRICH

"REFLECTIONS ON THE TREATMENT OF THE PEOPLES OF ALIEN RACES IN THE EAST"

A SECRET MEMORANDUM HANDED TO HITLER BY HIMMLER

MAY 25, 1940

[Handwritten] Dr. Gross of the Racial Policy Office has been informed 28 November 40

Wolff

For the files

[stamp] Top Secret

Concerning the treatment of peoples of alien races in the East we have to see to it that we acknowledge and cultivate as many individual ethnic groups as possible, that is, outside of the Poles and the Jews, also the Ukrainians, the White Russians, the Gorals [Goralen], the Lemcos [Lemken] and the Cashubos [Kaschuben]. If other small and isolated national groups can be found in other places, they should be treated the same way.

What I want to say is that we are not only most interested in not unifying the population of the East, but, on the contrary, in splitting them up into as many parts and fragments as possible.

But even within the ethnic groups themselves we have one interest in leading these to unity and greatness, or perhaps arouse in them gradually a national consciousness and national culture, but we want to dissolve them into innumerable small fragments and particles.

We naturally want to use the members of all these ethnic groups, especially of the small ones, in positions of police officials and mayors. Only the mayors and local police authorities will be allowed to head those ethnic groups. As far as the Gorals are concerned, the individual chieftains and elders of the tribes, who live in continuous feud with each other anyhow, should fill these positions. There must be no centralization toward the top, because only by dissolving this whole conglomeration of peoples of the General Government, amounting to fifteen million, and of the eight million of the eastern provinces, will it be possible for us to carry out the racial sifting which must be the basis for our considerations: namely selecting out of this conglomeration the racially valuable and bringing them to Germany and assimilating them there.

Within a very few years I should think about four to five years the name of the Cashubes, for instance, must be unknown, because at that time there won't be a Cashubian people any more (this also goes especially for the West Prussians). I hope that the concepts of Jews will be completely extinguished through the possibility of a large emigration of all Jews to Africa or some other colony. Within a somewhat longer period, it should also be possible to make the ethnic concepts of Ukrainians, Gorals and Lemcos disappear in our area. What has

Jews moving belongings into the ghetto. c. 1940. State Archive Kraków.

been said for those fragments of peoples is also meant on a correspondingly larger scale for the Poles.

A basic issue in the solution of all these problems is the question of schooling and thus the question of sifting and selecting the young. For the non-German population of the East there must be no higher school than the four-grade elementary school. The sole goal of this school is to be simple arithmetic—up to five hundred at the most; writing of one's name; the doctrine that it is a divine law to obey the Germans and to be honest, industrious, and good. I don't think that reading is necessary.

Apart from this school there are to be no schools at all in the East. Parents, who from the beginning want to give their children better schooling in the elementary school as well as later on in a higher school, must take an application to the Higher SS and police leaders. The first consideration in dealing with this application will be whether the child is racially perfect and conforming to our conditions. If we acknowledge such a child to be as of our blood, the parents will be notified that the child will be sent to a school in Germany and that it will permanently remain in Germany.

Cruel and tragic as every individual case may be, this method is still the mildest and best one if, out of inner conviction, one rejects as un-

German and impossible the Bolshevist method of physical extermination of a people.

The parents of such children of good blood will be given the choice to either give away their child; they will then probably produce no more children so that the danger of this subhuman people of the East [*Untermenschenvolk des Ostens*] obtaining a class of leaders which, since it would be equal to us, would also be dangerous for us, will disappear—or else the parents pledge themselves to go to Germany and become loyal citizens there. The love toward their child, whose future and education depends on the loyalty of the parents, will be a strong weapon in dealing with them.

Apart from examining the applications made by parents for better schooling of their children, there will be an annual sifting of all children of the General Government between the ages of six to ten years in order to separate the racially valuable and nonvaluable ones. The ones considered racially valuable will be treated in the same way as the children who are admitted on the basis of the approved application of their parents.

I consider it as a matter of course from an emotional as well as from a rational viewpoint that the moment children and parents come to Germany they are not treated like lepers in the schools and in everyday life, but, after having changed their names, they should, in full confidence, be incorporated into the German life, although attention and vigilance must be exercised with regard to them. It must not happen that the children be made to feel as outcasts, because, after all, we believe in this, our own blood, which, through the errors of German history has flowed into an alien nationality, and we are convinced that our ideology and our ideals will strike a chord of resonance in the racially equal soul of these children. Here teachers and

Hitler Youth leaders especially must do an out-and-out job, and the mistake that has been made in the past with the people from Alsace-Lorraine must never be repeated; namely, that on one side one wants to win the people as Germans, and on the other side one constantly hurts and repudiates their human value, their pride and honor through distrust and insults. Insults like "Polack" and "Ukrainian" or something like that must be made impossible.

The children will have to be educated in an elementary school and after those four grades it can be decided whether the children should continue to go to the German grammar school or should be transferred to a national political institution of education.

The population of the General Government during the next ten years, by necessity and after a consistent carrying out of these measures, will be composed of the remaining inferior population supplemented by the population of the eastern provinces deported there, and of all those parts of the German Reich which have the same racial and human qualities for instance, parts of the Sorbs [Sorben] and Wends [Wenden].

This population will, as a people of laborers without leaders, be at our disposal and will furnish Germany annually with migrant workers and with workers for special tasks (roads, quarries, buildings): they themselves will have more to eat and more to live on than under the Polish regime; and, though they have no culture of their own, they will, under the strict, consistent, and just leadership of the German people, be called upon to help work on its everlasting cultural tasks and its buildings and perhaps, as far as the amount of heavy work is concerned, will be the ones who make the realization of these tasks possible.

(Source: Translation of Document No.-1880 Prosecution Exhibit 1314)

File Note of Himmler Concerning the Handling and Distribution of His Memorandum on the Treatment of Alien Races in the East

May 28, 1940

The Reich Leader SS
Special Train, 28 May 1940
Top Secret

On Saturday, 25 May, I handed my memorandum on the treatment of peoples of alien race in the East to the Führer. The Führer read the six pages and considered them very good and correct. He directed, however, that only very few copies should be issued, that there should be no large edition, and that the report is to be treated with utmost secrecy. Minister Lammers was likewise present. The Führer wanted me to ask Governor General Frank to come to Berlin in order to show him this report and to tell him that the Führer considered it to be correct.

I suggested to the Führer that Minister Lammers, who had received one copy from me, be ordered to present this report to the four Gauleiters of the eastern Gaue: Koch; Forster; Greiser, the Oberpraesident of Silesia; the Governor General Frank; as well as to Reich Minister Darre, and to inform them that the Führer acknowledged and sanctioned this report as a directive.

Then a short file note should be made concerning the notification of the persons named as to the contents of the report. The Führer agreed and gave the order to Minister Lammers.

Reich Leader Bormann received another copy for notification of the deputy of the Führer.

One copy was given to the chief of my office, SS Brigadier General Greifelt, in his capacity as Reich Commissioner for the Strengthening of Germanism. I shall give him the order to inform in turn all chiefs of the Main Offices as well as the first five concerned Higher SS and Police Leaders East, North East, Vistula, Warta, and South East and to have a report made on this subject in the same manner. The notification to the chiefs of the Main Offices shall be effected by an SS Leader who will have to wait until the chief concerned of the Main Office has read the report and has acknowledged it by his signature. At the same time everyone has to confirm that he has been informed of the fact that this is to be considered as a directive, but that it shall never be laid down in an order of one of the Main Offices either in form of a mere excerpt or from memory.

Moreover SS Brigadier General Greifelt is authorized to bring the contents of the report to the attention of Mayor Winckler and his own main collaborators; the latter he shall suggest to me.

Furthermore, I will personally give one copy to the chief of the Security Police with the order to notify his main coworkers in the above described manner and without making any copies.

He has to suggest to me the circle of coworkers who are to be informed of the report.

[Handwritten by Himmler]

The same applies to the chief of the Race and Settlement Main Office.

The Reich Leader SS

(Source: Translation of Document No.-1881 Prosecution Exhibit 1313)

VIII. THE *JUDENRAT*

No aspect of Jewish behavior during the Holocaust is more controversial than that of the role of the *Judenrat*, the German initiated Jewish Councils, presiding over the ghetto population. Ghetto diary and memoir writers raised all of the hard questions during the Holocaust. What role did the *Judenrat* play? Whose interest did they serve? Were they helpful in assisting Jews to survive? Were they guilty of complicity with the enemy?

The questions were difficult. The answers were, more often than not, harsh; in part because the Jewish Councils were an available target for the ghettoized Jews and in part because they were in an impossible position, subject to criticism from all sides.

To the German authorities they were an instrument to dominate and rule the ghetto. Easy to manipulate, they were often a necessary annoyance, making representations on behalf of Jewish needs to the German rulers. To the Jews they were the representatives and enforcers of German decrees who did the Germans' dirty work for them. They were often criticized for freeing up German personnel for other tasks.

The role of the *Judenrat* reached public attention more than three decades ago with the publication of two works: Raul Hilberg's *The Destruction of the European Jews* and Hannah Arendt's *Eichmann in Jerusalem: A Report on the Banality of Evil*. Hilberg argued that the Jewish response pattern could be seen in four successive stages, which he described as Alleviation, Evasion, Paralysis and, ultimately, Compliance. "Preventative attack, armed resistance and revenge are almost completely absent in two thousand years of Jewish ghetto history," he wrote in 1961. "Both perpetrators and victims drew upon their age-old experience in dealing with the each other. The Germans did it with success. The Jews did it with disaster."

While the substance of Hilberg's magisterial work continues to command academic attention and profound respect despite the controversy surrounding his evaluation of Jewish behavior, the public outcry surrounding Hannah Arendt's work was far more intense and bitter.

Arendt wrote:

> Wherever Jews lived, there were recognized Jewish leaders, and this leadership, almost without exception, cooperated in one way or another, for one reason or another, with the Nazis. The whole truth was that if the Jewish people had really been unorganized and leaderless, there would have been chaos and plenty of misery but the total number of victims would hardly have been between four and a half and six million people.

Adam Czerniakow of Warsaw and Mordecai Chaim Rumkowski of Lodz exemplify the terrible problems faced by the German appointed Jewish Council leaders in the ghettos of Nazi-occupied eastern Europe.

Their daily dilemma: how to run a municipal government that could provide adequate food and shelter, heat, medicine, and work to a starving ghetto population. How to care for the young and sustain the elderly. How to make life bearable—even in the ghettos. Their resources were meager. Their power derived from German masters. Knowingly and unknowingly, they presided over doomed communities.

There were defining moments that tested the courage and character of *Judenrat* leaders. They were asked to provide lists of those to be deported. After all tactics of bribery, postponement, persuasion, and alleviation were exhausted, a decision had to be made.

Rumkowski cooperated. His reasoning: "I must cut off the limbs to save the body itself. I must take the children because if not, others will be taken as well." My duty, he would say, "is to preserve the Jews who remain—the part that can be saved is much larger than the part that must be given away."

Faced with similar choices, Jacob Gens, *Judenrat* chairman of Vilna, and Moshe Merin of Sosnowiec in Upper Silesia, also complied.

Yet other *Judenrat* leaders would not deliver their people to near-certain death. Dr. Joseph Parnas, first Jewish Council president in Lvov, refused to deliver several thousand Jews for deportation. He was shot. Leaders of the Jewish Council of Bilgoraj (Lublin District) met with the same fate when they refused to surrender their Jews.

The council chairman of Kovno (Lithuania), Dr. Elchanan Elkes, and his counterpart in

Dr. Elchanan Elkes, head of the Jewish council of the Kovno Ghetto, 1941. George Kadish/Courtesy USHMM-Photo Archives.

Minsk (Byelorussia), Eliyahu Mushkin, fully cooperated with the underground and the resistance. They assisted those who fled to the forests.

When the order was finally given to liquidate the entire ghetto, *Judenrat* leaders faced an even more agonizing dilemma.

Rumkowski pleaded with the Jews to go the trains in an orderly fashion. Those who came voluntarily could bring luggage, those who did not were to be rounded up by the Jewish police.

In Warsaw, Czerniakow swallowed a cyanide pill. The order for deportation was left unsigned by the chairman. He issued no call for resistance.

On October 14, 1942, the entire *Judenrat* of Bereza Kartuska committed suicide rather than participate in the deportation. The leader of the Jewish Council at Nesvizh, Megalif, marched to his death rather than turn Jews over to the Nazis. He said: "Brothers, I know you had not trust in me, you thought I was going to betray you. In this my last minute, I am with you—I and my family. We are the first ones to go to our death."

In his now classic work *Judenrat*, Isaiah Trunk demonstrated that the resources for understanding the Jewish Council are many.

In the readings below, we will read Mordecai Chaim Rumkowski's justification of his efforts in a speech of March 1942, at the House of Culture in Lodz to an audience consisting of those who ran the ghettos, managed its factories, and advised the chairman.

Rumkowski said: "When I received the deportation order, I was able to reduce it by half, that is to ten thousand people. Unfortunately, that did not end the deportation . . . The order [for deportation] must be carried out, or it will be carried out by others."

We will also read his fateful speech of September 4, 1942, in which with fear and trembling Rumkowski justifies the surrender of twenty thousand Jews—the young and the old.

> I must take the children, because if not others may be taken as well. I must tell you a secret: they requested twenty-four thousand victims . . . I succeeded in reducing the number to twenty thousand, but only on condition that these would be children below the age of ten . . .
>
> Help me carry out this action! I am trembling. I am afraid that others, God forbid, will do it themselves.

We will read the fateful description of October 28, 1941, in Kovno when the ghetto was to be separated between the labor force and those incapable of working. The Jewish Council was instructed to publish the order. To comply was to save some and endanger—perhaps even to doom—the others. Not to comply was to chose certain death for oneself and one's family, perhaps even for the community. They did not know what to do. They even approached the Chief Rabbi Abraham Dov Ber Kahana-Shapiro seeking advice. His decision: "Communal leaders were bound to summon their courage, take responsibility and save as many lives as possible."

We will read of two documents saved by the *Oneg Shabbos* group in Warsaw, a group of writers, historians, scholars, scientists, and artists assembled by Emanuel Ringelblum to document the destruction. When the ghetto was on the edge of destruction, these archives were buried; two milk cans have been recovered, one in 1946, the other in 1950. From this archive we will learn of the inner tension of the community to make life possible even under impossible situations—the dilemma they shared with the *Judenrat*.

And, finally, in this section on the Jewish Councils we read of Dr. Elchanan Elkes's final letter to his children. Elkes's reputation is unblemished by history. A leader of the Kovno Jewish Council, he cooperated with the resistance and worked well with all factions of the community as he presided over their destruction.

Elkes, who reluctantly accepted the office when he was drafted by the community, tried his best. The long-term results of his efforts were meager, as only two thousand Jews—8 percent of the ghetto's original population—survived.

In October 1943, just before his deportation, Elkes wrote to his children living in England. His verdict on his work:

> We are trying to steer our battered ship in furious seas, when waves of decrees and decisions threaten to drown it every day. Through my influence I succeeded, at times, in easing the verdict and scattering some of the dark clouds that hung over our heads.

He succeeded at times—for a time—in easing the verdict; but in the end the decree was issued, the fate of the Kovno Jews was sealed.

"WORK PROTECTS US FROM ANNIHILATION"
Speech by Mordecai Chaim Rumkowski*
MARCH 2, 1942

Uncertainty is worse than the bitter truth. Knowing this as well as I do, I've decided to call this meeting, to present the situation to you as it exists and to outline my plan for the immediate future. I stress that I shall speak about the situation as it is today. I cannot, of course, predict how things will develop later on. The explanations which I give today, and which are for the common good, should be repeated with the utmost accuracy throughout the ghetto. I shall be very grateful to you for this.

The legitimacy of my original basic slogan "Work" was confirmed from the minute I first issued it. We've seen many times now that we can have peace only through work. We live here in the ghetto; somehow we've been able to accommodate ourselves to our circumstances, modifying our existence and our behavior accordingly. Just last year I made jobs for all ghetto inhabitants a top priority. I therefore ordered a fifteen-day work assignment for those receiving welfare. You may remember that I stressed the importance of satisfying this requirement. Experience has made clear that the basic law of our times is: "Work protects us from annihilation." Unfortunately, there were Jews in the ghetto who laughed at this idea, preferring to evade their work obligation by manipulating the welfare system.

In the fall I reduced rations to force the shirkers receiving them to give them up and enter into productive work. But even this didn't

* This speech was delivered in the House of Culture to an invited audience of administrators, factory managers, and Rumkowski's advisers.

help, since those with big families felt it was still to their advantage to remain on relief. And there were other instances of people staying away from work, for one reason or another. I tried other incentives, all in order to ensure peace and a secure tomorrow. Peace of mind is more essential than food. Had my words been given their full due by a wide segment of the population, you and I would have it much easier now.

Cruel fate took over. First we had a shipment of new people into the ghetto, and later a series of deportations. When I received the deportation order, I was able to reduce it by half, that is to ten thousand people. As everyone knows, I included in that contingent the criminal and other undesirable elements. Unfortunately, that did not end the deportation. Thousands more were requested this time, in accordance with the agreement that only people who can work can remain in the ghetto. The order must be carried out, or it will be carried out by others.

After painful deliberation and inner struggle, I've decided to deport the people on relief. They too are at fault, if not fully, then partially, in that they stayed outside the ghetto workforce. I refer to the obvious disregard of the fifteen day per month work schedule. I stressed again and again that I needed a reserve work force, to keep it in readiness for a sudden need to fill orders. People willing to work had to register. It was secondary what kind of work it would be—whether in clothing factories, trolley transportation or public works.

It's not a bluff, and it's easy to see, how a person still unemployed but in the reserve workforce can use the indispensable work card for identification. This idea of mine grew out of reality, and I was proved right. But even then there were Jews who laughed at me, and unfortunately they've lived to see this calamity: more and more are being demanded for deportation. I've pointed out many times that a work card guarantees peace.

I'll outline for you the program I've carefully planned, as it relates to my current intentions. Children are always closest to my heart. How

my heart rejoiced when I saw the youngsters with their schoolbags on their way to school—the sight gave me hope and inspiration for my work. It was the best breakfast I could have, mornings on Baluty Square. But when there was a need to find housing for newcomers, I decided to close the schools, though it made my heart bleed. It was my hope that in two months the newcomers' housing problems would be solved and that the buildings occupied by them would revert to school use. Unfortunately, that did not come to pass. Even now, when the collectives are being disbanded and the school buildings where they've been located—including the big school building at Franciszkanska Street—are being vacated, new imperatives arise. These buildings have to be used as factories. The only thing that pleases me is that these buildings will enable us to set up large enterprises, in the full sense of the word. Again, my darling children will have to wait for their schools. But in April, with the first breath of spring, we shall take care of them properly.

I point out that the ghetto was assured it would receive orders for a great deal of work. I am implementing some work reform in factories and other enterprises. Many establishments work on a ten-hour or twelve-hour day. But with our meager sustenance, a double-digit number of hours per day can have a negative effect on productivity. My reform, therefore, will reduce the hours to eight, which will let us set up three shifts and triple our factory workforce.

Every employed person is a productive member of the workforce, regardless of the nature of his work: whether he's a laborer, office worker, policeman, or kitchen worker. As I've said, I shall put many new factories into operation, and by increasing the shifts to the maximum, I'll be able to increase our commercial capacity by twenty thousand people. Making use of public works, I shall attempt to have 90 percent or more of the population employed. My basic concern is and will be the care of the working class—or to put it another way, everybody who is employed in the ghetto.

Tomorrow I'll open a new office which

will be supervised by my most trusted advisors and which will conduct a survey of everyone employed. Each worker will have to supply information about each member of his family. This will enable the new office to assign work to unemployed members of a family: skilled workers to work in their fields of specialization, unskilled in unskilled work or to be reeducated. This is the way I shall solve today's most pressing problem. As far as older people are concerned, working people's parents who are unable to work, I trust that God will not forsake them. Seeking influence with regard to the work assignments will be useless. Everyone will have to be satisfied with the job he gets. Everyone fourteen years old and older must work for a living!

My plan is based on sound logic, and my well-founded hope is that once we have the most precise, accurate data, we'll be able to convince the higher authorities and emerge victorious from this difficult situation. I have no doubt that I can achieve this greatly desired goal if the whole ghetto unanimously, in closed ranks, reports to work. Don't be ashamed if many of you have to take jobs which aren't exactly prestigious, jobs which are to be performed in public. Especially you, my sisters who are getting on in years, remember that even if you're sent to sweep the streets or to cart refuse, it's only for your own good. We have a great task to accomplish: we have to find work for eighty thousand people. In spite of the immensity of this undertaking, I'm convinced that I'll be able to find a solution. With an eight-hour day in the factory and, subtracting an hour's preparation, closer to a seven-hour day, the odds are that productivity will keep increasing. I am assured that the ghetto will be supplied with sufficient food for all its inhabitants.

I may seem like an eavesdropping child, but I admit that news from "the street" reaches me. Fantastic lies are heard in the street. The latest gossip has it that I and my entire staff plan to flee to Warsaw. This is an ugly, total lie. I consider myself a soldier, staying faithfully at my post. I didn't think of running away at the beginning of the war, when practically all of the community's establishment left Lodz. My conviction that it was my duty to remain at my post didn't waver for a moment. And so it is today; I shall not abandon my post.

I shall try with all my might to realize 100 percent of the plan I've described. An atmosphere of calm is necessary, and I urge that everyone maintain it. Remember that this gossip mania makes my job more difficult. Gossip is like a terrible plague, and it's to blame for much of our difficulty.

Returning to the matter of provisions, I want to stress that the powers on which we depend wish to supply us with adequate food and are providing it as best they can. I was assured that when the potato storehouse is opened, the ghetto will be treated fairly. At this point, there is also a potato shortage in the city.

In order to improve the living conditions of the employed, special supplements will be given to this most important group when food is distributed. I had this in mind yesterday when I ordered that meat not be sold to the sick but to workers. I felt bad when I had to telephone yesterday to order the closing of Store R-III, the butcher shop for the sick. We must, alas, do everything to provide for the people who are well and who work. I do what I can, and I can say, with respect to food, that we're approaching a better tomorrow. As soon as it gets warm, my bare cupboards will be filled again.

I always hope and trust. I decided to speak to you because just today a ray of hope appeared, so that it may be possible to prevent the separation of families. That's how things look in a true light. The gossipmongers, however, are spreading lies that the ghetto will be liquidated.

Managers! I stand before you as a soldier on guard; I ask you to maintain calm and to devote yourselves to your work, and that's how you'll help me realize my important program. See that the questionnaires are fully completed as to the status of family members. It's this kind of paper, this document, presented to the commission that will decide human existence, because the commission will try to match people with jobs.

Nobody should try to avoid work because of poor health or other problems. You can expect nothing from me in this respect, for what can I do? Let's say I could save ten or one hundred people; it's meaningless when you take into consideration the overall numbers. We cannot treat each individual as a special case. That's why I hold all managers personally responsible for the careful completion of questionnaires. If a manager abuses this responsibility, I shall, without hesitating a moment, deport him and his entire family. Managers! You are equally responsible for the regular work in your workshops. If I ascertain the slightest attempt at sabotage, I will deport you without pity. I absolutely will not consider anyone indispensable.

Comrades and friends, I don't have anything more to say. I asked you to come today so I could explain the situation in which we find ourselves. I hope you understood me perfectly. Take pity on yourselves! Work as one man! Do not involve yourselves in politics! Do not shirk work because of sickness!

I shall try to protect first the families of those who have been working a long time. They obviously have priority over those who have just started working. Today in one of the shops

a shoemaker asked for a work certificate. He was asked how long he has been working, and he answered, "Since yesterday." This shoemaker is experienced and skilled, and yet he took advantage of the fact that with a family of seven he could remain idle and avail himself of welfare. Surely, individuals like this deserve to be deported. An unskilled person, or one for whom there is no work—that's an entirely different matter.

As of tomorrow, and until further notice, I forbid anyone to be hired for any job whatsoever. Hiring can be done only on the recommendation of the commission examining the family situation of workers. This commission will be in existence as of tomorrow and will work with the Labor Department. If you learn of anyone who violates my order, and hires someone on his own, please write to me about this. The only people to whom this order does not apply are those recently laid off because their workshops closed—for example, the workers in the straw-shoe factory. For these, all the doors of my factories are open. They have absolute priority. The work of the Education Department's Retraining Committee remains the same.

I assure you, personally and on behalf of my closest associates, that we'll do everything in our power for the good of the ghetto.

"GIVE ME YOUR CHILDREN!"

Speech by Mordecai Chaim Rumkowski

SEPTEMBER 4, 1942

A grievous blow has struck the ghetto. They are asking us to give up the best we possess—the children and the elderly. I was unworthy of having a child of my own, so I gave the best years of my life to children. I've lived and breathed with children. I never imagined I would be forced to deliver this sacrifice to the altar with my own hands. In my old age I must stretch out my hands and beg: Brothers and sisters, hand them over to me! Fathers and mothers, give me your children!

[Transcriber's note: Horrible, terrifying wailing among the assembled crowd.]

I had a suspicion something was about to befall us. I anticipated "something" and was always like a watchman on guard to prevent it. But I was unsuccessful because I did not know what was threatening us. I did not know the nature of the danger. The taking of the sick from the hospitals caught me completely by surprise. And I give you the best proof there is of this: I had my own nearest and dearest among them, and I could do nothing for them.

I thought that that would be the end of it, that after that they'd leave us in peace, the peace for which I long so much, for which I've always worked, which has been my goal. But something else, it turned out, was destined for us. Such is the fate of the Jews: always more suffering and always worse suffering, especially in times of war.

Yesterday afternoon, they gave me the order to send more than twenty thousand Jews out of the ghetto, and if not—"We will do it!" So, the question became: "Should we take it upon ourselves, do it ourselves, or leave it for others to do?" Well, we—that is, I and my closest associates—thought first not about "How many will perish?" but "How many is it possible to save?" And we reached the conclusion that, however hard it would be for us, we should take the implementation of this order into our own hands.

I must perform this difficult and bloody operation—I must cut off limbs in order to save the body itself! I must take children because, if not, others may be taken as well, God forbid.

[Horrible wailing.]

I have no thought of consoling you today. Nor do I wish to calm you. I must lay bare your full anguish and pain. I come to you like a bandit, to take from you what you treasure most in your hearts! I have tried, using every possible means, to get the order revoked. I tried—when that proved to be impossible—to soften the order. Just yesterday I ordered a list of children aged nine—I wanted, at least, to save this one age group, the nine- to ten-year-olds. But I was not granted this concession. On only one point did I succeed, in saving the ten-year-olds and

up. Let this be a consolation in our profound grief.

There are, in the ghetto, many patients who can expect to live only a few days more, maybe a few weeks. I don't know if the idea is diabolical or not, but I must say it: "Give me the sick. In their place, we can save the healthy." I know how dear the sick are to any family, and particularly to Jews. However, when cruel demands are made, one has to weigh and measure: who shall, can and may be saved? And common sense dictates that the saved must be those who can be saved and those who have a chance of being rescued, not those who cannot be saved in any case.

We live in the ghetto, mind you. We live with so much restriction that we do not have enough even for the healthy, let alone for the sick. Each

Mordecai Chaim Rumkowski, chairman of the Jewish Council in the Lodz Ghetto, with Hans Biebow, head of the German ghetto administration. Al Moss/Courtesy of USHMM–Photo Archives.

of us feeds the sick at the expense of our own health: We give our bread to the sick. We give them our meager ration of sugar, our little piece of meat. And what's the result? Not enough to cure the sick, and we ourselves become ill. Of course, such sacrifices are the most beautiful and noble. But there are times when one has to choose: sacrifice the sick, who haven't the slightest chance of recovery and who also may make others ill, or rescue the healthy.

I could not deliberate over this problem for long; I had to resolve it in favor of the healthy. In this spirit, I gave the appropriate instructions to the doctors, and they will be expected to deliver all incurable patients, so that the healthy, who want and are able to live, will be saved in their place.

[Horrible weeping.]

I understand you, mothers; I see your tears, all right. I also feel what you feel in your hearts, you fathers who will have to go to work the morning after your children have been taken from you, when just yesterday you were playing with your dear little ones. All this I know and feel. Since four o'clock yesterday, when I first found out about the order, I have been utterly broken. I share your pain. I suffer because of your anguish, and I don't know how I'll survive this—where I'll find the strength to do so.

I must tell you a secret: they requested twenty-four thousand victims, three thousand a day for eight days. I succeeded in reducing the number to twenty thousand, but only on the condition that these would be children below the age of ten. Children ten and older are safe. Since the children and the aged together equal only some thirteen thousand souls, the gap will have to be filled with the sick.

I can barely speak. I am exhausted; I only want to tell you what I am asking of you:

Help me carry out this action! I am trembling. I am afraid that others, God forbid, will do it themselves....

A broken Jew stands before you. Do not envy me. This is the most difficult of all the orders I've ever had to carry out at any time. I reach out to you with my broken, trembling hands and I beg: Give into my hands the victims, so that we can avoid having further victims, and a population of a hundred thousand Jews can be preserved. So they promised me: if we deliver our victims by ourselves, there will be peace....

[Shouts: "We all will go!" "Mr. Chairman, an only child should not be taken; children should be taken from families with several children!"]

These are empty phrases! I don't have the strength to argue with you! If the authorities were to arrive, none of you would shout.

I understand what it means to tear off a part of the body. Yesterday I begged on my knees, but it didn't work. From small villages with Jewish populations of seven to eight thousand, barely a thousand arrived here. So which is better? What do you want: that eighty to ninety thousand Jews remain, or, God forbid, that the whole population be annihilated?

You may judge as you please; my duty is to preserve the Jews who remain. I do not speak to hotheads. I speak to your reason and conscience. I have done and will continue doing everything possible to keep arms from appearing in the streets and blood from being shed. The order could not be undone; it could only be reduced.

One needs the heart of a bandit to ask from you what I am asking. But put yourself in my place, think logically, and you'll reach the conclusion that I cannot proceed any other way. The part that can be saved is much larger than the part that must be given away.

ON THE *JUDENRAT*'S DECISION TO ACCEPT WORK PERMITS

EXCERPTS FROM AVRAHAM TORY'S *SURVIVING THE HOLOCAUST: THE KOVNO GHETTO DIARY* *

OCTOBER 28, 1941

On Friday afternoon, October 24, 1941, a Gestapo car entered the ghetto. It carried the Gestapo deputy chief, Captain Schmitz, and Master Sergeant Rauca. Their appearance filled all onlookers with fear. The council was worried and ordered the Jewish Ghetto police to follow all their movements. Those movements were rather unusual. The two ghetto rulers turned neither to the council offices nor to the Jewish police, nor to the German labor office, nor to the armed commandant, as they used to in their visits to the Ghetto. Instead, they toured various places as if looking for something, tarried awhile in Demorkratu Square, looked it over, and left through the gate, leaving in their wake an ominously large question mark: what were they scheming to do?

The next day, Saturday afternoon, an urgent message was relayed from the ghetto gate to the council: Rauca, accompanied by a high-ranking Gestapo officer, was coming. As usual in such cases, all unauthorized persons were removed from the council secretariat room and from the hallway, lest their presence invoke the wrath of the Nazi fiends.

The two Germans entered the offices of the council—Rauca did not waste time. He opened with a major pronouncement: it is imperative to increase the size of the Jewish labor force in view of its importance for the German war

effort—an allusion to the indispensability of Jewish labor to the Germans. Furthermore, he continued, the Gestapo is aware that food rations allotted to the Ghetto inmates do not provide proper nourishment to heavy-labor workers and, therefore, he intends to increase rations for both the workers and their families so that they will be able to achieve greater output for the Reich. The remaining ghetto inmates, those not included in the Jewish labor force, would have to make do with the existing rations. To forestall competition and envy between them and the Jewish labor force, they would be separated from them and transferred to the small ghetto. In this fashion, those contributing to the war effort would obtain more spacious and comfortable living quarters. To carry out this operation a roll call would take place. The council was to issue an order in which all the ghetto inmates, without exception, and irrespective of sex and age, were called to report to Demokratu Square on October 28, at 6 A.M. on the dot. In the square they should line up by families and workplace of the family head. When leaving for the roll call they were to leave their apartments, closets, and drawers open. Anybody found after 6 A.M. in his home would be shot on the spot. The members of the council were shaken and overcome by fear. This order boded very ill for the future of the ghetto. But what did it mean? Dr. Elkes attempted to get Rauca to divulge some information about the intention behind this roll call, but his efforts bore no fruit. Rauca refused to add another word to his communication and, accompanied by his associate, left the council office and the ghetto.

The members of the council remained in a

---

* Avraham Tory's original description of the "action" of October 28, 1941, was written immediately after the event and buried in the ground. When, in August 1944, Tory dug out what he had buried, he felt that this entry was too short, so he expanded it. This second version, published here, was written three years after the event. It contains details Tory had learned during the war in discussions with survivors of the "action."

state of shock. What lay in wait for the ghetto? What was the true purpose of the roll call? Why did Rauca order the council to publish the order, rather than publish it himself? Was he planning to abuse the trust the ghetto population had in the Jewish leadership? And if so, had the council the right to comply with Rauca's order and publish it, thereby becoming an accomplice in an act which might spell disaster?

Some council members proposed to disobey the Gestapo and not publish the order, even if this would mean putting the lives of the council members at risk. Others feared that in the case of disobedience the arch-henchmen would not be contented with punishing the council alone, but would vent their wrath also on the ghetto inmates, and that thousands of Jews were liable to pay with their lives for the impudence of their leaders. After all, no one could fathom the intentions of Rauca and his men; why, then, stir the beasts of prey into anger? Was the council entitled to take responsibility for the outcome of not publishing the order? On the other hand, was the council entitled to take upon itself the heavy burden of moral responsibility and go ahead with publishing the order?

The council discussions continued for many hours without reaching a conclusion. In the meantime, the publication of the order was postponed and an attempt was made to inquire about Rauca's plans, using the contacts of Caspi Serebrovitz* in the Gestapo. Zvi Levin, who was Caspi's fellow party member (they were both

---

* Joseph Serebrovitz, a Jewish journalist, who wrote under the name Caspi. He had been imprisoned by the Soviet authorities in 1940 and released shortly after the German occupation. He at once offered the Germans his services against the Soviet Union. Later he tried to exert influence in the ghetto because of his special relationship with the Gestapo. Permitted not to wear the yellow Star of David, and allowed to live in the town with his family, he was a frequent visitor to the ghetto. In October 1941 he was sent to Vilna. He later returned to Kovno, but in July 1942 he was again transferred to Vilna. In June 1943 he once more appeared in the Kovno Ghetto; later in 1943 he was murdered by the Nazis, together with his wife and two daughters.

Revisionists), was asked to leave for the city, to call on him and ask him what he knew about Rauca's plans, and to ask Rauca to grant an audience to Dr. Elkes. Levin found Caspi packing his bags. The latter was stunned to learn about the order and exclaimed spontaneously: "Aha, now I understand why Rauca is sending me to Vilna for three days just at this time. He wants to keep me away from Kovno, especially now."

Complying with Levin's request, Caspi set out to inform Rauca that disquiet prevailed in the ghetto and that the council chairman wished to see him that very evening. Rauca responded favorably.

The council members agreed that the meeting with Rauca should take place in the modest apartment of Dr. Elkes, in order to keep the meeting as secret as possible. At 6 P.M. Rauca arrived at Dr. Elkes's apartment. Yakov Goldberg, a member of the council and head of the council's labor office, was also present. Dr. Elkes began by saying that his responsibilities as leader of the community and as a human being obliged him to speak openly. He asked Rauca to understand his position and not to be angry with him. Then he revealed his and the council members' fears that the decree spelled disaster for the ghetto, since, if the German authorities' intention was only to alter the food distribution arrangements, the council was prepared to carry out the appropriate decrees faithfully and to the letter. Therefore, he went on to say, there is no need for a roll call of the entire ghetto population, including elderly people and babes in arms, since such a summons was likely to cause panic in the ghetto. Moreover, the three roll calls that had taken place over the past three months had each ended in terrible "actions." Therefore, he, Dr. Elkes, pleaded with "Mr. Master Sergeant" to reveal the whole truth behind the roll call.

Rauca feigned amazement that any suspicion at all could have been harbored by the members of the council. He repeated his promise that a purely administrative matter was involved and that no evil intentions lurked behind it. He added that at the beginning the Gestapo had, in fact, considered charging the council with the distribution of the increased food rations for the Jewish labor force, but having given thought to the solidarity prevailing among the Jews, had suspected that the food distribution would not be carried out and that the food delivered to the council would be distributed among all ghetto residents—both workers and nonworkers—in equal rations. The Gestapo could not allow this to happen under the difficult conditions of the continuing war. Accordingly, the Gestapo had no choice but to divide the ghetto population into two groups. The roll call was a purely administrative measure and nothing more.

Dr. Elkes attempted to appeal to the "conscience" of the Gestapo officer, hinting casually that every war, including the present one, was bound to end sooner or later, and that if Rauca would answer his questions openly, without concealing anything, the Jews would know how to repay him. The council itself would know how to appreciate Rauca's humane approach. Thus, Dr. Elkes daringly intimated a possible defeat of Germany in the war, in which case Rauca would be able to save his skin with the help of the Jews. Rauca, however, remained unmoved: there was no hidden plan and no ill intention behind the decree. Having said this he left.

After this conversation, Dr. Elkes and Goldberg left for the council offices, where the other council members were waiting for them impatiently. Dr. Elkes's report of his conversation did not dispel the uncertainty and the grave fears. No one was prepared to believe Rauca's assertions that a purely administrative matter was involved. The question remained: why should the elderly and the infants, men and women, including the sick and feeble, be dragged out of their homes at dawn for a roll call by families and by workplace, if the purpose was simply the distribution of increased food rations to the workers? Even if the plan was just to transfer part of the ghetto population to the small ghetto, why was a total roll call needed? Was it not sufficient to announce

that such-and-such residents must move into those living quarters within the small ghetto which had been left empty after the liquidation of its residents and the burning of the hospital?

Even before Rauca ordered the council to publish the decree, rumors originating in various Jewish workplaces in the city where there was contact with Lithuanians had it that in the Ninth Fort large pits had been dug by Russian prisoners-of-war. Those rumors were being repeated by various Lithuanians and, naturally, they reached the council. When Rauca announced the roll call decree, the rumors and the roll call no longer seemed a coincidence.

As the rumors about digging of pits persisted, and the members of the council failed to give any indication of their apprehension, an atmosphere of fear pervaded the ghetto, growing heavier with each passing day. The very real apprehensions of the council were compounded by the fear that any revelation of its suspicions and doubts might lead many Jews to acts of desperation—acts which were bound to bring disaster both on themselves and on many others in the ghetto.

Since the members of the council could not reach any decision, they resolved to seek the advice of Chief Rabbi Shapiro. At 11 P.M. Dr. Elkes, Garfunkel, Goldberg, and Levin set out for Rabbi Shapiro's house. The unexpected visit at such a late hour frightened the old and sick rabbi. He rose from his bed and, pale as a ghost, came out to his guests. He was trembling with emotion.

The members of the council told Rabbi Shapiro about the two meetings with Rauca, and about the roll call decree. They also told him about their fears and asked him to rule on the question of whether they, as public leaders responsible for the fate of the Jews in the ghetto, were permitted or even duty bound to publish the decree.

The rabbi heaved a deep sigh. The question was complex and difficult; it called for weighty consideration. He asked them to come back to him at 6 A.M. the next day. Dr. Elkes and his colleagues replied by stressing the urgency of the matter, since the council had been told that it must publish the decree before that time. Each further delay was liable to provoke the ire of the Gestapo. The rabbi promised that he would not close his eyes all night; that he would consult his learned books and give them an early reply.

When the council members returned to the rabbi's house at 6 A.M. they found him poring over books which lay piled up on his desk. His face bore visible traces of the sleepless night and the great ordeal he had gone through to find scriptural support for the ruling on the terrible question facing the council. He lifted his head—adorned by white beard—and said that he had not yet found the answer. He asked them to come back in three hours' time. But at nine o'clock he was still engrossed in study and put off his answer for another two hours. At last, at eleven o'clock, he came up with the answer. In studying and interpreting the sources, he had found that there had been situations in Jewish history which resembled the dilemma the council was facing now. In such cases, he said, when an evil edict had imperiled an entire Jewish community and, by a certain act, a part of the community could be saved, communal leaders were bound to summon their courage, take the responsibility, and save as many lives as possible. According to this principle, it was incumbent on the council to publish the decree. Other rabbis, and a number of public figures in the ghetto, subsequently took issue with this ruling. They argued that it was forbidden for the council to publish the decree, since by doing so it inadvertently became a collaborator with the oppressor in carrying out his design—a design which could bring disaster on the entire ghetto. Those bereft of all hope added the argument that since the ghetto was doomed to perdition anyway, the council should have adopted the religious principle "*yehareg u'bal yaavor*" (to refuse compliance even on the pain of death), and refrained from publishing the decree.

Immediately after their visit to the chief rabbi, members of the council convened for a special meeting and decided to publish the decree. So it was that on October 27, 1941, announcements in Yiddish and in German were posted by the council throughout the ghetto. Their text was as follows:

> The council has been ordered by the authorities to publish the following official decree to the ghetto inmates:
> All inmates of the ghetto, without exception, including children and the sick, are to leave their homes on Tuesday, October 28, 1941, at 6 A.M., and to assemble in the square between the big blocks and the Demokratu Street, and to line up in accordance with police instructions.
> The ghetto inmates are required to report by families, each family being headed by the worker who is the head of the family.
> It is forbidden to lock apartments, wardrobes, cupboards, desks, etc....
> After 6 A.M. nobody may remain in his apartment.
> Anyone found in the apartments after 6 A.M. will be shot on sight.

The wording was chosen by the council so that everyone would understand that it concerned a Gestapo order; that the council had no part in it.

The ghetto was agog. Until the publication of this order everyone had carried his fears in his own heart. Now those fears and forebodings broke out. The rumors about the digging of pits in the Ninth Fort, which had haunted people like a nightmare, now acquired tangible meaning. The ghetto remembered well the way the previous "actions" had been prepared, in which some 2,800 people had met their deaths. An additional sign of the impending disaster was that on that very same day workers in various places were furnished with special papers issued by their German employers—military and paramilitary—certifying that their holders were employed on a permanent basis at such-and-such a German factory or workplace.

This category also included the airfield workers, who had been issued suitable cards and yellow armbands to be worn on their right sleeve, as well as members of the Jewish labor brigade which worked for the Gestapo. Workers in this brigade, headed by Lipzer,* were particularly conspicuous since, in addition to the documents certifying their employment by the Gestapo, they were provided by Lipzer with a sign bearing the word "Gestapo" as their workplace.

The overwhelming majority of the ghetto inmates did not have in their possession such privileged documents, or Jordan certificates. People kept flocking to street corners and into courtyards, making inquiries, hoping to hear something which might put them at their ease. Everyone was busy interpreting each word in the decree. Particularly ominous was the threat that anyone found in his apartment after 6 A.M. would be shot. The Gestapo also announced that, immediately after this deadline, armed German policemen would be deployed in every house and courtyard and would kill anyone found there regardless of the reason.

No one in the ghetto closed an eye on the night of October 27. Many wept bitterly, many others recited Psalms. There were also people who did the opposite: they decided to have a good time, to feast and gorge themselves on food, and use up their whole supply. Inmates whose apartments were stocked with wines and liquor drank all they could, and even invited neighbors and friends to the macabre drinking party "so as not to leave anything behind for the

Germans." There were also those who, despite everything, did not lose hope and kept themselves busy, hiding away money, jewelry, and other valuables in hiding places under floorboards or in door lintels, in pits they dug that night in their courtyards, and so on. Every unmarried woman looked for a family to adopt her, or for a bachelor who would present her as his wife. Widows with children also sought "husbands" for themselves and "fathers" for their children—all this in preparation for the roll call, in the hope of being able to save themselves.

I, too, adopted as my son an eleven-year-old boy, named Moishele Prusak, who was a remote relative of mine. His parents and the other members of his family were living in my native village of Lazdijai, whereas he lived alone in Slobodka, where he studied at the yeshiva.

Tuesday morning, October 28, was rainy. A heavy mist covered the sky and the whole ghetto was shrouded in darkness. A fine sleet filled the air and covered the ground in a thin layer. From all directions, dragging themselves heavily and falteringly, groups of men, women, and children, elderly and sick who leaned on the arms of their relatives or neighbors, babies carried in their mothers' arms, proceeded in long lines. They were all wrapped in winter coats, shawls, or blankets, so as to protect themselves from the cold and the damp. Many carried in their hands lanterns or candles, which cast a faint light, illuminating their way in the darkness.

Many families stepped along slowly, holding hands. They all made their way in the same direction—to Demokratu Square. It was a procession of mourners grieving over themselves. Some thirty thousand people proceeded that morning into the unknown, toward a fate that could already have been sealed for them by the bloodthirsty rulers.

A deathlike silence pervaded this procession tens of thousands strong. Every person dragged himself along, absorbed in his own thoughts, pondering his own fate and the fate of his family whose lives hung by a thread. Thirty thousand lonely people, forgotten by

---

* Benjamin (Benno) Lipzer, born in Grodno in 1896, in the Kovno Ghetto was head of the brigade (work group) of Jews employed by the Germans on various work details which served the headquarters building of the Gestapo in Kovno. After he had developed contacts with the upper echelons of the Gestapo, he attempted to gain control of the Jewish police. In June 1942 the ghetto authorized him to supervise the labor department of the Jewish Council. At the time of the liquidation of the ghetto in July 1944, he hid in the ghetto, but was driven from his hiding place by the Gestapo and killed.

God and by man, delivered to the whim of tyrants whose hands had already spilled the blood of many Jews.

All of them, especially heads of families, had equipped themselves with some sort of document, even a certificate of being employed by one of the ghetto institutions, or a high school graduation diploma, or a German university diploma—some paper that might perhaps, perhaps, who knows, bring them an "indulgence" for the sin of being a Jew. Some dug out commendations issued by the Lithuanian Army; perhaps these might be of help.

The ghetto houses were left empty, except for a handful of terminally ill persons who could not raise themselves from bed. In compliance with the instruction issued by the authorities, on every house in which a sick person had been left behind a note was posted giving his name and his illness. The council offices, as well as the offices of the Jewish Ghetto police, the labor office, and the ghetto workshops, were also left empty; doors of offices were left ajar, as well as closets, desks, and drawers, in compliance with Rauca's order, so that nobody could remain there in hiding. The storerooms containing the ghetto's food supplies and raw materials were left unattended on that day, as was the private property of the ghetto inmates.

As the ghetto inmates were assembling in Demokratu Square, armed Lithuanian partisans raided the ghetto houses, forcing their way into every apartment, every attic, every storage room, and every cellar, looking for who might be hiding Jews. Many of these Lithuanians took the opportunity to loot. Some carried with them suitcases stuffed with goods, but these looters were subsequently arrested by the German police officers, who disarmed them and removed them from the ghetto.

The ghetto fence was surrounded by machine guns and a heavy detachment of armed German policemen, commanded by Captain Tornbaum. He also had at his disposal battalions of armed Lithuanian partisans. A crowd of curious Lithuanian spectators had gathered on the hills overlooking the ghetto. They followed the events taking place in the square with great interest, not devoid of delight, and did not leave for many hours.

The ghetto inmates were lined up in columns according to the workplace of the family heads. The first column consisted of the council members, followed by the column of the Jewish policemen and their families. On both sides and behind stood the workers in the ghetto institutions, and many columns of the various Jewish labor brigades together with their families, since on that day the ghetto was sealed off. No one was allowed to go out to work. The airfield workforce, which had left for work the previous day and had stayed there for an additional shift in compliance with General Geiling's order,* were returned to the ghetto after the entire ghetto population had already been assembled in the square. Having completed two shifts of hard labor, these people hurried to and fro among the columns, tired, hungry, and dirty, in an effort to locate their families.

In the meantime, dawn broke. The grayish light of a rainy day replaced the nocturnal darkness. Old people, and those too weak to remain standing on their feet for long hours, collapsed on the ground. Others, having learned from past experience, had brought with them a chair or a stool on which they could sit and rest. Some had even equipped themselves with food before coming to the roll call, but the great majority of the ghetto inmates remained standing on their feet, hungry and tired, among them mothers and fathers with children in baby carriages or in their arms.

Three hours went by. The cold and the damp penetrated their bones. The endless waiting for the sentence had driven many people out of their minds. Religious Jews mumbled prayers and Psalms. The old and the sick whimpered. Babies cried aloud; in every eye the same horrible question stood out: "When will it begin?! When will it begin?!"

---

* General Geiling, supervisor of the construction of the large military airfield being built by the Germans in the suburb of Aleksotas.

At 9 A.M. a Gestapo entourage appeared at the square: the deputy Gestapo chief, Captain Schmitz, Master Sergeant Rauca, Captain Jordan, and Captain Tornbaum, accompanied by a squad of the German policemen and Lithuanian partisans.

The square was surrounded by machine-gun emplacements. Rauca positioned himself on top of a little mound from which he could watch the great crowd that waited in the square in tense and anxious anticipation. His glance ranged briefly over the column of the council members and the Jewish Ghetto police, and by a movement of his hand he motioned them to the left, which, as it became clear later, was the "good" side. Then he signaled with the baton he held in his hand and ordered the remaining columns: "Forward!" The selection had begun.

The columns of employees of the ghetto institutions and their families passed before Rauca, followed by other columns, one after another. The Gestapo man fixed his gaze on each pair of eyes and with a flick of the finger of his right hand passed sentence on individuals, families, or even whole groups. Elderly and sick persons, families with children, single women, and persons whose physique did not impress him in terms of labor power, were directed to the right. There, they immediately fell into the hands of the German policemen and the Lithuanian partisans, who showered them with shouts and blows and pushed them toward an opening especially made in the fence, where two Germans counted them and then reassembled them in a different place.

At first, nobody knew which was the "good" side. Many therefore rejoiced at finding themselves on the right. They began thanking Rauca, saying "Thank you kindly," or even "Thank you for your mercy." There were many men and women who, having been directed to the left, asked permission to move over to the right and join their relatives from whom they had been separated. Smiling sarcastically, Rauca gave his consent.

Those who tried to pass over from the right to the left, in order to join their families, or because they guessed—correctly, as it turned out—that that was the "good" side, immediately felt the pain of blows dealt by the hands and rifle butts of the policemen and the partisans, who brutally drove them back again to the right. By then everyone realized which side was the "good" and which the "bad" one.

When some old or sick person could not hold out any longer and collapsed on to the ground, the Lithuanians set upon him instantly, kicking him with their boots, beating him, and threatening to trample him underfoot if he did not get up at once. Drawing the last ounce of strength, he would rise to his feet— if he could—and try to catch up with his group. Those unable to get up were helped by their companions in trouble, who lifted them up, supported them, and helped them along to reach the assembly spot in the small ghetto, to which they were marched under heavy guard.

In most cases these were old people, women, and children, frightened and in a state of shock, turned by screams and blows into a panic-stricken herd which felt it was being driven by a satanic, omnipotent force. It was a force which banished all thought and seemed to allow no hope of escape.

In especially shocking cases where members of a family were separated, when pleas and cries were heartrending, Dr. Elkes tried to come to the rescue, and at times he even succeeded in transferring whole families to the left. Among others, he intervened on behalf of a veteran public figure, the director of the hospital, a skillful artisan, and a number of activists of Zionist and non-Zionist underground circles. Unfortunately he did not succeed in transferring everyone to the left.*

---

* In his book *Dem Goirel Antkegn (Facing Fate)*, published in Johannesburg in 1952, Professor Aharon Peretz, now of Haifa, writes that he and his family were already on the "bad" side when, all of a sudden, as a result of intervention of someone on the council, he was transferred to the "good" side and saved, together with his family. This "someone" was Dr. Elkes, who pointed him out to Rauca as a specialist needed in the hospital.

The commander of the Jewish police, Kopelman, who stayed with Dr. Elkes near Rauca, also succeeded in saving Jews and whole families. The number of such survivors, throughout this bitter and hurried day, reached into the hundreds.

Rauca directed the job of selection composedly, with cynicism, and with the utmost speed, by mere movements of the finger of his right hand. When the meaning of the movement of his finger was not grasped instantly, he would roar: "To the right!" or "To the left!" And when people failed to obey at once he shouted at them: "To the right, you lousy curs!" Throughout the selection he did not exhibit any sign of fatigue or sensitivity at the wailing, pleas, and cries, or at the sight of the heartrending spectacles which took place before his eyes when children were separated from their parents, or parents from their children, or husbands and wives from each other—all those tragedies did not penetrate his heart at all.

From time to time, Rauca feasted on a sandwich—wrapped in wax paper lest his bloodstained hands get greasy—or enjoyed a cigarette, all the while performing his fiendish work without interruption.

When a column composed mostly of elderly people, or of women or children, appeared before him, he would command contemptuously: "All this trash to the right!" or "All this pile of garbage goes to the right!" To Dr. Elkes, when he tried to intervene in an attempt to save their lives, he would say: "Wait, you'll be grateful to me for having rid you of this burden."

Whenever Rauca condescended to respond favorably to Dr. Elkes's intercession, he would say carelessly: "Well, as far as I am concerned . . ." and then order the German policeman: "This fat one, or this short one, or this one with the glasses on, bring him back to me."* Now and then Rauca would be handed a note with a number written on it, copied from the notebook kept by the German who diligently applied himself to the task of recording the number of Jews removed to the small ghetto.

Rauca was quick to dispense "mercy" to those who, having found themselves on the left side, asked to be reunited with their families motioned to the right. In such cases he would say: "You want to be together—all right, everybody to the right!"

Everyone passing in front of Rauca would wave a document he held in his hand. This brought a scornful smile to Rauca's lips. He acted in accordance with his own criteria.

Members of the Jewish labor brigades working at Gestapo headquarters, headed by Benno Lipzer, Rauca sent to the "good" side, together with their parents and children. He also motioned to the left the entire brigade of workers employed at German military installations whose commanders had contacted Rauca earlier. He also treated benevolently single women, and even women with children or aged parents, when that woman called out that she was employed by a high-ranking German officer, or by the German police commandant or by the German Ghetto commandant and such like. Their employers also had contacted Rauca in advance of the selection.

In contrast, there were cases where he paid no heed to the Jordan certificates, regarded thitherto as secure life permits in the ghetto, and sent their holders to the right.

The selection was a protracted affair. Hungry, thirsty, and dejected, thousands of people waited for their turn from dawn. Many had already undergone the selection process, yet the square still seemed full. No end to the torment seemed in sight. Many resigned themselves to their fate and sighed in despair: "Come what may, as long as this waiting comes to an end." Mothers clasped their little children to their broken hearts, hugging and kissing them as though aware they were doing so for the last time. As a

---

* Rauca did not mind transferring any Jew to the left, since, as was learned later on, a quota of ten thousand victims had been set for that day, and all he was concerned with was to know at any time how many had already been transferred to the right. Every so often he would turn to the German standing at his side and ask: "The number, give me the number, I want the exact number."

matter of fact, it was not clear what would happen to those sent to the right, but it was clear that it was the bad side and in the ghetto "bad" in most cases meant death.

Those who were weak—those who could not withstand the psychological tension and the bodily torment—collapsed and breathed their last even before their turn came to pass before Rauca.

Dr. Elkes stood there, his pale face bearing an expression of bottomless grief. Since 6 A.M this sixty-five-year-old man* had been standing on his feet, refusing to sit on the stool that had been brought to him. Now and then, when he was overcome by a fit of weakness, those near him asked him to sit down to regain his strength, or offered him a piece of bread. He refused, murmuring: "Thank you, thank you, gentlemen; terrible things are happening here; I must remain standing on guard in case I can be of assistance." Whenever he succeeded in transferring someone from the bad to the good side, and the person saved would try to shake his hand, he would refuse, saying: "Leave me alone, leave me alone." Sometimes, when in his efforts to transfer somebody to the left side he would inadvertently step too close to the guard unit charged with keeping order at the dividing line, he would be showered with curses and threats from the Lithuanian partisans: "Get away, you old, stupid Zhid, or else you'll go together with them."

_____
* Dr. Elkes was born in 1879.

THINGS I INTENDED TO SAY

A PRESENTATION TO THE JEWISH SOCIAL SELF-HELP CONFERENCE AT WARSAW

Rabbi Yitzhak Katz

MONDAY, JANUARY 6, 1942

One of the great philosophers, a prominent thinker, remarks about the Talmudic term of Charity (Tsedakah), which pertains to the giving of alms, that its meaning includes both Righteousness and Duty. It is not—he says—just philanthropy. And he is quite right. For, according to the Jewish Torah, the giving of alms for the poor is not dependent on the will of a person, but rather an obligation which turns into a law, and becomes a mandatory tax.

Thus the Law of Moses imposed obligations on the people to give offerings and tithes to priests and Levites in terms of produce, prescribed parts of meats and cattle; and to set aside for the poor gleanings, forgotten sheaves, corners of the field, gleanings of grapes from the vineyards, as well as poor tithe and charity. And the Torah specifies this share to be "suffi-cient for his need, in that which he wanteth." This states that it is an obligation to give to the poor as much as he needs. And an obligation it is, indeed, a law, for the Law of Moses imposes laws and statutes, warnings and rules upon humanity, unlike other religions which built their foundations upon utopias and believed the rules to be superfluous. One of the great thinkers even said that the purpose of rules is their destruction, by which he meant the rules should evolve to the point where they penetrate the heart and the thought of man. This idea is not strange to the Talmud either. But it pertains only to the future perfect world, in which, as the Talmud says, "commandments will be abolished." For in that future world rules will not be necessary, since duty felt in one's heart will suffice. Not so in the present, when "not grown is the generation." We need laws, and we need also constraint. Thus the Talmud ordains that "for the sake of alms one should pawn even on the Sabbath Day." For alms are a duty imposed.

One sage, in the Talmud, is known to have forced a person to get four hundred silver pieces in order to give them as alms. There is no relying on the pious will of man, particularly concerning issues which are the "foundations of the world." No, never. It is not lawful to tolerate one's dying of surfeit while the other dies of starvation, one's dying of overwork while the other dies of idleness. Each man has the right to live in this world, and therefore he has the right to eat. God, the Lord of the Universe, created the food for an ant just as He did for the elephant, so how could He not create it for man? Who would agree to tolerate crooks to grab all, letting others starve?

You, Jews of Warsaw, stand charged with a heavy guilt that you do not acquit yourself of your elementary duty of commiseration. In the streets we see people dying of hunger, starving, stumbling and falling in the street, without anyone showing compassion for them, the unfortunate who could be saved just with some tea and bread. Woe and pity, Jews! Where did you get this cruelty?

Let's turn again to the Talmud, where this problem is discussed: Two people in a desert are left with one small flask of water between the two of them; if both drink of it, both shall die; if one only, he may survive. Said one sage, both should drink and both should die so one does not witness the death of his companion. But Rabbi Akiba, quoting "one's life comes first," declared that one should save his own life. To this Rabbi Shneur Zaiman of Liady commented in one of his responsa that such is the case only in extreme necessity of life, never in anything above it. Never should one gorge on sweetmeats and another die like a pariah. Our legends tell of the time of the destruction of the Temple, when Betar fell to the enemy, people were feasting on one side while blood was running on the other, one side knowing not of the other. Is the same thing being repeated here? The ones, fully satiated, frequenting places of entertainment and absolutely refusing to take notice of those starving? Even worse, for this indifference is more blatant now than before the war. Man no longer preserves God's image, rather more like a rat he grabs his crumb and runs into his hole. This is how you look, Jews of Warsaw. The future historian will not extol your memory. The Law prescribes a rite for a single unaccounted death, with all the elders of a town participating in striking off the neck of a sacrificial heifer and taking an oath of innocence. How many rites like this would be necessary now for so many deaths? How sad to behold all this. Not even little children evoke compassion.

I want to mention a comment to the biblical phrase concerning an idolatrous city, namely: "And He shall show you mercy and have compassion on you." Rabbi Akiva in Tosefta Sanhedrin asks: How was compassion associated with an Idolatrous City? His answer is: Compassion was granted to small children. As I noted in my book, *Kerem Yavne*, that there is a difference between compassion and love. The latter is a lofty ideal for all mankind and all creation. The former, however, is no more than an instinct. If love can be felt only for a sound human being and not for one intellectually defective, pity, compassion can be felt for all living creatures. It is this which the Law of Moses states: In the Idolatrous City, inhabited by cruel idolaters, pity, but not love, can be shown for such creatures, and especially for children.

You, Jews of Warsaw, have no pity for little children, naked in the streets, entering stores to beg for crumbs only to be cruelly chased out. Those children hear the sated obese asking for rolls no other than Kagan's, and making anxiously sure that they are not yesterday's rolls. The same sated people look on, unmoved, when the little ones die of hunger and cold. This is blasphemy, as viewed by any race and any people.

So therefore I believe that at the present moment one must not play with illusions, conferences and house committees, all this waste of time. Rather, a compulsory tax must be imposed on those who have, for the sake of those who have not. I doubt whether people, who did not see their proper way clearly in the light of such thunder and such flames as are overhead, will respond to propaganda. This is just self-deception. The Jewish populace must be forced instead to tax itself for the sake of the hungry and the needy. And this must be done as soon as possible. The men of Sodom were said in our legends to have been moderate and slow in extending help. The response of Maimonides contains a verdict prohibiting the raising of questions in the face of emergency. A popular anecdote recalls the Rabbi, Reb Yoshe of Brisk who, examining a young candidate, asked him "What is the proper thing to do if one cuts his finger on the Shabbat?" As the young man stood thinking, the Rabbi shouted at him "Blood is running and you deliberate!?"

Well, this is precisely our present situation. With a flood of blood around us we must not deliberate but do. We must immediately resort to compulsion. The sooner we tackle the emergency and save some lives, the closer we come to salvation and consolation.

JEWISH WELFARE SOCIETY*

AUGUST 1941

Faced with the gruesome need and deprivation which threaten the very life of thousands of Jewish families and numerous individuals, among whom are many highly deserving persons who struggle with severest hunger in silence, mute and despairing, we must again solemnly appeal to the wide public for an immediate, voluntary rescue action to save a stratum of the Jewish population. We invoke the most ancient, most beautiful traditions of the Jewish Heart, the heart which responds not only to a loud alarming cry of pain, but to a muted moan of a veiled and resigned need as well.

The great tragedy of hunger and want does not take place nowadays only in the open. Far more acute is the one hidden in closed rooms, behind doors and windows, concealed from human eyes. There are thousands of people right here in Warsaw, who try their hardest to hide their utter want even while on the very brink of the abyss, unwilling to let a stranger's eye see their tragic situation. Their inborn decency and sense of personal honor keep them from reaching out for help. These are one-time professionals—engineers, lawyers, teachers, artists, intellectuals—people who worked all their lives and, unable to beg, succumb to hunger, sickness and death. A way must be found to offer help in a form which will not hurt their pride. Was not this the meaning of that ancient Jewish custom of *Mattan beSeter*—secret, concealed support?

Shocking cases of death from starvation among our intelligentsia cover all of us with shame, imprint the stigma of Cain on all of us. We bear, all together, the responsibility for the untimely death of many worthy men and women, who could be saved by a timely monetary support of a modest, small amount. No one of us may clear his or her conscience with the argument of one's own grave situation. With us these are excuses taken to silence the reproaches of our own hearts . . .

According to an old Jewish maxim "no public is poor." Had every one of us made the very

---

* In German: *Juedischer Wohlfahrtsverein in Warschau*; in Yiddish: *Yiddishe Geselshaft far Aleinhilf.*

The sign reads: "Jews! Donate old winter clothing and footwear that you don't need to the poor and naked. Give generously." George Kadish/Courtesy of USHMM–Photo Archives.

greatest effort possible in his circumstances, we would find it possible to save many from death, and even more than this from hunger and pain. And by saving the impoverished but most active members of our community, we should actually be saving ourselves, our own future, our honor and our right to live. Indifference to that part of our Jewish society dishonors us, degrades us to the level of a community which has signed its own death sentence . . .

The Jewish Welfare Society proclaims a campaign for an urgent individual collection for assistance. Our aim is to provide each honest Jewish family in need the necessary pressing particular support. We also strive to find the path to those who would not on their own turn for help for whatever reasons.

We trust that the importance of our initiative will move the Jewish public to the greatest

of voluntary sacrifices, the results of which should not fall behind other public collections conducted by us in the past.

We call upon all our welfare points and all our socially active supporters to cooperate with us to the fullest in this undertaking proclaimed here, and we impose on all of them the duty to go out on a most widespread publicity effort, in order to create an awareness in the Jewish society of the aims, the goals and the importance of this campaign, and to bring home to them the moral duty of the Jewish public to fully participate in rescuing the so deserving sections of our society.

Respectfully,
Jewish Welfare Society.
Warsaw, in August, 1941.

LAST TESTAMENT*

LETTER FROM DR. ELCHANAN ELKES TO HIS SON AND DAUGHTER IN LONDON[1]

OCTOBER 19, 1943

My beloved son and daughter!

I am writing these lines, my dear children, in the vale of tears of Vilijampole, Kovno Ghetto, where we have been for over two years. We have now heard that in a few days our fate is to be sealed. The ghetto is to be crushed and torn asunder. Whether we are all to perish or whether a few of us are to survive, is in God's hands. We fear that only those capable of slave labor will live; the rest, probably, are sentenced to death.

We are left, a few out of many. Out of the thirty-five thousand Jews of Kovno, approximately seventeen thousand remain; out of a quarter of a million Jews in Lithuania (including the Vilna district), only twenty-five thousand live plus five thousand who, during the last two days, were deported to hard labor in Latvia, stripped of all their belongings. The rest were put to death in terrible ways by the followers of the greatest Haman of all times and of all generations. Some of those dear and close to us, too, are no longer with us. Your Aunt Hannah and Uncle Arich were killed with 1,500 souls of the ghetto on October 4, 1941. Uncle Zvi, who was lying in the hospital suffering from a broken leg, was saved by a miracle. All the patients, doctors, nurses, relatives, and visitors who happened to be there were burned to death, after soldiers had blocked all the doors and windows of the hospital and set fire to it. In the provinces, apart from Siauliai, no single Jew survives. Your Uncle Dov and his son Shmuel were taken out and killed with the rest of the Kalvaria community during the first months of the war, that is, about two years ago.

Due to outer forces and inner circumstance, only our own ghetto has managed to survive and live out its diaspora life for the past two years, in slavery, hard labor, hunger, and deprivation. (Almost all our clothing, belongings, and books were taken from us by the authorities.)

The last massacre, when ten thousand victims were killed at one time, took place on October 28, 1941. Our total community had to go through the "selection" by our rulers: life or death. I am the man who, with my own eyes, saw those about to die. I was there early on the morning of October 29, in the camp that led to the slaughter at the Ninth Fort. With my own ears I heard the awe-inspiring and terrible symphony, the weeping and screaming of ten thousand people, old and young—a scream that tore at the heart of heaven. No ear had heard such cries through the ages and the generations. With many of our martyrs, I challenged my creator; and with them, from a heart torn in agony, I cried: "Who is like you in the universe, my Lord!" In my effort to save people here and there, I was beaten by soldiers. Wounded and bleeding, I fainted, and was carried in the arms of friends to a place outside the camp. There, a small group of about thirty or forty survived— witnesses to the fire.

---

* Dr. Elkes gave this testament, and the extra lines dated November 10, 1943, to Avraham Tory who took them with him when he escaped from the ghetto. After the war, Tory gave the testament and the letter to Dr. Elkes's widow, Miriam, in Israel. The original documents are now with the Elkes's son, Dr. Joel Elkes. This is the only testament of a Jewish Council chairman that has survived from those years.

[1] Dr. Elkes's son and daughter had gone to Britain in 1938 to study medicine: his son Joel in London, his daughter Sarah in Birmingham. Joel Elkes subsequently emigrated to the United States, where he became head of the Faculty of Psychiatry at Johns Hopkins University. Sarah Elkes, who divides her time between England and Israel, is a specialist in the problems of homeless children.

We are, it appears, one of the staging centers in the East. Before our eyes, before the very windows of our houses, there have passed over the last two years many, many thousands of Jews from southern Germany and Vienna, to be taken, with their belongings, to the Ninth Fort, which is some kilometers from us. There they were killed with extreme cruelty. We learned later that they were misled—they were told they were coming to Kovno, to settle in our ghetto.

From the day of the ghetto's founding, I stood at its head. Our community chose me and the authorities confirmed me as chairman of the Council of Elders, together with my friend, the advocate Leib Garfunkel, a former member of the Lithuanian Parliament, and a few other close and good people, concerned and caring for the fate of the surviving few. We are trying to steer our battered ship in furious seas, when waves of decrees and decisions threaten to drown it every day. Through my influence I succeeded, at times, in easing the verdict and in scattering some of the dark clouds that hung over our heads. I bore my duties with head high and an upright countenance. Never did I ask for pity; never did I doubt our rights. I argued our case with total confidence in the justice of our demands.

In these hardest moments of our life, you, my dear ones, are always before us. You are present in our deepest thoughts and in our hearts. In the darkest nights, your mother would sit beside me, and we would both dream of your life and your future. Our innermost desire is to see you again, to embrace you, and to tell you once again how close we are to you, and how our hearts beat as we remember you and see you before us. And is there any time, day or night, when your memory is not with us? As we stand here, at the very gates of hell, with a knife poised at our necks, only your images, dear ones, sustain us. And you, my children, how was your life these past five years, so hard and full of sorrow for the Jewry of Europe? I know that, far away from this place, you have shared our anguish and, in agony, listened to every slight rumor coming from this vale of tears; and that,

deep down, you have felt with us this unparalleled tragedy of our people.

With regard to myself, I have little to report. Last year I suffered an acute and severe attack of rheumatoid arthritis, which kept me bedridden for nine months. However, even in the most difficult days of my illness, I carried on in my community, and from my bedside participated actively in the work of my friends. Now I am better; it has been about six months since I ceased being regarded as sick. I am not fully well, either, but I continue to work ceaselessly, without rest or respite.

About six months ago we received a message from Uncle Hans, transmitted to us by way of the Red Cross; it said that you were all right. The little note, written by a stranger, took nine months to reach us. We have written and written to you by way of the Red Cross and private persons. Have any of our words reached you? We are desolate that during our stay here we could not contact you and tell you that we are still among the living. We know full well how heavily the doubt of our survival weighs upon you, and what strength and confidence you would draw from the news that we are alive. This would certainly give you courage, and belief in work and life with a firm and clear goal. I deeply fear despair, and the kind of apathy which tends to drive a person out of this world. I pray that this may not happen to you. I doubt, my beloved children, whether I will ever be able to see you again, to hug you and press you to my heart. Before I leave this world and you, my dear ones, I wish to tell you once again how dear you are to us, and how deeply our souls yearn for you.

Joel, my beloved! Be a faithful son to your people. Take care of your nation, and do not worry about the Gentiles. During our long exile, they have not given us an eighth of an eighth of what we have given them. Immerse yourself in this question, and return to it again and again.

Try to settle in the Land of Israel. Tie your destiny to the land of our future. Even if life there may be hard, it is a life full of content and meaning. Great and mighty is the power of faith and belief. Faith can move mountains. Do not look to the left or to the right as you pursue your path. If at times you see your people straying, do not let your heart lose courage, my son. It is not their fault—it is our bitter Exile which has made them so. Let truth be always before you and under your feet. Truth will guide you and show you the path of life.

And you, my dear daughter Sarah, read most carefully what I have just said to Joel. I trust your clear mind and sound judgment. Do not live for the moment; do not stray from your chosen path and pick flowers at the wayside. They soon wilt. Lead a life full of beauty, a pure life, full of content and meaning. For all your days, walk together: let no distance separate you, let no serious event come between you.

Remember, both of you, what Amalek has done to us. Remember and never forget it all your days; and pass this memory as a sacred testament to future generations. The Germans killed, slaughtered, and murdered us in complete equanimity. I was there with them. I saw them when they sent thousands of people—men, women, children, infants—to their death, while enjoying their breakfast, and while mocking our martyrs. I saw them coming back from their murderous missions—dirty, stained from head to foot with the blood of our dear ones. There they sat at their table—eating and drinking, listening to light music. They are professional executioners.

The soil of Lithuania is soaked with our blood, killed at the hands of the Lithuanians themselves; Lithuanians, with whom we have lived for hundreds of years, and whom, with all our strength, we hoped to achieve their own national independence. Seven thousand of our brothers and sisters were killed by Lithuanians in terrible and barbarous ways during the last days of June 1941. They themselves, and no others, executed whole congregations, following German orders. They searched—with special pleasure—cellars and wells, fields and forests, for those in hiding, and turned them over to the "authorities." Never have anything to do with them; they and their children are accursed forever.

I am writing this in an hour when many desperate souls—widows and orphans, threadbare and hungry—are camping on my doorstep, imploring us for help. My strength is ebbing. There is a desert inside me. My soul is scorched. I am naked and empty. There are no words in my mouth. But you, my most dearly beloved, will know what I wanted to say to you at this hour.

And now, for a moment, I close my eyes and see you both standing before me. I embrace and kiss you both; and I say to you again that, until my last breath, I remain your loving father,

Elchanan

IX. A MOSAIC OF VICTIMS: NON-JEWISH VICTIMS OF NAZISM

Throughout Nazi rule, Jews were the central Nazi target, but the Nazis did not confine their persecution to Jews alone. They attacked their political opponents, socialists and liberals, trade unionists, and dissident clergy. They attacked those who did not fit in with their notion of a racial theories; mentally retarded, physically handicapped, or emotionally disturbed Germans were not suitable raw material for breeding the "master race." They too suffered at the hands of the Nazis. By September 1939, a state-sponsored murder program was in place. Henry Friedlaner has argued that the roots of genocide must be seen in this so-called "euthanasia" program.

Jehovah's Witnesses, who would not swear allegiance to the state nor serve in the army of the Third Reich, were targeted as were pacifists.

Gypsies, traditional outsiders, were distrusted and despised. Regarded as a menace, they were deported and incarcerated. Still later, many were killed. Their fate parallels the fate of the Jews. They were the only other group—men, women, and children—killed in the gas chambers.

Male homosexuals were arrested and their institutions destroyed because of their sexual practices. Lesbians were often ignored. Thus, some groups were victimized for what they did, others for what they refused to do, still others, for what they were.

GYPSIES

Unlike the Jews, Gypsies were subjected to official discrimination long before 1933, yet no comprehensive Gypsy law was ever promulgated. Until 1942 pure Gypsies were not targeted. Only those who intermarried with Germans were considered a threat to the "purity of the race." In Germany, the persecution of the Gypsies began from the bottom up, not the top down. Local rules came before centralized decisions from Berlin.

Still, the initiatives from Berlin were forthcoming. In 1936 the Reich Interior Ministry issued guidelines "For Fighting the Gypsy Plague," which required the photographing and fingerprinting of the Gypsies. This information proved lethal when persecution and incarceration later gave way to murder. "Preventative custody"—concentration camp imprisonment—was authorized for Gypsies in 1937.

A leading professor proposed a biological solution: "In the long term the German people will only be freed from this public nuisance when . . . [the Gypsies'] fertility is completely eliminated."

JEHOVAH'S WITNESSES

Jehovah's Witnesses were isolated and harangued from 1933 onward. Suspicion and harassment turned into bitter persecution as the Witnesses refused to surrender. They refused to enlist in the army, undertake air raid drills, stop meeting or proselytizing. They were restrained in their social behavior and would not utter the words "Heil Hitler."

A tiny but determined minority, twenty thousand among sixty-five million Germans, they entered the spiritual battle against the Nazis as soldiers of Jehovah in the war between good and evil. They taught that Jehovah's forces will defeat Satan. The Nazis could not tolerate such "false gods."

Persecution began immediately in 1933, and continued until 1945. After 1937, Witnesses were sent to concentration camps. Outside the camps, Witnesses lost children, jobs, pensions, and all civil rights. Throughout their struggle, Witnesses continued to meet, to preach, to distribute literature. Five thousand Jehovah's Witnesses were sent to concentration camps where they alone were "voluntary prisoners," for the moment they recanted their views, they could be freed. Some lost their lives in the camps, but almost none renounced their faith. Because they understood why they were suffering, they maintained themselves spiritually to a degree unusual among prisoners.

HOMOSEXUALS

Even though homosexuality had been outlawed in Germany for centuries, it was tolerated in Weimar Germany. Works advocating homosexuality were published. Gay bars were found in each of Germany's major cities. Within weeks of taking office Hitler banned homosexual groups. On May 6, 1933—four days before the book burnings—Professor Magnus Hirschfeld's pro-homosexual Institute for Sexual Research was vandalized, its library and photo collections destroyed. By the summer of 1933, Storm Troopers were raiding gay bars. Homosexuals were soon sent to concentration camps marked with yellow bands with the letter A. Pink triangles would come later.

Political infighting and sexual politics were joined in June of 1934 when Hitler purged his SA and initiated the murder of his faithful lieutenant Ernst Röhm, a known homosexual, and three hundred of Röhm's subordinates. Nazi disdain for homosexuals made these early murders palatable to the populace. Shortly thereafter, Himmler created a special criminal police office to fight homosexuality. By December 1934, homosexual intent was sufficient to warrant criminal prosecution. We will read of the Nazi ambivalence toward lesbians.

THE MURDER OF THE HANDICAPPED

Mass murder began of the handicapped began slowly. At first authorization was informal and secret. Narrow in scope, it was limited only to the most serious cases. However, within months the T4 program involved virtually entire the German psychiatric community. Operating at the Berlin Chancellory Tiergarten 4, the program ordered a statistical survey of all psychiatric institutions, hospitals, and homes for chronic patients.

Three medical experts reviewed these forms without examining individual patients or reading detailed records. Theirs was the power to decide life or death. Patients ordered killed were transported to six killing centers: Hartheim, Sonnenstein, Grafeneck, Bernburg,

Hadamar, and Brandenburg. The SS donned white coats for the transports to impersonate a medical situation.

The first killings were by starvation. Starvation is passive, simple, natural. Injections were then used. Children were simply put to sleep, never again to awake. Sedatives became overdoses. Gassing soon became the preferred method of killing. False showers were constructed. Ph.D. chemists were employed. The process was administered by doctors; fifteen to twenty people were killed at a time.

A few doctors protested. Carl Bonhoffer, a leading psychiatrist, helped his son Dietrich contact church groups urging them not to turn patients over to the SS. A few physicians refused to fill out the forms. Only one psychiatrist, Professor Gottfried Ewald of Göttingen, openly opposed the killing.

Count von Galen, the bishop of Münster openly challenged the regime. We must oppose the taking of innocent human life even if it is to cost us our lives, he argued.

On August 24, 1941, almost two years after it began, the operation was seemingly discontinued. It was driven underground.

The killing did not end; mass murder was just beginning. And the physicians trained in the medical killing centers graduated to bigger tasks. Irmfriend Eberl, M.D., who began his career in the T4 program, became the commandant of Treblinka. His colleagues went on to Belzec, Sobibor, Treblinka, and Auschwitz where killing took on massive dimensions.

The murder of the handicapped was a prefiguration of the Holocaust. Killing centers for the handicapped were the antecedent of death camps. They were often staffed by the same physicians who received their specialized training—and lost their moral inhibitions—in this early training. Psychiatrists could save some patients for a time, but only if others were sent to their deaths. *Judenrat* leaders were later to face similar choices. The transport of the handicapped was the forerunner of deportations. Gas chambers were first developed at these killing centers. So, too, body disposal by burning. In the death camps, thousands could be killed at one time and their bodies burned within hours.

In the readings that follow, we will read Hitler's order to grant a "mercy killing" to patients deemed incurable. In response, a vast bureaucracy of murder was created. We will read of the deportations of Gypsies from Berlin and Vienna. We will see the form renouncing faith that a Jehovah's Witness would be asked to complete in order to be freed from arrest, and we will see the articulation of German policy toward male homosexuals and lesbians.

Hitler's Decree Authorizing "Mercy Killings"

September 1, 1939

Reich leader Bouhler and Dr. Brandt are charged with responsibility for expanding the authority of physicians to be designated by name, to the end that patients considered incurable according to the best available human judgment of their state of health, can be granted a mercy killing.

September 1, 1939
Adolf Hitler

HIMMLER'S GUIDELINES FOR THE RESETTLEMENT OF GYPSIES

BERLIN, 27 APRIL 1940

Reichsführer SS and Chief of the German Police
in the Reich Ministry of the Interior
V B No 95/40 secret

Guidelines for the Resettlement of Gypsies
(First transport from the western and north-western border region)

I. IDENTIFICATION OF AFFECTED PERSONS

I. Deported will be:
   A. Gypsies and part-Gypsies who were registered and reported pursuant to the Reich Security Main Office priority letter of 17 October 1939.
   B. The limit of 2,500 must not be exceeded under any circumstances.
   C. If this number cannot be reached within the actual border areas, Gypsies and part-Gypsies from adjoining areas may be tapped.
   D. In the case of c), only such families should be included which can be transported as a group, that is to say those which do not include any exceptions.

II. The following are exempt from the deportation:
   A. All infirm persons and those who cannot march, particularly persons older than seventy and higher, more than seven months' pregnant women.
   B. Gypsies who are married to persons of German blood. So-called "Gypsy [common-law] marriages" are only exempted if there are children.
   C. Gypsies with members of their immediate family (parents, children) who have been inducted into military service.
   D. Gypsies who own real estate, if recorded in land records, and those with extensive movables—e.g., larger theatrical enterprises if such enterprises cannot be sold or transferred. There is no legal basis for expropriation.
   E. Gypsies with foreign citizenship if definitely confirmed.

III. Gypsy men and women who stay behind on the basis of 2a are to be boarded with members of their family outside the actual border area. If necessary, the social welfare office should be notified.

FORM FOR JEHOVAH'S WITNESSES TO RENOUNCE THEIR FAITH

Concentration Camp _____

Department II

I,
(Mr./Mrs./Miss)_____

_____

born on_____

in_____

Herewith make the following declaration:

   1. I acknowledge that the International Jehovah's Witness Association is disseminating erro-

neous teachings and using religion as a disguise merely to pursue subversive goals against the interests of the state.

2. I have therefore completely left that organization and have also spiritually freed myself from the teachings of that sect.

3. I herewith pledge that I will never again participate in the International Jehovah's Witness Association. I will immediately denounce any individual who solicits me with the heresy of the Witnesses or who in any manner reveals his affiliation with the Witnesses. Should Jehovah's Witnesses publications be sent to me, I will immediately deliver them to the nearest police department.

4. In the future, I will obey the laws of the state, and particularly in the event of war, I will defend the Fatherland with weapon in hand and totally become part of the national community.

5. I have been informed that should I violate today's declaration, I will again be arrested.

_____(place)_____(date)

_____
(signature)

INSTRUCTIONS CONCERNING UNNATURAL SEXUAL OFFENSES [EXTRACT]

ISSUED BY THE REICH MINISTRY OF JUSTICE

1934?

[. . .] In the last few decades many furious attacks have been launched against Paragraph 175 of the Penal Code. Nevertheless, there can be no doubt that in the forthcoming penal code of the National Socialist State the threat of punishment will continue to apply to unnatural sexual acts.

It is interesting to start by considering the direction from which the fiercest attacks of Paragraph 175 have come.

When those who are themselves in the grip of the vice put up a fight against its criminalization, there is no cause for surprise. It must be noted, however, that it is precisely Jewish and Marxist circles which have always worked with special vehemence for the abolition of Paragraph 175 [. . .]

But if it has mainly been internationally oriented circles which have represented such tendencies, this is already an a priori reason to suppose that their struggle does not serve any goals which uphold the state and national traditions. This has to be said, even at the risk that such arguments might be described as "unscientific."

The opponents of Paragraph 175 set out a series of grounds for the ending of criminalization.

According to the opponents of Paragraph 175, homosexuality is not a vice into which one can fall through seduction or addiction; it is based rather upon an inborn disposition, a phenomenon of nature, against which the affected individual is powerless. This "natural riddle of uranism" [Assessor Ulrich's "uranism" (Urning) is derived from "Uranos," and he is also fond of the term "uranist" (Uranier) for male homosexuals] is based upon a "contrary sexual feeling" (Krafft-Ebing, Moll et al.). Just as a person with normal sexual feelings is not likely to become a "uranist," so a contrasexual is unable to resist his innate drive and to find satisfaction in intercourse with the other sex; indeed, he often feels an insuperable aversion to the other sex, which makes sexual intercourse with it psychologically and physically impossible for him. According to this view of things, it is the duty of everyone with this knowledge—which is the "result of secure research" (Hirschfeld)—to do all in their power to disseminate it. "Just as no one in Germany thinks any more of burning a heretic or a witch, so will immortal credit be due to men who have [. . .] fearlessly worked to ensure that it is the natural right also of uranists to live within their four walls as nature commands them to do" (van Erkelens, p. 20). In vain will one seek to compel these uranists—whom nature has made with different drives—not to obey their own nature; and innocent as they are, it would be judicial murder to brand the mark of the criminal on their brow. [. . .] The threat of punishment, moreover, is supposed to be unjust, because only a tiny proportion of punishable actions comes to the notice of the authorities for judgment to be passed upon them. But at the same time court sentences are said for this reason to be ineffectual, the result being simply that unfortunate people with contrary sexual feelings who are otherwise law-abiding spend their whole life on reprieve, subject to the undeserved psychological pressure of the threat of punishment.

It has been further objected that it is not at all clear which right is safeguarded through the threat of penalty; that violence, seduction of young people, etc. may be punished, exactly as they are in heterosexual relations, but there is no justification for the threat of punishment in the case of homosexual intercourse between freely consenting adults.

A final argument against the threat of penalty is that it is especially damaging because it constantly exposes the individuals concerned to the danger of blackmail, and experience shows that the threat of penalty actually breeds blackmailers. In the big cities, blackmail on the basis of the sanctions contained in Paragraph 175 is a commercial pursuit, whether in the form whereby wealthy homosexuals of high standing in society are forever at its mercy until in desperation they finally put an end to their life, or whether in the form of a partnership in which a "decoy"

leads a uranist to remote parts where, at a given moment, the other partner appears as a morally outraged third party who threatens to inform the police and is prepared to forget about it only after strong pleading and the handing over of an appropriate sum of money. This cancerous evil—so the argument goes—will be conquered only when the threat of punishment is lifted from love between men.

The main case against the penalization of pederasty is therefore based on the idea that it is not a vice but the result of an innate contrary direction of the sex drive. To decide on the legitimacy of this claim is, of course, the business not of jurists but of medical science. If one actually looks at scientific opinion, one cannot help but wonder at the self-assurance with which it is claimed that this opinion is the result of secure research. The conclusion at which one arrives is rather that Hirschfeld's "results of research" are anything but secure, and that there is no agreement at all among experts in the field. It is probably unnecessary to say any more here about the numerous and in part utterly contradictory theories. [. . .]

The dominant view of medical science is the following. The basis of homosexuality may be an innate predisposition (contrary sexuality), but it may also be a vice which causes normal sexual feelings to be lost over time. [. . .] From this it follows that there are cases where the psychological and physical possibility exists for both homosexual and heterosexual intercourse, and where the two forms of intercourse are actually practiced alongside each other. [. . .]

The mere possibility that contrary sexuality can be acquired through external circumstances [. . .], and not mainly the fact that homosexual intercourse is pursued purely as a vice, is enough to show that the demand for an end to all penalization of pederasty is without foundation. Insofar as the drive is so pathologically strong in the case of the innate, constitutional homosexuality that the free exercise of the will is excluded in the pursuit of a forbidden practice, the "poorest of the poor" (van Erkelens) are by no means at the mercy of a Paragraph 175 deriving from the "medieval darkness of jurists' heads" (Winzer, p. 17); for Paragraph 51 of the Penal Code protects them from punishment. The fact that a contrasexual may otherwise be a highly intellectual person does not contradict the assumption that in the specifically sexual domain he suffers from a pathological disturbance to the activity of the mind. [. . .]

In the interests of the others, however, for whom the drive is not irresistibly strong, it is not justified to drop the penal sanctions from Paragraph 175—even if they feel horror at the female sex and must therefore do completely without sexual satisfaction. One might just as well—although any comparison is inappropriate—call for a man with normal feelings to be left unpunished who commits an act of rape because no woman will give herself to him of her own free will.

What then of the argument that no right is violated by homosexual behavior, and that the threat of punishment in Paragraph 175 is therefore unjustified? It should be said that the old theory of Feuerbach, which restricted the concept of crime to direct violations of a right, has long been abandoned. [. . .] Moreover, it should not be open to doubt that the healthy moral sense of the overwhelming majority of the people would find it completely incomprehensible if the present-day state were, so to speak, to "recognize" the legitimacy of homosexual behavior by abolishing the threat of punishment. But the people do have a right to be protected against at least the grossest insults to that moral sense, just as it is expected of the state that it will defend against major insult the people's religious feelings and convictions. In the case of religious offenses one could say with much greater justice that they never directly cause harm to anyone—and yet the state punishes them. Besides, today more than ever, there should be a return to the belief that the stability of the people's moral thinking is the best guarantee of the stability of the state. Section Paragraph 175, then, protects a right that deserves to be protected unconditionally.

If it is thought illogical not to make lesbian-ism subject to penalty, this can at most lead to the demand that it too should be punished [. . .], but in no way that pederasty should also go unpunished. After what has been said, the other counterarguments can be dealt with more briefly. It cannot be denied that Paragraph 175 is often abused for the purposes of blackmail. It has been rightly pointed out, however, that abolition of the threat of penalty would not put an end to the blackmailing of homosexuals; for the fear of social disdain would just as before place a wealthy man at the mercy of blackmailers. Besides, other offenses known to a third party are used for the purposes of blackmail, and people do not consider that a reason to call for abolition of the penal code.

The same applies to the argument that the sanctions contained in Paragraph 175 are unjust and ineffectual, as only very few offenses under Paragraph 175 come up for sentence before the courts. With regard to the alleged ineffectuality, there can be no doubt that at least many who are not born homosexuals are held back by the threat of punishment from ever coming into contact with homosexual circles. [. . .] Nor can it be denied that the state's condemnation, contained in the threat of penalty under Paragraph 175, makes a strong impact precisely upon young people at the age of puberty with its inner uncertainty and lack of clarity, and influences their own judgment on such matters. Moreover, the demand has never yet been raised to abolish Paragraph 242 of the Penal Code on the grounds that not all thieves are caught and that it is unfair to punish only those who are.

That not any form of sexual dealings between men is punishable, but only intercourse-like behavior, has already been established by case law relating to Paragraph 175 and cannot be in doubt even de lege ferenda. It does not seem possible to give a more precise legal definition and delimitation of the concept, which would have to be brief and yet cover all punishable behavior. The text of the New York Penal Code [. . .] does not encourage one to make such an attempt. Further interpretation may be left to practice and to the sphere of jurisprudence.

Extracts from Discussions among Nazi Jurists Concerning the Prosecution of Lesbian Relations

1936-1937

Academy of German Law. Work preparation sub-committee of the Committee on Population Policy. Extracts from the minutes of discussions held on 2 March 1936.

Measures against sexual relations between persons of the female sex.

Professor Spiethoff reported that the director of the Reich Statistical Bureau, Dr. Ruttke, had asked him to raise the question of whether female homosexuality (tribadism)—which is apparently rising sharply—should not also be made a punishable offense. It is a striking fact, he argued, that Germany is one of the few countries which lets tribadism go unpunished, whereas most other countries—e.g., Austria—draw no distinction (at least in the penal code) between female and male homosexuality. A distinction should be drawn, he went on, between tribadism caused by circumstances and innate tribadism. The former is scarcely of any harm in terms of population policy, at least in the case of single and widowed women. But innate tribadism carries the danger of seduction, and if this is in reality a major danger—for which there is as yet hardly any accurate evidence—then it should certainly be considered in the context of population policy whether it should not be put on the same footing as male homosexuality.

The chairman expressed the view that there are so far no grounds for thinking that this matter is of sufficient importance for population policy to merit the presentation of proposals before the official Criminal Law Commission. But he declared his willingness to allow Director Ruttke the opportunity of presenting his point of view to the committee.

Assistant Secretary Dr. Schaefer argued that the Criminal Law Commission should have

been guided in its deliberations by the following considerations. The danger of seduction is itself not nearly as great in the case of innate tribadism as it is in that of male homosexuality. For it can generally be assumed that if a woman is seduced she will not for that reason lastingly withdraw from normal sexual relations, but will be useful as before in terms of population policy. Furthermore, the practice of this vice does not by any means do as much damage to a woman's psyche as in the case of a man, and the danger for the state is therefore by no means as great. A further reason to refrain from any penal sanctions lies in the danger of denunciations—one which is especially great because of woman's natural inclination toward effusiveness and caressing. It is not therefore proposed to make tribadism in general a punishable offense. But the criminal law will in future offer powerful instruments for the inclusion of cases that really do require punishment. Abuse or violation of the feeble-minded, as well as the making of an appointment depend on consent to illicit sex acts, will in future be made punishable offenses.

Whereas "seduction" through abuse of relations of dependence could previously be committed only by a man upon an unsullied virgin, the criminal law will in future provide more extensive protection by threatening to punish anyone, regardless of sex, who "induces a person into extramarital intercourse or intercourse-like acts by abusing his or her dependence based upon a relation of service or employment"; such inducement will thus also include the intercourse of a female employer or housewife with an employee or home help. Finally, in addition to the protection of young people up to the age of fourteen, it will also become a punishable offense for anyone "to induce a person under eighteen years of age to commit together an illicit sex act, or allow himself to be used for the purposes of an illicit sex act, by abusing his or her dependence based upon a relation of service or employment." The question largely remains open whether girls aged between fourteen and sixteen should be protected from seduction into homosexuality by a general defin- ition along the lines of: "Whoever seduces a person under sixteen years of age into extramarital intercourse or intercourse-like acts, etc." As a member of the subcommittee set up by the Criminal Law Commission to examine the text passed at the second reading, he would try to push this forward, but he could not say whether the Criminal Law Commission would be in agreement. […]

Himmler's Secret Directive on the Combating of Homosexuality and Abortion
October 10, 1936

The Reichsführer SS and Head of the German Police at the Reich Ministry of the Interior
Berlin, 10 October 1936
SV 1 24/36g
Secret!
Not to be printed in the RMBliV
To:
the Secret State Police Bureau, Berlin
the Prussian Land Criminal Police Bureau, Berlin
all regional and local headquarters of the State Police in the Reich
all regional and local headquarters of the Criminal Police in the Reich
Subject: The Combating of Homosexuality and Abortion

The serious danger to population policy and public health represented by the still relatively high number of abortions which are a major violation of the fundamental National Socialist worldview, as well as the homosexual activity of a not inconsiderable layer of the population which poses one of the greatest dangers to the youth, requires more than before the effective combating of these public scourges.

I. The handling of the above mentioned offenses is essentially the responsibility of the local police.

II. In order to ensure uniform guidelines for central registration and for effective combating of these offenses, I hereby establish within the Prussian Land Criminal Police Bureau a Reich Office for the Combating of Homosexuality and Abortion.

III. Where it becomes necessary for the state police to take certain measures, the Secret State Police Bureau should be informed and the necessary measures set in motion there. A special department II S is being created at the Secret State Police Bureau to deal with this area.

IV. In order to ensure swift cooperation, the special department II S at the Secret State Police Bureau and the Reich Office for the Combating of Homosexuality and Abortion attached to the Prussian Land Criminal Police Bureau shall be directed by the same officers.

V. From 15 October 1936 a report should be sent to the Reich Office for the Combating of Homosexuality and Abortion:

A. in cases coming under Paragraph 218 of the Penal Code,
   1. immediately after the initiation of proceedings, if the offense was not committed by the pregnant woman alone, on the enclosed form A a,
   2. for all convictions under Paragraph 218 on the enclosed form A b,
   3. for all acquittals on the charge of abortion on the enclosed form A b,
B. in criminal cases coming under Paragraphs 174, 176 and 253, where they are based on homosexuality, and under Paragraph 175, Paragraph 175a immediately after the initiation of proceedings on the enclosed form B,
   1. if the offender is a member of the NSDAP or one of its subdivisions or occupies a position of leadership,
   2. if the offender belongs to the armed forces,
   3. if the offender is a member of a religious order,
   4. if the offender is a civil servant,
   5. if the offender is a Jew,
   6. if persons are involved who held a leading position in the period before the taking of power.

   In reports per A a and B it should be indicated whether and on what grounds it appears necessary for the state police to take certain measures. State police measures shall be ordered by special department II S within the Secret State Police Bureau upon application by the Reich Office for the Combating of Homosexuality and Abortion.

VI. The Reich Office for the Combating of Homosexuality and Abortion shall maintain a national file on abortionists and rentboys. A report on individuals already known in this connection should be sent on the enclosed form I P to the Reich Office for the Combating of Homosexuality and Abortion, indicating precise personal particulars and, where possible, enclosing a photograph. Any change of address of such persons should also be notified at once.

VII. Reports under Paragraph 5 above to the Reich Office for the Combating of Homosexuality and Abortion do not relieve the local police authorities of their duty immediately to take all measures necessary to counter the offense. The Reich Office for the Combating of Homosexuality and Abortion is authorized, in agreement with special department II S, to issue instructions on the conduct of investigations or to continue them itself.

On behalf of:
SIGNED HEYDRICH

X. THE EINSATZGRUPPEN

On June 22, 1941, the German army invaded Soviet territory. They did not enter alone—small units of SS and police, some three thousand men in all, were also dispatched on special assignment. Their task to kill the Jews on the spot—Jews, but not only Jews; communists, Gypsies, political leaders, and the intelligentsia were also killed. Order Police battalions, Waffen SS units, the Higher SS, and Police Leaders also carried out these mass executions.

Their primary targets, Jews, were concentrated in the areas within easy reach of the German army. Almost nine in ten Jews were urbanized, living in large cities where the rapid advance of the army and the swift action of the mobile killing units left them unaware of their fate, paralyzed, unable to act.

Two Jewish women. 1941. Bilderdienst Suddeutscher Verlag.

There were five stages to the killing. The invasion was followed immediately by the roundup of Jews and other intended victims. Those rounded up were marched to the outskirts of the city where they were shot. Their bodies were buried in mass graves—large ditches were filled with bodies of people who had been shot one by one and buried layer upon layer.

The residents of these cities could see what was happening. They could hear the shots and the victims' cries. Most often, they remained neutral, neither helping the killer nor offering solace to the victim. Yet neutrality helped the killer, never his victim.

Frequently, local pogroms were encouraged by the Wehrmacht and the SS, especially in Lithuania and Latvia. Every Jew killed brought the Nazis closer to their goal.

Auxiliary police comprised of local natives became indispensable to the understaffed killing units. Local collaborators volunteered.

Before this phase of the killing ended, more than 1.2 million Jews were killed. Their bodies were piled high in mass graves throughout occupied Soviet territories.

Later still, in 1942 and 1943, when the war had turned against the Germans, SS kommando soldiers returned to these sites of infamy to unearth the graves and burn the bodies, thus leaving no trace of the crime.

The men who ran the mobile killing units that rounded up and murdered Jews were not German criminals but ordinary citizens. In scholarly literature, there is a current debate whether they were ordinary "men" or ordinary "Germans" imbued with an racist ideology that sanctified these killings. According to Raul Hilberg, the great majority of the officers of the Einsatzgruppen were professional men, who were in no sense hoodlums, delinquents, or sex maniacs; most were intellectuals, most were educated at universities. They brought to their new task all the skills and training which, as men of thought, they were capable of contributing. These men became efficient killers.

A handful of men had requested to be relieved of their unconscionable assignment; nothing happened to them. The rest went along performing a difficult and disciplined task. The killers drank heavily. Alcohol somehow made it easier.

They spoke in euphemisms, never quite saying what they were doing. Their language never spoke of murder and killing but of special actions, special treatment, executive measures, cleansing, resettlements, liquidation, finishing off, appropriate treatment.

The work of the Einsatzgruppen frightened the local inhabitants, "Today it's the Jews, tomorrow perhaps us."

In the documents, we will read the memo of Reinhard Heydrich authorizing the killing. We will read the Nuremberg Trial testimony of Otto Ohlendorf, commander of the Einsatzgruppe D, explaining the actions and motivations of the killer. He offered a simple explanation: he was just following orders. Asked his instructions, Ohlendorf replied directly: "The instructions were that in the Russian operational areas of the Einsatzgruppen the Jews as well as the Soviet political commissars were to be liquidated." He later clarified the meaning. "Yes I mean 'killed.'" He detailed the confiscation process. Valuables were sent to Berlin, gold to the Ministry of Finance. When asked how it was that the orders were carried out regardless of his personal scruples Ohlendorf replied: "Because to me it is inconceivable that a subordinate leader should not carry out an order given by the leaders of state."

Himmler personally witnessed executions at Minsk. As they proceeded, Himmler became more uncomfortable. Erich von dem Bach-Zelewski then stepped in to press for mercy, not for the victims, but for their executioners. He pleaded for the killers. Himmler was told by one of his commanders, "Look at the eyes of the men in this kommando, how deeply shaken they are. These men are finished for the rest of their lives. What kind of followers are we training here? Either neurotics or savages."

In part, it was to spare the perpetrators that a new and better form of killing—the concentration camp and its killing centers—was implemented.

EXTRACT FROM THE COMMISSAR'S ORDER FOR "OPERATION BARBAROSSA"
JUNE 6, 1941

Staff Command Secret Document
Chief Only
Only Through Officer
High Command of the Wehrmacht
WFST [Armed Forces Operational Staff] Div. L
(VI/Qu)
No. 44822/41 g.K Chiefs
June 6, 1941
Guidelines for the Treatment of Political
Commissars

In the fight against Bolshevism it is not to be expected that the enemy will act in accordance with the principles of humanity or international law. In particular, the political commissars of all kinds, who are the real bearers of resistance, can be expected to mete out treatment to our prisoners that is full of hate, cruel and inhuman.

The army must be aware of the following:

1. In this battle it would be mistaken to show mercy or respect for international law towards such elements. They constitute a danger to our own security and to the rapid pacification of the occupied territories.

2. The barbaric, Asiatic fighting methods are originated by the political commissars. Action must therefore be taken against them immediately, without further consideration, and with all severity. Therefore, when they are picked up in battle or resistance, they are, as a matter of principle, to be finished immediately with a weapon.

In addition, the following regulations are to be observed:

OPERATIONAL AREAS

1. Political commissars operating against our armies are to be dealt with in accordance with the decree on judicial provisions in the rank, even if they are only suspected of sabotage or incitement to sabotage . . .

Operational Situation Report USSR No. 107

The Chief of the Security
Police and Security Service
50 copies
(36th copy)
Operational Situation Report USSR No. 107

Berlin,
October 8, 1941

Einsatzgruppe B
Location: Smolensk

Oral Bolshevik-oriented propaganda continues as before. It is obviously systematically carried out by enemy agents and partisans as well as by the Jewish population. Together with the continually growing rumors and, due to the lack of effective counterpropaganda, this oral propaganda has the effects desired by the Bolsheviks.

Einsatzgruppe D
Location: Nikolayev

A small Vorkommando had entered Kherson on August 20, 1941, together with the army, and reported that the town was free of enemies. Consequently, a kommando consisting of two officers and thirteen men was sent to Kherson on August 22, 1941, in order to accomplish the task of Sonderkommando 11a. After the first two days, initial steps were taken towards the

The execution of Jews by members of the Einsatzkommando in the region near Kovno. Jewish State Museum of Lithuania.

solution of the Jewish question, the protection of the ethnic Germans, and the fight against Bolshevism. Then, a change occurred in the situation in this town of some 100,000 inhabitants. Artillery fire began on August 24, 1941, at about 15 o'clock, and lasted, with some interruptions, until September 6, 1941, reaching on some days extraordinary force. Because of that situation, a number of German officers left Kherson again....

OPERATIONAL SITUATION REPORT USSR NO. 108

Chief of the Security Police
and Security Service
50 copies
(36th copy)
Operational Situation Report USSR No. 108

Berlin,
October 9, 1941

Einsatzgruppe B
Location: Smolensk
Police activity

GENERAL SITUATION

In general, the situation at the front is unchanged, except for the southern part of the area of Einsatzgruppe B. This permitted, at the time of this report, the conduct once more of intensive searches in many areas and localities. General organizational measures were also continued, like the introduction of the Order Service, marking of the Jews, registration, putting up ghettos, planting of informants, and calling upon the population to cooperate with the police. We are also concerned with the fight against partisans and agitators who were hostile toward the Germans. The actions that were required were difficult because of the streets and roads that had turned into mire due to the bad and wet weather....

In any case, the endeavors and the attempts that were made to convert the partisan movement into a real popular movement to be used against German operations and plans have failed. This is without a doubt due to the enthusiasm of the German Security Police and the SD, the alertness of the army, and the systematic approach to these problems on the part of the army and the Security Force. This is by no means to belittle the danger of the partisan movement. First of all, attention will have to be paid to the effect of partisan activity on the feelings of the population. Partisans, Jews, and other Communists constantly try to intimidate the friendly population through Bolshevik pamphlets or whispering campaigns. They threaten that, as soon as the Reds return, they will take revenge on everyone who has rendered the smallest service to the Germans. Troop movements away from the front line cause the population to worry and to ask the German offices if they must really count on a return of the Red regime.

FIGHT AGAINST THE PARTISANS

The Vorkommando was urgently called to Khoslavichi by the local commander, since partisans were said to have invaded the place. After having shot a German soldier, the partisans retreated when the kommando arrived. Confidential information showed that several hundred partisans had committed their evil deeds in the localities and forests around Khoslavichi. Because of extremely bad road conditions, only two smaller places could be searched. In each of them two partisans were caught and liquidated.

SK 7a has repeatedly reported that a large number of partisans have carried out plunderous attacks from the dense forests south of Demidov. They caused considerable anxiety in the area as well as endangering the roads. According to reliable reports, one had to reckon with eight hundred to two thousand partisans. The 9th Army headquarters supplied two divisions for a thorough search of the area. Each male between the ages of fifteen and fifty-five was sent to the Demidov prison camp for an interrogation. The examination was conducted during several fire fights with the partisans. They resulted in the arrest of 493 people; 438, most of them kolkhoz farmers free of suspicion, were released. Seventy-two former Red Army members who lived in the area of the action, with no proven connection to the partisans, were brought into the prisoner-of-war camp. SK 7a uncovered 183 partisans and Communists. Interrogations revealed that they had repeatedly carried out attacks on members of the German Army. Five partisans admitted killing a total of fourteen German soldiers. One German soldier was strangled as he fetched eggs; the others were shot. They had also thrown hand grenades into trucks and cars.

In response, several kolkhoz farmers that had supported the partisans, even if only under duress, and five partisans who murdered fourteen German soldiers were hanged in the marketplace in the presence of about four hundred Kolkhozniki farmers. The other partisans were shot.

The SK 7a, in cooperation with a unit of the 9th Army, headquarters conducted, on different days, actions against the partisan groups that were known in the area of Trosty, Shitiki, Shlyki, Novi-Masyolok, Kupioly, Yanki, and Buly, some 20 km northwest of Velish. Also, the areas of Osinovka, Doroshkino, Prudok, Burshchina and Shility about 20 km north of Velish, were thoroughly combed. In these actions, a total of twenty-seven partisans were arrested and liquidated.

After careful investigations, eight partisans were taken by surprise as they were having their supper in the village of Mikhailovo. They were arrested and hanged together on the following morning in the place that was particularly infested with partisans.

Kommando 7b stated that "sabotage units" were posted prior to the occupation of Koseletz. Parts of these units were still in the surroundings of Koseletz at the time of the police activities. Systematically conducted searches led to the arrest of five persons belonging to these units according to concurrent testimonies.

ACTIONS AGAINST FUNCTIONARIES, AGENTS, SABOTEURS AND JEWS

In Khoslavichi, the Jews living in the ghetto there, according to reports of the Russian population, tried to create panic by spreading false rumors to the effect that the Bolsheviks were supposed to be advancing. Furthermore, they threatened to take revenge after the return of the Bolsheviks. Thereupon, the Vorkommando sent a kommando and liquidated 114 Jews....

SK 7a also reports of juvenile Communists who were liquidated. They intended to blow up a railway bridge nearing completion. Explosives had already been supplied and were at hand.

In Velikye Luki a group of juveniles intending to blow up a railway bridge was also rendered harmless. The ringleader of the group had persuaded the others to participate.

Sonderkommando 7a executed a local leading Bolshevik official and twenty-one Jewish plunderers and terrorists in Gorodnia. In Klintsy, eighty-three Jewish terrorists and three leading party officials were likewise liquidated. At another check, three Communist officials, one *Politruk*, and eighty-two Jewish terrorists were dealt with according to orders.

In Chernigov, nineteen Jews who were under suspicion of having either been Communists or of having committed arson were given special treatment. During the search operations in Beresna, east of Chernigov, eight Jews who had committed Bolshevik acts, that is to say, had sabotaged the regulations of the German authorities, were seized and shot. In Gomel, forty-one Jews and nine Russians were liquidated; they were equipped with firearms and carried out acts of sabotage and looting. In addition it was ascertained that two women started fires in houses by igniting wood shavings. The accused were shot after confessing their deeds. In Rechiza, 216 Jews were liquidated for having committed acts of sabotage and for refusing to work. They had, in addition, accommodated partisans and provided them with food.

Special stress is given to the fact that, according to information given by SK 7b, evacuated Jews in the towns where they were located reported that the Jews from Koseletz informed the remaining Ukrainians that they could plunder their [the Jews'] homes, since they would not return.

In Mogilev, eighteen persons who had been political functionaries, *Politruks*, and guerrillas were liquidated by Einsatzkommando 8. One of them was found at a Dnieper bridge with four Russian hand grenades in his pocket. The village of Krugloye, approximately 50 km west of Mogilev, was checked. While carrying out these operations, we were struck by the fact that practically the whole of the male Jewish population was missing. According to reports by the local Russian population, they were supposed to have left with the retreating Russian forces, that is to say, they are hiding in the surrounding woods. The Jewish women were extremely restive and not one was wearing the prescribed badge. In the course of the operations, twenty-eight Jewish women and three men were liquidated. In Mogilev as well, an increased resistance on the part of the Jews was noticeable, so that energetic measures, such as the shooting of eighty Jews and Jewesses, had to be taken. When even these measures did not suffice and the Jews continued to spread false rumors and sabotage the regulations of the German Occupation authorities, 215 Jews and 337 Jewesses were shot. In Minsk, at the city check points, 142 Jews were arrested and shot for loitering outside the ghetto without the prescribed identification badges.

According to reports received, large numbers of Jews of the district of Marina-Borka are supposed to have taken refuge in the woods, cooperating with the partisans and plundering in the vicinity of Marina-Borka. In some cases even Byelorussian mayors have been shot by these gangs. The mopping-up operations carried out in this area resulted in the arrest of seventy Uzbeks, Kirghizes, Tartars, and Jews. After a short interrogation, the arrested were liquidated; it had been proved that they had participated in the aforementioned acts of terrorism and violence.

Various acts of sabotage committed by Jews in Borisov were confirmed. At a mopping-up operation there, a total of 321 Jews were liquidated. Near Smolovich, the Jews were under suspicion as well of having several times, together with the partisans and other criminal elements, blown up the Minsk-Smolensk railway line. In conjunction with the kommando from Minsk, 1,401 Jews were shot during large-scale operations carried out in Smolovich. After these mopping-up operations, there were no more Jews left north, south and west of Borisov. In Borisov itself a further 118 Jews were liquidated because of sabotage at work and for having been engaged in plundering. In Bobruisk and its vicinity, about 1,380 persons were liquidated during the time of this report, twenty of them while escaping. The persons executed were mainly Jews, persons engaged in sabotage, and those who until the last minute were engaged in spreading hate propaganda against the German Occupation authorities.

MEASURES AGAINST CRIMINALS AND MARAUDERS

According to information obtained by SK 7b, the Red troops had, before leaving Chernigov, opened the door of the Asylum for the Insane and armed part of the inmates. These were marching down the streets marauding. Twenty-one of them were caught in the act and liquidated. Others left the town for the surrounding villages, probably in order to live there. The population, however, is cooperating with regard to the capture of these insane persons. Soon again there will be quite a few in the asylum. Then, they will be treated according to the usual procedure. In Minsk, 632 mentally deficient people and, in Mogilev, 836 were accorded special treatment.

LIQUIDATION

The liquidations carried out during the time of this report up to and including September 28, 1941, increased the final figures as follows:

A.	Staff and VKM	2,029
B.	SK 7a	1,252
C.	SK 7b	1,544
D.	EK 8	15,000
E.	EK 9	10,269
	Total	30,094 persons liquidated by the group.

Einsatzgruppe D
Location: Nikolayev
Construction work achieved so far by the kommandos of Einsatzgruppe D

PROTECTION

Strengthening of German consciousness in the different villages by bringing back the deported inhabitants [Germans]; removing Ukrainians and replacing them as far as possible with Germans mostly from Ukrainian communities.

ECONOMIC SAFEGUARDING

Distribution of Jewish possessions and Jewish property, in the first place to widows and families of deported persons.

OPERATIONAL SITUATION REPORT USSR No. 112

The Chief of the Security Police and Security Service
50 copies
(36th copy)
Operational Situation Report USSR No. 112

Berlin,
October 13, 1941

Einsatzgruppe C
Location: Kiev
Bolshevism and Jewry

The population's attitude towards these two problems in the areas of Kiev, Poltava, and Dnepropetrovsk is the same as has been observed elsewhere in the Ukraine. The population rejects Bolshevism almost without exception, since there is practically no family which has not lost one or more members through Bolshevik deportation or killing. Also, the Ukrainians had been free farmers and independent in ancient Russia and have not forgotten that everything was taken from them when forced into the collective farms. The number of Ukrainians who joined the Communist Party out of conviction is surprisingly low.

Only the young people who have neither seen nor heard of anything else but Communism and its "successes and achievements" allow themselves to be captivated by the Communist ideology. Yet even in this group one finds few fanatics and really convinced fighters. German propaganda will not have difficulty in promoting a complete change in this attitude. In order to begin the process of such a reeducation, and as long as the powerful battle is still fresh in the minds of the Ukrainians, propaganda, lectures, performances, films, radio and periodicals should be introduced.

The Ukrainian rejects Judaism together with Communism, as it was mainly Jews who were officials of the Communist Party. The Ukrainians had the opportunity to discover that practically only the Jews enjoyed the advantages connected with membership in the Communist Party, especially in its leading positions. The population is, however, unaware of real anti-Semitism based on rural and ideological principles. There are no leading personalities and no spiritual impetus within the Ukrainian population to trigger off persecution since all remember the harsh punishments inflicted by the Bolsheviks against anyone who attacked the Jews. For instance, whoever called the Jews "Zhid" (Yid) (which was at that time a curse word) and not "Evrei" (Hebrew), was sent to prison. However, if an impulse comes from any side and should the population be given a free hand, an extensive persecution of the Jews could result.

OPERATIONAL SITUATION REPORT USSR NO. 117

The Chief of the Security Police and Security Service
50 copies
(36th copy)
Operational Situation Report USSR No. 117

Berlin,
October 12, 1941

Einsatzgruppe A: Sonderkommando 1a
Location: Reval
Reports: Jews in Estonia

At the beginning of 1940, about 4,500 Jews were living in Estonia, of these, 1,900 to 2,000 lived in Reval; larger Jewish communities were in Dorpat, Narva, and Pernau, while only a few Jews lived in the countryside.

The deportations carried out by the Russians, as far as they concerned Jews, quantitatively cannot be established. According to inquiries made so far, the Jews were hardly affected by them.

With the advance of the German troops on Estonian territory about half of the Jews prepared to flee. As these Jews collaborated with the Soviet authorities, they left the country with them, going east. Only a few of them were seized in Reval because their escape route had been cut off. After the occupation of the country, there were probably still about 2,000 Jews left in the country.

The Estonian self-defense units which were formed when the [German] army marched in, immediately started to arrest Jews. Spontaneous demonstrations against the Jews did not take place because there was no known reason for the population to do so.

The following orders were therefore issued by us:

1. The arrest of all male Jews over sixteen;
2. The arrest of all Jewesses fit for work between the ages of sixteen and sixty, to be utilized to work in the peat bogs;
3. Collective billeting of female Jewish residents of Dorpat and vicinity in the synagogue and a tenement house in Dorpat;
4. Arrest of all male and female Jews fit for work in Pernau and vicinity;
5. Registration of all Jews according to age, sex, and fitness for work and billeting in a camp which is at present being built.

All male Jews over sixteen, with the exception of physicians and the appointed Jewish Elders, were executed by the Estonian self-defense units under supervision of the Sonderkommando. As for the town and country district of Reval, the action is still underway since the search for the Jewish hideouts has not yet been completed. So far, the total number of Jews shot in Estonia is 440.

When these measures are completed, about 500 to 600 Jewesses and children will still be alive.

The village communities are by now free of Jews.

For the Jews residing in Reval and vicinity, a camp is at present being prepared at Harku [Reval county], which, after receiving the Jews from Reval, will be expanded to contain all Jews from Estonia. All Jewesses fit for work are employed in farming and cutting of peat on the property of the nearby prison. Thus, the questions of feeding and financing are answered.

As an immediate measure, the following order was issued:

1. Marking of all Jews over six with a yellow star at least 10 cm large, to be attached to the left side of the breast and on the back;
2. Prohibition to engage in public trade;
3. Prohibition to use sidewalks, public communications, and to frequent theaters, cinemas and restaurants;
4. Seizure of all Jewish property;
5. Prohibition to attend schools.

TESTIMONY OF OTTO OHLENDORF AT NUREMBERG

JANUARY 3, 1946

COLONEL JOHN HARLAN AMEN (ASSOCIATE TRIAL COUNSEL FOR THE UNITED STATES): May it please the Tribunal, I wish to call as a witness for the Prosecution, Mr. Otto Ohlendorf....

[Witness Otto Ohlendorf took the stand]

THE PRESIDENT: Otto Ohlendorf, will you repeat this oath after me: "I swear by God the Almighty and Omniscient that I will speak the pure truth and will withhold and add nothing."

[The witness repeated the oath]

COL. AMEN: Will you try to speak slowly and pause between each question and answer.

OTTO OHLENDORF: Yes.

COL. AMEN: Where were you born?

OHLENDORF: In Hohen-Egelsen.

COL. AMEN: How old are you?

OHLENDORF: Thirty-eight years old.

COL. AMEN: When, if ever, did you become a member of the National Socialist Party?

OHLENDORF: 1925.

COL. AMEN: When, if ever, did you become a member of the SA?

OHLENDORF: For the first time in 1926.

COL. AMEN: When, if ever, did you become a member of the SS?

OHLENDORF: I must correct my answer to the previous question. I thought you were asking about my membership in the SS.

COL. AMEN: When did you become a member of the SA?

OHLENDORF: In the year 1925.

COL. AMEN: When, if ever, did you join the SD?

OHLENDORF: In 1936.

COL. AMEN: What was your last position in the SD?

OHLENDORF: Chief of Amt III in the RSHA....

COL. AMEN: Did you tell us for what period of time you continued to serve as chief of Amt III?

OHLENDORF: I was part-time chief of Amt III from 1939 to 1945.

COL. AMEN: Turning now to the designation "Mobile Units" with the army shown in the lower right hand corner of the chart, please explain to the Tribunal the significance of the terms "Einsatzgruppe" and "Einsatzkommando."

OHLENDORF: The concept "Einsatzgruppe" was established after an agreement between the chiefs of the RSHA, OKW, and OKH, on the separate use of Sipo units in the operational areas. The concept "Einsatzgruppe" first appeared during the Polish campaign.

   The agreement with the OKH and OKW, however, was arrived at only before the beginning of the Russian campaign. This agreement specified that a representative of the chief of the Sipo and the SD would be assigned to the army groups, or armies, and that this official would have at his disposal mobile units of the Sipo and the SD in the form of an Einsatzgruppe, subdivided into Einsatzkommandos. The Einsatzkommandos would, on orders from the army group or army, be assigned to the individual army units as needed.

COL. AMEN: State, if you know, whether prior to the campaign against Soviet Russia, any agreement was entered into between the OKW, OKH, and RSHA?

OHLENDORF: Yes, the Einsatzgruppen and Einsatzkommandos, as I have just described them, were used on the basis of a written agreement between the OKW, OKH, and RSHA.

COL. AMEN: How do you know that there was such a written agreement?

German soldiers with their murdered victims. Wartime date and place unknown. *Dokumentationarchiv des Osterreichischen Widestandes.*

OHLENDORF: I was repeatedly present during the negotiations which Albrecht and Schellenberg conducted with the OKH and OKW; and I also had a written copy of this agreement, which was the outcome of these negotiations, in my own hands when I took over the Einsatzgruppe.

COL. AMEN: Explain to the Tribunal who Schellenberg was. What position, if any, did he occupy?

OHLENDORF: Schellenberg was, at the end, chief of Amt VI in the RSHA; at the time when he was conducting as the representative of Heydrich, he belonged to the Amt VI.

COL. AMEN: On approximately what date did these negotiations take place?

OHLENDORF: The negotiations lasted several weeks. The agreement must have been reached one or two weeks before the beginning of the Russian campaign.

COL. AMEN: Did you yourself ever see a copy of this written agreement?

OHLENDORF: Yes!

COL. AMEN: Did you have occasion to work with this written agreement?

OHLENDORF: Yes.

COL. AMEN: On more than one occasion?

OHLENDORF: Yes; in all questions arising out of the relationship between the Einsatzgruppen and the army.

COL. AMEN: Do you know where the original or any copy of that agreement is located today?

OHLENDORF: No.

COL. AMEN: To the best of your knowledge and recollection, please explain to the Tribunal the entire substance of this written agreement.

OHLENDORF: First of all, the agreement stated that Einsatzgruppen and Einsatzkommandos would be set up and used in the operational areas. This created a precedent, because until that time the army had, on its own responsibility, discharged the tasks which would now fall solely to the Sipo. The second was the regulation as to competence.

THE PRESIDENT: You're going too fast. What is it that you say the Einsatzkommandos did under the agreement?

OHLENDORF: I said this was the relationship between the army and the Einsatzgruppen and the Einsatzkommandos. The agreement specified that the army groups or armies would be responsible for the movement and the supply of Einsatzgruppen, but that instructions for their activities would come from the chief of the Sipo and SD.

COL. AMEN: Let us understand. Is it correct that an Einsatz group was to be attached to each army group or army?

COL. AMEN: Every army group was to have an Einsatzgruppe attached to it. The army group in its turn would then attach the Einsatzkommandos to the armies of the army group.

COL. AMEN: And was the army command to determine the area within which the Einsatz group was to operate?

OHLENDORF: The operational area of the Einsatzgruppe was already determined by the fact that it was attached to a specific army group and therefore moved with it, whereas the operational areas of the Einsatzkommandos were then fixed by the army group or army.

COL. AMEN: Did the agreement also provide that the army command was to direct the time during which they were to operate?

OHLENDORF: That was included under the heading "movement."

COL. AMEN: And, also to direct any additional tasks they were to perform?

OHLENDORF: Yes. Even though the chiefs of the Sipo and SD had the right to issue instructions to them on their work, there existed a general agreement that the army was also entitled to issue orders to the Einsatzgruppen if the operational situation made it necessary.

COL. AMEN: What did this agreement provide with respect to the attachment of the Einsatz group command to this army command?

OHLENDORF: I can't remember whether anything specific was contained in the agreement about that. At any rate a liaison man between the army command and the SD was appointed.

COL. AMEN: Do you recall any other provisions of this written agreement?

OHLENDORF: I believe I can state the main contents of that agreement.

COL. AMEN: What position did you occupy with respect to this agreement?

OHLENDORF: From June 1941 to the death of Heydrich in June 1942, I led Einsatzgruppe D, and was the representative of the chief of the Sipo and the SD with the 11th Army.

COL. AMEN: And when was Heydrich's death?

OHLENDORF: Heydrich was wounded at the end of May 1942, and died on 4 June 1942.

COL. AMEN: How much advance notice, if any, did you have of the campaign against Soviet Russia?

OHLENDORF: About four weeks.

COL. AMEN: How many Einsatz groups were there, and who were their respective leaders?

OHLENDORF: There were four Einsatzgruppen, Groups A, B, C, and D. Chief of Einsatzgruppe A was Stahlecker; chief of Einsatzgruppe B was Nebe; chief of Einsatzgruppe C, Dr. Rasche, and later, Dr. Thomas; chief of Einsatzgruppe D, I myself, and later Bierkamp.

COL. AMEN: To which army was Group D attached?

OHLENDORF: Group D was not attached to any army group, but was attached directly to the 11th Army.

COL. AMEN: Where did Group D operate?

OHLENDORF: Group D operated in the southern Ukraine.

COL. AMEN: Will you describe in more detail the nature and extent of the area in which Group D originally operated, naming the cities or territories?

OHLENDORF: The northernmost city was Cernauti; then southward through Mohilev-Podolsk, Yampol, then eastward Zuvalje, Czervind, Melitopol, Mariopol, Taganrog, Rostov, and the Crimea.

COL. AMEN: What was the ultimate objective of Group D?

OHLENDORF: Group D was held in reserve for the Caucasus, for an army group which was to operate in the Caucasus.

COL. AMEN: When did Group D commence its move into Soviet Russia?

OHLENDORF: Group D left Duegen on 21 June and reached Pietra Namsk in Romania in three days. There the first Einsatzkommandos were already being demanded by the army, and they immediately set off for the destinations named by the army. The entire Einsatzgruppe was put into operation at the beginning of July.

COL. AMEN: You are referring to the 11th Army?

OHLENDORF: Yes.

COL. AMEN: In what respects, if any, were the official duties of the Einsatz groups concerned with Jews and Communist commissars?

OHLENDORF: On the question of Jews and Communists, the Einsatzgruppen and the commanders of the Einsatzkommandos were orally instructed before their mission.

COL. AMEN: What were their instructions with respect to the Jews and the Communist functionaries?

OHLENDORF: The instructions were that in the Russian operational areas of the Einsatzgruppen the Jews, as well as the Soviet political commissars, were to be liquidated.

COL. AMEN: And when you say "liquidated" do you mean "killed"?

OHLENDORF: Yes, I mean "killed."

COL. AMEN: Prior to the opening of the Soviet campaign, did you attend a conference at Pretz?

OHLENDORF: Yes, it was a conference at which the Einsatzgruppen and the Einsatzkommandos were informed of their tasks and were given the necessary orders.

COL. AMEN: Who was present at that conference?

OHLENDORF: The chiefs of the Einsatzgruppen and the commanders of the Einsatzkommandos and Streckenbach of the RSHA who transmitted the orders of Heydrich and Himmler.

COL. AMEN: What were those orders?

OHLENDORF: Those were the general orders on the normal work of the Sipo and the SD, and in addition the liquidation order which I have already mentioned.

COL. AMEN: And that conference took place on approximately what date?

OHLENDORF: About three or four days before the mission.

COL. AMEN: So that before you commenced to march into Soviet Russia you received orders at this conference to exterminate the Jews and Communist functionaries in addition to the regular professional work of the Security Police and SD; is that correct?

OHLENDORF: Yes.

COL. AMEN: Did you, personally, have any conversation with Himmler respecting any communication from Himmler to the chiefs of army groups and armies concerning this mission?

OHLENDORF: Yes. Himmler told me that before the beginning of the Russian campaign Hitler had spoken of this mission to a conference of the army groups and the army chiefs—no, not the army chiefs but the commanding generals—and had instructed the commanding generals to provide the necessary support.

COL. AMEN: So that you can testify that the chiefs of the army groups and the armies had been similarly informed of these orders for the liquidation of the Jews and Soviet functionaries?

OHLENDORF: I don't think it is quite correct to put it in that form. They had no orders for liquidation; the order for the liquidation was given to Himmler to carry out, but since this liquidation took place in the operational area of the army group or the armies, they had to be ordered to provide support. Moreover, without such instructions to the army, the activities of the Einsatzgruppen would not have been possible.

COL. AMEN: Did you have any other conversation with Himmler concerning this order?

OHLENDORF: Yes, in late summer of 1941 Himmler was in Nikolaiev. He assembled the leaders and men of the Einsatzkommandos, repeated to them the liquidation order, and pointed out that the leaders and men who were taking part in the liquidation bore no personal responsibility for the execution of this order. The responsibility was his, alone, and the Führer's.

COL. AMEN: And you yourself heard that said?

OHLENDORF: Yes.

COL. AMEN: Do you know whether this mission of the Einsatz group was known to the army group commanders?

OHLENDORF: This order and the execution of these orders were known to the commanding general of the army.

COL. AMEN: How do you know that?

OHLENDORF: Through conferences with the army and through instructions that were given by the army on the execution of the order.

COL. AMEN: Was the mission of the Einsatz groups and the agreement between OKW, OKH, and RSHA known to the other leaders in the RSHA?

OHLENDORF: At least some of them knew it, since some of the leaders were also active in the Einsatzgruppen and Einsatzkommandos in the course of time. Furthermore, the leaders who were dealing with the organization and the legal aspect of the Einsatzgruppen also knew of it.

COL. AMEN: Most of the leaders came from the RSHA, did they not?

OHLENDORF: Which leaders?

COL. AMEN: Of the Einsatz groups.

OHLENDORF: No, one can't say that. The leaders of in the Einsatzgruppen and Einsatzkommandos came from all over the Reich.

COL. AMEN: Do you know whether the mission and the agreement were also known to Kaltenbrunner?

OHLENDORF: After his assumption of office Kaltenbrunner had to deal with these questions and consequently must have known details of the Einsatzgruppen which were offices of his.

COL. AMEN: Who was the commanding officer of the 11th Army?

OHLENDORF: At first, Riter von Schober; later, Von Manstein.

COL. AMEN: Will you tell the Tribunal in what way or ways the command officer of the 11th Army directed or supervised Einsatz Group D in carrying out its liquidation activities?

OHLENDORF: An order from the 11th Army was sent to Nikolaiev that liquidations were to take place only at a distance of not less than two hundred kilometers from the headquarters of the commanding general.

COL. AMEN: Do you recall any other occasion?

OHLENDORF: In Simferopol the army command requested the Einsatzkommandos in its area to hasten the liquidations, because famine was threatening and there was a great housing shortage.

COL. AMEN: Do you know how many persons were liquidated by Einsatz Group D under your direction?

OHLENDORF: In the year between June 1941 to June 1942 the Einsatzkommandos reported ninety thousand people liquidated.

COL. AMEN: Did that include men, women, and children?

OHLENDORF: Yes.

COL. AMEN: On what do you base those figures?

OHLENDORF: On reports sent by the Einsatzkommandos to the Einsatzgruppen.

COL. AMEN: Were those reports submitted to you?

OHLENDORF: Yes.

COL. AMEN: And you saw them and read them?

OHLENDORF: I beg your pardon?

COL. AMEN: And you saw and read those reports, personally?

OHLENDORF: Yes.

COL. AMEN: And it is on those reports that you base the figures you have given the Tribunal?

OHLENDORF: Yes.

COL. AMEN: Do you know how those figures compare with the number of persons liquidated by other Einsatz groups?

OHLENDORF: The figures which I saw of other Einsatzgruppen are considerably larger.

COL. AMEN: That was due to what factor?

OHLENDORF: I believe that to a large extent the figures submitted by the other Einsatzgruppen were exaggerated.

COL. AMEN: Did you see reports of liquidations from the other Einsatz groups from time to time?

OHLENDORF: Yes.

COL. AMEN: And those reports showed liquidations exceeding those of Group D; is that correct?

OHLENDORF: Yes.

COL. AMEN: Did you personally supervise mass executions of these individuals?

OHLENDORF: I was present at two mass executions for purposes of inspection.

COL. AMEN: Will you explain to the Tribunal in detail how an individual mass execution was carried out?

OHLENDORF: A local Einsatzkommando attempted to collect all the Jews in its area by registering them. This registration was performed by the Jews themselves.

COL. AMEN: On what pretext, if any, were they rounded up?

OHLENDORF: On the pretext that they were to be resettled.

COL. AMEN: Will you continue?

OHLENDORF: After the registration the Jews were collected at one place; and from there they were later transported to the place of execution, which was, as a rule, an antitank ditch or a natural excavation. The executions were carried out in a military manner, by firing squads under command.

COL. AMEN: In what way were they transported to the place of execution?

OHLENDORF: They were transported to the place of execution in trucks, always only as many as could be executed immediately. In this way it was attempted to keep the span of time from the moment in which the victims knew what was about to happen to them until the time of their actual execution as short as possible.

COL. AMEN: Was that your idea?

OHLENDORF: Yes.

COL. AMEN: And after they were shot what was done with the bodies?

OHLENDORF: The bodies were buried in the antitank ditch or excavation.

COL. AMEN: What determination, if any, was made as to whether the persons were actually dead?

OHLENDORF: The unit leaders or the firing-squad commanders had orders to see to this and, if need be, finish them off themselves.

COL. AMEN: And who would do that?

OHLENDORF: Either the unit leader himself or somebody designated by him.

COL. AMEN: In what positions were the victims shot?

OHLENDORF: Standing or kneeling.

COL. AMEN: What was done with the personal property and clothing of the persons executed?

OHLENDORF: All valuables were confiscated at the time of the registration or the rounding up and handed over to the Finance Ministry, either through the RSHA or directly. At first the clothing was given to the population, but in the winter of 1941–42 it was collected and disposed of by the NSV.

COL. AMEN: All their personal property was registered at the time?

OHLENDORF: No, not all of it, only valuables were registered.

COL. AMEN: What happened to the garments which the victims were wearing when they went to the place of execution?

OHLENDORF: They were obliged to take off their outer garments immediately before the execution.

COL. AMEN: All of them?

OHLENDORF: The outer garments, yes.

COL. AMEN: How about the rest of the garments they were wearing?

OHLENDORF: The other garments remained on the bodies.

COL. AMEN: Was that true of not only your group but of the other Einsatz groups?

OHLENDORF: That was the order in my Einsatzgruppe. I don't know how it was done in other Einsatzgruppen.

COL. AMEN: In what way did they handle it?

OHLENDORF: Some of the unit leaders did not carry out the liquidation in the military manner, but killed the victims singly by shooting them in the back of the neck.

COL. AMEN: And you objected to that procedure?

OHLENDORF: I was against that procedure, yes.

COL. AMEN: For what reason?

OHLENDORF: Because, both for the victims and for those who carried out the executions, it was, psychologically, an immense burden to bear.

COL. AMEN: Now, what was done with the property collected by the Einsatzkommandos from these victims?

OHLENDORF: All valuables were sent to Berlin, to the RSHA or to the Reich Ministry of Finance. The articles which could be used in the operational area, were disposed of there.

COL. AMEN: For example, what happened to gold and silver taken from the victims?

OHLENDORF: That was, as I have just said, turned over to Berlin, to the Reich Ministry of Finance.

COL. AMEN: How do you know that?

OHLENDORF: I can remember that it was actually handled in that way from Simferopol.

COL. AMEN: How about watches, for example, taken from the victims?

OHLENDORF: At the request of the army, watches were made available to the forces at the front.

COL. AMEN: Were all victims, including the men, women, and children, executed in the same manner?

OHLENDORF: Until the spring of 1942, yes. Then an order came from Himmler that in the future women and children were to be killed only in gas vans.

COL. AMEN: How had the women and children been killed previously?

OHLENDORF: In the same way as the men—by shooting.

COL. AMEN: What, if anything, was done about burying the victims after they had been executed?

OHLENDORF: The kommandos filled the graves to efface the signs of the execution, and then labor units of the population leveled them.

COL. AMEN: Referring to the gas vans that you said you received in the spring of 1942, what order did you receive with respect to the use of these vans?

OHLENDORF: These gas vans were in future to be used for the killing of women and children.

COL. AMEN: Will you explain to the Tribunal the construction of these vans and their appearance?

OHLENDORF: The actual purpose of these vans could not be seen from the outside. They looked like closed trucks, and were so constructed that at the start of the motor, gas was conducted into the van causing death in ten to fifteen minutes.

COL. AMEN: Explain in detail just how one of these vans was used for an execution.

OHLENDORF: The vans were loaded with the victims and driven to the place of burial, which was usually the same as that used for the mass executions. The time needed for transportation was sufficient to insure the death of the victims.

COL. AMEN: How were the victims induced to enter the vans?

OHLENDORF: They were told that they were to be transported to another locality.

COL. AMEN: How was the gas turned on?

OHLENDORF: I am not familiar with technical details.

COL. AMEN: How long did it take to kill the victims ordinarily?

OHLENDORF: About ten to fifteen minutes; the victims were not conscious of what was happening to them.

COL. AMEN: How many persons could be killed simultaneously in one such van?

OHLENDORF: About fifteen to twenty-five persons. The vans varied in size.

COL. AMEN: Did you receive reports from those persons operating these vans from time to time?

OHLENDORF: I didn't understand the question.

COL. AMEN: Did you receive reports from those who were working on the vans?

OHLENDORF: I received the report that the Einsatzkommandos did not willingly use the vans.

COL. AMEN: Why not?

OHLENDORF: Because the burial of the victims was a great ordeal for the members of the Einsatzkommandos.

COL. AMEN: Now, will you tell the Tribunal who furnished these vans to the Einsatz groups?

OHLENDORF: The gas vans did not belong to the motor pool of the Einsatzgruppen but were assigned to the Einsatzgruppe as a special unit, headed by the man who had constructed the vans. The vans were assigned to the Einsatzgruppen by the RSHA.

COL. AMEN: Were the vans supplied to all of the different Einsatz groups?

OHLENDORF: I am not certain. I know only in the case of Einsatzgruppe D, and indirectly that Einsatzgruppe C also made use of these vans....

COL. AMEN: ... Referring to your previous testimony, will you explain to the Tribunal why you believe that the type of execution ordered by you, namely, military, was preferable to the shooting-in-the-neck procedure adopted by the other Einsatz groups?

OHLENDORF: On the one hand, the aim was that the individual leaders and men should be able to carry out the executions in a military manner acting on orders and should not have to make a decision of their own; it was, to all intents and purposes, an order which they were to carry out. On the other hand, it was known to me that through the emotional excitement of the executions ill treatment could not be avoided, since the victims discovered too soon that they were to be executed and could not therefore endure prolonged nervous strain. And it seemed intolerable to me that individual leaders and men should in consequence be forced to kill a large number of people on their own decision.

COL. AMEN: In what manner did you determine which were the Jews to be executed?

OHLENDORF: That was not part of my task; but the identification of the Jews was carried out by the Jews themselves, since the registration was handled by a Jewish Council of Elders.

COL. AMEN: Did the amount of Jewish blood have anything to do with it?

OHLENDORF: I can't remember the details, but I believe that half-Jews were also considered as Jews.

COL. AMEN: What organization furnished most off the officer personnel of the Einsatz groups and Einsatzkommandos?

OHLENDORF: I did not understand the question.

COL. AMEN: What organization furnished most of the officer personnel of the Einsatz groups?

OHLENDORF: The officer personnel was furnished by the State Police, the Kripo, and, to a lesser extent by the SD.

COL. AMEN: Kripo?

OHLENDORF: Yes, the State Police, the Criminal Police and, to a lesser extent, the SD.

COL. AMEN: Were there any other sources of personnel?

OHLENDORF: Yes, most of the men by the Waffen SS and the Ordnungspolizei. The State Police and the Kripo furnished most of the experts and the troops were furnished by the Waffen SS and the Ordungspolizei.

COL. AMEN: How about the Waffen SS.

OHLENDORF: The Waffen SS and the Ordungspolizei were each supposed to supply the Einsatzgruppen with one company.

COL. AMEN: How about the Order Police?

OHLENDORF: The Ordnungspolizei also furnished the Einsatzgruppen with one company.

COL. AMEN: What was the size of Einsatz Group D and its operating area as compared with other Einsatz groups?

OHLENDORF: I estimate that Einsatzgruppen D was one-half or two-thirds as large as the other Einsatzgruppen. That changed in the course of time since some of the Einsatzgruppen were greatly enlarged.

COL. AMEN: May it please the Tribunal, relating to organizational matters which I think would clarify some of the evidence which has already been in part received by the Tribunal. But I don't want to take the time of the Tribunal unless they feel that they want any more such testimony. I thought perhaps if any members of the Tribunal had any questions they would ask this witness directly because he is the best informed on these organizational matters of anyone who will be presented in court....

THE PRESIDENT: Colonel Amen, the Tribunal does not think that it is necessary to go further into the organizational questions at this stage, but it is a matter that must be really decided by you because you know what the nature of the evidence which you are considering is.

So far as the Tribunal is concerned, they are satisfied at the present stage to leave the matter where it stands, but there is one aspect of the witness's evidence which the Tribunal would like you to investigate, and that is whether the practices by which he has been speaking continued after 1942, and for how long.

COL. AMEN: [To the witness] Can you state whether the liquidation practices that you have described continued after 1942 and, if so, for how long a period of time thereafter?

OHLENDORF: I don't think that the basic order was ever revoked. But I cannot remember the details—at least not with regard to Russia— which would enable me to make concrete statements on this subject. The retreat began very shortly thereafter, so that the operational region of the Einsatzgruppen became ever smaller. I do know, however, that other Einsatzgruppen with similar orders had been envisaged for other areas.

COL. AMEN: Your personal knowledge extends up to what date?

OHLENDORF: I know that the liquidation of Jews was prohibited about six months before the end of the war. I also saw a document terminating the liquidation of Soviet commissary but I cannot recall a specific date.

COL. AMEN: Do you know whether in fact it was so terminated?

OHLENDORF: Yes, I believe so.

THE PRESIDENT: The Tribunal would like to know the number of men in your Einsatz group.

OHLENDORF: There were about five hundred men in my Einsatzgruppe, excluding those who were added to the group as assistants from the country itself....

COL. AMEN: May it please the Tribunal. The witness is now available to other counsel. I understand that Colonel Pokrovsky has some questions that he wishes to ask on behalf of the Soviets.

COLONEL Y. V. POKROVSKY (DEPUTY CHIEF PROSECUTOR FOR THE USSR): The testimony of the witness is important for the clarification of questions in a report on which the Soviet delegation is at present working. Therefore, with the permission of the Tribunal, I would like to put a number of questions to the witness.

[Turning to the witness] Witness, you said that you were present twice at the mass executions. On whose orders were you an inspector at the executions?

OHLENDORF: I was present at the executions on my own initiative.

COL. POKROVSKY: But you said that you attended as inspector.

OHLENDORF: I said that I attended for inspection purposes.

COL. POKROVSKY: On your initiative?

OHLENDORF: Yes.

COL. POKROVSKY: Did one of your chiefs always attend the executions for purposes of inspection?

OHLENDORF: Whenever possible I sent a member of the staff of the Einsatzgruppe to witness the executions but this was not always feasible since the Einsszgruppen had to operate over great distances.

COL. POKROVSKY: Why was some person sent for purposes of inspection?

OHLENDORF: Would you please repeat the question?

COL. POKROVSKY: For what purpose was an inspector sent?

OHLENDORF: To determine whether or not my instructions regarding the manner of the execution were actually being carried out.

COL. POKROVSKY: Am I to understand that the inspector was to make certain that the execution had actually been carried out?

OHLENDORF: No, it would not be correct to say that. He was to ascertain whether the conditions which I had set for the execution were actually been carried out.

COL. POKROVSKY: What manner of conditions had you in mind?

OHLENDORF: One: exclusion of the public; two: military execution by a firing-squad; three: arrival of the transports and carrying out of the liquidation in a smooth manner to avoid unnecessary excitement; four: supervision of the property to prevent looting. There may have been other details that I no longer remember. At any rate, all ill-treatment, whether physical or mental, was to be prevented through these measures.

COL. POKROVSKY: You wished so make sure that what you considered to be an equitable distribution of this property was effected, or did you aspire to complete acquisition of the valuables?

OHLENDORF: Yes.

COL. POKROVSKY: You spoke of ill-treatment. What did you mean by ill-treatment at the executions?

OHLENDORF: If, for instance, the manner in which the executions were carried out caused excitement and disobedience among the victims, so that the kommandos were forced to restore order by means of violence.

COL. POKROVSKY: What do you mean by "restore order by means of violence"? What do you mean by suppression of the excitement amongst the victims by means of violence?

OHLENDORF: If, as I have already said, in order to carry out the liquidation in an orderly fashion it was necessary, for example, to resort to beating.

COL. POKROVSKY: Was it absolutely necessary to beat the victims?

OHLENDORF: I myself never witnessed it, but I heard of it.

COL. POKROVSKY: From whom?

OHLENDORF: In conversations with members of other kommandos.

COL. POKROVSKY: You said that cars, autocars, were used for the executions?

OHLENDORF: Yes.

COL. POKROVSKY: Do you know where, and with whose assistance, the inventor, Becker, was able to put his invention into practice?

OHLENDORF: I remember only that it was done through Amt II of the RSHA; but I can no longer say that with certainty.

COL. POKROVSKY: How many persons were executed in these cars?

OHLENDORF: I did not understand the question.

COL. POKROVSKY: How many persons were executed by means of these cars?

OHLENDORF: I cannot give precise figures, but the number was comparatively very small—perhaps a few hundred.

COL. POKROVSKY: You said that mostly women and children were executed in these vans. For what reason?

OHLENDORF: That was a special order from Himmler to the effect that women and children were not to be exposed to the mental strain of the executions; and thus the men of the kommandos, mostly married men, should not be compelled to aim at women and children.

COL. POKROVSKY: Did anybody observe the behavior of the persons executed in these vans?

OHLENDORF: Yes, the doctor.

COL. POKROVSKY: Did you know that Becker had reported that death in these vans was particularly agonizing?

OHLENDORF: No. I learned of Becker's reports for the first time from the letter to Rauff, which was shown to me here. On the contrary, I know from the doctor's reports that the victims were not conscious of their impending death.

COL. POKROVSKY: Did any military units—I mean, army units—take part in these mass executions?

OHLENDORF: As a rule, no.

COL. POKROVSKY: And as an exception?

OHLENDORF: I think I remember that in Nikolaiev and in Simferopol a spectator from the Army High Command was present for a short time.

COL. POKROVSKY: For what purpose?

OHLENDORF: I don't know, probably to obtain information personally.

COL. POKROVSKY: Were military units assigned to carry out the executions in these towns?

OHLENDORF: Officially, the army did not assign any units for this purpose; the army as such was actually opposed to the liquidation.

COL. POKROVSKY: But in practice?

OHLENDORF: Individual units occasionally volunteered. However, at the moment I know of no such case among the army itself, but only among the units attached to the army (*Heeresgefolge*).

COL. POKROVSKY: You were the man by whose orders people were sent to their death. Were Jews only handed over for the execution by the Einsatzgruppe or were Communists— "Communist officials" you call them in your instructions—handed over for execution along with the Jews?

OHLENDORF: Yes, activists and political commissars. Mere membership in the Communist Party was not sufficient to persecute or kill a man.

COL. POKROVSKY: Were any special investigations made concerning the part played by persons in the Communist Party?

OHLENDORF: No, I said on the contrary that mere membership of the Communist Party was not, in itself, a determining factor in persecuting or executing a man; he had to have a special political function.

COL. POKROVSKY: Did you have any discussions on the murder vans sent from Berlin and on their use?

OHLENDORF: I did not understand the question.

COL. POKROVSKY: Had you occasion to discuss, with your chiefs and your colleagues, the fact that motor vans had been sent to your own particular Einsatzgruppe from Berlin for carrying out the executions? Do you remember any such discussions?

OHLENDORF: I do not remember any specific discussion.

COL. POKROVSKY: Had you any information concerning the fact that members of the execution squad in charge of the executions were unwilling to use the vans?

OHLENDORF: I knew that the Einsatzkommandos were using these vans.

COL. POKROVSKY: No, I had something else in mind. I wanted to know whether you received reports that members of the execution squads were unwilling to use the vans and preferred other means of execution?

OHLENDORF: That they would rather kill by means of the gas vans than by shooting?

COL. POKROVSKY: On the contrary, that they preferred execution by shooting to killing by means of the gas vans.

OHLENDORF: You have already said the gas van . . .

COL. POKROVSKY: And why did they prefer execution by shooting to killing in the gas vans?

OHLENDORF: Because, as I have already said, in the opinion of the leader of the Einsatzkommandos, the unloading of the corpses was an unnecessary mental strain.

COL. POKROVSKY: What do you mean by "an unnecessary mental strain"?

OHLENDORF: As far as I can remember the conditions at that time—the picture presented by the corpses and probably because certain functions of the body had taken place leaving the corpses lying in filth.

COL. POKROVSKY: You mean to say that the sufferings endured prior to death were clearly visible on the victims? Did I understand you correctly?

OHLENDORF: I don't understand the question; do you mean during the killing in the van?

COL. POKROVSKY: Yes.

OHLENDORF: I can only repeat what the doctor told me, that the victims were not conscious of their death in the van.

COL. POKROVSKY: In that case your reply to my previous question, that the unloading of the bodies made a very terrible impression on the members of the execution squad, becomes entirely incomprehensible.

OHLENDORF: And, as I said, the terrible impression created by the position of corpses themselves, and by the state of the vans which had probably been dirtied and so on.

COL. POKROVSKY: I have no further questions to put to this witness at the present stage of the trial . . .

THE TRIBUNAL (GEN. NIKITCHENKO): In your testimony you said that the Einsatz group had the object of annihilating the Jews and the commissars, is that correct?

OHLENDORF: Yes.

THE TRIBUNAL (GEN. NIKITCHENKO): And in what category did you consider the children? For what reason were the children massacred?

OHLENDORF: The order was that the Jewish population should be totally exterminated.

THE TRIBUNAL (GEN. NIKITCHENKO): Including the children?

OHLENDORF: Yes.

THE TRIBUNAL (GEN. NIKITCHENKO): Were all the Jewish children murdered?

OHLENDORF: Yes.

THE TRIBUNAL (GEN. NIKITCHENKO): But the children of those whom you considered as belonging to the category of commissars, were they also killed?

OHLENDORF: I am not aware that inquiries were ever made after the families of Soviet commissars.

THE TRIBUNAL (GEN. NIKITCHENKO): Did you send anywhere reports on the executions that the group carried out?

OHLENDORF: Reports on the executions were regularly submitted to the RSHA.

THE TRIBUNAL (GEN. NIKITCHENKO): No, did you personally send any reports on the annihilation of thousands of people which you effected? Did you personally submit any report?

OHLENDORF: The reports came from the Einsatzkommandos who carried out the actions, to the Einsatzgruppe and the Einsatzgruppe informed the RSHA.

THE TRIBUNAL (GEN. NIKITCHENKO): Whom?

OHLENDORF: The reports went to the chief of the Sipo personally.

THE TRIBUNAL (GEN. NIKITCHENKO): Personally?

OHLENDORF: Yes, personally.

THE TRIBUNAL (GEN. NIKITCHENKO): What was the name of this police officer? Can you give his name?

OHLENDORF: At that time, Heydrich.

THE TRIBUNAL (GEN. NIKITCHENKO): After Heydrich?

OHLENDORF: I was no longer there then, but that was the standing order.

THE TRIBUNAL (GEN. NIKITCHENKO): I am asking you whether you continued to submit reports after Heydrich's death or not?

OHLENDORF: After Heydrich's death I was no longer in the Einsatz, but the reports were, of course, continued.

THE TRIBUNAL (GEN. NIKITCHENKO): Do you know whether the reports continued to be submitted after Heydrich's death or not?

OHLENDORF: Yes.

THE TRIBUNAL (GEN. NIKITCHENKO): Yes?

OHLENDORF: No, the reports . . .

THE TRIBUNAL (GEN. NIKITCHENKO): Was the order concerning the annihilation of the Soviet people in conformity with the policy of the German government or the Nazi Party or was it against it? Do you understand the question?

OHLENDORF: Yes. One must distinguish here: the order for the liquidation came from the Führer of the Reich, and it was to be carried out by the Reichsführer SS Himmler.

THE TRIBUNAL (GEN. NIKITCHENKO): But was it in conformity with the policy conducted by the Nazi Party and the German government, or was it in contradiction to it?

OHLENDORF: A policy amounts to a practice so that in this respect it was a policy laid down by the Führer. If you were to ask whether this activity was in conformity with the idea of National Socialism, then I should say "no."

THE TRIBUNAL (GEN. NIKITCHENKO): I am talking about the practice.

THE PRESIDENT: I understood you to say that objects of value were taken from the Jewish victims by the Jewish Council of Elders.

OHLENDORF: Yes.

THE PRESIDENT: Did the Jewish Council of Elders settle who were to be killed?

OHLENDORF: The Jewish Council of Elders determined who was a Jew, and then registered the Jews individually.

THE PRESIDENT: And when they registered them did they take their valuables from them?

OHLENDORF: That was done in various ways. As far as I remember, the Council of Elders was given the order to collect valuables at the same time.

THE PRESIDENT: So that the Jewish Council of Elders would not know whether or not they were to be killed?

OHLENDORF: Yes. . . .

HERR BABEL: Now, a question concerning you personally. From whom did you receive your orders for the liquidation of the Jews and so forth? And in what form?

OHLENDORF: My duty was not the task of liquidation, but I did head the staff which directed the Einsatzkommandos in the field, and the Einsatzkommandos themselves had already received this order in Berlin on the instructions of Streckenbach, Himmler, and Heydrich. This order was renewed by Himmler at Nikolaiev.

HERR BABEL: You personally were not concerned with the execution of these orders?

OHLENDORF: I led the Einsatzgruppe, and therefore I had the task of seeing how the Einsatzkommandos executed the orders received.

HERR BABEL: But did you have no scruples in regard to the execution of these orders?

OHLENDORF: Yes, of course.

HERR BABEL: And how is it that they were carried out regardless of these scruples?

OHLENDORF: Because to me it is inconceivable that a subordinate leader should not carry out orders given by the leaders of the state.

HERR BABEL: This is your own opinion. But this must have been not only your point of view but also the point of view of the majority of the people involved. Didn't some of the men appointed to execute these orders ask you to be relieved of such tasks?

OHLENDORF: I cannot remember any one concrete case. I excluded some whom I did not consider emotionally suitable for executing these tasks and I sent some of them home.

HERR BABEL: Was the legality of the orders explained to these people under false pretenses?

OHLENDORF: I do not understand your question; since the order was issued by the superior authorities, the question of legality could not arise in the minds of these individuals, for they had sworn obedience to the people who had issued the orders.

HERR BABEL: Could any individual expect to succeed in evading the execution of these orders?

OHLENDORF: No, the result would have been a court martial with a corresponding sentence.

XI. BABI YAR

On September 19, 1941, the German Army captured Kiev, the capital of the Ukraine. Within days, a number of German buildings—both military and civilian—were blown up by the Soviet Secret Police. Retaliation was ordered and the Jews of Kiev were targeted.

An order was posted in Ukrainian and Russian:

Kikes of the city of Kiev and surroundings!

On Monday, September 29, you are to appear by 7:00 A.M. with your possessions, money, documents, valuables, and warm clothing at Dorogozhitshaya Street, next to the Jewish cemetery.

Failure to appear is punishable by death.

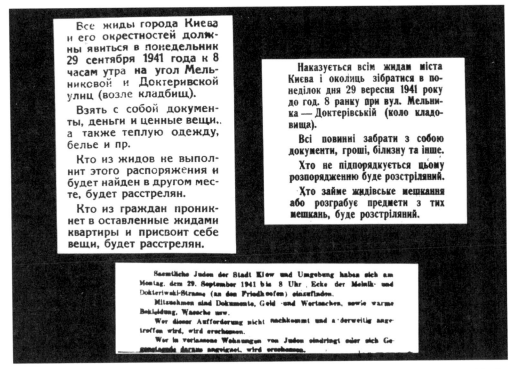

Copies in German, Ukrainian, and Russian of a sign posted in Kiev instructing Jews to assemble for what was termed a "resettlement action." Babi Yar Society, Kiev, courtesy of USHMM Photo Archives.

From the cemetery, Kiev's Jews were marched to the ravine at Babi Yar.

An outdoor office operation with desks had been set up at Babi Yar. The crowd waited behind barriers, unable to see the desks. Thirty to forty people at a time were led away under armed guard for "registration." Documents and valuables were taken away.

The Germans forced them to strip; no exceptions were made—men and women, boys and girls, old and young. Clothing was gathered and folded carefully. Rings were ripped from fingers of the naked. The shots could be heard in Kiev.

In a collection of reports on Babi Yar, we will read an account of one survivor, Nesya Elgort, who walked toward the ravine pressing her trembling son Ilya to her naked body. Her son in her arms, she walked up to the edge of the ravine filled with thousands of bodies. Only partially in control of her senses, she heard the shootings and the death cries. She fell untouched by the bullets. She lay under a heap of warm bloody bodies. The bodies of old men rested on the bodies of children who lay on their dead mothers.

At dawn, Kiev's Jews were moving slowly along the streets in the direction of the Jewish Cemetery at Lukyanovka. Many of them thought they were to be sent to provincial towns, but others realized that death awaited them.

Children were at their parents' side. Young people brought nothing, but elderly people tried to take as much with them from home as possible. The paralyzed and ill were borne on stretchers covered with sheets and blankets.

Streams of people flowed into the endless human current on Lvov Street. It was difficult to cross from one side of the street to the other. This procession of death continued for three days and three nights. Occasionally, people stopped, silently embraced, and said good-bye. Some prayed.

As the people approached Babi Yar the din of angry voices, groans, and sobs grew louder.

In a few days at the end of September 1941, between the Jewish New Year and the Day of Atonement, 33,771 Jews were killed at Babi Yar. In the months that followed, Babi Yar remained an execution site for other victims including Gypsies and Soviet prisoners of war.

In August 1943, as the Red Army was advancing, the mass graves of Babi Yar were dug up and the bodies burned. The evidence of mass murder was to be destroyed.

Paul Blobel, commander of Sonderkommando 4a, whose troops had slaughtered Kiev's Jews, returned to Babi Yar. For more than a month, his men and conscripted concentration camp inmates dug up the bodies. Bulldozers were required to reopen the mounds. Massive bone crushers were brought in. Bodies were piled on wooden logs doused with gas. The flames were seen in Kiev.

At the end of the assignment, the inmate workers were rewarded for their work. They too were murdered.

In the readings below, we read of Babi Yar from four perspectives. The first is the testimony of a truck driver who happened upon the slaughter. The second are a series of reports that were sent back from the field to Berlin headquarters. Einsatzgruppe C reports on October 2, 1941: "Sonderkommando 4a in collaboration with Einsatzgruppe HQ and two kommandos of Police Regiment South, executed 33,771 Jews in Kiev on September 29 and 30, 1941."

There was no more to be said.

Thirdly, we will read an affidavit by Paul Blobel who returned to burn the evidence of the crime. And finally we will read from the compilation of testimony documenting the

Nazi destruction of Jews in the Soviet Union compiled by Soviet writers Vasily Grossman and Ilya Ehrenburg that is known as *The Black Book* and represents the work of more than forty writers and journalists. *The Black Book* was compiled during and after the war and later suppressed by Joseph Stalin.

"IT TOOK NERVES OF STEEL"

Statement of Truck-Driver Höfer Describing the Murder of Jews at Babi Yar

One day I was instructed to drive my truck outside the town. I was accompanied by a Ukrainian. It must have been about ten o'clock. On the way there we overtook Jews carrying luggage marching on foot in the same direction that we were traveling. There were whole families. The farther we got out of town the denser the columns became. Piles of clothing lay in a large open field. These piles of clothing were my destination. The Ukrainian showed me how to get in there.

After we had stopped in the area near the piles of clothes the truck was immediately loaded up with clothing. This was carried out by Ukrainians. I watched what happened when the Jews—men, women and children—arrived. The Ukrainians led them past a number of different places where one after the other they had to remove their luggage, then their coats, shoes and overgarments and also underwear. They also had to leave their valuables in a designated place. There was a special pile for each article of clothing. It all happened very quickly and anyone who hesitated was kicked or pushed by the Ukrainians to keep them moving. I don't think it was even a minute from the time each Jew took off his coat before he was standing there completely naked. No distinction was made between men, women and children. One would have thought that the Jews that came later would have had a chance to turn back when they saw the others in front of them having to undress. It still surprises me today that this did not happen.

Once undressed, the Jews were led into a ravine which was about 150 meters long, 30 meters wide and a good 15 meters deep. Two or three narrow entrances led to this ravine through which the Jews were channeled. When they reached the bottom of the ravine they were seized by members of the Schutzpolizei and made to lie down on top of Jews who had already been shot. This all happened very quickly. The corpses were literally in layers. A police marksman came along and shot each Jew in the neck with a submachine gun at the spot where he was lying. When the Jews reached the ravine they were so shocked by the horrifying scene that they completely lost their will. It may even have been that the Jews themselves lay down in rows to wait to be shot.

There were only two marksmen carrying out the executions. One of them was working at one end of the ravine, the other at the other end. I saw these marksmen stand on the layers of corpses and shoot one after the other.

The moment one Jew had been killed, the marksman would walk across the bodies of the executed Jews to the next Jew, who had meanwhile lain down, and shoot him. It went on in this way uninterruptedly, with no distinction being made between men, women and children. The children were kept with their mothers and shot with them.

I only saw this scene briefly. When I got to the bottom of the ravine I was so shocked by the terrible sight that I could not bear to look for long. In the hollow I saw that there were already three rows of bodies lined up over a distance of about sixty meters. How many layers of bodies there were on top of each other I could not see. I was so astonished and dazed by the sight of the twitching, blood-smeared bodies that I could not properly register the details. In addition to the two marksmen there was a "packer" at either entrance to the ravine. These "packers" were Schutzpolizisten, whose job it was to lay the victim on top of the other corpses so that all the marksman had to do as he passed was fire a shot.

When the victims came along the paths to the ravine and at the last moment saw the terrible scene they cried out in terror. But at the very next moment they were already being knocked over by the "packers" and made to lie down with the others. The next group of people could not see this terrible scene because it took place round a corner.

Most people put up a fight when they had to undress and there was a lot of screaming and shouting. The Ukrainians did not take any notice. They just drove them down as quickly as possible into the ravine through the entrances.

From the undressing area you could not make out the ravine, which was about 150 meters away from the first pile of clothes. A biting wind was blowing; it was very cold. The shots from the ravine could not be heard at the undressing area. This is why I think the Jews did not realize in time what lay ahead of them. I still wonder today why the Jews did not try and do something about it. Masses kept on coming from the city to this place, which they apparently entered unsuspectingly, still under the impression that they were being resettled.

OPERATIONAL SITUATION REPORT USSR No. 97

The Chief of the Security   Berlin,
Police and Security Service   September 28, 1941
48 copies
(36th copy)
Operational Situation Report USSR No. 97

Einsatzgruppe C
Location: Kiev

Vorkommando 4a [operates] directly with the combat troops in Kiev since September 19. Einsatzgruppe HQ came up on September 24. Office Building NKVD, October 24th Street, assigned and commandeered as seat of Einsatzgruppe HQ. Building evacuated this morning to move into emergency quarters in the one-time tsar's castle. Town almost destroyed upon entry of troops. Numerous barricades and tank traps put up in main street. In addition, other strong defensive installations in the town area. On September 20, the citadel blew up and

the Artillery Commander and his chief of staff were killed. On September 24, violent explosions in the quarters of the Feldkommandatur; the ensuing fire has not yet been extinguished. Fire in the center of the town. Very valuable buildings destroyed. So far, fire fighting practically without any effect. Demolitions by blasting being carried out to bring the fire under control. Fire in the immediate neighborhood of this office. Had to be evacuated for this reason. Considerable damage done in and around the building by blasting. Blasts continuing. Also, fire breaking out. Up to now, 670 mines detected in buildings, according to a mine-laying plan which was discovered; all public buildings and squares are mined, among them, it is alleged, also the building assigned to this office for future use. Building being searched most assiduously. In the course of this search, sixty Molotov cocktails of explosives were detected and removed. In the Lenin Museum, seventy hundred weights of dynamite discovered which were to be touched off by wireless. It was repeatedly so observed that fires broke out the moment buildings were taken over.

As has been proved, Jews played a preeminent part. Allegedly 150,000 Jews living here. Verification of these statements has not been possible yet. In the course of the first action, 1,600 arrests, measures being evolved to check the entire Jewish population. Execution of at least 50,000 Jews planned. German Army welcomes measures and demands drastic proce-dure. Garrison commander advocates public execution of twenty Jews. A larger number of NKVD of finials, political commissary partisan leaders and partisans arrested. According to reliable information, demolition battalion of the NKVD and considerable number of NKVD men in Kiev. This morning, enemy plots detected. Contact established with German Army and authorities.

Participated preeminently in setting up town administration. Informants posted. Vorkommando of the Higher SS and Police Leaders arrived. Detailed reports to follow.

OPERATIONAL SITUATION REPORT USSR NO. 101

Chief of the Security Police
and Security Service
48 copies
(36th copy)
Operational Situation Report USSR No. 101

Berlin,
October 2, 1941

Einsatzgruppe C
Location: Kiev

Sonderkommando 4a in collaboration with Einsatzgruppe HQ and two kommandos of Police Regiment South, executed 33,771 Jews in Kiev on September 29 and 30, 1941.

Einsatzgruppe D
Location: Nikolayev

The kommandos continued the liberation of the area from Jews and Communist elements. In the period covered by the report, the towns of Nikolayev and Kherson in particular were freed of Jews. Remaining officials there were appropriately treated. From September 16 to 30, 22,467 Jews and Communists were executed. Total number, 35,782. Investigations again show that the high Communist officials everywhere have fled to safety. On the whole, leading partisans or leaders of sabotage detachments have been seized.

OPERATIONAL SITUATION REPORT USSR NO. 128

The Chief of the Security
Police and Security Service
50 copies
(50th copy)
Operational Situation Report USSR No. 128

Berlin
November 2, 1941

Einsatzgruppe C
Location: Kiev
Execution activities

As to purely execution matters, approximately 80,000 persons have been liquidated by now by the kommandos of the Einsatzgruppe.

Among these are approximately 8,000 persons convicted after investigation of anti-German or Bolshevist activities.

The remainder were liquidated in retaliatory actions.

Several retaliatory measures were carried out as large-scale actions. The largest of these actions took place immediately after the occupation of Kiev. It was carried out exclusively against Jews and their entire families.

The difficulties resulting from such a large-scale action, in particular concerning the round-up, were overcome in Kiev by requesting the Jewish population to assemble, using wall-posters. Although at first only the participation of approximately 5–6,000 Jews had been expected, more than 30,000 Jews arrived who, until the moment of their execution, still believed in their resettlement, thanks to extremely clever organization [propaganda]. Even though approximately 75,000 Jews have been liquidated in this manner, it is already evident at this time that this cannot be the best solution of the Jewish problem. Although we succeeded, particularly in smaller towns and villages, in bringing about a complete liquidation of the Jewish problem, nevertheless, again and again it has been observed in the larger cities that after such an action, all Jews have indeed been eradicated. But, when after a certain period of time a kommando returns, the number of Jews still found in the city always surpasses considerably the number of the executed Jews.

Besides, the kommandos have also carried out military actions in numerous cases. At the request of the army, separate platoons of the kommandos have repeatedly combed the woods searching for partisans, and have accomplished successful work there.

Besides, prisoners of war marching along the highways were systematically overtaken [by the kommandos of the EG]. All those elements were liquidated who did not possess identification papers and who were suspected, once set free, of [possibly] committing acts of sabotage against the German Army, the German authorities, or the population. In numerous cases, systematic searches for parachutists were carried out, with the result that approximately twenty parachutists were captured, among them a Russian who, at his interrogation, supplied extremely important information to the army.

Finally, it should be mentioned that prisoners of war were taken over from the prisoner assembly points and the prisoner-of-war transit camps, although, at times, considerable disagreements with the camp commander occurred.

COLLABORATION WITH THE WEHRMACHT AND THE SECRET FIELD POLICE

This concerns the relation of the Einsatzgruppe and its kommandos with other offices and authorities. Its relation to the army is especially noteworthy. From the outset, the Einsatzgruppe succeeded in establishing excellent terms with all army headquarters. This made it possible for the Einsatzgruppe never to operate in the rear of the military zone. On the contrary, the request was frequently made by the army to operate as far on the front as possible. In a great number of cases, it happened that the support of the Einsatzkommandos was requested by the fighting troops. Advance detachments of the Einsatzgruppe also participated in every large military action. They entered newly captured localities side by side with the fighting troops. Thus, in all cases, the utmost support was given. For example, in this connection, it is worth mentioning the participation in the capture of Zhitomir where the first tanks entering the city were immediately followed by three cars of Einsatzkommando 4a.

As a result of the successful work of the Einsatzgruppe, the Security Police is also held in high regard, in particular by the HQ of the German Army. The liaison officers stationed at Army HQ are loyally briefed on all military operations, and, besides, they receive the utmost cooperation. The commander of the 6th Army, General Field Marshal von Reichenau has repeatedly praised the work of the Einsatzkommandos and, accordingly, supported the interests of the SD with his staff. The extraordinary success of the kommandos was a contributing factor, for example, in the capture of Major-General Sokolov, the discovery of information concerning a plan by parachutists to blast a bridge, and the transmission of other important military information.

Only with respect to the Jewish problem could a complete understanding with junior army officers not be reached until quite recently. This was most noticeable during the taking over of prisoner-of-war camps. As a particularly clear example the conduct of a camp commander in Vinitsa is to be mentioned. He strongly objected to the transfer of 362 Jewish prisoners of war carried out by his deputy, and even started court martial proceedings against the deputy and two other officers. Unfortunately, it often occurred that the Einsatzkommandos had to suffer more or less hidden reproaches for their persistent stand on the Jewish problem. Another difficulty was added by the order from the Army High Command prohibiting entry by the SD into the POW transit camps. These difficulties have probably been overcome by now due to a new order from the Army High Command. This order clearly states that the Wehrmacht has to cooperate in the solution of this problem, and, in particular, that the necessary authorizations must he granted the SD to the fullest extent. However, it became evident in the in the past few days that this policy-making order still has not reached lower [military] authorities. In the future, further, cooperation and assistance by Wehrmact authorities can be expected. As far as the province of the 6th Army HQ is concerned, General Field Marshal von Reichenau issued an order on October 10, 1941, which states clearly that the Russian soldier has to he considered in principle to be a representative of Bolshevism and thus has to be treated accordingly by the Wehrmacht.

No difficulties whatsoever resulted from the cooperation with the Secret Military Police. To be sure, it was noted that the Security Military Police preferred to handle matters concerning the Security Police only, evidently because of a lack of other duties; however, these defects were always eliminated following consultation. Besides, the latest order of the chief of the Military Police has probably eliminated any remaining doubts. The exchange of informational material between the SD and the CFP took place without any disagreement. The original doubts whether the GFP would not retain some of the cases were not justified. Besides, it has already been ordered by Army HQ and its staff that matters concerning the Security Police have to be immediately transferred to the kommandos.

As for the counterintelligence offices in the rear, the work there is running smoothly. Counterintelligence officers regularly visit [EK Hqts] and kommandos in order to transfer files, as well as to receive orders.

Since the work of the Security Police has been carried out smoothly and has won high recognition, it can be assumed that this pleasant relationship will also be maintained in the future.

An Affadavit by Paul Blobel on the Burning of Bodies and Obliterating the Traces of Bodies of Jews Killed by the Einsatzgruppen

AFFIDAVIT

I, Paul Blobel, swear, declare and state in evidence:

1. I was born in Potsdam on August 13, 1894. From June 1941 to January 1942 I was the commander of Sonderkommando 4 A.
2. After I had been released from this command, I was to report in Berlin to SS Obergruppenführer Heydrich and Gruppenführer Müller, and in June 1942 I was entrusted by Gruppenführer Müller with the task of obliterating the traces of executions carried out by the Einsatzgruppen in the East. My orders were that I should report in person to the commanders of the Security Police and SD, pass on Müller's orders verbally, and supervise their implementation. This order was top secret and Gruppenführer Müller had given orders that owing to the need for strictest secrecy there was to be no correspondence in connection with this task. In September 1942 I reported to Dr. Thomas in Kiev and passed the order on to him. The order could not be carried out immediately, partly because Dr. Thomas was disinclined to carry it out, and also because the materials required for the burning of the bodies was not available. In May and June 1943 I

The ravine at Babi Yar near Kiev where 33,771 Jews were killed on September 29–30, 1941. Archiv Ernst Klee.

made additional trips to Kiev in this matter and then, after conversations with Dr. Thomas and with SS and Police Leader Hennecke, the order was carried out.

3. During my visit in August I myself observed the burning of bodies in a mass grave near Kiev. This grave was about 55 m. long, 3 m. wide and 2½ m. deep. After the top had been removed the bodies were covered with inflammable material and ignited. It took about two days until the grave burned down to the bottom. I myself observed that the fire had glowed down to the bottom. After that the grave was filled in and the traces were now practically obliterated.

4. Owing to the moving up of the front line it was not possible to destroy the mass graves farther south and east which had resulted from executions by the Einsatzgruppen. I traveled to Berlin in connection to this report, and was then sent to Estonia by Gruppenführer Müller. I passed on the same orders to Oberführer Achammer-Pierader in Riga, and also to Obergruppenführer Jeckeln.

I returned to Berlin in order to obtain fuel. The burning of the bodies began only in May or June 1944. I remember that incinerations took place in the area of Riga and Reval. I was present at such incinerations near Reval, but the graves were smaller here and contained only about twenty to thirty bodies. The graves in the area of Reval were about 20 or 30 kms. east of the city in a marshy district and I think that four or five such graves were opened and the bodies burned.

5. According to my orders I should have extended my duties over the entire area occupied by the Einsatzgruppen, but owing to the retreat from Russia I could not carry out my orders completely....

I have made this deposition of my own free will, without any kind of promise of reward, and I was not subjected to any form of compulsion or threat.

Nuremberg, June 18, 1947
SIGNED PAUL BLOBEL

THE BLACK BOOK

THE RUTHLESS MURDER OF JEWS BY GERMAN-FASCIST INVADERS

Kiev, Babi Yar.

... At dawn of September 29 Kiev's Jews were moving slowly along the streets in the direction of the Jewish Cemetery on Lukyanovka from various parts of the city. Many of them thought they were to be sent to provincial towns, but others realized that Babi Yar meant death. There were many suicides on that day.

Families baked bread for the journey, sewed knapsacks, rented wagons and two-wheeled carts. Old men and women supported each other while mothers carried their babies in their arms or pushed baby carriages. People were carrying sacks, packages, suitcases, boxes. Children were at their parents' side. Young people took nothing along, but elderly people tried to take as much with them from home as possible. Pale sighing old women were led by their grandchildren. The paralyzed and ill were borne on stretchers, blankets, and sheets.

Streams of people flowed into the endless human current on Lvov Street, while German patrols stood on the sidewalks. So enormous was the mass of people moving along the pavement from early morning until late at night that it was difficult to cross from one side of the street to the other. This procession of death continued for three days and three nights. People walked, stopping once in a while, embraced each other without words, said good-bye, and prayed. The town fell silent. Crowds of people flowed from Pavlovskaya Street, Dmitrievskaya Street, Volodarskaya and Nekrasovskaya Streets into Lvov Street, like streams into a river. Lvov Street led to Melnik Street, which led to a barren road through naked hills to the sheer ravines of Babi Yar. As the people approached Babi Yar the din of angry voices, groans and sobs grew louder.

Dmitry Orlov, an old resident of Kiev, watched the execution from the area of the Cable Factory. He was unable to look at the terrible picture more than for a few minutes and fled, overcome by dizziness.

An entire office operation with desks had been set up in an open area. The crowd waiting at the barriers erected by the Germans at the end of the street could not see the desks. Thirty to forty persons at a time were separated from the crowd and led under armed guard for "registration." Documents and valuables were taken away. The documents were immediately thrown to the ground, and witnesses have testified that the square was covered with a thick layer of discarded papers, torn passports, and union identification cards. Then the Germans forced everyone to strip naked: girls, women, children, old men. No exceptions were made. Their clothing was gathered up and carefully folded. Rings were ripped from the fingers of the naked men and women, and these doomed people were forced to stand at the edge of a deep ravine, where the executioners shot them at point-blank range. The bodies fell over the cliff, and small children were thrown in alive. Many went insane when they reached the place of execution.

Many Kievans did not know until the last minute what the Germans were doing in Babi Yar. Some said that this was a labor mobilization. Others believed that it was a resettlement. Still others claimed that the German High Command had arranged an exchange with a Soviet commission: one Jewish family for each captured German.

Tamara Mikhasev, a young Russian woman whose Jewish husband was a commander in the Red Army, also went to Babi Yar, planning to pass herself off as Jewish. She hoped to be exchanged and find her husband on free Soviet territory.

Tamara came to her senses only after she passed through the fence. First she got into line to hand in her belongings and then in another line to be registered. Next to her stood a tall woman with an ostrich plume in her hat, a young woman with a boy, and a tall broad-shouldered man.

The man picked up the boy.

Mikhasev walked up to them, and the man looked at her and asked:

"Are you a Jew?"

"My husband is Jewish."

"You should leave if you're not Jewish," he said. "Wait here and we'll leave together."

He picked up the boy again, kissed his eyes, and said farewell to his wife and mother-in-law. Then he said something abrupt and commanding in German, and the guard moved aside the board. The man was a Russified German and had accompanied his wife, son, and mother-in-law to Babi Yar. Mrs. Mikhasev left with him.

From the direction of Babi Yar could be heard the barking of many dogs, the crackle of automatic-rifle fire, and the cries of the dying. The crowd moved toward them, and the road was packed. Loud speakers bellowed dance melodies which drowned out the screams of the victims.

The following is the testimony of those who miraculously escaped: Nesya Elgort (40 Saksagansky Street) was moving toward the ravine pressing her trembling son Ilya to her naked body. Carrying her son in her arms, she walked up to the edge of the ravine. In only partial control of her senses, she heard the shooting and the death cries, and she fell. Untouched by the bullets, she lay under a heap of warm bloody bodies. All around hundreds and thousands of bodies lay piled on top of each other. The bodies of old men rested on the bodies of children who lay on the bodies of their dead mothers.

"It is now difficult for me to understand how I got out of that ravine of death," Nesya Elgort recalled, "but I crawled out, driven by an instinct for self-preservation. That evening I found myself in the Podol district with my son Ilya beside me. Truly, I cannot understand what miracle saved my son. It was as if he became part of me and didn't leave me for one second. I was taken in for the night by a Russian woman in Podol. I don't remember her surname, but her first name and patronymic was Marya Grigorievna. She helped me reach Saksagansky Street in the morning."

Another woman who was saved from death in Babi Yar was Yelena Yefimovna Borodyansky-Knysh. She arrived at Babi Yar carrying her child in her arms. It was already dark: "Along the way they added about one hundred and fifty people to our group—maybe more. I'll never forget one girl, Sara; she was about fifteen years old. I can't describe how beautiful she was. Her mother was pulling her own hair and screaming in a heartrending voice: 'Kill us together....' The mother was killed with a rifle butt, but they weren't in any hurry with the girl. Five or six Germans stripped her naked, but I didn't see what happened after that. I didn't see.

"They took our clothing, confiscating all our possessions, and led us about fifty meters away, where they took our documents, money, rings, earrings. They wanted to remove the gold teeth of one old man, and he tried to resist. Then one of the Germans grabbed him by the beard and threw him on the ground. There were tufts of beard in the German's hand, and the old man was covered with blood. When my child saw this, she started to cry.

"'Don't take me there, Mama. Look, they're killing the old man.'

"'Don't shout, sweety, because if you shout, we won't be able to run away, and the Germans will kill us.'

"She was a patient child, so she kept quiet, but she was shaking all over. She was four years old then. Everyone was stripped naked, but since I wore only old underwear, I didn't have to take it off.

"At about midnight the command was given in German for us to line up. I didn't wait for the next command, but threw my girl into the ditch and fell on top of her. A second later bodies started falling on me. Then everything fell silent. There were more shots, and again bloody dying and dead people began falling into the pit.

"I sensed that my daughter wasn't moving. I leaned up against her, covering her with my body. To keep her from suffocating, I made fists out of my hands and put them under her chin. She stirred. I tried to raise my body to keep from crushing her. The execution had been going on since 9:00 A.M. and there was blood all over the place. We were sandwiched between bodies.

"I felt someone walk across the bodies and swear in German. A German soldier was checking with a bayonet to make sure no one was still alive. By chance he was standing on me, so the bayonet blow passed me.

"When he left, I raised my head. The Germans were quarreling over the booty.

"I freed myself, got up, and took my unconscious daughter in my arms. I walked along the ravine. When I had put a kilometer between us and the execution spot, I sensed that my daughter was barely breathing. There was no water anywhere, so I wet her lips with my own saliva. I walked another kilometer and began to gather dew from the grass to moisten the child's mouth. Little by little she started to regain consciousness.

"I rested and moved on. Crawling my way over the ravines, I made my way to the village of Babi Yar. I entered the yard of the brick factory and hid in the basement. I remained there four days without any food or clothing. I would come out into the yard only at night to forage in the garbage can.

"My child and I both started to swell. I was no longer able to understand what was happening. Machine guns were firing somewhere. On the night of the fifth day I crept into an attic where I found a very worn knit skirt and two old blouses. I used one of the blouses as a dress for my little girl. I went then to Litoshenko, an acquaintance of mine. She was petrified when she saw me. She gave me a skirt and a dress and hid both me and my girl. I spent a week locked up in her house. She gave me some money to take with me, and I went to another acquaintance, Fenya Pliuyko, who also helped me a lot. Her husband died at the front. I spent a month at her apartment. Her neighbors didn't know me, and when they asked about me, Fenya said I was her sister-in-law from the village. After that I moved in with Shkuropadsky and I spent two weeks with her. But since everyone in the Podol district knew me, I couldn't go out in the daytime."

Dmitry Pasichny hid behind a gravestone at the Jewish Cemetery and saw the Germans shoot the Jews.

Pasichny's wife, Polina, and her mother, Yevgeniya Abramovna Shevelev, were Jewish. He hid both of them in a closet and spread the rumor that they had gone to the cemetery. Then both women were taken into the priest's house of the Pokrovskaya Church in Podol. The priest of that church, Glagolev, was the son of the priest who testified in the Beylis Trial. [Mendel Beylis was a Kievan Jew who was falsely accused of having murdered a Russian boy in 1913 for a religious ritual. He was acquitted.] Glagolev permitted Pasichny's wife to live in the rectory until August of 1942, and then he took her to Kamenets-Podolsk. Father Glagolev also saved many other Jews who turned to him for help.

The Germans and their (Ukrainian) policemen combed the countryside for new victims. Hundreds of Jews who had succeeded in avoiding execution in Babi Yar perished in their apartments, in the waters of the Dnieper, in the ravines of Pechersk and Demievka, on the city streets. The Germans were suspicious of anyone who looked like a Jew, and the documents of such persons were carefully checked. A single denunciation was sufficient to have anyone under suspicion shot. The Germans not only searched apartments, but also inspected cellars and caves, and even used explosives to blast open floors, suspicious walls, attics, and chimneys.

A handful of Kiev's Jews survived Babi Yar and have been preserved by fate so that mankind could hear the truth from the lips of victims and witnesses.

Two years later, when the Red Army was approaching the Dnieper, an order came from Berlin to destroy the bodies of the Jews buried in Babi Yar.

Vladimir Davydov, a prisoner in the Syrets Camp, related how the Germans realized they would have to give up Kiev and how, in the fall of 1943, they frantically covered up the evidence of the mass executions in Babi Yar.

On August 18, 1943, the Germans took three hundred prisoners from the Syrets Camp and shackled them in leg irons. Everyone in camp realized that some particularly important job lay ahead. This group of prisoners was accompanied only by regular officers and noncommissioned officers of the SS. The prisoners were taken from camp and transported to dark earthen bunkers surrounded by barbed wire. Germans stood duty day and night in machine-gun towers next to the bunkers. On August 19 the prisoners were led from the bunkers and taken under heavy guard to Babi Yar. There they were issued shovels. It was only then that the prisoners realized that they had been assigned the terrible job of digging up the bodies of the Jews shot by the Germans at the end of September 1941.

When the prisoners stripped off the upper layer of earth, they saw tens of thousands of bodies. The prisoner Gayevsky went mad. Since the bodies had been lying in the ground for a long time, they had fused together and had to be separated with poles. From 4:00 A.M. till late at night Vladimir Davydov and his comrades labored in Babi Yar. The Germans forced the prisoners to burn what was left of the bodies. Thousands of bodies were heaped on stacks of firewood and soaked with petrol. Enormous fires burned day and night. More than seventy thousand bodies were fed to the fire. The Germans forced the prisoners to grind up the remaining bones with large rollers, mix them with sand, and scatter them in the surrounding areas. During this terrible labor Himmler, the head of the Gestapo, came to inspect the quality of the work.

On September 28, 1943, when the destruction of the evidence was almost completed, the Germans ordered the prisoners to heat up the ovens again. The prisoners realized that they themselves were to be murdered. The Germans wanted to kill and then burn up the last living witnesses. Davydov had found a pair of rusty scissors in the pocket of a dead woman, and he used them to unlock his leg irons. The other prisoners followed suit. At dawn on September 29, 1943—exactly two years after the mass murder of Kiev's Jews—Germany's new victims rushed from their earthen bunkers toward the cemetery wall with a shout of "Hurrah!" Caught totally by surprise by the sudden escape, the SS men failed to open fire immediately with their machine guns. They did kill 280 persons. Vladimir Davydov and eleven other persons managed to climb the wall and escape. They were harbored by residents of Kiev's suburbs. Later Davydov was able to leave Kiev and lived in the village of Varovichi.

Not all the bodies were burned, and not all the bones were ground up; there were too many of them. Anyone who comes to Babi Yar—even now—will see fragments of skulls, bones mixed with coals. He might find a shoe with a decayed human foot, slippers, galoshes, rags, scarves, children's toys. And he will see the cast-iron grates ripped from the cemetery fence. It was this fence that provided the grates on which the exhumed bodies of the murdered were heaped for burning in those terrible September days of 1941.

(Source: This article is based on documental materials and testimony of Kievans. Prepared for publication by Lev Ozerov.)

XII. THE CALL TO ARMS

Jews fought the Nazis in the forests of the eastern Europe and in the ghettos of Poland; they fought as part of the Marquis in France and with Tito in Yugoslavia; they took up arms alone in Poland, and resisted alongside Soviet partisans.

Even in the death camps of Birkenau, Treblinka, and Sobibor, Jews resisted with arms; crematoria were blown up, escapes were organized.

Armed resistance was not the first response to Nazi oppression. Jews were more practiced in the art of spiritual resistance, thwarting Nazi intentions by nonviolent means, by

Ruins of crematorium No. II at Birkenau (Auschwitz II). Main Commission for the Investigation of Nazi Crimes/Courtesy of USHMM–Photo Archives.

less than all-out confrontation. Courage in the face of death—and valor—took many forms. It took courage—a different kind of courage—for a father to stay with his children and try to protect them for as long as possible and to remain with them even to the gas chamber. It took courage for Janusz Korczak, Poland's Mr. Rogers and Dr. Spock, to stay with the children in his orphanage and to march with them to the deportation point, refusing all entreaties that a man of his talents seek personal safety in hiding. So it was not for lack of courage that he did not join the resistance.

Jews fought against impossible odds. Unlike classical guerrilla fighters, Jews were often immobile. Confined to ghettos, they were captive and vulnerable to retaliation. Anti-Semitism was widespread, therefore Jewish resistance did not enjoy popular support. The Jewish fighters could not disappear among the Polish population. They were subject to betrayal. The ghettos in which they fought were subject to collective reprisals, collective responsibility. All could be killed for the decisions of a few.

Arms were difficult and dangerous to obtain; they had to be purchased and smuggled, pistol by pistol, rifle by rifle. Material assistance was not available from the Allies or even from underground armies in Poland.

Armed resistance was an act of desperation. It erupted when Jews understood Nazi intentions, when hope of survival had been abandoned. The motivation of the fighters was to protect Jewish honor, to avenge Jewish death. The call to arms in Bialystok read:

> Even if we are too weak to defend our lives, we are strong enough to defend Jewish honor and human dignity, and thus prove to the world that we are captive, but not defeated. Do not go freely to your death! Fight with your life until your last breath. . . . Make your enemies pay with blood for blood and death for death.

From 1942 to 1943, Jews took up arms in the ghettos when liquidation was imminent at a time when death camps were in full operation to keep pace with ghetto liquidations.

In one hundred ghettos in Poland, Lithuania, Byelorussia, and the Ukraine, underground organizations were formed whose purpose was to wage armed struggle. They had little hope for survival, less hope for victory; resistance was waged for its own sake.

The patterns of ghetto revolts differed. Young people, trained in Zionist or communist youth movements led the revolts. Jews could not fight together because their images of a future they would not live to see differed. Prewar politics continued to divide the fighters. Revisionists formed separate units. As a rule, Bundists and the Orthodox did not participate; the former because they would not cooperate with the Zionists, the latter because they would be forced to cooperate with secularists and sinners, antithetical to their values. The underground was at odds with those Jewish Councils that believed that the ghetto would survive because of the utility of its labor.

In Czestochowa, the revolt broke out on June 25, 1943. Planning had begun ten months earlier. In the summer of 1942, during the deportations, a decision was reached to create a Jewish fighting organization. During the winter deportation, resistance sprung into action; twenty-five Jews were executed, three hundred more were arrested. During the winter, weapons and chemicals for grenades were acquired. The arsenal, thirty grenades, eighteen revolvers, two rifles were turned over to the neighboring partisans for support, but to no avail.

In Bedzin and Sosnowiec, the revolt commenced on August 1. Bialystok rose in rebellion on August 6, 1943. It took several days to bring the ghetto under control. In September, Tarnow revolted.

In Lithuania and Byelorussia, ghetto residents faced a third choice between submission and full-scale revolt. Dense forests surrounded some ghettos; forests to which the population could flee.

Perhaps the most famous and most instructive document relating to resistance was authored by Abba Kovner, who was a leader of the resistance in Vilna, and later achieved added fame as a leader of *Bricha*, the attempt to bring Jews after the war from Soviet-held territories to American- and British-held territories, and thus eventually to Palestine. Kovner later became a figure in Israel comparable in stature to Elie Wiesel in the United States.

From a clandestine meeting in a convent on December 31, 1942, three weeks before the Wannsee Conference at which German leadership was informed of the decision to kill all Jews and practical steps toward the implementation of this decision were taken, Kovner wrote a public call for resistance:

> Jewish youth, do not believe those that are trying to deceive you. Out of eighty thousand Jews of Vilna only twenty thousand are left. Where are our own brethren from other ghettos? Those taken through the gate of the ghetto will never return. All the Gestapo roads lead to Ponary and Ponary means death. Let us not be led like sheep to the slaughter. True we are weak and helpless, but the only response to the murders is self defense. Brethren, it is better to die fighting like free men than to live at the mercy of the murderers. To defend oneself to the last breath. Take Courage!

> Manifesto of Zionist Youth
> by Abba Kovner
> December 31, 1941

Resistance began toward the end, after the major deportations. Vilna's prewar Jewish population was reduced from eighty thousand to twenty thousand people. Even then, armed resistance did not begin for another twenty-one months until the ghetto was on the verge of extinction.

Resistance only enjoyed popular support when the true nature of German intentions was understood. "All the Gestapo roads lead to Ponary, [the forest some seven miles outside of the city] and Ponary means death."

Resistance undermined traditional authority. "Do not believe those that are trying to deceive you."

It appealed to honor and revenge. It criticized those who went before. "Let us not walk like sheep to the slaughter."

Resistance was a choice between forms of dying, a choice between death and death. "To defend oneself to the last breath."

In the readings that follow, we will read of the call for resistance in Bialystok and Warsaw—late calls. The appeal in Warsaw was made after the great deportation of Jews to Treblinka, the appeal in Bialystok was made after they understood that "five million European Jews" had been murdered. The calls came many months after Gerhard Riegner had cabled secret information about the death camps to the West.

The calls are dramatically similar. There is a realization of impending death, anger at those who went to their deaths without resisting: "Know that escape is not be found walking to your death passively, like sheep to the slaughter," the Warsaw call proclaims. "Jews, we are being led to Treblinka! Like mangy animals we will be gassed and cremated. Let us not passively go to the slaughter like sheep," they proclaim in Bialystok. They are angry at Jewish leaders. Traitors, they call them in Warsaw. In Bialystok, they say: "Do not believe that labor will save you, for after the first liquidation, there will be a second and a third." Honor, strength, valor, war are the alternative values.

We will also read the calls that were issued in Vilna; first on January 1, 1942, and the battle orders of April 1943, and the manifesto of the uprising in September 1943.

In each, the choice was no longer how to live, but what statement to make with the fact of impending death.

CALL FOR RESISTANCE BY THE JEWISH MILITARY ORGANIZATION IN THE WARSAW GHETTO

JANUARY 1943

We are rising up for war!

We are of those who have set themselves the aim of awakening the people. Our wish is to take this watchword to our people:

Awake and fight! Do not despair of the road to escape!

Know that escape is not to be found by walking to your death passively, like sheep to the slaughter. It is to be found in something much greater: in war!

Whoever defends himself has a chance of being saved! Whoever gives up self-defense from the outset—he has lost already!

Nothing awaits him except only a hideous death in the suffocation machine of Treblinka.

Let the people awaken to war!

Find the courage in your soul for desperate action!

Put an end to our terrible acceptance of such phrases as: We are all under sentence of death!

It is a lie!!!

We also were destined to live! We too have a right to life! One only needs to know how to fight for it!

It is no great art to live when life is given to you willingly! But there is an art to life just when they are trying to rob you of this life.

Let the people awaken and fight for its life!

Let every mother be a lioness defending her young!

Let no father stand by and see the blood of his children in silence!

Let not the first act of our destruction be repeated! An end to despair and lack of faith!

An end to the spirit of slavery amongst us!

Let the tyrant pay with the blood of his body for every soul in Israel! Let every house become a fortress for us!

Let the People awaken to war!

In war lies your salvation!

Whoever defends himself has a hope of escape!

We are rising in the name of the war for the lives of the helpless masses whom we seek to save, whom we must arouse to action!

It is not for ourselves alone that we wish to fight. We will be entitled to save ourselves only when we have completed our duty! As long as the life of a Jew is still in danger, even one, single life, we have to be ready to fight!!!!

Our watchword is: Not even one more Jew is to find his end in Treblinka! Out with the traitors to the people!

War for life or death on the conqueror to our last breath!

Be prepared to act!
Be ready!

(Source: The appeal is attributed to the Jewish Military Organization, Zydowski Zwiazek Wojskowy [ZZW])

"AN APPEAL"

BIALYSTOK GHETTO RESISTANCE ORGANIZATION

AUGUST 15, 1943

Fellow Jews!

Fearsome days have come upon us. More than the ghetto and the yellow badge, hatred, humiliation and degradation—we now face death! Before our own eyes our wives and children, fathers and mothers, brothers and sisters are being led to the slaughter. Thousands have already gone; tens of thousands will shortly follow.

In these terrible hours, as we hover between life and death, we appeal to you as follows:

BE AWARE—five million European Jews have already been murdered by Hitler and his hangmen. All that remains of Polish Jewry is about 10 percent of the original Jewish community. In Chelmno and in Belzec, in Auschwitz and in Treblinka, in Sobibor and in other camps more than three million Polish Jews were tortured, suffering the most gruesome deaths.

BE AWARE—all those deported are going to their deaths! Do not believe the Gestapo propaganda about letters supposedly received from the evacuees. THAT IS A DAMNABLE LIE! The road on which the deportees have gone leads to gigantic crematoria and mass graves in the thicket of the Polish forests. Each one of us is condemned. We have nothing to lose!

Do not believe that labor will save you, for after the first liquidation there will be a second and a third—UNTIL THE LAST JEW IS KILLED!

Dividing the ghetto into various categories is a sophisticated Gestapo method of deceiving us and making their dirty work easier.

Jews, we are being led to Treblinka! Like mangy animals we will be gassed and cremated.

Let us not passively go to the slaughter like sheep! Even though we are too weak to defend our lives, still we are strong enough to preserve our Jewish honor and human dignity by showing the world that although we are in shackles, we have not yet fallen. DO NOT GO TO YOUR DEATH WILLINGLY!

Fight for your lives until your last breath! With tooth and nail, with axes and knives, with acid and iron we will greet our hangmen. Let the enemy pay for blood with blood! THEIR DEATH FOR OUR DEATH!

Will you cower in your corners when your nearest and dearest are humiliated and put to death? Will you sell your wives and children, your parents, your soul, for another few weeks of slavery?

Let us ambush the enemy, kill and disarm him, wage resistance against the murderers. And if necessary—DIE LIKE HEROES!

Except for our honor we have nothing to lose! DO NOT SELL YOUR LIVES CHEAPLY!

AVENGE the destroyed communities and uprooted settlements! When you leave your home—set fire to your households, burn and demolish the factories!

Do not let the hangmen inherit our possessions!

Jewish youth! Follow the example of generations of Jewish fighters and martyrs, dreamers and builders, pioneers and activists—go out and fight!

Hitler will lose the war. Slavery and murder will vanish from the face of the earth. The world will one day be cleansed and purified. For the sake of mankind's bright future—you must not die like dirty dogs! To the forest, to the resistance, fighters!

Do not flee the ghetto unarmed, for without weapons you will perish. Only after fulfilling your national obligation, go to the forest armed. Weapons can be seized from any German in the ghetto.

BE STRONG!

THE PROCLAMATION OF THE VILNA GHETTO RESISTANCE ORGANIZATION
JANUARY 1, 1942

Jewish youth!

Do not trust those who are trying to deceive you. Out of the eighty thousand Jews in the "Jerusalem of Lithuania" only twenty thousand are left. Before our eyes they took away our parents, our brothers and sisters. Where are the hundreds of men who were conscripted for labor? Where are the naked women and the children who were taken away from us on that dreadful night? Where are the Jews who were deported on Yom Kippur?

And where are our brethren in the second Ghetto?

Of those taken out through the gates of the Ghetto not a single one has returned. All the roads of the Gestapo lead to Ponar. And Ponar means death.

You who hesitate, cast aside all illusions. Your children, your wives and husbands are no longer alive.

Ponar is not a concentration camp. They have all been shot there. Hitler plans to destroy all the Jews of Europe, and the Jews of Lithuania have been chosen as the first in line.

We will not be led like sheep to the slaughter!

True, we are weak and defenseless, but the only reply to the murderer is revolt!

Brothers! Better to fall as free fighters than to live by the mercy of the murderers.

Arise! Arise with your last breath!

Ruins of crematorium No. III Birkenau (Auschwitz II). Main Commission for the Investigation of Nazi Crimes/Courtesy of USHMM–Photo Archives.

BATTLE ORDERS OF THE FPO (*FAREINIKTE PARTIZANER ORGANIZATZIE*)
APRIL 4, 1943

1. GENERAL

1. The fight we are about to start will serve as a touchstone of the moral and physical qualities of the FPO fighter and his individual ability to hold out and endure.
2. We shall have to go into battle after severe nervous strain, in an atmosphere of panic, after serious blows which the FPO may suffer even before the battle starts.
3. The FPO fighter must not lose his sangfroid under the most difficult battle conditions, and he must never recoil from personal danger.
4. Every company commander and every fighter must prepare for battle by undergoing conditions as close as possible to the future reality of battle, so that he should not be stunned or overwhelmed, so that a man who has never fired in his life should not panic at the sound of his own shots.
5. This will be achieved by continual training and careful thought to describe to every individual every possible situation he may face in the moment of battle.

3. AUTOMATIC MOBILIZATION

32. In case the command is put out of action for unforeseen reasons, the FPO

organization must carry out automatic mobilization.

33. What is the situation which calls for automatic mobilization? If the ghetto is suddenly endangered, if the population is gripped by panic, and that is accompanied by flight to places of concealment; that will be a "special situation."

34. In such a case, every FPO fighter must report to his post, ready for orders from the command, without waiting for a mobilization order ...

4. INDEPENDENT ACTION BEFORE BATTLE

42. If the command is arrested, the leadership of the FPO will be taken over by the deputy command, which will act according to prearranged orders ...

50. The battle must continue whatever the number of fighters, irrespective of the quantity of ammunition in their possession.

57. In time of danger, every member of the FPO must give an example of courage and heroism, arousing the largest possible number of men, by deed and word, to fight.

58. If the command falls into the hands of the Gestapo and all attempts to save it fail to succeed, the struggle must continue and the FPO be led independently into battle ...

SUPPLEMENT TO THE STANDING ORDERS

C. Should We Go Immediately to the Forests?

19. No. The desire to go to the forests immediately shows a lack of understanding of the FPO's ideas.

20. The idea of the Jewish United Partisans' Organization is national and social: to organize the struggle of the Jews and protect their lives and their honor.

22. We shall go to the forests only as the result of battle. After we carry out our mission, we shall take with us as large a number of Jews as possible and move to the forests, where we shall continue our struggle with the murderous occupant as part of the general partisan movement.

THE MANIFESTO OF THE COMMAND OF THE JEWISH UNITED PARTISANS ORGANIZATION, FPO, IN THE VILNA GHETTO

SEPTEMBER 1, 1943

Jews! Rise up in arms!

The German and Lithuanian butchers have reached the gates of the ghetto. They are going to murder us. Very soon they will lead us out through the gates in groups. So hundreds were led out on Yom Kippur. So they led people out in the days of the white, yellow, and pink *Scheine* [certificates]. So they led out our brothers and sisters, fathers and mothers, our children. So tens of thousands were led out to death.

But we will not go!

We will not be led like sheep to the slaughter.

Jews! Rise up in arms!

Do not believe in misleading promises of the murderers. Do not believe the traitors. For those led out through the gates of the ghetto there is only one destination: Ponar. And Ponar means death.

Jews! We have nothing to lose! Death will overtake us in any case. For who can still believe that he will live when the murderer is systematically taking our lives. The hands of the hangmen will overtake everyone. Concealment and cowardice will not save our lives.

Only by rising up in arms can we save our lives and our honor.

Brothers! Better to die fighting in the ghetto than be led like sheep to Ponar.

Let it be known: within the walls of the ghetto there is an organized Jewish force that will rise up with weapon in hand.

Join in the armed uprising!

Don't hide away in the bunkers, for in the end you will fall like mice into the murderers' hands. Jews! Go out into the streets in your masses!

If you have no arms, take hold of a pick, and if you have no pick, take hold of an iron bar, a stick.

For our parents, for our murdered children, for Ponar, strike at the murderers—in every street, in every yard, in every room in the ghetto and outside the ghetto. Beat the dogs!

Jews! We have nothing to lose. We can save our lives only by killing the murderers.

Long live freedom! Long live the armed uprising! Death to the murderers.

XIII. HITLER'S PLAN TO EXTERMINATE THE JEWS

When was the decision to murder all the Jews made?

Is it possible that Hitler's determination to kill all Jews evolved in a seamless progression from *Mein Kampf* onward? After all, Hitler indicated his goals and when opportunity made it possible, he carried out his plans. As early as 1919 he wrote: "Rational anti-Semitism must lead to systematic legal opposition. Its final objective must be the removal of the Jews altogether." We will read in this section three such statements by Adolf Hitler.

Adolf Hitler in the courtyard of Landsberg prison. The signature on the photograph is in Hitler's own hand. Landsberg, Germany. June 22, 1924. Bundesarchiv/Courtesy of USHMM–Photo Archives.

The first in a speech excerpted to the Reichstag on January 30, 1939, celebrating the sixth anniversary of his ascent to power; the second in 1942 when he reiterated his "prophecy" and spoke of his achievement; and the third, his final will and testament just prior to his suicide when the fallen leader charges his people to continue the struggle against the Jews.

Yet, the policy of genocide evolved over time. Until 1939, the basic aim of Nazi policy was the forced emigration of Jews. This policy failed as few countries were willing to offer the Jews a haven, and the expansion of the Reich brought more and more Jews under its control. Between 1933 and 1938, only 150,000 Jews had left Germany. When Austria joined the Reich in March 1938, its Jewish population was more than 200,000. With the conquest of Poland in September 1939, more than two million Jews came under German control. As Germany advanced eastward and westward, more Jews came under their control. Emigration would not work.

When the Germans invaded the Soviet Union in June 1941, the killing of Jews began immediately. The operations of the mobile killing units were planned well in advance of invasion. A decision to kill the Jews had been made—but was it some Jews or all?

By the summer of 1941, only months into the Soviet invasion, the infrastructure for the annihilation—the massive killing centers—was set in place. These were operational actions implementing a decision that had already been made.

The Wannsee Conference of January 20, 1942, produced the announcement of a policy decision—the Final Solution to the Jewish Problem—which was already in effect. Reinhold Heydrich, head of the SS Reich Security Main Office, invited the state secretaries of the most important government ministries to a villa in the affluent Berlin lake area named Wannsee. More than half of the fifteen invited guests held doctorates from German universities. They were well informed about the Jewish policy and the agencies they represented—the Department of Justice; the Foreign Ministry; the Gestapo; the SS Police; the Race and Resettlement Office; Hitler's office; the Nazi Party; the General Government; the Polish occupation administration, whose territory included more than two million Jews; and the office in charge of distributing Jewish property—were all essential to the implementation of so bold a policy. The director of Heydrich's Jewish Office, Adolf Eichmann, was present and prepared the conference protocols. He was later to testify about Wannsee at his trial in Jerusalem. The agenda was put forward by Heydrich.

> Another possible solution of the [Jewish] problem has now taken the place of emigra-tion, i.e. evacuation of the Jews to the East. . . . Such activities are, however, to be considered as provisional actions, but practical experience is already being collected, which is of greatest importance in relation to the future Final Solution of the Jewish problem.

Those at the conference fully understood the circumspect language. "Evacuation . . . to the East" was a euphemism for concentration camps, and "the Final Solution" really meant systematic murder. Some methods had already been tested. Since June, mobile killing units, Einsatzgruppen, had been hard at work killing hundreds of thousands of Jews in the East. Gas vans had been operating since December 8, 1941, at the Chelmno death camp. A farmhouse at Auschwitz/Birkenau was being converted into a gas cham-ber. Gas chambers using carbon monoxide from engine exhaust were under construction at the Belzec death camp. Experimentation with Cyclon-B had begun at Auschwitz. They spoke of eleven million Jews.

Within months of this meeting, three new killing centers—Belzec, Sobibor, and Treblinka—were in operation. They joined Auschwitz/Birkenau, Majdanek, and Chelmno. And the murder of Jews held in the ghettos had begun.

And in the end, on the eve of his own death, Hitler wrote two wills; one a private will, leaving his possessions, speaking of his wife. The other was a political document handing over the reins of power to his successors, rewarding those who were loyal and expelling those who were not. His final words were a warning to the German people about the threat of the Jews: "Above all, I enjoin the government and the people to uphold the race laws to the limit and to resist mercilessly the poisoner of all nations, international Jewry."

EXCERPTS FROM ADOLF HITLER'S SPEECH TO THE REICHSTAG

JANUARY 30, 1939

. . . In connection with the Jewish question I have this to say: it is a shameful spectacle to see how the whole democratic world is oozing sympathy for the poor tormented Jewish people, but remains hard-hearted and obdurate when it comes to helping them—which is surely, in view of its attitude, an obvious duty. The arguments that are brought up as an excuse for not helping them actually speak for us Germans and Italians.

For this is what they say:

1. "We," that is the democracies, "are not in a position to take in the Jews." Yet in these empires there are not even 10 people to the square kilometer. While Germany, with her 135 inhabitants to the square kilometer, is supposed to have room for them!
2. They assure us: We cannot take them unless Germany is prepared to allow them a certain amount of capital to bring with them as immigrants.

For hundreds of years Germany was good enough to receive these elements, although they possessed nothing except infectious political and physical diseases. What they possess today, they have by a very large extent gained at the cost of the less astute German nation by the most reprehensible manipulations.

Today we are merely paying this people what it deserves. When the German nation was, thanks to the inflation instigated and carried through by Jews, deprived of the entire savings which it had accumulated in years of honest work, when the rest of the world took away the German nation's foreign investments, when we were divested of the whole of our colonial possessions, these philanthropic considerations evidently carried little noticeable weight with democratic statesmen.

Today I can only assure these gentlemen that, thanks to the brutal education with which the democracies favored us for fifteen years, we are completely hardened to all attacks of sentiment. After more than eight hundred thousand children of the nation had died of hunger and undernourishment at the close of the War, we witnessed almost one million head of milking cows being driven away from us in accordance with the cruel paragraphs of a dictate which the humane democratic apostles of the world forced upon us as a peace treaty. We witnessed over one million German prisoners of war being retained in confinement for no reason at all for a whole year after the War was ended. We witnessed over one and a half million Germans being torn away from all that they possessed in the territories lying on our frontiers, and being whipped out with practically only what they wore on their backs. We had to endure having millions of our fellow countrymen torn from us without their consent, and without their being afforded the slightest possibility of existence. I could supplement these examples with dozens of the most cruel kind. For this reason we ask to be spared all sentimental talk. The German nation does not wish its interests to be determined and controlled by any foreign nation. France to the French, England to the English, America to the Americans, and Germany to the Germans. We are resolved to prevent the settlement in our country of a strange people which was capable of snatching for itself all the leading positions in the land, and to oust it. For it is our will to educate our own nation for these leading positions. We have hundreds of thousands of very intelligent children of peasants and of the working classes. We shall have them educated—in fact we have already begun—and we wish that one day they, and not the representatives of an alien race, may hold the leading positions in the state together with our educated classes. Above all, German culture, as its name alone shows, is German and not Jewish, and therefore its management and care will be entrusted to members of our own nation. If the rest of the world cries out with a hypocritical mien against this barbaric expulsion from Germany of such an irreplaceable and culturally eminently valuable element, we can only be astonished at the conclusions they draw from this situation. For how thankful they must be that we are releasing these precious apostles of culture, and placing them at the disposal of the rest of the world. In accordance with their own declarations they cannot find a single reason to excuse themselves for refusing to receive this most valuable race in their own countries. Nor can I see a reason why the members of this race should be imposed upon the German nation, while in the States, which are so enthusiastic about these "splendid people," their settlement should suddenly be refused with every imaginable excuse. I think that the sooner this problem is solved the better; for Europe cannot settle down until the Jewish question is cleared up. It may very well be possible that sooner or later an agreement on this problem may be reached in Europe, even between those nations which otherwise do not so easily come together.

The world has sufficient space for settlements, but we must once and for all get rid of the opinion that the Jewish race was only created by God for the purpose of being in a certain percentage a parasite living on the body and the productive work of other nations. The Jewish race will have to adapt itself to sound constructive activity as other nations do, or sooner or later it will succumb to a crisis of an inconceivable magnitude.

One thing I should like to say on this day which may be memorable for others as well as for us Germans: In the course of my life I have very often been a prophet, and have usually been ridiculed for it. During the time of my struggle for power it was in the first instance the Jewish race which only received my prophecies with laughter when I said that I would one day take over the leadership of the state, and with it that of the whole nation, and that I would then among many other things settle the Jewish problem. Their laughter was uproarious, but I think that for some time now they have been laughing on the other side of their face. Today I will once more be a prophet: If the international Jewish financiers in and outside Europe should succeed in plunging the nations once more into a world war, then the result will not be the Bolshevization of the earth, and thus the victory of Jewry, but the annihilation of the Jewish race in Europe!

. . . The nations are no longer willing to die on the battlefield so that this unstable international race may profiteer from a war or satisfy its Old Testament vengeance. The Jewish watchword "Workers of the world unite" will be conquered by a higher realization, namely "Workers of all classes and of all nations, recognize your common enemy!"

HITLER'S PRIVATE WILL

Because, in the years of my struggle, I thought it irresponsible to enter into marriage I have now, before the end of my life on earth, decided to take that girl for my wife who after many years of sincere friendship freely entered the beleaguered city to share her fate with mine. It is her express wish to join me in death as my wife. It will recompense us both for what both of us have sacrificed through my work in the service of my people.

All I own—if any of it is of value—belongs to the party. If the latter should no longer exist, it belongs to the state, and if the latter should be destroyed as well no further decision on my part is needed.

The paintings I have collected throughout the years were never meant for my private enjoyment but always for a gallery to be built in my native Linz on the Danube.

That this request be met is my sincerest wish.

As executor I appoint my most loyal party comrade, Martin Bormann whom I hereby authorize to make all final decisions. He is entitled to hand whatever may serve as a personal memento or help to sustain a simple middle-class life to my sisters and also to my wife's mother and to the faithful collaborators he knows so well, headed by my former secretaries, Frau Winter and others, who for years have assisted me in my work.

I myself and my wife have chosen death rather than suffer the disgrace of dismissal or capitulation. It is our wish to be burnt at once at the very place I have done the major part of my daily work in the service of my people during the past twelve years.

Berlin, 29 April, 1945, 4 A.M.
ADOLF HITLER

as witnesses:
MARTIN BORMANN

DR. GOEBBELS

as witness:
NICOLAUS VON BELOW

HITLER'S POLITICAL TESTAMENT

APRIL 29, 1945

More than thirty years have passed since 1914 when I made my modest contribution as a volunteer in the First World War, which was forced upon the Reich.

In these three decades love and loyalty to my people have guided all my thoughts, actions and my life. They gave me the strength to make the most difficult decisions ever to confront mortal man. In these three decades I have spent my strength and my health.

It is untrue that I or anyone else in Germany wanted war in 1939. It was wanted and provoked solely by international statesmen either of Jewish origin or working for Jewish interests. I have made too many offers for the limitation and control of armaments, which posterity will not be cowardly enough always to disregard, for responsibility for the outbreak of this war to be placed on me. Nor have I ever wished that, after the appalling First World War, there would be a second against either England or America. Centuries will go by, but from the ruins of our towns and monuments the hatred of those ultimately responsible will always grow anew against the people whom we have to thank for all this: international Jewry and its henchmen.

Only three days before the outbreak of the German-Polish war I proposed a solution of the German-Polish problem to the British ambassador in Berlin—international control as in the case of the Saar. This offer, too, cannot be lied away. It was only rejected because the ruling clique in England wanted war, partly for commercial reasons and partly because it was influenced by the propaganda put out by international Jewry.

I have left no one in doubt that if the people of Europe are once more treated as mere blocks of shares in the hands of these international money and finance conspirators, then the sole responsibility for the massacre must be borne by the true culprits: the Jews. Nor have I left anyone in doubt that this time millions of European children of Aryan descent will starve to death, millions of men will die in battle, and hundreds of thousands of women and children will be burned or bombed to death in our cities without the true culprits being held to account, albeit more humanely.

After six years of war which, despite all setbacks, will one day go down in history as the most glorious and heroic manifestation of the struggle for existence of a nation, I cannot abandon the city which is the capital of this Reich. Since our forces are too meager to withstand the enemy's attack and since our resistance is being debased by creatures who are as blind as they are lacking in character, I wish to share my fate with that which millions of others have also taken upon themselves by remaining in this city. Further, I shall not fall into the hands of the enemy who requires a new spectacle, presented by the Jews, for the diversion of the hysterical masses.

I have therefore decided to stay in Berlin and there to choose death voluntarily when I determine that the position of the Führer and the Chancellery itself can no longer be maintained. I die with a joyful heart in the knowledge of the immeasurable deeds and achievements of our peasants and workers and of a contribution unique in the history of our youth which bears my name.

That I am deeply grateful to them all is as self-evident as is my wish that they do not abandon the struggle but that, no matter where, they continue to fight the enemies of the Fatherland, faithful to the ideals of the great Clausewitz. Through the sacrifices of our soldiers and my own fellowship with them unto death, a seed has been sown in German history that will one day grow to usher in the glorious rebirth of the National Socialist movement in a truly united nation.

Many of our bravest men and women have sworn to bind their lives to mine to the end. I have begged, and finally ordered, them not to do so but to play their part in the further struggle of the nation. I ask the leaders of the army, the navy and the air force to strengthen the National Socialist spirit of resistance of our soldiers by all possible means, with special emphasis on the fact that I myself, as the founder and creator of this movement, prefer death to cowardly resignation or even to capitulation.

May it become a point of honor of future German army officers, as it is already in our navy, that the surrender of a district or town is out of the question and that, above everything else, the commanders must set a shining example of faithful devotion to duty unto death.

[SECOND PART OF THE POLITICAL TESTAMENT]

Before my death, I expel former Reichs Marshal Hermann Goering from the party and withdraw from him all the rights that were conferred upon him by the decree of 29 June, 1941 and by my Reichstag statement of 1 September, 1939. In his place I appoint Admiral Donitz as president of the Reich and supreme commander of the armed forces.

Before my death, I expel the former Reichsführer of the SS and the Minister of the Interior Heinrich Himmler from the party and from all his state offices. In his place I appoint Gauleiter Karl Hanke as Reichsführer of the SS and head of the German Police, and Gauleiter Paul Giesler as minister of the interior.

Apart altogether from their disloyalty to me, Goering and Himmler have brought irreparable shame on the whole nation by secretly negotiating with the enemy without my knowledge and against my will, and also by attempting illegally to seize control of the state.

In order to provide the German people with a government of honorable men who will fulfill the task of continuing the war with all the means at their disposal, I, as Führer of the nation, appoint the following members of the new cabinet:

President of the Reich: Donitz
Chancellor of the Reich: Dr. Goebbels
Party Minister: Bormann
Foreign Minister: Seyss-Inquart
Minister of the Interior: Gauleiter Gieser
Minister of War: Donitz
Supreme Commander of the Army: Schorner
Supreme Commander of the Navy: Donitz
Supreme Commander of the Air Force: Greim
Reichsführer of the SS and Head of the German Police: Gauleiter Hanke
Trade: Funk
Agriculture: Backe
Justice: Thierack
Culture: Dr. Scheel
Propaganda: Dr. Naumann
Finance: Schwerin-Crossigk
Labor: Dr. Hupfauer
Munitions: Saur
Leader of the German Labor Front and Minister without Portfolio: Dr. Ley.

Although a number of these men, including Martin Bormann, Dr. Goebbels and others together with their wives have joined me of their own free will, not wishing to leave the capital under any circumstances and prepared to die with me, I implore them to grant my request that they place the welfare of the nation above their own feelings. By their work and loyal companionship they will remain as close to me after my death as I hope my spirit will continue to dwell among them and accompany them always. Let them be severe but never unjust and let them never, above all, allow fear to preside over their actions, placing the honor of the nation above everything that exists on earth. May they, finally, always remember that our task, the consolidation of a National Socialist state, represents the work of centuries to come, so that every individual must subordinate his own interest to the common good. I ask of all Germans, of all National Socialists, men and women and all soldiers of the Wehrmacht, that they remain faithful and obedient unto death to the new government and its president.

Above all, I enjoin the government and the people to uphold the race laws to the limit and to resist mercilessly the poisoner of all nations, international Jewry.

Berlin, 29 April, 1945, 4 A.M.
ADOLF HITLER

Witnesses:
DR. JOSEPH GOEBBELS

MARTIN BORMANN

WILHELM BURGDORF

HANS KREBS

PROTOCOLS OF THE WANNSEE CONFERENCE

JANUARY 20, 1942

Translation of Document No. NG–2586
Office of Chief of Counsel for War Crimes

MINUTES OF DISCUSSION

I. The following persons took part in the discussion about the Final Solution of the Jewish question which took place in Berlin, *an grossen* Wannsee No. 56/58 on 20 January 1942.

Gauleiter Dr. MEYER and Reichsemtsleiter
Under Secretary of State Dr. STUCKART
Under Secretary of State NEUMANN
Under Secretary of State Dr. FREISLER
Under Secretary of State Dr. BUEHLER
Unterstaatssekretaer LUTHER
SS Oberführer KLOPPER
Ministeriadldirektor KRITZINGER
(handwritten note):
D III. 29 Top Secret.
SS Gruppenführer HOFMANN
SS Gruppenführer MUELLER
SS Oberführer Dr. SCHOENGARTH
SS Sturmbannführer Dr. LANGE
Reich Ministry for Dr. LEIBERANDT
Occupied Eastern territories

Reich Ministry for the Interior
Plenipotentiary for the Four-Year Plan
Reich Ministry of Justice
Office of the Government General
Foreign Office
Party Chancellory
Reich Chancellory
Race and Settlement Main Office
Reich Main Security Office
SS Obersturmbannführer EICHMANN
Security Police and Chief of the Security Police SD and the SD in the Government General
Security Police and Commander of the Security Police SD and the SD for the General district Latvia, as deputy of the Commander of the Security Police and the SD for the Reich Commissariat "Eastland."

II. At the beginning of the discussion SS Ober-gruppenführer HEYDRICH gave information that the Reich Marshal had appointed him delegate for the preparations for the Final Solution of the Jewish problem in Europe and pointed out that this discussion had been called for the purpose of clarifying fundamental questions. The wish of the Reich Marshal to have a draft sent to him concerning organizational, factual, and material interests in relation to the Final Solution of the Jewish problem in Europe, makes necessary an initial common action of all Central Offices immediately concerned with these questions in order to bring their general activities onto line.

He said that the Reichsführer-SS and the Chief of the German Police (Chief of the Security Police and the SD) was entrusted with the official handling of the Final Solution of the Jewish problem centrally without regard to geographic borders.

The Chief of the Security Police and the SD then gave a short report of the struggle which has been carried on against this enemy, the essential points being the following:

A. the expulsion of the Jews from every particular sphere of life of the German people,
B. the expulsion of the Jews from the *Lebensraum* of the German people.

In carrying out these efforts, an increased and planned acceleration of the emigration of Jews from the Reich territory was started, as the only possible present solution.

By order of the Reich Marshal a Reich Central Office for Jewish emigration was set up in January 1939, and the Chief of the Security Police and SD was entrusted with the management. Its most important tasks were:

A. to *make* all necessary arrangements for the *preparation* for an increased emigration of the Jews,
B. to *direct* the flow of immigration,
C. to hurry up the procedure of emigration in each *individual case.*

The aim of all this being that of clearing the German Lebensraum of Jews in a legal way.

All the offices realized the drawbacks of such enforced accelerated emigration. For the time being they had, however, tolerated it on account of the lack of other possible solutions to the problem.

The work concerned with emigration was, later on, not only a German problem, but also a problem with which the authorities of the countries to which the flow of emigrants was being directed would have a deal. Financial difficulties, such as the demand for increasing sums of money to be presented at the time of the landing on the part of various foreign governments, lack of shipping space, increasing restriction of entry permits, or canceling of such, extraordinarily increased the difficulties of emigration. In spite of these difficulties 537,000 Jews were sent out of the country between the day of the seizure of power and the deadline 31 October 1941. Of these as from 30 January from Germany proper approx. 360,000, from 15 March 1938 from Austria (Ostmark) approx. 147,000, from 15 March 1939 from the protectorate of Bohemia and Moravia approx. 30,000.

The Jews themselves, or rather their Jewish political organizations financed the emigration. In order to avoid the possibility of the impoverished Jews staying behind, action was taken to make the wealthy Jews finance the evacuation of the needy Jews. This was arranged by imposing a suitable tax, i.e. an emigration tax which was used for the financial arrangements in connection with the emigration of poor Jews, and was worked according to a ladder system.

Apart from the necessary reichsmark exchange, foreign currency had to be presented at the time of the landing. In order to save foreign exchange held by Germany, the Jewish financial establishments in foreign countries were—with the help of Jewish organizations in Germany—made responsible for arranging for an adequate amount of foreign currency. Up to 30 October 1941, the foreign Jews donated approx. $9,500,000.

In the meantime the Reichsführer-SS and

Chief of the German Police had prohibited emigration of Jews for reasons of the dangers of an emigration during wartime and consideration of the possibilities in the East.

III. Another possible solution of the problem has now taken the place of emigration, i.e. the evacuation of the Jews to the East, provided the Führer agrees to this plan.

Such activities are, however, to be considered as provisional actions, but practical experience is already being collected which is of greatest importance in relation to the future Final Solution of the Jewish problem.

Approx. 11,000,000 Jews will be involved in this Final Solution of the European problem, they are distributed as follows among the countries:

COUNTRY	NUMBER
Germany proper	131,800
Austria	43,700
Eastern territories	420,000
General Government	2,284,000
Bialystok	400,000
Protectorate of Bohemia & Moravia	74,000
Estonia	-no Jews-
Latvia	3,500
Lithuania	34,000
Belgium	43,000
Denmark	5,600
France/Occupied France	165,000
Unoccupied France	700,000
Greece	69,000
Netherlands	160,800
Norway	1,300
Bulgaria	48,000
England	330,000
Finland	2,300
Ireland	4,000
Italy incl. Sardinia	58,000
Albania	200
Croatia	40,000
Portugal	43,000
Romania incl. Bossarabia	342,000
Sweden	8,000
Switzerland	18,000
Serbia	10,000
Slovakia	88,000
Spain	6,000
Turkey (European Turkey)	55,500
Hungary	742,800
USSR	2,994,684
Ukraine/White Russia with exception of Bialystok	446,484
Total:	over 11,000,000

The number of Jews given here for foreign countries includes, however, only those Jews who still adhere to the Jewish faith as the definition of the term "Jew" according to racial principles is still partially missing there. The handling of the problem in the individual countries will meet with difficulties due to the attitude and conception of the people there, especially in Hungary and Romania. Thus, even today a Jew can buy documents in Hungary which will officially prove his foreign citizenship.

The influence of the Jews in all walks of life in the USSR is well known. Approximately five million Jews are living in the European Russia, and in Asiatic Russia scarcely one-quarter million.

The breakdown of Jews residing in the European part of the USSR, according to trades, was approximately as follows:

in agriculture	9.1%
communal workers	14.8%
in trade	20.0%
employed by the state	23.4%
in private occupations such as medical profession, newspapers, theater, etc.	32.7%

Under proper guidance the Jews are now to be allocated for labor to the East in the course of the Final Solution. Able-bodied Jews will be taken in large labor columns to these districts for work on roads, separated according to sexes, in the course of which action a great part will undoubtedly be eliminated by natural causes.

The possible final remnant will, as it must undoubtedly consist of the toughest, have to be treated accordingly, as it is the product of natural selection, and would, if liberated, act as a bud cell of a Jewish reconstruction (see historical experience).

In the course of the practical execution of this final settlement of the problem, Europe will be cleaned up from the West to the East. Germany proper, including the protectorate of Bohemia and Moravia, will have to be handled first because of reasons of housing and other social-political necessities.

The evacuated Jews will first be sent, group by group, into so-called transit ghettos from which they will be taken to the East.

SS Obergruppenführer HEYDRICH went on to say that an important provision for the evacuation as such is the exact definition of the group of persons concerned in the matter.

It is intended not to evacuate Jews of more than sixty-five years of age but to send them to an old-age ghetto—Theresienstadt is being considered for this purpose.

Next is these age groups—of the 280,000 Jews still in Germany proper and Austria on 31 October 1941, approximately 30 percent are over sixty-five; Jews disabled on active duty and Jews with war decorations (Iron Cross I) will be accepted in the Jewish old-age ghettos.

Through such an expedient solution the numerous interventions will be eliminated with one blow.

The carrying out of each single evacuation project of a larger extent will start at a time to be determined chiefly by the military developments. Regarding the handling of the Final Solution *in the European territories occupied and influenced* by us it was suggested that the competent officials of the Foreign Office working on these questions confer with the competent *Referenten* from the Security Police and the SD.

In Slovakia and Croatia the difficulties arising from this question have been considerably reduced, as the most essential problems in this field have already been brought near to a solution. In Romania the government in the meantime has also appointed a commissioner for Jewish questions. In order to settle the question in Hungary it is imperative that an *advisor in Jewish questions be pressed upon the Hungarian government without too* much delay.

As regards the taking of preparatory steps to settle the question in Italy SS Obergruppenführer HEYDRIDH considers it opportune to contact the chief of the police with a view to these problems.

In the occupied and unoccupied parts of France the registration of the Jews for evacuation can in all probability be expected to take place without great difficulties.

Assistant Under Secretary of State LUTHER in this connection calls attention to the fact that in some countries, such as the Scandinavian states, difficulties will arise if these problems are dealt with thoroughly and that it will be therefore advisable to defer action in these countries. Besides, considering the small number of Jews to be evacuated from these countries this deferment means not essential limitation.

On the other hand, the Foreign Office anticipated no great difficulties as far as the Southeast and the West of Europe are concerned.

SS Gruppenführer HOFMANN intends to send an official from the Main Race and Settlement Office to Hungary for general orientation at the time when the first active steps to bring up the question in this country will be taken by the Chief of the Security Police and the SD. It was determined officially to detail this official, who is not supposed to work actively, temporarily from the Main Race and Settlement Office as assistant to the police attaché.

IV. The implementation of the Final Solution is supposed to a certain extent to be based on the Nuremberg Laws, in which connection also the solution of the problems presented by the mixed marriages and the persons of mixed blood is seen to be conditional to an absolutely final clarification of the question.

The chief of the Security Police and the SD first discussed, with reference to a letter from the chief of the Reich Chancellery, the following points theoretically:

I. *Treatment of Persons of Mixed Blood of the First Degree.*

Persons of mixed blood of the first degree will, as regards the Final Solution of the Jewish questions, be treated as Jews. From this treatment the following persons will be exempt:

A. Persons of mixed blood of the first degree married to persons of German blood if their marriage has resulted in children (persons of mixed blood of the second degree). Such persons of mixed blood of the second degree are to be treated essentially as Germans.

B. Persons of mixed blood of the first degree to whom up till now in any sphere of life whatever exemption licenses have been issued by the highest party or state authorities.

Each individual case must be examined, in which process it will still be possible that a decision unfavorable to the persons of mixed blood can be passed. In any such case only *personal* essential merit of the person of mixed blood must be deemed a ground justifying the granting of an exemption. (Not merits of the parent or of the partner of German blood.)

Any person of mixed blood of the first degree to whom exception from the evacuation is granted will be sterilized—in order to eliminate the possibility of offspring and to secure a final solution of the problem presented by the persons of mixed blood. The sterilization will take place on a voluntary basis. But it will be conditional to a permission to stay in the Reich. Following the sterilizations the person of mixed blood will be liberated from all restrictive regulations which have so far been imposed upon him.

II. *Treatment of Persons of Mixed Blood of the Second Degree.*

Persons of mixed blood of the second degree will fundamentally be treated as persons of German blood, *with the exception of the following cases* in which persons of mixed blood of the second degree will be treated as Jews:

A. The person of mixed blood of the second degree is the result of a marriage where both parents are persons of mixed blood.

B. The general appearance of the person of mixed blood of the second degree is racially particularly objectionable so that he already outwardly must be included among the Jews.

C. The person of mixed blood of the second degree has a particularly bad police and political record sufficient to reveal that he feels and behaves like a Jew.

But also in these cases exceptions are not to be made if the person of mixed blood of the second degree is married to a person of German blood.

III. *Marriages between Full Jews and Persons of German Blood.*

Here it must be decided from one individual case to another whether the Jewish partner is to be evacuated, or whether in consideration of the effects produced by such measure upon the German relatives of the mixed marriage he is to be committed to a ghetto for aged Jews.

IV. *Marriages between Persons of Mixed Blood of the First Degree and Persons of German Blood.*

A. Without children:

If no children have resulted from the marriage the parents of mixed blood of the first degree will be evacuated or committed to a ghetto for old Jews. (The same treatment as in the case of marriages between full Jews and persons of German blood, Point 3).

B. With children:

If the marriage has resulted in children (persons of mixed blood of the second degree) these children will be evacuated or committed to a ghetto together with the parents of mixed blood of the first degree, *if they are to be* treated as Jews. If the children are to be *treated as Germans* (regular cases) they will be exempt from evacuation and in that case the same applies to the parent of mixed blood of the first degree.

V. *Marriages between Persons of Mixed Blood of the First Degree and Persons of Mixed Blood of the First Degree or Jews.*

In the case of these marriages (including the children) all members of the family will be treated as Jews, therefore, evacuated or committed to a ghetto for old Jews.

VI. *Marriages between Persons of Mixed Blood of the First Degree and Persons of Mixed Blood of the Second Degree.*

Both partners will be evacuated, regardless of whether or not they have children, or committed to a ghetto for old Jews, since as a rule these children will racially reveal the admixture of Jewish blood more strongly than persons of mixed blood of the second degree.

SS Gruppenführer HOFMANN advocated the opinion that sterilization must be applied on a large scale; in particular as the person of mixed blood placed before the alternative as whether to be evacuated or to be sterilized, would rather submit to the sterilization.

Under Secretary of State Dr. STUCKHART maintains that the possible solutions enumerated above for a clarification of the problems presented by mixed marriages and by persons of mixed blood when translated into practice in this form would involve endless administrative work. In the second place, as the biological facts cannot be disregarded in any case, it was suggested by Dr. STUCKHART to proceed to forced sterilization.

Further, for the purpose of simplifying the problem of mixed marriages it would be required to consider how it could be possible to attain the

object that the legislator can declare: "This marriage *has been* dissolved."

Regarding the question of the effects produced by the evacuation of Jews on the economic life, Under Secretary of State NEUMANN declared that the Jews assigned to work in plants of importance for the war could not be evacuated as long as no replacement was available.

SS Obergruppenführer HEYDRICH pointed out that, according to the directives approved by him governing the carrying out of the evacuation program in operation at that time, these Jews would not be evacuated.

Under Secretary of State Dr. BUEHLER stated that it would be welcomed by the Government General if the implementation of the final solution of this question could *start in the Government General,* because the transportation problem there was of no predominant importance and the progress of this action would not be hampered by considerations connected with the supply of labor. The Jews had to be removed as quickly as possible from the territory of the Government General because, especially there, the Jews represented an immense danger as carriers of epidemics, and on the other hand were permanently contributing to the disorganization of the economic system of the country through black market operations. Moreover, out of the two-and-a-half million Jews to be affected, the majority of cases were *unfit for work.*

Under Secretary of State BUEHLER further stated that the solution of the Jewish question in the Government General as far as the issuing of orders was concerned was dependent upon the chief of the Security Police and the SD, his work being supported by the administrative authorities of the Government General. He had this one request only, namely that the Jewish question in this territory be solved as quickly as possible.

Towards the end of the conference the various types of possible solutions were discussed; in the course of this discussion Gauleiter Dr. MEYER as well as Under Secretary of State Dr. BUEHLER advocated the view that certain preparatory measures incidental to the carrying out of the Final Solution ought to be initiated immediately in the very territories under discussion, in which process, however, alarming the population must be avoided.

With the request to the persons present from the chief of the Security Police and the SD that they lend him appropriate assistance in the carrying out of the tasks involved in the solution, the conference was adjourned.

XIV. THE KILLERS: A SPEECH, A MEMOIR, AND AN INTERVIEW

Any portrait of the killers is by its nature selective and limited. Who were the perpetrators? Were they the guards in the camps or the engineers who designed the crematoria? Were they the railroad men who brought 148 trains of Hungarian Jews—437,402 men, women, and children to Auschwitz between May and July 1944, or were the executioners those who made the selection and dropped the gas? Were they the bureaucrats who processed the booty and the men who went into the killing fields? Surely, one must portray all of them to begin to understand the perpetrators.

Still, apologies aside, in these readings we will attempt to understand the perpetrators by reading a speech by Heinrich Himmler; a selection from a memoir by Rudolf Höss,

Reinhard Heydrich in front of Prague's main railway station. April 20, 1942. Czechoslovak News Agency.

the commandant of Auschwitz; and an interview with Franz Stangl, his counterpart at Treblinka and Sobibor.

Richard Breitman entitled his masterful biography of Heinrich Himmler, the head of the SS, *The Architect of Genocide*. Himmler was the man responsible for the conception and implementation of the "Final Solution to the Jewish problem."

While historians can only piece together parts of Adolf Hitler's reflections on the annihilation of the Jews from fragments of evidence, Himmler's reflection can be more easily discerned from an address he gave to the SS Gruppenführer at Posen in October 1943, and another on June 21, 1944, the third anniversary of the German invasion of the Soviet Union. At Posen, still convinced that Germany would win the war, Himmler paused to assess with colleagues what had been achieved.

The speech was long, three hours and ten minutes. We know this with precision, for Himmler's speech was recorded for posterity and in a moment of anxiety he even paused to make certain the tape was recording before he continued.

Himmler spoke from notes. These notes were captured and preserved; they are in his distinctive handwriting and enunciate theme after theme. Breitman describes Himmler's voice as midrange. He spoke "clearly, deliberately, and emphatically, but for the most part dispassionately, much like a schoolmaster reviewing a long and somewhat complicated lesson."

Some two hours into his three-hour-ten-minute speech, Himmler paused to speak of the Jews. He spoke openly and directly. "The Jewish people is going to be annihilated."

He spoke with pride in his men, pride in their toughness, pride in their integrity: "Most of you know what it means to see a hundred corpses lie side by side, or five hundred, or a thousand. To have stuck this out and—excepting cases of human weakness—to have kept our integrity, that is what has made us hard."

He spoke the unspoken. He spoke but urged silence. "This is an unwritten and never-to-be-written page of glory [in German history]."

He spoke of the Jews, but not only the Jews. Of the Soviet POWs who were killed or allowed to die by the millions, he spoke with regret in the most utilitarian of tone. He regretted the loss of their labor potential. "At that time we did not value this human mass the way we value it today as raw material, as labor."

He spoke candidly, "What happens to others is a matter of total indifference." Germany is the center. Other nations concern him only insofar as needed. "It is a crime against our own blood to worry about them."

His expectations of SS men were high. It was imperative they be honest, decent, loyal, and comradely to members of their own blood—and nobody else.

By June 1944, Himmler was more wistful, but no less direct in his discussion on the annihilation of the Jews. "It is a good thing that we had the toughness to exterminate the Jews in our sphere. Don't ask how difficult it was."

The order was difficult but necessary. He described the mountain of gold that was captured, the cleansing of the Warsaw Ghetto of its five hundred thousand Jews, and the benefits of internal security for the Reich and the General Government.

"Moralist" that he was, Himmler addressed the moral question. "Well, you know, I understand very well that you are killing grown-up Jews, but how can you kill women and children! Then I say this: These children will grow up one day."

If the problem is not solved "finally," once and for all Himmler argues, German children will have to solve the problem again—"but at a time when Adolf Hitler no longer lives."

Auschwitz was the largest and most lethal of the Nazi death camps. Actually three camps in one, a killing center, a concentration camp, and a series of slave labor centers, Auschwitz has become emblematic of the Holocaust. Elie Wiesel has called it the "kingdom of Night." Others speak of "planet Auschwitz," a world apart. Auschwitz is linked with the career of its creator, commandant Rudolf Höss, who was in charge during its most formative stages. After reassignment because of widespread corruption under his command, Höss returned in time to personally coordinate the destruction of the Hungarian Jews. Code-named "Aktion Höss," more than 437,000 Hungarian Jews were deported en masse to Auschwitz between May 15 and July 8, 1944. Höss also managed the liquidation of sector BIIe in Birkenau in August 1944, which had been inhabited by Gypsies since February 1943.

After the collapse of the Nazi regime, Höss eluded capture for nine months. He was imprisoned in former army barracks at Heide, and then transferred to the main British center for interrogations of the most wanted war criminals. Surprisingly, Höss was candid in his testimony; he gave precise though passive answers. He corrected figures, when he knew them, and statements that he judged to be untrue.

Höss neither protected anyone nor evaded his own responsibility. Instead, he viewed his deeds as a technical challenge, a triumph of coping with unprecedented circumstances. In prison after conviction, he wrote his memoirs from which this section on gassing is taken.

A word of background is appropriate. Born on November 25, 1900, in Baden-Baden in southwest Germany, Höss was an only son, the oldest of three children of a prosperous merchant's clerk and a housewife. In high school he trained for the priesthood, yet his father's death and the onset of war changed these plans. In 1916, he joined the army. Wounded three times, he was twice awarded the Iron Cross. He joined the East Prussian Free Corps (Freikorps) and took part in the suppression of disturbances in Latvia, and in quelling workers who were staging a revolt in the Ruhr in 1920. A reunion of the Freikorps in the early 1920s introduced him to Adolf Hitler for the first time. Höss immediately joined the Nazi Party and renounced his affiliation with the Catholic Church. He was to become a priest in another "church." When France and Belgium entered and occupied the Upper Rhein region on January 1923, and extremist German elements responded with terror, Höss participated in the assassination of Freikorpsman Walter Kadow on the estate of the man who was later to serve as Hitler's secretary, Martin Bormann. Höss was captured and sentenced to ten years in prison. When Hitler came to power, Höss joined the SS guard battalion at Dachau, serving under Camp Inspector (and future SS Gruppenführer) Theodor Eicke. Höss's rise was rapid: first sergeant in March 1936, second lieutenant in September 1936, first lieutenant in September 1938, and captain in November 1938.

In 1939, he was named director of the concentration camp at Sachsenhausen. By 1940, Höss headed the commission charged with deciding how to use the Polish army barracks at Auschwitz. His recommendations prompted Heinrich Himmler's order on April 27, 1940, that established KL Auschwitz to house about ten thousand prisoners. Höss seized the opportunity to display his organizational talents, and was appointed commandant of the new camp on May 1, 1940. He tackled the tasks at hand with a passion, impressing Himmler with his skills. In March 1941, Himmler instructed Höss to expand Auschwitz to hold the thirty thousand prisoners expected to arrive during the course of the anticipated war with the Soviet Union. In addition, Himmler ordered that a camp for one hundred thousand prisoners of war be set up in nearby Brzezinka (KL Auschwitz-Birkenau), and that a labor force of ten thousand prisoners be placed at the disposal of I.G. Farben to construct a chemical works.

When Hitler limited Himmler's grand plans for Auschwitz in 1941, Auschwitz was assigned a special role in the plan to liquidate European Jews, euphemistically termed the "Final Solution of the Jewish question." In his autobiography, Höss maintained that he first learned of the plan, and the designation of Auschwitz as the hub of the Holocaust, in the summer of 1941. Accordingly, he modified his plans for Birkenau, and began implementing installations of mass extermination. An experiment was conducted at Auschwitz on September 3, 1941, using the gas, prussic (hydrocyanic) acid, known commercially as Cyclon-B. Six hundred Soviet POWs and 250 camp prisoners were gassed in the cellars of Block 11 with Höss personally viewing the experiment.

During the lethal six months from July to December of 1942, Auschwitz served as a killing center. The killing process and the treasures looted from the victims led to widespread reports of corruption. Seven hundred SS men from various camps were either discharged from active service or put under arrest.

In Auschwitz, an investigation uncovered massive corruption: willful, unauthorized killing of prisoners (authorized killing by gas, hanging, and execution was permissible—indeed rewarded) and a special fund through which monies were funneled for officer-corps banquets. As a result, Höss was reassigned—kicked upstairs—as chief of the Department DI, the Central Office within SS-WVHA, in January 1944, where he coordinated all undertakings within the entire camp system. He now controlled the activities of camp commandants, and could submit proposals for personnel changes in the camps. Höss's length of service and loyalty to the Nazi cause was rewarded by a mere mild punishment, which on paper looked like a promotion.

After Adolf Eichmann ordered the deportation of several hundred thousand Jews from Hungary to Auschwitz in mid–1944, Höss arranged for his successor at Auschwitz, Arthur Liebenhenschel, to be appointed commandant of the Lublin/Majdanek camp. Höss then returned to Auschwitz where he assumed the command of the SS garrison for several months. As such, the commandants of all the Auschwitz camps (KL Auschwitz I, II, and III) answered directly and formally to him. Thus, he was responsible for the murder of Hungarian Jews.

His last words once again acknowledged his responsibility for all that occurred in Auschwitz. He did not appeal for leniency. He only asked for permission to send a farewell letter to his family and to return his wedding ring to his wife. On the morning of April 16, 1947, several dozen yards from his former villa near Crematorium I in the main camp, Rudolf Höss was hanged.

He left behind a legacy of obedience to the Nazi cause, and initiative at the implementation of the Final Solution. He left behind more than a million people murdered by gas and a memoir, which is remarkable for its detail and its detachment.

In what has become a classic document, we read segments of the 1971 interview by journalist and Holocaust scholar Gitta Sereny with Franz Stangl, who was the commandant of both Sobibor and Treblinka, the deaths camps that consumed more than a million Jews (approximately 850,000 at Treblinka and 250,000 at Sobibor). Since she comments in her own interview, suffice it to say that the dialogue offers unparalleled insight into the killers, their motivations, and self-justifications. It would be wise to read these two testimonies not as acts by men without conscience, but as statements by men who must adjust their conscience to take cognizance of the deeds they committed.

EXTRACTS FROM THE SPEECH OF HEINRICH HIMMLER AT A POZNAN MEETING OF SS MAJOR GENERALS

OCTOBER 4, 1943

Partial Translation of Document 1919_PS
Prosecution Exhibit 2368

MEMORIAL SERVICE FOR THE WAR DEAD

In the months that have gone by since we met in June 1942 many of our comrades were killed, giving their lives for Germany and the Führer. In the first rank—and I ask you to rise in his honor and in honor of all our dead SS men, soldiers, men, and women—in the first rank our old comrade and friend from our ranks, SS Lieutenant General Eicke. [The SS Gruppenführers have risen from their seats.] Please be seated.

One basic principle must be the absolute rule for the SS men—we must be honest, decent, loyal, and comradely to members of our own blood and to nobody else. What happens to a Russian or to a Czech does not interest me in the slightest. What the nations can offer in the way of good blood of our type we will take, if necessary by kidnapping their children and raising them here with us. Whether nations live in prosperity or starve to death interests me only so far as we need them as slaves for our culture; otherwise, it is of no interest to me. Whether ten thousand Russian females fall down from exhaustion while digging an antitank ditch interests me only so far as the antitank ditch for Germany is finished. We shall never be rough and heartless when it is not necessary, that is clear. We Germans, who are the only people in the world who have a decent attitude toward animals, will also assume a decent attitude toward these human animals. But it is a crime against our own blood to worry about

them and give them ideals, thus causing our sons and grandsons to have a more difficult time with them. When somebody comes to me and says: "I cannot dig the antitank ditch with women and children, it is inhuman, for it would kill them," then I have to say, "You are a murderer of your own blood because if the antitank ditch is not dug, German soldiers will die, and they are sons of German mothers. They are our own blood." That is what I want to instill into this SS—and what I believe have instilled into them—as one of the most sacred laws of the future. Our concern, our duty is our people and our blood. It is for them that we must provide and plan, work and fight, nothing else. We can be indifferent to everything else. I wish the SS to adopt this attitude to the problem of all foreign, non-Germanic peoples, especially Russians. All else is vain, fraud against our own nation, and an obstacle to the early winning of the war.

RUSSIAN SOLDIERS ON OUR SIDE

One thing must be understood in this war—it is better that a Russian dies than a German. When we employ Russians, the principle is to mix them in a ratio of one to two or one to three with Germans. The best thing is that you use Russians singly, then you can ride with them in a tank. One Russian with two or three Germans in a tank, marvelous, nothing at all. The only thing you have to avoid is letting the Russian meet other Russian tank drivers, lest these fellows conspire. If for some reason, however, you desire companies made up entirely of Russians, then gentlemen take care—and this is not just an idea, but this is an order—that this company has your informer set-up, your NKVD organization. Then you can rest quietly. Besides—this is one of the earliest lessons that I have taught—-take care that these subhuman beings always look in your face, that they always have to look their superiors in the eye. That is as with animals. As long as it looks its tamer in the eye it won't do anything. But never forget—it is a beast. With this attitude we can make use of the Russian, with this attitude we shall always be superior to the Slav.

FOREIGNERS IN THE REICH

We must also realize that we have six to seven million foreigners in Germany. Perhaps it is even eight million now. We have prisoners in Germany. None of them are dangerous so long as we take severe measures at the merest trifles. It is a mere nothing today to shoot ten Poles, compared with the fact that we might later have to shoot tens of thousands in their place and compared to the fact that the shooting of these tens of thousands would then be carried out even at the cost of German blood. Every little fire will immediately be stamped out and quenched, and extinguished otherwise—as in the case of a real fire—a political and psychological surface fire may spring up among the people.

THE COMMUNISTS IN THE REICH

I don't believe the Communists could attempt any action, for their leading elements, like most criminals, are in our concentration camps. And here I must say this—that we shall be able to see after the war what a blessing it was for Germany that in spite of the silly talk about humanitarianism, we imprisoned all this criminal substratum of the German people in concentration camps. I'll answer for that. If they were going about free, we would be worse off. For then the subhumans would have their NCOs and commanding officers, then they

would have their councils of workers and military. As it is, however, they are locked up and are making shells or projectile cases or other important things and are very useful members of human society.

CHIEF OF THE ANTI-PARTISAN UNITS BANDENKAMPF-VERBAENDE

In the meantime I have also set up the department of Chief of the Anti-Partisan Units. Our comrade SS Lieutenant General von dem Bach [Bach-Zelewski] is chief of the Anti-Partisan Units. I considered it necessary for the Reich Leader SS to be in authoritative command in all these battles, for I am convinced that we are best in a position to take action against this enemy struggle, which is a decidedly political one. Except where the units have been supplied and which we had formed for this purpose were taken from us to fill in gaps at the front, we have been very successful.

It is notable that, by setting up this department we have gained for the SS in turn a division, a corps, an army, and the next step, which is the headquarters of an army or even of a [army] group—if you wish to call it that.

UNIFORMED POLICE AND THE SECURITY POLICE

Now to deal briefly with the tasks of the regular Uniform Police and the Security Police. They still cover the same field. I can see that great things have been achieved. We have formed roughly thirty police regiments from police reservists and former members of the police—police officials, as they used to be called. The average age in our police battalions is not lower than that of the security battalions of the armed forces. Their achievements are beyond all praise. In addition, we have formed police rifle regiments by merging the indigenous security battalions of the "savage peoples" [wilden Voelker]. Thus, we did not leave these police battalions untouched but blended them in the ratio of about one to three. That is why we have, at the present moment of crisis, a far greater stability than could be seen among the other units made up of natives or local inhabitants.

THE EVACUATION OF THE JEWS

I also want to talk to you, quite frankly, on a very grave matter. Among ourselves it should be mentioned quite frankly, and we will never speak of it publicly. Just as we did not hesitate on 30 June 1934 to do the duty we were bidden and stand comrades who had lapsed up against the wall and shoot them, so we have never spoken about it and will never speak of it. It was that tact which is a matter of course and which I am glad to say, inherent in us, that made us never discuss it among ourselves, nor speak of it. It appalled everyone, and yet everyone was certain that he would do it the next time if such orders are issued and if it is necessary.

I mean the evacuation of the Jews, the extermination of the Jewish race. It's one of those things it is easy to talk about, "The Jewish race is being exterminated," says one party member, "that's quite clear, it's in our program—elimination of the Jews and we're doing it, exterminating them." And then they come to me, eighty million worthy Germans, and each one has his decent Jew. Of course the others are vermin, but this one is an A-1 Jew. Not one of all those who talk this way has watched it, not one of them has gone through it. Most of you must know what it means when one hundred corpses are lying side by side, or five hundred, or one thousand. To have stuck it out and at the same time—apart from exceptions caused by human weakness—to have remained decent fellows, that is what has made us hard. This is a page of glory in our history which has never been written and is never to be written, for we know how difficult we should have made it for ourselves, if with the bombing raids, the burdens and the deprivations of war we still had Jews today in every town as secret saboteurs, agitators, and troublemakers. We would now probably have reached the 1916-1917 stage when the Jews were still in the German national body.

We have taken from them what wealth they had. I have issued a strict order, which SS Lieutenant General Pohl has carried out, that this wealth should, as a matter of course, be handed over to the Reich without reserve. We have taken none of it for ourselves. Individual men who have lapsed will be punished in accordance with an order I issued at the beginning which gave this warning: whoever takes so much as a mark of it is a dead man. A number of SS men—there are not very many of them—have fallen short, and they will die without mercy. We had the moral right, we had the duty to our people, to destroy this people which wanted to destroy us. But we have not the right to enrich ourselves with so much as a fur, a watch, a mark, or a cigarette, or anything else. Because we have exterminated a germ, we do not want in the end to be infected by the germ and die of it. I will not see so much as a small area of sepsis appear here or gain a hold. Wherever it may form, we will cauterize it. Altogether, however, we can say that we have fulfilled this most difficult duty for the love of our people. And our spirit, our soul, our character has not suffered injury from it....

THE PRINCIPLE OF SELECTION

We are a product of the law of selection. We have made our choice from a cross section of our people. This people came into being eons ago, through generations, and centuries, by the throw of the dice of fate and of history. Alien peoples have swept over this people and left their heritage behind them. Alien blood streams have flowed into this people, but it has, nevertheless in spite of horrible hardships and terrible blows of fate, still had strength in the very essence of its blood to win through. Thus, this whole people is saturated with and held together by Nordic-Phalian-Germanic blood, so that after all one could and can still speak of a German people. From this people of such varied hereditary tendencies as it emerged from the collapse after the years of the battle of liberation, we have now consciously tried to select the Nordo-Germanic blood, for we could best expect this section of our blood to contain the creative, heroic, and life-preserving qualities of our people. We have gone partly by outward appearances and for the rest have kept these outward appearances in review by making constantly new demands, and by repeated tests both physical and mental, both of the character and the soul. Again and again we have sifted out and cast aside what was worthless, what did not suit us. Just as long as we have strength to do, thus will this organization *[Orden]* remain healthy. The moment we forget the law which is the foundation of our race and the law of selection and austerity toward ourselves, we all have the germ of death in us and will perish, just as every human organization, every blossom in this world, does some time perish. It must be our endeavor, our inner law, to make this blossoming and fructifying last for our people as long as possible, bringing as much prosperity as possible and—don't be alarmed—if possible for thousands of years. That is why, wherever we meet and whatever we do, we must be mindful of our principle blood, selection, and austerity. The law of nature is just this. What is hard is good, what is vigorous is good; whatever wins through in the battle of life, physically, purposefully, and spiritually, that is what is good—always taking the long view. Of course sometimes—and this has happened often in history—someone can get to the top by deceit and cheating. That makes no difference to nature, to the fate of the earth, or to the fate of the world. Really, that is nature. Fate removes the impostor after a time—time not reckoned in generations of man but in historical periods. It must be our endeavor never to deceive ourselves but always to remain genuine, that is what we must continually preach and instill into ourselves, and into every boy and each one of our subordinates.

THE SS AFTER THE WAR

One thing must be clear. One thing I would like to say to you today, the moment the war is over we will really begin to weld together our organization, this organization which we have built up for ten years, which we imbued and indoctrinated with the first most important principles during the ten years before the war. We must continue to do this—we if I may say so, we older men—for twenty years full of toil and work, so that a tradition thirty, thirty-five, forty years, a generation, may be created. Then this organization will march forward into the future young and strong, revolutionary and efficient, to fulfill the task of giving the German people, the Germanic people, the superstratum of society that will combine and hold together this Germanic people and this Europe, and from which the brains the people need for industry, farming, politics, and as soldiers, statesmen, and technicians, will emerge. In addition, this superstratum must be so strong and vital that every generation can unreservedly sacrifice two or three sons from every family on the battlefield, and that nevertheless the continued flowing of the bloodstream is assured....

When the war is won—then, as I have already told you, our work will start. We do not know when the war will end. It may be sudden, or it may be long delayed. We shall see. But I say to you now, if an armistice and peace comes suddenly, let no one think that he can then sleep the sleep of the just. Get all your commanders, chiefs, and SS Führers attuned to this; only then, gentlemen, shall we be awake, for then, so many others will fall into this sleep. I am going to rouse the whole SS, and keep it so wide awake that we can tackle reconstruction in Germany immediately. Then Germanic work will be begun immediately in the General SS, for then the harvest will be ripe to be taken into the granary. We shall then call up age groups there by law. We shall then immediately put all our Waffen SS units into excellent form, both as regards equipment and training. We shall go on working in this first six months after the war, as though the big offensive were starting on the next day. It will make all the difference, if Germany has an operative reserve, an operative backing, at the peace or armistice negotiations, of twenty, twenty-five, or thirty SS divisions intact.

If the peace is a final one, we shall be able

to tackle our great work of the future. We shall colonize. We shall indoctrinate our boys with the laws of the SS organization. I consider it to be absolutely necessary to the life of our peoples, that we should not only impart the meaning of ancestry, grandchildren, and future, but feel these to be a part of our being. Without there being any talk about it, without our needing to make use of rewards and similar material things, it must be a matter of course that we have children. It must be a matter of course that the most copious breeding should be from this racial superstratum of the Germanic people. In twenty to thirty years we must really be able to present the whole of Europe with its leading class. If the SS, together with the farmers—we together with our friend Backe—then run the colony in the East on a grand scale, without any restraint, without any question about any kind of tradition, but with nerve and revolutionary impetus, we shall in twenty years push the national boundary *[Volkstumsgrenze]* five hundred kilometers eastward.

I requested of the Führer already today, that the SS—if we have fulfilled our task and our duty by the end of the war—should have the privilege of holding Germany's easternmost frontier as a defense frontier. I believe this is the only privilege for which we have no competitors. I believe not one person will dispute our claim to this privilege. We shall be in a position there to train every young age group in the use of arms. We shall impose our laws on the East. We will charge ahead and push our way forward little by little to the Urals. I hope that our generation will successfully bring it about that every age group has fought in the East, and that every one of our divisions spends a winter in the East every second or third year. Then we shall never grow soft, then we shall never get SS members who only come to us because it is distinguished or because the black coat will naturally be very

attractive in peacetime. Everyone will know that "if I join the SS, there is the possibility that I might be killed." He has contracted in writing that every second year he will not dance in Berlin, attend the carnival in Munich, but that he will be posted to the eastern frontier in an ice-cold winter. Then we will have a healthy elite for all time. Thus, we will create the necessary conditions for the whole Germanic people and the whole of Europe: controlled, ordered, and led by us, the Germanic people, to be able in generations to stand the test in her battles of destiny against Asia which will certainly break out again. We do not know when that will be.

Then, when the mass of humanity of one to one and one-half billions line up against us, the Germanic people numbering, I hope, 250 to 300 millions and the other European peoples making a total of 600 to 700 millions (and with an outpost area stretching as far as the Urals or a hundred miles beyond the Urals) must stand the test in its vital struggle against Asia. It would be an evil day if the Germanic people did not survive it. It would be the end of beauty and culture, of the creative power of this earth. That is the distant future. It is for that we are fighting, pledged to hand down the heritage of our ancestors.

We see into the distant future because we know what it will be. That is why we are doing our duty more fanatically than ever, more devoutly than ever, more bravely, more obediently, and more thoroughly than ever. We want to be worthy of being permitted to be the first SS men of the Führer Adolf Hitler in the long history of the Germanic people which stretches before us.

Now let us remember the Führer Adolf Hitler who will create the Germanic Reich and will lead us into the Germanic future. Our Führer, Adolf Hitler, Sieg Heil, Sieg Heil, Sieg Heil.

EXCERPTS FROM *DEATH DEALER: THE CONFESSIONS OF RUDOLPH HÖSS, COMMANDANT OF AUSCHWITZ*

THE FINAL SOLUTION TO THE JEWISH PROBLEM

. . . Experience had shown that the prussic acid called Cyclon-B caused death with far greater speed and certainty, especially if the rooms were kept dry and airtight with the people packed closely together, and provided they were fitted with as large a number of intake vents as possible. So far as Auschwitz is concerned, I have never known or heard of a single person being found alive when the gas chambers were opened half an hour after the gas had been poured in.[1]

The extermination process in Auschwitz took place as follows: Jews selected for gassing

---

[1] Dr. Miklos Nyiszli, a Hungarian prisoner who worked as Mengele's assistant and had access to the gas chamber areas, relates a story of a teenage girl who miraculously survived the gassing process. Unconscious, yet still alive, she was revived and fed; then came the question of what to do with her. SS Master Sergeant Mussfeld happened by and discovered Nyiszli and the Sonderkommando occupied with helping the girl to full consciousness. After a discussion with Nyiszli as to what to do with the girl, Mussfeld carried her to the furnace room hallway where another SS soldier shot her to death. Miklos Nyiszli, *Auschwitz*, 1960, pp. 88–96.

Heinrich Himmler speaking with a Soviet prisoner during an official visit to the POW camp in Minsk. His chief of staff, Karl Wolff, stands over Himmler's left shoulder. July 1941. National Archives/Courtesy of USHMM–Photo Archives.

were taken as quietly as possible to the crematories. The men were already separated from the women. In the undressing chamber, prisoners of the Sonderkommandos, who were specially chosen for this purpose, would tell them in their own language that they were going to be bathed and deloused, and that they must leave their clothing neatly together, and, above all, remember where they put them, so that they would be able to find them again quickly after the delousing. The Sonderkommando had the greatest interest in seeing that the operation proceeded smoothly and quickly.[2] After undressing, the Jews went into the gas chamber, which was furnished with showers and water pipes and gave a realistic impression of a bathhouse.

The women went in first with their children, followed by the men, who were always fewer in number. This part of the operation nearly always went smoothly since the Sonderkommando would always calm those who showed any anxiety or perhaps even had some clue as to their fate. As an additional precaution, the Sonderkommando and an SS soldier always stayed in the chamber until the very last moment.

The door would be screwed shut and the waiting disinfection squads would immediately pour the gas [crystals] into the vents in the ceiling of the gas chamber down an air shaft which went to the floor. This ensured the rapid distribution of the gas. The process could be observed through the peep hole in the door. Those who were standing next to the air shaft were killed immediately. I can state that about one-third died immediately. The remainder staggered about and began to scream and struggle for air. The screaming, however, soon changed to gasping and in a few moments everyone lay still. After twenty minutes at the most no movement could be detected. The time required for the gas to take effect varied according to weather conditions and depended on whether it was damp or dry, cold or warm. It also depended on the quality of the gas, which was never exactly the same, and on the composition of the transports, which might contain a high proportion of healthy Jews, or the old and sick, or children. The victims became unconscious after a few minutes, according to the distance from the air shaft. Those who screamed and those who were old, sick, or weak, or the small children died quicker than those who were healthy or young.

The door was opened a half hour after the gas was thrown in and the ventilation system was turned on. Work was immediately started to remove the corpses. There was no noticeable change in the bodies and no sign of convulsions or discoloration. Only after the bodies had been left lying for some time—several hours—did the usual death stains appear where they were laid. Seldom did it occur that they were soiled with feces. There were no signs of wounds of any kind. The faces were not contorted.

The Sonderkommando now set about removing the gold teeth and cutting the hair from the women. After this, the bodies were taken up by an elevator and laid in front of the ovens, which had meanwhile been fired up. Depending on the size of the bodies, up to three corpses could be put in through one oven door at the same time. The time required for cremation also depended on the number of bodies in each retort, but on average it took twenty minutes. As previously stated, Crematories II and III could cremate two thousand bodies in twenty-four hours, but a higher number was not possible without causing damage to the installations. Crematories IV and V should have been able to cremate fifteen

---

[2] Although the Sonderkommando were themselves killed off after a period of time, enough veterans of different commandos survived because they were transferred from one to the other. They knew very well from past experiences that to try to inform the victims would only lead to a bloody end. Many did try to whisper to the victims what lay ahead, but were looked at in total disbelief. Although there were some riots during the undressing they only added to the horror because the SS would beat or shoot to death anyone who showed the slightest indication that they might cause problems. Besides, how brave can one be when one is naked and the oppressor is clothed and armed? The psychology of the undressing phase helped to cow the groups of people. Massed together in their nakedness clinging to their children or parents, they were in no position to revolt.

hundred bodies in twenty-four hours, but as far as I know this figure was never reached.[3]

During the period when the fires were kept continuously burning without a break, the ashes fell through the grates and were constantly removed and crushed to powder. The ashes were taken by trucks to the Vistula [River], where they immediately dissolved and drifted away. The ashes taken from the burning pits near Bunker II and from Crematory V were handled in the same way. The process of destruction in Bunkers I and II was exactly the same as in the crematories, except that the effects of the weather on the operation were more noticeable.

THE GASSINGS

While I was on an official trip, my second-in-command, Camp Commander Fritzsch, experimented with gas for these killings. He used a gas called Cyclon-B, prussic acid, which was often used as an insecticide in the camp to exterminate lice and vermin. There was always a supply on hand. When I returned Fritzsch reported to me about how he had used the gas. We used it again to kill the next transport.

The gassing was carried out in the basement of Block 11. I viewed the killings wearing a gas mask for protection. Death occurred in the crammed-full cells immediately after the gas was thrown in. Only a brief choking outcry and it was all over.[4] This first gassing of people did not really sink into my mind. Perhaps I was much too impressed by the whole procedure.

I remember well and was much more impressed by the gassing of nine hundred Russians which occurred soon afterwards in the old crematory because the use of Block 11 caused too many problems. While the unloading took place, several holes were simply punched from above through the earth and concrete ceiling of the mortuary. The Russians had to undress in the antechamber, then everyone calmly walked into the mortuary because they were told they were to be deloused in there. The entire transport fit exactly in the room. The doors were closed and the gas poured in

through the openings in the roof. How long the process lasted, I don't know, but for quite some time sounds could be heard. As the gas was thrown in some of them yelled "Gas!" and a tremendous screaming and shoving started toward both doors, but the doors were able to withstand all the force. It was not until several hours later that the doors were opened and the room aired out. There for the first time I saw gassed bodies in mass. Even though I imagined death by gas to be much worse, I still was overcome by a sick feeling, a horror. I always imagined death by gas a terrible choking suffocation, but the bodies showed no signs of convulsions. The doctor explained to me that prussic acid paralyzes the lungs.[5] The effect is sudden and so powerful that symptoms of suffocation never appear in cases of death by coal gas or by lack of oxygen.

At the time I really didn't waste any thoughts about the killings of the Russian POWs. It was ordered, I had to carry it out. But I must admit

---

[3] According to expert evidence by Dr. Roman Dawidowski, professor at the Academy of Mining and Metallurgy in Kraków, the average number of bodies cremated within twenty-four hours in the thirty ovens of the two largest crematories was about five thousand. The figure of three thousand could be reached in smaller Crematories IV and V. This total allows for a break of three hours in every twenty-four-hour period to allow for deslagging the generators and for smaller stoppages caused by the constant use. Similar numbers were given as evidence by eyewitness Sonderkommando members, namely Henryk Tauber and Alter Feinsilber, and also by Stanislaw Kankowski. KL-PMO, p. 134.

[4] Death is caused by the cyanide gas combining with red blood cells, thus prohibiting them from carrying needed oxygen to the body. Victims of this gas first fall unconscious due to lack of oxygen. As the body struggles to save the vital organs, it cuts off the flow to the extremities, attempting to bring the oxygen-full blood to the heart, brain, and other vital organs. If the victim is not removed or given the amino nitrate antidote, he will die of oxygen starvation. This explains the many descriptions of the Sonderkommandos who worked pulling out bodies from the gas chambers. They reported that the victims' lips, fingers, toes, and even ears were purple or dark blue. The gas is noticeable in the air by a bitter almond smell; some have described it as a peach pit smell. Two hundred five parts per million of air for thirty minutes is usually fatal. Interview Craig Skaggs, Dupont Chemical Company, Wilmington, Delaware.

[5] Höss and the doctors are incorrect. See footnote 2.

openly that the gassings had a calming effect on me, since in the near future the mass annihilation of the Jews was to begin. Up to this point it was not clear to me, nor to Eichmann how the killing of the expected masses was to be done. Perhaps by gas? But how, and what kind of gas? Now we had discovered the gas and the procedure. I was always horrified of death by firing squads, especially when I thought of the huge numbers of women and children who would have to be killed. I had had enough of hostage executions, and the mass killings by firing squad ordered by Himmler and Heydrich.

Now I was at ease. We were all saved from these bloodbaths, and the victims would be spared until the last moment. That is what I worried about the most when I thought of Eichmann's accounts of the mowing down of the Jews with machine guns and pistols by the Einsatzgruppe.[6] Horrible scenes were supposed to have occurred: people running away even after being shot, the killing of those who were only wounded, especially the women and children. Another thing on my mind was the many suicides among the ranks of the SS Special Action Squads who could no longer mentally endure wading in the bloodbath. Some of them went mad. Most of the members of the Special Action Squads drank a great deal to help get through this horrible work. According to [Captain] Hoffie's accounts, the men of Globocnik's extermination section drank tremendous quantities of alcohol.

In the spring of 1942 [January] the first transports of Jews arrived from Upper Silesia. All of them were to be exterminated. They were led from the ramp across the meadow, later named section B-II of Birkenau, to the farmhouse called Bunker I. [Camp Commander] Aumeier, Palitzsch, and a few other block leaders led them and spoke to them as one would in casual conversation, asking them about their occupations and their schooling in order to fool them. After arriving at the farmhouse they were told to undress. At first they went very quietly into the rooms where they were supposed to be disinfected. At that point some of them

became suspicious and started talking about suffocation and extermination. Immediately a panic started. Those still standing outside were quickly driven into the chambers, and the doors were bolted shut. In the next transport those who were nervous or upset were identified and watched closely at all times. As soon as unrest was noticed these troublemakers were inconspicuously led behind the farmhouse and killed with a small caliber pistol which could not be heard by the others. The presence of the Sonderkommando[7] and their soothing behavior also helped calm the restless and suspicious. Some of the Sonderkommando even went with them into the rooms and stayed until the last moment to keep them calm while an SS soldier stood in the doorway. The most important thing, of course, was to maintain as much peace and quiet as possible during the process of arriving and undressing. If some did not want to undress, some of those already undressed as well as the Sonderkommando had to help undress them.

With quiet talk and persuasion even those who resisted were soothed and undressed. The Sonderkommando, which was composed of prisoners, took great pains that the process of undressing took place very quickly so that the victims had no time to think about what was happening. Actually the eager assistance of the

---

[6] The infamous *Einsatzgruppen* (special action squads) were a contingent of the SS who followed behind the *Wehrmacht* (regular German Army) and arrested Communist Party members, those connected with the Soviet government (*Politruks*) and Jews. These were usually marched to a wooded area, machine gunned to death, then buried in shallow mass graves. If the number was small, they would be shot in town and their bodies left.

[7] The *Sonderkommando* were special squads of men in Auschwitz-Birkenau who worked exclusively in the gas chambers and were kept separate from all the other camp prisoners. They were usually Jews who were selected or sent to the *Kommando* (work detail) as punishment, as in the case of Fillip Müller. They helped the SS get the victims undressed and into the gas chambers. After the people were gassed they went into the chambers and pulled out bodies and dragged them to be checked for gold teeth. Others pulled the teeth, while still others worked near the ovens or the open-pit trenches making sure the bodies were consumed by the flames. Fillip Müller.

Sonderkommando during the undressing and the procession into the gas chambers was very peculiar. Never did I see or ever hear even a syllable breathed to those who were going to be gassed as to what their fate was. On the contrary, they tried everything to fool them. Most of all, they tried to calm those who seemed to guess what was ahead. Even though they might not believe the SS soldiers, they would have complete trust in those of their own race. For this reason the Sonderkommando was always composed of Jews from the same country as those who were being sent to the gas chamber.

The new arrivals asked about life in the camp and most of them asked about their relatives and friends from earlier transports. It was interesting to see how the Sonderkommando lied to them and how they emphasized these lies with convincing words and gestures. Many women hid their babies under piles of clothing. Some of the Sonderkommando watched carefully for this and would talk and talk to the woman until they persuaded her to take her baby along. The women tried to hide the babies because they thought the disinfection process would harm their infants. The little children cried mostly because of the unusual setting in which they were being undressed. But after their mothers or the Sonderkommando encouraged them, they calmed down and continued playing, teasing each other, clutching a toy as they went into the gas chamber.

I also watched how some women who suspected or knew what was happening, even with the fear of death all over their faces, still managed enough strength to play with their children and to talk to them lovingly. Once a woman with four children, all holding each other by the hand to help the smallest ones over the rough ground, passed by me very slowly. She stepped very close to me and whispered, pointing to her four children, "How can you murder these beautiful, darling children? Don't you have any heart?"

Another time an old man hissed while passing me, "Germany will pay a bitter penance for the mass murder of the Jews." His eyes glowed with hatred as he spoke. In spite of this he went bravely into the gas chamber without worrying about the others.

Another young woman stands out in my mind. While constantly running back and forth, she helped to undress the little children and old women with great care. At the point of selection she had two little children at her side and she caught my attention by her agitated behavior and her appearance. She didn't look Jewish at all. At this point the children were no longer with her. Staying until the end with several other children, she kept speaking softly and calming those who weren't finished undressing. She then went into the bunker with the last group. In the doorway she stopped and said, "I knew from the beginning that we were destined to be gassed at Auschwitz. I got through the selection of those who were chosen to work by taking children in my hands. I wanted to experience the process fully conscious and accurately. I hope it will be quick. Farewell!"

Occasionally some women would suddenly start screaming in a terrible way while undressing. They pulled out their hair and acted as if they had gone crazy. Quickly they were led behind the farmhouse and killed by a bullet in the back of the neck from a small caliber pistol. Sometimes, as the Sonderkommando were leaving the room, the women realized their fate and began hurling all kinds of curses at us. As the doors were being shut, I saw a woman trying to shove her children out of the chamber, crying out, "Why don't you at least let my precious children live?" There were many heartbreaking scenes like this which affected all who were present.

In the spring of 1942 hundreds of people in the full bloom of life walked beneath the budding fruit trees of the farm into the gas chamber to their death, most of them without a hint of what was going to happen to them. To this day I can still see these pictures of the arrivals, the selections, and the procession to their death.

As the selection process continued at the unloading ramps, there were an increasing number of incidences. Tearing apart families, separating the men from the women and children, caused great unrest and excitement in the entire transport. Separating those who were able to work only increased the seriousness of the situation. No matter what, the families wanted to stay together. So it happened that even those selected to work ran back to the other members of their family, or the mothers with their children tried to get back to their husbands, or to the older children. Often there was such chaos and confusion that the selection process had to be started all over again. The limited amount of standing room did not permit better ways to separate them. There was no way to calm down these overly excited masses. Oftentimes order was restored by sheer force.

EXCERPTS FROM GITTA SERENY'S INTERVIEWS WITH FRANZ STANGL, THE COMMANDANT OF TREBLINKA AND SOBIBOR

"What did the camp look like when you got there?"

"It was just the Sobibor railway station. The station building and across from it the forester's hut and a barn, that's all; just those three wooden buildings."

"And who did you find at Sobibor?"

"That was a surprise for me," he said the first time, "because there were several people there I already knew: they'd been in the . . . you know . . . the Euthanasia Program. Especially one Michel, he'd been the head nurse at Hartheim."

(He repeated this answer on a second occasion, but when I asked him the same question yet again, six weeks later, he suddenly said that Michel had actually traveled to Sobibor with him.)

"Weren't you a bit surprised to see Michel there? What did you think a nurse was doing at this supply camp site?"

"Well, I didn't really think about it. I knew of course that as the Aktion was over, the staff had become available—something had to be done with them. Also, it was very nice for me to have a friend there."

It was of course quite clear at the time that the story of his beginnings in Poland and, of some of the euthanasia phase, was at least partly fabrication, partly rationalization and partly evasion. But having pressed him about this repeatedly—on each occasion when we went through it again—I hoped that if I didn't press him too hard, he would find it possible later on to revert to telling me the truth about the rest of it, however difficult.

He went on to describe the Polish workers, whom he found a "lackadaisical lot." "They lived in the neighborhood and went home at night— no doubt to get drunk on their slivovitz. Anyway, they always arrived late in the morning."

Within two or three days he obtained a Jewish kommando "work kommando" of twenty-five men, he said, and some Ukrainian guards from a nearby training camp, Trawniki. "At that time we really had nothing, no amenities for anybody," he said. "Those first weeks we all bunked in together."

"What do you mean 'all together'? The German staff, the Ukrainian guards and the Jews?"

"At first we just used one hut but while we were working on the others: we slept on

the floor in the kitchen, and the others in the loft. Everything had to be built from scratch."

"When did you first find out what the camp was really for?"

"Two things happened: when we'd been there about three days I think, Michel came running one day and said he'd found a funny building back in the woods. 'I think there is something fishy going on here,' he said. 'Come and see what it reminds you of.'"

"What did he mean, 'in the woods'?"

"It was about ten or even fifteen minutes' walk away from the railway station where we were building the main camp. It was a new brick building with three rooms, three meters by four. The moment I saw it I knew what Michel meant: it looked exactly like the gas chamber at Schloss Hartheim."

"But who had built this? How could you possibly not have noticed it before? Or seen it on the plans?"

"The Poles had built it—they didn't know what it was to be. Neither Michel nor I had had any time yet to go for walks in the woods. We were very busy. Yes—it was on the plans, but so were lots of other buildings . . ." The sentence trailed off.

"All right, you hadn't known, but now you knew. What did you do?"

His face had gone red. I didn't know whether because he had been caught out in a lie or because of what he was about to say next; it was much more usual for him to blush in advance than in retrospect.

"The second thing I mentioned happened almost simultaneously: a transport officer, a sergeant, arrived from Lublin—he was drunk—and said to me [he sounded angry even now] that Globocnik was dissatisfied with the progress of the camp and had said to tell me that 'If these Jews don't work properly, just kill them off and we'll get others.'"

"What did that indicate to you?"

"I went the very next day to Lublin to see Globocnik. He received me at once. I said to him, 'How can this sergeant be permitted to give me such a message? And anyway, I am a police officer, how can I be expected to do anything like that?' Globocnik was very friendly. He said I had misunderstood: I was just overwrought. He said, 'We'd better get you some leave. You just go back for the moment and get on with the building. You are doing fine.' And then he said, 'Perhaps we can arrange to have your family come out for a bit.' So I went back. What else could I do?"

"Did you ask Globocnik about the gas chambers?"

"There was no opportunity," he said firmly. "I went back to Sobibor and talked it over with Michel. We decided that somehow we had to get out. But the very next day Wirth came. He told me to assemble the German personnel and made a speech—just as awful, just as vulgar as his speeches had been at Hartheim. He said that any Jews who didn't work properly here would be 'eliminated.' 'If any of you don't like that,' he said to us, 'you can leave. But under the earth,'—that was his idea of being humorous—'not over it.' And then he left. I went back to Lublin the next morning. Sturmbannführer (Major) Höfle, Globocnik's aide then, kept me waiting in the office all day, and again the next morning. Then he finally told me that the General would not be available for me. I went back to Sobibor. Four days later a courier came from Lublin with a formal letter from Globocnik informing me—in ice-cold language—that Wirth had been appointed inspector of camps and that I was to report to him at Belzec forthwith."

Wirth had by then commanded both Chelmno and Belzec, a much larger establishment. At Chelmno it was found that the method of gas vans was impracticable for the huge task on hand, and he claimed to have invented the Jewish Sonderkommandos (probably falsely, as this idea, reverting to the legend of the pharaonic tombs, seems more likely to have emanated from Heydrich's fertile intellectual brain). At Belzec the first large scale exterminations with engine exhaust gas in gas chambers were begun in March 1942.

"I can't describe to you what it was like," Stangl said. *He spoke slowly now, in his more formal German, his face strained and grim. He passed his hand over his eyes and rubbed his forehead. "I went there by car. As one arrived, one first reached Belzec railway station, on the left side of the road. The camp was on the same side, but up a hill. The Kommandantur was two hundred meters away, on the other side of the road. It was a one-story building. The smell . . ." he said, "Oh God, the smell. It was everywhere. Wirth wasn't in his office. I remember, they took me to him . . . he was standing on a hill, next to the pits . . . the pits . . . full . . . they were full. I can't tell you; not hundreds, thousands, thousands of corpses . . . oh God. That's where Wirth told me—he said that was what Sobibor was for. And that he was putting me officially in charge."*

Although I have never doubted that Stangl's first experience of a death camp in operation was—as he claimed—that day in Belzec, he did give me, here too, two versions of this experience, although they were only marginally different. (His giving different versions of events is not too important from the point of view of facts. It is, however, of psychological relevance, for the gradual decrease in evasions, embellishments, and anxiety to project a favorable image

of himself reflects significantly and accurately the intensity of his emotion, and possibly the psychological changes these conversations produced in him.)

The second time I asked him to tell me this story, he said:

"Wirth wasn't in his office; they said he was up in the camp. I asked whether I should go up there and they said, 'I wouldn't if I were you—he's mad with fury. It isn't healthy to go near him.' I asked what was the matter. The man I was talking to said that one of the pits had overflowed. They had put too many corpses in it and putrefaction had progressed too fast, so that the liquid underneath had pushed the bodies on top up and over and the corpses had rolled down the hill. I saw some of them— oh God, it was awful. A bit later Wirth came down. And that's when he told me. . . ."

The historical record provides a number of horrifyingly graphic descriptions of Wirth's Belzec where the installations constantly broke down, causing unimaginable suffering to the deportees who were either left waiting, naked and without food or water, in the open, sometimes for days, or else were crammed into railway cars, the floors of which had been covered with lime, and left to suffocate on sidings only a few hundred meters from the camp. These conditions—the beginnings of which Stangl obviously saw in April 1942—have been described by Jan Karski in *The Story of a Secret State* and by Kurt Gerstein. Both men visited Belzec.[1] Gerstein did

---

[1] Editors note: In their fine biography of Jan Karski, *Karski: How One Man Tried to Stop the Holocaust*, E. Thomas Wood and Stanilaw M. Jankowski clear up one misidentification in Karski's testimony. Prior to his departure from Poland, Karski was sent to a concentration camp previously identified as Belzec, but the story of his visit was not credible. Small details did not add up and they called into question his entire testimony, which was clearly so valuable and verifiable. The authors identify the town as Izbica Lubelska, the midway point between Lublin and Belzec, some forty miles from each locality, and a sorting point.

so in his official capacity as Obersturmführer (lieutenant) in the SS Health Department and his description of the gas chambers is probably the most terrible that has emerged from that approximate period. Gerstein's somewhat ambiguous but undoubtedly tortured personality has been amply described in the literature (although his death, in Fresnes prison on July 17, 1945, remains clouded in mystery). Karski (now professor emeritus at Georgetown University in Washington, D.C.), who was an indomitable courier for the Polish government in exile, spent a day at Belzec disguised as a Ukrainian guard. Karski's description of the extermination of the Jews in Poland reached London and Washington as early as October 1942 (presumably, at least through the diplomatic post, also the Vatican in Rome). Although the fact of the physical extermination of the Jews in Poland was by then thoroughly known to the Allies—and to the Vatican—Karski's detailed description to the world press, MPs, members of Congress and religious leaders in London and Washington, and his meetings with Anthony Eden and President Roosevelt, provided the first testimony of an eyewitness. If previously there had been any doubt, after meeting Karski or reading his report, the Allied leaders knew precisely what was happening in Poland.

I had no doubt whatever of Stangl's sincerity when he described his reaction to Belzec. Nor could one doubt that this was the real moment of decision for him: the time when he might have braved what he certainly considered the deadly dangers of taking a stand . . . and didn't because it wasn't in him to do so.

"I said [to Wirth] I couldn't do it," he said. "I simply wasn't up to such an assignment. There wasn't any argument or discussion. Wirth just said my reply would be reported to HQ and I was to go back to Sobibor. In fact I went to Lublin, tried again to see Globocnik, again in vain. He wouldn't see me. When I got back to Sobibor, Michel and I talked and talked about it. We agreed that what they were doing was a crime. We considered deserting—we discussed it for a

long time. But how? Where could we go? What about our families?" He stopped. He stopped at that point, when he told me about it, just as he and Michel must have stopped talking about it at that point, because, if there was nothing they could or dared do, there was nothing else to say.

"But you knew that day that what was being done was wrong?"

"Yes, I knew. Michel knew. But we also knew what had happened in the past to other people who had said no. The only way out that we could see was to keep trying in various and devious ways to get a transfer. The direct way was impossible. As Wirth had said, that led 'under the earth.' Wirth came to Sobibor the next day. He ignored me; he stayed several days and organized everything. Half the workers were detailed to finish the gas chambers."

"While Wirth was organizing, what were you doing?"

"I just went on with other construction work," he said wearily. "And then one afternoon Wirth's aide, Oberhauser, came to get me. I was to come to the gas chamber. When I got there, Wirth stood in front of the building wiping the sweat off his cap and fuming. Michel told me later that he'd suddenly appeared, looked around the gas chambers on which they were still working and said, 'Right, we'll try it out right now with those twenty-five work-Jews. Get them up here.' They marched our twenty-five Jews up there and just pushed them in, and gassed them. Michel said Wirth behaved like a lunatic, hit out at his own staff with his whip to drive them on. And then he was livid because the doors hadn't worked properly."

"What did he say to you?"

"Oh, he just screamed and raved and said the doors had to be changed. After that he left."

"And after he was gone, what did you do?"

"The same thing; I continued the construction of the camp. Michel had been put in charge of the gassings."

"Put in charge by whom?"

"By Wirth."

"So now the exterminations had really started; they were happening right in front of you. How did you feel?"

"At Sobibor one could avoid seeing almost all of it—it all happened so far away from the camp buildings. All I could think of was that I wanted to get out. I schemed and schemed and planned and planned. I heard there was a new police unit at Mogilev. I went again to Lublin and filled out an application form for transfer. I asked Hofle to help me get Globocnik's agreement. He said he would do what he could, but I never heard of it again. Two months later—in June—my wife wrote that she had been requested to supply details about the children's ages: they were going to be granted a visit to Poland."

The exact date on which Sobibor became fully operational is not quite certain; it was either May 16 or May 18, 1942. It is certain, however, that in the first two months, the period when Stangl was administering the camp, about one hundred thousand people were killed there. Soon after that, the machinery broke down for a while and exterminations did not recommence until October.

I drove to Sobibor by way of Lublin on a cold Friday in March 1972, and we passed the site of the camp before we realized what it was. It is marked by a light-brown stone monument, ten feet tall, on which are engraved the words: "In this place from May 1942 until October 1943 there existed a Hitler extermination camp. At this camp 250,000 Russian, Polish, Jewish and Gypsy prisoners were murdered. On the 4th of October 1943 an armed rebellion took place, with several

hundred prisoners taking part who, after a battle with the Hitler guards, escaped." Facing the monument is Sobibor railway station. The station building has probably been improved, but the forester's cottage—built of timber and painted green and dark brown—in which Stangl lived, appears to be unchanged. It is now inhabited by the families of two foresters, and the little room in which Stangl worked and slept is still a bedroom. It overlooks the railway track, which was known in the camp as "the ramp." Transports may have halted slightly farther back rather than directly opposite his window, but it would still have been impossible for Stangl to avoid seeing them.

The site—about 160 acres of forest—is quiet. The big clumps of pines and other trees are thick enough even in March to hide all open spaces. It is dark in the woods, with a musty, damp smell. "In Sobibor," Franz Suchomel had said, "one couldn't do any killing after the snow thawed because it was all under water. It was very damp at the best of times, but then it became a lake."

There is a road about thirty feet wide, still in good condition, stretching from the railway track into the woods. It was constructed under either Stangl or his successor Reichleitner, and the SS called it the *Himmelfahrtsstrasse*—the Road to Heaven. The area adjoining the disembarkation ramp, no larger than a medium-sized football ground, was called Camp 10. Cunningly divided by means of blind fences into squares and corridors, with many narrow "doors" from one square into another, it allowed the systematic separation of the arriving deportees, usually without arousing their suspicion. From the arrival point at the ramp, all that was visible were the fences, tightly camouflaged with evergreen branches; the distant trees; and, to the left, the small cluster of barracks (now a bare and open space) known as Camp I where the SS staff, the Ukrainian guards and the "work-Jews" lived and worked. This was all the 250,000 who were killed in Sobibor ever saw.

I walked along the road they had to take—except that now there was complete solitude and silence. After perhaps half a mile it ends in a large tract of open land. In the center, facing the road, is a huge mound of earth, an artificial hill thirty feet high, the bottom half of which is faced with glass laid over millions of tiny pebbles. Inset in the middle is a small square filled with dried wild flowers. This mound, now overgrown with grass and bushes, marks the place where the three gas chambers stood and symbolizes the graves of those who died there.

The air is clear and clean. There is the sound of birds, the occasional whistle and clatter of a train, the far-away clucking of chickens; familiar sounds which, thirty years ago, must have offered momentary illusions of reassurance. But the earth round the mound is dark and terribly fine while the soil over the rest of Sobibor is a light brown sand which gives underfoot. And one is jolted out of any effort at detachment by the sickening shock of realizing that—even these three decades later—one must be walking on ashes.

The custodian of the site is Wladzimier Gerung, head forester of the region, who lives with his wife in a new house on the other side of the railway, about twenty-five yards from the station. We went to see them, unannounced. The Gerungs, tall, easy-moving people with open faces and quietly courteous manners, came to Sobibor eighteen years ago. But as a girl, throughout the war, Pani Gerung lived near Chelm. "Oh yes," she said, "people in Chelm knew what was going on in Sobibor—how could they not? They could smell it—the air was rancid even though it was twenty miles away. And their terrible fires lit up the sky at night."

I asked whether she and the people who lived around her had feelings against the Jews. She shook her head. "No—it was just . . . there was nothing one could do. Except, I think sometimes, what our neighbors did."

The neighbors—farmers—had taken in two children of a Jewish peddler, a girl of five and a boy of fourteen, when both parents were put into a ghetto. The boy, on hearing that his parents and all the rest of the ghetto "had been taken away," had disappeared, but the farmer adopted the girl

legally and kept her as his own child. The little girl, said Pani Gerung, looked very Jewish, and to start with both children had to be passed from one house to another to keep them hidden: "Relatives and friends, everyone took them," said Pani Gerung. "The little girl's name was Elisabetta. In 1947 relations turned up and took her to Israel. She wrote to the farmers for several years. Then the letters stopped. Now they are old and deaf. They missed her terribly."

Any Pole who, during the occupation, was found assisting or hiding a Jew was summarily shot; the *Sondergerichte* (special courts) who tried such people accepted no pleas in defense. The penalty was automatic. Nonetheless, in spite of the strong anti-Semitism of large sections of the population, there are a number of documented examples of families, like the one quoted by Pani Gerung, who did extend such help. And there were also some Jewish children who were hidden by nuns in convents although the Catholic Church in Poland was immeasurably more pressured than anywhere else in Europe; ninety-five per cent of the priests held in concentration camps were Poles. In the government-sponsored *History of Help to the Jews in Occupied Poland*, the Polish writer Wladyslaw Bartoszewski (who is by no means only wedded to the party line) cites a number of examples; the account he gives is, perhaps, made all the more convincing because the figure he finally has to cite for the number of Polish Jews actually rescued by his compatriots is so pitifully small that it heavily underlines the heroism of the relatively few who were willing or felt able to take the risk.

It was difficult to remember Polish anti-Semitism when talking to these two people who belonged to the very region—the extreme east of Poland—where it was most rampant. Their manner of speaking, their caring for the Sobibor Memorial and their protectiveness of the mementos they have collected (two flags, some documents, a map of the camp, and the visitors' book with its pathetically few signatures) has a reverent, tender quality.

At Stangl's trial, his activities at Sobibor were, for administrative reasons, not included in the prosecution's case. But, even so, his behavior and attitude while there became part of the trial record and one of the matters brought up by each of the few Sobibor survivors who came to Düsseldorf as witnesses was the fact that he often attended the unloading of transports "dressed in white riding clothes." It was when he tried to explain this to me that I became aware for the first time of how he had lived—and was still living when we spoke—on two levels of consciousness, and conscience.

"When I came to Poland," he said, "I had very few clothes: one complete uniform, a coat, an extra pair of trousers and shoes, and an indoor jacket, that's all. I remember, during the very first week I was there, I was walking from the forester's hut—my quarters—to one of the construction sites and suddenly I began to itch all over. I thought I was going crazy; it was awful. I couldn't even reach everywhere at once to scratch. Michel said, 'Didn't anybody warn you? It's sand flies, they are all over the place. You shouldn't have come out without boots.' [This would appear to indicate that Michel was there ahead of Stangl.] I rushed back to my room and took everything off. I remember just handing all the stuff to somebody out of the door, and they boiled and disinfected everything. My clothes and almost every inch of me was covered with the things; they attach themselves to all the hair on your body. I had water brought in and bathed and bathed."

It was difficult at that point not to recall that in these camps the prisoners retained as "work-Jews" had to stand at rigid attention, caps off, whenever a German passed. Anyone who moved, for any reason whatever—cramps, itches or anything else—was more likely than not to be hit or beaten with a whip, and the consequences of being struck could go far beyond momentary pain. Any prisoner who, at the daily roll call, was found to be—as they called it—"marked" or "stamped," was a candidate for immediate gassing.

"These sand flies must have been an awful problem for the prisoners, weren't they?" I asked.

"Not everyone was as sensitive to them as I. They just liked me," he said, and smiled. "Anyway, what I wanted to tell you, with all this wear and tear, and the heat—it was very hot you know—my clothes fell apart. Well, one day, in a small town not far away, I found a weaving mill. I was interested in it because, you remember, that had been my profession once. So I went in. They were making very nice linen—off-white. I asked whether they'd sell me some. And that's how I got the white material; I had a jacket made right away and a little later jodhpurs and a coat."

"But even so, how could you go into the camp in this getup?"

"The roads were very bad," he explained blankly. "Riding was the best mode of transport."

I tried once more: "Yes, but to attend the unloading of these people who were about to die, in white riding clothes . . . ?"

"It was hot," he said. . . .

At Christmas 1942 Stangl ordered the construction of the fake railway station. A clock (with painted numerals and hands which never moved, but no one was thought likely to notice this), ticket-windows, various timetables and arrows indicating train connections "To Warsaw," "To Wolwonoce," and "To Bialystock" were painted on to the facade of the "sorting barracks"; all for the purpose of lulling the arriving transports—an increasing number of whom were to be from the West—into a belief that they had arrived in a genuine transit camp. "It is possible," Stangl agreed at his trial, "that I ordered the construction of the fake station."

"You've been telling me about your routines," I said to him. "But how did you feel? Was there anything you enjoyed, you felt good about?"

"It was interesting to me to find out who was cheating," he said. "As I told you, I didn't care who it was; my professional ethos was that if something wrong was going on, it had to be found out. That was my profession; I enjoyed it. It fulfilled me. And yes, I was ambitious about that; I won't deny that."

"Would it be true to say that you got used to the liquidations?"

He thought for a moment. "To tell the truth," he then said, slowly and thoughtfully, "one did become used to it."

"In days? Weeks? Months?"

"Months. It was months before I could look one of them in the eye. I repressed it all by trying to create a special place: gardens, new barracks, new kitchens, new everything; barbers, tailors, shoemakers, carpenters. There were hundreds of ways to take one's mind off it; I used them all."

"Even so, if you felt that strongly, there had to be times, perhaps at night, in the dark, when you couldn't avoid thinking about it?"

"In the end, the only way to deal with it was to drink. I took a large glass of brandy to bed with me each night and I drank."

"I think you are evading my question."

"No, I don't mean to; of course, thoughts came. But I forced them away. I made myself concentrate on work, work and again work."

"Would it be true to say that you finally felt they weren't really human beings?"

"When I was on a trip once, years later in—Brazil," he said, his face deeply concentrated, and obviously reliving the experience, "my train stopped next to a slaughterhouse. The cattle in the pens hearing the noise of the train, trotted up to the fence and stared at the train. They were very close to my window, one crowding the other, looking at me through that fence. I thought then, 'Look at this, this reminds me of Poland; that's just how the people looked, trustingly, just before they went into the tins—'"

"You said tins," I interrupted. "What do you mean?" But he went on without hearing or answering me.

". . . I couldn't eat tinned meat after that. Those big eyes . . . which looked at me . . . not knowing that in no time at all they'd all be dead." He paused. His face was drawn. At this moment he looked old and worn and real.

"So you didn't feel they were human beings?"

"Cargo," he said tonelessly. "They were cargo." He raised and dropped his hand in a gesture of despair. Both our voices had dropped. It was one of the few times in those weeks of talks that he made no effort to cloak his despair, and his hopeless grief allowed a moment of sympathy.

"When do you think you began to think of them as cargo? The way you spoke earlier, of the day when you first came to Treblinka, the horror you felt seeing the dead bodies everywhere—they weren't 'cargo' to you then, were they?"

"I think it started the day I first saw the Totenlager in Treblinka. I remember Wirth standing there, next to the pits full of blue-black corpses. It had nothing to do with humanity, it couldn't have; it was a mass— a mass of rotting flesh. Wirth said, 'What shall we do with this garbage?' I think unconsciously that started me thinking of them as cargo."

"There were so many children, did they ever make you think of your children, of how you would feel in the position of those parents?"

"No," he said slowly, "I can't say I ever thought that way." He paused. "You see," he then continued, still speaking with this *extreme seriousness and obviously intent on finding a new truth within himself, "I rarely saw them as individuals. It was always a huge mass. I sometimes stood on the wall and saw them in the tube. But—how can I explain it—they were naked, packed together, running, being driven with whips like ..."* the sentence trailed off. ("Stangl often stood on the earthen wall between the [two] camps," said Samuel Rajzman in Montreal. "He stood there like a Napoleon surveying his domain.")

"Could you not have changed that?" I asked. "In your position, could you not have stopped the nakedness, the whips, the horror of the cattle pens?"

"No, no, no. This was the system. Wirth had invented it. It worked. And because it worked, it was irreversible."

Suchomel remembered Stangl telling the SS personnel that an order had come from Hitler that nobody was to be beaten or tortured. "But then he said, 'It's impossible. But when the bigwigs come from Berlin you must hide the whips.'"

At the Treblinka trial Richard Glazar testified that the beatings often had distinctly sexual overtones and Suchomel's account seems to confirm this, if confirmation were needed. "When Kurt Franz beat them," Suchomel recounted, "it was on their bare buttocks [the crasser German word he used was *Hintern*]. They had to drop their trousers and count the blows of the whip. The others didn't insist on that, though."

Joe Siedlecki, too, talked about Kurt Franz's beatings. "He'd give them fifty strokes," he said. "They'd be dead at the end. He'd be half dead himself, but he'd beat and beat. Oh, some of the others, they were just weaklings—two strokes and they'd collapse—but Franz and Miete and some of them, they could go on and on."

"Stangl did improve things," Suchomel said later. "He alleviated it a bit for people, but he could have done more, especially from Christmas 1942. He could have stopped the whipping

post, the 'races,' 'sport,' and what Franz did with that dog; Barihe was Stangl's dog originally. He could have stopped all that without any trouble for himself. [The dog, originally harmless, had been trained to attack people, and specifically their genital regions, on command.] He had the power to do that—and he didn't. I don't think he cared. All he did was look after the death camp, the burning and all that; there everything had to run just so because the whole camp organization depended on it. I think what he really cared about was to have the place run like clockwork."

Gustav Munzberger, who was more incriminated than Suchomel, put it differently. "Do I think that Stangl could have done something to change things at Treblinka?" he said. "No. Well, perhaps a little, the whipping post and all that; but, on the other hand, if he had, then Franz would have told Wirth, and he would just have countermanded it. So what was the use?"

"What was the worst place in the camp for you?" I asked Stangl.

"The undressing barracks," he said at once. "I avoided it from my innermost being; I couldn't confront them; I couldn't lie to them; I avoided at any price talking to those who were about to die. I couldn't stand it."

It became clear that as soon as the people were in the undressing barracks—that is, as soon as they were naked—they were no longer human beings for him. What he was "avoiding at any price" was witnessing the transition. And when he cited instances of human relations with prisoners, it was never with any of those who were about to die.

"But were there never moments when this wall you built around yourself was breached? When the sight of a beautiful child, perhaps, or a girl, brought you up against the knowledge that these were human beings?"

"There was a beautiful red-blonde girl," he said. "She usually worked in the clinic but

when one of the maids in our living quarters was ill, she replaced her for a time. . . . It was just around the time when I had put up new barracks with single rooms for quite a few of the work-Jews," he said (a claim confirmed by Suchomel but put in doubt by Richard Glazar who says that only just before the revolt were two couples, both stooges for the SS, given single rooms).

"This girl—I knew one of the Kapos was her boyfriend . . . one always knew about things like that. . . ."

"What nationality was she?"

"Polish, I think. But she spoke German well. She was a—you know—a well-educated girl. Well, she came to my office that day to dust or something. I suppose I thought to myself, 'What a pretty girl she is and now she can have some privacy with her boyfriend.' So I asked her, just to say something nice, you know, 'Have you chosen a room for yourself yet?' I remember she stopped dusting and stood very still looking at me. And then she said, very quietly, you know, 'Why do you ask?'"

His tone of voice even now reflected the astonishment he felt twenty-nine years ago when this young girl responded to him not as a slave to her master, but as a free human being to a man she rejected. Not only that, she responded as to a social inferior, and the wording and tone of his reply confirm that he was immediately aware of this. "I said, 'Why shouldn't I ask? I can ask, can't I?' And again she just stood there, very straight, not moving, just looking right at me. And then she said, 'Can I go?' And I said, 'Yes, of course.' She went. I felt so ashamed. I realized she thought I'd asked because—well, you know, because I wanted her myself. I so admired her for facing up to me, for saying 'Can I go?' I felt ashamed for days because of the way she had misunderstood."

"Do you know what happened to her?" I asked this question each time he spoke of any of the prisoners in individual terms. But each time the answer was precisely the same, in the same tone of detachment, with the same politely aloof expression in his face.

"I don't know."

In this case I persisted. "But here was a girl who had enormously impressed you. Didn't you ever want to find out what happened to her?"

He looked uncomfortable. "I heard something about her having been transferred to the Totenlager." (The life expectancy of prisoners working in that part of the camp rarely exceeded two months.)

"How did that happen?"

"I am not really sure. You see, when our usual maid returned—I was on leave at that time—this girl went back to her work at the clinic. The doctor—I can't remember his name—had a run-in with Kurt Franz. It was never very clear what had happened. But the doctor killed himself. He took poison. And the girl was there when this happened and Franz sent her up to the Totenlager."

Later, when I tried to identify the girl Stangl had talked about, no one could say for certain who she was.

"Why don't you ask Otto Horn?" said Gustav Munzberger. "He was always larking about with the girls in the laundry in Camp II."

"Yes, I sometimes went into the laundry and talked to the girls," said Horn. "But I don't know of any red-blonde girl who was sent up to the upper camp by Franz. There was one amongst the six in the laundry who had red hair. But I don't know what her name was. All the girls spoke German. What did they do when they weren't working? I don't know. They had their own barracks and were locked in there at night. Later on, I sometimes let them out on a Sunday to go for a walk in the wood behind the camp; it was fenced in, you know...."

But the last word, as often, was Suchomel's, for whom recalling the details of Treblinka has become something of a passion.

"The only red-blonde was Tchechia, who had been Kapo Rakowski's girlfriend," he said. "A very proud and courageous girl. It would certainly have been her who would have said no to Stangl. But she was never sent up to the *Totenlager*. Otherwise, there was Sabina, but she was sent 'up' much earlier on—by Kuttner, not by Franz— after her affair with Kapo Kuba; it can't have been her. And it can't have been Irka, the doctor's assistant; she was dark. No, it was Tchechia Mandel from Lemberg. But she never worked at the clinic; she always worked in the kitchen...."

It has been generally agreed that although Stangl drank heavily at Treblinka, women, other than his wife, played no part in his life. Therefore, although we will never know for sure who this exceptionally brave and proud young girl was, it is probable, and corresponds with the overall impression he gave me, that his description of his impulsive attempt to communicate with her was accurate.

"Couldn't you have ordered her to be brought back?" I asked him.

He shook his head. "No."

I spent a good deal of time investigating this sequence of events, interesting for several reasons but particularly as this was the first instance of Stangl reacting personally or emotionally to any of the Treblinka inmates. As often happened, each of the people I questioned gave a different version of what happened.

The circumstances surrounding the death of the doctor, Dr. Choronzycki, sadly misrepresented in at least one much-discussed book on Treblinka, are in general agreed on by all those who were in Treblinka at the time—prisoners or guards—though there is a curious difference of opinion concerning Dr. Choronzycki's medical

specialty (not to speak of the spelling of his name). Stangl told me that this physician had been a "famous Warsaw internist." In Steiner's book, *Treblinka*, Dr. Choronzycki is described as "the doctor of the Germans." Suchomel says, "Of course, I remember him well; he was a nose and throat specialist. I talked with him many times; my son was physically handicapped, you know, and Dr. Choronzycki often advised me about him. He was a converted Jew, you know. He wore a golden necklace with a cross. He said his Polish colleagues in the hospital in Warsaw had given him away...." Richard Glazar says: "Choronzycki was a dentist, or at least that is what he claimed to be in Treblinka. That is why the SS picked him out of the transport for their own so-called SS *Revierstube*. This SS dental clinic was almost exactly opposite the room of the gold-Jews. The money for the revolt was to go from one of the gold-Jews via Choronzycki...."

All the survivors I spoke to agreed on the essential part the doctor was playing in the preparations for the revolt. But Suchomel said, "Dr Choronzycki had nothing to do with the revolt. That was just invention, like the book by Jean-Francois Steiner."

On the other hand, Suchomel agrees that Kurt Franz surprised the doctor in possession of gold, and that after the doctor attacked Franz with a surgical knife (surely an extraordinary act of courage) and the latter fled out of the window, he had time to take poison before being apprehended.

"Stangl was away," Suchomel says. "Franz sent for me and said, 'Get that woman doctor on the double.'" The woman doctor, Dr. Choronzycki's assistant, was Dr. Irena (Irka) Lewkowski.

"I ran," said Suchomel. "The old bitch pretended she couldn't walk quickly. Anyway, when we got there, the doctor's eyes were still open— he was still alive—she pumped his stomach out. Then Franz told me to assemble all the gold-Jews. The doctor could no longer speak. Franz was wild...."

"Kurt Franz kept beating him with his whip even when Choronzycki was quite obviously dead," said Glazar. "He had him dragged to the

Lazarett—all the gold-Jews had been brought there; he told them they'd be shot, one after the other, unless they told where the doctor got the gold. I remember, Willie Furst was there, he was a hotel owner from Slovakia; and little Edek, the accordion player, they'd picked him up too. After a while Edek, I was told, cried and begged the others to tell what they knew. 'I don't want to die,' he is supposed to have cried. Well, none of them told anything—the doctor was dead—and in the end Franz let them all go. He knew perfectly that they were the most valuable specialists they had, more important to them than anyone else in the camp."

"I didn't actually hear the end," said Suchomel. "I went out. Though before leaving the Lazarett I called out in Czech telling the gold-Jews that Franz was faking, he wasn't going to kill them, and for them not to tell...."

"I have never heard anything about Suchomel calling out something like that to the gold-Jews," said Glazar.

"I did have contact with the work-Jews," Stangl said. "You know, quite friendly relations. You asked me a while ago whether there was anything I enjoyed. Beyond my specific assignment, that's what I enjoyed; human relations. Especially with people like Singer and Blau. They were both Viennese. I always tried to give as many jobs as possible to Viennese Jews. It made for a lot of talk at the time, I know. But after all, I was Austrian.... Singer I had made the chief of the *Totenjuden*; I saw a lot of him. I think he was a dentist in Vienna. Or perhaps an engineer," he reflected. "He was killed during the revolt; it started in the upper camp you know." (He was wrong about Singer, who was a German, not a Viennese, and a businessman, not a dentist; and also about the revolt, which started in the lower camp.)

"Blau was the one I talked to most, he and his wife. No, I don't know what his profession had been, business I think. I'd made him the cook in the lower camp. He knew I'd help whenever I could.

"There was one day when he knocked at the door of my office about mid-morning and stood to attention and asked permission to speak to me. He looked very worried. I said, 'Of course, Blau, come on in. What's worrying you?' He said it was his eighty-year-old father; he'd arrived on that morning's transport. Was there anything I could do. I said, 'Really, Blau, you must understand, it's impossible. A man of eighty....' He said quickly that, yes, he understood, of course. But could he ask me for permission to take his father to the *Lazarett* rather than the gas chambers. And could he take his father first to the kitchen and give him a meal. I said, 'You go and do what you think best, Blau. Officially I don't know anything, but unofficially you can tell the Kapo I said it was all right.' In the afternoon, when I came back to my office, he was waiting for me. He had tears in his eyes. He stood to attention and said, 'Herr Hauptsturmführer, I want to thank you. I gave my father a meal. And I've just taken him to the *Lazarett*—it's all over. Thank you very much.' I said, 'Well, Blau, there's no need to thank me, but of course if you want to thank me, you may.'"

"What happened to Blau and his wife?"

That same vagueness—"I don't know."

This story and the way it was told represented to me the starkest example I had ever encountered of a corrupted personality, and it came very near to making me stop these conversations. I broke off early that lunchtime and went to sit for nearly two hours in a pub across the street, wrestling with the most intense malaise I'd ever felt at the thought of listening further to these disclosures.

I think the reason I finally did return to the little room in the prison was because I came to realize—perhaps as a result of the intensity of my own reaction—that for a man whose view was so distorted he could tell the story in that way, the relatively simple terms "guilt" or "innocence," "good" or "bad" no longer applied; what was important was that he had found in himself the need—or strength—to speak. Even as I acknowledged my own apprehension at continuing with these talks, I also knew for certain, at that moment, that if I did he would end by telling me the truth.

All the Treblinka survivors I talked to affirmed—with the fatalistic lack of vehemence of those who have come to terms with the inevitability of human failings in everyone, themselves included—that "Blau" was an informer. But it was Suchomel, in his chosen role of an objective observer, who put this into cogent words.

"Oh, Blau," he said. "He was Oberkapo at first. You see, he had known Stangl in Austria; he told me himself. No, I don't think he was lying. Stangl made no secret of having known him previously. He was Austrian, but by origin I think Polish and I think he had been sent from Vienna to a Polish ghetto. He told me about his arrival in Treblinka; apparently he got off the train and saw Stangl standing there. He said, 'I threw my arms around him.' In Austria he had been a cattle or horse trader. He said Stangl had said to him, 'Listen, I am going to appoint you Chief Kapo; you help me now and I'll see that you survive this. And after the war I'll get you a farm in Poland.' That's how Blau became Oberkapo. When he arrived he had a big stomach—he was a big fat man; in two weeks he had shrunk by half. Yes, he was hated, of course he was; he certainly "collaborated," so naturally they feared and hated him. He didn't just carry an ordinary whip, he had one of the long ones and he'd stand there swinging it and shouting in his broad Viennese, 'You pigs, you shit sows, get on with it, let's see how quick you can learn to be.' He behaved as if he wanted to outdo the worst of the Ukrainians. I suppose he did it to survive; who am I to accuse or blame him? He stayed Kapo till early spring, I think. Then he asked Stangl to relieve him on medical grounds. He complained of heart flutters or something and Stangl made him and his wife cooks for the Jews. Old Frau Blau, she was a good cook; she cooked many a meal for me. I hated the food in our mess, so quite often she'd cook me something special. After the revolt, they were amongst the hundred or so who were left over, and who were evacuated to Sobibor. I went there too.

"One day I heard they were going to shoot these hundred the next day. So I went to see old Blau and warned him. I just asked him whether he had some poison and he understood. He and his wife took poison and so did a doctor and his wife who had been in this group; they had helped to put out the fire in the Ukrainian barracks after the revolt. Well, they too died that day. It was better that way than being shot."

"In the midst of all the horror that surrounded you," I said to Stangl the afternoon of the day he told me the story about Blau, "and of which you were so aware that you drank yourself to sleep each night, what kept you going? What was there for you to hold on to?"

"I don't know. Perhaps my wife. My love for my wife?"

"How often did you see her?"

"After that first time in Poland they let me go on leave quite regularly—every three or four months."

"Did you feel close to your wife when so much had to remain hidden, remain unsaid between you?"

"The little time we had together, we usually talked about the children and ordinary everyday things. But it is true, things changed between us after that time when Ludwig told her about Sobibor. There was tension. And I knew she was terribly worried about me...."

"The first time I saw Paul again after Sobibor," said Frau Stangl, "was five months later when he came home for Christmas. It was so wonderful to see him, and at Christmas, too. In Austria, at home, what with Christmas and everything, what I knew was happening in Poland seemed utterly unreal. I asked about Treblinka, of course, but he said he was only responsible for the valuables, construction and discipline. No, he didn't pretend then that it wasn't the same sort of place as Sobibor, but he said that he was doing everything he could to get out. He stayed home for eight or ten days, but he'd only been there a couple of days when he said he'd run over and see Fraulein Hintersteiner [in Linz] who had been a secretary at Hartheim and who afterwards worked for a man called Kaufmann who went out to the Crimea as police chief. Paul wanted her to help him get a transfer to the Crimea. When he came back from seeing her, he was very happy and said it was all right—all he had to do now was wait to be notified of the transfer. So we had a good Christmas after all. I can still see his happy, relieved face."

Perhaps in the end it was easier for her husband to tell the truth because, I think, he knew he would die when he had told it.

The last day I spent with Stangl was Sunday, June 27, 1971. He had felt faintly unwell much of that week with stomach trouble, and on that day I had brought him some special soup in a thermos. It was an Austrian soup he had said his wife used to make for him when he didn't feel well. When I came back to the prison after a half-hour lunch break, he looked quite different: elated, his face smooth, his eyes fresh.

"I can't tell you," he said, "how wonderful I suddenly feel. I ate that wonderful soup and then I lay down. And I rested so deeply, somehow like never before. Oh, I feel wonderful," he repeated.

As my time for these talks was running out and I only intended coming back once more—the following Tuesday for an hour or two, to recapitulate anything important before flying back to London—the prison governor had said I could stay later than usual this Sunday. We spent four hours that afternoon, going back over many questions we had discussed before.

He talked again, at length, about the fairy-tale book by Janusz Korczak; he became fascinated with the subject of what children should, and should never again, be taught. He spoke for a long time in a decisive but thoughtful and quiet manner. Then he turned to stupidity in general. As he warmed to the subject and went back to relating it to his own experiences, as often before during

these talks, his personality changed brusquely and startlingly; his voice became harder and louder, his accent more provincial and his face coarse. ("It happened," his wife had said to me. "God help me, I saw it again here in Brazil—not for years, but then just in the last two years. It happened most often when he was driving and got angry about other drivers—stupidity, he called it—and it frightened me to see his face like that.")

"In Brazil," he said, his voice harsh, his accent almost vulgar, "at VW, the stupidity of some of the people there had to be seen to be believed. It sometimes drove me wild." He gestured with his hands. "There were idiots amongst them— morons. I often opened my mouth too wide and let them have it. 'My God,' I'd say to them, 'euthanasia passed you by, didn't it?' and I'd tell my wife when I got home, 'These morons got overlooked by the euthanasia.'"

"Do you think," I finally asked—it had become very late—"that that time in Poland taught you anything?"

Yes, he said, his voice once again calm and pensive—the increasing abruptness of these repeated metamorphoses becoming ever more disconcerting. *"That everything human has its origin in human weakness."*

"You said before that you thought perhaps the Jews were 'meant' to have this 'enormous jolt': when you say 'meant to' are you speaking of God?"

"Yes."

"What is God?"

"God is everything higher which I cannot understand but only believe."

The awful distortion in his thinking had shown up time after time as we had talked. And now here it was again, as we came to the end of these talks.

"Was God in Treblinka?"

"Yes," he said. *"Otherwise, how could it have happened?"*

"But isn't God good?"

"No," he said slowly, "I wouldn't say that. He is good and bad. But then, laws are made by men; and faith in God too depends on men—so that doesn't prove much of anything, does it? The only thing is, there are things which are inexplicable by science, so there must be something beyond man. Tell me, though, if a man has a goal he calls God, what can he do to achieve it? Do you know?"

"Don't you think it differs for each man? In your case, could it be to seek truth?"

"Truth?"

"Well, to face up to yourself? Perhaps as a start, just about what you have been trying to do in these past weeks?"

His immediate response was automatic, and automatically unyielding. "My conscience is clear about what I did, myself," he said, in the same stiffly spoken words he had used countless times at his trial, and in the past weeks, when we had always come back to this subject, over and over again. But this time I said nothing. He paused and waited, but the room remained silent. "I have never intentionally hurt anyone myself," he said, with a different, less incisive emphasis, and waited again—for a long time. For the first time, in all these many days, I had given him no help. There was no more time. He gripped the table with both hands as if he was holding on to it. "But I was there," he said then, in a curiously dry and tired tone of resignation. These few sentences had taken almost half an hour to pronounce. "So, yes" he said finally, very quietly, "in reality I share the guilt.... Because my guilt ... my guilt ... only now in these talks ... now that I have talked about it all for the first time...." He stopped.

He had pronounced the words "my guilt," but more than the words, the finality of it was in the sagging of his body, and on his face.

After more than a minute he started again, a half-hearted attempt, in a dull voice. "My guilt," he said, "is that I am still here. That is my guilt."

"Still here?"

"I should have died. That was my guilt."

"Do you mean you should have died, or you should have had the courage to die?"

"You can put it like that," he said, vaguely, sounding tired now.

"Well, you say that now. But then?"

"That is true," he said slowly, perhaps deliberately misinterpreting my question. "I did have another twenty years—twenty good years. But, believe me, now I would have preferred to die rather than this...." He looked around the little prison room. "I have no more hope," he said then, in a factual tone of voice, and continued, just as quietly: "And anyway—it is enough now. I want to carry through these talks we are having and then—let it be finished. Let there be an end."

It was over. I got up. Usually a prison guard had come to fetch him; this time, because we had continued much later than usual, the instructions were that he was to come downstairs with me to the entrance of the prison block, from where a guard would take him back to his cell. When we stood up he became suddenly very gay, fatigue appeared to have gone; he helped me pick up my papers and insisted on carrying the coffee cups.

When we got downstairs, we stood for a moment near the door which was opened for me to leave the block. He stuck his head out. "Nice air," he said, "let me smell it a moment. I'll be glad to see the lady out," he jested to the officer on duty who smiled and pressed the button that closed the electronic door. When I waved from outside, he smiled and waved back. It was just after five o'clock.

Stangl died nineteen hours later, just after noon the next day, Monday, of heart failure. He had seen no one since I left him except a prison officer who had taken the food trolley around. On a piece of paper tacked to his wall he had jotted down a name he had been trying to remember. On his table everything was in perfect order. Inside the book of fairy tales by Jasnusz Korczak, the sheet of paper with which he had marked a page he wanted to show me was no longer blank as I had seen it, but covered with emphatically underlined quotes from the book, each headed by the appropriate page number. The prison library book he was reading at the time of his death was *Laws and Honour* by Josef Pilsudski.

The possibility was certainly in everybody's mind—including mine—that he might have killed himself, and he was carefully examined at the obligatory postmortem.

He had not committed suicide. His heart was weak and he would no doubt have died quite soon anyway. But I think he died when he did because he had finally, however briefly, faced himself and told the truth. It was a monumental effort to reach that fleeting moment when he became the man he should have been.

EPILOGUE

I do not believe that all men are equal, for what we are above all other things, is individual and different. But individuality and difference are not only due to the talents we happen to be born with. They depend as much on the extent to which we are allowed to expand in freedom.

There is an as yet ill-defined, little-understood essential core to our being which, given this freedom, comes into its own, almost like birth, and which separates or even liberates us from intrinsic influences, and thereafter determines our moral conduct and growth. A moral monster, I believe, is not born, but is produced by interference with this growth. I do not know what this core is: mind, spirit, or perhaps a moral force as yet unnamed. But I think that, in the most fundamental sense, the individual personality only exists, is only valid, from the moment when it emerges; when, at whatever age (in infancy, if we are lucky), we begin to be in charge of and increasingly responsible for our actions.

Social morality is contingent upon the individual's capacity to make responsible decisions, to make the fundamental choice between right and wrong; this capacity derives from this mysterious core—the very essence of the human person.

This essence, however, cannot come into being or exist in a vacuum. It is deeply vulnerable and profoundly dependent on a climate of life, on freedom in the deepest sense, not license, but freedom to grow: within family, within community, within nations, and within human society as a whole. The fact of its existence therefore—the very fact of our existence as valid individuals—is evidence of our interdependence and of our responsibility for each other.

XV: CHOICELESS CHOICES

In a painful and powerful work, *Versions of Survival*, Lawrence Langer, the distinguished literary critic, introduced the notion of "choiceless choices" as a way of comprehending the victim's dilemma. The victims were caught in the horns of an impossible dilemma. They were forced to choose between the unimaginable and the impossible. The choices they made exceed our capacity for moral judgment. Langer argues that in the concentration camps, the Nazi's so dominated the victim that we cannot speak of moral choice. In the universe of choiceless choices, one could not choose between good and bad or even a lesser of two evils, but between the impossible and the unacceptable. In the morally denuded atmosphere of the death camps, a system of meaning evaporated and we have no means by which to judge the behavior of the victim. In the readings that follow, one by a Jewish physician who found herself in Auschwitz and the other by a rabbi who tried to make decisions on the basis of precedent whether a father could ransom his son from a *selektion*, knowing that another would be chosen in his place, we will find it impossible to judge.

The fate of Gisella Perl paralleled that of Hungarian Jewry. As an ally of Nazi Germany, Hungary remained independent through March of 1944. While Jews were subject to persecution and discrimination under Hungarian rule, they were not deported. Until 1944, Hungary would not participate in "the Final Solution to the Jewish problem"—at least not with respect to Jews within Hungarian territory.

By March of 1944, it was certain that Germany would lose the World War. The Soviet army was pushing westward, and the Allies had moved from North Africa into Italy. An invasion of the continent from the West was imminent. Distrustful of their ally, the Germans feared that Hungary would seek a separate peace and switch sides. Thus, in March, the Germans took effective control of Hungary and immediately implemented the Final Solution at a breathtaking pace. Between March and May, Jews were defined according to the Nuremberg law, based on the religion of their grandparents. Their property and wealth was expropriated; they were forced to wear the yellow star. Finally they were herded into ghettos.

Enter Adolf Eichmann, whose herculean logistical efforts succeeded in deporting more than four hundred thousand Jews in seven weeks beginning on May 15, destination Auschwitz.

A native of Sighet, Elie Wiesel's hometown, Perl was an accomplished physician when she was deported to Auschwitz in the spring of 1944. Trained as a gynecologist, she continued to serve as a doctor in Auschwitz and thus to struggle with the life and death decisions characteristically faced by all physicians under unprecedented, extreme conditions. Her memoir, *I Was A Doctor in Auschwitz*, pains the reader for it illustrates the anguish of the victims. She writes of the basics: life and death, hunger and cold, survival and despair, inhumanity and dignity.

Primo Levi, an Italian Jew who was a contemporary of Perl's in Auschwitz, wrote of the need for a new language of atrocity.

> Just as hunger is not that feeling of missing a meal so our way of being cold has need of a new word. We say "hunger," we say "tiredness," "fear," "pain," we say "winter" and they are different things. They are free words created and used by free men who lived in comfort and suffering in their homes. If the Lagers had lasted longer, a new, harsh language would have been born, and only this language could express what it means to toil the whole day in the wind, with the temperature below freezing, wearing only a shirt, underpants, cloth jacket and trousers, and in one's body nothing but weakness, hunger and the knowledge of the end drawing near.

If such a language were to be developed, Gisella Perl's experience would be essential to its creation.

She writes of hunger:

> We waited for food with the same burning impatience, the same excited imagination with which a young girl waits for a lover, the only moment worth waiting for . . .
>
> Our tortured stomachs hurt more and more at the thought of food, our salivary glands worked overtime and we could already feel the smell of food in our noses before it arrived. . . .
>
> The containers were dirty and smelly. . . . We didn't care. It was warm and it was food, even if there were pieces of wood, potato peeling and unrecognizable substances swimming in it. . . .
>
> Ten miserable mouthfuls and it was over. We were hungrier than before.

Dr. Perl writes as a woman of the fate that befell her gender. She writes directly of sexual exploitation, rape, the trading of favors, and of the singular suffering of mothers and children.

Perl is at once a healer and a murderer. She describes in vivid detail the birth of Yolanda's little boy. She hid the child for two days, "unable to destroy him."

> Then I could hide him no longer. I knew that if he were discovered it would mean death to Yolanda, to myself and to all these pregnant women whom my skill could still save. I took the little body in my hands, kissed the smooth faced, caressed the long hair—then strangled him and buried his body under a mountain of corpses, waiting to be cremated.

Her tone bespeaks love, gentility, softness; her deed is infanticide, or is it? The healer must chose between one child and many women. The physician's ordinary responsibility is, "above all do no harm." There is safety in such guidance, moral protection, but what of its applicability to the world of Auschwitz?

Perl also depicts the arbitrariness, the whimsical, unpredictability of life in Auschwitz. For a time, women with infants are both condemned to die. Thus, the women are saved and the infants discarded. Then Dr. Mengele—another sort of physician—announced a new policy, women with children are not to be killed, thus both the mother and her offspring can be saved. Shortly thereafter, both were shipped to their deaths and no efforts could alter the fate of those condemned to die.

Rabbi Zevi Hirsch Meisels of Vac, Hungary, was asked to decide an impossible question. He was approached by a father whose son was chosen in a *selektion* with an inquiry. Was it permissible, the father asked, for him to ransom his son. Unspoken was the certainty that another child would be chosen in his stead so that the number of victims were equal and no guard was in trouble. The rabbi refused to respond; he begged the question repeatedly refusing to answer. He could neither sanction the deed nor did he wish to prohibit the switch and force the father to accept the death of his son. His refusal was understood by the pious Jew. What could not be sanctioned was forbidden. For Rabbi Meisels, not to decide was to decide. His silence illustrates the choiceless choice; the father asked for a choice and for clarity. He accepted the loss of his son as a sacrifice required for faith.

The third document is a letter written by a mother to an unknown woman on how to care for her child. The mother understood that she and her husband could no longer protect the child, that remaining with the child was to condemn the child. Her choice was to let the child go to an unknown destination, to the care of someone she did not know, whom she could not know. She pleads that the child be taken care of. She provides incentive for such care—a promise for payment in the future—and she cannot resist being a mother, giving specific instructions for her child's care.

EXCERPTS FROM *I WAS A DOCTOR IN AUSCHWITZ*
Gisella Perl

BLOCK VII: THE LATRINE

Before we knew what went on in there, it was the ardent desire of all of us to be admitted to Block VII. This block was considerably cleaner, and better built than the others. Rain did not seep through the roof, the cages were more solid and even the air was cleaner. Block VII was the "Worker Block" and it housed fewer women than the others.

One morning a group of unknown SS officers and women appeared at the morning roll call. Their visit resulted in a new kind of "selection," in which the young, the pretty, the well-built were pulled out of the ranks, not the weak, the old and the sick-looking. Out of the thirty thousand inhabitants of Camp C about

seven hundred young women were selected. The others watched in silence, not knowing whether to pity or envy the chosen ones. We followed them with our eyes and saw that they were being herded into Block VII, the Worker Block.

The camp was soon seething with rumors. We heard that somewhere, far away, there was a radio factory in the middle of a forest and that's where these women would go to work. We did not know that the story about the radio factory was carefully planted among us. We did not know that all these fairy tales about the privileges accorded to those who were taken away for work were only part of the ghastly joke played on us.

About four weeks later an SS physician

came to Camp C and with a group of strong-arm SS men entered Block VII and locked the door from the inside. No one was permitted to go near the block. We still had no idea of what was happening, but waited with fear and curiosity in our hearts.

A few hours later the doctors of the hospital were sent for. The sight which greeted us when we entered Block VII is one never to be forgotten. From the cages along the walls about six hundred panic-stricken, trembling young women were looking at us with silent pleading in their eyes. The other hundred were lying on the ground, pale, faint, bleeding. Their pulse was almost inaudible, their breathing strained and deep rivers of blood were flowing around their bodies. Big, strong SS men were going from one to the other sticking tremendous needles into their veins and robbing their undernourished, emaciated bodies of their last drop of blood. The German army needed blood plasma! The guinea pigs of Auschwitz were just the people to furnish that plasma. *Rassenschande* or contamination with "inferior Jewish blood" was forgotten. We were too "inferior" to live, but not too inferior to keep the German army alive with our blood. Besides, nobody would know. The blood donors, along with the other prisoners of Auschwitz would never live to tell their tale. By the end of the war fat wheat would grow out of their ashes and the soap made of their bodies would be used to wash the laundry of the returning German heroes . . .

We were ordered to put these women back on their feet before they returned to camp so as to make place for others. What could we do without disinfectants, medicines, liquids? How could we replace the brutally stolen blood? All we had were words, encouragement, tenderness. And yet, under our care, these unfortunate creatures slowly returned to life and they even smiled when saying: "This is still better than the crematory . . ."

Block VII was always full. Once it was the women with beautiful eyes who were told to come forward, once the women with beautiful hands . . . And the poor wretches always believed the stories they were told, came forward, and to the amusement of the SS henchmen gave their last drops of precious blood for the German soldiers who used the strength robbed from us to murder our friends, our relatives, our allies . . .

One of the basic Nazi aims was to demoralize, humiliate, ruin us, not only physically but also spiritually. They did everything in their power to push us into the bottomless depths of degradation. Their spies were constantly among us to keep them informed about every thought, every feeling, every reaction we had, and one never knew who was one of their agents.

There was only one law in Auschwitz—the law of the jungle—the law of self-preservation. Women who in their former lives were decent self-respecting human beings now stole, lied, spied, beat the others and—if necessary—killed them, in order to save their miserable lives. Stealing became an art, a virtue, something to be proud of. We called it "organization." Those who were working near the crematories had an opportunity to "organize" an occasional can of food, a pair of shoes, a dress, a cooking pot, a comb, which they then sold on the black market operating in the latrine for food, for special favors, and—if the buyers were men—for "love."

But among those who had no connections among the crematory workers there were many who "organized" the piece of bread of their neighbor, regardless of whether she might starve to death as a consequence, or "organized" their bedfellow's shoes, no matter if her bleeding feet would condemn her to be cremated. By stealing bread, shoes, water, you stole a life for yourself, even if it was at the expense of other lives. Only the strong, the cruel, the merciless survived. The SS were, of course, greatly amused by these practices and encouraged them by showing special favors to some, so as to awaken the jealousy, the hatred, the greed of the others.

A few privileged persons were tacitly permitted to own small aluminum drinking cups stolen from the crematory. Such a cup made it possible for them to get more water than the others who could only drink from their cupped hands. These cups were jealously guarded, their owners carried them on a piece of string tied around their waist. After they filled it with water, they would seek out a quiet corner where they could enjoy their long drink in peace. But more likely than not, they would not succeed. No sooner had they found a lonely spot than one of the strongest, most brutal fellow prisoners would sneak up behind them, hit them over the head to rob them of their water and their cup. Many survived these attacks, but others, who had a thin skull or had no resistance left, lost their lives for a drink of water and an aluminum cup ...

The latrine—without water, of course—was one of the most important places in Camp C. It was our community hall, the center of our social activities and our news-room. In the second month of my stay in Auschwitz the tiny hut which served as a latrine was closed down and a whole block was consecrated to this worthy purpose. Ditches were dug along the walls and wooden planks thrown across the ditches. In the middle of the building ran a wide passage and this is where the latrine superintendents walked up and down with filthy clubs in their hands, hitting those who spent too much time satisfying their urges or talking to their friends.

The latrine was also our black market, our commodity exchange building. Here you could buy bread for your sausage, margarine for your bread, exchange food, shoes, a piece of cloth for "love" ... It was here that we made plans for the future, gave expression to our despair, to our thirst for vengeance, our hatred. It was here that we heard all rumors, the good and the bad, and sometimes, miraculously, they proved to be true. Sometimes I feel that if it hadn't been for the latrine we would all have gone crazy in the deadly monotony of camp life.

Once in a while an SS woman came to inspect the latrine and chased us out with her whip and gun. Such an inspection had many victims, many casualties, but the next day our club life would continue, as if nothing had happened.

The latrine also served as a "love nest." It was here that male and female prisoners met for a furtive moment of joyless sexual intercourse in which the body was used as a com-

modity with which to pay for the badly needed items the men were able to steal from the warehouses. The saltpeter mixed into our food was not strong enough to kill sexual desire. We did not menstruate, but that was more a consequence of psychic trauma caused by the circumstances we lived in than of saltpeter. Sexual desire was still one of the strongest instincts and there were many who lacked the moral stamina to discipline themselves.

Detachments of male workers came into Camp C almost daily, to clean the latrines, build streets, and patch up leaking roofs. These men were trusted old prisoners who knew everything there was to know about camp life, had connections in the crematories and were masters at "organizing." Their full pockets made them the Don Juans of Camp C. They chose their women among the youngest, the prettiest, the least emaciated prisoners and in a few seconds the deal was closed. Openly, shamelessly, the dirty, diseased bodies clung together for a minute or two in the fetid atmosphere of the latrine—and the piece of bread, the comb, the little knife wandered from the pocket of the man into the greedy hands of the woman.

At first I was deeply shocked at these practices. My pride, my integrity as a woman revolted against the very idea. I begged and preached and, when I had my first cases of venereal disease, I even threatened to refuse treatment if they didn't stop prostitution. But later, when I saw that the pieces of bread thus earned saved lives, when I met a young girl whom a pair of shoes, earned in a week of prostitution, saved from being thrown into the crematory, I began to understand and to forgive.

Our SS guards knew very well what was going on in the latrine. They even knew who was whose *kochana* (lover), and were much amused by it all. They were always amused by what was insane, filthy, bestial, horrible . . . The man-eating furnaces were burning, their flames were licking the sky . . . Millions were dying on their feet eaten up alive by lice, hunger, disease—and in the latrines, lying in human excrement before the eyes of their fellow prisoners, men and women were writhing in sexual paroxysm. Hitler's dream of a New Order.

CHILDBIRTH IN CAMP C

The poor, young women who were brought to Auschwitz from the various ghettos of Hungary did not know that they would have to pay with their lives and the lives of their unborn children for that last, tender night spent in the arms of their husbands.

A few days after the arrival of a new transport, one of the SS chiefs would address the women, encouraging the pregnant ones to step forward, because they would be taken to another camp where living conditions were better. He also promised them double bread rations so as to be strong and healthy when the hour of delivery came. Group after group of pregnant women left Camp C. Even I was naive enough, at that time, to believe the Germans, until one day I happened to have an errand near the crematories and saw with my own eyes what was done to these women.

They were surrounded by a group of SS men and women, who amused themselves by giving these helpless creatures a taste of hell, after which death was a welcome friend. They were beaten with clubs and whips, torn by dogs, dragged around by the hair and kicked in the stomach with heavy German boots. Then, when they collapsed, they were thrown into the crematory—alive. I stood, rooted to the ground, unable to move, to scream, to run away. But gradually the horror turned into revolt and this revolt shook me out of my lethargy and gave me a new incentive to live. I had to remain alive. It was up to me to save all the pregnant women in Camp C from this infernal fate. It was up to me to save the life of the mothers, if there was no other way, then by destroying the life of their unborn children. I ran back to camp and going from block to block told the women what I had seen. Never again was anyone to betray their condition. It was to be denied to our last breath, hidden from the SS, the guards and even the Blockova, on whose good will our life depended.

On dark nights, when everyone else was sleeping—in dark corners of the camp, in the toilet, on the floor, without a drop of water, I delivered their babies. First I took the ninth-month pregnancies, I accelerated the birth by the rupture of membranes, and usually within one or two days spontaneous birth took place without further intervention. Or I produced dilatation with my fingers, inverted the embryo and thus brought it to life. In the dark, always hurried, in the midst of filth and dirt. After the child had been delivered, I quickly bandaged the mother's abdomen and sent her back to work. When possible, I placed her in my hospital, which was in reality just a grim joke. She usually went there with the diagnosis of pneumonia, which was a safe diagnosis, not one that would send her to the crematory. I delivered women pregnant in the eighth, seventh, sixth, fifth month, always in a hurry, always with my five fingers, in the dark, under terrible conditions.

No one will ever know what it meant to me to destroy these babies. After years and years of medical practice, childbirth was still to me the most beautiful, the greatest miracle of nature. I loved those newborn babies not as a doctor but as a mother and it was again and again my own child whom I killed to save the life of a woman. Every time when kneeling down in the mud, dirt and human excrement which covered the floor of the barracks to perform a delivery without instruments, without water, without the most elementary requirements of hygiene, I prayed to God to help me save the mother or I would never touch a pregnant woman again. And if I had not done it, both mother and child would have been cruelly murdered. God was good to me. By a miracle, which to every doctor must sound like a fairy tale, every one of these women recovered and was able to work, which, at least for a while, saved her life.

My first such case was the delivery of a young woman called Yolanda. Yolanda came from my hometown. She was the child of an impoverished family and made a living by doing fine embroidery on expensive underwear, handkerchiefs and baby clothes. To make beautiful baby clothes was the greatest pleasure in her life and, while working on them until late into the night, she would dream about the baby she, herself, would one day have. Then she got married. Month after month she waited and prayed, but Nature refused to grant her most ardent wish. This is when she began coming to me. I treated her for a long time until finally my treatment showed results and Yolanda became pregnant. She was radiant. "I shall give you the most beautiful present in the world when my baby arrives ..." she would then tell me every time we met.

In the end it was I who gave her a present—the present of her life—by destroying her passionately desired little boy two days after his birth. Day after day I watched her condition develop, fearing the moment when it could be hidden no longer. I bandaged her abdomen, hid her with my body at roll call and hoped for a miracle which would save her and her baby.

The miracle never came, but one horribly dark, stormy night Yolanda began having birth pains. I was beside her, waiting for the moment when I could take a hand in the delivery, when I saw to my horror that she fell into convulsive seizures. For two days and nights the spasms shook her poor, emaciated little body and I had to stand by, without drugs, without instruments to help her, listening to her moans, helpless. Around us, in the light of a few small candles I could see the thirteen-hundred women of her barracks look down upon us from their cages, thirteen-hundred death-masks with still enough life left in them to feel pity for Yolanda and to breathe the silent but ever-present question: Why?

The third day Yolanda's little boy was born. I put her into the hospital, saying that she had pneumonia—an illness not punishable by death—and hid her child for two days, unable to destroy him. Then I could hide him no longer. I knew that if he were discovered, it would mean death to Yolanda, to myself and to all these pregnant women whom my skill could still save. I took the warm little body in my hands, kissed the smooth face, caressed the long hair—then strangled him and buried his body under a mountain of corpses waiting to be cremated.

Then, one day, Dr. Mengele came to the hospital and gave a new order. From now on Jewish women could have their children. They were not going to be killed because of their pregnancy. The children, of course, had to be taken to the crematory by me, personally, but the women would be allowed to live. I was jubilant. Women, who delivered in our so-called hospital, on its clean floor, with the help of a few primitive instruments that had been given to me, had a better chance to come out of this death camp not only alive but in a condition to have other children later.

I had two hundred ninety-two expectant mothers in my ward when Dr. Mengele changed his mind. He came roaring into the hospital, whip and revolver in hand, and had all the two hundred ninety-two women loaded on a single truck and tossed alive into the flames of the crematory.

In September 1944, Camp C was liquidated to make place for new arrivals. I shall tell, later, what this liquidation meant. All I want to say here is that out of thirty thousand women only ten thousand remained alive to be put into other blocks or taken to Germany to work.

As soon as we were installed in Camps F, K and L, a new order came from Berlin. From now on, not only could Jewish mothers have their children in the "maternity ward" of the hospital but the children were to be permitted to live.

Eva Benedek was eighteen years old. She was a violinist from Budapest, a beautiful, talented young woman who was separated from her husband only a few days after her wedding. Eva Benedek believed with an unconquerable faith that her life and the life of her child would be saved. The child, growing in her womb, was her only comfort, her only pleasure, her only concern. When the SS organized an orchestra among the prisoners Eva became the violinist of that orchestra. I bandaged her abdomen and in her formless rags, amidst women whose stomachs were constantly bloated with undernourishment, her condition went unnoticed.

Then came the "liquidation" of Camp C and Eva Benedek came with me to Camps F, K and L. When the order for the conservation of Jewish children came, nobody was happier than she. Her delivery was only a day or two off and we both believed that the miracle had happened, a miracle of God for the sake of Eva Benedek. She smiled all day and in the evening, in our barracks, she whistled Mozart concertos and Chopin waltzes for us to bring a little beauty into our terror-filled, hopeless lives. Two days later she had her baby, a little boy, in the "maternity ward." But when the baby was born, she turned her back on it, wouldn't look at it, wouldn't hold it in her arms. Tears were streaming down her cheeks incessantly, terrible, silent tears, but she wouldn't speak to me. Finally I succeeded in making her tell what was on her mind.

"I dare not take my son in my arms, Doctor," she said. "I dare not look at him, I dare not kiss him, I dare not get attached to him. I feel it, I know it, that somehow they are going to take him away from me . . ."

And she was right. Twenty-four hours after Eva Benedek had her son, a new order came, depriving Jewish mothers of the additional food, a thin, milky soup mixed with flour, which swelled their breasts and enabled them to feed their babies. For eight days Eva Benedek had to look on while her son starved slowly to death.

His fine, white skin turned yellow and blotched, his smooth face got wrinkled and shriveled and on the eighth day I had to take him out and throw him on a heap of rotting corpses.

A RESPONSUM BY RABBI ZEVI HIRSCH MEISELS

Whether a Father May Ransom His Son from Certain Death at the Expense of Another Life

INTRODUCTION

Whether one life may be spared at the possible or certain expense of another is one of the most chronic and agonizing questions to emerge from the responsa of the Holocaust era. The complex aggregate of legal sources bearing upon this question and its intrinsic dilemmas are discussed in responsum 6 by R. Shimon Efrati. Since R. Efrati's opinion was solicited some time after the fact, he had both the time and the clarity of mind to formulate a thoughtful and thorough reply. In contrast, the following account by R. Zevi Hirsch Meisels of Vac (Hungary) describes how the ultimate question of whose life takes precedence was submitted to him twice in a situation of utter extremity requiring immediate response. In such circum-

stances the rabbi's ruling is obviously no mere theory but a prescription for action (*Halakah le-mu'aseh*). R. Meisels's decision, in these two instances, was literally a matter of life or death.

The descendant of a distinguished line of rabbis, R. Meisels lived in Vac (Ger. Weitzen), Hungary, before the war. After the German invasion (19 March 1944) the Jews of Vac were deported to Auschwitz. Of the prewar population of two thousand Jews, only a few survived including R. Meisels. After the war he was appointed chief rabbi of the British zone in Bergen-Belsen. Later he emigrated to Chicago where his volume of responsa, *Mekaddeshei ha-Shem*, was published.

DIGEST

R. Meisels describes a "selection" conducted by the Nazis at Auschwitz in which some fourteen hundred boys of less than an arbitrary height were singled out for death. Some camp inmates sought to ransom certain boys by bribing the guards. However, the guards would not release any boy without capturing another to take his place. This trading in lives went on throughout the day.

The father of one of the condemned boys, aware that his son could be ransomed only at the expense of another life, asked R. Meisels whether under the circumstances the Torah permitted a father to save his son's life. R. Meisels did not wish to render an explicit decision in a capital case, especially without access to books of law, the counsel of other rabbis, or the calm objectivity necessary to make such a ruling.

Still, R. Meisels wonders whether or not there might be some rationale for permitting the ransom. The isolated block in which the boys were confined was guarded by Jewish inmates who presumably might refrain from the grave sin of condemning another boy in the place of the ransomed one. As long as the exchange had not yet occurred, it might be permissible for the father A. Zevi Hirsch Meisels to ransom his son on the assumption that another boy might never be captured.

However, it was the guards' procedure to capture a replacement before releasing a ransomed captive, nullifying this line of argument.

Reluctant to render a definite Halakic ruling (*pesak din*), especially in such a calamitous circumstance, R. Meisels refuses to answer the father's question. From the rabbi's refusal the father concludes that the ransom of his son is Halakically forbidden.

TEXT

One thousand four hundred imprisoned children condemned to be burned.

May the generations be horrified and consciences stirred to turn the hearts of the children to their fathers, as I tell publicly of the fearful and exalted things my eyes beheld at Auschwitz on Rosh Hashanah and Simhat Torah; the magnitude of self-sacrifice, the sanctifica-

tion of God's name by fourteen hundred boys, fourteen to eighteen years old, who were chosen on the day of the eve of Rosh Hashanah (in a "selection") to be sacrificed upon the altar, to be burned for the sanctification of God's name.

I will not go on at length with stories like these, for the paper would run out and they would still not suffice. Much ink has already been spilled in writing about the events and calamities of the days of the Nazis, may their names be blotted out. Each person writes according to his intellect, understanding, and perception in order to derive benefit from the fruits of his pen. But I will not refrain, for the sake of the glory of the sanctification of His blessed name, from bringing up here in the introduction to *Mekaddeshei ha-Shem* this incident that I myself saw, from among an ocean of incidents and events that were engraved upon my heart and mind, which I personally witnessed while under the yoke of the Nazis. I promise to be brief even though it is possible to go on and on. So I begin with the help of God, may He be blessed.

On the eve of Rosh Hashanah [17 September 1944], the Nazi guards and their helpers in the camp seized and assembled the boys of eighteen years of age or less who were still scattered throughout the camp, who by various methods and pretexts had managed to elude the inspection of the Nazi camp commander, may his name be blotted out, when [the Nazis] entered the camp. About sixteen hundred boys were assembled in an empty lot behind the camp blocks, and all of them knew the destiny that awaited them. (My dear son Zalman Leib, may his light shine, a boy of fourteen years who was with me at Auschwitz, was saved by a miracle with the help of God, may He be blessed. He was not taken with the other youths.)

Then the Nazi camp commander came there and ordered that a wood pole be sunk into the ground, and at the top of the pole a board laid [horizontally across] and fastened with nails so that it appeared like a kind of letter daleth [ד]. He then gave the order that all the boys pass by one by one under the board. Those whose heads touched the board remained alive and were sent back inside the camp; but those whose heads did not touch the board were taken separately into a closed block. In this way the enemy estimated for himself their ages and their fitness for work. Since the boys knew what the failure to touch the board meant—that whoever failed to touch it was considered a child and condemned to be burned—many of them rose up on their toes at the moment they passed beneath the board so that their head would touch it. But this oppressor stood near them, and the instant he saw anything like this—a boy elevating himself to touch the board—he struck him hard on the head with the heavy rubber club in his hand, with such force that the unfortunate boy would drop to the ground covered with blood and die right there; or else if he were still barely alive they would take him this way straight to the crematorium. This happened to many of the boys.[1]

After this examination and procedure, about fourteen hundred boys remained on the site, and they were taken immediately to an isolated locked block until the next day when their doom would be sealed. They received nothing more to eat or drink. The Kapo[2] guards stood at the entrance, and no one could go out or in.

Trading Lives with the Kapos

The next day, the first day of Rosh Hashanah, when all the people of the world pass before [God] like sheep, there was panic and confusion. By word of mouth the news spread throughout the camp that on that evening they would take the boys away to the crematorium (since during the day they did not bring new victims to the ovens, but only during the night). In the case of many people in the camp, their only children, the only survivors left to them, were among these boys condemned to be burned; or else they had close relatives or beloved friends from their own towns [among the condemned boys]. These people ran around bewildered all day outside the closed block. Perhaps a ray of light would appear to rescue their beloved child from there before the sun went down.

But the Kapo guards paid no attention to all their pleas and tears to release this or that boy from among the prisoners condemned to burn. As is known, most of these Kapos were wicked and hardhearted, the dregs of the wicked among our people. Yet in this instance their argument was somewhat justified, since they were liable for the number of boys they had been ordered to guard, which was a precise number. In the evening it would be their responsibility to deliver to the SS[3] the same number that had been delivered to them. If one was missing, they themselves would be held accountable and would be taken away to be burned, a life for a life.

Even so, at last after much effort and bargaining between the relatives and the Kapos, the Kapos' greed conquered them and they agreed—in exchange for large payments—to free this or that boy. But immediately they snatched another boy in his place from those they could capture inside the camp (who had managed to elude yesterday's roundup, or who had been freed during the selection because their heads touched the board). Then they shut up the new captive in the block in place of the ransomed boy in order to meet the quota.

Many people had money or gold pieces or jewels concealed in hiding places or in their shoes for a time of emergency, and of course

---

[1] According to the testimony of Joseph Kleinman at the Eichmann trial (cited by Gideon Hausner, *Justice in Jerusalem* [New York, 1966], p. 172), a nearly identical selection ritual was conducted at Auschwitz on Yom Kippur, when two thousand boys were assembled on the SS football grounds and forced to pass under a plank nailed to the goalpost. Since there are many striking similarities between Kleinman's account and that of R. Meisels, it is possible that despite the confusion of dates they are describing the same incident.

[2] *Kapo* was concentration camp slang for a Jewish prisoner in charge of a section of Jewish inmates. There are different theories of the word's origin, e.g.: an abbreviated form of the French *caporal*; a German slang word for "foreman"; a borrowing from the Italian *capo*, "head"; or an abbreviation of *Kamp Polizei*.

[3] One of the subdivisions of the SS (*Schutzstaffel*, defense corps) was the *Totenkopfverband* (death's head units) who were assigned to the concentration camps.

there were some simple people of little understanding who gave no thought to what would be done to replace the ransomed boy. At great sacrifice they collected all the wealth that remained to them, or else managed to gather the required amount from friends or acquaintances, and ransomed their imprisoned child from certain annihilation. This trading continued throughout most of the Day of Judgment [Rosh Hashanah] before the eyes of all the people in the camp. (For it was known that the SS men did not walk around inside the camp during the day, but only around its perimeter. Within the camp itself the Jewish *Kapos* ruled.)

However, there were of course many people of conscience in the camp who would not run to ransom their children at the expense of another boy's life, in accord with the statement of our sages of blessed memory [Pes. 25b], "What [reason] do you see [for thinking your blood is redder? Perhaps his blood is redder]."[4] Never will I forget one fearful incident that I myself witnessed during the time described above, an incident that symbolizes the holiness of the Jews and their sacrifice for the ways of the holy Torah offered in perfect piety, even in the time of their anguish and fearful suffering.

The Self-Sacrifice of a Father by Not Saving His Only Son

I was approached by a Jewish man who appeared to be a simple Jew from Oberland.[5] In innocent piety he said to me something like this: "Rabbi! My only son, my dear one so precious to me, is over there among the boys condemned to be burned; and I have the ability to ransom him. Yet we know without a doubt that the *Kapos* will seize another in his place. Therefore I ask of the rabbi a question of law and practice:[6] According to the Torah, am I permitted to save him? Whatever you decide, I will do."

When I heard this question I was seized by trembling. Could I decide a matter of life and death? I answered him: "My dear friend, how can I render a clear decision for you on a question like this? In such a situation, even when the Temple stood, a question concerning matters of life and death came before the Sanhedrin.[7] But I am here in Auschwitz without any books of law, without any other rabbis [to consult or join in a *bet din*], and without a clear mind because of so much suffering and grief."[8]

If it were the way of the wicked *Kapos* to release the ransomed prisoner first and afterward take another in his place, it might be possible to incline a little toward permitting [the ransom], since after all the *Kapos* were Jews, and for them it was certainly forbidden by law to do such a thing with their own hands and endanger another life whose fate had not been to burn. Such an act is included in the prohibition, "One should suffer death rather than transgresses."[9] If so, it is possible to assume that it was not certain that the *Kapos* would take another life in place of the ransomed one. For perhaps at the last moment their Jewish soul would be stirred and they would not transgress

4 Cf. Pes. 25b, Sanh. 74a. The issue is discussed at length in responsum 6.

5 Part of Slovakia occupied by Hungary.

6 The rabbis differentiate between the purely theoretical study of a legal question and its common application. Only decisions handed down in connection with an actual case constitute practical law. Cf. Bez. 28b, BK 30b; Boaz Cohen, *Law and Tradition in Judaism* (New York, 1969), p. 49.

7 The Talmud (Yer. Sanh. 1:1, 7:2; Shab. 15a; Sanh. 41a) records that Jewish courts lost authority over capital cases forty years before the destruction of the Second Temple in Jerusalem (70 C.E.). See Hugo Mantel, *Studies in the History of the Sanhedrin* (Cambridge, 1965 pp. 291-94, 316). Cf. the possibly contradictory texts cited by Alexsander Guttmann, *Rabbinic Judaism in the Making* (Detroit, 1970) pp. 20-21.

8 There is Halakic warrant for R. Meisels' reluctance to make a ruling in this instance. While it is a positive commandment for a duly qualified Torah scholar to render Halakic decisions when asked (Lev. 10:11; cf. *Sefer Mizvot ha-Katan* 111), it is forbidden to decide the law while intoxicated or otherwise disoriented (Rashi, Lev. 10:11; Ker. 13b; Ket. 10b; Er. 64a).

9 See Sanh. 74a: "R. Yohanan said in the name of R. Shimon b. Yehozedek: They decided by vote in the upper chamber of Bet Niza in Lod: [Concerning] all of the prohibitions of the Torah, if they say to a man, 'Transgress or you will be killed,' he should transgress rather than be killed, with the exception of [the prohibitions of idolatry, unchastity, and murder]."

a severe prohibition like this. See Tosafot to Ket. (72a) s.v. "If . . ." in the name of the Rashba[10] that even if a wife wanted to feed her husband a forbidden thing, she does not leave [the marriage] without her *ketubbah* [the sum guaranteed by her marriage contract], for she could say, "I was only joking, and if you had actually started to eat I would have stopped you." Likewise one could say that as long as the sin was not actually committed, it could be that it would never be committed at all, that the Jewish soul would awaken and a severe prohibition like this would not be violated.

However, to my sorrow I knew with certainty that it was the *Kapos'* practice to first take someone else from the camp and only afterward release the ransomed prisoner. Thus they would be sure that none was lacking from the exact number delivered to them by the SS, for which they were responsible. If they released the ransomed prisoner and did not succeed in taking another in his place, they would pay with their own lives when the SS found that one was missing from the number handed over to them. Obviously there were not [sufficient] grounds to allow anything.[11]

Still the man mentioned above wept and pleaded with me. He said to me: "Rabbi, you must decide for me now what the law is in this case, for it is very urgent that I save my only son while it is still possible to save him." I begged him, "My dear, precious friend, leave off from asking this question, for I cannot say a thing at all to you without studying a book, [especially] in a situation as fearful and dreadful as this." But he continued to plead with me and said the following: "Rabbi, does this mean that you cannot permit me to ransom my only child? Is it not so? Then I will accept with love the decision."

I entreated him and protested, saying, "Dear Jew, I did not say this either, that I do not permit you to ransom your child. I cannot decide either yes or no. Do as you wish as if you had not asked me at all." But still he stood there and pleaded with me to give him a clear answer. When he saw that I stood firm in my opinion that I did not want to render a legal decision,[12]

he responded with emotion and great fervor: "Rabbi, I did what I could, what the Torah obligated me to do: I asked a question of a rabbi, and there is no other rabbi here. Since you cannot answer me that I am allowed to ransom my child, this is a sign that according to the law you may not permit it. Were it permitted without any hesitation, you surely would have answered me that it is permitted. This means to me that the verdict is that by law I am not allowed to do it. This is enough for me. It is clear that my only child will be burned according to the Torah and the law, and I accept this with love and rejoicing. I will do nothing to ransom him, for so the Torah has commanded."

Nothing I said to him was of any use. I urged him not to lay the responsibility for this upon me, that it was as if I had never heard his question. But he repeated once again with pious fervor and weeping what he had said, which tore the heart into twelve pieces.[13] So he carried out his words and did not ransom his son. All that day of Rosh Hashanah he walked around talking to himself, murmuring joyfully that he had the merit to sacrifice his only son to God, for even though he could have ransomed him, nevertheless he did not because he saw that the Torah

---

[10] Referring not to R. Shlomo b. Adret but to R. Shimshon b. Abraham of Sens (late twelfth to early thirteenth century, France).

[11] In his own gloss to this account, R. Meisels cites the view of Rema Sh. Ar. (HM 388:2) that one may save himself from impending danger even if his action may endanger others. However, this appears to apply only in the case of potential danger; if one is in immediate peril, he may not save himself at the certain expense of another. The Shakh (HM 163:11) cites the view that if a man is imprisoned and held for ransom, he may not be rescued if another will be sent in his place; but, according to Yad Avraham, YD 157, the prisoner himself may certainly try to escape. In the present case, it might be argued that father and son should be considered the same person; thus permitting the father to bribe the *Kapo*. But R. Meisels finds no definitive warrant for such a view.

[12] Shlomo Rozman, an eyewitness to this encounter, understood R. Meisels to render a definite decision forbidding the father to ransom his son. See Irving Rosenbaum, *The Holocaust and Halakah* (New York, 1976), p. 158.

[13] Cf. Jud. 19:29.

did not permit him to do so; and that his sacrificial act should be considered by God like the binding of Isaac which also occurred on Rosh Hashanah.[14]

And you, my dear brother, look closely and consider the righteousness and perfect piety of this Jewish man. I have no doubt that his words caused a great commotion among the celestial host; and the Holy One, blessed be He, gathered together all the host of heaven and was, so to speak, very proud: "Behold the creatures that I created in my world." Justifiably it is said of this man [Is. 49:3]: "Thou art My servant, Israel, in whom I will be glorified."

ZEVI HIRSCH MEISELS [*MEKADDESHEI HA-SHEM* 1:7].

---

[14] One of the explanations given by the Talmud (RH 16a) for the sounding of the ram's horn on Rosh Hashanah is to recall the ram substituted for Isaac. The biblical account of the binding of Isaac (Genesis 22: 1-19) is read on the second day of Rosh Hashanah (Meg. 31a).

A LETTER TO THE WOMAN WHO WILL FIND MY DAUGHTER

Dear Lady:

I leave in your care my child, my treasure! I beg of you, as you are a mother yourself save my *Baby.* God will reward you for the good deed—and I and my family will reward you as well.

Please remember that this child comes from a very rich family, and if and when we survive the war we promise to reward you generously. However, if we don't survive then my little daughter will be able to compensate you for saving her life. (I enclose a document which shows that she will be heir to the estate, property and all the wealth.) My child will bring you luck, and good health!! Please I beseech you dear lady, have pity on my child and save her from annihilation!

She does not need much, just feed her, and keep her clean.

I bathe her every evening, then feed her and she sleeps the night through till six o'clock in the morning.

She is being fed every three hours.

A buttered roll and warm milk with sugar.
Oatmeal with butter and milk.
Once a day carrot juice with sugar.
When she cries please give her a little light tea with sugar.
She also cries when wet.
Dear, Dear, lady we—my husband and I—hope that you will save our precious baby!!!

Please have mercy, take her into your heart like a mother, and give her warmth and love which her own unhappy and tormented mother is not able to give her.

I will try and send you the baby's clothes as soon as possible.

Meanwhile I am sending pillow cases which can be made into little shirts, and sheets into diapers and towels after the bath.

Also for you a few of my good dresses. If the child should—God forbid—get sick, please contact the doctor immediately. When she cries please give her a pacifier dipped in sugar, and lots of talcum powder after the bath.

XVI. THE END OF A GHETTO: DEPORTATION FROM WARSAW

In January 1942, the decision on the "Final Solution to the Jewish problem" was announced and its implementation ordered. The infrastructure of the death camps was built, most especially the Aktion Reinhard Camps: Treblinka, Sobibor, and Belzec.

By July, the camps were ready and on July 19 Himmler ordered the completion of the "Final Solution" in the Government General, the central area of Poland containing large Jewish ghettos. The task was to be completed by the end of the year and the ghettos were to remain solely as collection camps. Jewish labor was to conclude by the end of the year. Other arrangements for necessary work would have to be made. The cleansing was to be carried out. Himmler was to personally approve all exemptions.

The order for the "Evacuation of the Jews from the Warsaw Ghetto," July 22, 1942, was simple: "All Jewish persons living in Warsaw regardless of age and sex will be reset-

Deportation from the Warsaw ghetto. Jerzy Tomaszewski/Courtesy of USHMM–Photo Archives.

tled in the East." Certain categories of exclusion were specified: those employed by the German Authorities, the *Judenrat*, German companies, hospital staff, the Jewish Police and their wives and children.

The instructions for the evacuations were precise: fifteen kilograms of property, three days of food. The resettlement will begin at 11:00 A.M. on July 22 and the *Judenrat* is responsible for its execution under penalty of their lives.

We will read the order, appearing without a signature, and then a description from *The Warsaw Diary of Adam Czerniakow*, leader of the Warsaw Jewish Council, of his last days before the July 23, 1942, deportation of Warsaw's Jews to Treblinka. Czerniakow describes the ordinary burdens of his everyday life. His attempts to manage the unmanageable, to solve today's problems knowing full well that tomorrow will bring more grave situations. Contrast his writing with what we have already read regarding the *Judenrat*. The chairman depicts the false reassurances he received from German leaders as he went from office to office. We will read a description of his final days. Chaim Kaplan, another of the ghetto's chroniclers described these very same days. On July 20, 1942—three days before the deportation—Kaplan wrote: "The ghetto is quiet. All the rumors are false. *Judenrat* circles deny them."

Two days later when the truth of the massive deportation was learned, he wrote: "I haven't the strength to hold a pen in my hand. I'm broken, shattered. My thoughts are jumbled." And then we will read of what Czerniakow did not live to see—the actual deportation in the desperate, despondent postmortem written by the Warsaw Ghetto's most important chronicler, Emanuel Ringelblum, who organized the clandestine collection of archives by a group of several dozen writers, teachers, rabbis, and historians. The secret operation's code name was *Oneg Shabbos* (Joy of the Sabbath). They wrote diaries, collected documents, commissioned papers, and preserved the posters and decrees—the memory of the doomed community. The Jews of Warsaw were without illusions. Their only hope was that the memory of the Warsaw Ghetto would endure. On the eve of destruction, when all seemed lost, the archive was buried in several milk cans deep beneath the streets of Warsaw. One can was found in 1946. It is now on display at the Jewish Historical Institute in Warsaw. The other can—on display at the United States Holocaust Memorial Museum—was discovered on December 12, 1950, at Nowolipki 58, Warsaw. Despite repeated searches, no one knows what else remains buried in the rubble.

Ringelblum is angry, reflective, descriptive, and disappointed. His feelings reflect those of the surviving remnants of the once vibrant Warsaw Jewish community. His writings also show how the spirit of resistance developed.

Himmler's Order for the "Resettlement" of Jews in the General Government

I order that the resettlement of the entire Jewish population of the General Government be carried out and completed by December 31, 1942.

By December 31, 1942, no persons of Jewish extraction are to be found in the General Government, except if they are in the assembly camps of Warsaw, Kraków, Czestochowa, Radom, Lublin. All other work projects employing Jewish labor must be completed by then or, if completion is not possible, must be transferred to one of the assembly camps.

These measures are necessary for the ethnic separation of races and peoples required in the context of the New Order of Europe, as well as in the interest of the security and purity of the German Reich and the spheres of its interest.

Any breach in this proceeding constitutes a threat to peace and order in the entire sphere of German interest, a starting point for the resistance movement, and a center of moral and physical contagion.

For all these reasons, a total cleanup is necessary and is accordingly to be carried out. Anticipated delays beyond the deadline are to be reported to me in time for early remedial measures. All requests from other agencies for alterations or for permission to make exceptions are to be submitted to me personally.

Heil Hitler!
[SIGNED]

H. HIMMLER

Announcement of the Evacuation of the Jews from the Warsaw Ghetto

JULY 22, 1942

The *Judenrat* is informed of the following:

I. All Jewish persons living in Warsaw, regardless of age and sex, will be resettled in the East.

II. The following are excluded from the resettlement:

    A. All Jewish persons employed by German authorities or enterprises, and who can show proof of this fact;

    B. All Jewish persons who are members or employees of the *Judenrat* (on the day of the publication of this regulation);

    C. All Jewish persons who are employed by a Reich-German company and can show proof of this fact;

    D. All Jews capable of work who have up to now not been brought into the labor process are to be taken to the barracks in the Jewish quarter;

    E. All Jewish persons who belong to the staff of the Jewish hospitals. This applies also to the members of the Jewish Disinfection Team;

    F. All Jewish persons who belong to the Jewish Police [*Judischer Ordnungsdienst*];

G. All Jewish persons who are first-degree relatives of the person listed under a) through f). Such relatives are exclusively wives and children;

H. All Jewish persons who are hospitalized in one of the Jewish hospitals on the first day of the resettlement and are not fit to be discharged. Fitness for discharge will be decided by a doctor to be appointed by the *Judenrat*.

III. Every Jew being resettled may take 15 kgs [kilograms] of his property as baggage. All valuables such as gold, jewelry, money, etc., may be taken. Food is to be taken for three days.

IV. The resettlement will begin at 11:00 on July 22, 1942. In the course of the resettlement the *Judenrat* will have the following tasks, for the precise execution of which the members of the *Judenrat* will answer with their lives....

EXCERPTS FROM *THE WARSAW DIARY OF ADAM CZERNIAKOW*

JUNE 30, 1942 I was summoned to Auerswald for 4:45 P.M. to receive a text for a poster to be printed. On my arrival he handed me a written order announcing that one hundred Jews and ten Order Service men would be executed for having physically opposed orders of German policemen. Later in the afternoon I telephoned Auerswald that—not to mention the others—the ten patrolmen were guilty of no crime. Some of them were seized in the street.

I sent First and Lejkin to A[uerswald]; they returned at 10:30 reporting the A[uerswald] has invited me for eight o'clock tomorrow morning on the matter of the execution. Perhaps there is still some hope! In the meantime the courtyard has become black [with people]. Panic in the whole Quarter.

The cemetery has been ordered to stop work on a large grave. The gravediggers are to report with their spades at 1 P.M. tomorrow to the Schutzpolizei [German City Police].

JULY 1, 1942 In the morning, at eight o'clock, with Lejkin to the *Kommissar.* I submitted to him a petition for the release of ten functionaries of the Order Service [sentenced to death]. Auerswald informed me that he would pass on my petition to the German police.

I argued that three of those involved were taken from the street as hostages in place of others who were summoned but who had disappeared. Moreover, there are names on the list (of the ten) who had nothing to do with [the] poster announcing the execution of the one hundred prisoners and ten functionaries, adding that he was going to alter its contents.

In the afternoon he came to the detention facility with Galuba. Later he informed me that I was mistaken, since the police had proven to him that all the arrested functionaries were guilty. First was told to call Auerswald at 7:30 tomorrow morning about the possible printing of the announcement. I suppose the execution will be carried out tonight or tomorrow morning.

I submitted my own report on the workers' altercation at the Eastern Railroad Station, presenting the incident in a different light. I also spoke to Brandt about the impending execution. He promised no help. I talked with his chief Bohm on the matter Szerynski. He promised to ask for a pardon.

There was a roundup of Jews for work in the streets today. There are very few volunteers. Panic in the Quarter. Both yesterday and today rumors about deportation of seventy thousand Jews. The rumors are groundless (so far).

They say the three smugglers died tonight. The wives would not leave the bodies.

JULY 2, 1942 In the morning at the Community. In three convoys the 110 persons were driven out of the detention facility between four and six in the morning. The *Kommissar* amended the text of the announcement. Later in the afternoon three hundred copies of his orders were posted. I requested the *Kommissar* to issue an order about extending the curfew hour until ten o'clock at night. He telephoned Brandt and told me that the matter would be taken care of.

Nikolaus, the SD *Kommissar*, arrived at the Community on the matter of three children who are to be brought to Pawiak [prison] with small suitcases and enough food for five days. An exchange is to take place. Their parents are said to be already abroad.

I received a letter from the Commission on Religious Affairs to the effect that during the traditional weeks of mourning there should be no parties or musical and singing performances. I said to Ekerman, who was supporting this position, what I often repeat, that "one cannot wind one's watch with tears" [Dickens]. To which he replied that it is precisely with tears that a Jewish watch can be wound. He did not edify me with these words.

In the evening the [Order] Service was stopping pedestrians and directing all of them not to go along Zelazna Street but through Ogrodowa Street and across the overpass, in order to avoid Burchard's [a sadistic guard] abuse on the corner of Zelazna and Chlodna Streets.

JULY 3, 1942 In the morning at the Community. Later at the Children's Home at Wolnosc Street. During the night a bag of smuggled goods was thrown over the wall. When the police arrived, the night janitor fled. The police took the name of the headmistress, Mrs. Polman. I issued instructions for enlarging the walls separating the Children's Home from other buildings and for nailing up the door leading through the courtyard to another street. I inspected our new playgrounds under construction at Nowolipki Street and at the corner of Franciszkanska and Nalewki Streets.

JULY 4, 1942 In the morning with Lejkin to Brandt and Mende. At my request Brandt released the sixty-four-year-old Heller, the *Obmann* [chairman of the Jewish Council] from Stoczek. Encouraging hints about the Szerynski case.

I was summoned by Nikolaus, the head of the Emigration Section. Nikolaus was concerned that Jozef Ehrlich interfered several days ago with an order to bring three children to the Pawiak [prison] (the children were to be sent abroad to their parents for exchange). Ehrlich had told the escort to bring the children to his apartment. Nikolaus informed me that Ehrlich has been rendering certain services, but not with regard to emigration.

Brandt told me that he had gotten in touch with Auerswald on the issue of an extended curfew hour. I sent First to A[uerswald] to get the text of the announcement. A[uerswald] said that he was preparing it for Monday.

JULY 5, 1942 In the morning at the Community. The Order Service band played at the playground. A program was offered by six hundred boys and girls from elementary schools. From among the performers, I invited to sit at the stand with me a little girl who was made up as Chaplin (great applause). The religionists are opposed to merrymaking with music and signing during the current three weeks (a period of mourning).

JULY 6, 1942 In the morning at the Community. We are to provide five hundred workers for Lublin. A roundup for one thousand people. In the afternoon a conference with Dr. Milejkowski. The findings of scientific research on hunger. Papers were given by Dr. Apfelbaum, Dr. Stein, Dr. Fliderbaum, and Dr. Drein (?).

Today is our twenty-ninth wedding anniversary.

JULY 7, 1942 In the morning at the Community. A delegation from the Order Service arrived (Niunia was present) and presented 32,900 zlotys, the proceeds of the charity concert to aid the prisoners. I discussed the question of a welfare council with Gepner and Sztolcman. G[epner] suggested a permanent body which could be of value also after the war. I expressed the viewpoint that a nucleus of seven to nine persons would be formed with ten or more advisors around it.

I asked G[epner] to speed up the deliberations of the Children's Aid Committee (reformatories, etc.); the children will be sent over by the Polish police from the Aryan side.

The *Kommissar* is sick today. (The problem of an extended curfew hour still unsettled.) I borrowed 300,000 zlotys in town.

The Gypsies who are involuntary residents of the ghetto submit to me their "humble and loyal" petitions. Lately some Gypsies who claim to have been born in Hamburg and have lived there for centuries, came to me on the matter of their return to Germany. They are the Weiss family. One of them fought in the Great War [World War I] and received numerous decorations for valor. They added that several of their close relatives were at that very moment serving in the German Army.

JULY 8, 1942 In the morning with Lejkin to Brandt and Mende. B[randt] claims that he had done his best with the *Kommandeur* on the subject of extending the curfew hour. The rest depends on Auerswald. For tactical reasons he does not feel that he should intercede on behalf of Szerynski. Mende asked for *die Grundlagen des XIX Jahrhunderts,* [*The Foundation of the 19th Century*] by Chamberlain.

I proceeded to the *Kommissar.* Speaking or the curfew, he told me that he had to refer to legal sources. Although not asked, I sent him his legal sources in the afternoon. I raised the subject of the homeless children. I added that if he signs the decree on the basis of which those employed would be paying a tax for their exemption from [camp] labor—I would be in possession of funds for rebuilding the ruined houses. In this way we will have enough accommodations for at least five thousand children. Another solution to the problem: setting up several children's correction homes outside the ghetto. Auerswald replied that he could not publish a decree yet. When asked what his rea-

sons were, he replied that they had to do with need for workers in the East. Discussions of this matter are continuing.

He incidentally raised the subject of women. He had indeed issued instructions to the *Arbeitsamt* [labor office] to register all women who were working. I asked whether housewives fall into this category. Would the volunteers in social work be registered? I did not get a clear answer. As usual, I perceived a lack of sympathy for this class of people.

He added that the definition of export would be revised. Exportation for its own sake, that is to balance the imports, should stop. Exportation profitable to the authorities should remain. Mirrors, etc. are unnecessary.

Concerning finances, it turns out that he again appropriated 700,000 zlotys. He is to give us 300,000 zlotys of it. Today, he ordered that several hundred thousand zlotys are to be transferred from the discretionary fund to the reserve fund. The purpose of the latter is unclear. For a dire emergency? A long time ago (several weeks) he ordered the checking of credentials of all the members of the Order Service. The list was submitted to him. He asked me today whether we have received it back. Unfortunately, we have not. He promised to talk to Fribolin about our funds. I do not expect much from this conversation.

Mende has prohibited answering letters arriving in Warsaw in which questions are asked about the Jews.

About eleven at night some seven hundred people (many of them women and children) from Rawa, etc., were brought to the Community building. The residents of Grzybowska Street helped with tea, etc. A hundred loaves of bread were distributed to the deportees.

Many people hold a grudge against me for organizing play activity for the children, for arranging festive openings of playgrounds, for the music, etc. I am reminded of a film: a ship is sinking and the captain, to raise the spirit of the passengers, order the orchestra to play a jazz piece. I had made up my mind to emulate the captain.

JULY 9, 1942 In the morning at the Community. I sent the *Kommissar* the legal references as grounds for his announcement about the curfew. It is now up to him alone to contrive a few lines and sign a *Trägheitsmoment* [moment of inertia].

I invited Gepner, Sztolcman, Jaszunski, and Altberg, and proposed a shift of exports to commodities most in demand [by the Germans]. I reported on my recent conversations and the thinking of the decision-making authorities. I informed my guests that I would spare no efforts to get in touch with the highest authorities responsible for the Jewish question.

At eight in the morning I went to the little square at Ceglana Street to see about eight hundred deportees from Rawa Mazowiecka and surroundings who were brought there during the night. Small children, babies, women. The sight would break my heart, had it not been hardened by three years of misery.

In the afternoon Polish urchins [keep] throwing stones over the little wall on Chlodna Street. Ever since we removed the bricks and stones from the middle of Chlodna Street, they have not got much ammunition left.

I have often asked myself the question whether Poland is Mickiewicz and Slowacki or whether it is that urchin. The truth lies in the middle. I was informed in the evening that someone had hidden a fur coat, a shabby one at that, in a cellar. In view of the possible consequences I instructed the Order Service to turn the coat over to the Polish police.

Brandt turned up at the prison and wanted to be shown Mrs. Judt. Out of sheer curiosity, I think.

JULY 10, 1942 In the morning at the community. I toured a ceramics studio and workshop, accompanied by Heyman, etc., who used to own a ceramics factory at Wloclawek. I have suggested that bowls and cups be produced there. So far to no avail. I visited the playgrounds at Nalewski and Nowolipki Streets. They will be ready by Sunday. At 2 P.M. I inaugurated an [in-service] training course for teachers in the Community auditorium. Besides me, Mrs. Wolf and Brandszteter addressed the gathering. The room was overflowing.

The *Arbeitsamt* is supposed to have received a letter stating the SS is going to take over the Labor Office function of processing workers for the labor camps.

JULY 11, 1942 In the morning with Lejkin to Brandt to Mende. I asked B[randt] whether it would be possible for him to talk over the question of the Quarter with the *Kommandeur* of the SS in Brühl [Palace].

No progress in the Szerynski case. Mende repeated his order forbidding supplying information about individual Jews in the ghetto. I went to see Rodeck. He informed me that he would allocate to the Council part of the tax money he received from the *Finanzinspektor*. I drew his attention to the fact that the sums I received are insignificant in relation to our needs. I pointed to the necessity of rebuilding the orphanage etc., to move children out of the streets. Also I am supposed to set up the fire department.

I raised the issue of social insurance which does nothing for the Quarter but which at any time can call upon me to make huge payments. It transpired that they are planning to open a *Nebenstelle* [branch office] in the Quarter. In the course of the conversation I mentioned the rumors: resettlement, directing tens of thousands to East. I received the answer that these matters are under discussion. An order may be issued any day.

On my way out I encountered Auerswald. He asked me to postpone our conversation until Monday. He has not yet settled the matter of the curfew hour.

The economic situation in the Quarter is as follows. In January 1942, 1,268 men and 165 women obtained jobs through the *Arbeitsamt*; in June 9,250 men and 1,802 women. All together [for 1942] 24,357 men and 5,739 women.

At the end of April the number of those gainfully employed was 79,000 (not counting those persons whose employment we are not allowed to control). As of now, 95,000 people work (without the 2nd group); of these 4,500 outside the Quarter, 50,000 in industry, crafts, and self employed.

In December 1941 our exports amounted to 2 million zlotys; in June, 12 million zlotys.

JULY 12, 1942 In the morning at the Community. At 9:30 the opening of the playground at the corner of Franciszkanska and Nalewki Streets for the schoolchildren. Crowds of people: in the streets, on the roofs, on the chimneys, on the balconies, Orchestras, choirs, ballet. I addressed the children. In the street the children gave me an ovation. At noon the opening or workshops at the prison. I spoke. The first anniversary of the Jewish detention facility.

JULY 13, 1942 In the morning at the Community. After a heat wave, there has been a significant drop of temperature in the last few days. Rains. Several days ago the guards [at the gates] were replaced by the military police but not for long. An incident with Wundheiler.

Kon arrived yesterday and reported that there was chaos in the Provisioning Authority. I summoned Gepner and we came to the conclusion that Kon might be right.

Auerswald withdrew the armband exemption from Rechthand and Graf; also from Haendel to whom he had granted this right himself and which he had extended not so long ago.

JULY 14, 1942 In the morning at the Community. Later with the *Kommissar*. I want to introduce the raising of rabbits in the ghetto. A[uerswald] retorted that we would not be given oats.

He told me that the question of burying Protestants in the Jewish cemetery should be postponed until Grassler's return. He agreed that the children in the detention facility could be placed in orphanages until the children's reformatory is ready to receive them.

I made a request for the release of the condemned, present and future, in the same way as it had already been done once. He refused. I suggested then a labor camp right in prison. He agreed provided that Toebbens, Schultze or the

brush makers set up the workshop. I summoned Gepner, Rechtland, Wielikowski, Lejkin, Lichtenbaum, and Lindenfeld for a meeting. I asked Lindenfeld to make up a list of prisoners. I ordered Lichtenbaum to prepare an estimate for construction of barracks on the prison grounds, or for the conversion of a Community-owned building at Ceglana Street (baths). Rechthand is to talk to the brush makers, etc.

JULY 15, 1942 In the morning with Lejkin and Brandt and Mende. Later with Mueller about Schmied who had come from Berlin to arrange a barter involving a variety of goods from us for something that is unspecified. The *Kommissar* called and ordered that we take away the German Jews from the quarantine at 109/11 Leszno Street since he wanted to use the premises as an assembly area for the workers on their way to camps (next transport 620 people). I issued instructions for the Housing Department to find accommodations for the German Jews. I visited a commercial establishment at 31 Nalewski Street. In a sort of coffeehouse, I found more than fifty young people playing dominoes and cards. I will use the premises for the children from the detention facility (a reformatory). On my way I stopped to visit the playground at the corner of Francizkanska Street (full of children). Nikolaus arrived at the Community and issued orders for (over eighty) foreign Jews to be brought to Pawiak [prison] on Friday morning from where they are to be sent abroad. Schmied came. The problem of delivery of goods was discussed. He declared the prisoners would be released in exchange.

It does not seem that the Jews will be able to take advantage of Fischer's decree permitting certain food purchases even though Fischer did not exclude Jews from his enactment. Neither shall we obtain the buildings outside the ghetto for industrial workshops. I made arrangements for a conference on this matter tomorrow at 9 A.M. Auerswald's announcement extending the curfew to 10 P.M. was posted throughout the Quarter.

JULY 16, 1942 In the morning at the Community. Later with the *Kommissar*. He instructed me to meet with Schmied. When I asked who S[chmied] was, Auerswald answered that he could not tell me. I decided to seek advice for tomorrow's session with Schmied from Gepner, Sztolcman, Rechthand, etc.

I went to see Galuba and arranged a meeting with him for nine tomorrow morning. He will inspect the premises (reformatory) for the children from the detention facility and will probably release the children.

I gave instructions for the transfer of German refugees from area of 109/11 Leszno Street to make room for the camp assembly area.

Rumors about the deportation of Jews from the Quarter, with 120,000 to be left behind. We have drafted a short memorandum about our economic situation, about Jewish production in the Quarter, and delivered copies of it to the several authorities on who our fate depends.

In the evening our welfare building at Ogrodowa Street was forcibly occupied by someone from Toebens' Co. for German-Jewish employees evicted from 109 Leszno Street. I asked Wielikowski to call the *Kommissar*.

Evening (the second day of the extended curfew hour): rickshaws were being stopped and not allowed to cross under the overpass at the corner of Chlodna and Zelazna Streets.

JULY 17, 1942 At seven o'clock in the morning, a list of condemned prisoners, etc., was brought to my apartment for discussion with Schmied.

In the morning at the Community, Miss Glass from the *Kommissar*'s office telephoned saying that today we must empty the synagogue of the refugees. The building is to be at the disposal of the SS. I dispatched First to Brühl Palace in this matter. The day has started badly. Fortunately, it turned out that the synagogue is needed for foreign Jews. I must empty it today to make room for the emigrants to America, etc.

Two Germans came at 11 A.M. and offered a barter transaction if we supply shoes, etc., we will be permitted to purchase rye flour and some prisoners will be released. In a conference with Gepner, Sztolcman, Rechtman, and Altberg, the main points were agreed upon. Maybe on Monday the matter will be definitely settled. I will make an appointment with the *Kommissar* tomorrow. The evacuation of seventeen hundred of the German Jews from 109 Leszno Street took place in an orderly manner. Sixty or more apartments were taken for that purpose.

JULY 18, 1942 In the morning with Lejkin to Brandt and Mende. A day full or foreboding. Rumors that the deportations will start on Monday evening (All?!). I asked the *Kommissar* whether he knew anything about it. He replied that he did not believe the rumors. In the meantime panic in the Quarter; some speak of deportations, others of a pogrom. Today and tomorrow we are to empty the synagogue for the foreign Jews to move in.

When I was sitting in Mende's office a Polish girl, sixteen or eighteen years old, came in and reported that a converted Jewish woman had been living in the house.

JULY 19, 1942 In the morning at the Community. Incredible panic in the city. Kohn, Heller and Ehrlich are spreading terrifying rumors creating the impression that it is all false propaganda. I wish it were so. On the other hand, there is talk of about forty railroad cars ready and waiting. It transpired that twenty of them had been prepared on SS orders for 720 workers leaving tomorrow for a camp.

Kohn claims that the deportation is to commence tomorrow at 8 P.M. with three thousand Jews from the Little Ghetto (Sliska Street?). He himself and his family slipped away to Otwock. Others did the same.

A Czerniakow, allegedly a relative of mine, is a fixer (a small-scale influence peddler) in the labor department where he used to work for a long while. I ordered that he be put in prison.

Because of the panic, I drove through the streets of the entire Quarter. I visited three playgrounds. I do not know whether I managed to calm the population, but I did my best. I try to hearten the delegations which come to see me. What it costs me they do not see. Today I took two headache powders, another pain reliever, and a sedative, but my head is still splitting. I am trying not to let the smile leave my face.

JULY 20, 1942 In the morning at 7:30 at the Gestapo. I asked Mende how much truth there was in the rumors. He replied that he had heard nothing. I turned to Brandt; he also knew nothing. When asked whether it *could* happen, he replied that he knew of no such scheme. Uncertain, I left his office. I proceeded to his chief, *Kommissar* Böhm. He told me that this was not his department but Hoeheman [Höhmann] might say something about the rumors. I mentioned that, according to rumor, the deportation is to start tonight at 7:30. He replied that he was bound to know something if it were about to happen. Not seeing any other way out, I went to the deputy chief of Section III, Scherer. He expressed his surprise at hearing the rumor and informed me that he too knew nothing about it. Finally, I asked whether I could tell the population that their fears were groundless. He replied that I could and that all the talk was *Quatsch* and *Unsinn* [utter nonsense].

I ordered Lejkin to make the public announcement through the precinct police stations. I drove to Auerswald. He informed me that he reported everything to the SS Polizeiführer. Meanwhile, First went to see Jesuiter and Schlederer who expressed their indignation that the rumors were being spread and promised an investigation.

I returned to the Community and found Dr. Schmied. The barter deal, shoes, etc., for rye is being concluded (1,250,000 zlotys).

Today I discussed with the *Kommissar* the problem of children in the detention center. He ordered me to write him a letter for their release, on the condition that they be placed in reformatories and that a guarantee would be given that they would not escape. I suggested that the prisoners' aid committee be charged with the care of the children. The *Kommissar* demanded a person be designated who would be responsible for guarding them. It is to be someone from the Order Service.

I talked this over with Kaczka, the manager of the transit center on Dzika Street. Some of the children would be placed there. I am also planning to complete alterations in a building at Ceglana Street (the baths) to provide additional accommodations. It appears that about two thousand children will qualify for reformatories.

JULY 21, 1942 In the morning at the Community. Just before noon officers of the SP ordered me to detain in my office those councilors who were present in the Community building. Besides, they asked for a list of the remaining councilors. Soon the members of the council in my office were arrested in groups. At the same time the senior officials of the Provisioning Authority, with Gepner heading the list, were also seized. I wanted to leave with those arrested but was instructed to stay in the office. In the meantime others reached my apartment looking for my wife. They were told that she was at the Children's Home at Wolnosc Street. They left only to return to the apartment with an order that my wife should be home by 3 P.M. Some of the council members were freed today.

I contacted Brandt who told me that everyone would be released tomorrow or the day after tomorrow. I interceded with Auerswald on behalf of Gepner and his colleagues at the Provisioning Authority. He promised to see to it tomorrow morning and asked who exactly was involved. I had the impression that he hesitated about Gepner. I stressed that Gepner was the heart and soul of the Provisioning Authority.

I decided to stay at the Community until 6 P.M. having brought my wife there earlier. The evening was quiet. During the night deaths.

JULY 22, 1940 [*SIC*] In the morning at 7:30 at the Community. The borders of the Small Ghetto surrounded by a special unit in additional to the regular one.

Sturmbannführer Höfle and associates came at ten o'clock. We disconnected the telephone. Children were moved from the playground opposite the community building.

We were told that all the Jews irrespective of sex and age, with certain exceptions, will be deported to the East. By 4 P.M. today a contingent of six thousand people must be provided. And this (at the minimum) will be the daily quota.

We were ordered to vacate a building at 103

Zelazna Street for the German personnel who will be carrying out the deportation. I asked that the JSS personnel, craftsmen, and garbage collectors, etc. also be excluded. This was granted.

I requested the release of Gepner, Rozen, Sztolcman, Drybinski, Winter, Kobryner, which was approved. By 3:45 P.M. everyone but Rozen is already back in the ghetto.

In the afternoon Lejkin sent a message that a piece of glass had allegedly been thrown at a police car. They warned us that if this were to happen again hostages would be shot.

The most tragic dilemma is the problem of children in orphanages, etc. I raised the issue—perhaps something can be done.

At 5:30 one of the officials Forwort (?) drove in and demanded that Jozef Ehrlich should be named Lejkin's deputy. Ehrlich is already wearing three stars.

Sturmbannführer Höfle (*Beauftragter* [plenipotentiary] in charge of deportation) asked me into his office and informed me that for the time being my wife was free, but if the deportation were impeded in any way, she would be the first to be shot as a hostage.

JULY 23, 1942 In the morning at the Community. Worthoff from the deportation staff came and we discussed several problems. He exempted the vocational school students from deportation. The husbands of working women as well. He told me to take up the matter of the orphans with Höfle. The same with reference to craftsmen. When I asked for the number of days per week in which the operation would be carried on, the answer was seven days a week.

Throughout the town a great rush to start new workshops. A sewing machine can save a life.

It is three o'clock. So far four thousand are ready to go. The orders are that there must be nine thousand by four o'clock. Some officials came to the post office and issued instructions that all incoming letters and parcels be diverted to the Pawiak [prison].

Excerpts from Emanuel Ringelblum's *Notes from the Warsaw Ghetto*

WHY? OCT. 15

Why didn't we resist when they began to resettle thirty thousand Jews from Warsaw? Why did we allow ourselves to be led like sheep to the slaughter? Why did everything come so easy to the enemy? Why didn't the hangmen suffer a single casualty? Why could fifty SS men (some people say even fewer), with the help of a division of some two hundred Ukrainian guards and an equal number of Letts, carry the operation out so smoothly?

The shops are traps. They took the best specialists away. "A couple of porters" laughed—they were taken away. The professionals were taken away. They looked at their hands, clean palms.

Office employees taken away only wearing work clothes—wearing slippers. Accompanied on the way [to the *Umschlagplatz*, or deportation point] by Ukrainians—they kept shooting.

Selection for deportation in the street among whole blocks. At first on the basis of working papers, later on the basis of appearance (people dyed their gray hair).

They shaved off all the beards, tore off all the frock coats, ear locks. The street dead all day, except for after the barricade and from five in the morning to seven—the movement from one street to another, where there had already been a barricade. But the Others kept barricading the same neighborhood day after day. The Jewish agents informed the Others about the populace's mood, about the hideout methods.

The role the shop owners played in the barricades—their cooperation with the SS—how they fooled people. For example [the shop owner] Toebbens at 65 Niska Street. He said he wanted to avoid a barricade, so he took away all the workers' laundry. Another example: Jewish [work] directors helped catch the illegals at Hallman's shop.

THE *UMSCHLAGPLATZ*—WHAT IT LOOKED LIKE

The heroic nurses—the only ones who saved people from deportation without [asking for] money. Szmerling—the hangman with the whip.

The scenes when the wagons were loaded—the industriousness of the Jewish Police, the tearing of parents from their children, wives from their husbands, Rabbi Kanal, Lubliner.

The shooting on the spot of those who tried to escape through holes in the Wall at night, the exemption of people who pretended to be doctors. Nurses' kerchiefs saved hundreds of professionals, employees of the Jewish Council.

The great Pursuit. Szmerling currying the Others' favor. More than once he tore the badges off policemen who had saved Jews from the *Umschlag*.

Faithful executor of their orders—introduced a check of the nurses because they allowed people to escape without paying money.

Great grafter—took more than one hundred zlotys per head. Most of those who were exempted bought off the watch at the gate. The police made enormous sums.

["The Thirteen"] Special Service made a lot of money exempting people too; [community] institutions set up a fund to save the professionals.

The tragedy of those seized two, three, and five times. The mother who wouldn't go without her child. The husband who wouldn't go without his wife, etc.—and afterward they all went in the same wagon. Hundreds of families went to the *Umschlag* together because of the children.

Because the quota wasn't met, the Germans seized people on the street, drove them directly into the wagons, not to the *Umschlag* but straight into the wagons. Twelve thousand killed during the resettlement.

THE POT ON NISKA STREET

The 6th of September—the cruelty. In the middle of the night Lejkin was instructed to have all the Jews in the quadrangle bounded on one side by Gesia, on another by Smocza, on a third by Niska, and on the fourth by Zamenhofa to select [deportees] and round up illegals. Massacre of twenty-five thousand people, perhaps even more. Of the barracks that were emptied out (everyone ordered out of the barracks) two or three houses set aside for each shop, most of them in the country. Some shops' [workers] got back into their apartments that day—others not till the next day, or the day after.

"Ah, but we had a fine pot!" said Witasek, who directed the resettlement operation.

The tens of thousands who remained on Niska Street—the continual slaughtering—seventy people killed in one apartment on Wolanska Street. In two days, one thousand people killed, taken to the graveyard—hundreds killed in the street during the selections, all forced to kneel on the pavement [to be killed].

Hundreds and thousands of people lay in their hiding places all week, without water (a water main burst), without food....

YOM KIPPUR, SEPT. 22

The day there was a selection in the shops. The slaughter of women, children, illegals. The practice of torturing Jews in the cities on Yom Kippur. The barricade of the German and Jewish householders—selection supposedly on the basis of craft actually on the basis of graft. The "good Germans" turned bad, e.g., Toebbens.

HOW THE SELECTION TOOK PLACE

In the Jewish Council, around three thousand employees, elsewhere [in other community institutions] entire departments were sent to the *Umschlag*. At Hallmans's [shop] seven hundred were numbered off and [exempted] on the spot; the remaining thirty carpenters with their wives and children were taken away. At the brush factory, twelve hundred were numbered off [and exempted], the rest sent away, mechanically, including the shop where the *chalultzim* worked, valuable human material, the young.

Thousands of people who had managed to save their lives by staying in their hiding places all the time went to the Niska [quadrangle] because they believed they would be leaving the ghetto for good.

The goal [of the Niska Pot]: to get the secret Jews—the ones in hiding—to come out. [It] succeeded. Tens of thousands taken in the Niska Pot.

PREHISTORY OF THE RESETTLEMENT

Letter from Lublin: [warning about] Szamek Grayer, about sixty thousand Jews [to be left] in Warsaw, about a work ghetto [to be set up in Warsaw]. Letter from Wlodasa about the sacrificial "altar" being set up in Warsaw neighborhood, the rumor about Pelcowizne, Kohn and Heller's warnings, the SS threat to stifle bloodily those who spread the rumor.

The arrival of [Oscar] Lotisz [a Lett collaborator, to help in the extermination], the readying of special wagons to Treblinka.

WHY WERE 10 PERCENT OF THE JEWS OF WARSAW ALLOWED TO REMAIN?

Many people have attempted to answer this question, because the answer to a series of fundamental questions hangs on it. How long shall we remain in the ghetto? How long shall we live? How long shall we survive? When shall we be done away with? The opinion of a large group of perceptive persons is that the motive behind their allowing 10 percent of the Jews to remain in Warsaw is not economic but political. It matters little to them that the Jews are pro-

ducing, even for the Wehrmacht. Germany, which dominates all Europe, can easily make up the [economic] loss sustained by a deportation of Jews. If they took the economic factor into account at all, they would not so casually have sent thousands of first-class craftsmen to the *Umschlagplatz* (incidentally the SS are literally searching high and low for Jewish craftsman now—carpenters, apprentices—and [offering] good work conditions). The same was true in the provinces, where complete cities were cleaned out of Jews, although the entire Jewish populations was engaged in working for the Wehrmacht—as for example in Zamosc.

The fact remains that, insofar as Jews are concerned, economic criteria do not apply—only political criteria, propaganda. This being so, the question poses itself even more strongly: Why, then, has a "saving remnant" been allowed to remain in Warsaw? The answer is political. If all the Jews were to be cleared out of Warsaw and out of the Government General [of Poland] as a whole, they would lose the Jewish argument. It would be hard for them then to attribute all their difficulties and failures to the Jews. The Jews have to remain, in keeping with the proverb: "God grant that all your teeth fall out, except one to give you a toothache!"

There is another factor that influences the Germans to allow a handful of Jews to remain in Warsaw for a while. It is world public opinion. They have not publicly acknowledged the massacre of millions of Jews. When forty thousand Lublin Jews were liquidated, the Warsaw newspaper published a news item describing how well off the Jews were in Majdan[ek], how wonderfully they have turned smugglers and fences into "productive elements," living respectable lives in Majdan[ek].

The same is true of Warsaw. They don't want to admit to the world that they have murdered all the Jews of Warsaw, so they leave a handful behind, to be liquidated when the hour strikes twelve—not just for the toothache, but also for the world to see. Hitler will use every means in his power to "free" Europe of all the Jews. Only a miracle can save us from complete extermination; only a speedy and sudden downfall can bring us salvation.

Hence the bitter pessimism dominating the Jewish populace. *Morituri*, that is the best description of our mood. Most of the populace is set on resistance. It seems to me that people will no longer go to the slaughter like lambs. They want the enemy to pay dearly for their lives. They'll fling themselves at them with knives, staves, coal gas. They'll permit no more blockades. They'll not allow themselves to be seized in the street, for they know that work camp means death these days. And they want to die at home, not in a strange place. Naturally, there will only be a resistance if it is organized, and if the enemy does not move like lightning, as [they did] in Kraków, where, at the end of October, 5,500 Jews were packed into wagons in seven hours one night. We have seen the confirmation of the psychological law that the slave who is completely repressed cannot resist. The Jews appear to have recovered somewhat from the heavy blows they have received; they have shaken off the effects of their experiences to some extent, and they calculate now that going to the slaughter peaceably has not diminished the misfortune, but increased it. Whomever you talk to, you hear the same cry: The resettlement should never have been permitted. We should have run out into the street, have set fire to everything in sight, have torn down the walls, and escaped to the Other Side. The Germans would have taken their revenge. It would have cost tens of thousands of lives, but not three hundred thousand. Now we are ashamed of ourselves, disgraced in our own eyes, and in the eyes of the world, where our docility earned us nothing. This must not be repeated now. We must put up a resistance, defend ourselves against the enemy, man and child.

Deportation from the Warsaw ghetto during the ghetto uprising. Jews are led to the *Umschlagplatz* (deportation point) passing "Opus" travel agency. 1943. National Archives/Courtesy of USHMM–Photo Archives.

GERMAN WAR STRATEGY AS APPLIED TO THE JEWS IN WARSAW

The German fear of approaching the large Jewish settlement [in Warsaw]. Fear of [an] uprising, with the help of Poles and paratroopers.

"Divide and rule" [the German strategy] poisons relations between Jews and Poles and makes any help from that [Polish] quarter impossible. [The Germans] fooled the populace about [the meaning of the] resettlement. Chelmno remained a secret to the greater part of the Jews.

[The Germans] set the Warsawers against the refugees. Supposedly the resettlement was to free Warsaw of its "nonproductive elements." [The Germans] promised the Law and Order Service that they and the members of their families, even uncles, mothers-in-law, brothers-in-law, would be secure.

Afterward, they reassured certain trades of their priority over other trades. Afterward, one shop was promised priority over another. Afterward, women and children in the shops themselves became dispensable—afterward, poor workers as compared with good workers. Better shops were opposed to poorer shops—red stamps—continually contracting the circle, continually deceiving, declaring that the resettlement operation was over, in order to prevent a revolt.

The Niska Street Pot: the hermetic sealing of the ghetto limits to keep out help. Hermetic sealing of communications inside and outside the country by stopping the post.

Continual blockades throughout the city. To make any kind of counteraction impossible. Propaganda lies about the resettlement to the East, to make opposition impossible. Supporting the Law and Order Service until the operation was over, when 1,300 Jewish policemen were rounded up and herded into wagons for deportations—the liquidation of the Jewish Gestapo agents.

Moral "attrition" of the Jewish populace in the course of the three war years.

Suddenness—they denied all the rumors about resettlement in order suddenly to surprise the Jewish Council and give it no opportunity for thought.

POLICE

The Jewish Police had a very bad name even before the resettlement. The Polish police didn't take part in the forced work press-gangs, but the Jewish Police engaged in that ugly business. Jewish policemen also distinguished themselves with their fearful corruption and immorality. But they reached the height of viciousness during the resettlement.

They said not a single word of protest against this revolting assignment to lead their own brothers to the slaughter. The police were psychologically prepared for the dirty work and executed it thoroughly. And now people are wracking their brains to understand how Jews, most of them men of culture, former lawyers (most of the police officers were lawyers before the war), could have done away with their brothers with their own hands. How could Jews have dragged women and children, the old and the sick to the wagons, knowing they were all being driven to the slaughter? There are people who hold that every society has the police it deserves, that the disease—cooperation with the occupying power in the slaughter of three hundred thousand Jews—is a contagion affecting the whole of our society and is not limited to the police, who are merely an expression of our society. Other people argue that the police is the haven of morally weak psychological types, who do everything in their power to survive the difficult times, who believe that the end determines all means, and the end is to survive the war—even if survival is bound up with the taking of other people's lives.

In the presence of such nihilism, apparent in the whole gamut of our society, from the highest to the lowest, it is no surprise that the Jewish Police executed the German resettlement operation with the greatest of zeal. And yet the fact remains that most of the time during the resettlement operation the Jewish Police exceeded their daily quotas. That meant they were preparing a reserve for the next day. No sign of sorrow or pain appeared on the faces of the policemen. On the contrary, one saw satisfied and happy individuals, well-fed, loaded with the loot they carried off in company with the Ukrainian guards.

Very often, the cruelty of the Jewish Police exceeded that of the Germans, Ukrainians, and Letts. They uncovered more than one hiding place, aiming to be *plus catholique que le pope* and so curry favor with the occupying power. Victims who succeeded in escaping the German eye were picked up by the Jewish Police. I watched the procession to the wagons on the *Umschlagplatz* for several hours and noted that many Jews who were fortunate enough to work their way toward the spot where the exempted people were standing were forcibly dragged back to the wagons by the Jewish Police. Scores, and perhaps hundreds, of Jews were doomed by the Jewish Police during those two hours. The same thing happened during the blockades. Those who didn't have enough money to pay off the police were dragged to the wagons, or put on the lines going to the *Umschlagplatz*.

A scene I witnessed at 3 Dzszika Street, opposite the *Umschlagplatz*, one day when every policeman had to meet a quota of four "heads" (this was several days before the end of the "operation") will remain in my mind as the symbol for the Jewish Police in Warsaw. I saw a Jewish policeman pulling an old woman by the arm to the *Umschlagplatz*. He had a hatchet on his shoulder. He used the hatchet to break down locked apartment doors. As he approached the *Umschlagplatz* where the watch was stationed, the policeman shamefacedly took the hatchet off his shoulder and transferred it to his hand. It was the general rule those days to see individual policemen dragging men, women, and children to the *Umschlag*. They took the sick there in rickshaws.

For the most part, the Jewish Police showed an incomprehensible brutality. Where did Jews get such murderous violence? When in our history did we ever before raise so many hundreds of killers, capable of snatching children off the street, throwing them on the wagons, dragging

them to the *Umschlag*? It was literally the rule for the scoundrels to fling women onto the Kohn-Heller streetcars, or onto ordinary trucks, by grabbing them by the hands and legs and heaving. Merciless and violent, they beat those who tried to escape.

They weren't content simply to overcome the resistance, but with the utmost severity punished the "criminals" who refused to go to their death voluntarily. Every Warsaw Jew, every woman and child, can cite thousands of cases of the inhuman cruelty and violence of the Jewish Police. Those cases will never be forgotten by the survivors, and they must and shall he paid for.

Beside the police, another group of [Jewish] organizations shared in the resettlement operation. Gancwajch's red-capped Special Ambulance Service was the worst. This organization of swindlers had never given a single Jew the medical aid they promised. They limited their activity to issuing authorization cards and caps, for thousands of zlotys. Possession of these, together with Gancwajch's personal assistance, exempted the owner from forced labor and was a defense against all kinds of trouble and taxes in general. Besides, a Special Service uniform enabled its wearer to perpetrate a variety of swindles and blackmail associated with sanitation (informing on typhus cases, disinfection of steam baths, and the like). It was this pretty gang that now voluntarily reported for the assignment of sending Jews to the hereafter—and they distinguished themselves with their brutality and inhumanity. Their caps were covered with the bloodstains of the Jewish people.

The officials of the Jewish Council also cooperated in the "operation," as did the service of the KAM—City Aid Committee.

HATRED OF THE POLICE. OCT. 15

So long as the "operation" was in progress (that was the name for the massacre of the Warsaw Jews), the populace was silent. They allowed themselves to be led to the slaughter like sheep. I know that porters from the CENTOS

(Children's Aid Society) warehouses, who had many a time displayed courage in the face of danger, allowed themselves to be led off like lambs during the "operation." The same can be said of most of the men and women taken to the *Umschlag* at that time. This will be an eternal mystery—this passivity of the Jewish populace even toward its own police. Now that the populace has calmed down somewhat, and they are reviewing what took place, they are becoming ashamed of having put up no resistance at all. People remember who was responsible for the mass slaughter, and conclude that it was the Jewish Police who were the chief culprits; some people go so far as to lay the whole guilt on the police's shoulders. Now people are taking their revenge. They pass up no opportunity to remind the Jewish Police of their crime. Every policeman you talk to nowadays acts as innocent as a newborn babe. He never took part in the operation. He was assigned to this or that institution. Or else, if he was there, he saved people from the *Umschlag*. Others did the seizing, not he. From these protestations, one would gather that those who seized people for the *Umschlag* were themselves deported to various labor camps or to Treblinka, since none of them are around. We know the truth is exactly the opposite. It is the hoodlum and criminal element in the police that has remained among the three hundred policemen who are now on guard duty in the ghetto, while, on the contrary, the less diligent, who didn't have enough money for "protection," have gone either to Treblinka or to camps like those at Lublin.

So the time for soul-searching has come, the time for revenge. A secret hand did away with Lejkin, the police chief in charge of the resettlement. The Jewish Police are persecuted at every step. Not only by the Jews—the Poles, too, demonstrate their hatred for the Jewish Police. The ex-Jewish policemen working on the streetcar platforms are constantly persecuted by the Polish workers. In Rembertow, even German soldiers persecute them. Many shops protested against hiring policemen. One shop voted to have all former policemen dismissed. I know for a fact that ex-policemen in one outside work detail wore their caps until they reach the watch at the ghetto wall, because a cap is a sign of importance in the ghetto. Once outside the ghetto, they take their caps off, because they are afraid of the Polish populace, who hate the Jewish Law and Order Service for what they did during the resettlement. A man recognized a policeman in the street who had taken away his parents, and attacked him. In Hallman's shop the relief committee distributed dole to a sick ex-policeman. The furor against the relief committee cannot be imagined. This happens everywhere—ex-policemen are persecuted at every step.

People keep bringing up instances of the Jewish Police's brutality during the resettlement. They tell this story: A Jew was killed at 50 Lecszno Street. His body lay there in front of the gate. Two undertakers came along in a wagon to remove the corpse. That day, the police were scurrying around like poisoned rats, because their quota for the day was five "heads." If they didn't meet it, they and their families faced the threat of deportation. Without thinking overlong, the police took away the two undertakers, leaving the corpse to lie unattended in the middle of the street. Another incident, one that took place at 24 Leszno Street: A sixteen-year-old baker's boy beat up a policeman who was trying to take away the boy's mother. The boy tore the policeman's short coat. He was taken to the courtyard of the police headquarters, and there given twenty-five stripes, as a result of which he died.

Still another, no less horrible, instance: A policeman enters, or rather, to be precise about it, breaks into an apartment. All the tenants are hiding somewhere or other, leaving only a three-month-old baby in his cradle. Without a moment's thought, the policeman calls the German who is supervising the operation in from the courtyard. The German makes a face at being offered such a victim. He beats the policeman up badly and shoots the baby. A number of people have assured me this is true.

There are any number of horrifying stories about the conduct of the Jewish Police at the

Umschlag. To them, nobody was a person, only a "head" that could be blackmailed. The only way to escape was by buying the police off with money, diamonds, gold, and the like. The price per head varied. At first it was one thousand or two thousand zlotys. Later it went up, until it reached ten thousand zlotys per head. The exact sum depended on a complex of subjective and objective factors, into which the Jewish Police had sometimes to draw "Yunakes" as partners, as well as the Letts or Ukrainians who were on service in the *Umschlagplatz.* The Jewish Police were without mercy. You could be the most worthy of persons, if you didn't have ransom money, or relatives to pay the asking price, you would he sent away. There are known cases where the police, in addition to money, demanded payment in the form of a woman's body. My friend Kalman Zylberberg knows the badge numbers of the policemen, and the names of the women who paid for freedom with their bodies. The police had a special room in the hospital for this purpose. As a general rule, the police were beside themselves during the resettlement. They were always furious at the recalcitrant who refused to allow themselves to be resettled. The police themselves were continually threatened with being sent to the *Umschlag* with their wives and children. And then, they were demoralized from before the resettlement. Those seized for the *Umschlag*, particularly the women, put up resistance. All these things created an impossible situation for the police, who reacted like beasts....

XVII. THE WARSAW GHETTO UPRISING

From July to September 1942, 265,000 Jews were shipped from Warsaw to Treblinka; only 50,000 Jews remained in the ghetto. For the most part, they were young, able-bodied, shocked, and angry. The old and the very young had been deported and those who remained were not bound by family responsibilities. They were responsible for themselves alone—and for Jewish history. They felt betrayed. They were furious at fate

A clandestine photograph of a burning building in the Warsaw Ghetto during the uprising. May 1943. National Archives/Courtesy of USHMM–Photo Archives.

and at themselves, for they had not resisted the Germans nor even struck out against the Jewish Police.

Despair soon gave way to a firm determination to resist. The Jewish Fighting Organization, the ZOB (*Zydowska Organizacja Bojowa*), slowly took effective control of the ghetto.

The ZOB proclaimed:

Jewish masses, the hour is drawing near. You must be prepared to resist. Not a single Jew should go to the railroad cars. Those who are unable to put up active resistance should resist passively, should go into hiding. . . . Our slogan must be: All are ready to die as human beings.

On January 9, 1943, Heinrich Himmler visited the Warsaw Ghetto. He ordered the deportation of eight thousand more Jews. Ghetto residents assumed this was the end. The resistance sprung into action. There were battles in the streets, near the *Umschlagplatz* [the deportation point], and in buildings. The *Aktion* ended within a matter of days.

Those who remained believed that resistance had brought the deportations to a halt. Hideouts were fortified, resistance units were strengthened. In actuality, Himmler had only ordered a thinning out of the ghetto.

On April 18, 1943, the ghetto received word of an impending *Aktion*. The population was alerted immediately; in fifteen minutes ZOB forces were at their positions.

The Warsaw Ghetto uprising began on April 19, 1943, the second night of Passover, and continued for more than a month until the ghetto was destroyed by fire and its inhabitants killed or captured.

At 6:00 A.M. on April 19, Col. von Sammern initiated the *Aktion*. Within ninety minutes his troops were routed. There were casualties. Open warfare had begun. Jewish fighters were exhilarated. The Nazis were vulnerable to attack. Supermen had fallen.

On April 20, the Germans attacked the factory area where five ZOB squads of fighters were stationed. A mine was set off and the Germans again were forced to retreat. When they reappeared, Jewish fighters opened fire. Hand-to-hand fighting ensued. The Germans raised a white flag—requesting a fifteen minute reprieve. The Jews answered with a volley of fire.

The Germans tightened the siege. They cut off electricity, water, and gas. Police dogs were brought in to uncover shelters.

On the third day, they changed their tactics. The Germans no longer entered the ghetto in large groups. Small bands roamed throughout the ghetto. Resistance also broke into small mobile squads. The German commander, General Jurgen Stroop, changed his strategy. The ghetto was to be burned, building after building, street after street.

On April 22, he reported:

The fire that raged all night drove the Jews who, despite all the search operations, were still hiding under roofs, in cellars and other hiding places. Scores of burning Jews jumped from windows or tried to slide down sheets. We took pains to ensure that those Jews, as well as others, were wiped out immediately.

The Germans had planned to liquidate the ghetto within three days. The Jews held out for more than a month.

On May 8, at ZOB command headquarters at Mila 18, the Germans sent gas inside the bunkers. According to one account, Aryeh Wilner was the first to cry out: "Come let us destroy ourselves. Let's not fall into their hands alive." The suicides began. Pistols jammed and their owners begged their friends to kill them. But no one dared take the life of a comrade. Then someone discovered a hidden exit. But only a few succeeded in escaping. The others suffocated.

Some escaped through the sewers and searched for a hiding place on the Aryan side.

The uprising was literally a revolution in Jewish history. Its importance and scope cannot be conveyed by the results, which were an overwhelming rout of the Jews, a massacre and slaughter. It was understood by those who fought. They saw themselves as freedom fighters, willing to risk all, to lose all, yet not to surrender.

To the Poles, who lived on the Aryan side of Warsaw, they proclaimed: "Long live freedom. Death to the hangman and torturers."

The most expressive sense of the Warsaw Ghetto uprising was given by its commandant, Mordecai Anielewicz, who, at the age of twenty-four, was at the helm of the battle. Resistance was the province of the young, those who were not burdened by responsibilities for elderly parents or young children, those who were responsible solely to themselves and to history. Anielewicz wrote to Yitzhak Zuckerman, a unit commander:

> What really matters is that the dream of my life has become true. Jewish self-defense in the Warsaw Ghetto has become a fact. Jewish armed resistance and the retaliation have become a reality. I have been witness to the magnificent heroic struggle of the Jewish fighters.

This heroism must be read in quite a different context, determined by the perpetrators. So alongside fragmentary documents, the Call for Resistance, Anielewicz's last letter, the call of the Warsaw Resistance Fighters, and diary accounts of the actual battle, we will read the Stropp Report—cool, calculating, precise, it describes a massacre with precision. Numbers, dates, statistics, and then the final announcement: "The Jewish quarter is no longer." To the killer, a battle won. To the victim, a world lost, shattered forever. We will also read Samuel Zygelbojm's letter of protest before he set himself aflame in front of the British Parliament in an act of solidarity with the victims of the Warsaw Ghetto. Zygelbojm, the Jewish representative to the London-based Polish government-in-exile had met on the evening of May 12 with Major Arthur J. Goldberg, who was then working for the OSS in London. Goldberg informed him that no American aid would be forthcoming to the Jews of Warsaw. "In my death I wish to express my strongest protest against mankind, which looks on and accepts the annihilation of the Jewish people," Zygelbojm wrote.

Heinrich Himmler Orders the Destruction of the Warsaw Ghetto

February 16, 1943

Reichsführer SS
Journal No. 38/33/43 g.
Field Command
February 16, 1943
Secret!
To:
Higher SS and Police Leader (Hoher SS- und Polizeiführer), Ea[?] SS Obergruppenführer Kruger, Kraków

For reasons of security I herewith order that the Warsaw Ghetto be pulled down after the concentration camp has been moved. All parts of houses that can be used, and other materials all kinds, are first to be made use of.

The razing of the ghetto and the relocation of the concentration camp are necessary, as otherwise we would probably never establish quiet in Warsaw, and the prevalence of crime cannot be stamped out as long as the ghetto remains.

An overall plan for the razing of the ghetto is to be submitted to me. In any case we must achieve the disappearance from sight of the living space for 500,000 subhumans (*Untermenschen*) that has existed up to now, but could never be suitable for Germans, and reduce the size of this city of millions—Warsaw—that has always been a center of corruption and revolt.

SIGNED H. HIMMLER
NO-2494

Call for Resistance by the Jewish Military Organization in the Warsaw Ghetto

January 1943

ARII/333
Number 1 Warsaw Ghetto January 1943

TO THE JEWISH MASSES IN THE GHETTO

On January 22, 1943 it will be six months since the deportation from Warsaw began. All of us remember well the terrible days in which 300,000 of our brothers and sisters were deported and brutally murdered in the death camp of Treblinka. During the past six months we have been living in constant mortal fear, never knowing what the coming day would bring. News has reached us from all sides, about the extermination of Jews in the General Government, in Germany and in the occupied countries. Having heard the sad news, we have been waiting for our turn, every day, every hour. Today, we must understand that the Hitlerite murderers have allowed us to live only because they want to exploit our labor to the last drop of blood and sweat, to the last breath. We are slaves and when slaves no longer bring profit, they are killed. Each one of us must realize this and each one of us must remember this constantly.

During the last few weeks, certain persons have spread information about letters alleged to have come from Jews deported from Warsaw who are supposedly in labor camps near Pinsk or in Bobruisk.

JEWISH MASSES, DO NOT BELIEVE THOSE STORIES. They are spread by Jews who are in the service of the Gestapo. The bloody murderers are thereby pursuing a certain objective: to calm the Jewish population so that the coming deportation will be carried out without difficulties, with minimal forces and without loss of German lives. They do not want the Jews to prepare hiding places or offer resistance. Jews, do not repeat these lies. Do not help the agents. The criminal Gestapo men will receive their punishment.

JEWISH MASSES! The hour is drawing near. You must be prepared to offer resistance and not let yourselves be slaughtered like sheep. No Jew must enter a boxcar. People unable to resist actively should offer passive resistance, that means hide themselves.

We have received information from Lemberg (Lvov) that Jewish Police—unassisted—carried out a deportation of three thousand Jews there. In Warsaw this will not take place anymore.

The attempt on Lejkin proves it.

Our motto must be:

EVERYBODY SHOULD BE PREPARED TO DIE LIKE A HUMAN BEING.

We are rising to struggle!

We are the ones who will make it our aim to arouse the people. We want to proclaim our slogan in public:

ARISE AND FIGHT!

Do not lose hope in the possibility of rescue!

You should know that rescue is not to be found in going to death passively like a flock of sheep.

It lies in something considerably higher: In struggle!

He who fights for his life stands a chance of saving himself!

He who in advance gives up has lost straightaway! Only disgraceful death in the asphyxiating machine of Treblinka awaits him.

ARISE, PEOPLE, AND FIGHT!

Summon up courage to do reckless deeds!

Down with the shameful acceptance of statements such as "We are all doomed to death!"

This is a lie! For us, too, a future life was destined!

We, too, have the right to it!

It is only necessary to fight for it!

It is no achievement to live when your life is spared only as a favor!

It is an achievement to live when someone else wants to wrest this life from you.

ARISE, PEOPLE, AND FIGHT FOR YOUR LIVES!

Let no father acquiesce at the death of his children!

Let the disgrace of the first act of our extermination never repeat itself!

Down with resignation and self-distrust!

Let the enemy pay with his own blood for every Jewish life!

Let your homes become fortresses!

ARISE, PEOPLE, AND FIGHT!

Your survival is in struggle!

He who fights for his life has a chance to save himself.

We are rising to struggle for the lives of those helpless masses to whose rescue we want to come, whom we must rouse to action!

We do not want to fight for our own lives only. We shall be permitted to save ourselves only after we have fulfilled our duty!

SO LONG AS THE LIFE OF EVEN ONE JEW IS IN DANGER WE MUST BE ON OUR GUARD AND FIGHT!!!

OUR SLOGAN:

Not one Jew will perish in Treblinka anymore!

Down with the traitors of the nation!

Relentless struggle against the invader to the last drop of our blood!

Prepare for action!

BE ON YOUR GUARD!

JEWS!!

The invader is about to carry out the second act of your extermination.

Do not go to death unresisting.

Defend yourselves.

Take hold of an axe, a crowbar, knife, barricade your house.

LET THEM CAPTURE YOU LIKE THAT . . .

In fighting you stand a chance to survive . . .

FIGHT . . .

FOR YOUR FREEDOM AND OURS

WARSAW GHETTO: APRIL 23, 1943

Poles, citizens, freedom fighters!

From out of the roar of the cannon with which the German Army is battering our homes, the dwellings of our mothers, children, and wives;

From out of the reports of machine guns which we have captured from the cowardly police and SS men;

From out of the smoke of fires and the blood of the murdered Warsaw Ghetto, we—imprisoned in the ghetto—send you our heartfelt fraternal greetings. We know that you watch with pain and compassionate tears, with admiration and alarm, the outcome of this war which we have been waging for many days with the cruel occupant.

Let it be known that every threshold in the ghetto has been and will continue to be a fortress, that we may all perish in this struggle, but we will not surrender; that, like you, we breathe with desire for revenge for all the crimes of our common foe.

A battle is being waged for your freedom as well as ours.

For your and our human, civic, and national honor and dignity.

We shall avenge the crimes of Auschwitz, Treblinka, Belzec, Majdanek!

Long live the brotherhood of arms and blood of fighting Poland!

Long live freedom!

Death to the hangmen and torturers.

Long live the struggle for life and death against the occupant.

THE LAST LETTERS OF MORDECAI ANIELEWICZ, WARSAW GHETTO REVOLT COMMANDER

APRIL 1943

This letter, which bears the date April 23, was written in Hebrew and sent to the emissary in the Aryan district, Yitzhak Zukerman. It was then transmitted in Polish on the clandestine radio Swit (Dawn) and published in the illegal organ of Polish Catholic circles, In *the Eyes of the World. Publications in various countries gave an inexact text of this important document. The text which we give here must be considered authentic because it is taken from the direct translation in Yiddish preserved in the archives of Doctor Berman, at that time a member of the National Jewish Committee, who lives today in Israel. This letter was published in the Israeli weekly* Smol (The Left), *April 16, 1953.*

Shalom, Ishak:

I don't know what to write to you. Excuse me if this time I do not write to you of personal matters. To express what I and my friends feel, I will say that we have succeeded beyond our wildest dreams.

On two occasions the Germans were forced to flee from the ghetto. One of our contingents managed to remain in its position for forty minutes and another for more than six hours. One of our mines exploded in the enclosure of the brush factory.

We had only one casualty, Iechiel. He died heroically firing a machine gun.

Yesterday when we read the notice that our comrades of the PPR had attacked the Germans and that the radio station Swit had transmitted the magnificent news of our self-defense, I had a feeling that our work had not been entirely in vain. We still have a great deal of work ahead of us, but so far all has gone well. The general situation is as follows: All the factories in the ghetto and outside are closed with the exception of the Wertverfassung, the Transavia and the Dohring. I have no information on the position in the Toebbens and Schulz factory; communications have been broken. The brush factory has been burning for three days. I have no contact with the troops. In the ghetto fires are raging. Yesterday the hospital was blazing. Whole blocks of houses are enveloped in flames. The Wertverfassung is still working. Schmerling has appeared once more. Lichtenbaum has been released from the U*mschlagplatz.* Not many people have been taken away from the ghetto and therefore not from the shops. I have no details. By day we go into hiding.

From today we are beginning to adopt partisan tactics. This evening three groups will go into action. They have a twofold mission: to locate and capture weapons. Remember, a revolver has no value for us; its use is limited. We have urgent need of hand grenades, sub-machine guns and explosives.

It is impossible to describe the conditions reigning in the ghetto. Very few could bear all this. All the others are destined to perish sooner or later. Their fate has been sealed. In most of the bunkers where thousands of Jews are hiding it is impossible to light a candle because of the lack of air.

I greet you, my dear friend. Who knows whether we shall meet again? My life's dream has now been realized: the Jewish self-defense in the ghetto is now an accomplished fact. Armed resistance on the part of the Jews has been realized.

This letter from the leader of the revolt to his comrade in the Aryan quarter, written on April 26, must be considered as the last authentic document from the H.Q. Staff of the Ghetto Resistance, and the most important. We give it here according to the text published in the previously quoted review, Smol.

For a week we have been involved in a life-and-death struggle. The Warsaw Ghetto, the last of all the ghettos, was suddenly surrounded on the night of April 19th by the regular German Army which has begun the liquidation of the remaining Jews. In the first two days the Germans, after suffering great losses, were forced to beat a retreat. Later, after receiving reinforcements of tanks, armored cars, guns and finally aircraft, they began a regular siege of the ghetto and the systematic burning of all the houses. Our losses are enormous, taking into account the number of victims of shooting and of the fires in which men, women and children perished. Our end is imminent. But while we are in possession of arms we shall continue to resist.

We have rejected a German ultimatum to capitulate because the enemy knows no pity and we have no choice.

As we feel our last days approaching, we ask you to remember how you have betrayed us. The day will come for us to be avenged for the shedding of our innocent blood. Help those who at the last moment will slip through the enemy hands to carry on the struggle.

EXCERPTS FROM *THE STROPP REPORT*

For Führer and Fatherland

FORCES USED	AVERAGE NUMBER OF PERSONNEL USED PER DAY
Waffen SS	
SS Panzer Grenadier Training and Reserve Battalion No. 3	4 officers/440 men
Warsaw	
SS Cavalry Training and Reserve Division, Warsaw	5 officers/381 men
Order Police	
SS Police Regiment No. 22, 1st Battalion	3 officers/94 men
SS Police Regiment No. 22, 3rd Battalion	3 officers/134 men
Technical Emergency Corps	1 officer/6 men
Polish Police	4 officers/363 men
Polish Fire Brigade	166 men
Security Police	3 officers/32 men
Wehrmacht (Armed Forces)	
Light Anti-aircraft Alarm Battery No. III/8, Warsaw	2 officers/22 men
Engineers Detail of the Railway	
Armored Trains-Reserve Division	2 officers/42 men
Rembertow	
Reserve Engineer Battalion No. 14, Gora-Kalwaria	1 officer/34 men
Foreign Ethnic Units	
1 Battalion Trawniki Men	32 officers/335 men

I

The creation of Jewish quarters and the imposition of residential and economic restrictions on the Jews are nothing new in the history of the East. These practices began as far back as the Middle Ages and have continued through the last few centuries. These restrictions were imposed with the intention of protecting the Aryan population from the Jews.

By February 1940, the same considerations led to the idea of creating a Jewish quarter in Warsaw. The original plan called for the establishment of a Jewish quarter in the part of Warsaw that is bounded on the east by the Vistula River. The situation prevailing in the city of Warsaw at first seemed to make this plan unworkable. There were also objections from various parties, especially from the city administration, which claimed that the establishment of a Jewish quarter would cause extensive disruptions in industry and the economy, and that it would be impossible to assure food supplies for Jews who were concentrated in an enclosed quarter.

HALT! STOJ!
SPERRGEBIET! STREFA ZAKAZANA!

Das Betreten des ehemaligen jüdischen Wohnbezirkes ist strengstens erboten.

Jeder der ohne einen gültigen Aus weis
im ehemaligen jüdischen Wohn
angetroffen wird, wird erschossen.

Alle vor dem 2 April 1943 ausge-
stellten Ausweis zum Betreten des
ehem. jüdischen Wohnbezirkes haben
ihre Gültigkeit verloren.

gez. Stroop

Wstęp do byłej żydowskiej dzielnicy miuszka-
jowej jest najsurowiej zakazany.

Każdy, kto bez nowej ważnej przepustki będzie
napotkany w b. żydowskiej dzielnicy mieszkaniowej, będzie zastrzelony.

Wszystkie przepustki, uprawniające do wstępu do byłej
żydowskiej dzielnicy mieszkaniowej, wystawione przed
23 kwietnia 194 tracą swą ważność.

Dowódca SS i Policji w Okręgu Warszawskim
(-) Stroop

An announcement signed by General Stropp, forbidding entrance to the area of the Warsaw Ghetto under pun-ishment of death. All previous permits are declared void. Credit: Main Commission for the Investigation of Nazi Crimes/Courtesy of USHMM–Photo Archives.

Due to these objections, the plan to create a ghetto was set aside at a conference in March 1940. At the same time, consideration was given to making the Lublin District a reservation for all Jews in the General Government [General-gouvernement], particularly for evacuated and fleeing Jews arriving from the Reich. But the Higher SS and Police Leader East in Kraków informed us in April 1940 that such a concentra-tion of Jews in the Lublin District was not intended.

In the interim, the number of arbitrary and unwarranted frontier crossings by Jews increased. This was especially true at the border of the Lowicz and Skierniewice districts. These illegal migrations of Jews began to threaten not only

hygienic but also security conditions in the town of Lowicz. In order to avert these dangers, the senior district official began to create Jewish quar-ters in his district.

The experiences derived from the establish-ment of Jewish quarters in the Lowicz District showed that these methods were the only suit-able ones to banish the dangers which emanate from the Jews.

The need to create a Jewish quarter in the city of Warsaw as well became more and more pressing in the summer of 1940, when, with the end of the French campaign, even larger num-bers of troops assembled in the district of Warsaw. At this point, the Department of Health strongly urged the establishment of a Jewish quarter in order to preserve the health of the German troops as well as that of the civilian population. Considering that a regrouping of almost six hundred thousand people was required, implementation of the original plan of February 1940 to establish a Jewish quarter in the suburb of Praga would have taken four to five months. Since experience indicated that a high incidence of epidemics could be expected in the winter months, the plan for a suburban ghetto in Praga was dropped; and the city's quarantine district was chosen instead for use as a Jewish quarter. On the advice of the district medical officer, resettlement had to be completed by 15 November 1940 at the latest. The governor ordered the plenipotentiary of the Warsaw District Chief to complete the resettlements necessary to the creation of a Jewish quarter within the city of Warsaw by this date.

About four hundred thousand Jews lived in this Jewish quarter. It contained twenty-seven thousand apartments, averaging two and one-half rooms. It was separated from the rest of the city by fire and partition walls and by walled-up thoroughfares, windows, doors, and empty lots.

The Jewish Council [*Aeltestenrat*] administered the new Jewish quarter. It received its instructions from the Commissioner for the Jewish quarter, who was directly subordinate to the Governor. The Jews had administrative autonomy, and German supervision was limited to occasions when German interests were affected. A Jewish Police [*Ordnungsdienst*] was established to implement orders of the Jewish Council. They were identified by special armbands and caps, and were armed with rubber truncheons. This Jewish Police force was responsible for maintaining order and security within the Jewish quarter and was subordinate to the German and Polish Police.

II

It soon became clear that not all dangers had been banished by confining the Jews to one district. Security considerations necessitated that Jews be completely removed from the city of Warsaw. The first large removal occurred during the period from 22 July to 3 October 1942, when 310,322 Jews were removed. In January 1943, another resettlement operation was carried out, which encompassed a total of 6,500 Jews.

On the occasion of his visit to Warsaw in January 1943, the Reichsführer SS ordered the SS and Police Leader of the Warsaw District to transfer from the ghetto to Lublin all armament and defense industries inclusive of their work force and machines. The implementation of this command proved to be very difficult, since the managers as well as the Jews resisted in every conceivable way. Therefore, the SS and Police Leader decided that forced transfer be carried out by means of a three-day grand operation [*Grossaktion*]. The preparation and combat orders for the grand operation were initiated by my predecessor. I arrived in Warsaw on 17 April 1943 and took command of the grand operation on 19 April 1943 at 0800 hours. The operation had already started the same day at 0600 hours.

To prevent the Jews from escaping, the borders of the former Jewish quarter were secured from the outside by a barricade before the start of the grand operation. This barricade was maintained from start to finish of the operation and was reinforced at night.

The Jews and Polish bandits succeeded in repelling the first penetration of the ghetto by ambushing the participating units, which included tanks and armored cars. During the second attack, at about 0800 hours, I committed the attack units to various predetermined battle sectors with orders to sweep the entire ghetto. Despite a second ambush, the blocks of buildings were swept according to plan. The enemy was forced to withdraw from roofs and from strongholds above ground level into basements, bunkers, and sewers. The sewer system was dammed up below the Jewish quarter and flooded to prevent escape into the sewers. Most of this plan, however, proved illusory when the Jews blew up the cutoff valves. Heavy resistance was encountered on the first evening but was quickly broken by a special battle unit. During further operations, the Jews were driven out of their furnished nests of resistance, sniper holes, etc. During 20 and 21 April, the greater part of the so-called remnant ghetto came under our control, and resistance within these blocks could no longer be termed very substantial.

The main Jewish fighting unit, which was intermingled with Polish bandits, had already withdrawn during the first or second day to the so-called Muranowski Square. They were reinforced there by a considerable number of Polish bandits. Their plan was to entrench themselves in the ghetto by every means in order to prevent our penetration. The Jewish and Polish flags were hoisted on top of a concrete building in a call to battle against us. But both flags became the booty of a special battle unit on the second day of the engagement. During this skirmish with the bandits, SS Second Lieutenant Dehmke was killed when the hand grenade he held was triggered by enemy fire, exploded, and injured him fatally.

After the first few days, I realized that the original plan could not be carried out without dissolving the armament and military enterprises that were located throughout the ghetto. It was therefore necessary to set a suitable deadline and to request these enterprises to proceed with an evacuation and immediate transfer. One firm after another was dealt with in this way, and Jews and bandits were quickly deprived of the opportunity to relocate to those enterprises supervised by the Wehrmacht. Thorough inspections were necessary in order to decide how much time was needed to evacuate these enterprises. The conditions discovered during these inspections are indescribable. I cannot imagine another place as chaotic as the Warsaw Ghetto. The Jews controlled everything, from chemical substances used in the manufacture of explosives to items of clothing and equipment for the Wehrmacht. The managers oversaw their operations so poorly that it was possible for the Jews to produce all kinds of weapons, especially hand grenades, Molotov cocktails, etc.

Furthermore, the Jews succeeded in establishing pockets of resistance in these enterprises. One such place, located in a plant under the jurisdiction of the Quartermaster's office, had to be attacked as early as the second day of operations by an Engineers' unit, equipped with flame throwers and artillery. The Jews were so entrenched in this enterprise that it was not possible to induce them to leave voluntarily. I therefore resolved to destroy this enterprise by fire the next day.

In almost all instances, the plant managers, who were usually still supervised by a Wehrmacht officer, were not able to provide precise data about their stocks and storage locations. Their declarations about the number of Jews in their employ were incorrect in every case. Repeatedly, it was discovered that in these labyrinths of buildings, which served as housing blocks of the armament plants, rich Jews disguised as defense workers had found accommodations for themselves and their families and were leading magnificent lives. Despite all orders to request the Jews to leave the enterprises, it was frequently discovered that managers simply included the Jews in their expectation that the operation would last only a few days, after which they expected to continue work with the remaining Jews. According to statements by arrested Jews, owners of enterprises were said to have gone on drinking sprees with Jews. Women allegedly played a prominent part in this. It was said that Jews endeavored to keep up good relations with officers and men of the Wehrmacht. Business deals are said to have been concluded between Jews and Germans during frequent drinking sprees.

The number of Jews who were removed from houses and apprehended was relatively small during the first days. It was apparent that the Jews were hiding in sewers and specially-constructed bunkers. During the first days, it was assumed that there were only scattered bunkers. However, during the grand operation, the whole ghetto was found to be systematically equipped with cellars, bunkers, and passages. These bunkers and passages were all connected to the sewer system. Thus, the Jews were able to maintain an undisturbed subterranean traffic.

They also used this sewer network to escape underground into the Aryan part of the city of Warsaw. Reports were continuously received that Jews attempted to get away through manholes. Under the pretext of building air-raid shelters, they had been constructing bunkers in the former Jewish quarter since late autumn 1942. The bunkers were intended to shelter the Jews during the new resettlement, which had long been anticipated, and to serve as their base of resistance against our troops. Using posters, leaflets, and word-of-mouth propaganda, the Communist resistance movement in the former Jewish quarter was able to man the bunkers occupied as soon as the new grand operation commenced. The skillful construction of the bunkers proved how providentially the Jews had prepared themselves. The bunkers were furnished for entire families and equipped with washing and bathing facilities, toilets, storage rooms for arms and ammunition, and food supplies sufficient for several months. There were different bunkers for poor and rich Jews. Because of camouflage, the discovery of individual bunkers by the troops was extremely difficult. In many cases, discovery was possible only through betrayal by Jews.

After the first few days, it was clear that the Jews no longer considered voluntary resettlement but were determined to resist with all weapons and means at their disposal. So-called fighting groups had been formed under Polish-Bolshevik leadership. They were armed and paid any price for available weapons.

During the grand operation, Jews were caught who had already been transferred to Lublin or Treblinka, had escaped from there, and had returned to the ghetto, equipped with arms and ammunition. Polish bandits continually found refuge in the ghetto and remained there almost unmolested, since no forces were available to penetrate this chaos. While it was possible at the beginning to catch considerable numbers of Jews, who are inherently cowardly, it proved increasingly difficult to capture Jews and bandits in the second half of the grand operation. Repeatedly, fighting groups of twenty to thirty or more Jewish youths, aged eighteen to twenty-five, accompanied by a corresponding number of females, unleashed new resistance. These fighting groups had orders to offer armed resistance to the last person and, if necessary, to commit suicide to escape capture. After ascending from a sewer opening in the so-called Prosta, one such fighting group (circa thirty to thirty-five bandits) succeeded in escaping in a truck. One bandit, who had arrived with this truck, exploded two hand grenades as a prearranged signal for the waiting bandits to emerge from the sewer. The Jews and bandits climbed into the truck and drove away in an unknown direction. These groups always included Polish bandits armed with carbines, small arms, and one light machine gun. The last member of the gang, who was on guard in the sewer and was assigned to replace the manhole cover, was captured. It was he who provided the above information. The search for the truck was unfortunately without result.

During the armed resistance, females belonging to fighting groups were armed just like the men. Some of them were members of the He-halutz movement. Not infrequently, these females fired pistols from both hands. Repeatedly, they concealed pistols or hand grenades (oval Polish hand grenades) in their underpants to use at the last minute against the men of the Waffen SS, police, or Wehrmacht.

The resistance offered by the Jews and bandits could be broken only by the energetic and relentless day and night commitment of our assault units. On 23 April 1943, the Reichsführer SS promulgated his order, transmitted through the Higher SS and Police Leader East in Kraków, to complete the sweeping of the Warsaw Ghetto with greatest severity and unrelenting tenacity. I therefore decided to embark on the total destruction of the Jewish quarter by burning down every residential block, including the housing blocks belonging to the armament enterprises. One enterprise after another was systematically evacuated and destroyed by fire. In almost every instance, the Jews then emerged from their hiding places and bunkers. It was not unusual for Jews to remain in the burning houses until the heat and their fear of being cremated forced them to jump from the upper floors. They did so after throwing mattresses and other upholstered items into the street. With broken bones, they still tried to crawl across the street into housing blocks that had not yet been set on fire or were only partly in flames. Jews often changed their hiding places during the night, moving into already burned-out ruins and finding refuge there until they were found by one of our assault units. Nor was their stay in the sewers very pleasant after the first eight days. Frequently, the sewer shafts carried loud voices upward to the streets, whereupon men of the Waffen SS, Police, or Wehrmacht Engineers courageously climbed down the shafts to bring out Jews. Not infrequently the Engineers would stumble over dead Jews or be shot at. It was always necessary to use smoke candles to drive out the Jews. On one day alone, at a predetermined hour, 183 sewer gates were opened and smoke candles lowered. The bandits fled from what they thought was gas toward the center of the former Jewish quarter, where they were pulled out of the sewer holes. An indeterminable number of Jews were finished off when sewers and bunkers were blown up.

The longer the resistance lasted, the tougher became the men of the Waffen SS, police, and Wehrmacht, who tirelessly fulfilled their duties in true comradeship and stood together as exemplary soldiers. Their mission often lasted from early morning to late at night. Nightly search patrols, with rags wrapped around their feet, dogged the Jews and gave them no respite. Jews who used the night to supplement their provisions from abandoned bunkers and to make contact or exchange news with neighboring groups were often brought to bay and finished off.

Considering that the greater part of the men of the Waffen SS had been trained for only three or four weeks before this operation, they must be given special recognition for their daring, courage, and devotion to duty. It must be noted that the Wehrmacht Engineers also executed their tasks of blowing up bunkers, sewers, and concrete houses with tireless devotion. The officers and men of the police, many already with experience at the front, again acquitted themselves with devil-may-care valor.

Only the continuous and tireless commitment of all forces made it possible to apprehend and/or destroy 56,065 Jews. To this confirmed number must be added the Jews who lost their lives in explosions, fires, etc., whose number could not be ascertained.

During the grand operation, the Aryan population was informed through posters that it was strictly forbidden to enter the former Jewish quarter and that anyone caught within the former Jewish quarter without a valid pass would be shot. Simultaneously, these posters instructed the Aryan population once again that anyone who knowingly gave refuge to a Jew, especially if they provided shelter, food, or a hiding place to a Jew outside the Jewish quarter, would be sentenced to death.

The Polish police was authorized to pay Polish policemen one-third of the cash belonging to any Jew they arrested within the Aryan part of Warsaw. This measure has already produced results.

The Polish population has by and large welcomed the measures implemented against the Jews. Toward the end of the grand operation, the governor issued a special proclamation to the Polish population that was submitted to the undersigned for approval before publication. This proclamation informed them of the reasons for destroying the former Jewish quarter by referring to the recent assassinations in the city of Warsaw and the mass graves found in Katyn. They were asked to assist in the fight against Communist agents and Jews .

The grand operation was terminated on 16 May 1943, with the dynamiting of the Warsaw Synagogue at 2015 hours.

Now there are no enterprises left in the former Jewish quarter. Everything of value, the raw materials, and machines have been transferred. The buildings and whatever else there was have been destroyed. The only exception is the so-called Dzielna Prison of the Security Police, which was exempted from destruction.

III

Since it must be assumed that even with the grand operation complete a few Jews are still living in the ruins of the former Jewish quarter. This area must be guarded and firmly sealed off from the Aryan residential section for immediate future. Police Battalion III/23 has been assigned this duty.

Police Battalion has instructions to keep watch over the former Jewish quarter, especially to prevent anyone from entering the former ghetto and shoot immediately any unauthorized person found there. The Commander the Police Battalion will continue to receive further direct orders from SS and Police Leader. In this way, it should be possible to keep the small number of Jews who might remain there under constant pressure and to destroy them. The remaining Jews and bandits must be deprived of every chance of survival through the destruction of all buildings and refuges, and the cutting of the water supply.

It is proposed to change Dzielna Prison into a concentration camp and to use the prisoners to strip down and collect the millions of bricks, scrap iron, and other materials for further utilization.

Warsaw 16 May 1943
SS and Police Leader in the
Warsaw District
(SIGNED) STROOP

SS Major General and Major General
of the Police

"A PROTEST AGAINST THE INDIFFERENCE OF THE WORLD"
Samuel Zygelbojm

Samuel Zygelbojm was one of the leaders of the Bund, the Jewish Socialist Party in Poland. In 1940 he managed to flee from Poland. When he reached London in 1942, he, as representative of the Polish Jews, joined the National Polish committee, which became the Polish government-in-exile. Zygelbojm and others tried desperately to draw the attention of the Allied governments to the fate of the Jews in Poland. When the news of the revolt in the Warsaw Ghetto came, and with it the final phase of the extermination, Zygelbojm committed suicide as an act of protest against the indifference of the Allied governments to the fate of his people. Before his death he addressed to the Polish government the following letter, which was transmitted to the British and American governments.

With these, my last words, I address myself to you, the Polish government, the Polish people, the Allied governments and their peoples, and the conscience of the world.

News recently received from Poland informs us that the Germans are exterminating with unheard-of savagery the remaining Jews in that country. Behind the walls of the ghetto is taking place today the last act of a tragedy which has no parallel in the history of the human race. The responsibility for this crime—the assassination of the Jewish population in Poland—rests above all on the murderers themselves, but falls indirectly upon the whole human race, on the Allies and their governments, who so far have taken no firm steps to put a stop to these crimes. By their indifference to the killing of millions of hapless men, to the massacre of women and children, these countries have become accomplices of the assassins.

Furthermore, I must state that the Polish government, although it has done a great deal to influence world public opinion, has not taken adequate measures to counter this atrocity which is taking place today in Poland.

Of the three and a half million Polish Jews (to whom must be added the seven hundred thousand deported from the other countries) in April, 1943, there remained alive not more than three hundred thousand Jews according to news received from the head of the Bund organization and supplied by government representatives. And the extermination continues.

I cannot remain silent. I cannot live while the rest of the Jewish people in Poland, whom I represent, continue to be liquidated.

My companions of the Warsaw Ghetto fell in a last heroic battle with their weapons in their hands. I did not have the honor to die with them but I belong to them and to their common grave.

Let my death be an energetic cry of protest against the indifference of the world which witnesses the extermination of the Jewish people without taking any steps to prevent it. In our day and age human life is of little value; having failed to achieve success in my life, I hope that my death may jolt the indifference of those who, perhaps even in this extreme moment, could save the Jews who are still alive in Poland.

My life belongs to my people in Poland and that is why I am sacrificing it for them. May the handful of people who will survive out of the millions of Polish Jews achieve liberation in a

First page of the *Stropp Report*. The text reads: "The Jewish Quarter is no more." National Archives/Courtesy of USHMM–Photo Archives.

world of liberty and socialist justice together with the Polish people.

I think that there will be a free Poland and that it is possible to achieve a world of justice. I am certain that the president of the Republic and the head of the government will pass on my words to all concerned. I am sure that the Polish government will hasten to adopt the necessary political measures and will come to the aid of those who are still alive.

I take my leave of all those who have been dear to me and whom I have loved.

SAMUEL ZYGELBOJM

XVIII. WHAT WAS KNOWN IN THE WEST

THE RIEGNER TELEGRAM

On August 11, 1942, Dr. Gerhart Riegner, World Jewish Congress representative in Bern, Switzerland, sent a cable to the State Department and to Rabbi Stephen S. Wise, president of the World Jewish Congress, informing them that there was being considered in Hitler's headquarters a plan to exterminate all Jews from Germany and German-controlled areas in Europe once they had been concentrated in the East. He reported

Third meeting of the board of directors of the War Refugee Board in the office of Secretary of State Cordell Hull. *Left to right* are Hull, Secretary of Treasury Henry Morgenthau, Jr., and Secretary of War Henry L. Stimson. March 21, 1944. Credit: FDR Library/Courtesy of USHMM–Photo Archives.

that the numbers involved was between three and a half and four million and the object was to permanently settle the Jewish question in Europe.

Riegner had been interviewed by Howard Etling, Jr., American Vice Consul in Bern before the cable had been sent. It was Etling's personal opinion that Riegner "is a serious and balanced individual and that he would never have come to the Consulate . . . if he had not had confidence in his informant's reliability and if he did not seriously consider the report might well contain an element of truth." Etling passed on this information to the State Department "for what it is worth." After reviewing the Bern telegram the State Department concluded that "it does not appear advisable in view of the Legation's comments, the fantastic nature of the allegations, and the impossibility of our being of any assistance if such action were taken" to give the telegram to Stephen Wise.

Unbeknownst to the State Department, Riegner had also sent a telegram to Samuel Silverman, a Member of Parliament in London, who passed on the very same information to Rabbi Wise who in turn transmitted it to the State Department. He was asked not to make the information public until it could be confirmed by additional sources. By mid-September, the information was confirmed.

THE MISSION OF JAN KARSKI

In October 1942, Jan Karski [Kozielewski], a secret courier for the London-based Polish government-in-exile met with Jewish leaders Menachem Kirschenbaum of the General Zionists and Leon Feiner of the German Bund. These leaders were the final remnant of what had once been the largest and most influential Jewish community in Europe, Warsaw. More than 250,000 of these Jews had been deported to the death camp of Treblinka some sixty kilometers away in the summer of 1942; only 50,000 desperate Jews, mostly young men and women without families, remained alive.

Two meetings were arranged. The leaders representing different parties and divergent ideologies stressed that they were speaking on behalf of all Polish Jews, regardless of political differences. Their requests were urgent. Preventing the physical extermination of the Jews, they insisted, must become part of the Allied war strategy. Public appeals must be made to the German people to pressure their government to stop the extermination. The full facts regarding the murder of European Jews—concentration and death camps, ghettos, the number of dead—must be made public. Finally, the German nation must be held responsible if the killings did not stop.

> Germany can be impressed only by power and violence. The cities of Germany ought to be bombed mercilessly and with every bombing leaflets should be dropped informing the Germans fully of the fate of Polish Jewry.

To add greater weight to his testimony, Karski was urged to visit the ghetto. Karski recalled: "as an eyewitness I would be much more convincing than a mere mouthpiece." Years later he could still recount the horror: "It was not a world. There was not humanity. Streets full, full. Apparently all, they lived in the street, exchanging what was most important. . . . Selling. Begging each other. Crying. Hungry."

He was admonished. "Look at him. Tell them over there. You saw it. Don't forget."

Jewish leaders in Warsaw made demands as bold as they were despairing: bomb the German cities with direct public announcements that the bombing was in retaliation for the extermination of Jews. They demanded that Jewish leaders in London, Samuel Zygelbojm of the Bund and Dr. Ignace Szwarcbard of the Zionists, be informed of the plight of Polish Jewry and be urged to take effective action. Karski was a faithful messenger. He told Zygelbojm:

> This is what they want from their leaders in the free countries of the world, this is what they told me to say. Let them go to all important English and American offices and agencies. Tell them not to leave until they have obtained guarantees that a way has been decided upon to save the Jews. Let them accept no food or drink, let them die a slow death while the world looks on. Let them die. This may shake the conscience of the world.

As we have read Zygelbojm wrote his final note of despair just before setting himself aflame.

Karski himself pressed this program in meetings with English and American leaders. In London, he met with four members of the British War Cabinet including Foreign Minister Anthony Eden. A meeting with Winston Churchill was not arranged. In July 1943, Karski was sent to Washington where he met with President Roosevelt, Secretary of State Cordell Hull, Secretary of War Henry Stimson, Attorney General Francis Biddle, OSS Chief William Donovan, [OSS, or Office of Strategic Services, the forerunner of the CIA], and Justice Felix Frankfurter, as well as with Jewish leaders such as Rabbi Wise, and Nahum Goldman, president of the World Jewish Congress.

Karski's meeting with Justice Frankfurter may contain a key to understanding Allied inaction to reports of the mass murders. Meeting at the home of the Polish Ambassador to the United States, Karski recounted his story, omitting no details, and Frankfurter listened attentively. At the conclusion he rose with great agitation. "I can't believe you," the Justice said to the young courier. The ambassador interrupted, vouching for Karski's integrity. Frankfurter responded that he did not doubt that Karski was telling the truth, he merely couldn't believe him. There was a difference.

Historians know that there was an abundance of timely and accurate information about the "Final Solution to the Jewish problem," available as events were developing. However, available information did not translate into accepted knowledge which could be acted upon. Most often, the information was not even believed.

Karski also briefed prominent journalists in an effort to convey the severity of the situation. This effort had no better result than his other attempts to spread information. "The Lord assigned me a role," Karski said, "to speak and write during the war, when—as it seemed to me—it might help. It did not."

ON THE ACQUIESCENCE OF THIS [UNITED STATES] GOVERNMENT

On January 13, 1944, Secretary of Treasury Henry Morgenthau received an explosive memo from his staff—General Counsel Randolph Paul, Josiah DuBois, and John Pehle—entitled "Report to the Secretary on the Acquiescence of This Government in the Murder of the Jews." They wrote:

> State Department officials:
>   have not only failed to use the governmental machinery at their disposal to rescue Jews from Hitler, but have even gone so far as to use this governmental machinery to prevent the rescue of these Jews.

They have not only failed to cooperate with private organizations . . . but have taken steps designed to prevent these [rescue] programs from being put into effect.

They not only have failed to facilitate the obtaining the information concerning Hitler's plans to exterminate the Jews of Europe but in their official capacity have gone so far as to surreptitiously attempt to stop obtaining of information concerning the murder of the Jewish population of Europe.

They have tried to cover up their guilt by:

A. concealment and misrepresentation;
B. the giving of false and misleading explanations for their failures to act and their attempts to prevent action; and
C. the issuance of false and misleading statements

DuBois made grave charges, noting, "I fully recognize the graveness of this statement. I make it only after having most carefully weighed the shocking facts which have come to my attention during the last months."

The descendant of a prominent Jewish family, Secretary of the Treasury Morgenthau read the memo with mounting rage. He condensed the memo originally drafted by Paul's assistant, Josiah DuBois from eighteen to nine pages, and neutralized its title to "Personal Report to the President"—adding some charges of his own and making sure that the president fully understood the political consequences of what he was reading—1944 was an election year.

Three days later, on Sunday morning January 16, 1944, Morgenthau went to see the President Roosevelt, who read the report, but to protect the president from leaks to the press—perhaps even from the judgment of history—no copy was left at the White House.

Four words, deliberately omitted from the copy of Memo 354 sent to the Treasury Department, revealed the intent and scope of the State Department's activities: "Your 482, January 21." The missing words could have been an innocent omission. To DuBois, it unraveled a mystery.

The four words referred to an earlier cable sent through secret channels informing the State Department and Jewish organization of the Final Solution to the Jewish question—the German decision to murder all the Jews.

Memo 354 shut down the secret channel of communication from Switzerland to cable from Reigner. The State Department intended to prevent access to information concerning the Jews, and thus diminish political pressure from Jewish organizations.

For three weeks, the young Treasury Department official dictated to his secretary by day and wrote at home at night. Even on Christmas day—after having spent time with his family—DuBois went back to the office to unlock a consistent, systematic pattern of deception and delay by high-ranking State Department officials.

Only in the eleventh year of the Nazi regime, thirty months after the systematic killing of Jews began, months after Treblinka, Sobibor, and Belzec had completed their task of murdering the Jews of Poland, did the sleeping giant fully awake from its slumber and dedicate national energies toward rescue.

Secretary Morgenthau presented President Roosevelt with a concrete proposal to actively involve the United States in the business of rescue. Within days of the January 16, 1944, meeting Roosevelt established the War Refugee Board (WRB) consisting of the

Secretaries of State, Treasury, and War, and charged it to implement an American policy of rescue.

Headed by John Pehle, a young Treasury Department lawyer who had helped DuBois and Paul unravel the State Department cover-up, the WRB tried to find a haven for Jews, it forced presidential platforms, pushed for war-crimes trials, and pressed to have Auschwitz bombed. Through its European and Asian operatives, including Raoul Wallenberg, the WRB played a crucial role in saving perhaps as many as two hundred thousand Jews.

Yet when John Pehle viewed the work of the WRB from the perspective of twelve years of American efforts, he commented: "What we did was little enough. It was late. Late and little, I would say."

LETTER OF TRANSMISSION OF GERHART RIEGNER'S TELEGRAM

Air Mail Pouch
No. 35 Political
AMERICAN CONSULATE
Geneva, Switzerland, August 10, 1942
Subject: Transmitting Memorandum of
Conversation with Secretary of Jewish
Congress, Geneva, concerning Report that
Germans are Considering Wholesale
Extermination of Jews.
The Honorable
The Secretary of State,
Washington.

SIR:

At the suggestion of the Legation of Bern, I have the honor to enclose a copy of a memorandum in the above entitled matter.

I desire to reiterate my belief in the utter seriousness of my informant.

Respectfully yours,
Howard Elting, Jr.
American Vice Consul
Enclosure:
Copy of memorandum, as stated.
In sextuplicate to Department
800
HE/db

MEMORANDUM

Subject: Conversation with Mr. Gerhart M. Riegner, Secretary of World Jewish Congress

This morning Mr. Gerhart M. RIEGNER, secretary of the World Jewish Congress in Geneva, called in great agitation. He stated that he had just received a report from a German businessman of considerable prominence, who is said to have excellent political and military connections in Germany and from whom reliable and important political information has been obtained on two previous occasions, to the effect that there has been and is being considered in Hitler's headquarters a plan to exterminate all Jews from Germany and German-controlled areas in Europe after they have been concentrated in the east (presumably Poland). The number involved is said to be between three-and-a-half and four millions and the object is to permanently settle the Jewish question in Europe. The mass execution if decided upon would allegedly take place this fall.

Riegner stated that according to his informant the use of prussic acid was mentioned as a means of accomplishing the executions. When I mentioned that this report seemed fantastic to me, Riegner said that it had struck him in the same way but that from the fact that mass deportation had been taking place since July 16 as confirmed by reports received by him from Paris, Holland, Berlin, Vienna, and Prague it was always conceivable that such a diabolical plan was actually being considered by Hitler as a corollary.

According to Riegner, 14,000 Jews have already been deported from occupied France and 10,000 more are to be handed over from occupied France in the course of the next few days. Similarly from German sources 56,000 Jews have already been deported from the protectorate together with unspecified numbers from Germany and other occupied countries.

Riegner said this report was so serious and alarming that he felt it his duty to make the following requests: (1) that the American and other Allied governments be informed with regard thereto at once; (2) that they be asked to try by every means to obtain confirmation or denial; (3) that Dr. Stephen Wise, the president of his organization, be informed of the report.

I told Riegner that the information would be passed on to the Legation at once but that I was not in a possible to inform his as to what action, if any, the Legation might take. He hoped that he might be informed in due course that the information had been transmitted to Washington.

For what it is worth, my personal opinion is that Riegner is a serious and balanced individual and that he would never have come to the Consulate with the above report if he had not had confidence in his informant's reliability and if he did not seriously consider that the report might well contain an element of truth. Again it is my opinion that the report should be passed on to the Department for what it is worth.

There is attached a draft of a telegram prepared by Riegner giving in his own words a telegraphic summary of his statements to me.

Howard Elting, Jr.
American Vice Consul
American Consulate
Geneva, Switzerland
800
HE/db

THE RIEGNER TELEGRAM TO DR. STEPHEN WISE THAT WAS NOT DELIVERED

DR. STEPHEN WISE PRESIDENT AMERICAN
JEWISH CONGRESS
330 WEST 42ND STREET ROOM 809
NEW YORK

RECEIVED ALARMING REPORT STATING THAT IN FUHRERS HEADQUARTERS A PLAN HAS BEEN DISCUSSED AND BEING UNDER CONSIDERATION ACCORDING WHICH TOTAL OF JEWS IN COUNTRIES OCCUPIED CONTROLLED BY GERMANY NUMBERING THREE AND HALF TO FOUR MILLIONS SHOULD AFTER DEPORTATION AND CONCENTRATED IN EAST BE AT ONE BLOW EXTERMINATED IN ORDER RESOLVE ONCE FOR ALL JEWISH QUESTION IN EUROPE STOP ACTION IS REPORTED TO BE PLANNED FOR AUTUMN WAYS OF EXECUTION STILL DISCUSSED STOP IT HAS BEEN SPOKEN OF PRUSSIC ACID STOP IN TRANSMITTING INFORMATION WITH ALL NECESSARY RESERVATION AS EXACTITUDE CANNOT BE CONTROLLED BY US BEG TO STATE THAT INFORMER IS REPORTED HAVE CLOSE CONNECTIONS WITH HIGHEST GERMAN AUTHORITIES AND HIS REPORTS TO BE GENERALLY RELIABLE

WORLD JEWISH CONGRESS
GERARD RIEGNER

DEPARTMENT OF STATE
DIVISION OF EUROPEAN AFFAIRS

MEMORANDUM

August 13, 1942.

With reference to Bern's telegram no. 3697, August 11, 3 P.M. transmitting information from Mr. Gerhart M. Riegner, secretary of the World Jewish Congress, Geneva, regarding the alleged plan of the Nazis to exterminate three and a half to four million Jews, it does not appear advisable in view of the Legation's comments, the fantastic nature of the allegation, and the impossibility of our being of any assistance if such action were taken, to transmit the information to Dr. Stephen Wise as suggested.

Eu: EDurbrow:LS

LETTER FROM DR. STEPHEN WISE TO SECRETARY OF STATE SUMNER WELLES

1200 CNY 89035 AG
AMERICAN JEWISH CONGRESS
330 WEST 42nd STREET NEW YORK CITY
STEPHEN S. WISE, PRESIDENT
CARL SHERMAN, CHAIRMAN, EXECUTIVE COMMITTEE
NATHAN D. PERLMAN VICE-PRESIDENT
LEO H. LOWITZ, VICE-PRESIDENT
LOUIS LIPSKY, CHAIRMAN, GOVERNING COUNCIL
M. MALDWIN FERTIG, CHAIRMAN, ADMINISTRATION COMMITTEE
JACOB LEICHTMAN, TREASURER
Office of Dr. Wise
40 West 68 Street,
September 2, 1942.
Hon. Sumner Welles
State Department
Washington, D.C.

My dear Secretary Welles,

I trust that you understand how loath I am to bring the following matter to your attention on the eve of your abundantly deserved holiday. But as you will see from the reading of the enclosure, my associates and I of the American and the World Jewish Congress have been reduced to consternation by this cable. May I say that it comes from Mr. Silverman, who is a member of the House of Commons, and Riegner, whom he quotes, is a representative of the World Jewish Congress at Geneva, who appears to have gotten this information directly from someone who knows within Nazi circles.

I have these suggestions to offer. One, that you be good enough to ask either our Ambassador at Berne, or our Consul General in Geneva, to talk to Dr. M. Riegner, whose address is 52 rue de Paquis, and learn from him whatever may be learned in substantiation of this appalling rumor. Dr. Riegner is a scholar of entire reliability, who would not have cabled through the Foreign Office to Silverman unless he believed the situation to be one of the gravest urgency. He is not an alarmist but a conservative and equable person, whose reports ordinarily are entirely trustworthy. Two, if through your inquiry we get further information, it may then become necessary for us to ask the administration chiefly and your department especially to take such action as may seem wisest.

If you are leaving almost immediately, would you be good enough to tell me with whom I am to deal after I shall have heard from you?

May I venture to suggest that you consider whether the matter is not of such immediate importance as to merit it being brought to the attention of the president himself.

Finally, may I expect a telephone call from you, through your secretary, tomorrow morning before you leave. My telephone number is Trafalgar 7–4050.

I know you will help in every way you think wise.

Faithfully yours,
SSW:S   *PRESIDENT*

CABLE FROM SAMUEL SILVERMAN TO DR. STEPHEN WISE

COPY OF
WESTERN UNION
CABLEGRAM
NV 15 CABLE–LIVERPOOL 122 1/63 NFD

NLT STEPHEN WISE
WORLD JEWISH CONGRESS
330 West 42 Street

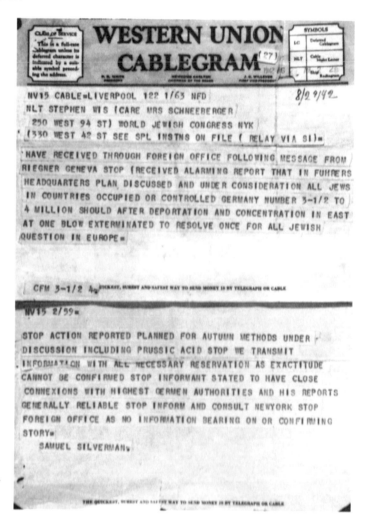

Cable from Samuel Silverman to Dr. Stephen Wise, president of the American Jewish Congress, informing him of plans for the Final Solution and the use of Cyclon-B gas. August 29, 1942. American Jewish Archives/Courtesy of USHMM–Photo Archives.

HAVE RECEIVED THROUGH FOREIGN OFFICE FOLLOWING MESSAGE FROM RIEGNER STOP (RECEIVED ALARMING REPORT THAT IN FUHRERS HEADQUARTERS PLAN DISCUSSED AND UNDER CONSIDERATION ALL JEWS IN COUNTRIES OCCUPIED OR CONTROLLED GERMANY NUMBER 3-1/2 TO 4 MILLION SHOULD AFTER DEPORTATION AND CONCENTRATION IN EAST AT ONE BLOW BE EXTERMINATED TO RESOLVE ONCE FOR ALL JEWISH QUESTION IN EUROPE STOP ACTION REPORTED PLANNED FOR AUTUMN METHODS UNDER DISCUSSION INCLUDING PRUSSIC ACID STOP WE TRANSMIT INFORMATION WITH ALL NECESSARY RESERVATION AS EXACTITUDE CANNOT BE CONFIRMED STOP INFORMANT STATED TO HAVE CLOSE CONNECTION WITH HIGHEST GERMAN AUTHORITIES AND HIS REPORTS GENERALLY RELIABLE STOP INFORM AND CONSULT NEW YORK STOP FOREIGN OFFICE HAS NO INFORMATION BEARING ON OR CONFIRMING STORY

SAMUEL SILVERMAN

MEMO TO THE SECRETARY OF STATE

BY AIR POUCH
NO. 44-Political
AMERICAN CONSULATE
Geneva, Switzerland, September 28, 1942.
Subject: Jewish Persecutions
THE HONORABLE
THE SECRETARY OF STATE,
WASHINGTON.

SIR:

I have the honor to transmit herewith two memoranda concerning persecutions of the Jews based on data furnished by Mr. Gerhart M. RIEGNER, secretary of the World Jewish Congress at Geneva.

The first memorandum deals with the utilization of corpses after their arrival in Germany while the second reproduces extracts from letters posted at Warsaw containing veiled information concerning the extermination of the Jews confined in the ghettos there. The latter memorandum is supported by photostat copies of letters dated September 4 and 12, 1942. It is imperative that the identity of the sender in Warsaw and the recipient in Switzerland be guarded in the strictest confidence, as well as the dates of the letters and the registration number. The underscoring appearing in these photostats was made by the recipient.

Information reaching me from a German source regarded as trustworthy and to which I am accustomed to refer to my Political Notes as "Frank" would seem to reconfirm that the program of extermination embraces not only the Jews but the Polish people. I quote "Frank" as follows:

"There is no longer the slightest doubt that it is the objective if the Nazi leaders to exterminate the Polish people. High Party officials who have to do with Governor General Frank confirm this aim."

If no objection is perceived it is requested that the enclosed letter with enclosures, after perusal, be forwarded to Dr. Stephen S. WISE, President of the American and World Jewish Congress, 330 West 42nd Street, New York City.

Respectfully yours,
PAUL C. SQUIRE

American Consul

Enclosures:
1. and 2. Two memoranda.
3. Photostat copies of letters, as stated.
4. Letter dated September 24, 1942, addressed to Dr. Stephen S. Wise from Geneva Office of the World Jewish Congress.
In sextuplicate to Department.
Copy of Legation, Bern
PCS/lc

REPORT ON MY MISSION

Jan Karski

The subject "Discovering the Final Solution" requires consideration of the following questions:

1. What and when did the western leaders as well as western public opinion learn about the Jewish tragedy?
2. In what way did the information reach them?
3. What was the reaction? According to evidence?

I, among many, did play a part in this story, and my usefulness to this conference lies in reporting on it for the record.

In the middle of the summer 1942, I received a message from the delegate of the Polish government-in-exile for the homeland, Cyril Ratajski, that he approved of my request to be sent secretly to London as a courier for the leaders of political parties organized in the Central Political Committee, and for the delegate himself. The coming expedition was to be my fourth secret trip between Warsaw, Paris, and London.

Sometime in September 1942, the delegate informed me that the leaders of two Jewish underground organizations, the Socialist Bund and the Zionists, learned about my mission and requested permission to use my services for their own communications to their representatives in London, to the Polish government, and to the Allied authorities. The delegate was sympathetic and I agreed.

Soon after, I met the two Jewish leaders on two occasions. They met me jointly to emphasize that their communications were on behalf of all Polish Jews regardless of their political differences. They identified themselves by their functions (naturally, no names). All postwar literature identifies them as Leon Feiner (Bund leader) and Adolf Berman (Zionist). For the record, I must add that Walter Laqueur, in his recently published book, *The Terrible Secret*,

suggests that the Zionist leader might have been Menachem Kirschenbaum.

The Jewish leaders sent through me various messages, instructions, and appeals to various quarters.

The message given to me to relay to the Polish and Allied governments is as follows:

The unprecedented destruction of the entire Jewish population is not motivated by Germany's military requirements. Hitler and his subordinates aim at the total destruction of the Jews before the war ends and regardless of its outcome. The Polish and Allied governments cannot disregard this reality. The Jews in Poland are helpless. They have no country of their own. They have no independent voice in the Allied councils. They cannot rely on the Polish underground or population-at-large. They might save some individuals—they are unable to stop the extermination. Only the powerful Allied governments can help effectively. The Polish Jews appeal to the Polish and Allied governments to undertake measures in an attempt to stop the extermination. They place historical responsibility on the Polish and Allied governments if they fail to undertake those measures.

1. A public announcement that prevention of the physical extermination of the Jews become a part of the overall Allied war strategy, at the same time informing the German nation through radio, air-dropped leaflets, and other means about their government's crimes committed against the Jews.
2. All available data on the Jewish ghettos; concentration and extermination camps; names of the German officials directly involved in the crimes; statistics; facts and methods used should be spelled out. And public and formal demand for evidence that such a pressure has been exercised and Nazi practices directed against the Jews stopped.

3. Public and formal appeals to the German people to exercise pressure on their government to make it stop the exterminations.
4. Placing the responsibility on the German nation as a whole if they fail to respond and if the extermination continues.
5. Public and formal announcement that, in view of the unprecedented Nazi crimes against the Jews and in hope that those crimes would stop, the Allied governments were to take unprecedented steps.

These steps would include:

1. Certain areas and objects in Germany would be bombed in retaliation. The German people would be informed before and after each action that the Nazis' continued extermination of the Jews prompted bombing.
2. Certain German war prisoners who, having been informed about their government's crimes, and who still profess solidarity with and allegiance to the Nazis, would be held responsible for the crimes committed against the Jews as long as those crimes continued.
3. Certain German nationals living in the Allied countries who, having been informed about the crimes committed against the Jews and who still profess solidarity with the Nazi government, would be held responsible for those crimes.
4. Jewish leaders in London, particularly Samuel Zygelbojm (Bund) and Dr. Ignace Szwarcbard (Zionist), are solemnly charged to make all efforts so as to make the Polish government formally forward these demands at the Allied councils.

The message to the prime minister and commander in chief (General Wladyslaw Sikorski), minister of interior (Stanislaw Mikolajczyk), Zygelbojm, and Szwarcbard was as follows:

Although the Polish people at large sympathize or try to help the Jews, many Polish criminals blackmail, rob, denounce, or murder the Jews in hiding. The underground authorities must apply punitive sanctions against them, exe-cutions included. In the last case, the identity of the guilty ones and the nature of their crimes should be publicized in the underground press.

Zygelbojm and Szwarcbard must use all their pressure so that pertinent instructions would be issued.

In order to avoid any risk of anti-Polish propaganda, I was explicitly forbidden to discuss that subject with any non-Polish Jewish leaders. I was to inform Zygelbojm and Szwarcbard about that part of my instructions.

The message to the Allied individual government/civic leaders as well as to international Jewish leaders was as follows:

There is a possibility to save some Jews if money were available. The Gestapo is corrupted not only on the low level, but also on the medium and even high level. They would cooperate for gold or hard currency. The Jewish leaders are able to make appropriate contact.

Some Jews might be allowed to leave Poland semiofficially in exchange for gold, dollars, or delivery of certain goods.

Some Jews would be allowed to leave Poland provided they have original foreign passports. Origins of those passports are unimportant. As large a supply of such passports as possible should be sent. They must be blank. Forged names, identification, data, etc., would be overlooked by the German authorities—for money, of course.

Provisions must be made that those Jews who do succeed in leaving Poland would be accepted by the Allied or neutral countries.

Some Jews of non-Semitic appearance could leave the ghettos, obtain false German documents, and live among other Poles under assumed names.

Money to bribe the ghetto's guards and various officials as well as subsistence funds are needed.

Many Christian families would agree to hide the Jews in their homes. But they risk instant execution if discovered by the Germans. All of them are in dire need themselves. Money is needed, at least for subsistence.

Money, medicines, food, and clothing are

most urgently needed by the survivors in the ghettos. Subsidies obtained from the delegate of the Polish government as well as other funds sent through various channels by the Jewish international organizations are totally insufficient. More hard currency, sent without any delay, is a question of life or death for thousands of Jews.

In addition to all the messages I was to carry, both Jewish leaders solemnly committed me to do my utmost in arousing the public opinion in the free world on behalf of the Jews. I solemnly swore that, should I arrive safely in London, I would not fail them.

At the end of the second meeting, the Bund leader confronted me with the following. He knew the English people. My report might seem incredible. My mission would be enhanced if I were able to say that I witnessed the Jewish tragedy. The Jewish underground does have some contact, even with Gestapo. They are able to smuggle me to the Warsaw Ghetto. They are even able to smuggle me—in disguise—to the Belzec camp. In the ghetto, he himself, would be me guide. In Belzec a Nazi official would take care of my expedition. Both trips are dangerous, but they are feasible. He has no right to ask me to undertake them. But he said, "Witold (my pseudonym at the time), I know much about you and your work. Who knows—perhaps you will volunteer to help our Jewish cause." I agreed.

I visited the Jewish Ghetto twice in the middle of October 1942. A few days later, I visited Belzec. All three trips proved successful. These trips became the last items in collecting data, messages, instructions, and complaints of various political leaders in the underground. Two or three days later, I embarked on my secret journey to London.

Again, my trip was successful. This fourth secret mission between Paris, London, and Warsaw lasted twenty-one days: Warsaw-Berlin-Brussels-Paris-Lyon-Perpignan-Pyrenees Mountains on foot-Barcelona-Madrid-Algeciras-Gibraltar. In Gibraltar I had a ceremonious dinner with the governor and a good night's sleep. The next day a plane was waiting.

In the last week of November 1942, I already began reporting in London. Now one must realize that my Jewish reports were only a part of my overall mission. In addition I was supposed to go back to Poland—on my fifth mission. The Polish prime minister's office, which organized all of my contacts, asked every individual I had been sent to not to identify me publicly.

As to my Jewish materials, I was not the only informant. Since 1941, secret radio contacts with London functioned. Coded data on the Jewish ghettos, deportations, and extermination had been regularly transmitted from Poland to London for information and public distribution. Most of the messages, however, were considered as lacking credibility. The head of the secret radio service, throughout the entire war, was Stefan Korbonski, who was eventually the last head of the Polish underground state.

To whom did I report the Jewish material in England during the period November 1942–June 1943? Because of time constraints, I give here only the most important personalities.

1. The Poles: All government and political leaders; Liaison to Cardinal Hlond (at the time residing in the Vatican): Monsignor Kacynski; Jewish leaders: Zygelbojm (Bund); Szwarcbard (Zionists); Grosfeld (Socialist).
2. The English: four members of the War Cabinet: Anthony Eden, foreign secretary; Arthur Greenwood, Labour Party; Lord Cranborne, Conservative Party; Hugh Dalton, president of the Board of Trade.

I also talked with Lord Selbourne, War Office, European underground resistance; Miss Ellen Wilkinson, Labour, Member of Parliament; William Henderson, Labour Party leader, Member of Parliament; Owen O'Malley, British ambassador to the Polish government; Anthony D. Biddle, American ambassador to the Polish government; and Sir Cecil Hurst, chairman of the United Nations War Crime Commission.

I pressed for and did contact several non-government English personalities: H.G. Wells, world-known author; Arthur Koestler, world-known author; Victor Gollancz, Penguin publishing firm; Allen Lane, Penguin; Kingsley Martin, editor-in-chief, *New Statesman* and *Nation*; Ronald Hyde, editor, *Evening Standard*; and Gerard Berry, editor, *News Chronicle*.

Actions resulting from my mission and, no doubt, other reports are as follows:

1. On December 7, 1942, two weeks after I began reporting, the Polish National Council passed a resolution dealing with the Jewish extermination and committing the government to act without any delay.
2. Three days later, on December 10, 1942, the Polish government issued a formal appeal to the Allied governments concerning the extermination of the Jews in Poland.
3. On December 17, 1942, the Allied Council (which included representatives of all Allied governments) unanimously passed a public appeal of the Allied Nations on behalf of the Jews.
4. Two days later, on December 19, 1942, the president of the Polish Republic sent a note to Pope Pius XII asking for intervention on behalf of the Jews.
5. Then, one month later, on January 18, 1943, the Polish foreign minister, Edward Raczynski, presented his government's demands on behalf of the Polish Jews at the Allied Nations' Council. They asked for the bombing of Germany as reprisals for the continued extermination of the Jews, the forwarding of demands to Berlin to let the Jews out of the German-dominated countries.

He did not advance demands for reprisals against German war prisoners and German nationals living in the Allied countries, considering them contrary to the acceptable practices of international relations.

British foreign secretary, Anthony Eden, in the name of His Majesty's government, rejected all demands, offering vague promises to intervene in some neutral countries.

Beginning in March 1943, secret executions of the Polish hoodlums who acted against the Jews were carried out. The names of the criminals and the nature of their crimes were publicized in the underground press.

The Directorate of the Civil Resistance which organized Underground courts had been established already in 1942. It was headed again by Korbonski. Last April—thirty-six years after the war ended—he was decorated by the Israeli ambassador with a Yad Vashem Medal for the Righteous Among the Nations.

In early 1943, numerous articles based on my information appeared in the British press. Public demonstrations had been organized. In May 1943, a pamphlet was published, authored by a prominent Soviet writer, Alexey Tolstoy; German writer Thomas Mann; and myself (described as a "Polish Underground Worker"). The pamphlet was entitled "The Fate of the Jews."

With regard to my mission in the USA, in June 1943, at the suggestion of American Ambassador Biddle, I was sent to Washington, still secretly, under a false name—Jan Karski. I stayed there until August 1943, living on the premises of the [Polish] embassy. The Polish ambassador, Jan Ciechanowski, supervised my activities and organized my contacts.

I reported to the following individuals (only the most important will be mentioned): Franklin Delano Roosevelt, president of the United States; Cordell Hull, secretary of state; Henry Stimson, secretary of war; Francis Biddle, attorney general; Colonel Donovan, chief, Office of Strategic Services (OSS); Apostolic Delegate, Cardinal Ameleto, Giovanni Cicognani; Archbishop Mooney; Archbishop Spellman; Archbishop Strich; Dr. Nahum Goldman, president, World Jewish Congress; Rabbi Stephen Wise, president, American Jewish Congress; Louis Waldman, American Jewish Congress; Felix Frankfurter, Justice of the Supreme Court; and Mr. Backer, Joint Distribution Committee.

Among the prominent journalists with whom I spoke were: Mrs. Ogden Reed, publisher, *New York Herald Tribune*; Walter Lippmann; George Sokolsky; Leon Dennen, editor, *The American Mercury*; Eugene Lyons; Dorothy Thompson; William Prescott, *The New York Times*; Frederick

Kuh, *Chicago Sun*; and George Creel, former chief, Office of War Information.

Upon my return to London, Prime Minister Mikolajczyk informed me that he would not send me to Poland for the duration of the war. I had seen too many people in the United States and I had become too well-known. The German radio had mentioned my activities in America, describing me, by the way, as a "Bolshevik agent on the payroll of American Jews."

Two months later, in October 1943, I was sent to the United States—for the second time but this time openly and again as Karski—to speak, to write, to report, to inform the public-at-large—openly.

From October 1943 until the end of the war, I delivered some two hundred lectures in the United States from coast to coast, from Rhode Island to Florida. In all of them I spoke about the Jewish tragedy. Every lecture was reviewed in the local press.

Then came my articles on what the Jews demanded, on what I saw in the Warsaw Ghetto and Belzec. These were published in *Colliers, New York Times, American Mercury, La France Libre, The Jewish Forum, Common Cause, Herald Tribune, New Europe,* and *Harper's Bazaar.* Many of them were illustrated—several under my personal supervision: "No phony inspiration! Paint as I am telling you." Various exhibitions were organized.

Then, in 1944, still during the war, I published a book, *Story of a Secret State.* Its central theme was my visits to the Warsaw Ghetto and Belzec. The book became a Book-of-the-Month Club Selection. It was published simultaneously also in Great Britain, Sweden, Switzerland, and France.

Letter from the War Refugee Board

EXECUTIVE OFFICE OF THE PRESIDENT
WAR REFUGEE BOARD
WASHINGTON, D.C.

GERMAN EXTERMINATION CAMPS—
AUSCHWITZ AND BIRKENAU

It is a fact beyond denial that the Germans have deliberately and systematically murdered millions of innocent civilians—Jews and Christians alike—all over Europe. This campaign of terror and brutality, which is unprecedented in all history and which even now continues unabated, is part of the German plan to subjugate the free peoples of the world.

So revolting and diabolical are the German atrocities that the minds of civilized people find it difficult to believe that they have actually taken place. But the governments of the United States and of other countries have evidence which clearly substantiates the facts.

The War Refugee Board is engaged in a desperate effort to save as many as possible of Hitler's intended victims. To facilitate its work the Board has representatives in key spots in Europe. These representatives have tested contracts throughout Europe and keep the Board fully advised concerning the German campaign of extermination and torture.

Recently the Board received from a representative close to the scene two eyewitness accounts of events which occurred in notorious extermination camps established by the Germans. The first report is based upon the experiences of two young Slovakian Jews who escaped in April, 1944 after spending two years in the Nazi concentration camps at Auschwitz and Birkenau in southwestern Poland. The second report is made by a non-Jewish Polish major, the only survivor of one group imprisoned at Auschwitz.

The two reports were prepared independently and are reproduced exactly in the form they were received by the War Refugee Board, except for a few deletions necessary for the protection of persons who still be alive. The figures concerning the size of the Jewish convoys and the numbers of men and women admitted to the two camps cannot be taken as mathematically exact; and, in fact, are declared by the authors to be no more than reliable approximations. They are accepted as such by the Board.

The Board has every reason to believe that these reports present a true picture of the frightful happenings in these camps. It is making the reports public in the firm conviction that they should be read and understood by all Americans.

November, 1944
No. 1

The Extermination Camps of Auschwitz (Oswiecim) and Birkenau in Upper Silesia

FOREWORD

Two young Slovak Jews—whose names will not be disclosed for the time being in the interest of their own safety—have been fortunate enough to escape after spending two years in the concentration camps of BIRKENAU, AUSCHWITZ and LUBLIN-MAJDANEEK, where they had been deported in 1942 from SLOVAKIA.

One of them was sent on April 13, 1942 from the assembly camp of SERED directly to AUSCHWITZ and then to BIRKENAU, while the other was sent from the camp of NOVAKY to LUBLIN on June 14, 1942 and, after a short stay there, transferred to AUSCHWITZ and, later, to BIRKENAU.

The following report does not contain everything these two men experienced during their captivity, but only what one or both together underwent, heard, or experienced at first hand. No individual impressions or judgments are recorded and nothing passed on from hearsay.

The report starts with the story of the young Jew who was removed from SERED. The account of his experiences in BIRKENAU begins at the time the second Jew arrived there and is, therefore, based on the statements of both. Then follows an individual narrative of the second Jew who was sent from NOVAKY to LUBLIN and from there to AUSCHWITZ.

The declarations tally with all the trustworthy yet fragmentary reports hitherto received, and the dates given with regard to transports to various camps agree with the official records. These statements can, therefore, be considered as entirely credible.

I. AUSCHWITZ AND BIRKENAU

On the 13th April, 1942 our group, consisting of one thousand men, was loaded into railroad cars at the assembly camp of SERED. The doors were shut so that nothing would reveal the direction of the journey, and when they were opened after a long while we realized that we had crossed the Slovak frontier and were in ZWARDON. The train had until then been guarded by Hlinka men, but was now taken over by SS guards. After a few of the cars had been uncoupled from our convoy, we continued on our way arriving at night at AUSCHWITZ, where we stopped on a sidetrack. The reason the other cars were left behind was apparently the lack of room at AUSCHWITZ. They joined us, however, a few days later. Upon arrival we were placed in rows of five and counted. There were 643 of us. After a walk of about twenty minutes with our heavy packs (we had left Slovakia well equipped), we reached the concentration camp of AUSCHWITZ.

We were at once led into a huge barrack where on the one side we had to deposit all our luggage and on the other side completely undress, leaving our clothes and valuables behind. Naked, we then proceeded to an adjoining barrack, where our heads and bodies were shaved and disinfected with lysol. At the exit every man was given a number which began with 28,600 in consecutive order. With this number in hand we were then herded to a third barrack where so-called registration took place. This consisted of tattooing the numbers we had received in the second barrack on the left side of our chests. The extreme brutality with which this was effected made many of us faint. The particulars of our identity were also recorded. Then we were led in groups of a hundred into a cellar, and later to a barrack where we were issued striped prisoners' clothes and wooden clogs. This lasted until 10 A.M. In the afternoon our prisoners' outfits were taken away from us again and replaced by the ragged and dirty remains of Russian uniforms. Thus equipped we were marched off to BIRKENAU.

AUSCHWITZ is a concentration camp for political prisoners under so-called "protective custody." At the time of my arrival, that is in April of 1942, there were about fifteen thousand prisoners in the camp, the majority of whom were Poles, German, and civilian Russians under protective custody. A small number of prisoners came under the categories of criminals and "work-shirkers."

AUSCHWITZ camp headquarters controls, at the same time, the work camp of BIRKENAU, as well as the farm labor camp of HARMENSE. All the prisoners arrive first at AUSCHWITZ where they are provided with prisoners' matriculation numbers and then are either kept there, sent to BIRKENAU or, in very small numbers, to HARMENSE. The prisoners receive consecutive numbers upon arrival. Every number is only used once so that the last number always corresponds to the number of prisoners actually in the camp. At the time of our escape, that is to say at the beginning of April, 1944, the number had risen up to 180,000. At the outset the numbers were tattooed on the left breast, but later, due to their becoming blurred, on the left forearm.

All prisoners, irrespective of category or nationality, are treated the same. However to facilitate identification, they are distinguished by various colored triangles sewed on the clothing on the left breast under the matriculation number. The first letter indicated the nationality of the prisoner. The letter (for instance "P" for Poles) appears in the middle of the triangle. The colored triangles have the following meaning:

red triangle "political prisoners under protective custody"
green "professional criminals"
black "dodgers" (labor slackers), "anti-socials" (mostly Russians)
pink "homosexuals"
violet "members of the religious sect of *Bibelforscher*"

The Jewish prisoners differ from the Aryan prisoners in that their triangle (which in the majority of cases is red) is turned into a David's star by adding yellow points.

Within the enclosure of the camp of AUSCHWITZ there are several factories: a war production plant, Deutscher Aufrustungswerk (DAW), a factory belonging to the KRUPP works and on to the SIEMENS concern. Outside the boundary of the camp is a tremendous plant covering several square kilometers named "BUNA." The prisoners work in all the aforementioned factories.

The prisoners' actual living quarters, if such a term may at all be used, inside the camp proper cover an area of approximately 500 by 300 meters surrounded by a double row of concrete posts, about 3 meters high, which are connected (both inside and outside) with one another by a dense netting of high-tension wires fixed into the posts by insulators. Between these two rows of posts, at intervals of 150 meters, there are 5-meters-high watchtowers, equipped with machine guns and searchlights. In front of the inner high-tension circle there is further an ordinary wire fence. Merely touching this fence is answered by a stream of bullets from the watchtowers. This system is called "small or inner chain of sentry posts." The camp itself is composed of three rows of houses. Between the first and second row is the camp street, and between the second and third there used to be a wall. The Jewish girls deported from Slovakia in March and April 1942, over seven thousand of them, lived in the houses separated by this wall up to the middle of August, 1942. After these girls had been removed to BIRKENAU, the wall between the second and third row of houses was removed. The camp entry road cuts across the row of houses, while over the entrance gate, which is of course always heavily guarded, stands the ironic inscription: "Work brings freedom."

At a radius of some 2,000 meters the whole camp is encircled by a second line called "the big or outer chain of sentry posts" also with watchtowers every 150 meters. Between the inner and outer chain of sentry posts are the factories and other workshops. The towers of the inner chain are only manned at night when the high-tension current is switched into the double row of wires. During daytime the garrison of the inner chain of sentry posts is withdrawn, and the men take up duty in the outer chain. Escape through these sentry posts—and many attempts have been made—is practically impossible. Getting through the inner circle of posts at night is completely impossible, and the towers of the outer chain are so close to one another (one every 150 meters, i.e., giving each tower a sector with a 75-meter radius to watch) that approaching unnoticed is out of the question. The guards shoot without warning. The garrison of the outer chain is withdrawn at twilight, but only after it has been ascertained that all the prisoners are within the inner circle. If the roll call reveals that a prisoner is missing, sirens immediately sound the alarm.

The men in the outer chain remain in their towers on the lookout, the inner chain is manned, and a systematic search is begun by hundreds of SS guards and bloodhounds. The siren brings the whole surrounding countryside to a state of alarm, so that if by miracle the escapee has been successful in getting through the outer chain he is nearly certain to be caught by one of the numerous German police and SS patrols. The escapee is furthermore handicapped by his clean-shaven head, his striped prisoner's outfit or red patch sewn on his clothing, and the passiveness of the thoroughly intimidated inhabitants. The mere fact of neglecting to give information on the whereabouts of a prisoner, not to speak of extending help, is punished by death. Provided that the prisoner has not been caught sooner, the garrison of the outer chain of sentry posts remains on the watch for three days and nights after which delay it is presumed that the escapee has succeeded in breaking through the double circle. The following night the outer guard is withdrawn. If the escapee is caught alive, he is hanged in the presence of the whole camp; but if he is found dead, his body—wherever it may have been located—is brought back to camp (it is easy to identify corpse by means of the tattooed number) and seated at the entrance gate, a small notice clasped in his hands, reading: "Here I am." During our two years' imprisonment many attempts to escape were made by prisoners but, with the exception of two or three, all were brought back dead or alive. It is not known whether the two or three escapees who were not caught actually managed to get away. It can, however, be asserted that among the Jews who were deported from SLOVAKIA to AUSCHWITZ or BIRKENAU we are the only two who were lucky enough to save ourselves.

As stated previously, we were transferred from AUSCHWITZ to BIRKENAU on the day of our arrival.

Actually there is no such district as BIRKE-NAU. Even the word BIRKENAU is new in that it has been "adopted" from the nearby Birch Forest (BREZINSKY). The district now called BIRKENAU was, and is still, called "RAJSKA" by the local population. The existing camp center of BIRKENAU lies four kilometers distant from AUSCHWITZ. The outer control zones of both BIRKENAU and AUSCHWITZ meet and are merely separated by a railway track. We never found anything out about NEW-BERUN, probably about thirty to forty kilometers away which, oddly enough, we had to indicate as postal district for BIRKENAU.

At the time of our arrival in BIRKENAU we found there only one huge kitchen for fifteen thousand people and three stone buildings, two of which were completed and one under construction. The buildings were surrounded by an ordinary barbed wire fence. The prisoners were housed in these buildings and in others later constructed. All are built according to a standard model. Each house is about thirty meters long and eight to ten meters wide. Whereas the height of the walls hardly exceeds two meters, the roof is disproportionately high—about five meters—so that the house gives the impression of a stable surmounted by a large hayloft. There is no inner ceiling, so that the room reaches a height of seven meters in the center; in other words the pointed roof rests directly on the four walls. The room is divided in two by a partition running its whole length down the middle and fitted with an opening to enable communication between the two parts thus separated. Along both side walls, as well as along the middle partition, two parallel floors, some eighty centimeters apart, have been built which are in turn divided into small cells by vertical partitions. Thus there are three floors: the ground floor and the two built in the side walls. Normally three people live in each cubicle. As can be judged from the dimensions indicated, these cubicles are too narrow for a man to lie stretched out and not high enough for him to sit upright. There is no question of having enough space to stand upright. In this way some four hundred to five hundred people are accommo-dated in one house or block, as they are also called.

The present camp of BIRKENAU covers an area of some 1,600 by 500 meters which is sur-rounded—similar to AUSCHWITZ—by a so-called small or inner chain of sentry posts. Work is now proceeding on a still larger compound which is to be added later on to the already exiting camp. The purpose of this extensive planning is not known to us.

Within a radius of two kilometers, as with AUSCHWITZ, BIRKENAU is also surrounded by an outer chain of sentry posts with the same type of watch system as at AUSCHWITZ.

The building we found on our arrival had been erected by twelve thousand Russian pris-oners of war brought there in December 1941. In severe winter weather they had to work under inhuman conditions as a result of which most of them, with the exception of a small number employed in the kitchen, died of expo-sure. They were numbered from one to twelve thousand in a series which had no connection with the ordinary camp numbering system pre-viously described. Whenever fresh convoys of Russian prisoners arrived, they were not issued the current AUSCHWITZ prisoner numbers, but received those of deceased Russians in the one to twelve thousand series. It is, therefore, diffi-cult to estimate how many prisoners of this cat-egory passed through the camp. Apparently Russians were transferred to AUSCHWITZ or BIRKENAU on disciplinary grounds from regular prisoner-of-war camps. We found what remained of the Russians in a terrible state of destitution and neglect living in the unfinished building without the slightest protection against cold or rain. They died "en masse." Hundreds and thou-sands of their bodies were buried superficially, spreading a stench of pestilence. Later we had to exhume and burn the corpses.

A week before our arrival in AUSCHWITZ the first group of Jews reached the camp; (the women were dealt with separately and received numbers parallel to those of the men; the Slovak women received serial numbers from one to eight thousand) 1,320 naturalized French Jews from Paris. They were numbered from 27,500 onwards. It is clear, therefore, that between this French group and our convoy no other men arrived in AUSCHWITZ, since we have already pointed out that our numbers started with 28,600. We found the seven hundred French Jews who were still alive in terrible condition, the missing six hundred having died within a week after their arrival.

The following categories were housed in the three completed buildings:

1. The so-called "prominencia": professional criminals and older Polish political prisoners who were in charge of the administration of the camp.
2. The remainder of the French Jews, namely some seven hundred.
3. The 643 original Slovak Jews to whom were added a few days later those who had been left at ZWARDON.
4. Those Russians who were still alive and housed in the unfinished building as well as in the open air and whose numbers diminished so rapidly that as a group they are scarcely worth mentioning.

Together with the remaining Russian prisoners the Slovak Jews worked at the construction of buildings, whereas the French Jews had to do spade work. After three days I was ordered, together with two hundred other Slovak Jews, to work in the German armament factories at AUSCHWITZ, but we continued to be housed in BIRKENAU. We left early in the morning returning at night and worked in the carpentry shop as well as on road construction. Our food consisted of one liter of turnip soup at midday and three hundred grams of bad bread in the evening. Working conditions were inconceivably hard, so that the majority of us, weakened by starvation and the inedible food, could not stand it. The mortality was so high that every day our group of two hundred had thirty to thirty-five dead. Many were simply beaten to death by the overseers—the "Capos"—during work, without the slightest provocation. The gaps in our ranks caused by these deaths were replaced daily by prisoners from BIRKENAU. Our return at night was extremely painful and dangerous, as we had to drag along over a distance of five kilometers our tools, fire wood, heavy caldrons, and the bodies of those who had died or had been killed during the working day. With these heavy loads we were forced to maintain a brisk pace, and anyone incurring the displeasure of one of the "Capos" was cruelly knocked down, if not beaten to death. Until the arrival of the second group of Slovak men some fourteen days later, our original number had dwindled to 150. At night we were counted, the bodies of the dead were piled up on flat, narrow-gauge cars or in a truck and brought to the Birch Forest (BREZINSKY) where they were burned in a trench several meters deep and about fifteen meters long. Every day on our way to work we met a working party of three hundred Jewish girls from Slovakia who were employed on ground work in the vicinity. They were dressed in old Russian uniform rags and wore wooden clogs. Their heads were shaven and, unfortunately, we could not speak to them.

Until the middle of May, 1942, a total of four convoys of male Jews from Slovakia arrived at BIRKENAU and all received similar treatment to ours.

From the first and second transports 120 men were chosen (including myself) and placed at the disposal of the administration of the camp of AUSCHWITZ, which was in need of doctors, dentists, intellectuals, and clerks. This group consisted of ninety Slovak and thirty French Jews. As I had in the meantime managed to work my way up to a good position in BIRKENAU—being in command of a group of fifty men, which had brought me considerable advantage—I at first felt reluctant to leave for AUSCHWITZ. However, I was finally persuaded to go and left. After eight days, eighteen doctors and attendants as well as three further persons were selected from this group of 120 intellectuals. The doctors were used in the "sick building" or "hospital" at AUSCHWITZ, while we three were sent back to BIRKENAU. My two comrades, Ladislav Braun from Trnava and Gross from Vrbove (?), both of whom have since died, were sent to the Slovak block while I was ordered to the French section where we were employed at collecting "personal data" and at "nursing the sick." The remaining ninety-nine persons were sent to work in the gravel pit where they all died within a short time.

Shortly thereafter, a so-called "sick-building" (Krankenbau) was set up. It was destined to become the much dreaded Block 7 where at first I was chief attendant and later administrator. The chief of this "infirmary" was a Pole. Actually this building was nothing else than an assembly center for death candidates. All prisoners incapable of working were sent there. There was no question of any medical attention or care. We had some 150 dead daily and their bodies were sent for cremation to AUSCHWITZ.

At the same time the so-called "selections" were introduced. Twice weekly, Mondays and Thursdays, the camp doctor indicated the number of prisoners who were to be gassed and then burned. These "selectees" were loaded into trucks and brought to the Birch Forest. Those still alive upon arrival were gassed in a big barrack erected near the trench used for burning the bodies. The weekly "draft" in dead from Block 7 was about 2,000, of whom 1,200 died of "natural death," and about 800 through "selection." For those who had *not* been "selected" a death certificate was issued and sent to the central administration at ORANIENBURG; whereas for the "selectees" a special register was kept with the indication "S.B." (*Sonderbehandelt*—special treatment). Until January 15, 1943, up to which time I was administrator of Block 7 and therefore in a position to directly observe happenings, some fifty thousand prisoners died of "natural death" or by "selection."

As previously described, the prisoners were numbered consecutively so that we are able to reconstruct fairly clearly their order of succession and the fate which befell each separate convoy on arrival.

The first male Jewish transport reaching AUSCHWITZ from BIRKENAU was composed, as mentioned, of 1,320 naturalized French Jews bearing *approximately* the following numbers:

27,400–28,600	
28,600–29,600	In April, 1942 the first convoy of Slovak Jews (our convoy).
29,600–29,700	100 men (Aryans) from various concentration camps.
29,700–32,700	3 complete convoys of Slovak Jews.
32,700–33,100	400 professional criminals (Aryans) from Warsaw prisons.
33,100–35,100	1,900 Jews from Kraków.
35,100–36,000	1,000 Poles (Aryans)—political prisoners.
36,000–37,300	In May, 1942—1,300 Slovak Jews from LUBLIN MAJDANEK.
37,300–37,900	600 Poles (Aryans) from RADOM, amongst them a few Jews.
37,900–38,000	100 Poles from the concentration camp of DACHAU.
38,000–38,400	400 French naturalized Jews who arrived with their families.

This whole convoy consisted of about sixteen hundred individuals of whom approximately two hundred girls and four hundred men were admitted to the camp, while the remaining one thousand persons (women, old people, children as well as men) were sent without further procedure from the railroad siding directly to the Birch Forest, and there gassed and burned. From this moment on all Jewish convoys were dealt with in the same manner. Approximately 10 percent of the men and 5 percent of the women were allotted to the camps and the remaining members were immediately gassed. This process of extermination had already been applied earlier to the Polish Jews. During long months, without interruption, trucks brought thousands of Jews from the various "ghettos" direct to the pit in the "Birkenwald."

38,400–39,200	800 naturalized French Jews, the remainder of the convoy was—as previously described—gassed.
39,200–40,000	800 Poles (Aryans), political prisoners.
40,000–40,150	150 Slovak Jews with their families.
	Outside of a group of 50 girls sent to the women's camp, all other members were gassed in the Birch Forest. Among the 150 men who came to camp there were a certain Zucker (Christian name unknown) and Sonnenschein, Villiam, both from Eastern Slovakia.
40,150–43,800	Approximately 4,000 French naturalized Jews, almost all intellects; 1,000 women were directed to the women's camp, while the balance of about 3,000 persons were gassed in the usual manner.
43,800–44,200	400 Slovak Jews from LUBLIN, including Matej Klein and no. 43820, Meiloch Laufer from Eastern Slovakia. This convoy arrived on June 30, 1942.
44,200–45,000	200 Slovak Jews. The convoy consisted of 1,000 persons. A number of women were sent to the women's camp, the rest gassed in the Birch Wood. Among the prisoners sent to camp were: Jozef Zelmanovic, Snina; Adolf Kahan, Bratislava; Walter Reichmann, Sucany; Esther Kahan, Bratislava.
45,000–47,000	2,000 Frenchmen (Aryans), Communists and other political prisoners, among whom were the brother of Thorez and the young brother of Leon Blum. The latter was atrociously tortured, then gassed and burned.
47,000–47,500	500 Jews from Holland, in the majority German emigrants. The rest of the convoy, about 2,500 persons, gassed.
47,500–47,800	About 300 so-called Russians under protective custody.
48,300–48,620	320 Jews from Slovakia. About 70 girls were transferred to the women's camp, the remainder, some 650 people, gassed in the Birch Wood. This convoy included about 80 people who had been handed over to the Hungarian police to the camp of SERED. Others from this convoy were: Dr. Zoltan Mandel (since deceased); Holz (Christian name unknown), butcher from Piestany; Miklos Engel, Zilina; Chaim Katz, Snina, (his wife and 6 children were gassed).
49,000–64,800	15,000 naturalized French, Belgian, and Dutch Jews. This figure certainly represents less than 10 percent of the total convoy. This was between July 1 and September 15, 1942. Large family convoys arrived from various European countries and were at once directed to the Birch Wood. The special squad (Sonderkommando) employed for gassing and burning worked in day and night shifts. Hundreds of thousands of Jews were gassed during this period.
64,800–65,000	200 Slovak Jews. Out of this transport about 100 women were admitted to the camp, the rest of them gassed and burned. Among the newly arrived were: Ludwig Katz, Zilina; Avri Burger, Bratislava; Poprad (wife dead); Mikulas Steiner, Povazska Bystrica; Juraj Fried, Trencin; Buchwald; Josef Rosenwasser, Eastern Slovakia; Julius Neuman, Bardejov; Sandor Wertheimer, Vrbove; Misi Wertheimer, Vrbove; Bela Blau, Zilina.
65,000–68,000	Naturalized French, Belgian, and Dutch Jews. Not more than 1,000 women were "selected" and sent to the camp. The others, at the lowest estimate 30,000 were gassed.
71,000–80,000	Naturalized French, Belgian, and Dutch Jews. The prisoners brought to the camp hardly represent 10 percent of the total transport. A conservative estimate would be that approximately 65,000 to 70,000 persons were gassed.

On December 17, 1942, the two hundred young Slovak Jews, the so-called "special squad" employed in gassing and burning the condemned, were in turn executed at BIRKENAU. They were executed for having planned to mutiny and escape. A Jew betrayed their preparations. This frightful job had to be taken over by a group of two hundred Polish Jews who had just arrived at camp from MAKOW.

The men belonging to the "special squad" lived separately. On account of the dreadful smell spread by them, people had little contact with them. Besides they were always filthy, destitute, half wild and extraordinarily brutal and ruthless. It was not uncommon to see one of them kill another. This was considered by the others a sensation, a change. One simply recorded that number so-and-so had died.

Once I was an eyewitness when a young Polish Jew named Jossel demonstrated "scientific" murder on a Jew in the presence of an SS guard. He used no weapon, merely his bare hands, to kill his victim.

No. 80,000 marks the beginning of the systematic extermination of the Polish ghettos.

80,000–85,000	Approximately 5,000 Jews from various ghettos in MLJAWA, MAKOW, ZICHENOW, LOMZA, GRODNO, HIALOSTOK.
	For fully 30 days truck convoys arrived without interruption. Only 5,000 persons were sent to the concentration camp; all the others were gassed at once. The "special squad" worked in two shifts, twenty-four hours daily and was scarcely able to cope with the gassing and burning. Without exaggerating, it may be said that out of these convoys some 30,000 to 90,000 received "special treatment." These transports also brought in a considerable amount of money, valuables, and precious stones.
85,000–92,000	6,000 Jews from GRODNO, BIALOSTOK and CRACÓW as well as 1,000 Aryan Poles. The majority of the Jewish convoys were directly gassed and daily about 4,000 Jews were driven into the gas chambers.
	During mid-January, 1943 three convoys of 2,000 persons each from THERESIENSTADT arrived. They bore the designations "CU" "CR" and "R." (The meaning of these signs is unknown to us). These markings were also stamped on their luggage. Out of these 6,000 persons only 600 men and 300 women were admitted to the camp. The remainder were gassed.
99,000–100,000	End of January, 1943 large convoys of French and Dutch Jews arrived; only a small proportion of them reached the camp.
100,000–102,000	In February, 1943, 2,000 Aryan Poles, mostly intellectuals.
102,000–103,000	700 Czech Aryans. Later, those still alive were sent to BUCHENWALD.
103,000–108,000	3,000 French and Dutch Jews and 2,000 Poles (Aryans).
	During the month of February, 1943, two contingents arrived daily. They included Polish, French, and Dutch Jews who, in the main, were sent to the gas chambers. The number gassed during this month can well be estimated at 90,000.

At the end of February, 1943 a new modern crematorium and gassing plant was inaugurated at BIRKENAU. The gassing and burning of the bodies in the Birch Forest was discontinued, the whole job being taken over by the four specially built crematoria. The large ditch was filled in, the ground leveled, and the ashes used as before for fertilizer at the farm labor camp of HERMENSE, so that today it is almost impossible to find traces of the dreadful mass murder which took place here.

At present there are four crematoria in operation at BIRKENAU, two large ones, I and II, and two smaller ones, III and IV. Those of types I and II consist of 3 parts, i.e.: (A) the furnace room; (B) the large hall; and (C) the gas chamber. A huge chimney rises from the furnace room around which are grouped nine furnaces, each having four openings. Each opening can take three normal corpses at once and after an hour and a half the bodies are completely burned. This corresponds to a daily capacity of about two thousand bodies. Next to this is a large "reception hall" which is arranged so as to give the impression of the antechamber of a bathing establishment. It holds two thousand people and apparently there is a similar waiting room on the floor below. From there a door and a few steps lead down into the very long and narrow gas chamber. The walls of this chamber are also camouflaged with simulated entries to shower rooms in order to mislead the victims. The roof is fitted with three traps which can be hermetically closed from the outside. A track leads from the gas chamber towards the furnace room. The gassing takes place as follows: the unfortunate victims are brought into hall (B) where they are told to undress. To complete the fiction that they are going to bathe, each person receives a towel and a small piece of soap issued by two men clad in white coats. Then they are crowded into the gas chamber (C) in such numbers that there is, of course, only standing room. To compress this crowd into the narrow space, shots are often fired to induce those already at the far and to huddle still closer together. When everybody is inside, the heavy doors are closed. Then there is a short pause, presumably to allow the room temperature to rise to a certain level, after which SS men with gas masks climb on the roof, open the traps, and shake down a preparation in powder form out of tin cans labeled "CYKLON," "For use against vermin," which is manufactured by a Hamburg concern. It is presumed that this is a CYANIDE mixture of some sort which turns into gas at a certain temperature. After three minutes everyone in the chamber is dead. No one is known to have survived this ordeal, although it was not common to discover signs of life after the primitive measures employed in the Birch Wood. The chamber is then opened, aired, and the "special squad" carts the bodies on flat trucks to the furnace rooms where the burning takes place. Crematoria III and IV work on nearly the same principle, but their capacity is only half as large. Thus the total capacity of the four cremating and gassing plants at BIRKENAU amounts about six thousand daily.

On principle only Jews are gassed; Aryans very seldom, as they are usually given "special treatment" by shooting. Before the crematoria were put into service, the shooting took place in the Birch Wood and the bodies were burned in the long trench; later, however, executions took place in the large hall of one of the crematoria which has been provided with a special installation for this purpose.

Prominent guests from BERLIN were present at the inauguration of the first crematorium in March, 1943. The "program" consisted of the gassing and burning of eight thousand Kraków Jews. The guests, both officers and civilians, were extremely satisfied with the results and the special peephole fitted into the door of the gas chamber was in constant use. They were lavish in their praise of this newly erected installation.

109,000–119,000	At the beginning of March, 1943, 45,000 Jews arrived from Saloniki. 10,000 of them came to the camp, including a small percentage of the women; some 30,000 however went straight to the cremating establishment. Of the 10,000 nearly all died a short time later from a contagious illness resembling malaria. They also died of typhus due to the general conditions prevailing in the camp.

Malaria among the Jews and typhus took such a toll among the prisoners in general that the "selections" were temporarily suspended. The contaminated Greek Jews were ordered to present themselves and in spite of our repeated warnings many of them did. They were all killed by intracardial phenol injections administered by a lance-corporal of the medical corps.

Out of the ten thousand Greek Jews, some one thousand men remained alive and were later sent, together with five hundred other Jews, to do fortification work in Warsaw. A few weeks later several hundred came back in a pitiful state and were immediately gassed. The remainder presumably died in Warsaw. Four hundred Greek Jews suffering from malaria were sent for "further treatment" to LUBLIN after the phenol injections had been stopped, and it appears that they actually arrived. Their fate is not known to us, but it can be taken for granted that out of the original number of ten thousand Jews not one eventually remained in the camp.

Simultaneously with the stopping of the "selections" the murdering of prisoners was forbidden. Prominent murderers such as: the Reich German professional criminals Alexander Neumann, Zimmer, Albert Haemmerle, Rudi Osteringer, Rudi Bechert, and the political prisoners Alfred Kien and Alois Stahler, were punished for repeated murder and had to make written declarations that they had killed so and so many prisoners.

At the beginning of 1943 the political section of AUSCHWITZ received five hundred thousand discharge certificates and we thought with ill-concealed joy, that at least a few of us would be liberated. But the forms were simply filled out with the names of those gassed and filed away in the archives.

119,000–120,000	1,000 Poles (Aryans) from the PAWIAK penitentiary in Warsaw.
120,000–123,000	3,000 Greek Jews, part of whom were sent to replace their comrades in Warsaw. The remainder quickly died off.
123,000–124,000	1,000 Poles (Aryans) from RADOM and TARNOW.
124,000–126,000	2,000 from mixed Aryan convoys.

In the meantime, ceaseless convoys of Polish and a few French and Belgian Jews arrived and, without exception, were dispatched to the gas chambers. Among them was a transport of one thousand Polish Jews from MAJDANEK which included three Slovaks, one of whom was a certain Spira from Stropkow or Vranov.

The flow of convoys abruptly ceased at the end of July, 1943 and there was a short breathing space. The crematoria were thoroughly cleaned, the installations repaired and prepared for further use. On August 3 the killing machine again went into operation. The first convoys consisted of Jews from HENZBURG and SOS-NOWITZ and others followed during the whole month of August.

132,000–136,000	Only 4,000 men and a very small number of women were brought to the camp. Over 35,000 were gassed. Of the aforementioned 4,000 men, many died as a result of bad treatment, hunger or illness; some were even murdered. The main responsibility for these tragedies lies with the concentration camp of SACHSEN-HAUSEN and the Polish political prisoner No. 8516, Mieczislav KATERZINSKI, from Warsaw.

The "selections" were introduced again and this time to a murderous extent, especially in the women's camp. The camp doctor, an SS Hauptsturnführer and the son or nephew of the police president of Berlin (we forgot his name) outdid all the others in brutality. The selection system has been continued ever since, until our escape.

137,000–138,000	At the end of August 1,000 Poles came from the PAWIAK prison and 80 Jews from Greece.
138,000–141,000	3,000 men from various Aryan transports.
142,000–145,000	At the beginning of September, 1943, 3000 Jews arrived from Polish working camps and Russian prisoners of war.
148,000–152,000	During the week following September 7, 1943 family transports of Jews arrived from THERESIENSTADT. They enjoyed quite an exceptional status which was incomprehensible to us. The families were not separated and not a single one of them received the customary and "normal" gas treatment. Their heads were not even shaven, they were able to keep their luggage, and were lodged in a separate section of the camp, men, women and children together. The men were not forced to work and a school was even set up for the children under the direction of Fredy HIRSCH (Makabi, Prague). They were allowed to correspond freely. The worst they had to undergo was mistreatment at the hands of their "camp eldest," a certain professional criminal by the name of Arno BOHM, prisoner No. 8. Our astonishment increased when we learned of the official indication given to this special transport:

"SB—transport of Czech Jews with six months' quarantine"

We very well knew what "SB" meant *(Sonderbehandlung)*, but could not understand the long period of six months' quarantine and the generally clement treatment this group received. The longest quarantine period we had witnessed so far only three weeks. Towards the end of the six months' period, however, we became convinced that the fate of these Jews would be the same as that of most of the others—the gas chamber. We tried to get in touch with the leader of this group and explain their lot and what they had to expect. Some of them declared (especially Fredy HIRSCH who seemed to enjoy the full confidence of his companions) that if our fears took shape they would organize resistance. Thus, some of them hoped to instigate a general revolt in the camp. On March 6, 1944 we heard that the crematoria were being prepared to receive the Czech Jews.

I hastened to inform Fredy HIRSCH and begged him to take immediate action as they had nothing to lose. He replied that he recognized his duty. Before nightfall I again crept over to the Czech camp where I learned that Fredy HIRSCH was dying; he had poisoned himself with luminol. The next day, March 7, 1944, he was

taken, unconscious, along with his 3,791 comrades who had arrived at BIRKE-
NAU on September 7, 1943 on trucks, to the crematoria and gassed. The young
people went to their death singing, but to our great disappointment nobody
revolted. Some 500 elderly people had died during quarantine. Of all these Jews
only 11 twins were left alive. They are being subjected to various medical tests at
AUSCHWITZ and when we left BIRKENAU they were still alive. Among the
gassed was Rozsi FURST, from SERED. A week before the gassing, that is to say on
March 1, 1944, everyone in the Czech group in the camp had been asked to
inform his relatives about his well being. The letters had to be dated March 23 to
25, 1944 and they were requested to ask for food parcels.

153,000–154,000	1,000 Polish Aryans from the PAVIAK penitentiary.
155,000–159,000	During October and November, 1943, 4,000 persons from various prisons and smaller transports of Jews from BENZBURG and vicinity, who had been driven out of their hiding places; also a group of Russians under protective custody from the MINSK and VITEBSK regions. Some more Russian prisoners of war arrived and, as stated, they as usual received numbers between 1 and 12,000.
160,000–165,000	In December, 1943, 5,000 men originated from Dutch, French, Belgian transports and, for the first time, Italian Jews from FIUME, TRIESTE and ROME. Of these at least 30,000 were immediately gassed. The morality among these Jews was very high and, in addition, the "selection" system was still decimating all ranks. The bestiality of the whole procedure reached its culminating point between January 10 and 24, 1944 when even young and healthy persons irrespective of profession or working classification—with the exception of doctors—were ruthlessly "selected."

Every single prisoner was called up, a strict control was established to see that
all were present, and the "selection" proceeded under the supervision of the same
camp doctor (son or nephew of the police president of Berlin) and of the commandant of BIRKENAU, SS Unterstürmführer SCHWARZHUBER. The "infirmary"
had in the meantime been transferred from Block 7 to a separate section of the
camp where conditions had become quite bearable. Its inmates, nevertheless,
were gassed to the last man. Apart from this group, this general action cost some
2,500 men and over 6,000 women their lives.

165,000–168,000	On December 20, 1943 a further group of 3,000 Jews arrived from THERESIEN-STADT. The convoy was listed under the same category as the one which had reached the camp on September 7, i.e., "SB—transport Czech Jews with six months' quarantine." On their arrival, men, women and children all joined the September group. They enjoyed the same privileges as their predecessors. Twenty-four hours before the gassing of the first group took place, the latest arrivals were placed in another part of the camp where they still are at present. Their quarantine ends on June 20, 1944.
169,000–170,000	1,000 people in small groups, Jews, Poles, and Russians under protective custody.
170,000–171,000	1,000 Poles and Russians and a number of Yugoslavs.
171,000–174,000	At the end of February and beginning of March, 3,000 Jews from Holland, Belgium, and for the first time long-established French Jews (not naturalized) from VICHY, in France. The greater part of this transport was gassed immediately upon arrival.

Small groups of BENZBURGER and SOSNOWITZER Jews, who had been dragged from hiding, arrived in the middle of March. One of them told me that many Polish Jews were crossing to Slovakia and from there to Hungary and that the Slovak Jews helped them on their way through.

After the gassing of the THERESIENSTADT transport there were no further arrivals until March 15, 1944. The effective strength of the camp rapidly diminished and men of later incoming transports, especially Dutch Jews, were directed to the camp. When we left on April 7, 1944 we heard that large convoys of Greek Jews were expected.

The camp of BIRKENAU consists of three building areas. At present only sections I and II are guarded by the inner chain of sentry posts, whereas section III is still under construction and uninhabited. At the time of our departure from the camp (the beginning of April, 1944), the following categories of prisoners were in BIRKENAU:

Section I (Women's concentration camp)

	Slov. Jews	Other Jews	Aryans	Remarks
Ia and Ib	app. 300	app. 7,000	app. 6,000	In addition to the 300 Slovak Jewish girls, approx. 100 are employed in the administration building of AUSCHWITZ.

Section II (Women's concentration camp)

		Slov. Jews	Other Jews	Aryans	Remarks
IIa	Quarantine Camp	2	app. 200	app. 800	One of the two Slovak Jews is Dr. Andreas MULLER from Podolinec (block eldest).
IIb	Jews from THERESIENSTADT	–	app. 3,500	–	With a six months' quarantine.
IIc	At present uninhabited	–	–	–	
IId	"Stammlager"	58	app. 4,000	app. 6,000	
IIe	Gypsy camp	–	–	app. 4,500	This is the remainder of some 16,000 gypsies. They are not used for work and die off rapidly.
IIf	Infirmary	6	app. 1,000	app. 500	The six Slovak Jews are all employees of the building, namely:

No. 36,832   Walter SPITZER, block eldest from NEMSOVA, came to LUBLIN from BIRKENAU.
No. 29,867   Jozef NEUMANN, ("overseer" of the "corpse crew") from SNINA.
No. 44,989   Josef ZELMANOVIC, "staff" from SNINA.
   –   Cham KATZ, "staff" from SNINA.
No. 30,049   Ludwig SOLMANN, "clerk" from KESMAREK.
No. 32,407   Ludwig EISENSTADTER, tattooist from KREMPACHY.

The internal administration of the camp of BIRKENAU is run by specially selected prisoners. The blocks are not inhabited according to nationalities but rather according to working categories. Each block is supervised by a staff of five, i.e., a block eldest, a block recorder, a male nurse, and two attendants.

The block eldest

He wears an arm band with the number of his block, and is responsible for order there. He has power over life and death. Until February, 1944 nearly 50 percent of the block eldests were Jews but this was stopped by order of BERLIN. They all had to resign with the exception of three Jews who, in spite of this order, were able to keep their posts.

The block recorder

He is the block eldest's right hand, does all the clerical work, keeping the index cards and records. His work is of great responsibility and he has to keep his ledgers with painful exactitude as the index cards only indicate the number and not the name of the prisoners; errors are fatal. For instance, if the recorder has noted down a death by mistake—and this often occurs with the unusually high mortality—the discrepancy is simply straightened out by killing the bearer of the corresponding number. Corrections are not admitted. The block recorder occupies a key post which is often misused.

Nursing and room duties

They consist in keeping the inside of the barracks clean and carrying out small manual jobs in and around the block. Of course there is no question of really taking care of the sick.

The camp eldest supervises the whole camp; he is also a prisoner. This post is at present held by:

Franz DANISCH, No. 11,182, a political prisoner, from KONIGSHUTTE, Upper Silesia. He is undisputed master of the whole camp and has power to nominate or dismiss block eldests and block recorders, hand out jobs, etc.

Further we have a chief recorder whose position is undoubtedly one of the most powerful in the camp. He is in direct contact with camp headquarters, receiving their orders and reporting on all matters. All camp recorders are directly subordinated to him and have to submit all their reports to him. The chief recorder of BIRKENAU is:

Kasimir GORK, No. 31,029, a Pole from WARSAW, a former bank clerk.

The supreme control over the blocks lies in the hands of six to eight "block leaders," all SS men. Every night they hold roll call, the result of which is communicated to:

The Camp Leader, Unterstürmführer SCHWARZHUBER, from the Tyrol. This individual is an alcoholic and a sadist. Over him is the camp commander who also controls AUSCHWITZ where there is a second subordinate camp leader. The camp commander's name is: HÖSS.

The chief of a work squad or group is called the "Capo."

During work the "Capo" has full authority over his group of prisoners and not infrequently one of these "Capos" kills a man working under him. In larger squads there may be several "Capos" who are then under the orders of a "Capo-in-chief." At first there were many Jewish "Capos," but an order from BERLIN prohibited their being employed.

Supreme control over work is carried out by German specialists.

II. MAJDANEK

On June 14, 1942 we left NOVAKY, passed through ZILINA and arrived at ZWARDON toward five o'clock in the evening. We were assembled, counted, and SS men took over our convoy. One of these guards voiced his surprise at the fact we had made the journey without water by shouting: "Those Slovak barbarians, give them no water!" The journey continued and we reached LUBLIN two days later. Here the following order was issued: "Those fit for work aged between fifteen and fifty are to leave the cars. Children and old people remain."We struggled out of the freight car and discovered that the station was surrounded by Lithuanians in SS uniforms, all armed with automatic pistols. The cars containing the children and old people were immediately closed and the train moved on. We do not know where they went and what happened to them.

The SS troop leader in command informed us that we had a long way ahead of us, but that whoever wanted to take his luggage with him could do so. Those who preferred to put it on a truck would certainly receive it later. So some of us dragged along our luggage, whereas others loaded it on the truck.

Behind the town stood a clothing factory called the "Bekleidungserke." In the courtyard waiting for their noon meal some one thousand prisoners in dirty stripped clothing, obviously Jews, were lined up and the sight of them was none too encouraging. Arriving on a small hill we suddenly sighted the vast barrack camp of MAJDANEK surrounded by a three-meter-high barbed-wire fence. No sooner had we gone through the entrance gate than I met a prisoner who warned me that all our personal belongings would be taken away. Around us stood Slovak Jews in a wretched condition, their heads shaven, in dirty prison clothes and wooden clogs or simply bare-footed, many of them having swollen feet. They begged us for food and we gave them what we could spare, knowing very well that everything would be confiscated anyway. We were then conducted to the stock room where we had to leave everything we possessed. At double time we were herded into another barrack where we had to undress, were shaven, and given a shower. After this we were issued convict outfits, wooden clogs and caps.

I was assigned to "working section No. 2" as the whole camp was divided into three such sections separated by wire fences. Section No. II was occupied by a number of Slovak and Czech Jews. For two full days we were taught how to remove and put on our caps when we met a German. Then in the pouring rain we practiced roll calling for hours.

The barrack accommodations were quite original to say the least. Three long tables (nearly as long as the barrack itself) had been placed one on top of the other. These comprised our "bunks" (four floors of them, that is ground floor plus the three tables). A small passage was kept open along the walls.

Our food consisted of a fairly thick "soup" early in the morning which had to be eaten with the hands. We got the same soup again at lunch. The evening meal consisted of a brew called "tea," 300 grams of bad bread and some 20 to 30 grams of marmalade or artificial fat of the worst quality.

Great importance was attributed during the first few days to the learning of the "camp song." For hours we stood singing:

From the whole of Europe
We Jews to Lublin
Much work has to be done
And this is the beginning
To manage this duty
Forget all about the past
For in fulfillment of duty
There is community.
Therefore on to work with vigor
Let everyone play his part
Together we want to work
At the same pace and rhythm.
Not all will understand
Why we stand here in rows
Those must we soon force
To understand its meaning.
Modern times must teach us
Teach us all along
That it is to work
And only to work we belong.
Therefore on to work with vigor
Let everyone play his part
Together we want to work
At the same pace and rhythm.

(This is a literal translation of the song.)

Working section No. I was occupied by
 Slovak Jews
Working section No. II was occupied by
 Slovak and Czech Jews

Working section No. III was occupied by partisans

Working section Nos. IV & V were being built by the Jews of Sectors I & II

The partisans in section III were locked up in their barracks without having to work and their food was thrown at them as if they had been dogs. They died in great numbers in their overcrowded barracks and were shot at the slightest excuse by the guards who did not dare venture too near them.

The "Capos" were Reich Germans and Czechs; whereas the Germans were brutal, the Czechs helped whenever they could. The camp eldest was a Gypsy from HOLIC by the name of GAL-BAVY. His adjutant, a Jew from SERED called MIT-TLER, certainly owed his post to his brutal actions. He took full advantage of the power conferred upon him to torment the Jews who, as it was, already had their full share of hardships. The evening roll call brought us more brutal treatment from the SS men and for hours we had to stand in the open after a hard day's work and sing the camp song. A Jewish orchestra leader was forced to conduct from the roof of one of the barracks. This was the occasion of much hilarity among the SS men.

During these "concert parties" the SS guards were very generous with blows and physical punishment. A tragic end befell Rabbi ECKSTEIN from SERED who was suffering from dysentery and once came a few minutes too late to roll call. The group leader had him seized and dipped head first into one of the latrines, then poured cold water over him, drew his revolver and shot him.

The crematorium was located between working sections I and II and all the bodies were burned there. With an effective strength of six thousand to eight thousand men per working section, the mortality was about thirty a day. This figure later increased five and sixfold. In other instances ten to twenty inmates were removed from the sick room, brought to the crematorium and burned, after having been put to death in a manner which I have not been able to

find out. This crematorium was electrically heated and the attendants were Russians.

Illnesses increased as a result of the bad food and intolerable living conditions. Serious stomach troubles and a seemingly incurable foot disease spread throughout the camp. The feet of the victims swelled up to the point where they could not walk. More and more of the sick were now being taken to the crematorium and when on June 26, 1942 the number thus treated rose to seventy, I decided to take an opportunity which was offered to me and applied for a transfer to AUSCHWITZ.

On June 27, 1942 I discarded my prisoner's outfit and travelled to AUSCHWITZ in civilian clothes.

After a journey of forty-eight hours during which we were coupled up in freight cars without food or water, we arrived at AUSCHWITZ half dead. At the entrance gate the huge poster, "Work brings freedom," greeted us. As the courtyard was clean and well kept, and the brick buildings made a good impression after the dirty and primitive barracks of LUBLIN, we thought that the change was for the best. We were taken to a cellar and received tea and bread. Next day, however, our civilian clothes were taken away, our heads were shaved, and our numbers were tattooed on our forearms in the usual way. Finally, we were issued a set of prisoner's clothes similar to those we had worn in LUBLIN and were enrolled as "political prisoners" in the concentration camp of AUSCHWITZ.

We were billeted in "Block 17" and slept on the floor. In an adjoining row of buildings separated from ours by a high wall, the Jewish girls from Slovakia, who had been brought there in March and April of 1942, were quartered. We worked in the huge "BUNA" plant to which we were herded every morning about 3 A.M. At midday our food consisted of potato or turnip soup and in the evening we received some bread. During work we were terribly mistreated. As our working place was situated outside the large chain of sentry posts, it was divided into small sectors of ten by ten meters, each guarded by an SS man. Whoever stepped outside these squares during working hours was immediately shot without warning for having "attempted to escape." Often it happened that out of pure spite an SS man would order a prisoner to fetch some given object outside his square. If he followed the order, he was shot for having left his assigned place. The work was extremely hard and there were no rest periods. The way to and from work had to be covered at a brisk military trot; anyone falling out of line was shot. On my arrival about three thousand people, of whom two thousand were Slovak Jews, were working on this emplacement. Very few could bear the strain and although escape seemed hopeless, attempts were made every day. The result was several hangings a week.

After a number of weeks of painful work at the "BUNA" plant a terrible typhus epidemic broke out. The weaker prisoners died in hundreds. An immediate quarantine was ordered and work at the "BUNA" stopped. Those still alive were sent, at the end of July, 1942, to the gravel pit but there work was even still more strenuous. We were in such a state of weakness that, even in trying to do our best, we could not satisfy the overseers. Most of us got swollen feet. Due to our inability to perform the heavy work demanded of us our squad was accused of being lazy and disorderly. Soon after a medical commission inspected all of us; they carried out their job very thoroughly. Anyone with swollen feet or particularly weak was separated from the rest. Although I was in great pain, I controlled myself and stood erect in front of the commission who passed me as physically fit. Out of three hundred persons examined, two hundred were found to be unfit and immediately sent to BIRKENAU and gassed. I was then detailed for work at the DAW (Deutsche Aufrustungswerke) where we had to paint skis. The prescribed minimum to be painted each day was 120. Anyone unable to paint this many was thoroughly flogged in the evening. Another group was employed at making cases for hand grenades. At one time fifteen thousand had been completed but it was found that they were a few centimeters too small. As punishment several Jews were shot for sabotage.

Somewhere around the middle of August, 1942 all the Jewish girls from Slovakia who lived next to our quarters, on the other side of the wall, were transferred to BIRKENAU. I had the opportunity to talk to them and was able to see how weak and half-starved all of them were. They were dressed in old Russian uniform rags and wore wooden clogs. Their heads were shaven clean. The same day we again had to undergo a strict examination and those suspected of having typhus were removed to the Birch Wood. The remainder were shaven afresh, bathed, issued a new set of clothes and finally billeted in the barracks the girls had just left. By chance I learned that there was an opening in the "clearance squad" and I handed in my application. I was detailed to this task.

This squad consisted of about a hundred Jewish prisoners. We were sent to a far corner of the camp, away from all our comrades. Here we found huge sheds full of knapsacks, suitcases, and other luggage. We had to open each piece of baggage and sort the contents into large cases specially prepared for each category of goods, i.e. combs, mirrors, sugar, canned food, chocolate, medicines, etc. The cases were then stored away. Underwear, shirts and clothes of all kinds went to a special barrack, where they were sorted out and packed by Jewish girls. Old and worn clothes were addressed to the "TEXTILE FACTORY" at MEMEL, whereas the usable garments were dispatched to a collecting center in BERLIN. Gold, money, bank notes, and precious stones had to be handed over to the political section. Many of these objects were, however, stolen by the SS guards or by prisoners. A brutal and vile individual who often struck the women is commander of this squad. He is SS Scharführer WYKLEFF.

Every day the girls who came to their work from BIRKENAU described to us the terrible conditions prevailing there. They were beaten and brutalized and their mortality was much higher than among the men. Twice a week "selections" took place, and every day new girls replaced those who had disappeared.

During a night shift I was able to witness for

the first time how incoming convoys were handled. The transport I saw contained Polish Jews. They had received no water for days and when the doors of the freight cars were open we were ordered to chase them out with loud shouts. They were utterly exhausted and about a hundred of them had died during the journey. The living were lined up in rows of five. Our job was to remove the dead, dying, and the luggage from the cars. The dead, and this included anyone unable to stand on his feet, were piled in a heap. Luggage and parcels were collected and stacked up. Then the railroad cars had to be thoroughly cleaned so that no trace of their frightful load was left behind. A commission from the political department proceeded with the "selection" of approximately 10 percent of the men and 5 percent of the women and had them transferred to the camps. The remainder were loaded on trucks, sent to BIRKENAU, and gassed while the dead and dying were taken directly to the furnaces. It often happened that small children were thrown alive into the trucks along with the dead. Parcels and luggage were taken to the warehouses and sorted out in the previously described manner.

Between July and September, 1942 a typhus epidemic had raged in AUSCHWITZ, especially in the women's camp of BIRKENAU. None of the sick received medical attention and in the first stages of the epidemic a great many were killed by phenol injections, and later on others were gassed wholesale. Some fifteen to twenty thousand, mostly Jews, died during these two months. The girls' camp suffered the most, as it was not fitted with sanitary installations, and the poor wretches were covered with lice. Every week large "selections" took place and the girls had to present themselves naked to the "selection committee," regardless of weather conditions. They waited in deadly fear whether they would be chosen or given another week's grace. Suicides were frequent and were mostly committed by throwing one's self against the high tension wires of the inner fence. This went on until they had dwindled to 5 percent of their original number. Now there are only four hundred of these girls left and most of them have been able to secure some sort of clerical post in the women's camp. About one hundred girls hold jobs at the staff building in AUSCHWITZ where they do all the clerical work connected with the administration of the two camps. Thanks to their knowledge of languages they are also used as interpreters. Others are employed in the main kitchen and laundry. Of late these girls have been able to dress themselves quite well as they have had opportunities to complete their wardrobes which, in some cases, even include silk stockings. Generally speaking they are reasonably well off and are even allowed to let their hair grow. Of course this cannot be said of the other Jewish inmates of the women's camp. It just so happens that these Slovak Jewish girls have been in the camp the longest of all. But if today they enjoy certain privileges, they have previously undergone frightful sufferings.

I was not to hold this comparatively good job with the "clearance squad" for long. Shortly afterwards I was transferred to BIRKENAU on disciplinary grounds and remained there over a year and a half. On April 7, 1944 I managed to escape with my companion.

Poland (transported by trucks)	approximately	300,000
" " " train	"	600,000
Holland	"	100,000
Greece	"	45,000
France	"	150,000
Belgium	"	50,000
Germany	"	60,000
Yugoslavia, Italy and Norway	"	50,000
Lithuania	"	50,000
Bohemia, Moravia and Austria	"	30,000
Slovakia	"	30,000
Various camps for foreign Jews in Poland	"	300,000

approximately 1,765,000

III.

On August 6, 1944 a report was received in Switzerland covering the happenings in BIRKE-NAU during the period April 7 and May 27. This second report was drawn up by two other young Jews who succeeded in escaping from this camp and reaching Slovakia. Their declarations complete the first report, particularly in regard to the arrival of the Hungarian Jews in BIRKENAU. They also add certain new details not contained in the previous accounts. It has not been possible, however, to check the origin of this "second report" as closely as it was the first.

After the flight of the two Slovak Jews from BIRKENAU on April 7, 1944 great excitement reigned in the camp. The "Political Division" of the Gestapo instituted a thoroughgoing investigation, and the friends and superiors of the two escapees were closely questioned, although in vain. Since the two had held posts as block recorders, all Jews exercising such functions, by way of punishment and also as a precautionary measure, were removed and, as the Gestapo suspected that they had succeeded in escaping through Building No. 3, the outer chain of sentry posts was considerably shortened so that now it cuts through the middle of Building No. 3.

At the beginning of the month of April, a transport of Greek Jews arrived, of whom about two hundred were admitted to the camp. The remainder of circa 1,500 were immediately gassed.

Between the 10th and 15th of April some five thousand Aryans arrived in BIRKENAU, mainly Poles, some two to three thousand women among them being from the abandoned camp of LUBLIN-MAJDANEK. They were given numbers running from approximately:

| 176,000 to 181,000 | Among the women were about 300 Jewish girls from Poland. The greater part of the new arrivals were ill, weak, and very run down. According to their information the healthy ones had been sent from LUBLIN to German concentration camps. Concerning the fate of the Jews held in the camp of LUBLIN-MAJDANEK, we learned from them, especially from the Jewish girls, that on November 3, 1943 all Jews in this camp, that is some 11,000 men and 6,000 women, were killed. |

We realized that about this time the SS in BIRKENAU had reported that LUBLIN had been attacked by partisans and, in order to fight against the latter, a number of the SS personnel from BIRKENAU had been temporarily transferred to LUBLIN. It was now clear to us for what purpose our SS had gone to LUBLIN.

Apparently the Jews had been compelled to dig a long, deep grave in Field V of the camp MAJDENEK and on November 3 they were brought out in groups of 200 to 300, shot and thrown into the grave. Within twenty-four hours everything was over. During the execution loud music was played to drown out the shots.

Three hundred girls who were active in LUBLIN on the Kommando "clearing-up kommando" and as recorders were left alive. Three days after their arrival in BIRKENAU they were all gassed and burned on special order of BERLIN. Through an error on the part of the recorder two of the girls were not sent to the gas chamber. This was discovered, however, the next day, and the girls were immediately shot and the recorder replaced.

The fate of the LUBLIN Jews caused great depression among the Jews in the camp of BIRKENAU who became afraid that one day the whole of BIRKENAU would suddenly be "liquidated" in the same way.

| Approximately 183,000 to 185,000 | Toward the end of April more Greek No. 182,000 Jews were brought to BIRKENAU. Some 200 were admitted to the camp and about 3,000 exterminated. At the beginning of May, 1944 smaller transports of Dutch, French, Belgian, and Greek Jews arrived, as well as Polish Aryans. Most of them were put to work in the BUNA plant. |

On May 10, 1944 the first transport of Hungarian Jews arrived in BIRKENAU. They were principally from the prisons of Budapest, including those who had been arrested in the streets and railroad stations of the city. Among the women were:

1. Ruth Lorant
2. Mici Lorant
3. Ruth Quasztler
4. Irene Roth
5. Barna Fuchs

The transport was received in AUSCHWITZ and BIRKENAU according to the well-known procedure (heads shaven, numbers tattooed, women were placed in the women's camp. About 600 men, of whom some 150 were between the ages of forty-five and sixty, were brought to BIRKENAU where they were divided up among various work detachments. The remainder stayed in AUSCHWITZ where they worked in the BUNA plant.

The members of the transport were all left alive and none of them, as had been customary, were sent directly to the crematoria. In the postcards which they were allowed to write, they had to give "Waldsee" as a return address.

On May 15 mass transports from Hungary began to arrive in BIRKENAU. Some fourteen to fifteen thousand Jews arrived daily. The spur railroad track which ran into the camp to the crematoria was completed in great haste, the crews working night and day, so that the transports could be brought directly to the crematoria. Only about 10 percent of these transports were admitted to the camp; the balance were immediately gassed and burned. Never had so many Jews been gassed since the establishment of BIRKENAU. The KommandoSpecial Kommando had to be increased to 600 men and, after two or three days, to 800 (people being recruited from among the Hungarian Jews who had arrived first). The size of the Kommando "Clearing Kommando" was stepped up from 150 to 700 men. Three crematoria worked day and night (the 4th was being repaired at the time) and, since the capacity of the crematoria was not enough, great pits thirty meters long and fifteen meters wide were once more dug in the "Birkenwald" (as in the time before the crematoria) where corpses were burned day and night. Thus the "exterminating capacity" became almost unlimited.

The Hungarian Jews who were left alive (about 10 percent) were not included in the normal camp enrollment. Although they were shaved and shorn and received convict's clothing, they were not tattooed. They were housed in a separate section of the camp, section "C," and were later transferred to various concentration camps in the German Reich: Buchenwald, Mauthausen, Grossrosen, Gusen, Flossenburg, Sachsenhausen, etc. The women were temporarily quartered in the "Gypsy camp" in separate blocks and then also transferred elsewhere. Jewish girls from Slovakia were block eldests there.

The first Hungarian transport came from: Wunkacs, Magyszollos, Nyiregyhaza, Ungvar, Huszt, Kassau, Beregszasz, Marmarossziget, Nagyberezna. Among those remaining alive were:

1. Robert and Ervin Waizen
2. Stark
3. Ehrenreich
4. Katz, Chaim

The last two have already been transferred. The parents of the Waizen brothers were gassed.

The transports of Hungarian Jews under the particular control of the former Camp Commander Hauptsturmbannführer HÖSS, who travelled continually between AUSCHWITZ and Budapest. The Commandant of Birkenau at this time was HÖSS's former adjutant, Hauptsturmführer KRAMER.

| 187,000 to 189,000 | 1,600 French Aryans, almost exclusively intellectuals and prominent persons, including a small number of Polish "emigrés." Among the French were high officers, members of leading French financial circles, well-known journalists and politicians, and even, it was said, former ministers. On their arrival some of them rebelled but were put down in an exceedingly brutal fashion by the SS, some of them being shot on the spot. The French were very courageous and self-possessed. They were strictly isolated in BIRKENAU and no one was allowed to have any contact with them. After two weeks, on orders form Berlin, they were sent to Mauthausen (near Linz, in Austria.) |

Since the middle of May the newly arrived Jews no longer received consecutive numbers, as formerly. A new numbering system was inaugurated beginning with No. 1 preceded by the tattooed letter "A." We do not know the reason for this measure. At the time of our flight on May 27, 1944 about four thousand Jews had received these new numbers. The four thousand were composed of one thousand Dutch, French, and Italian Jews and three thousand Jews from THERESIENSTADT who reached BIRKENAU on May 23, 1944. These were treated exactly as the previous two transports from THERESIENSTADT. They were quartered (unshorn) with the members of the previous convoy from THERESIENSTADT (who have been in BIRKENAU since December 20, 1943 and whose "quarantine" is due to be up on June 20, 1944) in Section IIB.

According to the statement of a Jew from the KommandoSpecial Kommando, Reichsführer Himmler was said to have visited BIRKENAU on the 15th or 16th of May. On one of these days I myself saw three automobiles and five men in civilian clothing drive toward the crematoria. The Jew who made this statement declared that he, as well as others, recognized Himmler, who had visited crematorium No. 1 and after a stay of about half an hour had again there was an account in the Silesian newspapers of Himmler's visit to Kraków, so that this report could be true.

One other happening should not be forgotten which was told to us by the men of the KommandoSpecial Kommando. In the late summer of 1943 a commission of four Dutch Jews—distinguished looking men—came to AUSCHWITZ. Their visit had already apparently been announced to the Camp Commander, for the Dutch Jews in AUSCHWITZ received better clothes, as well as regular eating equipment (plates, spoons, etc.) and better food. The commission of four were very politely received and were shown over the camp buildings and particularly those portions which were clean and made a good impression. Dutch Jews from the camp were brought to them who reported that only a portion of the Dutch Jews were in this camp, the others being in other similar camps. In this manner the four men were satisfied and signed a statement according to which the commission had found everything in good order in AUSCHWITZ. After the signing the four Dutch Jews expressed a desire to see the camp of BIRKENAU and particularly the crematoria about which they had heard some stories. The camp authorities declared themselves quite willing to show them both BIRKENAU and the crematoria, the latter being used, they said, to cremate those who died in the camp. The commission was then taken to BIRKENAU, accompanied by the camp leader, Aumayer, and immediately to crematoria No. 1. Here they were shot from behind. A telegram was supposedly sent to Holland reporting that after leaving AUSCHWITZ the four men had been victims of an unfortunate automobile accident.

There is a biological laboratory in AUSCHWITZ where SS, civilian, and internee doctors are occupied. The women and girls on whom experiments are performed are housed in Block 10. For a long time the block eldest there was Magda Hellinger from Michalovce and a girl named Rozsi (family name unknown) from Hummene. Experiments were carried out only on Jewish girls and women, although to date no Slovakian girls have been used.

Experiments were also performed on men but the latter were not housed separately. A great many died as a result of these experiments. Often Gypsies were used. Block 10, where the subjects of the experiments are housed, is completely isolated, and even the window openings are walled up. No one whatsoever had admission to it.

The commandants of AUSCHWITZ and BIRKENAU have been to date the following: AUMAYER, SCHWARZHUBER, WEISS, HARTENSTEIN, HÖSS, and KRAMER.

Report to the Secretary on the Acquiescence of This Government in the Murder of the Jews

One of the greatest crimes in history, the slaughter of the Jewish people in Europe, is continuing unabated.

This government has for a long time maintained that its policy is to work out programs to save those Jews of Europe who could be saved.

I am convinced on the basis of the information which is available to me that certain officials in our State Department, which is charged with carrying out this policy, have been guilty not only of gross procrastination and willful failure to act, but even of willful attempts to prevent action from being taken to rescue Jews from Hitler.

I fully recognize the graveness of this statement and I make it only after having most carefully weighed the shocking facts which have come to my attention during the last several months.

Unless remedial steps of a drastic nature are taken, and taken immediately, I am certain that no effective action will be taken by this government to prevent the complete extermination of the Jews in German controlled Europe, and that this government will have to share for all time responsibility for this extermination.

The tragic history of this government's handling of this matter reveals that certain State Department officials are guilty of the following:

1. They have not only failed to use the *governmental machinery* at their disposal to rescue Jews from Hitler, but have gone so far as to use this government machinery to prevent the rescue of these Jews.
2. They have not only failed to cooperate with *private organizations* in the efforts of these organizations to work out individual programs of their own, but have taken steps designed to prevent these programs from being put into effect.

3. They not only have failed to facilitate the obtaining of information concerning Hitler's plans to exterminate the Jews of Europe but in their official capacity have gone so far as to surreptitiously attempt to stop the obtaining of information concerning the murder of the Jewish population of Europe.
4. They have tried to cover up their guilt by:
    A. concealment and misrepresentation;
    B. the giving of false and misleading explanations for their failures to act and their attempts to prevent action; and
    C. the issuance of false and misleading statements concerning the "action" which they have taken to date.

Although only part of the facts relating to the activities of the State Department in this field are available to us, sufficient facts have come to my attention from various sources during the last several months to fully support the conclusions at which I have arrived.

I. *State Department officials have not only failed to use the governmental machinery at their disposal to rescue the Jews from Hitler, but have even gone so far as to use their governmental machinery to prevent the rescue of these Jews.*

The public record, let alone the facts which have not as yet been made public, reveals the gross *procrastination and willful failure to act* of those officials actively representing this government in this field.

A. A long time has passed since it became clear that Hitler was determined to carry out a policy of exterminating the Jews in Europe.

B. Over a year has elapsed since this government and other members of the United Nations publicly acknowledged and denounced this policy of extermination; and since the president gave assurances that the United States would make every effort together with the United Nations to save those who could be saved.

C. Despite the fact that time is most precious in this matter, State Department officials have been kicking the matter around for over a year without producing results; giving all sorts of excuses for delays upon delays; advancing no specific proposals designed to rescue Jews, at the same time proposing that the whole refugee problem be "explored" by this government and Intergovernmental Committees. While the State Department as been thus "exploring" the whole refugee problem, without distinguishing between those who are in imminent danger of death and those who are not, hundreds of thousands of Jews have been allowed to perish.

As early as August 1942 a message from the secretary of the World Jewish Congress in Switzerland (Riegner), transmitted through the British Foreign Office, reported that Hitler had under consideration a plan to exterminate all Jews in German controlled Europe. By November 1942 sufficient evidence had been received, including substantial documentary evidence transmitted through our Legation in Switzerland, to confirm that Hitler had actually adopted and was carrying out his plan to exterminate the Jews. Sumner Welles accordingly authorized the Jewish organization to make the facts public.

Thereupon, the Jewish organizations took the necessary steps to bring the shocking facts to the attention of the public through mass meetings, etc., and to elicit public support for governmental action. On December 7, 1942, a joint statement of the United States and the European members of the United Nations was issued calling attention to and denouncing the fact that Hitler was carrying into effect his oft-repeated intention to exterminate the Jewish people in Europe.

Since the time when this government knew that the Jews were being murdered, our State Department has failed to take any positive steps reasonably calculated to save any of these people. Although State has used the devices of setting up inter-governmental organizations to survey the whole refugee problem, and calling conferences such as the Bermuda Conference to explore the whole refugee problem, making it appear that positive action could be expected, in fact nothing has been accomplished.

Before the outcome of the Bermuda Conference, which was held in April 1943, was made public, Senator Langer prophetically stated in an address in the Senate on October 6, 1943:

> "As yet we have had no report from the Bermuda Refugee Conference. With the best goodwill in the world and with all latitude that could and should be accorded to diplomatic negotiations in time of war, I may be permitted to voice the bitter suspicion that the absence of a report indicates only one thing—the lack of action.
>
> "Probably in all 5703 years, Jews have hardly had a time as tragic and hopeless as the one which they are undergoing now. One of the most tragic factors about the situation is that while singled out for suffering and martyrdom by their enemies, they seem to have been forgotten by the nations which claim to fight for the cause of humanity. We should remember the Jewish slaughterhouse of Europe and ask what is being done— and I emphasize the word 'done'—to

get some of these suffering human beings out of the slaughter while yet alive.

"Perhaps it would be necessary to introduce a formal resolution or to ask the secretary of state to report to an appropriate congressional committee on the steps being taken in this connection. Normally it would have been the job of the government to show itself alert to this tragedy; but when a government neglects a duty it is the job of the legislature in a democracy to remind it of that duty. It is not important who voices a call for action, and it is not important what procedure is being used in order to get action. It is important that action be undertaken."

Similar fears were voiced by Representatives Celler, Dickstein, and Klein. Senator Wagner and Representative Sadowski also issued calls for *action*.

The widespread fears concerning the failure of the Bermuda Conference were fully confirmed when Breckinridge Long finally revealed some of the things that had happened at the conference in his statement before the Committee on Foreign Affairs of the House on November 26, 1943.

After Long's "disclosure" Representative Celler stated in the House on December 20, 1943:

"He discloses some of the things that happened at the so-called Bermuda Conference. He thought he was telling us something heretofore unknown and secret. What happened at the Bermuda Conference could not be kept executive. All the recommendations and findings could not be kept executive. All the recommendations and findings of the Bermuda Conference were made known to the Intergovernmental Committee on Refugees in existence since the Evian Conference on Refugees in 1938 and which has been functioning all this time in London. How much has that committee accomplished in the years of its being. It will be remembered that the Intergovernmental Committee functions through an executive committee composed of six countries, the United States, United Kingdom, the Netherlands, France, Brazil, and Argentina. True, no report of the Bermuda Conference was made public. But a strangely ironical fact will be noted of the presence of Argentina on this most trusted of committees, Argentina that provoked the official reprimand of the President Roosevelt by its banning of the Jewish Press, and within whose borders Nazi propagandists and falangists now enjoy a Roman holiday. I contend that by the very nature of its composition the Intergovernmental Committee on Refugees cannot function successfully as the instrumentality to rescue the Jewish people of Europe. The benefits to be derived from the Bermuda Conference like those of the previous Evian Conference can fit into a tiny capsule."

One of the best summaries of the whole situation is contained in one sentence of a report submitted on December 20, 1943, by the Committee on Foreign Relations of the Senate, recommending the passage of a Resolution (S.R. 203) favoring the appointment of a commission to formulate plans to save the Jews of Europe from extinction of Nazi Germany. The Committee stated:

"We have talked; we have sympathized; we have expressed our horror; the time to act is long past due."

The Senate Resolution had been introduced by Senator Guy M. Gillette in behalf of himself and eleven colleagues, Senators Taft, Thomas, Radcliffe, Murray, Johnson, Guffey, Ferguson, Clark, Van Nuys, Downey, and Ellender.

The House Resolutions (H.R.'s 350 and 352), identical with the Senate Resolution, were introduced by Representatives Baldwin and Rogers.

The most glaring example of the use of the machinery of this government to *actually prevent the rescue of Jews* is the administrative restrictions which have been placed upon the granting of visas to the United States. In the note which the State Department sent to the British on February 25, 1946 it was stated:

> "Since the entry of the United States into the war there have been no new restrictions placed by the government of the United States upon the number of aliens of any nationality permitted to proceed to this country under existing laws, except for the more intensive examination of aliens required for security reasons." [Underscoring supplied]

The exception "for security reasons" mentioned in this note is the joker. Under the pretext of security reasons so many difficulties have been placed in the way of refugees obtaining visas that is no wonder that the admission of refugees to this country does not come anywhere near the quota, despite Long's statement designed to create the impression to the contrary. The following administrative restrictions which have been applied to the issuance of visas since the beginning of the war are typical.

D. Many applications for visas have been denied on the grounds that the applicants have close relatives in Axis controlled Europe. They theory of this is that the enemy would be able to put pressure on the applicant as a result of the fact that the enemy has the power of life or death over his immediate family.

E. Another restriction greatly increased the red tape and delay involved in getting the visa and requires among other things two affidavits of support and sponsorship to the furnished with each application for a visa. To each affidavit of support and sponsorship there must be attached two letters of references from two reputable American citizens.

If anyone were to attempt to work out a set of restrictions specifically designed to prevent Jewish refugees from entering this country it is difficult to conceive of how more of active restrictions could have been imposed than have already been imposed on grounds of "security."

It is obvious of course that these restrictions are not essential for security reasons. Thus refugees upon arriving in this country could be placed in internment camps similar to those used for the Japanese on the West Coast and released only after a satisfactory investigation. Furthermore, even if we took these refugees and treated them as prisoners of war it would be better than letting them die.

Representative Dickstein stated in the House on December 15:

> "If we consider the fact that the average admission would then be at the rate of less than 50,000 per year, it is clear that the organs of our government have not done their duty. The existing quotas call for the admission of more than 150,000 every year, so that if the quotas themselves had been filled there would have been a

total of one-half million and not 50,000 during the period mentioned.

"But that is not the whole story. There was no effort of any kind made to save from death many of the refugees who could have been saved during the time that transportation lines were available and there was no obstacle to their admission to the United States. But the obstructive policy of our organs of government, particularly the State Department, which saw fit to hedge itself about the rules and regulations, instead of lifting rules and regulations, brought about a condition so that not even the existing immigration quotas are filled."

Representative Celler stated in the House on June 30:

"Mr. Speaker, nations have declared war on Germany, and their high-ranking officials have issued pious protestations against the Nazi massacre of Jewish victims, but not one of those countries thus far has said they would be willing to accept these refugees either permanently or as visitors, or any of the minority peoples trying to escape the Hitler prison and slaughterhouse.

"Goebbels says: 'The United Nations won't take any Jews. We don't want them. Let's kill them.' And so he and Hitler are making Europe *Judenrein*.

"Without any change in the immigration statutes we could receive a reasonable number of those who are fortunate enough to escape the Nazi hellhole, receive them as visitors, the immigration quotas notwithstanding. They could be placed in camps or cantonments and held there in such havens until after the war. Private charitable agencies would be willing to pay the entire cost thereof. They would be no expense to the government whatsoever. These agencies would even pay for transportation by ships to and from this country.

"We house and maintain Nazi prisoners, many of them undoubtedly responsible for Nazi atrocities. We should do no less for the victims of the rage of the Huns."

Again, on December 20, he stated:

"According to Earl G. Harrison, commissioner of the Immigration and Naturalization Service, not since 1862 have there been fewer aliens entering the country.

"Frankly, Breckinridge Long, in my humble opinion, is least sympathetic to refugees in all the State Department. I attribute to him the tragic bottleneck in the printing of visas.

"The Interdepartmental Review Committees which review the applications for visas are composed of one official, respectively, from each of the following departments: War, Navy, FBI, State, and Immigration. That committee has been glacierlike in its slowness and cold-bloodedness. It take months and months to grant the visas and then it usually applies to a corpse.

"I brought this difficulty to the attention of the president. He asked Long to investigate at once. No, there has been no change in conditions. The gruesome bottleneck still exists."

II. *State Department officials have not only failed to cooperate with private organizations in the efforts of these organizations to work out individual programs of their own, but have taken steps designed to pre-*

vent these programs from being put into effect.

The best evidence in support of this charge are the facts relating to the proposal of the World Jewish Congress to evacuate thousands of Jews from Romania and France. The highlights relating to the efforts of State Department officials to prevent this proposal from being put into effect are the following:

A. On *March 13, 1943,* a cable was received from the World Jewish Congress representative in London stating that information reaching London indicated the possibility of rescuing Jews provided funds were put at the disposal of the World Jewish Congress representation in Switzerland.

B. On *April 10, 1943,* Sumner Welles cabled our Legation in Bern and requested them to get in touch with the World Jewish Congress representative in Switzerland, whom Welles had been informed was in possession of important information regarding the situation of the Jews.

C. On *April 20, 1943,* a cable was received from Bern relating to the proposed financial arrangements in connection with the evacuation of the Jews from Romania and France.

D. On *May 25, 1943,* State Department cabled or a clarification of these proposed financial arrangements. This matter was not called to the attention of the Treasury Department at this time.

E. This whole question of financing the evacuation of the Jews from Romania and France was first called to the attention of the Treasury Department on *June 25, 1943.*

E. A conference was held with the State Department relating to this matter on *July 15, 1943.*

G. One day after this conference, on *July 16, 1943,* the Treasury Department

advised the State Department that it was prepared to issue a license in this matter.

H. The license was not issued until *December 13, 1943.*

During this five-month period between the time that the Treasury stated that it was prepared to issue a license and the time when the license was actually issued delays and objections of all sorts were forthcoming from officials in the State Department, our Legation in Bern, and finally the British. The real significance of these delays and objections was brought home to the State Department in letters which you sent to Secretary Hull on November 24, 1943, and December 17, 1943, which completely devastated the "excuses" which State Department officials had been advancing. On December 18 you made an appointment to discuss the matter with Secretary Hull on December 20. And then an amazing but understandable thing happened. On December 13, the day after you sent your letter and the day on which you requested an appointment with Secretary Hull, the State Department sent a telegram to the British Foreign Office expressing astonishment with the British point of view and stating that the department was unable to agree with that point of view (in simple terms, the British point of view referred to by the State Department is that they are apparently prepared to accept the possible—even probable—death of thousands of Jews in enemy territory because of "the difficulties of disposing of any considerable number of Jews should they be rescued"). On the same day, the State Department issued a license notwithstanding the fact that the objections of our Legation in Bern were still outstanding and that British disapproval had already been expressed. State Department officials were in such a hurry to issue this license that they not only did not ask the Treasury to draft the license (which would have been normal procedure) but they drafted the license themselves and issued it without even consulting the Treasury as to its terms. Informal discussions with certain State Department officials have confirmed what is obvious from the above mentioned facts.

Breckinridge Long knew that his position was so indefensible that he was unwilling to even try to defend it at your pending conference with Secretary Hull on December 20. Accordingly, he took such action as he felt was necessary to "cover up" his previous position in this matter. It is, of course, clear that if we had not made the record against the State Department followed by your request to see Secretary Hull, the action which the State Department officials took on December 18 would either never have been taken at all or would have been delayed so long that any benefits which it might have had would have been lost.

III. *State Department officials not only have failed to facilitate the obtaining of information concerning Hitler's plans to exterminate the Jews of Europe but in their official capacity have gone so far as to surreptitiously attempt to stop the obtaining of information concerning the murder of the Jewish population in Europe.*

The evidence supporting this conclusion is so shocking and so tragic that it is difficult to believe.

A. *Sumner Welles as acting secretary of state requests confirmation of Hitler's plan to exterminate the Jews.* Having already received various reports on the plight of the Jews, on *October 5, 1942* Sumner Welles as acting secretary of state sent a cable (2314) for the personal attention of Minister Harrison in Bern stating that leaders of the Jewish Congress has received reports from their representatives in Geneva and London to the effect that many thousands of Jews in eastern Europe were being slaughtered pursuant to a policy embarked upon by the German government for the complete extermination of the Jews in Europe. Welles added that he was trying to obtain further information from the Vatican but that other than this he was unable to secure confirmation of these stories. He stated that Rabbi Wise believed that information was available to his representatives in Switzerland but that they were in all likelihood fearful of dispatching any such reports through open cables or mail. He then stated that Riegner and Lichtheim were being requested by Wise to call upon Minister Harrison; and Welles requested Minister Harrison to advise him by telegram of all the evidence and facts which he might secure as a result of conferences with Riegner and Lichtheim.

B. *State Department received confirmation and shocking evidence that the extermination was being rapidly and effectively carried out.* Pursuant to Welles's cable of October 5 Minister Harrison forwarded documents from Riegner confirming the fact of extermination of the Jews (in November 1942), and in a cable of January 21, 1943 (482) relayed a message from Riegner and Lichtheim which Harrison stated was for the information of the under secretary of state (and was to be transmitted to Rabbi Stephen Wise if the under secretary should so determine). *This message described a horrible situation concerning the plights of Jews in Europe.* It reported mass executions of Jews in Poland; according to one source 6,000 Jews were being killed daily; the Jews were required before execution to strip themselves of all their clothing which was then sent to Germany; the remaining Jews in Poland were confined to ghettos, etc.; in Germany deportations were continuing; many Jews were in hiding and there had been many cases of suicide; Jews were being deprived of rationed foodstuffs; no Jews would be left in Prague or Berlin by the end of March, etc.; and in Romania 180,000 Jews were deported to Transnistria; about 60,000 had already died and the remaining 70,000 were starving; living conditions were indescribable; Jews were deprived of all their money, foodstuffs and possessions; they were housed in deserted cellars, and occasionally twenty to thirty people slept on the floor of one unheated room; disease was prevalent, particularly fever; urgent assistance was needed.

C. *Sumner Welles furnished this information to the Jewish organizations.* Sumner Welles furnished the documents received in November to the Jewish organizations in the United States and authorized them to make the facts public. On *February 9, 1943* Welles forwarded the horrible message contained in cable 432 of January 21 to Rabbi Stephen Wise. In his letter of February 9 Welles stated that he was pleased to be of assistance in this matter.

Immediately upon the receipt of this message, the Jewish organizations arranged for a public mass meeting in Madison Square Garden in a further effort to obtain effective action.

D. *Certain State Department officials surreptitiously attempt to stop this government from obtaining further information from the very source from which the above evidence was received.* On February 10, the day after Welles forwarded the message contained in cable 482 of January 21 to Rabbi Wise, and in direct response to this cable, a most highly significant cable was dispatched. This cable, 354 of February 10, read as follows:

Your 482, January 21

In the future we would suggest that you do not accept reports submitted to you to be transmitted to private persons in the United Stated unless such action is advisable because of extraordinary circumstances. Such private messages circumvent neutral countries' censorship and it is felt that by sending them we risk the possibility that steps would necessarily be taken by the neutral countries to curtail or forbid our means of communication for confidential official matter.

Hull (SW)

Although this cable on its face is most innocent and innocuous, when read together with the previous cable I am forced to conclude it is nothing less than an attempted suppression of information requested by this government concerning the murder of Jews by Hitler.

Although this cable was signed for Hull by "SW" (Sumner Welles), *it is significant that there is not a word in the cable that would even suggest to the person signing it that it was designed to countermand the department's specific requests for information on Hitler's plan to exterminate the Jews.* The cable appeared to be a normal routine message which a busy official would sign without question.

I have been informed that the initialed file copy of the cable bears the initials of Atherton and Dunn as well as of Durbrow and Hickerson.

E. Thereafter Sumner Welles again requested our Legation on April 10, 1943 (cable 877) for information, apparently not realizing that in cable 354 (to which he did not refer) Harrison had been instructed to cease forwarding reports of this character. Harrison replied on April 20 (cable 280) and indicated that he was in most confused state of mind as a result of the conflicting instructions he had received. Among other things he stated: "May I suggest that message of this character should not (repeat not) be subjected to the restriction imposed by your 354, February 10, and that I be permitted to transmit messages from R more particularly in view of the helpful information which they may frequently contain?"

The fact that cable 354 is not the innocent and routine cable that it appears to be on its face is further highlighted by the efforts of State Department officials to prevent this department from obtaining the cable and learning its true significance.

The facts relating to this attempted concealment are as follows:

1. Several men in our department had requested State Department officials for a copy of the cable of February 10 (354). We had been advised that it was a department communication; a strictly political communication, which had nothing to do with economic matters; that it had only had a very limited distribution within the department, the only once having anything to do with it being the European Division, the political Advisor and Sumner Welles; and that a copy could not be furnished to the Treasury.

2. At the conference in Secretary Hull's office on December 20 in the presence of Breckinridge Long asked Secretary Hull for a copy of cable 354, which you [Henry Morgenthau] were told would be furnished to you.

3. By note to you of December 30, Breckinridge Long enclosed a paraphrase of cable 354. This paraphrase of cable 354 specifically *omitted*

any reference to cable 482 of January 21—thus destroying the only tangible clue to the true meaning of the message.

4. You would never have learned the true meaning of cable 354 had it not been for the fact that one of the men in my office whom I had asked to obtain all the facts on this matter for me had previously called one of the men in another division of the State Department and requested permission to see the cable. In view of the Treasury interest in this matter this State Department representative obtained cable 354 and the cable of January 21 to which it referred and showed these cables to my man.

IV. *The State Department officials have tried to cover up their guilt by:*

A. *concealment and misrepresentation.*

In addition to concealing the true facts from and misrepresenting these facts to the public, State Department officials have even attempted concealment and misrepresentation within the government. The most striking example of this is the above mentioned action taken by State Department officials to prevent this department from obtaining a copy of cable 354 of February 10 (which stopped the obtaining of information concerning the murder of Jews); and the fact that after you had requested a copy of this cable, State Department officials forwarded the cable to us with its most significant part omitted, thus destroying the whole meaning of the cable.

B. *the giving of false and misleading explanations for their failures to act and their attempts to prevent action.*

The outstanding explanation of a false and misleading nature which the State Department officials have given for their failures to work out programs to rescue Jews, and their attempts to prevent action, are the following:

1. The nice sounding but vicious theory that the *whole* refugee problem must be explored and consideration given to working out problems for the relief of *all* refugees—thus failing to distinguish between those refugees whose lives are in imminent danger and those whose lives are not in imminent danger.

2. The argument that various proposals cannot be acted upon promptly by this government but must be submitted to the Executive Committee of the Intergovernmental Committee on Refugees. This Committee had taken no effective action to actually evacuate refugees from enemy territory and it is at least open to doubt whether it has the necessary authority to deal with the matter.

3. The argument that the extreme restrictions which the State Department has placed on the granting of visas to refugees is necessary for "security reasons." The falsity of this argument has already been dealt with in the memorandum.

The false and misleading explanations, which the State Department officials gave for delaying for over six months the program of the World Jewish Congress for the evacuation of thousands of Jews from Romania and France, are dealt with in your letter to Secretary Hull of December 17, 1943.

A striking example is the argument of the State Department officials that the proposed financial arrangements might benefit the enemy. It is of course not surprising that the same State Department officials who usually argue that economic warfare considerations are not important should in this particular case attempt to rely on economic warfare considerations to kill the proposed program.

In this particular case, the State Department officials attempted to argue that the relief plan might benefit the enemy by facilitating the acquisition of funds by the enemy. In addition to the fact that this contention had no merit whatsoever by virtue of the conditions under which the local funds were to be acquired, it is significant that this consideration had not been regarded as controlling in the past by the State Department officials, even where no such conditions had been imposed.

Thus, in cases involving the purchase, by branches of United Stated concerns in Switzerland, of substantial amounts of material in enemy territory, State Department officials have argued that in view of the generous credit supplied by the Swiss to the Germans "transactions of this type cannot be regarded as actually increasing the enemy's purchasing power in Switzerland which is already believed to be at a maximum." It is only when these State Department officials really desire to prevent a transaction that they advance economic warfare considerations as a bar.

C. *the issuance of false and misleading statements concerning the "action" which they have taken to date.*

It is unnecessary to go beyond Long's testimony to find many examples of misstatements. His general pious remarks concerning what this government has done for the Jews of Europe; his statement concerning the powers and functions of the Intergovernmental Committee on Refugees; his reference to the "screening process" set up to insure wartime security, etc., have already been publicly criticized as misrepresentations.

A statement which is typical of the way Long twists facts is his remarks concerning the plan of a Jewish agency to send money to Switzerland to be used through the International Red Cross to buy food to take care of Jews in parts of Czechoslovakia and Poland. Long indicated that the Jewish agency requested that the money be sent through the instrumentality of the Intergovernmental Committee. I am informed that the Jewish agency wished to send the money immediately to the Intergovernmental Red Cross and it was Long who took the position that the matter would have to go through the Intergovernmental Committee, thereby delaying the matter indefinitely. Long speaks of an application having been filed with the Treasury to send some of this money and that the State Department was supporting this application to the Treasury. The facts are that no application has ever been filed with the Treasury and the State Department has at no time indicated to the Treasury that it would support any such application.

The most patent instance of a false and misleading statement is that part of Breckinridge Long's testimony before the Committee of Foreign Affairs of the House (November 26, 1948) relating to the admittance of refugees into this country. Thus, he stated:

> "We have taken into this country since the beginning of the Hitler regime and the persecution of the Jews, until today, approximately 580,000 refugees. The whole thing has been under the quota, during the period of ten years—all under the quota—except the generous gesture we made with visitors' and transit visas during an awful period."

Congressman Emanuel Celler, in commenting upon Long's statement in the House on December 20, 1943, stated:

> "In the first place these 500,000 refugees were in the main ordinary quota immigrants coming in from all countries. The majority were not Jews. His statement drips with sympathy for the persecuted Jews, but the tears he sheds are crocodile. I would like to a ask him how many Jews were admitted during the last three years in comparison with the number seeking entrance to preserve life and dignity. . . . One gets the impression from Long's statement that the United States has gone out of its way to help refugees fleeing death at the hands of Nazis. I deny this. On the contrary, the State Department has turned its back on the time-honored principle of granting havens to refugees. The tempest-tossed get little comfort from men like Breckinridge Long. . . . Long says that the door to the oppressed is open but that it 'has been carefully screened.' What he should have said is 'barlocked and bolted.' By the act of 1924, we are permitted to admit approximately 150,000 immigrants each year. During the last fiscal year only 23,725 came as immigrants. Of these only 4,705 were Jews fleeing Nazi persecution. . . .

> "If men of the temperament and philosophy of Long continue in control of immigration administration, we may as well take down that plaque from the Statue of Liberty and black out the 'lamp beside the golden door.'"

XIX. WHY AUSCHWITZ WAS NOT BOMBED

During the spring and summer of 1944, hundreds of thousands of Hungarian Jews were deported to Auschwitz/Birkenau. As many as ten thousand people a day were killed in its gas chambers.

Jewish leaders in Slovakia implored that Auschwitz be bombed. Requests were forwarded from American Jewish organizations, and the U.S. government's War Refugee

An American B-17 bomber over Auschwitz during a bombing run at the I.G. Farben refinery at Auschwitz III. Smithsonian Institution.

Board asked the Allies to take action. Though independently made, their requests were identical: Auschwitz must be bombed, or at the very least, the railway lines leading to death.

There were fierce debates among world Jewish leaders as to whether Auschwitz should be bombed. Some feared killing innocent civilians; some were afraid that the Germans would have a major propaganda advantage in blaming the Allies for Jewish casualties. Others did not—could not—fully perceive the reality of Auschwitz even as they were receiving accurate information confirming the worst of their fears, describing events beyond their imagination. The Jewish Agency in Palestine debated the issue at length and would not endorse the request. It instructed its chief proponent of bombing Auschwitz, Isaac Gruenbaum, to cease his activities. Even Leon Kubowitzki who forwarded the formal request to bomb Auschwitz to Assistant Secretary of War John J. McCloy was known to personally oppose the bombing. He wrote to the War Refugee Board opposing the bombing on July 1, 1944. Thus if Richard Levy, who has revisited the controversy is correct, the very fact that Kubowitzki forwarded this request, weakened it.

The requests to bomb Auschwitz were denied. Why?

The Americans offered several reasons: Auschwitz was not within the range of Allied bombers. . . . Resources should not be diverted from the war effort. . . . Bombing Auschwitz might provoke even more vindictive German actions.

There is a debate among historians and military analysts whether Auschwitz could have been bombed. In *The Abandonment of the Jews* David Wyman has argued that as early as May 1944, the U.S. Air Force could have struck Auschwitz at will. The rail lines from Hungary were also within range. On July 7, 1944, over four hundred American bombers traveled along the railway lines to Auschwitz. On August 20, 1944, 127 Flying Fortresses escorted by 100 Mustang fighters dropped 1,336 five-hundred-pound bombs on a factory less than five miles east of Auschwitz. However, Wyman's readings of military capacity have been disputed. Others have argued that the operation would have been hazardous, bombing impossible, and it would have been uncertain at best if the planes could have returned to base.

Still, the industrial targets at Auschwitz III, Buna-Monowitz were targeted, yet the death camp and the railway lines leading to it remained untouched.

In August 1944, Assistant Secretary of War John J. McCloy wrote to Leon Kubowitzki of the World Jewish Congress:

> The War Department has been approached by the War Refugee Board which raised the question of the practicability of this suggestion [of bombing Auschwitz]. After a study it became apparent that such an operation could be executed only by the diversion of considerable air forces now engaged in decisive operations elsewhere and would be of such doubtful efficacy that it would not warrant the use of our resources. There has been considerable opinion to the effect that such an effort, even if practicable, might provoke even more vindictive action by the Germans.

McCloy was less than candid: there had been no study on bombing Auschwitz.

Instead, the War Department had decided, in January 1944, that units of the Armed Forces would not be "employed for the purpose of rescuing victims of enemy oppression" unless such rescues arose in the course of routine military operations.

An internal U.S. War Department memo of February 1944 further advised: "We must constantly bear in mind that the most effective relief which can be given the victims of enemy persecution is to insure the speedy defeat of the Axis."

Yet, the defeat of the Axis fifteen months later came too late for the two million murdered in 1944–45. Bombing Auschwitz may have retarded the killing process and saved lives. It may have expressed an American outrage.

By 1944, American government officials had been informed about the details of the killing centers. One wonders how much more vindictive could the Nazis have become?

In his memoir, *Night*, Elie Wiesel recalled the bombing of Buna-Monowitz, which was also called Auschwitz III, the slave labor camp some five kilometers from Auschwitz:

> Then we began to hear the airplanes. Almost at once, the barracks began to shake.
>
> "They're bombing Buna!" someone shouted. I thought of my father. But I was glad all the same. To see the whole works go up in fire—what revenge.
>
> . . . We were not afraid. And yet if a bomb had fallen on the blocks, it would have claimed hundreds of victims on the spot. But we were no longer afraid of death; at any rate, not of that death. Every bomb that exploded filled us with joy and gave us new confidence in life.

In the documents below, we reprint the correspondence between Kubowitzki and McCloy; the report of the discussion between the United States Consul General in Palestine and Isaac Gruenbaum; an internal document of the War Refugee Board that pressed for the bombing; the letter of Kubowitzki to John Pehle, head of the War Refugee Board opposing the bombing; a note on the proposal for bombing the death camps; and a report of the Jewish Agency opposing the bombing saying, "We should not ask the Allies to bomb places where there are Jews."

REPORT ON A DISCUSSION BETWEEN ISAAC GRUENBAUM AND MR. PINKERTON, AMERICAN CONSUL GENERAL IN THE LAND OF ISRAEL [PALESTINE].

THURSDAY, JUNE 2, 1944, AT THE AMERICAN CONSULATE

JUNE 7, 1944, JERUSALEM

Mr. Gruenbaum opened the discussion by stating that Mr. A. Dubkin informed him of Mr. P. Lakavmal's [?] desire from a while ago to obtain authoritative information on the development of matters relating to the question of rescue. Thus he [Gruenbaum] is now passing on the latest pieces of news received, and requesting that the [American] consul, Mr. Pinkerton, pass these on to his government. He [Gruenbaum] passed on a detailed description of how things are going in Romania, and on the rescue activities of Jews from there. He expressed his opinion that the widespread publicity given to Mr. Hirschmann's activities have hurt him in a significant way, in terms of his own work. And especially his talking about *"gesher aniyot"* (bridge of ships) that took Jews out of countries of oppression to countries of freedom. It is they who angered the Germans, and it is now as if they are eager to show that the Americans are not able to give real aid to the Jews under the yoke of the Nazis. He requested that the consul pass this information on to his government.

The consul commented that this matter was already known to him. He requested that what was said on individuals involved in rescue should not turn into an attack on the War Refugee Board of the U.S. Attacks such as these could only serve to hurt the efforts. It is permissible for me—he said—to attack Mr. Gruenbaum, but it is not permissible for me to talk against the Jewish Agency.

Mr. Gruenbaum switched to the matter of the Turkish ship intended to transport Jewish refugees from Romania. The agreement on this ship was reached on the basis of American responsibility [America as guarantor] that if the ship sinks another one will be supplied to Turkey in its place. Mr. Gruenbaum claimed that after all the publicity given to the ship, he is doubtful as to whether there is really anything to this offer. Instead of this arrangement, he would suggest that pressure be put on the Turks to provide another Turkish ship, under the same conditions, for the very same goal, in order that it should sail without a guarantee from an enemy party, so that they shouldn't [intentionally] sink it. The American consul wrote down these remarks and promised to present them to his government.

Mr. Gruenbaum switched to the matter of Hungary. He described the situation according to the latest news received. He focused primarily on the expulsion [deportation] of Jews from Hungary to Poland and emphasized the peril foreseen for these Jews, which the Germans began by deportation and persecution the same way they did in Poland [to the Jews in Poland]. He suggests:

A. that a stringent warning be given to Hungary (the American consul writes this down to pass on to Washington)

B. that the American air force receive instructions to bomb the death camps in Poland.

On this matter, Pinkerton brought up the following point: Won't bombing the camps also cause the death of many Jews? And isn't there the concern that German propaganda will spread news that here also Americans are taking part in the destruction of the Jews?

Mr. Gruenbaum answered, that in spite of all this, he sees this operation [the bombing of the death camps] as desirable, because in any event the Jews concentrated in the death camps are destined to die, and maybe with the havoc that would be caused by bombing the camp, some Jews will be able to escape. This and more: The establishment of the camps cost the Germans greatly in financial expense and labor forces, and thus the camps' destruction might disrupt the mass killing process and deter the Germans from building similar death camps in the future, and what's more, bombing the camps will cost the Germans the loss of their manpower who guard the camps.

After a brief argument over this suggestion, Mr. Pinkerton stated that he will *not* pass on this suggestion to Washington. Pinkerton advises Gruenbaum to present his suggestion [to bomb the death camps] in writing.

Gruenbaum then suggested bombing the railroad lines between Budapest and Poland. This suggestion, Mr. Pinkerton promised to pass on to his government.

Mr. Gruenbaum suggested to make all efforts to influence Marshall Tito to permit Jews from Hungary and neighboring countries to cross over the borders into his country. The consul mentioned the lack of coordination of labor among the various divisions of the Jewish Agency. A separate division should deal with the issue at hand and he hopes to receive a detailed memo on this issue. Mr. Gruenbaum stated that he was aware of the situation. In any event he wanted to emphasize the point [of bombing the tracks].

Gruenbaum suggested, in relation to the situation in Hungary, that the Allied powers request from the International Red Cross that its employees in Budapest come up with authorized, documented and detailed pieces of news on what is taking place there with the Jews, for this will serve as a pipeline for the passing on of material aid (e.g. food, etc.) for Jews in Hungary. The consul promised to do this.

Within this discussion, Mr. Gruenbaum spoke of the situation in Bulgaria, which also may take on a serious character in the near future. Gruenbaum suggested that a warning be given to Bulgaria, and that it be made possible to send boats over there—since this is being done with Romania. The consul also wrote down this request.

At the conclusion of the discussion, Mr. T[?] Shimsor[?] stated that all these suggestions for the War Refugee Board in Washington were not in his name, but rather in that of Mr. Gruenbaum.

PROTOCOL OF THE JEWISH AGENCY EXECUTIVE MEETING

JERUSALEM, JUNE 11, 1944

Confidential
No. 51
PROTOCOL
Meeting of the Executive of the Jewish Agency.
Jerusalem, June 11, 1944.

Present at meeting: Mr. Ben-Gurion, chairman; Mr. Gruenbaum; Dr. Santor; Rabbi Fishman; Mr. Kaplan; Dr. Schmorak; Dr. Yosef; Mr. Shapira; Mr. Ben-Zvi; Dr. Hentke; Dr. Granovsky; Mr. Eisenberg
    Agenda:

1. Rescue Matters
2. Conversation between Mr. Gruenbaum and Mr. Pinkerton on Rescue Matters
3. Section on Immigrant Absorption

2. CONVERSATION BETWEEN MR. GRUENBAUM AND MR. PINKERTON [AMERICAN CONSUL] ON RESCUE MATTERS

MR. GRUENBAUM: I sent to [Jewish Agency] Executive members notes of my meeting on rescue matters with the General American Consul [Pinkerton]. Among other things I proposed that the Allies bomb the railroad tracks between Hungary and Poland. The Germans are expelling [deporting] twelve thousand Jews a day from Hungary to Poland. If they [the Allies] would destroy the railroad tracks, the Germans would be unable for a protracted period of time to carry out their plan.

Mr. Pinkerton promised to relay the proposal to the War Refugee Board.

Also proposed to Mr. Pinkerton was that the Allied air forces bomb the death camps in Poland, such as: Oswiecim, Treblinka, etc. Mr. Pinkerton claimed that if this would be carried out the Allies will be blamed in the murder of Jews and thus requested that the proposal be presented to him in writing. I [Gruenbaum] promised to consult my colleagues on this matter.

According to our information thousands of Jews are murdered daily in the death camps in Poland. Only the forced laborers are left alive for a certain amount of time. The victims' bodies are not left to be buried [they're cremated]. Even if we also take into account the fact that if the tracks are bombed while there are Jews on them a portion of them will be killed, the other portion will be able to disperse [run away] and be saved. By the destruction of buildings, they [the Germans] will be unable for a number of months to implement their systematic murder plans.

We received today a piece of information that during ten days 120,000 Jews were expelled [deported] from Hungary.

MR. BEN-GURION: We do not know the truth concerning the entire situation in Poland, and it seems that we will be unable to propose anything concerning this matter.

RABBI FISHMAN: Concurs with Ben-Gurion on this point.

DR. SCHMORAK: It is currently relayed that in Oswiecim exists a large labor camp. It is forbidden for us to take responsibility for a bombing that could very well cause the death of even one Jew.

DR. YOSEF: Also opposes the proposal to request that the Americans bomb the camps, and thus cause the murder of Jews.

Mr. Gruenbaum is not speaking as a private individual, but rather as an institution spokesman. It seems that also the institution to which we are connected should be prohibited from making such a proposal.

DR. SANTOR: Concurs with Dr. Yosef on this point. It is regrettable that Mr. Gruenbaum spoke at all on this matter with the American consul.

CHAIRMAN BEN-GURION: [Summation] The opinion of the Jewish Agency's Executive Committee is not to propose to the Allies the bombing of sites in which Jews are located.

Selection on the ramp of Auschwitz-Birkenau. An SS man examines a Hungarian Jew to determine if he is strong enough for labor. A Jewish women is walking to the right, to slave labor and not immediate gassing. Yad Vashem/Courtesy of USHMM–Photo Archives.

INTERNAL MEMO OF THE WAR REFUGEE BOARD PRESSING FOR THE BOMBING OF AUSCHWITZ

Letterhead—Executive Office of the President,
WAR REFUGEE BOARD, Inter-office
Communication
To: L.S. Lesser
From: B. Akzin
Dated June 29, 1944

By Cable No. 4041 of June 21, from Bern, McClelland, reporting on the deportation and extermination of Hungarian Jews, states that "there is little doubt that many of these Hungarian Jews are being sent to the extermination camps of AUSCHWITZ (OSWIECIM) and BIRKENAU (RAJSKA) in Western Upper Silesia where xZaccording to recent reports, since early summer 1942 at least 1,500,000 Jews have been killed. There is evidence that already in January 1944 preparations were being made to receive and exterminate Hungarian Jews in these camps."

In view of the preeminent part evidently played by these two extermination camps in the massacre of Jews, equipped to kill 125,000 people per month, it would seem that the destruction of their physical installations might appreciably slow down the systematic slaughter at least temporarily. The methodical German mind might require some time to rebuild the installations or to evolve elsewhere equally efficient procedures of mass slaughter and of disposing of the bodies. Some saving of lives would therefore be a most likely result of the destruction of the two extermination camps.

Though no exaggerated hopes should be entertained, this saving of lives might even be quite appreciable, since, in the present stage of the war, with German manpower and material resources gravely depleted, German authorities might not be in a position to devote themselves to the task of equipping new large-scale extermination centers.

Aside from the preventive significance of the destruction of the two camps, it would also seem correct to mark them for destruction as a matter of principle, as the most tangible—and perhaps only tangible—evidence of the indignation aroused by the existence of these charnel houses. It will also be noted that the destruction of the extermination camps would presumably cause many deaths among their personnel—certainly among the most ruthless and despicable of the Nazis.

It is suggested that the foregoing be brought to the attention of the appropriate political and military authorities, with a view to considering the feasibility of a thorough destruction of the two camps by aerial bombardment. It may be of interest, in this connection, that the two camps are situated in the industrial region of Upper Silesia, near the important mining and manufacturing centers of Katowice and Chorzow (Oswiecim lies about fourteen miles southeast of Katowice), which play an important part in the industrial armament of Germany. Therefore, the destruction of these camps could be achieved without deflecting aerial strength from an important zone of military objectives.

Presumably, a large number of Jews in these camps may be killed in the course of such bombings (though some of them may escape in the confusion). But such Jews are doomed to death anyhow. The destruction of the camps would not change their fate, but it would serve as visible retribution on their murderers and it might save the lives of future victims.

It will be noted that the inevitable fate of Jews herded in ghettos near the industrial and railroad installations in Hungary has not caused the United Nations to stop bombing these installations. It is submitted, therefore, that refraining from bombing the extermination centers would be sheer misplaced sentimentality, far more cruel than a decision to destroy these centers.

[signed B.A.]

LETTER FROM LEON KUBOWITZKI TO JOHN PEHLE

letterhead of the WORLD JEWISH CONGRESS
July 1, 1944
In reply refer
to No. 126
Hon. John W. Pehle
War Refugee Board
Treasury Building
Washington, D.C.

Dear Mr. Pehle:

May I come back to the suggestion I made to Mr. Lesser in the course of the conference I had with him on June 28.

Discussing the apparent determination of the German government to speed up the extermination of the Jews, I wondered whether the pace of the extermination could not be considerably slowed down if the instruments of annihilation—the gas chambers, the gas vans, the death baths—were destroyed. You will remember that in August and October, 1943, respectively, revolting Jews set fire to installations in Treblinka and Sobibor. The revolt culminated in the escape of a large number of Jews from these camps.

Three governments are directly interested in stopping the massacres: the Soviet government, whose captured soldiers are being exterminated in the Oswiecim gas chambers, according to a cable received by the Polish Information Center on June 22, a copy of which is attached; the Czechoslovak government, whose citizens are being murdered in Birkenau; and the Polish government, for obvious reasons.

The destruction of the death installations cannot be done by bombing from the air, as the first victims would be the Jews who are gathered in these camps, and such a bombing would be a welcome pretext for the Germans to assert that their Jewish victims have been massacred not by their killers, but by the Allied bombings.

I submitted to Mr. Lesser that the Soviet government be approached with the request that it should dispatch groups of paratroopers to seize the buildings, to annihilate the squads of murderers, and to free the unfortunate inmates. Also that the Polish government be requested to instruct the Polish underground to attack these and similar camps to destroy the instruments of death.

May I add that it would be useful to approach also the Czechoslovak government, so that it may use its influence with the Soviet and Polish governments to support our request.

May I express the hope that you will consider the suggestion made in this letter as deserving to be acted upon without delay.

Sincerely yours,
[signed]
A. LEON KUBOWITZKI

Head, Rescue Department
ALE:bg
P.S. I attach a report, "Three Years in Oswiecim Hell," published by the Polish Jewish Observer *on June 16.*

NOTE ON THE PROPOSAL FOR BOMBING THE DEATH CAMPS

1. According to reports received, most, if not practically all, of the 400,000 Jews deported from Hungary, have been or are being sent to the death camps of Birkenau and Oswiecim in Upper Silesia, there to be put to death. A message received via Geneva puts the number of Jews killed in these camps during last year at 2,500,000 and states that the four crematoria at Birkenau have a capacity for gassing and burning 60,000 a day (this may be an error in transmission, the real figure being possibly 6,000). A report which has reached the Polish government from underground sources speaks of Hungarian Jews being killed by gas in two chambers, each holding 1,000 persons, the corpses being burnt in four crematoria and on piles. According to the same report, the deportees believe that they are being taken to Germany eventually to be exchanged against German prisoners of war, and let out into Allied territories; this belief being strengthened by optimistic letters received in Hungary from a group of 2,000 Hungarian Jews kept for the time being at Gliwice. All information points to the fact that deportees are put to death immediately on arrival. A detailed description of the two camps, contained in a report submitted to Allied governments and published by the Jewish Telegraphic Agency, is attached. It is understood that this report (received since the original suggestion for bombing was made) emanated from Czech underground sources. Its reading repays the effort.

2. The bombing of the death camps is thus hardly likely to achieve the salvation of the victims to any appreciable extent. Its physical efforts can only be the destruction of plant and personnel, and possibly the hastening of the end of those already doomed. The resulting dislocation of the machinery for systematic wholesale murder may possibly cause delay in the execution of those still in Hungary (over 300,000 in and around Budapest). This in itself is valuable as far as it goes, it may not go very far, as other means of extermination can be quickly improvised. The main purpose of the bombing should be its many-sided and far-reaching moral effect.

3. It would seem, in the first instance, that the Allies waged direct war on the extermination of the victims of Nazi oppression—today Jews, tomorrow Poles, Czechs, or whatever race may become the victim of mass murder during the German retreat and collapse. Secondly, it would give the lie to the oft-repeated assertions of Nazi spokesmen that the Allies are not really so displeased with the work of the Nazis in ridding Europe of Jews. Thirdly, it would go far towards dissipating the incredulity which still persists in Allied quarters with regard to the reports of mass extermination perpetrated by the Nazis. Fourthly, it would give weight to the threats of reprisals against the murders, by showing that the Allies are taking the extermination of Jews so seriously as to warrant the allocation of aircraft resources for this particular operation, and thus have a deterrent effect. Lastly, it would convince the German circles still hopeful of Allied mercy of the genuineness of Allied opposition to the murder of Jews, and possibly result in some internal pressure against a continuation of the massacres. The first report that the RAF or the American air force had bombed the death camps in Upper Silesia is bound to have a demonstration value in all these directions.

4. Special attention may be drawn to the fact (mentioned in the enclosed report) that the Oswiecim camp contains workshops of the German armament concerns and Krupp.

London,
11.7.44.

An Exchange of Letters between Leon Kubowitzki and John J. McCloy

WORLD JEWISH CONGRESS
CONGRESS JUIF MONDIAL CONGRESO JUDIO
   MUNDIAL
1834 BROADWAY
NEW YORK, 25, N.Y.
August 9, 1944
Hon. John J. McCloy
Assistant Secretary of War
War Department
Washington, D.C.

My dear Mr. Secretary:

I beg to submit to your consideration the following excerpt from a message which we received under date of July 29 from Mr. Ernest Frischer of the Czechoslovak State Council through the War Refugee Board:

> I believe that destruction of gas chambers and crematoria in Oswiecim by bombing would have a certain effect now. Germans are now exhuming and burning corpses in an effort to conceal their crimes. This could be prevented by destruction of crematoria and then Germans might possibly stop further mass exterminations especially since so little time is left to them. Bombing of railway communications in this same area would also be of importance and of military interest.

Sincerely yours,
A. LEON KUBOWITZKI

Head, Rescue Department
ALK:dl

14 August 1944

Dear Mr. Kubowitski:

I refer to your letter of August 9 in which you request considerations of a proposal made by Mr. Ernest Frischer that certain installations and railroad centers be bombed.

This War Department has been approached by the War Refugee Board, which raised the question of the practicability of this suggestion. After a study it became apparent that such an operation could be executed only by the diversion of considerable air support essential to the success of our forces now engaged in decisive operations elsewhere and would in any case be of such doubtful efficacy that it would not warrant the use of our resources. There has been considerable opinion to the effect that such an effort, even if practicable, might provoke even more vindictive action by the Germans.

The War Department fully appreciated the humanitarian motives which prompted the suggested operations, but for the reasons stated above it has not been felt that it can or should be undertaken, at least at this time.

Sincerely,
JOHN J. MCCLOY

Assistant Secretary of War
MR. A. LEON KUBOWITSKI

Head, Rescue Department
World Jewish Congress
1834 Broadway
New York 29, N.Y.

XX. LIBERATION AND ITS AFTERMATH

AMERICANS ENTER THE CONCENTRATION CAMPS

In the final days of the war in April and May 1945, American soldiers entered the Nazi concentration camps. Ohrdruf, Nordhausen, Buchenwald, Dachau, and Mauthausen—these were not ordinary stops in the march to victory. American soldiers happened upon the camps in the course of battle; the concentration camps were not their targets, they were unexpected, accidental discoveries. After years of combat, veterans thought they

Corpses in Gunkirchen, a subcamp of Mauthausen, Austria, shortly after the camp was liberated by the 71st Infantry Division of the 3rd U.S. Army on May 6, 1945. National Archives/Courtesy of USHMM–Photo Archives.

had seen the worst, yet when they came upon these camps, they discovered something for which they were totally unprepared emotionally or psychologically.

They should not have been unprepared. Soviet soldiers had liberated Majdanek in July 1944, and Auschwitz in January 1945, months before the Americans came across the western camps.

Yet American troops were unprepared for what they were to see. They saw piles of corpses stacked like cordwood, bodies strewn, rotting in the April sun, and the living skeletons of those who had survived. Everywhere the stench of death.

Numbness set in. A liberator reported: "I saw death everywhere, and before I left the camp that evening I saw it reduced to such ordinariness that it left me with nothing, not even sickness in my stomach."

We will read the firsthand account of a man who entered the camps: the testimony of an ordinary soldier, Captain J. D. Pletcher of Berwyn, Illinois, who happened to come upon Gunskirchen, a subcamp of Mauthausen, on liberation day.

Liberation was the first step; the end of one stage, the beginning of another. As one survivor, Hadassah Bimko Rosensaft, put it, "We [survivors of Bergen-Belsen] had been liberated from death and from the fear of death, but we were not free from the fear of life."

DISPLACED PERSONS

As the war ended, Allied armies found approximately seven to nine million people displaced from their countries of origin as a result of the war. But within months, more than six million people returned to their native lands.

More than one million refused repatriation; they were mainly Poles, Estonians, Latvians, Lithuanians, Ukrainians, and Yugoslavs. Non-Jews feared political retaliation for their wartime activities—some had collaborated—while others were wary of persecution by Communist regimes.

Jewish survivors could not return home. Their communities were decimated, their homes destroyed or occupied by strangers, the lands of their birth inhospitable to their return. Some returned home briefly to search for relatives. They were confronted with the magnitude of their losses. Their families were gone, their towns were without Jews, their neighbors were less than neighborly. With nowhere to go, they were forced to stay in the camps adjacent to the places of their liberation. For most survivors, that entailed a prolonged stay in Germany, living alongside those who had sought to impose the Final Solution.

The American army was beleaguered. Trained for war, they had to juggle multiple assignments: the occupation, the cold war, and the problems of survivors who were naturally distrustful of all authority and in need of medical and psychological attention.

Short-term problems, such as housing, medical treatment, food, and family reunification, were acute. The army had no long-term strategy. The survivors had nowhere to go. Britain was unwilling to permit Jewish immigration to Palestine and the United States was not ready to receive refugees.

Within weeks of taking office President Harry Truman dispatched Earl Harrison, a law school dean, to report on the Displaced Persons Camp.

His conclusions were harsh, even overstated:

We appear to be treating the Jews as the Nazis treated them except that we do not exterminate them. They are in concentration camps in large numbers under our military guard instead of SS troops. One is led to wonder whether the German people seeing this are not supposing that we are following or at least condoning Nazi policy.

His recommendations were equally dramatic: "Jews must be recognized as Jews. They should be evacuated from Germany quickly. One hundred thousand Jews should be admitted to Palestine." President Truman endorsed the report, rebuked the army, and intensified pressure on Britain. He opened up the United States for limited immigration.

In response to growing international pressure the British called for an Anglo-American Commission of Inquiry consisting of six Americans and six British commissioners.

The commission was deeply shocked by conditions in the camps. But they were impressed by the desire of Jewish DPs to go to Palestine. They, too, recommended that one hundred thousand Jews be admitted immediately to Palestine.

The British government demurred. Foreign Minister Bevin wryly commented "the Americans wanted one hundred thousand Jews in Palestine because they didn't want them in New York."

On December 22, 1945, President Truman authorized preferential treatment to DPs to immigrate to the United States. Within eighteen months 22,950 DPs were admitted to the U.S.; 15,478 of them Jews.

In the summer of 1946 one hundred thousand Polish Jews released from Russia and Jews escaping from Eastern Europe after the Kielce pogrom flooded the American Zone of occupation. The DP problem could not be solved merely by adjusting quotas. Congressional action was required.

The American Jewish community successfully marshaled its allies at home to overcome domestic nativistic and anti-Semitic forces that wanted to limit immigration. The Protestant Federal Council of Churches and the Catholic publication *Commonweal* endorsed a liberalized immigration law to bring four hundred thousand DPs to the United States within four years. The political struggle was intense.

The first bill to pass Congress in 1948, which called for two hundred thousand displaced persons to be admitted over four years, was, in the words of President Truman, "flagrantly discriminatory against Jews." In 1950, Congress amended the bill to make it slightly less discriminatory. A year earlier, most of the Jewish DPs had gone to the newly established state of Israel.

Of the forty-one thousand emigrés admitted to the United States up until 1948 two-thirds were Jews. Over the next four years 365,223 displaced persons were brought to American shores—47 percent were Roman Catholic and only 16 percent Jews. Some displaced persons admitted to the United States had openly collaborated with the Nazis.

Altogether fewer than one hundred thousand Jews reached the United States in the postwar years before the last DP camp was closed in Foerhrenwald on February 28, 1957.

Yet in retrospect, the 1948 legislation was a turning point in American policy. The DP legislation was a precedent for subsequent responses to refugee crises such as the Hungarians in 1957, the Cubans in 1960, and the Vietnamese in 1979.

In the documents that follow we will read accounts of liberation and its aftermath: the Harrison Report, the response of President Truman to General Eisenhower, and Eisenhower's reply. We will also read sections from General Patton's *Diary* which depict his response to a visit to a DP camp and his physical revulsion at the appearance of its inhabitants. Perhaps Patton's writings tell us much of what led to the situation in the camps.

A REPORT FROM GUNSKIRCHEN BY CAPTAIN J. D. PLETCHER
MAY 1945

Capt. J. D. Pletcher, Berwyn, Ill, of the 71st Division Headquarters and Cpl. James DeSpain, Allegan, Michigan, arrived at Gunskirchen Lager the same morning the camp was found by elements of the Division. Capt. Pletcher's account of the scenes he witnessed follows.

When the German SS troops guarding the concentration camp at Gunskirchen heard the Americans were coming, they suddenly got busy burying the bodies of their victims—or rather having them buried by inmates—and gave the prisoners who were still alive what they considered an extremely liberal food ration: one lump of sugar per person and one loaf of bread for every seven persons. Then, two days or a day and half before we arrived, the SS left. All this I learned from talking to inmates of the camp, many of whom spoke English. Driving up to the camp in our jeep, Cpl. DeSpain and I first knew we were approaching the camp by the hundreds of starving, half-crazed inmates lining the roads, begging for food and cigarettes. Many of them had been able to get only a few hundred yards from the gate before they keeled over and died. As weak as they were, the chance to be free, the opportunity to escape was so great they couldn't resist, though it meant staggering only a few yards before death came.

Then came the next indication of the camp's nearness—the smell. There was something about the smell of Gunskirchen I shall never forget. It was strong, yes, and permeating, too. Some six hours after we left the place, six hours spent riding in a jeep, where the wind was whistling

around us, we could still detect the Gunskirchen smell. It had permeated our clothing, and stayed with us.

Of all the horrors of the place, the smell, perhaps, was the most startling of all. It was a smell made up of all kinds of odors: human excreta, foul bodily odors, smoldering trash fires, German tobacco—which is a stink in itself—all mixed together in a heavy dank atmosphere, in a thick, muddy woods, where little breeze could go. The ground was pulpy throughout the camp, churned to a consistency of warm putty by the milling of thousands of feet, mud mixed with feces and urine. The smell of Gunskirchen nauseated many of the Americans who went there. It was a smell I'll never forget, completely different from anything I've ever encountered. It could almost be seen and hung over the camp like a fog of death.

As we entered the camp, the living skeletons still able to walk crowded around us and, though we wanted to drive farther into the place, the milling, pressing crowd wouldn't let us. It is not an exaggeration to say that almost every inmate was insane with hunger. Just the sight of an American brought cheers, groans and shrieks. People crowded around to touch an American, to touch the jeep, to kiss our arms—perhaps just to make sure that it was true. The people who couldn't walk crawled out toward our jeep. Those who couldn't even crawl propped themselves up on an elbow, and somehow, through all their pain and suffering, revealed through their eyes the gratitude and joy they felt at the arrival of Americans.

An English-speaking inmate offered to show

us around the camp. We accepted his offer. Another inmate organizer asked me if he could climb on the jeep to say a few words to his people. We helped him up on the hood and he yelled for order. He spoke in his native tongue—Hungarian, I believe—and my guide interpreted for us. He was asking the inmates to remain in the camp and not clutter up the roads, some three thousand had already left, and he wanted his fellow prisoners to help the Yanks by staying off the roads. He told them that the Americans were bringing food and water and medical help. After every sentence he was interrupted by loud cheers from the crowd. It was almost like a political speech. Everyone was hysterical with joy at being found by the Americans, yet in a frenzy of hunger, for they had had no food since the Germans left two days before, and not enough to keep anyone alive for months before.

During the talk of the man on our jeep hood, a tall, blond-haired man approached me. He spoke excellent English. He was an engineer, educated in New York. He had committed the crime of letting Jewish blood infiltrate into his family stream some generations back. As hungry as he was for food, he was hungry for news. He said the camp inmates had known all about the movements of the Yanks for the past five days. Every day they had known we were coming closer, and as we approached, the anticipation in the stinking hole of Gunskirchen heightened. Through the last few, foodless days, the inmates had lived on faith alone, he said. Faith that the Americans would come soon. He was vitally interested in knowing about all phases of the European War. He asked about the other armies, how far they had advanced, how fast they were moving, about the Russians. He eagerly listened to all the news I could give him.

The man on the jeep hood spoke for about five minutes. At the completion he asked the people to clear the road so that we might proceed. Many of the more energetic waved the cheering crowds back to clear a path just wide enough for our vehicle.

All wanted to get close enough to see and many wanted to touch us as we moved slowly on. It was like a triumphal procession with the milling crowd cheering and waving their arms in exaltation.

The thousands of prisoners had been crammed into a few low, one-story, frame buildings with sloppy, muddy floors. Those who were able had come out of the buildings, but there were hundreds left in them—the dead, the near-dead, and those too weak to move. Sometimes, my guide said, it was so crowded in the buildings that people slept three-deep on the floor, one on top of the other. Often, a man would awake in the morning and find the person under him dead. Too weak to move even the pathetically light bodies of their comrades, the living continued sleeping on them.

I want to make it clear that human beings subjected to the treatment these people were given by the Germans results in a return to the primitive. Dire hunger does strange things. The inmates of Gunskirchen were a select group of prisoners—the intellectual class of Hungarian Jews, for the most part, professional people, many distinguished doctors, lawyers, representatives of every skilled field. Yet, these people, who would naturally be expected to maintain their sense of values, their human qualities, longer than any others, had been reduced to animals by the treatment of the Germans. The deliberate prolonged starvation, the indiscriminate murder on little or no provocation, the unbelievable living conditions gradually brought about a change in even the strongest.

The camp was littered with bodies. Since the Germans had left, the inmates had been unable to cope with the swiftly mounting death rate. As long as the SS men were in charge, they made the stronger inmates dig crude pits and bury the dead, not for sanitary reasons, but in an attempt to hide some of the evidence of the inhuman treatment given their prisoners.

For the thousands of prisoners in Gunskirchen, there was one twenty-hole latrine. The rule of the SS men was to shoot on sight anyone seen relieving himself in anyplace but the latrine. Many of the persons in the camp had diarrhea. There were always long lines at the latrine and it was often impossible for many to reach it in time because of hours spent waiting. Naturally, many were shot for they could not wait in line. Their bodies were still lying there in their own filth. The stench was unbelievable.

Cpl. DeSpain and I both remarked later about the appearance of the inmates—that they all seemed to look alike. When men are reduced to skeletons, as these men were, they all resembled one another—the only difference being in their height and the color of their hair.

My guide explained that many of the new prisoners at Gunskirchen had recently been forced to march from the vicinity of Hungary to Gunskirchen. There was very little food. They died like flies. If they fell out and were too weak to continue, the SS men shot them. The air-line distance from the Hungarian border to Gunskirchen is 150 miles. The intervening territory is full of mountains and winding roads, so the actual distance these people walked was far greater than 150 miles. It is not hard to imagine the thousands of skeletons that mark their route.

The hunger in evidence is hard to imagine. We found huge animal bones in camp—the bones of a horse or cow the prisoners had found and smuggled into camp. Usually these prizes were eaten raw, the flesh torn from the bones and swallowed in great gulps.

Rarely did a prisoner have the strength to curb his hunger long enough to cook what food he got. Outside the gate of the camp was the carcass of a horse that had been killed by shellfire. There was a great gaping wound in his belly. As we passed it, one of the inmates was down on his knees, eating off the carcass. It had been dead several days. The next day when we came back, the whole side had been sliced away. Though our troops got food to them as soon as possible, many could not wait. Of course, we quickly gave away all the rations and cigarettes we had. It was strange to see them eat the cigarettes instead of smoking them. Not one cigarette did I see smoked. They were all swallowed in a hurry.

American troops soon organized things. Water was hauled in German tank wagons. All horses and wagons in the vicinity were put on a food hauling detail. We found a German food warehouse three miles from Gunskirchen stocked with dried noodles, potatoes, soups, meats and other food. German civilians took it to Gunskirchen under the supervision of American military government personnel, and before we could establish proper control some of the prisoners had gobbled down the food, gorged themselves and died. A starving person must learn to eat all over again.

None of the inmates of Gunskirchen will ever be the same again. I doubt if any of us who saw it will ever forget it—the smell, the hundreds of bodies that looked like caricatures of human beings, the frenzy of the thousands when they knew the Americans had arrived at last, the spark of joy in the eyes of those who lay in the ditches and whispered a prayer of thanks with their last breaths. I felt, the day I saw Gunskirchen Lager, that I finally knew what I was fighting for. What the war was all about.

Excerpts of Report by Earl G. Harrison to President Harry S Truman

Text of Report By Earl G. Harrison
London, England
The White House, Washington.

Dear Mr. President:

Pursuant to your letter of June 22, 1945, I have the honor to present to you a partial report upon my recent mission to Europe to inquire into (1) the conditions under which displaced persons, and particularly those who may be stateless or non-repatriable, are at present living, especially in Germany and Austria, (2) the needs of such persons, (3) how those needs are being met at present by the military authorities, the governments of residence, and international and private relief bodies, and (4) the views of the possibly non-repatriable persons as to their future destinations.

My instructions were to give particular attention to the problems, needs and views of the Jewish refugees among the displaced people, especially in Germany and Austria. The report, particularly this partial report, accordingly deals in the main with that group.

On numerous occasions appreciation was expressed by the victims of Nazi persecution for the interest of the United States government in them. As my report shows, they are in need of attention and help. Up to this point, they have been "liberated" more in a military sense than actually.

For the reasons explained in the report their particular problems to this time have not been given attention to any appreciable extent; consequently, they feel that they, who were in so many ways the first and worst victims of Nazism, are being neglected by their liberators.

Upon my request the Department of State authorized Dr. Joseph J. Schwartz to join me in the mission. Dr. Schwartz, European director of the American Joint Distribution Committee, was granted a leave of absence from that organization for the purpose of accompanying me. His long and varied experience in refugee problems, as well as his familiarity with the Continent and the people, made Dr. Schwartz a most valuable associate: this report represents our joint views, conclusions and recommendations.

During various portions of the trip I had, also, the assistance of Mr. Patrick M. Malin, vice-director of the Inter-Governmental Committee on Refugees and Mr. Herbert Katzski of the War Refugee Board. These gentlemen, likewise, have had considerable experience in refugee matters. Their assistance and cooperation were most helpful in the course of the survey.

I. GERMANY AND AUSTRIA

Conditions

1. Generally speaking, three months after V-E Day, and even longer after the liberation of individual groups, many Jewish displaced persons and other possibly non-repatriables are living under guard behind barbed-wire fences in camps of several descriptions (built by the Germans for slave laborers and Jews), including some of the most notorious of the concentration camps, amid crowded, frequently unsanitary and generally grim conditions, in complete idleness, with no opportunity, except surreptitiously, to communicate with the outside world, waiting, hoping, for some word of encouragement and action on their behalf.

2. While there has been marked improvement in the health of survivors of the Nazi starvation and persecution program, there are many pathetic malnutrition cases both among the hospitalized and in the general population of

the camps. The death rate has been high since liberation, as was to be expected. One army chaplain, a rabbi, personally attended, since liberation, twenty-three thousand burials at Bergen-Belsen alone, one of the largest and most vicious of the concentration camps, where, incidentally, despite persistent reports to the contrary, fourteen thousand displaced persons are still living, including over seven thousand Jews. At many of the camps and centers, including those where serious starvation cases are, there is a marked and serious lack of needed medical supplies.

3. Although some camp commandants have managed, in spite of the many obvious difficulties, to find clothing of one kind or another for their charges, many of the Jewish displaced persons, late in July, had no clothing other than their concentration camp garb—a rather hideous striped pajama effect—while others, to their chagrin, were obliged to wear German SS uniforms. It is questionable which clothing they hate the more.

4. With a few notable exceptions, nothing in the way of a program of activity or organized effort toward rehabilitation has been inaugurated, and the internees, for they are literally such, have little to do except to dwell upon their plight, the uncertainty of their future and, what is more unfortunate, to draw comparisons between their treatment "under the Germans" and "in liberation."

Beyond knowing that they are no longer in danger of the gas chambers, torture and other forms of violent death, they see—and there is—little change; the morale of those who are either stateless or who do not wish to return to their countries of nationality is very low. They have witnessed great activity and efficiency in returning people to their homes, but they hear or see nothing in the way of plans for them and consequently they wonder and frequently ask what "liberation" means.

This situation is considerably accentuated where, as in so many cases, they are able to look from their crowded and bare quarters and see the German civilian population, particularly in the rural areas, to all appearances living normal lives in their own homes.

5. The most absorbing worry of these Nazi and war victims concerns relatives, wives, husbands, parents, children. Most of them have been separated for three, four or five years and they cannot understand why the liberators should not have undertaken immediately the organized effort to reunite family groups. Most of the very little which has been done in this direction has been informal action by the displaced persons themselves with the aid of devoted army chaplains, frequently rabbis, and the American Joint Distribution Committee.

Broadcasts of names and locations by the Psychological Warfare Division at Luxembourg have been helpful, although the lack of receiving sets has handicapped the effectiveness of the program. Even where, as has been happening, information has been received as to relatives living in other camps in Germany, it depends on the personal attitude and disposition of the camp commandant whether permission can be obtained or assistance received to follow up on the information. Some camp commandants are quite rigid in this particular while others lend every effort to join family groups.

6. It is difficult to evaluate the food situation fairly because one must be mindful of the fact that quite generally food is scarce and is likely to be more so during the winter ahead. On the other hand, in presenting the factual situation, one must raise the question as to how much longer many of these people, particularly those who have over such a long period felt persecution and near starvation, can survive on a diet composed principally of bread and coffee, irrespective of the caloric content.

In many camps, the 2,000 calories included 1,250 calories of a black, wet and extremely unappetizing bread. I received the distinct impression and considerable substantiating information that large numbers of the German population—again principally in the rural areas—have a more varied and palatable diet in their requisitions with the German burgomaster, and many seemed to accept whatever he turned over as being the best that was available.

7. Many of the buildings in which displaced persons are housed are clearly unfit for winter use and everywhere there is great concern about the prospect of a complete lack of fuel. There is every likelihood that close to a million displaced persons will be in Germany and Austria when winter sets in. The outlook in many areas so far as shelter, food and fuel are concerned is anything but bright.

II. NEEDS OF THE JEWS

While it is impossible to state accurately the number of Jews now in that part of Germany not under Russian occupation, all indications point to the fact that the number is small, with one hundred thousand probably the top figure; some informed persons contend the number is considerably smaller. The principal nationality groups are Poles, Hungarians, Romanians, Germans and Austrians.

The first and plainest need of these people is a recognition of their actual status and by this I mean their status as Jews. Most of them have spent years in the worst of the concentration camps. In many cases, although the full extent is not yet known, they are the sole survivors of their families and many have been through the agony of witnessing the destruction of their loved ones. Understandably, therefore, their present condition, physical and mental, is far worse than that of other groups.

While SHAEF (now Combined Displaced Persons Executive) policy directives have recognized formerly persecuted persons, including enemy and ex-enemy nationals, as one of the special categories of displaced persons, the general practice thus far has been to follow only nationality lines. While admittedly it is not normally desirable to set aside particular racial or religious groups from their nationality categories, the plain truth is that this was done for so long by the Nazis that a group has been created which has special needs. Jews as Jews (not members of their nationality groups) have been more severely victimized than the non-Jewish members of the same or other nationalities.

When they are now considered only as members of nationality groups, the result is that special attention cannot be given to their admittedly greater needs because, it is contended, doing so would constitute preferential treatment and lead to trouble with the non-Jewish portion of the particular nationality group.

Thus there is a distinctly unrealistic approach to the problem. Refusal to recognize the Jews as such has the effect, in this situation, of closing one's eyes to their former and more barbaric persecution, which has already made them a separate group with greater needs.

Their second great need can be presented only by discussing what I found to be their wishes as to future destinations.

1. For reasons that are obvious and need not be labored, most Jews want to leave Germany and Austria as soon as possible. That is their first and great expressed wish and while this report necessarily deals with other needs present in the situation, many of the people themselves fear other suggestions or plans for their benefit because of the possibility that attention might thereby be diverted from the all-important matter of evacuation from Germany.

   Their desire to leave Germany is an urgent one. The life which they have led for the past ten years, a life of fear and wandering and physical torture, has made them impatient of delay. They want to be evacuated to Palestine now, just as other national groups are being repatriated to their homes. They do not look kindly on the idea of waiting around in idleness and in discomfort in a German camp for many months until a leisurely solution is found for them.

2. Some wish to return to their countries of nationality, but as to this there is considerable nationality variation. Very few Polish or Baltic Jews wish to return to their countries; higher percentages of the Hungarian and Romanian groups want to return, although some hasten to add that it may be only temporarily, in order to look for relatives. Some of the German Jews, especially those who have intermarried, prefer to stay in Germany.

3. With respect to possible places of resettlement for those who may be stateless or who do not wish to return to their homes, Palestine is definitely and preeminently the first choice. Many now have relatives there while others, having experienced intolerance and persecution in their homelands for years, feel that only in Palestine will they be welcomed and find peace and quiet and be given an opportunity to live and work. In the case of the Polish and Baltic Jews, the desire to go to Palestine is based in a great majority of the cases on a love for the country and devotion to the Zionist ideal. It is also true, however, that there are many who wish to go to Palestine because they realize that their opportunity to be admitted into the United States or into other countries in the western hemisphere is limited, if not impossible. Whatever the motive which causes them to turn to Palestine, it is undoubtedly true that the great majority of the Jews now in Germany do not wish to return to those countries from which they came.

4. Palestine, while clearly the choice of most, is not the only named place of possible emigration. Some, but the number is not large, wish to emigrate to the United States, where they have relatives, others to England, the British Dominions, or to South America.

Thus, the second great need is the prompt development of a plan to get out of Germany and Austria as many as possible of those who wish it.

Otherwise the needs and wishes of the Jewish groups among the displaced persons can be simply stated: among their physical needs are clothing and shoes (most sorely needed), more varied and palatable diet, medicine, beds and mattresses, reading materials. The clothing for the camps, too, is requisitioned from the German population, and whether there is not sufficient quantity to be had or the German population has not been willing or has not been compelled to give up sufficient quantity, the internees feel particularly bitter about the state of their clothing when they see how well the German population is still dressed. The German population today is still the best dressed population in all of Europe.

III. MANNER IN WHICH NEEDS ARE BEING MET

Aside from having brought relief from the fear of extermination, hospitalization for the serious starvation cases and some general improvement in conditions under which the remaining displaced persons are compelled to live, relatively little beyond the planning stage has been done, during the period of mass repatriation, to meet the special needs of the formerly persecuted groups.

UNRRA, being neither sufficiently organized or equipped or authorized to operate displaced persons camps or centers on any large scale, has not been in a position to make any substantial contribution to the situation. Regrettably there has been a disinclination on the part of many camp commandants to utilize UNRRA personnel even to the extent available, though it must be admitted that in many situations this resulted from unfortunate experiences army officers had with UNRRA personnel who were unqualified and inadequate for the responsibility involved. Then, too, in the American and British Zones, it too frequently occurred that UNRRA personnel did not include English-speaking members and this hampered proper working relationships.

Under these circumstances UNRRA, to which has been assigned the responsibility for coordinating activities of private social welfare agencies, has been in an awkward position when it came to considering and acting upon proposals of one kind or another submitted by well-qualified agencies which would aid and supplement military and UNRRA responsibilities. The result has been that, up to this point, very few private social agencies are working with displaced persons, including the Jews, although the situation cries out for their services in many different ways.

It must be said, too, that because of their preoccupation with mass repatriation and because of housing, personnel and transport difficulties, the military authorities have shown considerable resistance to the entrance of voluntary agency representatives, no matter how qualified they might be to help meet existing needs of displaced persons.

IV. CONCLUSIONS ANY RECOMMENDATIONS

I. Now that the worst of the pressure of mass repatriation is over, it is not unreasonable to suggest that in the next and perhaps more difficult period those who have suffered most and longest be given first and not last attention.

Specifically, in the days immediately ahead, the Jews in Germany and Austria should have the first claim upon the conscience of the people of the United States and Great Britain and the military and other personnel who represent them in work being done in Germany and Austria.

II. Evacuation from Germany should be the emphasized theme, policy and practice.

A. Recognizing that repatriation is most desirable from the standpoint of all concerned, the Jews who wish to return to their own countries, should be aided to do so without further delay. Whatever special action is needed to accomplish this, with respect to countries of reception or consent of military or other authorities, should be undertaken with energy and determination. Unless this and other action, about to be suggested,

is taken, substantial unofficial and unauthorized movements of people must be expected, and these will require considerable force to prevent, for the patience of many of the persons involved is, and in my opinion with justification, nearing the breaking point. It cannot be overemphasized that many of these people are now desperate, that they have become accustomed under German rule to employ every possible means to reach their end, and that the fear of death does not restrain them.

B. With respect to those who do not, for good reason, wish to return to their homes, prompt planning should likewise be undertaken. In this connection, the issue of Palestine must be faced. Now that such large numbers are no longer involved and if there is any genuine sympathy for what these survivors have endured, some reasonable extension or modification of the British White Paper of 1939 ought to be possible without too serious repercussions. For some of the European Jews, there is no acceptable or even decent solution for their future other than Palestine. This is said on a purely humanitarian basis with no reference to ideological or political considerations so far as Palestine is concerned.

It is my understanding, based upon reliable information, that certificates for immigration to Palestine will be practically exhausted by the end of the current month (August, 1945). What is the future to be? To xanyone who has visited the concentration camps and who has talked with the despairing survivors, it is nothing short of calamitous to contemplate that the gates of Palestine should be soon closed.

The Jewish Agency of Palestine has submitted to the British government a petition that one hundred thousand additional immigration certificates be made available. A memorandum accompanying the petition makes a persuasive showing with respect to the immediate absorptive capacity of Palestine and the current, actual manpower shortages there.

While there may be room for difference of opinion as to the precise number of such certificates which might under the circumstances be considered reasonable, there is no question but that the request thus made would, if granted, contribute much to the sound solution for the future of Jews still in Germany and Austria and even other displaced Jews, who do not wish either to remain there or to return to their countries of nationality.

No other single matter is, therefore, so important from the viewpoint of Jews in Germany and Austria and those elsewhere, who have known the horrors of the concentration camps, as is the disposition of the Palestine question.

Dr. Hugh Dalton, a prominent member of the new British government, is reported as having said at the Labour Party conference in May, 1945:

> This party has laid it down and repeated it so recently as last April . . . that this time, having regard to the unspeakable horrors that have been perpetrated upon the Jews of Germany and other occupied countries in Europe, it is morally wrong and politically indefensible to impose obstacles to the entry into Palestine now of any Jews who desire to go there....
>
> We have also stated clearly that this is not a matter which should be regarded as one for which the British government alone should take responsibility, but as it comes, as do many others, in the international field, it is indispensable that there should be close agreement and cooperation among the British, American and Soviet governments, particularly if we are going to get a sure settlement in Palestine and the surrounding countries....

If this can be said to represent the viewpoint of the new government in Great Britain, it certainly would not be inappropriate for the United States government to express its interest in and support of some equitable solution of the question, which would make it possible for some reasonable number of Europe's persecuted Jews, now homeless under any fair view, to resettle in Palestine. That is their wish and it is rendered desirable by the generally accepted policy of permitting family groups to unite or reunite.

C. The United States should, under existing immigration laws, permit reasonable numbers of such persons to come here, again particularly those who have family ties in this country. As indicated earlier, the number who desire emigration to the United States is not large.

If Great Britain and the United States were to take the actions recited, it might the more readily be that other countries would likewise be willing to keep their doors reasonably open for such humanitarian considerations and to demonstrate in a practical manner their disapproval of Nazi policy which unfortunately has poisoned so much of Europe.

III. To the extent that such emigration from Germany and Austria is delayed, some immediate temporary solution must be found. In any event there will be a substantial number of persecuted persons who are not physically fit or otherwise presently prepared for emigration.

Here I feel strongly that greater and more extensive effort should be made to get them out of camps, for they are sick of living in camps. In the first place, there is real need for such specialized places as (a) tuberculosis sanitaria and (b) rest homes for those who are mentally ill or who need a period of readjustment before living again in the world at large—anywhere. Some will require at least short periods of training or retraining before they can be really useful citizens.

But speaking more broadly, there is an opportunity here to give some real meaning to the policy agreed upon at Potsdam. If it be true, as seems to be widely conceded, that the German people at large do not have any sense of guilt with respect to the war and its causes and results, and if the policy is to be "to convince the German people that they have suffered a total military defeat and that they cannot escape responsibility for what they have brought upon themselves," it is difficult to understand why so many displaced persons, particularly those who have so long been persecuted and whose repatriation or resettlement is likely to be delayed, should be compelled to live in crude, overcrowded camps while the German people, in rural areas, continue undisturbed in their homes.

As matters now stand, we appear to be treating the Jews as the Nazis treated them, except that we do not exterminate them. They are in concentration camps in large numbers under our military guard instead of SS troops. One is led to wonder whether the German people, seeing this, are not supposing that we are following or at least condoning Nazi policy.

It seems much more equitable, and as it should be, to witness the very few places where fearless and uncompromising military officers have either requisitioned an entire village for the benefit of displaced persons, compelling the German population to find housing where they can, or have required the local population to billet a reasonable number of them.

Thus the displaced persons, including the persecuted, live more like normal people and less like prisoners or criminals or herded sheep. They are in Germany, most of them and certainly the Jews, through no fault or wish of their own. This fact is, in this fashion, being brought home to the German people, but it is being done on too small a scale.

At many places, however, the military government officers manifest the utmost reluctance or indisposition, if not timidity, about inconveniencing the German population. They even say that their job is to get communities working properly and soundly again, that they must "live with the Germans while the DPs (displaced persons) are a more temporary problem."

Thus (and I am ready to cite the example) if a group of Jews are ordered to vacate their temporary quarters, needed for military purposes, and there are two possible sites, one a block of flats (model apartments) with conveniences and the other a series of shabby buildings with outside toilet and washing facilities, the Burgomaster readily succeeds in persuading the town mayor to allot the latter to the displaced persons and to save the former for returning German civilians.

This tendency reflects itself in other ways, namely, in the employment of German civilians in the offices of Military Government when equally qualified personnel could easily be found among the displaced persons whose repatriation is not imminent. Actually, there have been situations where displaced persons, especially Jews, have found it difficult to obtain audiences with military government authorities because ironically they have been obliged to go through German employers who have not facilitated matters.

Quite generally, insufficient use is made of the services of displaced persons. Many of them are able and eager to work, but apparently they are not considered in this regard. While appreciating that language difficulties are sometimes involved, I am convinced that, both within and outside camps, greater use could be made of the personal services of those displaced persons who in all likelihood will be on hand for some time. Happily, in some camps every effort is made to utilize the services of the displaced persons and these are apt to be the best camps in all respects.

IV. To the extent that (a) evacuation from Germany and Austria is not immediately possible and (b) the formerly persecuted groups cannot be housed in villages or billeted with the German population, I recommend urgently that separate camps be set up for Jews, or at least for those who wish, in the absence of a better solution, to be in such camps. There are several reasons for this: (1) A great majority want it; (2) it is the only way in which administratively their special needs and problems can be met without charges of preferential treatment or (oddly enough) charges of "discrimination" with respect to Jewish agencies now prepared and ready to give them assistance.

In this connection, I wish to emphasize that it is not a case of singling out a particular group for special privileges. It is a matter of raising to a more normal level the position of a group which has been depressed to the lowest depths conceivable by years of organized and inhuman oppression. The measures necessary for their restitution do not come within any reasonable interpretation of privileged treatment and are required by considerations of justice and humanity.

There has been some tendency at spots in the direction of separate camps for those who might be found to be stateless or non-repatriable or whose repatriation is likely to be deferred some time. Actually, too, this was announced some time ago as SHAEF policy, but in practice it has not been taken to mean much, for there is (understandably if not carried too far) a refusal to contemplate possible statelessness and an insistence, in the interests of the large repatriation program, to consider all as repatriable. This results in a resistance to anything in the way of special planning for the "hard core," although all admit it is there and will inevitably appear.

While speaking of camps, this should be pointed out: While it may be that conditions in Germany and Austria are still such that certain control measures are required, there seems little justification for the continuance of barbed-wire fences, armed guards and prohibition against leaving camp except by passes, which at some places are illiberally granted. Prevention of looting is given as the reason for these stern measures, but it is interesting that in portions of the Seventh Army area, where greater liberty of movement in and out of camps is given, there is actually much less plundering than in other areas where people, wishing to leave camp temporarily, do so by stealth.

V. As quickly as possible the actual operation of such camps should be turned over to a civilian agency—UNRRA. That organization is aware of weaknesses in its present structure and is pressing to remedy them. In that connection, it is believed that greater assistance could be given by the military authorities, upon whom any civilian agency in Germany and Austria today is necessarily dependent, so far as housing, transport and other items are concerned. While it is true the military have been urging UNRRA to get ready to assume responsibility, it is also the fact that insufficient cooperation of an active nature has been given to accomplish the desired end.

VI. Since, in any event, the military authorities must necessarily continue to participate in the program for all displaced persons, especially with respect to housing, transport, security and certain supplies, it is recommended that there be a review of the military personnel elected for camp commandant positions. Some serving at present, while perhaps adequate for the mass repatriation job, are manifestly unsuited for the longer-term job of working in a camp composed of people whose repatriation or resettlement is likely to be delayed. Officers who have had some background or experience in social welfare work are to be preferred, and it is believed there are some who are available. It is most important that the officers selected be sympathetic with the program and that they be temperamentally able to work and to cooperate with UNRRA and other relief and welfare agencies.

VII. Pending the assumption of responsibility for operations by UNRRA, it would be desirable if a more extensive plan of field visitation by appropriate army group headquarters be instituted. It is believed that many of the conditions now existing in the camps would not be tolerated if more intimately known by supervisory officers through inspection tours.

VIII. It is urgently recommended that plans for tracing services, if on open postal card only, be made available to displaced persons within Germany and Austria as soon as possible. The difficulties are appreciated but it is believed that, if the anxiety of the people, so long abused and harassed, were fully understood, ways and means could be found within the near future to make such communication and tracing of relatives possible. I believe also that some of the private agencies could be helpful in this direction if given an opportunity to function.

V. "THE MAIN SOLUTION—PALESTINE"

While I was instructed to report conditions as I found them, the following should be added to make the picture complete:

1. A gigantic task confronted the occupying armies in Germany and Austria in getting back to their homes as many as possible of the more than six million displaced persons found in those countries. Less than three months after V-E Day, more than four million of such persons have been repatriated—a phenomenal performance. One's first impression, in surveying the situation, is that of complete admiration for what has been accomplished by the military authorities in so materially reducing the time as predicted to be required for this stupendous task. Praise of the highest order is due all military units with respect to this phase of post-fighting jobs. In directing attention to existing conditions which unquestionably require remedying, there is no intention or wish to detract one particle from the preceding statements.

2. While I did not actually see conditions as they existed immediately after liberation, I had them described in detail sufficient to make entirely clear that there had been, during the intervening period, some improvement in the conditions under which most of the remaining displaced persons are living. Reports which have come out of Germany informally from refugees themselves and from persons interested in refugee groups indicate something of a tendency not to take into account the full scope of the overwhelming tasks and responsibilities facing the military authorities. While it is understandable that those who have been persecuted and otherwise mistreated over such a long period should be impatient at what appears to them to be undue delay in meeting their special needs, fairness dictates that, in evaluating the progress made, the entire problem and all its ramifications be kept in mind. My effort has been, therefore, to weigh quite carefully the many complaints made to me in the course of my survey, both by displaced persons themselves and in their behalf, in the light of the many responsibilities which confronted the military authorities.

3. While for the sake of brevity this report necessarily consisted largely of general statements, it should be recognized that exceptions exist with respect to practically all such generalizations. One high-ranking military authority predicted, in advance of my trip through Germany and Austria, that I would find, with respect to camps containing displaced persons, "some that are quite

good, some that are very bad, with the average something under satisfactory." My subsequent trip confirmed that prediction in all respects.

In order to file this report promptly so that possibly some remedial steps might be considered at as early a date as possible, I have not taken time to analyze all of the notes made in the course of the trip or to comment on the situation in France, Belgium, Holland or Switzerland, also visited. Accordingly, I respectfully request that this report be considered as partial in nature. The problems present in Germany and Austria are much more serious and difficult than in any of the other countries named and this fact, too, seemed to make desirable the filing of a partial report immediately upon completion of the mission.

In conclusion, I wish to repeat that the main solution, in many ways the only real solution, of the problem lies in the quick evacuation of all non-repatriable Jews in Germany and Austria, who wish it, to Palestine. In order to be effective, this plan must not be long delayed. The urgency of the situation should be recognized. It is inhuman to ask people to continue to live for any length of time under their present conditions. The evacuation of the Jews of Germany and Austria to Palestine will solve the problem of the individuals involved and will also remove a problem from the military authorities who have had to deal with it.

The army's ability to move millions of people quickly and efficiently has been amply demonstrated. The evacuation of a relatively small number of Jews from Germany and Austria will present no great problem to the military. With the end of the Japanese war, the shipping situation should also become sufficiently improved to make such a move feasible.

The civilized world owes it to this handful of survivors to provide them with a home where they can again settle down and begin to live as human beings.

PRESIDENT HARRY S TRUMAN'S DIRECTIVE TO GENERAL DWIGHT D. EISENHOWER REGARDING THE HARRISON REPORT

AUGUST 31, 1945

My dear General Eisenhower:

I have received and considered the report of Mr. Earl G. Harrison, OUI representative on the Intergovernmental Committee on Refugees, upon his mission to inquire into the condition and needs of displaced persons in Germany who may be stateless or non-repatriable, particularly Jews. I am sending you a copy of that report. I have also had a long conference with him on the same subject matter.

While Mr. Harrison makes due allowance for the fact that during the early days of liberation the huge task of mass repatriation required main attention, he reports conditions which now exist and which require prompt remedy. These conditions are not in conformity with policies promulgated by SHAEF, now Combined Displaced Persons Executive. But they are what actually exists in the field. In other words, the policies are not being carried out by some of your subordinate officers.

For example, military government officers have been authorized and even directed to requisition billeting facilities from the German population for the benefit of displaced persons. Yet, from this report, this has not been done on any wide scale. Apparently it is being taken for granted that all displaced persons, irrespective of their former persecution or the likelihood that their repatriation or resettlement will be delayed, must remain in camps—many of which are overcrowded and heavily guarded. Some of these camps are the very ones where these people were herded together, starved, tortured and made to witness the death of their fellow-inmates and friends and relatives. The announced policy has been to give such persons preference over the German civilian population in housing. But the practice seems to be quite another thing.

We must intensify our efforts to get these people out of camps and into decent houses until they can be repatriated or evacuated. These houses should be requisitioned from the German civilian population. That is one way to implement the Potsdam policy that the German people "cannot escape responsibility for what they have brought upon themselves."

I quote this paragraph with particular reference to the Jews among the displaced persons:

> As matters now stand, we appear to be treating the Jews as the Nazis treated them except that we do not exterminate them. They are in concentration camps in large numbers under our military guard instead of SS troops. One is led to wonder whether the German people, seeing this, are not supposing that we are following or at least condoning Nazi policy.

You will find in the report other illustrations of what I mean.

I hope you will adopt the suggestion that a

Survivors cluster around U.S. Sergeant Fredrick W. Peacock upon arrival of the 71st Infantry in the Gunkirchen concentration camp. May 6, 1945. Ghetto Fighters' House/Courtesy of USHMM–Photo Archives.

more extensive plan of field visitation by appropriate Army Group Headquarters be instituted, so that the inhumane policies which have been enunciated are not permitted to be ignored in the field. Most of the conditions now existing in displaced persons camps would quickly be remedied if through inspection tours they came to your attention or to the attention of your supervisory officers.

I know you will agree with me that we have a particular responsibility toward these victims of persecution and tyranny who are in our zone. We must make clear to the German people that we thoroughly abhor the Nazi policies of hatred and persecution. We have no better opportunity to demonstrate this than by the manner in which we ourselves actually treat the survivors remaining in Germany.

I hope you will report to me as soon as possible the steps you have been able to take to clean up the conditions mentioned in the report.

I am communicating directly with the British government in an effort to have the doors of Palestine opened to such of these displaced persons as wish to go there.

Very sincerely yours,
HARRY S TRUMAN

GENERAL DWIGHT D. EISENHOWER'S RESPONSE TO PRESIDENT TRUMAN
18 SEPTEMBER 1945

The Hon. Harry S Truman
The White House
Washington, D.C.

Dear Mr. President:

During my absence from this Headquarters, receipt of your letter concerning the problem of displaced persons was acknowledged. I was then on a trip during which I made an inspection of a number of the installations in which we have displaced persons. This letter deals primarily with my own observations and will be supplemented, either immediately or in the near future, by a more extensive report comprehending the findings of subordinate commanders and staffs and of a special Jewish investigator.

As to the seriousness of the problem, there is not the slightest doubt. The hopelessness of the ordinary displaced person comes about from fear of the future, which involved questions, always of international politics, and from the practical impossibility of participating, at this time, in any useful occupation.

To speak very briefly about the psychological attitude of these people, I give you a few impressions gained by direct conversations with them. A very large percentage of the persons from the Baltic States, as well as from Poland and Romania, definitely do not want to return to their own countries *at this time*. Although such a return represents the height of their ultimate ambitions, they constantly state, "We cannot go back until there is a change in the political situation—otherwise we will all be killed." They state that the government of all these states will persecute them to the point of death, although they insist that they bitterly opposed German domination of their respective states just as they opposed domination by any other government.

With respect to the Jews, I found that most want to go to Palestine. I note in your letter that you have already instituted action in the hope of making this possible. All these matters are, of course, distinctly outside my military responsibility or authority and there is nothing whatsoever that I or my subordinates would be justified in promising or intimating in regard to them. However, this matter draws practical importance for us out of the possibility that caring for displaced persons may be a long-time job. Since I assume that most countries would be unwilling to absorb masses of these people as citizens in their countries, the only alternative is that of hoping they will gradually voluntarily disperse in the areas of Western Europe and try to establish themselves in a self-sustaining life. To this end we encourage everybody to go out and get a job if he possibly can, and have been trying to explore the possibilities of agriculture and small business in the hopes of establishing small colonies of these people near their present locations. One great difficulty is that they do not desire to look upon their present location as any form of permanent home. They prefer to sit and wait rather than to attempt, as they say, "forcing themselves into a population where they would never be welcome."

With regard to the actual living condition; I personally visited five camps, two of which were exclusively Jewish and a third largely so. Two of the camps were villages taken from the Germans. Two others were city suburbs which had been taken over and occupied, one by the Jews, one by the Poles. In one camp, which was Jewish, I found conditions less than satisfactory, but found also that the camp and local authorities were taking over additional houses in the immediate vicinity, throwing the Germans out of these houses in order to provide more and better accommodations for the displaced persons. You will understand that to provision these people adequately they must be housed in the same general vicinity; an impossible administrative problem would be presented if they are scattered indiscriminately throughout the German population. All the feeding of displaced persons is under military or UNRRA control; whereas, with few exceptions, the German population has to look out for itself. You will understand, also that when we speak of "camp" we do not mean either a tent camp or one made of huts. Speaking generally, every displaced person is in a permanent building of some sort, either an ordinary dwelling or building that was once used for other purposes. In the camp where I found conditions unsatisfactory, there were still guards on the entrance and passes were required for visits to any distant spot. This practice is stopped, but the Jewish leaders within order, as they said, that "all of us do not get a bad name." I found no instances of displaced persons still living in the old "horror" camps.

In one camp we have experienced, on the part of a considerable minority of the displaced persons, a distinct lack of cooperation. I am still reporting on evidence given me by these people themselves. The most simple of sanitary regulations were constantly violated to a degree that in some instances could be termed nothing less than revolting, although much improved.

The voluntary police begged me to permit them to have arms. Upon my flat refusal to entertain such an idea I received the reply, "We have some very mean men here and they can get us all in trouble." However, I am certain that since these people are completely dependent upon us for food, the necessary standard of conduct can be maintained without any resort to harsh methods.

At no place did I find any timidity on the part of any officer to throw a German out of a house in order to give better accommodations to displaced persons, but, as before mentioned, problems of feeding, distribution and medical care for this completely helpless group, make it imperative that they be sufficiently concentrated in order that these services can be performed. In those instances where I believe officers have overemphasized the administration difficulties, vigorous steps are being taken and improvement will be prompt.

When it is realized that the army in this area has been faced with the most difficult types of redeployment problems; has had to preserve law and order; furnish a multitude of services for itself and for the thousands of people it employs; and on top of this has had this question of displaced persons with unusual demands upon transportation, housing, fuel, food, medical care and security, you can well understand that there have been undeniable instances of inefficiency. Commanders of all grades are engaged in seeking these out and I am confident that if you could compare conditions with what they were three months ago, you would realize that your army here has done an admirable and almost unbelievable job in this respect.

Respectfully,

Excerpts from the *Diary of George S. Patton*
September 15-21, 1945

SEPTEMBER 15

Late yesterday afternoon I was notified that General Eisenhower would arrive ...near Munich at 0930 this morning, having flown from the Riviera....

I later found out that the purpose of his visit was to inspect the DP camps, particularly at least one occupied by Jews, to determine the condition of these Jews in order that he may write a letter to Mr. Truman.

Harkins and I went there to greet him in spite of the fact he had suggested that I not put myself out. I have always felt that an officer should be present to meet in person an officer of the next higher grade and, in this case, General Eisenhower was also my friend.

Harkins and I waited until 19:00 o'clock, at which time we heard that General Eisenhower had been unable to land and had had to go to Paris to get down, using the beam at the field there.

While waiting, I talked to Brigadier General Mickelsen who is G-S for Eisenhower's headquarters [in charge of DP affairs], and he showed me a letter from President Truman to General Eisenhower which was unnecessarily harsh and in much less considerate language than I would have used in cussing out a second lieutenant.

Mickelsen also showed me the report of a man named Harrison (which report was enclosed in the president's letter) on the condition of Displaced Persons in Europe, particularly Jews. Harrison is a member of the State Department [*sic*]. The report contained many allegations against General Eisenhower, the army, and the various commanders.

One of the chief complaints is that the DPs are kept in camps under guard. Of course Harrison is ignorant of the fact that if they were not kept under guard they would not stay in the camps, would spread over the country like locusts and should eventually have to be rounded up after quite a few of them had been shot and quite a few Germans murdered and pillaged.

The brilliant Mr. Harrison further objected to the sanitary conditions. Again being ignorant of the fact that we frequently have to use force in order to prevent the inmates—Germans, Jews and other people—from defecating on the floor when ample facilities are provided outside.

Evidently the virus started by Morgenthau and Baruch of a Semitic revenge against all Germans is still working. Harrison and his associates indicate that they feel German civilians should be removed from houses for the purpose of housing Displaced Persons.

There are two errors in this assumption. First, when we remove an individual German, we punish an individual German while the punishment is not intended for the individual but for the race. Furthermore, it is against my Anglo-Saxon conscience to remove a person from a house, which is a punishment, without due process of law. In the second place, Harrison and his ilk believe that the Displaced Person is a human being which he is not, and this applies particularly to the Jews who are lower than animals. I remember once at Troina in Sicily, General Gay said that it wasn't a question of the people living with the dirty animals but of the animals living with the dirty people. At that time he had never seen a Displaced Jew.

Furthermore, I do not see why Jews should be treated any better or any worse than Catholics, Protestants, Mohammedans or Mormons. However, it seems apparent that we will have to do this, and I am going to do it as painlessly as possible by taking a certain group of buildings in several cities and placing the Jews, who do not exceed twenty thousand, in sort of improved ghettos.

To put the Jews on farms would be disastrous because it would break up the agricultural economy of Bavaria on which we depend for providing what food is provided which is not paid for by American taxpayers.

We arranged a good itinerary for General Eisenhower which we will put into effect when he comes. Unquestionably he is just as much under fire as is anyone else and, in this particular case, very unjustly so.

If the people in Washington would stop trying to find fault with others and wake up to the extent of making the Russians take back the Poles and other people whom they have not permitted to return, the situation in Displaced Persons would be much ameliorated....

It seems to be quite a hell of a mess.

SEPTEMBER 17

Eisenhower and I drove to Munich where we inspected a Baltic Displaced Persons camp. The Baltic people are the best of the Displaced Persons and the camp was extremely clean in all respects.... We were both, I think, very much pleased with the conditions here ...

We drove for about forty-five minutes to a Jewish camp ... established in what had been a German hospital. The buildings were therefore in a good state of repair when the Jews arrived but

were in a bad state of repair when we arrived, because these Jewish DPs, or at least a majority of them, have no sense of human relationships. They decline, where practicable, to use latrines, preferring to relieve themselves on the floor ...

This happened to be the feast of Yom Kippur, so they were all collected in a large wooden building which they called a synagogue. It behooved General Eisenhower to make a speech to them. We entered the synagogue which was packed with the greatest stinking bunch of humanity I have ever seen. When we got about half way up, the head rabbi, who was dressed in a fur hat similar to that worn by Henry VIII of England and in a surplice heavily embroidered and very filthy, came down and met the general. Also a copy of the Talmud, I think it is called, written on a sheet and rolled around a stick, was carried by one of the attending physicians.

First, a Jewish civilian made a very long speech which nobody seemed inclined to translate. Then General Eisenhower mounted the platform and I went up behind him, and he made a short and excellent speech, which was translated paragraph by paragraph.

However, the smell was so terrible that I almost fainted and actually about three hours later lost my lunch as the result of remembering it.

From here we went to the Headquarters of the XX Corps, where General Craig gave us an excellent lunch which I, however, was unable to partake of owing to my nausea.

After lunch we visited a . . . model German workers' village. . . . It was my purpose to turn this over into a Jewish concentration camp. Here we met the most talkative Jewish female, an American who was running the UNRRA part of the camp. . . .

After inspecting this and making another speech, which I avoided, General Eisenhower directed that sufficient Germans be evicted from houses contiguous to the concentration camp so that the density per capita of DPs and Germans should be approximately the same. Also that the American guards be removed from the camp except for a standby guard in case of a riot, and that guards composed of Allied inmates take over the police of the camp proper. . . .

After this we returned home and went for a fishing trip on the lake which, while not successful, at least removed from our minds the nauseous odors and aspects of the camps we had inspected.

We then took as long and as hot a bath as we could stand to remove from our persons the germs which must have accumulated during the day.

I believe this was the first time General Eisenhower had inspected or seen much of Displaced Persons. Of course, I have seen them since the beginning and marveled that beings alleged to be made in the the image of God can look the way they do or act the way they act.

SEPTEMBER 21

General Louis Craig came in to see me this morning to explain how he had arranged for taking care of the Jews. It has been necessary for him, against his and my instincts, to move twenty-two rich German families from their houses in order to put the animals in them. I told Craig to take pictures of the houses before they were occupied by the Jews and then subsequently. I also told him to move the Germans with as much consideration as possible and to give them transportation to move as much of their decent property out as they could.

Craig … told me he had inspected another Jewish camp yesterday in which he found men and women using adjacent toilets which were not covered in any way although screens were available to make the toilets individually isolated, which the Jews were too lazy to put up.

He said the conditions and filth were unspeakable. In one room he found ten people, six men and four women, occupying four double beds. Either the Displaced Persons never had any sense of decency or else they lost it all during their period of internment by the Germans. My personal opinion is that no people could have sunk to the level of degradation these have reached in the short space of four years.

XXI. THE NUREMBERG TRIALS

In the winter of 1943, Franklin Roosevelt, Winston Churchill, and Joseph Stalin declared their determination to bring the Nazi leaders to justice. Allied outrage at Nazi wartime behavior only intensified after the discovery of killing centers.

Within a fortnight of the war's end, an agreement was reached to conduct joint trials. President Truman took the unusual step of asking Supreme Court Justice Robert Jackson to lead the American effort. Nuremberg, the site of annual Nazi Party pageants, was chosen for practical reasons. It was one of the few German cities that did not lie in ruins.

Three forms of crimes were specified in the indictment:

At 10:00 A.M. on November 21, 1946, Walter Beals, the presiding judge opened the trial of twenty-three German physicians who had conducted experiments on human "guinea pigs." Wilhelm Beiglbock is pleading "not guilty." National Archives/Courtesy of USHMM–Photo Archives.

Crimes against the Peace—planning, preparation, initiation, or waging of a war of aggression;

War Crimes—violations of laws and customs of war such as the murder, ill-treatment, or deportation of slave labor or for any other purpose of civilian populations . . . killing of hostages, prisoners of war, plunder of private property, destruction of towns and cities;

Crimes Against Humanity—murder, extermination, enslavement, deportation . . . against any civilian population . . . persecution on political, racial, or religious grounds . . . whether or not in violation of domestic laws of the country where perpetrated.

The first series of trials were International Military Tribunals. Twenty-two major Nazi leaders were placed on trial by the victors. The accused included Hitler's trusted lieutenant Hermann Goering; Nazi Party officials; cabinet ministers including the foreign minister, and the ministers of armaments and labor; ranking bureaucrats; military leaders; and German occupation officials.

After the first trials were concluded in 1946, a second series of trials at Nuremberg commenced, 185 defendants were divided into twelve groups.

Doctors were tried for their participation in selection, murder, and medical experimentation. Mobile killing units officers, such as Otto Ohlendorf, were prosecuted for their slaughter of civilians in the East. Concentration camps leaders, such as Rudolph Höss, commandant of Auschwitz, faced trial for the systematic murder that occurred in their camps, on their watch.

Judges were tried for their role in the facade of German legality. The generals who invaded the USSR and whose armies ravaged eastern Europe were placed on trial; so too, corporate leaders of I.G. Farben for the sale of Cyclon-B and the construction of industrial plants at Auschwitz. Entrepreneurs such as Alfred Krupp and the directors of his company were tried for the employment of slave labor.

Those on trials did not claim innocence. They shifted the burden of responsibility. Some claimed they did not know. Their comrades argued that they were following legal orders given by a superior officer. Others complained that they were being singled out; they had behaved just as everyone else had behaved. In essence, they argued "Why me?"

Judges and generals spoke of their sacred oath to the Führer. They were men of honor to the end.

Proximity to the crime was a measure of one's responsibility. The closer one came to the actual killing, the greater the accountability. Officers of the Einsatzgruppen, concentration camp commandants, and doctors who presided over experiments were regarded as more responsible than the corporate and industrial structure that made their activities possible. The architects who designed the camp, the engineers who modified the crematoria, the chemists who made the gas were not held accountable. Industrialists were given lighter sentences. Thirty-five defendants were acquitted.

In the midst of the trials, public attention shifted to the cold war, the struggle between capitalism and communism. The American government was anxious to win the Germans over to their side and the trials soon became a nuisance, the activities of idealistic do-gooders in a difficult war. No sooner had they ended than clemency boards were introduced, sentences were reduced, pardons were granted; time off was given for good behavior.

By 1951, the High Commissioner for Germany, John J. McCloy, who as assistant secretary of war had pushed for the War Crimes' trials in 1944, commuted death sentences and freed seventy-seven Nazi officials including the leading industrialists.

The trials only touched a few of those who perpetrated the crime—mostly top leaders whose role was immediately visible. Most of those responsible escaped judgment.

Some Nazi officials established new identities in Germany and Austria. Others fled to South America. Some Nazi leaders sought refuge in the Middle East among the enemies of Israel. Still others availed themselves of Vatican help. It is estimated that ten thousand Nazi war criminals came to the United States; heralded as anticommunists they arrived through the front door with their papers in order.

Those who dismiss the trials argue that little was accomplished—most especially in proportion to the crime. And yet, for the first time in history, leaders of a regime were held legally accountable for crimes committed within the framework of their policy. Individuals were held responsible for their deeds; they could not seek shelter in the defense that they were merely carrying out orders. New standards were introduced into the world community, standards often breached, but standards nevertheless.

And the trials led to early actions by the United Nations. A Convention for the Prevention of Crimes of Genocide was adopted by the United Nations on December 9, 1948. A Universal Declaration of Human Rights followed the next day. The Geneva Convention on the Laws and Customs of War was enacted a year later.

Fearful of a loss of national sovereignty, the United States postponed the ratification of the convention. Almost four decades after its adoption, the treaty was ratified by the U.S. Senate.

In the documents that follow we will read excerpts from Justice Jackson's opening statement at the Nuremberg Trials, which defines the nature of the crime and the unique situation of the "victors' justice." While, over the years, the attention given to the Nuremberg Trials has shifted to the crimes against humanity, Jackson is specific in his priorities and his goals.

We will also read parts of Chief Prosecutor Telford Taylor's opening statement to the Doctors' Trial of December 9, 1946, in which he summarizes the medical experimentation conducted during the Holocaust and specifies a code of individual responsibility for the physician. His argument is sustained by the judges in their decision, which lists the ten principles of permissible human experimentation, a code of conduct for the physician that is honored to this day.

Excerpts from the Opening Statement of the Prosecution (Justice Robert Jackson) at the First Nuremberg Trial

November 21, 1945

Opening Statement for the United States of America By Robert H. Jackson, Chief of Counsel for the United States at Palace of Justice, Nuremberg, Germany, November 21, 1945.

May It Please Your Honors:

The privilege of opening the first trial in history for crime against the peace of the world imposes a grave responsibility. The wrongs which we seek to condemn and punish have been calculated, so malignant and so devastating, that civilization cannot tolerate their being ignored because it cannot survive their being repeated. That four great nations, flushed with victory and stung with injury, stay the hand of vengeance and voluntarily submit their captive enemies to the judgment of the law is one of the most significant tributes that Power ever has paid to Reason.

This Tribunal, while it is novel and experimental, is not the product of abstract speculations nor is it created to vindicate legalistic theories. This inquest represents the practical effort of four of the most mighty of nations, with the support of seventeen more, to utilize international law to meet the greatest menace of our times—aggressive war. The common sense of mankind demands that law shall not stop with the punishment of petty crimes by little people. It must also reach men who possess themselves of great power and make deliberate and concerted use of it to set in motion evils which leave no home in the world untouched. It is a cause of this magnitude that the United Nations will lay before Your Honors.

In the prisoners' dock sit twenty-odd broken men. Reproached by the humiliation of those they have led almost as bitterly as by the desolation of those they have attacked, their personal capacity for evil is forever past. It is hard now to perceive in these miserable men as captives the power by which as Nazi leaders they once dominated much of the world and terrified most of it. Merely as individuals, their fate is of little consequence to the world.

What makes this inquest significant is that these prisoners represent sinister influences that will lurk in the world long after their bodies have returned to dust. They are living symbols of racial hatreds, of terrorism and violence, and of the arrogance and cruelty of power. They are symbols of fierce nationalism and of militarism, of intrigue and war-making which have embroiled Europe generation after generation, crushing its manhood, destroying its homes, and impoverishing its life. They have so identified themselves with the philosophies they conceived and with the forces they directed that any tenderness to them is a victory and an encouragement to all the evils which are attached to their names. Civilization can afford no compromise with the social forces which would gain renewed strength if we deal ambiguously or indecisively with the men in whom those forces now precariously survive.

What these men stand for we will patiently and temperately disclose. We will give you undeniable proofs of incredible events. The catalogue of crimes will omit nothing that could be conceived by a pathological pride, cruelty, and lust for power. These men created in Germany, under the *Führerprinzip*, a National Socialist despotism equaled only by the dynasties of the ancient East. They took from the German people all those dignities and freedoms that we hold natural and inalienable rights in every human being. The people were compensated by inflaming and gratifying hatreds toward those who were marked as "scapegoats." Against their opponents, including Jews, Catholics, and free labor, the Nazis directed such a campaign of arrogance, brutality, and annihilation as the world has not witnessed since the pre-Christian ages. They excited the German ambition to be a "master race," which of course implies serfdom for others. They led their people on a mad gamble for domination. They diverted social energies and resources to the creation of what they thought to be an invincible war machine. They overran their neighbors. To sustain the "master race" in its war-making, they enslaved millions of human beings and brought them into Germany, where these hapless creatures now wander as displaced persons. At length bestiality and bad faith reached such excess that they aroused the sleeping strength of imperiled Civilization. Its united efforts have ground the German war machine to fragments. But the struggle has left Europe a liberated yet prostrate land where a demoralized society struggles to survive. These are the fruits of the sinister forces that sit with these defendants in the prisoners' dock.

In justice to the nations and the men associated in this prosecution, I must remind you of certain difficulties which may leave their mark on this case. Never before in legal history has an effort been made to bring within the scope of a single litigation the developments of a decade, covering a whole continent, and involving a score of nations, countless individuals, and innumerable events. Despite the magnitude of the task, the world has demanded immediate action. This demand has had to be met, though perhaps at the cost of finished craftsmanship. In my country, established courts, following familiar procedures, applying well-thumbed precedents, and dealing with the legal consequences of local and limited events seldom commence a trial within a year of the event in litigation. Yet less than eight months ago today the courtroom in which you sit was an enemy fortress in the hands of German SS troops. Less than eight months ago nearly all our witnesses and documents were in enemy hands. The law had not been codified, no procedures had been established, no Tribunal was in existence, no usable courthouse stood here, none of the hundreds of tons of official German documents had been

examined, no prosecuting staff had been assembled, nearly all the present defendants were at large, and the four prosecuting powers had not yet joined in common cause to try them. I should be the last to deny that the case may well suffer from incomplete research and quite likely will not be the example of professional work which any of the prosecuting nations would normally wish to sponsor. It is, however, a completely adequate case to the judgment we shall ask you to render, and its full development we shall be obliged to leave to historians.

Before I discuss particulars of evidence, some general considerations which may affect the credit of this trial in the eyes of the world should be candidly faced. There is a dramatic disparity between the circumstances of the accusers and of the accused that might discredit our work if we should falter, in even minor matters, in being fair and temperate.

Unfortunately, the nature of these crimes is such that both prosecution and judgment must be by victor nations over vanquished foes. The worldwide scope of the aggressions carried out by these men has left but few real neutrals. Either the victors must judge the vanquished or we must leave the defeated to judge themselves. After the First World War, we learned the futility of the latter course. The former high station of these defendants, the notoriety of their acts, and the adaptability of their conduct to provoke retaliation make it hard to distinguish between the demand for a just and measured retribution, and the unthinking cry for vengeance which arises from the anguish of war. It is our task, so far as humanly possible, to draw the line between the two. We must never forget that the record on which we judge these defendants today is the record on which history will judge us tomorrow. To pass these defendants a poisoned chalice is to put it to our own lips as well. We must summon such detachment and intellectual integrity to our task that this trial will commend itself to posterity as fulfilling humanity's aspirations to do justice.

At the very outset, let us dispose of the contention that to put these men to trial is to do them an injustice entitling them to some special consideration. These defendants may be hard pressed but they are not ill-used. Let us see what alternative they would have to being tried.

More than a majority of these prisoners surrendered to or were tracked down by forces of the United States. Could they expect us to make American custody a shelter for our enemies against the just wrath of our allies? Did we spend American lives to capture them only to save them from punishment? Under the principles of the Moscow Declaration, those suspected war criminals who are not to be tried internationally must be turned over to individual governments for trial at the scene of their outrages. Many less responsible and less culpable American-held prisoners have been and will be turned over to other United Nations for local trial. If these defendants should succeed, for any reason, in escaping the condemnation of this Tribunal, or if they obstruct or abort this trial, those who are American-held prisoners will be delivered up to our continental allies. For these defendants, however, we have set up an International Tribunal and have undertaken the burden of participating in a complicated effort to give them fair and dispassionate hearings. That is the best-known protection to any man with a defense worthy of being heard.

If these men are the first war leaders of a defeated nation to be prosecuted in the name of the law, they are also the first to be given a chance to plead for their lives in the name of the law. Realistically, the Charter of this Tribunal, which gives them a hearing, is also the source of their only hope. It may be that these men of troubled conscience, whose only wish is that the world forget them, do not regard a trial as a favor. But they do have a fair opportunity to defend themselves—a favor which these men, when in power, rarely extended to their fellow countrymen. Despite the fact that public opinion already condemns their acts, we agree that here they must be given a presumption of innocence, and we accept the burden of proving criminal acts and the responsibility of these defendants for their commission.

When I say that we do not ask for convictions unless we prove crime, I do not mean mere technical or incidental transgression of international conventions. We charge guilt on planned and intended conduct that involves moral as well as legal wrong. And we do not mean conduct that is a natural and human, even if illegal, cutting of corners, such as many of us might well have committed had we been in the defendants' positions. It is not because they yielded to the normal frailties of human beings that we accuse them. It is their abnormal and inhuman conduct which brings them to this bar.

We will not ask you to convict these men on the testimony of their foes. There is no count of the Indictment that cannot be proved by books and records. The Germans were always meticulous record keepers, and these defendants had their share of the Teutonic passion for thoroughness in putting things on paper. Nor were they without vanity. They arranged frequently to be photographed in action. We will show you their own films. You will see their own conduct and hear their own voices as these defendants reenact for you, from the screen, some of the events in the course of the conspiracy.

We would also make clear that we have no purpose to incriminate the whole German people. We know that the Nazi Party was not put in power by a majority of the German vote. We know it came to power by an evil alliance between the most extreme of the Nazi revolutionists, the most unrestrained of the German reactionaries, and the most aggressive of the German militarists. If the German populace had willingly accepted the Nazi program, no Storm Troopers would have been needed in the early days of the party and there would have been no need for concentration camps or the Gestapo, both of which institutions were inaugurated as soon as the Nazis gained control of the German state. Only after these lawless innovations proved successful at home were they taken abroad.

The German people should know by now that the people of the United States hold them in no fear, and in no hate. It is true that the Germans have taught us the horrors of modern warfare, but the ruin that lies from the Rhine to the Danube shows that we, like our allies, have not been dull pupils. If we are not awed by German fortitude and proficiency in war, and if we are not persuaded of their political maturity, we do respect their skill in the arts of peace, their technical competence, and the sober, industrious and self-disciplined character of the masses of the German people. In 1933, we saw the German people recovering prestige in the commercial, industrial and artistic world after the setback of the last war. We beheld their progress neither with envy nor malice. The Nazi regime interrupted this advance. The recoil of the Nazi aggression has left Germany in ruins. The Nazi readiness to pledge the German word without hesitation and to break it without shame has fastened upon German diplomacy a reputation for duplicity that will handicap it for years. Nazi arrogance has made the boast of the "master race" a taunt that will be thrown at Germans the world over for generations. The Nazi nightmare has given the German name a new and sinister significance throughout the world which will retard Germany a century. The German, no less than the non-German world, has accounts to settle with these defendants.

The fact of the war and the course of the war, which is the central theme of our case, is history. From September 1, 1939, when the German armies crossed the Polish frontiers, until September 1942, when they met epic resistance at Stalingrad, German arms seemed invincible. Denmark and Norway, the Netherlands and France, Belgium and Luxembourg, the Balkans and Africa, Poland and the Baltic States, and parts of Russia, all had been overrun and conquered by swift, powerful, well-aimed blows. That attack upon the peace of the world is the crime against international society which brings into international cognizance crimes in its aid and preparation which otherwise might be only internal concerns. It was aggressive war, which the nations of the world had renounced. It was war in violation of treaties, by which the peace of the world was sought to be safeguarded.

This war did not just happen—it was planned and prepared for over a long period of time and with no small skill and cunning. The world has perhaps never seen such a concentration and stimulation of the energies of any people as that which enabled Germany twenty years after it was defeated, disarmed, and dismembered to come so near carrying out its plan to dominate Europe. Whatever else we may say of those who were the authors of this war, they did achieve a stupendous work in organization, and our first task is to examine the means by which these defendants and their fellow conspirators prepared and incited Germany to go to war.

In general, our case will disclose these defendants all uniting at some time with the Nazi Party in a plan which they well knew could be accomplished only by an outbreak of war in Europe. Their seizure of the German state, their subjugation of the German people, their terrorism and extermination of dissident elements, their planning and waging of war, their calculated and planned ruthlessness in the conduct of warfare, their deliberate and planned criminality toward conquered peoples—all these are ends for which they acted in concert; and all these are phases of the conspiracy, a conspiracy which reached one goal only to set out for another and more ambitious one. We shall also trace for you the intricate web of organizations which these men formed and utilized to accomplish these ends. We will show how the entire structure of offices and officials was dedicated to the criminal purposes and committed to use of the criminal methods planned by these defendants and their co-conspirators, many of whom war and suicide have put beyond reach.

It is my purpose to open the case, particularly under Count One of the Indictment, and to deal with the common plan or conspiracy to achieve ends possible only by resort to crimes against peace, war crimes, and crimes against humanity. My emphasis will not be on individual barbarities and perversions which may have occurred independently of any central plan. One of the dangers ever present is that this trial may be protracted by details of particular wrongs and that we will become lost in a wilderness of single instances.

Nor will I now dwell on the activity of individual defendants except as it may contribute to exposition of the common plan.

The case as presented by the United States will be concerned with the brains and authority in back of all the crimes. These defendants were men of a station and rank which does not soil its own hands with blood. They were men who knew how to use lesser folk as tools. We want to reach the planners and designers, the inciters and leaders without whose evil architecture we would not have been for so long scourged with the violence, lawlessness, and wracked with the agonies and convulsion this terrible war. . . .

CRIMES AGAINST THE JEWS

The most savage and numerous crimes planned and committed by the Nazis were those against the Jews. These in Germany, in 1933, numbered about five hundred thousand. In the aggregate, they had made for themselves positions which excited envy, and had accumulated properties which excited the avarice of the Nazis. They were few enough to be helpless and numerous enough to be held up as a menace.

Let there be no misunderstanding about the charge of persecuting Jews. What we charge against these defendants is not those arrogances and pretensions which frequently accompany the intermingling of different peoples and which are likely, despite the honest efforts of government, to produce regrettable crimes and convulsions. It is my purpose to show a plan and design, to which all Nazis were fanatically committed, to annihilate all Jewish people. These crimes were organized and promoted by the party leadership, executed and protected by the Nazi officials, as we shall convince you by written orders of the Secret State Police itself.

The persecution of the Jews was a continuous and deliberate policy. It was a policy directed against other nations as well as against the Jews themselves. Anti-Semitism was promoted to divide and embitter the democratic peoples and to soften their resistance to the Nazi aggression. As Robert Ley declared in *Der Angriff*, on May 14, 1944, "The second German secret weapon is anti-Semitism because if it is constantly pursued by Germany, it will become a universal problem which all nations will be forced to consider."

Anti-Semitism also has been aptly credited with being a "spearhead of terror." The ghetto was the laboratory for testing repressive measures. Jewish property was the first to be expropriated. The custom grew and included similar measures against anti-Nazi Germans, Poles, Czechs, Frenchmen, and Belgians. Extermination of the Jews enabled the Nazis to bring a practiced hand to similar measures against Poles, Serbs, and Greeks. The plight of the Jew was a constant threat to opposition or discontent among other elements of Europe's population—pacifists, conservatives, communists, Catholics, Protestants, socialists. It was, in fact, a threat to every dissenting opinion and to every non-Nazi's life.

The persecution policy against the Jews commenced with nonviolent measures, such as disenfranchisement and discriminations against their religion, and the placing of impediments in the way of success in economic life. It moved rapidly to organized mass violence against them, physical isolation in ghettos, deportation, forced labor, mass starvation, and extermination. The government, the party formations indicted before you as criminal organizations, the Secret State Police, the army, private and semipublic associations, and spontaneous mobs that were carefully inspired from official sources, were all agencies concerned in this persecution. Nor was it directed against individual Jews for personal bad citizenship or unpopularity. The avowed purpose was the destruction of the Jewish people as a whole, as an end in itself, as a measure of preparation for war, and as a discipline of conquered peoples.

The conspiracy or common plan to exterminate the Jew was so methodically and thoroughly pursued that despite the German defeat and Nazi prostration, this Nazi aim largely has succeeded. Only remnants of the European Jewish population remain in Germany, in the countries which

Germany occupied, and in those which were her satellites or collaborators. Of the 9,600,000 Jews who lived in Nazi-dominated Europe, 60 percent are authoritatively estimated to have perished. Five million seven hundred thousand Jews are missing from the countries in which they formerly lived, and over 4,500,000 cannot be accounted for by the normal death rate nor by immigration; nor are they included among displaced persons. History does not record a crime ever perpetrated against so many victims or one ever carried out with such calculated cruelty.

You will have difficulty, as I have, to look into the faces of these defendants and believe that in this twentieth century human beings could inflict such sufferings as will be proved here on their own countrymen as well as upon their so-called "inferior" enemies. Particular crimes, and the responsibility of defendants for them, are to be dealt with by the Soviet Government's Counsel, when committed in the East, and by Counsel for the Republic of France when committed in the West. I advert to them only to show their magnitude as evidence of a purpose and a knowledge common to all defendants, of an official plan rather than of a capricious policy of some individual commander, and to show such a continuity of Jewish persecution from the rise of the Nazi conspiracy to its collapse as forbids us to believe that any person could be identified with any part of Nazi action without approving this most conspicuous item of its program.

The Indictment itself recites many evidences of the anti-Semitic persecutions. The defendant Streicher led the Nazis in anti-Semitic bitterness and extremism. In an article appearing in *Der Stürmer* on March 19, 1942, he complained that Christian teachings have stood in the way of "radical solution of the Jewish question in Europe," and quoted enthusiastically as the twentieth-century solution the Führer's proclamation of February 24, 1942, that "the Jew will be exterminated." And on November 4, 1943, Streicher declared in *Der Stürmer* that the Jews "have disappeared from Europe" and that "the Jewish 'Reservoir of the East' from which the Jewish plague has for centuries beset the people of Europe, has ceased to exist." Streicher now has the effrontery to tell us he is "only a Zionist"—he says he wants only to return the Jews to Palestine. But on May 7, 1942, his newspaper had this to say: "It is also not only an European problem! The Jewish question is a world question! Not only is Germany not safe in the face of the Jews as long as one Jew lives in Europe, but also the Jewish question is hardly solved in Europe so long as Jews live in the rest of the world."

And the defendant Hans Frank, a lawyer by profession I say with shame, summarized in his diary in 1944 the Nazi policy thus: "The Jews are a race which has to be eliminated; whenever we catch one, it is his end." And earlier, speaking of his function as Governor General of Poland, he confided to his diary this sentiment: "Of course I cannot eliminate all lice and Jews in only a year's time." I could multiply endlessly this kind of Nazi ranting but I will leave it to the evidence and turn to the fruit of this perverted thinking.

The most serious of the actions against Jews were outside of any law, but the law itself was employed to some extent. There were the infamous Nuremberg decrees of September 15, 1935. (*Reichsgesetzblatt*, 1935, Part I, p. 1146.) The Jews were segregated into ghettos and put into forced labor; they were expelled from their professions; their property was expropriated; all cultural life, the press, the theater, and schools were prohibited them; and the SD was made responsible for them. This was an ominous guardianship, as the following order for "The Handling of the Jewish Question" shows:

The competency of the Chief of the Security Police and Security Service, who is charged with the mission of solving the European Jewish question, extends even to the occupied eastern provinces....

An eventual act by the civilian population against the Jews is not to be prevented as long as this is compatible with the maintenance of order and security in the rear of the fighting troops....

The first main goal of the German measures must be strict segregation of Jewry from the rest of the population. In the execution of this, first of all is the seizing of the Jewish populace by the introduction of a registration order and similar appropriate measures....

Then immediately, the wearing of the recognition sign consisting of a yellow Jewish star is to be brought about and all rights of freedom for Jews are to be withdrawn. They are to be placed in ghettos and at the same time are to be separated according to sexes. The presence of many more or less closed Jewish settlements in White Ruthenia and in the Ukraine makes this mission easier. Moreover places are to be chosen which make possible the full use of the Jewish manpower in case labor needs are present....

The entire Jewish property is to be seized and confiscated with exception of that which is necessary for a bare existence. As far as the economic situation permits, the power of disposal of their property is to be taken from the Jews as soon as possible through orders and other measures given by the commissariat, so that the moving of property will quickly cease.

Any cultural activity will be completely forbidden to the Jew. This includes the outlawing of the Jewish press, the Jewish theaters and schools.

The slaughtering of animals according to Jewish rites is also to be prohibited....

The anti-Jewish campaign became furious in Germany following the assassination in Paris of the German Legation Councilor von Rath. Heydrich, Gestapo head, sent a teletype to all Gestapo and SD offices with directions for handling "spontaneous" uprisings anticipated for the nights of November 9 and 10, 1938, so as to aid in destruction of Jewish-owned property and protect only that of Germans. No more cynical document ever came into evidence. Then there is a report by an SS Brigade Leader, Dr. Stahlecker, to Himmler, which recites that:

... Similarly, native anti-Semitic forces were induced to start pogroms against Jews during the first hours after capture, though this inducement proved to be very difficult. Following our orders, the Security Police was determined to solve the Jewish question with all possible means and most decisively. But it was desirable that the Security Police should not put in an immediate appearance, at least in the beginning, since the extraordinarily harsh measures were apt to stir even German circles. It had to be shown to the world that the native population itself took the first action by way of natural reaction against the suppression by Jews during several decades and against the terror exercised by the Communists during the preceding period....

... In view of the extension of the area of operations and the great number of duties which had to be performed by the Security Police, it was intended from the very beginning to obtain the cooperation of the reliable population for the fight against vermin—that is mainly the Jews and Communists. Beyond our directing of the first spontaneous actions of self-cleansing, which will be reported elsewhere, care had to be taken that reliable people should be put to the cleansing job and that they were appointed auxiliary members of the Security Police....

... Kovno ... To our surprise it was not easy at first to set in motion an extensive pogrom against Jews. Klimatis, the leader of the partisan unit, mentioned above, who was used for this purpose primarily, succeeded in starting a pogrom on the basis of advice given to him by a small advanced detachment acting in Kovno, and in such a way that no German order or German instigation was noticed from the outside. During the first pogrom in the night from 25. to 26.6 the Lithuanian partisans did away with more than 1,500 Jews, set fire to several synagogues or destroyed them by other means, and burned down a Jewish dwelling district consisting of about sixty houses. During the following nights about 2,300 Jews were made harmless in a similar way. In other parts of Lithuania similar actions followed the example of Kovno, though smaller and extending to the Communists who had been left behind.

These self-cleansing actions went smoothly because the army authorities who had been informed showed understanding for this procedure. From the beginning it was obvious that only the first days after the occupation would offer the opportunity for carrying out pogroms. After the disarmament of the partisans the self-cleansing actions ceased necessarily.

It proved much more difficult to set in motion similar cleansing actions in Latvia.…

… From the beginning it was to be expected that the Jewish problem in the East could not be solved by pogroms alone. In accordance with the basic orders received, however, the cleansing activities of the Security Police had to aim at a complete annihilation of the Jews.…

The sum total of the Jews liquidated in Lithuania amounts to 71,105.…

Of course, it is self-evident that these "uprisings" were managed by the government and the Nazi Party. If we were in doubt we could resort to Streicher's memorandum of April 14, 1939, which says, "The anti-Jewish action of November 1938 did not arise spontaneously from the people. … Part of the party formation have been charged with the execution of the anti-Jewish action." Jews as a whole were fined a billion reichsmarks. They were excluded from all businesses, and claims against insurance companies for their burned properties were confiscated, all by decree of the defendant Goering. (*Reichsgesetzblatt*, 1938, Part I, pp. 1579–1582.)

Synagogues were the objects of a special vengeance. On November 10, 1938, the following order was given: "By order of the Group Commander, all Jewish synagogues in the area of Brigade 50 have to be blown up or set afire. … The operation will be carried out in civilian clothing. … Execution of the order will be reported.…" Some forty teletype messages from various police headquarters will tell the fury with which all Jews were pursued in Germany on those awful November nights. The SS troops were turned loose and the Gestapo supervised. Jewish-owned property was authorized to be destroyed. The Gestapo ordered twenty to thirty thousand "well-to-do Jews" to be arrested. Concentration camps were to receive them. Healthy Jews, fit for labor, were to be taken. As the German frontiers were expanded by war, so the campaign against the Jews expanded. The Nazi plan never was limited to extermination in Germany; always it contemplated extinguishing the Jew in Europe and often in the world. In the West, the Jews were killed and their property taken over. But the campaign achieved its zenith of savagery in the East. The eastern Jew has suffered as no people ever suffered. Their sufferings were carefully reported to the Nazi authorities to show faithful adherence to the Nazi design. I shall refer only to enough of the evidence of these to show the extent of the Nazi design for killing Jews.

If I should recite these horrors in words of my own, you would think me intemperate and unreliable. Fortunately, we need not take the word of any witness but the Germans themselves. I invite you now to look at a few of the vast number of captured German orders and reports that will be offered in evidence, to see what a Nazi invasion meant. We will present such evidence as the report of "Einsatzgruppe (Action Group) A" of October 15, 1941, which boasts that in overrunning the Baltic States, "native anti-Semitic forces were induced to start pogroms against the Jews during the first hours after occupation …" The report continues:

From the beginning it was to be expected that the Jewish problem in the East could not be solved by pogroms alone. In accordance with the basic orders received, however, the cleansing activities of the Security Police had to aim at a complete annihilation of the Jews. Special detachments reinforced by selected units—in Lithuania partisan detachments, in Latvia units of the Latvian auxiliary police—therefore performed extensive executions both in the towns and in rural areas. The actions of the execution detachments were performed smoothly.

The sum total of the Jews liquidated in Lithuania amounts to 71,105. During the pogroms in Kovno 3,800 Jews were eliminated, in the smaller towns about 1,200 Jews.

In Latvia, up to now a total of 30,000 Jews were executed. Five hundred were eliminated by pogroms in Riga.

This is a captured report from the commissioner of Sluzk on October 30, 1941, which describes the scene in more detail. It says:

> . . . The first lieutenant explained that the police battalion had received the assignment to effect the liquidation of all Jews here in the town of Sluzk, within two days. . . . Then I requested him to postpone the action one day. However, he rejected this with the remark that he had to carry out this action everywhere and in all towns and that only two days were allotted for Sluzk. Within these two days, the town of Sluzk had to be cleared of Jews by all means. . . . All Jews without exception were taken out of the factories and shops and deported in spite of our agreement. It is true that part of the Jews was moved by way of the ghetto where many of them were processed and still segregated by me, but a large part was loaded directly on trucks and liquidated without further delay outside of the town. . . . For the rest, as regards the execution of the action, I must point out to my deepest regret that the latter bordered already on sadism. The town itself offered a picture of horror during the action. With indescribable brutality on the part of both the German police officers and particularly the Lithuanian partisans, the Jewish people, but also among them White Ruthenians, were taken out of their dwellings and herded together. Everywhere in the town shots were to be heard and in different streets the corpses of shot Jews accumulated. The White Ruthenians were in greatest distress to free themselves from the encirclement. Regardless

of the fact that the Jewish people, among whom were also tradesmen, were mistreated in a terribly barbarous way in the face of the White Ruthenian people, the White Ruthenians themselves were also worked over with rubber clubs and rifle butts. There was no question of an action against the Jews any more. It rather looked like a revolution. . . .

There are reports which merely tabulate the numbers slaughtered. An example is an account of the work of Einsatzgruppen of Sipo and SD in the East, which relates that:

> In Estonia, all Jews were arrested immediately upon the arrival of the Wehrmacht. Jewish men and women above the age of sixteen and capable of work were drafted for forced labor. Jews were subjected to all sorts of restrictions and all Jewish property was confiscated.
>
> All Jewish males above the age of sixteen were executed, with the exception of doctors and elders. Only 500 of an original 4,500 Jews remained.
>
> Thirty-seven thousand, one hundred and eighty persons have been liquidated by the Sipo and SD in White Ruthenia during October.
>
> In one town, 337 Jewish women were executed for demonstrating a "provocative attitude." In another, 380 Jews were shot for spreading vicious propaganda.

And so the report continues, listing town after town, where hundreds upon hundreds of Jews were murdered.

In Witebsk 3,000 Jews were liquidated because of the danger of epidemics.

In Kiev, 33,771 Jews were executed on September 29 and 30 in retaliation for some fires which were set off there.

In Shitomir, 3,145 Jews "had to be shot" because, judging from experience, they had to be considered as the carriers of Bolshevik propaganda.

In Cherson, 410 Jews were executed in reprisal against acts of sabotage.

In the territory east of the Dnepr, the Jewish problem was "solved" by the liquidation of 4,891 Jews and by putting the remainder into labor battalions of up to 1,000 persons.

Other accounts tell not of the slaughter so much as of the depths of degradation to which the tormentors stooped. For example, we will show the report made to defendant Rosenberg about the army and the SS in the area under Rosenberg's jurisdiction, which recited the following:

Details: In presence of SS man, a Jewish dentist has to break all gold teeth and fillings out of mouth of German and Russian Jews before they are executed.

Men, women and children are locked into barns and burned alive.

Peasants, women and children are shot on pretext that they are suspected of belonging to bands.

We of the Western world heard of gas wagons in which Jews and political opponents were asphyxiated. We could not believe it. But here we have the report of May 16, 1942, from the German SS officer, Becker, to his supervisor in Berlin which tells this story:

Gas vans in C group can be driven to execution spot, which is generally stationed 10 to 15 kms. from main road only in dry weather. Since those to be executed become frantic if conducted to this place, such vans become immobilized in wet weather.

Gas vans in D group camouflaged as cabin trailers, but vehicles well known to authorities and civilian population which calls them Death Vans.

Writer of letter (Becker) ordered all men to keep as far away as possible during gassing. Unloading van has "atrocious spiritual and physical effect" on men and they should be ordered not to participate in such work.

I shall not dwell on this subject longer than to quote one more sickening document which evidences the planned and systematic character of the Jewish persecutions. I hold a report written with Teutonic devotion to detail, illustrated with photographs to authenticate its almost incredible text, and beautifully bound in leather with the loving care bestowed on a proud work. It is the original report of the SS Brigadier General Stroop in charge of the destruction of the Warsaw Ghetto, and its title page carries the inscription, "The Jewish Ghetto in Warsaw no longer exists." It is characteristic that one of the captions explains that the photograph concerned shows the driving out of Jewish "bandits"; those whom the photograph shows being driven out are almost entirely women and little children. It contains a day-by-day account of the killings mainly carried out by the SS organization, too long to relate, but let me quote General Stroop's summary:

The resistance put up by the Jews and bandits could only be suppressed by energetic actions of our troops day and night. The Reichsführer SS ordered, therefore, on 23 April 1943 the cleaning out of the ghetto with utter ruthlessness and merciless tenacity. I, therefore, decided to destroy and burn down the entire ghetto without regard to the armament factories. These factories were systematically dismantled and then burned. Jews usually left their hideouts, but frequently remained in the burning buildings and jumped out of the windows only when the heat became unbearable. They then tried to crawl with broken bones across the street into buildings which were not afire. Sometimes they changed their hideouts during the night into the ruins of burned buildings. Life in the sewers was not pleasant after the first week. Many times we could hear loud voices in the sewers. SS men or policemen climbed bravely through the manholes to capture these Jews.

Sometimes they stumbled over Jewish corpses; sometimes they were shot at. Tear gas bombs were thrown into the manholes and the Jews driven out of the sewers and captured. Countless numbers of Jews were liquidated in sewers and bunkers through blasting. The longer the resistance continued the tougher became the members of the Waffen SS police and Wehrmacht who always discharged their duties in an exemplary manner. Frequently Jews who tried to replenish their food supplies during the night or to communicate with neighboring groups were exterminated.

"This action eliminated," says the SS commander, "a total of 56,065. To that we have to add the number of those killed through blasting, fire, etc., which cannot be counted."

We charge that all atrocities against Jews were the manifestation and culmination of the Nazi plan to which every defendant here was a party. I know very well that some of these men did take steps to spare some particular Jew for some personal reason from the horrors that awaited the unrescued Jew. Some protested that particular atrocities were excessive, and discredited the general policy. While a few defendants may show efforts to make specific exceptions to the policy of Jewish extermination, I have found no instance in which any defendant opposed the policy itself or sought to revoke or even modify it.

Determination to destroy the Jews was a binding force which at all times cemented the elements of this conspiracy. On many internal policies there were differences among the defendants. But there is not one of them who has not echoed the rallying cry of Nazism—"*Deutschland erwache, Juda verrecke*." (Germany awake, Jewry perish.)

…I dislike to encumber the record with such morbid tales, but we are in the grim business of trying men as criminals, and these are the things their own agents say happened. We will show you these concentration camps in motion pictures, just as the Allied armies found them when they arrived, and the measures General Eisenhower had to take to clean them up. Our proof will be disgusting and you will say I have robbed you of your sleep. But these are the things which have turned the stomach of the world and set every civilized hand against Nazi Germany.

Germany became one vast torture chamber. Cries of its victims were heard round the world and brought shudders to civilized people everywhere. I am one who received during this war most atrocity tales with suspicion and skepticism. But the proof here will be so overwhelming that I venture to predict not one word I have spoken will be denied. These defendants will only deny personal responsibility or knowledge.

Under the clutch of the most intricate web of espionage and intrigue that any modern state has endured, and persecution and torture of a kind that has not been visited upon the world in many centuries, the elements of the German population which were both decent and courageous were annihilated. Those which were decent but weak were intimidated. Open resistance, which had never been more than feeble and irresolute, disappeared. But resistance, I am happy to say, always remained, although it was manifest in only such events as the abortive effort to assassinate Hitler on July 20, 1944. With resistance driven underground, the Nazi had the German state in his own hands.

But the Nazis not only silenced discordant voices. They created positive controls as effective as their negative ones. Propaganda organs, on a scale never before known, stimulated the party and party formations with a permanent enthusiasm and abandon such as we democratic people can work up only for a few days before a general election. They inculcated and practiced the *Führerprinzip* which centralized control of the party and of the party-controlled state over the lives and thought of the German people, who are accustomed to look upon the German state by whomever controlled with a mysticism that is incomprehensible to my people.

All these controls from their inception were exerted with unparalleled energy and single-mindedness to put Germany on a war footing. We will show from the Nazis' own documents their secret training of military personnel, their secret creation of a military air force. Finally, a conscript army was brought into being. Financiers, economists, industrialists, joined in the plan and promoted elaborate alterations in industry and finance to support an unprecedented concentration of resources and energies upon preparations for war. Germany's rearmament so outstripped the strength of her neighbors that in about a year she was able to crush the whole military force of continental Europe, exclusive of that of Soviet Russia, and then to push the Russian armies back to the Volga. These preparations were of a magnitude which surpassed all need of defense and every defendant, and every intelligent German, well understood them to be for aggressive purposes....

CRIMES IN THE CONDUCT OF WAR

Even the most warlike of peoples have recognized in the name of humanity some limitations on the savagery of warfare. Rules to that end have been embodied in international conventions to which Germany became a party. This code had prescribed certain restraints as to the treatment of belligerents. The enemy was entitled to surrender and to receive quarter and good treatment as a prisoner of war. We will show by German documents that these rights were denied, that prisoners of war were given brutal treatment and often murdered. This was particularly true in the case of captured airmen, often my countrymen.

It was ordered that captured English and American airmen should no longer be granted the status of prisoners of war. They were to be treated as criminals and the army was ordered to refrain from protecting them against lynching by the populace. The Nazi government, through its police and propaganda agencies, took pains to incite the civilian population to attack and kill airmen who crash-landed. The order, given by the SS Reichsführer, Himmler, on August 10, 1943, directed that "It is not the task of the police to interfere in clashes between Germans and English and American flyers who have bailed out."

This order was transmitted on the same day by SS Obersturmbannführer Brand of Himmler's Personal Staff to all Senior Executive SS and Police officers, with these directions:

> I am sending you the enclosed order with the request that the chief of the Regular Police and of the Security Police be informed. They are to make this instruction known to their subordinate officers verbally.

Similarly, we will show Hitler's top secret order, dated October 18, 1942, that kommandos, regardless of condition, were "to be slaughtered to the last man" after capture. We will show the circulation of secret orders, one of which was signed by Hess, to be passed orally to civilians, that enemy fliers or parachutists were to be arrested or liquidated. By such means were murders incited and directed.

This Nazi campaign of ruthless treatment of enemy forces assumed its greatest proportions in the fight against Russia. Eventually all prisoners of war were taken out of control of the army and put in the hands of Himmler and the SS. In the East, the German fury spent itself. Russian prisoners were ordered to be branded. They were starved. I shall quote passages from a letter written February 28, 1942, by defendant Rosenberg to defendant Keitel:

> The fate of the Soviet prisoners of war in Germany is on the contrary a tragedy of the greatest extent. Of 3.6 millions of prisoners of war, only several hundred thousand are still able to work fully. A large part of them has starved, or died, because of the hazards of the weather. Thousands also died from spotted fever. The camp commanders have forbidden the civilian population to put food at the disposal of the prisoners, and they have rather let them starve to death.

In many cases, when prisoners of war could no longer keep up on the march because of hunger and exhaustion, they were shot before the eyes of the horrified civilian population, and the corpses were left.

In numerous camps, no shelter for the prisoners of war was provided at all. They lay under the open sky during rain or snow. Even tools were not made available to dig holes or caves.

Finally, the shooting of prisoners of war must be mentioned: For instance, in various camps, all the "Asiatics" were shot.

Civilized usage and conventions to which Germany was a party had prescribed certain immunities for civilian populations unfortunate enough to dwell in lands overrun by hostile armies. The German occupation forces, controlled or commanded by men on trial before you, committed a long series of outrages against the inhabitants of occupied territory that would be incredible except for captured orders and the captured reports showing the fidelity with which these orders were executed.

We deal here with a phase of common criminality designed by the conspirators as part of the common plan. We can appreciate why these crimes against their European enemies were not of a casual character but were planned and disciplined crimes when we get at the reason for them. Hitler told his officers on August 22, 1939, that "the main objective in Poland is the destruction of the enemy and not the reaching of a certain geographical line." The project of deporting promising youth from occupied territories was approved by Rosenberg on the theory that "a desired weakening of the biological force of the conquered people is being achieved." To Germanize or to destroy was the program. Himmler announced, "Either we win over any good blood that we can use for ourselves and give it a place in our people or, gentlemen—you may call this cruel, but nature is cruel—we destroy this blood." As to "racially good types" Himmler further advised, "Therefore, I think that it is our duty to take their children with us, to remove them from their environment, if necessary by robbing or stealing them." He urged deportation of Slavic children to deprive potential enemies of future soldiers.

The Nazi purpose was to leave Germany's neighbors so weakened that even if she should eventually lose the war, she would still be the most powerful nation in Europe. Against this background, we must view the plan for ruthless warfare, which means a plan for the commission of war crimes and crimes against humanity.

Hostages in large numbers were demanded and killed. Mass punishments were inflicted, so savage that whole communities were extinguished. Rosenberg was advised of the annihilation of three unidentified villages in Slovakia. In May 1943, another village of about forty farms and 220 inhabitants was ordered wiped out. The entire population was ordered shot, the cattle and property impounded, and the order required that "the village will be destroyed totally by fire." A secret report from Rosenberg's Reich Ministry of Eastern Territory reveals that:

> Food rations allowed the Russian population are so low that they fail to secure their existence and provide only for minimum subsistence of limited duration. The population does not know if they will still live tomorrow. They are faced with death by starvation.
>
> The roads are clogged by hundreds of thousands of people, sometimes as many as one million according to the estimate of experts, who wander around in search of nourishment.
>
> Sauckel's action has caused great unrest among the civilians. Russian girls were deloused by men, nude photos in forced positions were taken, women doctors were locked into freight cars for the pleasure of the transport commanders, women in night shirts were fettered and forced through the Russian towns to the railroad station, etc. All this material has been sent to the OKH.

Perhaps the deportation to slave labor was the most horrible and extensive slaving operation in history. On few other subjects is our evidence so abundant or so damaging. In a speech made on January 25, 1944, the defendant Frank,

Governor General of Poland boasted, "I have sent 1,300,000 Polish workers into the Reich." The defendant Sauckel reported that "out of the five million foreign workers who arrived in Germany not even two hundred thousand came voluntarily." This fact was reported to the Führer and defendants Speer, Goering, and Keitel. Children of ten to fourteen years were impressed into service by telegraphic order from Rosenberg's Ministry for Occupied Eastern Territories:

The Command is further charged with the transferring of worthwhile Russian youth between 10–14 years of age, to the Reich. The authority is not affected by the changes connected with the evacuation and transportation to the reception camps of Bialystok, Krajewo, and Olitei. The Führer wishes that this activity be increased even more.

When enough labor was not forthcoming, prisoners of war were forced in war work in flagrant violation of international conventions. Slave labor came from France, Belgium, Holland, Italy, and the East. Methods of recruitment were violent. The treatment of these slave laborers was stated in general terms, not difficult to translate into concrete deprivations, in a letter to the defendant Rosenberg from the defendant Sauckel, which stated:

All prisoners of war, from the territories of the West as well of the East, actually in Germany, must be completely incorporated into the German armament and munition industries. Their production must be brought to the highest possible level....

The complete employment of all prisoners of war as well as the use of a gigantic number of new foreign civilian workers, men and women, has become an undisputable necessity for the solution of the mobilization of labor program in this war.

All the men must be fed, sheltered and treated in such a way as to exploit them to the highest possible extent at the lowest conceivable degree of expenditure....

In pursuance of the Nazi plan permanently to reduce the living standards of their neighbors and to weaken them physically and economically, a long series of crimes were committed. There was extensive destruction, serving no military purpose, of the property of civilians. Dikes were thrown open in Holland almost at the close of the war not to achieve military ends but to destroy the resources and retard the economy of the thrifty Netherlanders. There was carefully planned economic syphoning off of the assets of occupied countries. An example of the planning is shown by a report on France dated December 7, 1942 made by the Economic Research Department of the Reichsbank. The question arose whether French occupation costs should be increased from fifteen million reichsmarks per day to twenty-five million reichsmarks per day....

THE LAW OF INDIVIDUAL RESPONSIBILITY

The Charter also recognizes individual responsibility on the part of those who commit acts defined as crimes, or who incite others to do so, or who join a common plan with other persons, groups or organizations to bring about their commission. The principle of individual responsibility for piracy and brigandage, which have long been recognized as crimes punishable under International Law, is old and well established. That is what illegal warfare is. This principle of personal liability is a necessary as well as logical one if International Law is to render real help to the maintenance of peace. An International Law which operates only on states can be enforced only by war because the most practicable method of coercing a state is warfare. Those familiar with American history know that one of the compelling reasons for adoption of our Constitution was that the laws of the Confederation, which operated only on constituent states, were found ineffective to maintain order among them. The only answer to recalcitrance was impotence or war. Only sanctions which reach individuals can peacefully and effectively be enforced. Hence, the principle of the criminality of aggressive war is implemented by the Charter with the principle of personal responsibility.

Of course, the idea that a state, any more than a corporation, commits crimes is a fiction. Crimes always are committed only by persons. While it is quite proper to employ the fiction of responsibility of a state or corporation for the purpose of imposing a collective liability, it is quite intolerable to let such a legalism become the basis of personal immunity.

The Charter recognizes that one who has committed criminal acts may not take refuge in superior orders nor in the doctrine that his crimes were acts of states. These twin principles working together have heretofore resulted in immunity for practically everyone concerned in the really great crimes against peace and mankind. Those in lower ranks were protected against liability by the orders of their superiors. The superiors were protected because their orders were called acts of state. Under the Charter, no defense based on either of these doctrines can be entertained. Modern civilization puts unlimited weapons of destruction in the hands of men. It cannot tolerate so vast an area of legal irresponsibility.

Even the German Military Code provides that:

If the execution of a military order in the course of duty violates the criminal law, then the superior officer giving the order will bear the sole responsibility therefor. However, the obeying subordinate will share the punishment of the participant: (1) if he has exceeded the order given to him, or (2) if it was within his knowledge that the order of his superior officer concerned an act by which it was intended to commit a civil or military crime or transgression. (*Reichsgesetzblatt*, 1926, No. 87, p. 278, Art. 47.)

Of course, we do not argue that the circumstances under which one commits an act should be disregarded in judging its legal effect. A conscripted private on a firing squad cannot expect to hold an inquest on the validity of the execution. The Charter implies common sense limits to liability just as it places common sense limits upon immunity. But none of these men before you acted in minor parts. Each of them was entrusted with broad discretion and exercised great power. Their responsibility is correspondingly great and may not be shifted to that fictional being, "the state," which cannot be produced for trial, cannot testify, and cannot be sentenced.

The Charter also recognizes a vicarious liability, which responsibility is recognized by most modern systems of law, for acts committed by others in carrying out a common plan or conspiracy to which a defendant has become a party. I need not discuss the familiar principles of such liability. Every day in the courts of countries associated in this prosecution, men are convicted for acts that they did not personally commit but for which they were held responsible because of membership in illegal combinations or plans or conspiracies. . . .

. . . The refuge of the defendants can be only their hope that International Law will lag so far behind the moral sense of mankind that conduct which is crime in the moral sense must be regarded as innocent in law.

Civilization asks whether law is so laggard as to be utterly helpless to deal with crimes of this magnitude by criminals of this order of importance. It does not expect that you can make war impossible. It does expect that your juridical action will put the forces of International Law, its precepts, its prohibitions and, most of all, its sanctions, on the side of peace, so that men and women of goodwill in all countries may have to live by no man's leave, underneath the law.

Excerpts from the Opening Statement of the Prosecution (Telford Taylor) at the Medical Trials

December 9, 1946

The defendants in this case are charged with murders, tortures, and other atrocities committed in the name of medical science. The victims of these crimes are numbered in the hundreds of thousands. A handful only are still alive; a few of the survivors will appear in this courtroom. But most of these miserable victims were slaughtered outright or died in the course of the tortures to which they were subjected.

For the most part they are nameless dead. To their murderers, these wretched people were not individuals at all. They came in wholesale lots and were treated worse than animals. They were two hundred Jews in good physical condition, fifty Gypsies, five hundred tubercular Poles, or one thousand Russians. The victims of these crimes are numbered among the anonymous millions who met death at the hands of the Nazis and whose fate is a hideous blot on the page of modern history.

The charges against these defendants are brought in the name of the United States of America. They are being tried by a court of American judges. The responsibilities thus imposed upon the representatives of the United States, prosecutors and judges alike, are grave and unusual. It is owed, not only to the victims and to the parents and children of the victims, that just punishment be imposed on the guilty, but also to the defendants that they be accorded a fair hearing and decision. Such responsibilities are the ordinary burden of any tribunal. Far wider are the duties which we must fulfill here.

These larger obligations run to the peoples and races on whom the scourge of these crimes was laid. The mere punishment of the defendants or even of thousands of others equally guilty, can never redress the terrible injuries which the Nazis visited on these unfortunate peoples. For them it is far more important that these incredible events be established by clear and public proof, so that no one can ever doubt that they were fact and not fable and that this court, as the agent of the United States and as the voice of humanity, stamp these acts, and the ideas which engendered them, as barbarous and criminal.

We have still other responsibilities here. The defendants in the dock are charged with murder, but this is no mere murder trial. We cannot rest content when we have shown that crimes were committed and that certain persons committed them. To kill, to maim, and to torture is criminal under all modern systems of law. These defendants did not kill in hot blood, nor for personal enrichment. Some of them may be sadists who killed and tortured for sport, but they are not all perverts. They are not ignorant men. Most of them are trained physicians and some of them are distinguished scientists. Yet these defendants, all of whom were fully able to comprehend the nature of their acts, and most of whom were exceptionally qualified to form a moral and professional judgment in this respect, are responsible for wholesale murder and unspeakably cruel tortures.

It is our deep obligation to all peoples of the world to show why and how these things happened. It is incumbent upon us to set forth with conspicuous clarity the ideas and motives which moved these defendants to treat their fellow men as less than beasts. The perverse thoughts and distorted concepts which brought about these savageries are not dead. They cannot be killed by force of arms. They must not become a spreading cancer in the breast of humanity. They must be cut out and exposed, for the reason so well stated by Mr. Justice Jackson in this courtroom a year ago. "The wrongs which we seek to condemn and punish have been so calculated, so malignant, and so devastating, that civilization cannot tolerate their being ignored because it cannot survive their being repeated."

To the German people we owe a special responsibility in these proceedings. Under the leadership of the Nazis and their warlords, the German nation spread death and devastation throughout Europe. This the Germans now know. So, too, do they know the consequences to Germany: defeat, ruin, prostration, and utter demoralization. Most German children will never, as long as they live, see an undamaged German city.

To what cause will these children ascribe the defeat of the German nation and the devastation that surrounds them? Will they attribute it to the overwhelming weight of numbers and resources that was eventually leagued against them? Will they point to the ingenuity of enemy scientists? Will they perhaps blame their plight on strategic and military blunders by their generals?

If the Germans embrace those reasons as the true cause of their disaster, it will be a sad and fatal thing for Germany and for the world. Men who have never seen a German city intact will be callous about flattening English or American or Russian cities. They may not even realize that they are destroying anything worthwhile, for lack of a normal sense of values. To reestablish the greatness of Germany they are likely to pin their faith on improved military techniques. Such views will lead the Germans straight into the arms of the Prussian militarists to whom defeat is only a glorious opportunity to start a new war game. "Next time it will be different." We know all too well what that will mean.

This case, and others which will be tried in this building, offer a signal opportunity to lay before the German people the true cause of their present misery. The walls and towers and churches of Nuremberg were, indeed, reduced to rubble by Allied bombs, but in a deeper sense Nuremberg had been destroyed a decade earlier, when it became the seat of the annual Nazi Party rallies, a focal point for the moral disintegration in Germany, and the private domain of Julius Streicher. The insane and malignant doctrines that Nuremberg spewed forth account alike for the crimes of these defendants and for the terrible fate of Germany under the Third Reich.

A nation which deliberately infects itself with poison will inevitably sicken and die. These defendants and others turned Germany into an infernal combination of a lunatic asylum and a charnel house. Neither science, nor industry, nor the arts could flourish in such a foul medium. The country could not live at peace and was fatally handicapped for war. I do not think the German people have as yet any conception of how deeply the criminal folly that was Nazism bit into every phase of German life, or of how utterly ravaging the consequences were. It will be our task to make these things clear.

These are the high purposes which justify the establishment of extraordinary courts to hear and determine this case and others of comparable importance. That murder should be punished goes without the saying, but the full performance of our task requires more than the just sentencing of these defendants. Their crimes were the inevitable result of the sinister doctrines which they espoused, and these same doctrines sealed the fate of Germany, shattered Europe, and left the world in ferment. Wherever those doctrines may emerge and prevail, the same terrible consequences will follow. That is why a bold and lucid consummation of these proceedings is of vital importance to all nations. That is why the United States has constituted this Tribunal.

I pass now to the facts of the case in hand. There are twenty-three defendants in the box. All but three of them—Rudolf Brandt, Sievers, and Brack—are doctors. Of the twenty doctors, all but one—Pokorny—held positions in the medical services of the Third Reich. To understand this case, it is necessary to understand the general structure of these state medical services, and how these services fitted into the overall organization of the Nazi state. [The material on the organization of the military medical personnel, and where the individual defendants fit into it, has been deleted.]

CRIMES COMMITTED IN THE GUISE OF SCIENTIFIC RESEARCH

. . . . A sort of rough pattern is apparent on the face of the indictment. Experiments concerning high altitude, the effect of cold, and the potability of processed sea water have an obvious relation to aeronautical and naval combat and rescue problems. The mustard gas and phosphorus burn experiments, as well as those relating to the healing value of sulfanilamide for wounds, can be related to air-raid and battlefield medical problems. It is well known that malaria, epidemic jaundice, and typhus were among the principal diseases which had to be combated by the German Armed Forces and by German authorities in occupied territories. To some degree, the therapeutic pattern outlined above is undoubtedly a valid one, and explains why the Wehrmacht, and especially the German Air Force, participated in these experiments. Fanatically bent upon conquest, utterly ruthless as to the means or instruments to be used in achieving victory, and callous to the sufferings of people whom they regarded as inferior, the German militarists were willing to gather whatever scientific fruit these experiments might yield.

But our proof will show that a quite different and even more sinister objective runs like a red thread through these hideous researches. We will show that in some instances the true object of these experiments was not how to rescue or to cure, but how to destroy and kill. The sterilization experiments were, it is clear, purely destructive in purpose. The prisoners at Buchenwald who were shot with poisoned bullets were not guinea pigs to test an antidote for the poison; their murderers really wanted to know how quickly the poison would kill. This destructive objective is not superficially as apparent in the other experiments, but we will show that it was often there.

Mankind has not heretofore felt the need of a word to denominate the science of how to kill prisoners most rapidly and subjugated people in large numbers. This case and these defendants have created this gruesome question for the lexicographer. For the moment we will christen this macabre science thanatology, the science of producing death. The thanatological knowledge, derived in part from these experiments, supplied the techniques for genocide, a policy of the Third Reich, exemplified in the "euthanasia" program and in the widespread slaughter of Jews, Gypsies, Poles, and Russians. This policy of mass extermination could not have been so effectively carried out without the active participation of German medical scientists. . . .

STERILIZATION EXPERIMENTS

In the sterilization experiments conducted by the defendants at Auschwitz, Ravensbrueck, and other concentration camps, the destructive nature of the Nazi medical program comes out most forcibly. The Nazis were searching for methods of extermination, both by murder and sterilization, of large population groups by the most scientific and least conspicuous means. They were developing a new branch of medical science which would give them the scientific tools for the planning and practice of genocide. The primary purpose was to discover an inexpensive, unobtrusive, and rapid method of sterilization which could be used to wipe out Russians, Poles, Jews, and other people. Surgical sterilization was thought to be too slow and expensive to be used on a mass scale. A method to bring about an unnoticed sterilization was thought desirable.

Medicinal sterilizations were therefore carried out. A Dr. Madaus had stated that caladium sequinum, a drug obtained from a North American plant, if taken orally or by injection, would bring about sterilization. In 1941 the defendant Pokorny called this to Himmler's attention, and suggested that it should be developed and used against Russian prisoners of war. I quote one paragraph from Pokorny's letter written at that time:

> If, on the basis of this research, it were possible to produce a drug which, after a relatively short time, effects an imperceptible steriliza-

tion on human beings, then we would have a powerful new weapon at our disposal. The thought alone that the three million Bolsheviks, who are at present German prisoners, could be sterilized so that they could be used as laborers but be prevented from reproduction, opens the most far-reaching perspectives.

As a result of Pokorny's suggestion, experiments were conducted on concentration camp inmates to test the effectiveness of the drug. At the same time, efforts were made to grow the plant on a large scale in hothouses.

At the Auschwitz concentration camp sterilization experiments were also conducted on a large scale by a Dr. Karl Clauberg, who had developed a method of sterilizing women, based on the injection of an irritating solution. Several thousand Jews and Gypsies were sterilized at Auschwitz by this method.

Conversely, surgical operations were performed on sexually abnormal inmates at Buchenwald in order to determine whether their virility could be increased by the transplantation of glands. Out of fourteen subjects of these experiments, at least two died.

The defendant Gebhardt also personally conducted sterilizations at Ravensbrueck by surgical operation. The defendant Viktor Brack, in March 1941, submitted to Himmler a report on the progress and state of X-ray sterilization experiments. Brack explained that it had been determined that sterilization with powerful X rays could be accomplished and that castration would then result. The danger of this X-ray method lay in the fact that other parts of the body, if they were not protected with lead, were also seriously affected. In order to prevent the victims from realizing that they were being castrated, Brack made the following fantastic suggestion in his letter written in 1941 to Himmler, from which I quote:

One way to carry out these experiments in practice would be to have those people who are to be treated line up before a counter. There they would be questioned and a form would be given them to be filled out, the whole process taking two or three minutes. The official attendant who sits behind the counter can operate the apparatus in such a manner that he works a switch which will start both tubes together (as the rays have to come from both sides). With one such installation with two tubes about 150 to 200 persons could be sterilized daily, while twenty installations would take care of 3,000 to 4,000 persons daily. In my opinion the number of daily deportations will not exceed this figure.

In this same report the defendant Brack related that, and I quote, "the latest X-ray techniques and research make it easily possible to carry out mass sterilization by means of X rays. However, it appears to be impossible to take these measures without having those who were so treated finding out sooner or later that they definitely had been either sterilized or had been castrated by X rays."

Another letter from Brack to Himmler, in June 1942, laid [out] the basis for X-ray experiments which were subsequently carried out at Auschwitz. The second paragraph of this letter forms a fitting conclusion to this account of Nazi depravity and I quote:

Among ten millions of Jews in Europe there are, I figure, at least two to three millions of men and women who are fit enough to work. Considering the extraordinary difficulties the labor problem presents us with, I hold the view that these two to three millions should be specially selected and preserved. This can, however, only be done if at the same time they are rendered incapable to propagate. About a year ago I reported to you that agents of mine have completed the experiments necessary for this purpose. I would like to recall these facts once more. Sterilization, as normally performed on persons with hereditary diseases, is here out of the question because it takes too long and is too expensive. Castration by X rays, however, is not only relatively cheap but can also be performed on many thousands in the shortest time. I think that at this time it is already irrelevant whether the people in question become aware of having been castrated after some weeks or months, once they feel the effects....

JEWISH SKELETON COLLECTION

I come now to charges stated in paragraphs 7 and 11 of the indictment. These are perhaps the most utterly repulsive charges in the entire indictment. They concern the defendants Rudolf Brandt and Sievers. Sievers and his associates in the Ahnenerbe Society were completely obsessed by all the vicious and malignant Nazi racial theories. They conceived the notion of applying these nauseous theories in the field of anthropology. What ensued was murderous folly.

In February 1942, Sievers submitted to Himmler, through Rudolf Brandt, a report, from which the following is an extract:

We have a nearly complete collection of skulls of all races and peoples at our disposal. Only very few specimens of skulls of the Jewish race, however, are available, with the result that it is impossible to arrive at precise conclusions from examining them. The war in the East now presents us with the opportunity to overcome this deficiency. By procuring the skulls of the Jewish-Bolshevik commissars, who represent the prototype of the repulsive but characteristic subhuman, we have the chance now to obtain a palpable, scientific document.

The best practical method for obtaining and collecting this skull material could be handled by directing the Wehrmacht to turn over alive all captured Jewish-Bolshevik commissars to the Field Police. They, in turn, are to be given special directives to inform a certain office at regular intervals of the number and place of detention of these captured Jews and to give them special close attention and care until a special delegate arrives. This spe-

cial delegate, who will be in charge of securing the "material," has the job of taking a series of previously established photographs, anthropological measurements, and in addition has to determine, as far as possible, the background, date of birth, and other personal data of the prisoner. Following the subsequently induced death of the Jew, whose head should not be damaged, the delegate will separate the head from the body and forward it to its proper point of destination in a hermetically sealed tin can, especially produced for this purpose and filled with a conserving fluid.

Having arrived at the laboratory, the comparison tests and anatomical research on the skull, as well as determination of the race membership of pathological features of the skull form, the form and size of the brain, etc., can proceed. The basis of these studies will be the photos, measurements, and other data supplied on the head, and finally the tests of the skull itself.

After extensive correspondence between Himmler and the defendants Sievers and Rudolf Brandt, it was decided to procure the skulls from inmates of the Auschwitz concentration camp instead of at the front. The hideous program was actually carried out, as is shown by a letter from Sievers written in June 1943, which states in part:

I wish to inform you that our associate, Dr. Beger, who was in charge of the above special project, has interrupted his experiments in the concentration camp Auschwitz because of the existing danger of epidemics. Altogether 115 persons were worked on, 79 were Jews, 30 were Jewesses, 2 were Poles, and 4 were Asiatics. At the present time these prisoners are segregated by sex and are under quarantine in the two hospital buildings of Auschwitz.

After the death of these wretched Jews had been "induced" their corpses were sent to Strasbourg. A year elapsed, and the Allied armies were racing across France and were nearing Strasbourg where this monstrous exhibit of the culture of the master race reposed. Alarmed, Sievers sent a telegram to Rudolf Brandt in September 1944, from which I quote:

According to the proposal of 9 February 1942, and your approval of 23 February 1942, Professor Dr. Hirt has assembled a skeleton collection which has never been in existence before. Because of the vast amount of scientific research that is connected with this project, the job of reducing the corpses to skeletons has not yet been completed. Since it might require some time to process eighty corpses, Hirt requested a decision pertaining to the treatment of the collection stored in the morgue of the Anatomy, in case Stras-

bourg should be endangered. The collection can be defleshed and rendered unrecognizable. This, however, would mean that the whole work had been done for nothing—at least in part—and that this singular collection would be lost to science, since it would be impossible to make plaster casts afterwards. The skeleton collection, as such, is inconspicuous. The flesh parts could be declared as having been left by the French at the time we took over the Anatomy and would be turned over for cremating. Please advise me which of the following three proposals is to be carried out:

(1) The collection as a whole is to be preserved. (2) The collection is to be dissolved in part. (3) The collection is to be completely dissolved.

Opening of the proceedings against the major war criminals, some of whom are seated at left (*first on left:* Hermann Goering). Chart showing organizational scheme is displayed on wall. November 22, 1945. National Archives/Courtesy of USHMM–Photo Archives.

The final chapter of this barbaric enterprise is found in a note in Himmler's files addressed to Rudolf Brandt stating that:"During his visit at the Operational Headquarters on 21 November 1944, Sievers told me that the collection in Strasbourg had been completely dissolved in conformance with the directive given him at the time. He is of the opinion that this arrangement is for the best in view of the whole situation."

These men, however, reckoned without the hand of fate. The bodies of these unfortunate people were not completely disposed of, and this Tribunal will hear the testimony of witnesses and see pictorial exhibits depicting the charnel house that was the Anatomy Institute of the Reich University of Strasbourg.

I have now completed the sketch of some of the foul crimes that these defendants committed in the name of research. The horrible record of their degradation needs no underlining. But German medical science was in past years honored throughout the world, and many of the most illustrious names in medical research are German. How did these things come to pass? I will outline briefly the historical evidence which we will offer and which, I believe, will show that these crimes were the logical and inevitable outcome of the prostitution of German medicine under the Nazis....

SUMMARY

I have outlined the particular charges against the defendants under counts two, three, and four of the indictment; and I have sketched the general nature of the evidence that we will present. But we must not overlook that the medical experiments were not an assortment of unrelated crimes. On the contrary, they constituted a well-integrated criminal program in which the defendants planned and collaborated among themselves and with others.

We have here, in other words, a conspiracy and a common design, as is charged in count one of the indictment, to commit the criminal experiments set forth in paragraphs 6 and 11 thereof. There was a common design to discover, or

improve, various medical techniques. There was a common design to utilize for this purpose the unusual resources which the defendants had at their disposal, consisting of numberless unfortunate victims of Nazi conquest and Nazi ideology. The defendants conspired and agreed together to utilize these human resources for nefarious and murderous purposes, and proceeded to put their criminal design into execution. Numbered among the countless victims of the conspiracy and the crimes are Germans, and nationals of countries overrun by Germany, and Gypsies, and prisoners of war, and Jews of many nationalities. All the elements of a conspiracy to commit the crimes charged in paragraphs 6 and 11 are present, and all will be clearly established by the proof.

There were many co-conspirators who are not in the dock. Among the planners and leaders of this plot were Conti and Grawitz, and Hippke whose whereabouts is unknown. Among the actual executioners, Dr. Ding is dead and Rascher is thought to be dead. There were many others.

Final judgment as to the relative degrees of guilt among those in the dock must await the presentation of the proof in detail. Nevertheless, before the introduction of evidence, it will be helpful to look again at the defendants and their part in the conspiracy. What manner of men are they, and what was their major role?

The twenty physicians in the dock range from leaders of German scientific medicine, with excellent international reputations, down to the dregs of the German medical profession. All of them have in common a callous lack of consideration and human regard for, and an unprincipled willingness to abuse their power over, the poor, unfortunate, defenseless creatures who have been deprived of their rights by the ruthless and criminal government. All of them violated the Hippocratic commandments which they had solemnly sworn to uphold and abide by, including the fundamental principle never to do harm—"primum non nocere."

Outstanding men of science, distinguished for their scientific ability in Germany and abroad, are the defendants Rostock and Rose. Both exemplify, in their training and practice alike, the highest traditions of German medicine. Rostock headed the Department of Surgery at the University of Berlin and served as dean of its medical school. Rose studied under the famous surgeon, Enderlen, at Heidelberg and then became a distinguished specialist in the fields of public health and tropical diseases. Handloser and Schroeder are outstanding medical administrators. Both of them made their careers in military medicine and reached the peak of their profession. Five more defendants are much younger men who are nevertheless already known as the possessors of considerable scientific ability, or capacity in medical administration. These include the defendants Karl Brandt, Ruff, Beiglboeck, Schaefer, and Becker-Freyseng.

A number of the others such as Romberg and Fischer are well-trained, and several of them attained high professional positions. But among the remainder few were known as outstanding scientific men. Among them at the foot of the list is Blome who has published his autobiography, entitled *Embattled Doctor*, in which he sets forth that he eventually decided to become a doctor because a medical career would enable him to become "master over life and death."

The part that each of these twenty physicians and their three lay accomplices played in the conspiracy and its execution corresponds closely to his professional interests in his place in the hierarchy of the Third Reich, as shown in the chart. The motivating force for this conspiracy came from two principal sources. Himmler, as head of the SS, a most terrible machine of oppression with vast resources, could provide numberless victims for the experiments. By doing so, he enhanced the prestige of his organization and was able to give free rein to the Nazi racial theories of which he was a leading protagonist and to develop new techniques for mass exterminations which were dear to his heart. The German military leaders, as the other main driving force, caught up the opportunity which Himmler presented them with and ruthlessly capitalized on Himmler's hideous overtures in an endeavor to strengthen their military machine.

And so the infernal drama was played just as it had been conceived in the minds of the authors. Special problems which confronted the German military or civilian authorities were, on the orders of the medical leaders, submitted for solution in the concentration camps. Thus we find Karl Brandt stimulating the epidemic jaundice experiments, Schroeder demanding "forty healthy experimental subjects" for the sea-water experiments, Handloser providing the impetus for Ding's fearful typhus researches, and Milch and Hippke at the root of the freezing experiments. Under Himmler's authority, the medical leaders of the SS—Grawitz, Genzken, Gebhardt, and others—set the wheels in motion. They arranged for the procurement of victims through other branches of the SS and gave directions to their underlings in the SS medical service such as Hoven and Fischer. Himmler's administrative assistants, Sievers and Rudolf Brandt passed on the Himmler orders, gave a push here and a shove there and kept the machinery oiled. Blome and Brack assisted from the side of the civilian and party authorities.

The Wehrmacht provided supervision and technical assistance for those experiments in which it was most interested. A low-pressure chamber was furnished for the high-altitude tests, the services of Weltz, Ruff, Romberg, and Rascher for the high-altitude and freezing experiments, and those of Becker-Freyseng, Schaefer, and Beiglboeck for sea water. In the important but sinister typhus researches, the eminent Dr. Rose appeared for the Luftwaffe to give expert guidance to Ding.

The proper steps were taken to ensure that the results were made available to those who needed to know. Annual meetings of the consulting physicians of the Wehrmacht held under Handloser's direction were favored, with lectures on some of the experiments. The report on the high-altitude experiment was sent to Field Marshal Milch, and a moving picture about them was shown at the Air Ministry in Berlin. Weltz spoke on the effects of freezing at a medical conference in Nuremberg, the same symposium at which Rascher and others passed on their devilish knowledge.

There could, we submit, be no clearer proof of conspiracy. This was the medical service of the Third Reich at work. Among the defendants in the box sit the surviving leaders of that service. We will ask the Tribunal to determine that neither scientific eminence nor superficial respectability shall shield them against the fearful consequences of the orders they gave.

I intend to pass very briefly over matters of medical ethics, such as the conditions under which a physician may lawfully perform a medical experiment upon a person who has voluntarily subjected himself to it, or whether experiments may lawfully be performed upon criminals who have been condemned to death. This case does not present such problems. No refined questions confront us here.

None of the victims of the atrocities perpetrated by these defendants were volunteers, and this is true regardless of what these unfortunate people may have said or signed before their tortures began. Most of the victims had not been condemned to death, and those who had been were not criminals, unless it be a crime to be a Jew, or a Pole, or a Gypsy, or a Russian prisoner of war.

Whatever book or treatise on medical ethics we may examine, and whatever expert on forensic medicine we may question, will say that it is a fundamental and inescapable obligation of every physician under any known system of law not to perform a dangerous experiment without the subject's consent. In the tyranny that was Nazi Germany, no one could give such a consent to the medical agents of the state; everyone lived in fear and acted under duress. I fervently hope that none of us here in the courtroom will have to suffer in silence while it is said on the part of these defendants that the wretched and helpless people whom they froze and drowned and burned and poisoned were volunteers. If such a shameless lie is spoken here, we need only remember the four girls who were taken from the Ravensbrueck concentration camp and made to lie naked with the frozen and all but dead Jews who survived Dr. Rascher's tank of ice water. One of these women, whose hair and eyes and figure

were pleasing to Dr. Rascher, when asked by him why she had volunteered for such a task, replied, "rather half a year in a brothel than half a year in a concentration camp."

Were it necessary, one could make a long list of the respects in which the experiments that these defendants performed departed from every known standard of medical ethics. But the gulf between these atrocities and serious research in the healing art is so patent that such a tabulation would be cynical.

We need look no further than the law which the Nazis themselves passed on the 24th of November 1933 for the protection of animals. This law states explicitly that it is designed to prevent cruelty and indifference of man towards animals and to awaken and develop sympathy and understanding for animals as one of the highest moral values of a people. The soul of the German people should abhor the principle of mere utility without consideration of the moral aspects. The law states further that all operations or treatments which are associated with pain or injury, especially experiments involving the use of cold, heat, or infection, are prohibited, and can be permitted only under special exceptional circumstances. Special written authorization by the head of the department is necessary in every case, and experimenters are prohibited from performing experiments according to their own free judgment. Experiments for the purpose of teaching must be reduced to a minimum. Medico-legal tests, vaccinations, withdrawal of blood for diagnostic purposes, and trial of vaccines prepared according to well-established scientific principles are permitted, but the animals have to be killed immediately and painlessly after such experiments. Individual physicians are not permitted to use dogs to increase their surgical skill by such practices. National Socialism regards it as a sacred duty of German science to keep down the number of painful animal experiments to a minimum.

If the principles announced in this law had been followed for human beings as well, this indictment would never have been filed. It is perhaps the deepest shame of the defendants that it probably never even occurred to them that human beings should be treated with at least equal humanity.

This case is one of the simplest and clearest of those that will be tried in this building. It is also one of the most important. It is true that the defendants in the box were not among the highest leaders of the Third Reich. They are not the warlords who assembled and drove the German military machine, nor the industrial barons who made the parts, nor the Nazi politicians who debased and brutalized the minds of the German people. But this case, perhaps more than any other we will try, epitomizes Nazi thought and the Nazi way of life, because these defendants pursued the savage premises of Nazi thought so far. The things that these defendants did, like so many other things that happened under the Third Reich, were the result of the noxious merger of German militarism and Nazi racial objectives. We will see the results of this merger in many other fields of German life; we see it here in the field of medicine.

Germany surrendered herself to this foul conjunction of evil forces. The nation fell victim to the Nazi scourge because its leaders lacked the wisdom to foresee the consequences and the courage to stand firm in the face of threats. Their failure was the inevitable outcome of that sinister undercurrent of German philosophy that preaches the supreme importance of the state and the complete subordination of the individual. A nation in which the individual means nothing will find few leaders courageous and able enough to serve its best interests.

Individual Germans did indeed give warning of what was in store, and German doctors and scientists were numbered among the courageous few. At a meeting of Bavarian psychiatrists held in Munich in 1931, when the poisonous doctrines of the Nazis were already sweeping Germany, there was a discussion of mercy killings and sterilization, and the Nazi views on these matters, with which we are now familiar, were advanced. A German professor named Oswald Bumke rose and made a reply more eloquent and prophetic than anyone could have possibly realized at the time. He said:

I should like to make two additional remarks. One of them is please for God's sake leave our present financial needs out of all these considerations. This is a problem which concerns the entire future of our people, indeed, one may say without being overemotional about it, the entire future of humanity. One should approach this problem neither from the point of view of our present scientific opinion nor from the point of view of the still more ephemeral economic crises. If by sterilization we can prevent the occurrence of mental disease then we should certainly do it, not in order to save money for the government but because every case of mental disease means infinite suffering to the patient and to his relatives. But to introduce economic points of view is not only inappropriate but outright dangerous because the logical consequence of the thought that for financial reasons all these human beings, who could be dispensed with for the moment, should be exterminated, is a quite monstrous logical conclusion; we would then have to put to death not only the mentally sick and the psychopathic personalities but all the crippled, including the disabled veterans, all old maids who do not work, all widows whose children have completed their education, and all those who live on their income or draw pensions. That would certainly save a lot of money but the probability is that we will not do it.

The second point of advice is to use utmost restraint, at least until the political atmosphere here in this country shall have improved, and scientific theories concerning heredity and race can no longer be abused for political purposes. Because, if the discussion about sterilization today is carried into the arena of political contest, then pretty soon we will no longer hear about the mentally sick but, instead, about Aryans and non-Aryans, about the blond Germanic race and about inferior people with round skulls. That anything useful could come from that is certainly improbable; but science in general and genealogy and eugenics in particular would suffer an injury which could not easily be repaired again.

I said at the outset of this statement that the Third Reich died of its own poison. This case is a striking demonstration not only of the tremendous degradation of German medical ethics which Nazi doctrine brought about, but of the undermining of the medical art and thwarting of the techniques which the defendants sought to employ. The Nazis have, to a certain extent, succeeded in convincing the peoples of the world that the Nazi system, although ruthless, was absolutely efficient; that although savage, it was completely scientific; that although entirely devoid of humanity, it was highly systematic— that "it got things done." The evidence which this Tribunal will hear will explode this myth. The Nazi methods of investigation were inefficient and unscientific, and their techniques of research were unsystematic.

These experiments revealed nothing which civilized medicine can use. It was, indeed, ascertained that phenol or gasoline injected intravenously will kill a man inexpensively and within sixty seconds. This and a few other "advances" are all in the field of thanatology. There is no doubt that a number of these new methods may be useful to criminals everywhere and there is no doubt that they may be useful to a criminal state. Certain advances in destructive methodology we cannot deny, and indeed from Himmler's standpoint this may well have been the principal objective.

Apart from these deadly fruits, the experiments were not only criminal but a scientific failure. It is indeed as if a just deity had shrouded the solutions which they attempted to reach with murderous means. The moral shortcomings of the defendants and the precipitous ease with which they decided to commit murder in quest of "scientific results" dulled also that scientific hesitancy, that thorough thinking-through, that responsible weighing of every single step which alone can ensure scientifically valid results. Even if they had merely been forced to pay as little as two dollars for human experimental subjects, such as American investigators may have to pay for a cat, they might have thought twice before wasting unnecessary numbers and thought of simpler and better ways to solve their problems. The fact that these investigators had free and unrestricted access to human beings to be experimented upon misled them to the dangerous and fallacious conclusion that the results would thus be better and more quickly obtainable than if they had gone through the labor of preparation, thinking, and meticulous preinvestigation....

Guilt for the oppression and crimes of the Third Reich is widespread, but it is the guilt of the leaders that is deepest and most culpable. Where could German medicine look to keep the profession true to its traditions and protect it from the ravaging inroads of Nazi pseudoscience? This was the supreme responsibility of the leaders of German medicine—men like Rostock and Rose and Schroeder and Handloser. That is why their guilt is greater than that of any of the other defendants in the dock. They are the men who utterly failed their country and their profession, who show neither courage nor wisdom nor the vestiges of moral character. It is their failure, together with the failure of the leaders of Germany in other walks life, that debauched Germany and led to her defeat. It is because of them and others like them that we all live in a stricken world.

(Sources: 4f War Criminals Before the Nuremberg Military Tribunals Under ConLaw 10, Vol. I (Washington, D.C.: Superintendent of Documents, U.S. at Printing Office, 1950); Military Tribunal, Case 1, United States v. Karl Fol. (October 1946-April 1949, pp. 27–74.)

JUDGMENT AND AFTERMATH

PERMISSIBLE MEDICAL EXPERIMENTS

The great weight of the evidence before us is to the effect that certain types of medical experiments on human beings, when kept within reasonably well-defined bounds, conform to the ethics of the medical profession generally. The protagonists of the practice of human experimentation justify their views on the basis that such experiments yield results for the good of society that are unprocurable by other methods or means of study. All agree, however, that certain basic principles must be observed in order to satisfy moral, ethical and legal concepts:

1. The voluntary consent of the human subject is absolutely essential.

    This means that the person involved should have legal capacity to give consent; should be so situated as to be able to exercise free power of choice, without the intervention of any element of force, fraud, deceit, duress, overreaching, or other ulterior form of constraint or coercion; and should have sufficient knowledge and comprehension of the elements of the subject matter involved as to enable him to make an understanding and enlightened decision. This latter element requires that before the acceptance of an affirmative decision by the experimental subject there should be made known to him the nature, duration, and purpose of the experiment; the method and means by which it is to be conducted; all inconveniences and hazards reasonably to be expected; and the effects upon his health or person which may possibly come from his participation in the experiment.

    The duty and responsibility for ascertaining the quality of the consent rests upon each individual who initiates, directs, or engages in the experiment. It is a personal duty and responsibility which may not be delegated to another with impunity.

2. The experiment should be such as to yield fruitful results for the good of society, unprocurable by other methods or means of study, and not random and unnecessary in nature.

3. The experiment should be so designed and based on the results of animal experimentation and a knowledge of the natural history of the disease or other problem under study that the anticipated results will justify the performance of the experiment.

4. The experiment should be so conducted as to avoid all unnecessary physical and mental suffering and injury.

5. No experiment should be conducted where there is an *a priori* reason to believe that death or disabling injury will occur; except, perhaps, in those experiments where the experimental physicians also serve as subjects.

6. The degree of risk to be taken should never exceed that determined by the humanitarian importance of the problem to be solved by the experiment.

7. Proper preparations should be made and adequate facilities provided to protect the experimental subject against even remote possibilities of injury, disability, or death.

8. The experiment should be conducted only by scientifically qualified persons. The highest degree of skill and care should be required through all stages of the experiment of those who conduct or engage in the experiment.

9. During the course of the experiment the human subject should be at liberty to bring the experiment to an end if he has reached the physical or mental state where continuation of the experiment seems to him to be impossible.

10. During the course of the experiment the scientist in charge must be prepared to termi-

nate the experiment at any stage, if he has probable cause to believe, in the exercise of the good faith, superior skill and careful judgment required of him that a continuation of the experiment is likely to result in injury, disability, or death to the experimental subject.

Of the ten principles which have been enumerated, our judicial concern, of course, is with those requirements which are purely legal in nature—or which at least are so clearly related to matters legal that they assist us in determining criminal culpability and punishment. To go beyond that point would lead us into a field that would be beyond our sphere of competence. However, the point need not be labored. We find from the evidence that in the medical experiments which have been proved, these ten principles were much more frequently honored in their breach than in their observance. Many of the concentration camp inmates who were the victims of these atrocities were citizens of countries other than the German Reich. They were non-German nationals, including Jews and "asocial persons," both prisoners of war and civilians, who had been imprisoned and forced to submit to these tortures and barbarities without so much as a semblance of trial. In every single instance appearing in the record, subjects were used who did not consent to the experiments; indeed, as to some of the experiments, it is not even contended by the defendants that the subjects occupied the status of volunteers. In no case was the experimental subject at liberty of his own free choice to withdraw from any experiment. In many cases, experiments were performed by unqualified persons; were conducted at random for no adequate scientific reason, and under revolting physical conditions. All of the experiments were conducted with unnecessary suffering and injury and very little, if any, precautions were taken to protect or safeguard the human subjects from the possibilities of injury, disability, or death. In every one of the experiments the subjects experienced extreme pain or torture, and in most of them they suffered permanent injury, mutilation, or death, either as a direct result of the experiments or because of lack of adequate follow-up care.

Obviously all of these experiments involving brutalities, tortures, disabling injury, and death were performed in complete disregard of international conventions, the laws and customs of war, the general principles of criminal law as derived from the criminal laws of all civilized nations, and Control Council Law No. 10. Manifestly inhuman experiments under such conditions are contrary to "the principles of the law of nations as they result from the usage established among civilized peoples, from the laws of humanity, and from the dictates of public conscience."

✦ AUTHOR AND TITLE INDEX

COPYRIGHT ACKNOWLEDGMENTS

1989). Copyright © 1989 by The Jewish Heritage Writing Project. Used with permission of Viking Penguin, a division of Penguin Books USA, Inc.

Avraham Tory, *Surviving the Holocaust: The Kovno Ghetto Diary* (Cambridge: Harvard University Press, 1990). Copyright © 1990 by the President and Fellows of Harvard College. Reprinted with permission of Harvard University Press.

Yitzhak Arad, Yisrael Gutman, and Abraham Margaliot, *Documents on the Holocaust* (Jerusalem: Yad Vashem Holocaust Martyrs' and Heroes Remembrance Authority, 1981). Reprinted with permission.

"The Good Old Days": The Holocaust as Seen by Its Perpetrators and Bystanders, Ernst Klee, Willi Dressen, and Voer Reiss, eds. (New York: The Free Press, 1991). Reprinted with permission.